The
COLUMBIA
History of
AMERICAN
POETRY

JAY PARINI, EDITOR
BRETT C. MILLIER, ASSOCIATE EDITOR

MJF BOOKS
NEW YORK

Published by MJF Books
Fine Communications
Two Lincoln Square
60 West 66th Street
New York, NY 10023

The Columbia History of American Poetry
ISBN 1-56731-276-4
Library of Congress Card Catalog No. 98-66481

Manufactured in the United States of America on acid-free paper

MJF Books and the MJF colophon are trademarks of Fine Creative Media, Inc.

10   9   8   7   6   5   4   3   2   1

Contents

Introduction

THE relationship between poetry and national culture is always an intimate if troubled one, and to a large extent what American poets have accomplished as a whole is a measure of what American culture itself has accomplished. One can track the evolution of a national consciousness in the poems, as American poets, who begin as English Metaphysical poets abroad, gradually test their own voices and learn ways to absorb and embody the vision—the outer and inner landscapes—that spread out before them.

As one might expect, the story of American poetry involves our struggle as a people to achieve a national identity. "Nationalism," says an African character in a novel by Raymond Williams, "is in this sense like class. To have it, and to feel it, is the only way to end it. If you fail to claim it, or give it up too soon, you will merely be cheated, by other classes and other nations." In an essay called "Nationalism: Irony and Commitment" (1990) Terry Eagleton notes that nationalism, like class, inevitably involves an impossible irony. "It is sometimes forgotten," he writes, "that social class, for Karl Marx at least, is itself a form of alienation, canceling the particularity of an individual life into collective anonymity." Marx separates himself from the usual liberal view here in his notion that to undo this alienation one has to go, not around class, but through it. The same might be said for nationalism: one must go through it, not around it, grasping all forms of national feeling (including alienation from the nation state or the national mood or ethos of a particular time or region, as in the war protest poetry of the 1960s).

The poet's job in such a context of national self-realization has always been to lay claim to a voice that reflects the genuineness and separateness of a particular culture. The poets seize the given day, giving a "local habitation and a name" to what otherwise remains ineluctable—ever more alien. While the ultimate goal, as Eagleton would argue, is to go "through" to some point beyond nationalism, to create a poetry reflecting not an "American" consciousness but something like a "human" consciousness, we must still go through every stage of nationalism as a culture, feel each stage fully, in order to transcend them.

Adrienne Rich, one of our most essential contemporary poets, has written about what she calls "the dream of a common language." In her terms this dream is deeply feminist, involving "women's struggle to name the world." She says, movingly, that "a whole new poetry is beginning here" in a poem called "Transcendental Etude." Although Rich might well object, I would generalize from these observations to suggest that in fact the struggle of American poetry from the beginning has been this dream of a common language, and that there has always been in our best poets a sense that a "whole new poetry is beginning here."

The Columbia History of American Poetry offers a fresh testament to this "whole new poetry." While poets in this country have been far removed from the most visible centers of political and even cultural power, their poems have consistently taken the measure of the culture as a whole. They have done so in remarkably different ways (although one might argue that superficial differences of style are as not as important as underlying drives and motives reflected in striking thematic consistencies).

As a quick perusal of this text will suggest, the stylistic range of American poetry is unusually broad. If anything, one hestitates even to refer to "an American style in poetry." A poet like Edward Taylor, for instance, looks very like an English Metaphysical poet of the seventeenth century "gone native," while many of our early African American poets seem to belong to the traditions of oral poetry that have roots in a variety of West African tribal cultures. More recently one can hardly imagine poets with styles as different as James Merrill and John Ashbery. Nevertheless, as so many of the chapters in this book suggest, the wish to speak for the American people at large—for them and to them—is always present in the American poet: a brave and bold assumption that underlies each visionary project as it unfolds from Anne Bradstreet and Phyllis Wheatley to Adrienne Rich, Charles Wright, and Mary Oliver.

The reader will find in this collection a rich variety of responses to many different "traditions" of American poetry by some of our strongest critics. These chapters are arranged chronologically, and represent what the editors consider important aspects of American poetry. Nevertheless, each chapter should be taken as one critic's point of view: necessarily subjective, rooted in the critic's position in the evolution of the culture as a whole. The reader will discover a considerable variety of critical methods in this "history." The only thing we, as editors, have consistently discouraged is obscurity of language and the excessive use of critical jargon.

The achievement of two of our most well-known Puritan poets, Anne Bradstreet and Edward Taylor, is examined by Frank Murphy. Bradstreet, he says, "wrote the best American poems on human love before the middle of the nineteenth century." He finds "an openness in her writing that is directly related to her role as an understanding mother." Edward Taylor, her younger contemporary, was an Englishman who came to America as a young man in the seventeenth century and remained an English Metaphysical poet in temperament and style; his work recalls the poetry of Donne, Herbert, Quarles, and others. Like many of the Metaphysical poets, he was also a clergyman, serving a parish in the frontier town of Westfield, Massachusetts, until his retirement in 1725, when he wrote the last of his brilliant "Preparatory Meditations."

What is interesting is how important these early American poets, especially Bradstreet and Taylor, have been for twentieth-century poets. John Berryman, in *Homage to Mistress Bradstreet*, acknowledges his debt directly. Poets such as Sylvia Plath, Anne Sexton, Adrienne Rich, and Anne Stevenson—each of whom in different ways has confronted the issue of motherhood in her work—can also be seen to have learned a great deal from their distant precursor. Poets as diverse as T. S. Eliot, Allen Tate, Hart Crane, John Crowe Ransom, and Robert Lowell are in debt to Edward Taylor—as Murphy suggests—for the style of meditative poetry that he brought to this continent from England and naturalized in his own powerful way.

One of the chief tasks of criticism in the past decades has been the recovery of lost traditions. Women and African Americans, in particular, have been occluded, pushed to the margins, forgotten. The reasons why this happened are complex and go beyond any simple formulations involving patriarchy and racism, although these are certainly the places to begin. North America was, first, a land of indigenous people turned imperial colony. A whole native population was "erased" in a collective act of genocide in which millions of native people suffered and died. A further "colonization" took place when African slaves were forceably brought to this country, and many more millions suffered and died. Meanwhile, poets worked—at the center of the culture and in the margins.

In her chapter on "Early African American Poetry" Carolivia Herron performs an act of cultural archaeology, reaching into the margins for the origins of what has become one of our strongest "traditions." More specifically, she locates the origins of contemporary African American "polyphonic poetry" in the lyrics attached to "field hollers, ring shouts, rudimentary work songs, and songs of familial entertainment in the early colonies of the Americas—in the North, in the South, and in the Caribbean." She points to early African American lyric poets such as Lucy Terry, Phyllis Wheatley, and Jupiter Hammon, and she discusses several epics by African American poets, such as "The Sentinel of Freedom" by John Sella Martin, an apocalyptic poem that prophesies a "second coming after the United States is swept clean from the corruption of slavery," and *Moses* by Frances Ellen Watkins Harper, a popular abolitionist poet who turns Moses into a mulatto who "freely chooses to return to the aid of his enslaved people." Moving from Lucy Terry through Wheatley, Hammon, Paul Laurence Dunbar, Frances Harper, and others, Herron notes: "The end of the immediate political requirements of the Civil War gave African American poets the freedom to write on all human themes: racism and flowers, wars and love, lynching and childhood."

At the center of American poetry has been the obsession with the long poem: the poem equal in size, power, and scope to the growing power of the nation state as a whole. John McWilliams and Lynn Keller each took upon themselves the formidable task of confronting this American obsession. McWilliams examines the work of epic poets such as Joel Barlow, Timothy Dwight, Alfred Mitchell, and a dozen others, moving right up through Stephen Vincent Benét's once popular but now rarely acknowledged narrative poem, *John Brown's Body*, a poem that addresses one of the critical moments in the history of the abolitionist movement. McWilliams wonders in the end if the "disappearance of *John Brown's Body* from public view . . . suggests that a narrative verse epic will lose its impact whenever a poet fabricates characters said to embody cultural legend."

Lynn Keller, in her answering chapter on the long poem in the twentieth century, argues that the "long poem is a central—even obsessive— form for twentieth-century American literature." She demonstrates the peculiarly "contestatory form" of the long poem in this century, looking at the major Modernist attempts to create the long poem, such as Pound's *Cantos* and *The Waste Land*, as well as some lesser known but no less powerful works, which include Melvin Tolson's *Harlem Gallery* and H.D.'s *Helen in Egypt*. Keller's encyclopedic chapter takes the long poem right up to the present, looking at contemporary long poems by James Merrill, A. R. Ammons, and others; she locates "several characteristics that typify the varied and experimental history of the twentieth-century long poem: a liberating mixture of genres, an enlargement beyond the postromantic lyric's focus on a moment of subjective experience, and an accompanying exploration of social and historical materials, often in service to a fresh understanding of the self and its construction."

In the postcolonial era American poetry began to move in fresh directions, as the urge to overthrow the English political yoke moved from the literal cancellation of British imperial power to an attempt to embody this freedom imaginatively in something like a separate national voice. William Cullen Bryant was probably our first national poet in this sense; he published *Thanatopsis and Other Poems* in 1921, and it was greatly prized by readers of poetry through the nineteenth and early twentieth century as the first flowering of a distinctly American expression. One can still return to Bryant with pleasure, hearing in him the first cadence of a truly national literature, one that would embody the American voice in all its grainy particularity.

The same may be said for John Greenleaf Whittier. As Jeffrey Meyers notes in his chapter on Edgar Allan Poe, "When Poe came to maturity William Cullent Bryant and John Greenleaf Whittier were the leading American poets." It is interesting to note that Poe himself turned away from them, preferring instead the English Romantic poets. His *Poems* (1831) was an impressive volume for a young man (Poe was twenty-two at the time, and this was already his third collection). This book signaled to the reading public an original genius, one who would receive world acclaim, though Poe's early verse does not have the mesmerizing power of the poems included in *The Raven and Other Poems* (1845). Ezra Pound, a founding father of Modernism, would eventually say that "no one who has tried to write like Poe . . . has done anything good." Nevertheless, the impact of Poe has lingered, as Meyers observes: "His extensive influence on later writers has been quite out of proportion to the extremely uneven quality of his hundred poems." He locates the source of Poe's strength in his appeal to "basic feelings" and his natural gravitation toward "universal themes common to everyone in every language: dreams, love, loss; grief, mourning, alienation; terror and insanity, disease and death."

Poe was immensely popular in his own time, and he remains so. This cannot be said for Henry Wadsworth Longfellow, who became the most widely admired poet of nineteenth-century America but whose work is now infrequently read and rarely studied. Dana Gioia, however, makes a compelling case here for Longfellow as the most talented of the Fireside poets, a group that includes Bryant, Oliver Wendell Holmes, and James Russell Lowell. Gioia looks in particular at Longfellow's narrative poems: *Evangeline* (1847), *The Song of Hiawatha* (1855), *The Courtship of Miles Standish* (1858), and *Tales of a Wayside Inn* (1863–1873). "These were the poems that earned him a preeminent position among his contemporaries," Gioia writes. "They were also the works most utterly rejected by Modernism." Much of Gioia's chapter is concerned with the issue of Longfellow in the postmodern age, concluding that the task for American poetry is "not to reject Modernism, which was our poetry's greatest period, but to correct its blindspots and biases." Furthermore, he argues, a "reevaluation of Longfellow will be an important part of this enterprise."

For modern and postmodern poets Ralph Waldo Emerson and Walt Whitman might be considered the most profoundly generative voices. As poet, this is more true of Whitman than Emerson, yet Emerson has probably had more influence on American thinking in general than anyone else. In an essay called "Emerson: The American Religion" (published in a collection called *Agon: Towards a Theory of Revisionism* in 1982), Harold Bloom makes the case for Emerson's priority:

The lengthened shadow of our American culture is Emerson's, and Emerson indeed saw everything in everything, and spoke with the tongue of a daemon. His truest achievement was to invent the American religion. . . . Starting from Emerson we came to where we are, and from that impasse, which he prophesied, we will go by a path that most likely he marked out also. The mind of Emerson is the mind of America.

This "American religion" is self-reliance, not in any common sense but as reliance on the alien God within us. Bloom writes: "*Self*-reliance . . . is the religion that celebrates and reveres what in the self is before the Creation, a whatness which from the perspective of religious orthodoxy can only be the primal Abyss." In his chapter on Emerson and other poets of the Transcendental movement Lawrence Buell examines Emerson's major poems carefully in relation to the gnostic urge toward self-definition in the face of the abyss that Bloom cites. "More often than not," says Buell, "the development of the subjective mood in Transcendentalist poetry expresses loss or lack of self-integration."

That vulnerability, for instance, is expressed in "Days," one of Emerson's finest poems:

> Daughters of Time, the hypocritic Days,
> Muffled and dumb like barefoot dervishes,
> And marching single in an endless file,
> Bring diadems and fagots in their hands.
> To each they offer gifts after his will,
> Bread, kingdoms, stars, and sky that holds them all.
> I, in my pleached garden, watched the pomp,
> Forget my morning wishes, hastily
> Took a few herbs and apples, and the Day
> Turned and departed silent. I, too late,
> Under her solemn fillet saw the scorn.

This memorable poem reenacts the Blakean myth of the fall into individuality, and thus frames what begins to emerge in Emerson as a central conflict in American poetry: the self versus the abyss, a dialectic later characterized explicitly by Edward Arlington Robinson in his poem "Man Against the Sky" and by Wallace Stevens in his "Notes Toward a Supreme Fiction," where he writes: "Soldier, there is a war between the mind / And sky, between thought and day and night."

Late in life, in the winter of 1866 Emerson noted in his journal that "for every seeing soul there are two absorbing facts,—*I and the Abyss.*" But his poetry from the first was a formal meditation on this crucial dialectic, and the work of fellow Transcendentalist poets such as William Ellery Channing, Christopher Pearse Cranch, and Jones Very continues the Emersonian project of working through this dialectic. For the most part, as Buell notes, the Transcendentalists preferred tight poetic forms, a sense of what he calls "liberty-within-restraint," and he cites their influence on such later poets as Robinson, Frost, Bishop, and Wilbur. In a startling conclusion Buell suggests a major revision of our notion of American poesis. He would review the whole of American poetry in the light of what he calls "a transatlantic Anglophone community almost as interlinked in the nineteenth century as in the High Modernist era." In his narrative of American poetic development he eschews "the autochthonous myth of American poetic history that winds up dancing around a selective version of Whitman, fathered perhaps by an even more selective version of Emerson." Transcendentalist poetry must not, Buell suggest, merely be seen as a "proto-Whitmanian artifact." In effect, Transcendentalism becomes part and parcel of the larger movement from Puritan meditative poetry to Frost, Moore, Bishop, and many of our best contemporary poets.

Even a cursory reading of the chapters gathered in this *Columbia History* will reveal the centrality of Whitman, who has been and remains our most influential poet. We must all, as poets and readers of poetry, "make a pact," as Pound says, with Whitman, and many books have been written about the attempts by some of our best poets to come to terms with Whitman's expansive visionary challenge to posterity. Listen, for a moment, to Whitman's unmistakable voice:

> As Adam early in the morning
> Walking forth from the bower refresh'd with sleep,
> Behold me where I pass, hear my voice, approach,
> Touch me, touch the palm of your hand to my body as I pass,
> Be not afraid of my body.

This poem leads directly to the solitary singer by the sea in Wallace Stevens' majestic "Idea of Order at Key West" via Hart Crane's invocation of Whitman in the "Cape Hatteras" section of *The Bridge*, where he writes:

> O Walt!—Ascensions of thee hover in me now
> As thou at junctions elegiac, there, of speed,
> With vast eternity, dost wield the rebound seed!

Likewise, Theodore Roethke, in a moment of crisis in a late poem, calls out with piercing directness: "Be with me, Whitman, maker of catalogues!" More recently, one hears the Whitmanian note vividly reborn in Mary Oliver's astonishing "When Death Comes," where she considers what it will be like when one has stepped through the door of life into the eternal night of death:

> I want to step through the door full of curiosity, wondering:
> what is it going to be like, that cottage of darkness?
>
> And therefore I look upon everything
> as a brotherhood and a sisterhood,
> and I look upon time as no more than an idea,
> and I consider eternity as another possibility,
>
> and I think of each life as a flower, as common
> as a field daisy, as singular,
> and each name a comfortable music in the mouth,
> tending, as all music does, toward silence,
>
> and each body a lion of courage, and something
> precious to the earth.

One can hardly imagine our debt, as a culture, to Walt Whitman, who was able to summon a vision as defiantly idiosyncratic yet as thoroughly central and representative as any in the history of our poetry. He did it in *Leaves of Grass,* his lifetime project, which is discussed and alluded to by a dozen different critics in this book. And Whitman is the primary focus of Donald E. Pease's chapter, which surveys the whole of this poet's career, moving chronologically through the major poems of *Leaves of Grass.* Pease begins with Ezra Pound's famous homage to Whitman called "A Pact." In this poem Pound recognizes Whitman as the true father of American poetry, the poet who broke new ground and found a voice equal to the vast new continent that it celebrated. Pease sees Whitman as a radical democrat whose inclusive vision of an American future repositions the Emersonian dialectic as not just self versus the abyss but *included* versus *excluded* figures. He identifies the Whitmanian project as one that cleverly absorbs, even appropriates, the reader in an ongoing and expansive dialectic in which the poet returns us, always, to the democratic principles on which this country was founded.

While the expansive Whitman responded to Emerson's call in one way, Emily Dickinson's response took another turn. In her chapter on Dickinson Cynthia Griffin Wolff suggests that "Dickinson's unique turn upon Emerson's injunction that "the poet" ought to be "representative" was "to write as a woman in an explicitly domestic realm." Dickinson, the isolated spinster living in her father's house in Amherst, Massachusetts, had none of Whitman's robust contact with the "real" world; she nevertheless felt intensely, thought deeply, read widely, and managed to become our other central poet: a brilliant counterpoint to Whitman. Indeed, each poet is incomparably enhanced by the presence of the other. Where Whitman proceeds by flinging his fire in every direction, Dickinson's movement is ever inward, a centripetal motion that generates a poetry of compression and power. Her compacted poems are bullets aimed straight at the heart, and they kill.

Dickinson has also been crucial in the development of an American consciousness from the viewpoint of women. She was able, as Wolff says, "to exploit this issue of gender in a wide variety of ways." She constructs an image of the housewife as soldier, for instance, one who " 'mans' the front lines of our engagement with the forces of destruction." Chaos and dissolution underlie Dickinson's fierce, intensely wrought lyrics, which splinter in the reader's eye. In this sense, she anticipates the painful darkness of Modernist and postmodern poetry. There is indeed a natural line from Dickinson to Sylvia Plath, Anne Sexton, and Louise Glück. The Emersonian dialectic between self and the abyss seems all but lost to the abyss much of the time in Dickinson, but there are moments of rebellion, too. "Emily Dickinson espoused an openly rebellious attitude toward God and toward the various forms of male authority that He epitomized," Wolff observes. She rightly places Dickinson in the direct line of major American poets.

Many of the chapters in the book address issues that have been raised by feminist scholars in the past two decades. In her chapter on women poets and the emergence of Modernism, for instance, Margaret Dickie examines the role of women in the Modernist movement as not mere adjuncts to male poets but as innovators themselves: "Simply inserting the women Modernists into the movement . . . will not offer a better understanding of the women's work unless they are considered not as adjuncts to the men but as original experimenters on their own terms." The great male Modernists—Eliot, Pound, Frost, Stevens—were almost all political reactionaries, she points out. "The women," says Dickie, "were more radical in their sexual choices as well as in their social and political views." She studies, in particular, the neglected yet profoundly experimental poetry of Gertrude Stein as well as the poetry of H.D. and Marianne Moore.

Moore, again, is the subject of Jeredith Merrin's chapter, which compares her to Elizabeth Bishop in unconventional ways. To consider Moore and Bishop as "subspecies of female American poet is," writes Merrin, "to persist in a kind of marginalization." Merrin is more interested in identifying their individual poetic personalities and noting their impact on younger American poets. Inevitably, she finds that these writers have something in common as "describers of nature and natural creatures," an aspect they also have in common with many of the best poets this country has produced.

Jeanne Larsen treats an often bypassed group of women lyric poets from the first half of this century: Amy Lowell, Sara Teasdale, Elinor Wylie, Edna St. Vincent Millay, and Louise Bogan. These poets have in common, she argues, "passionate expression of emotion, revelation of personal sensibility, apparent delicacy overlying sensuality and self-assertion, musicality created by diction and cadence, a vigorous grace of form." Each of these women was unique and a compelling poet, but they wrote without much of a sense of themselves *as* women except in the most conventional ways. Bogan, for instance, "struggled with assimilated misogynist attitudes of her times." Like most women, she learned to read by reading against herself as a woman and identifying with the presiding male subject in the text. But her struggle, like that of the other poets examined here, eventually revealed to her "a profound awareness of [gender as a] molding force," one that shapes and transforms a woman's experience of what is true. In a very real sense Bogan's work anticipates the work of contemporary women poets like Linda Pastan and Margaret Atwood, the Canadian poet, novelist, and short story writer, both of whom have written movingly about domestic life.

Literary historians love movements—catch-all terms in which a wide variety of poets can shelter—but there is something unsettling about the use of such giant categories as Romanticism, Modernism, and postmodernism. Just as there were almost as many varieties of romanticisms as there were romantics, it is also true of Modernism that each poet responded to this complex international movement in his or her own way. One of the most visible poets of the early Modernist period was Vachel Lindsay, for instance. In such poems as "General William Booth Enters into Heaven" and "The Congo," Lindsay created poems that were entertaining as performance pieces, and they are still worth reading. But Lindsay's version of modern poetry, though ear-catching, proved a cul-de-sac. It did not inspire the best younger poets of the day, and Lindsay remains a curiosity in the history of our poetry, no more read than his slightly older contemporary Trumbull Stickney, whose poem "Mnemosyne" caught the imagination of many readers in the late nineteenth century, with its haunting evocation of "the long sun-sweetened summer-days" of his boyhood.

The mainstream of American literary Modernism went in a different and often more esoteric direction; it included poets as diverse as Ezra Pound, T. S. Eliot, Robert Frost, Wallace Stevens, William Carlos Williams, and Hart Crane; they are each treated at length in separate chapters in this book. J. T. Barbarese, himself a poet, considers Pound in relation to the Imagist movement, which he, H.D., and Amy Lowell helped to found. The influence of this aesthetic, with its emphasis on "direct treatment of the thing itself," can hardly be overestimated. Twentieth-century American poetry is largely image-centered, even when there is an overarching narrative. There is an overriding concern with concreteness—an emphasis, again, that has its origins in Emerson, who argued consistently against abstraction in language.

Pound, of course, was a "difficult" poet who adored allusions. In many ways he—like the Eliot of *The Waste Land*—wrote a poetry of quotation, drawing on world literature with the adventurousness of an amateur reader. Nothing daunted him, and it shows. From his first early lyrics, which owe so much to the Greek lyric, through the famous imitations of Chinese poetry, found in *Cathay*, and on through *Hugh Selwyn Mauberly* and the *Cantos*, Pound remained a teacher as much as a poet. The last work, a multivolume project that continues to daunt readers of American poetry, is treated by several critics in this collection, including Keller and poet W. S. DiPiero. (Barbarese's focus is early to mid-career Pound, though he does briefly discuss the *Cantos*.)

T. S. Eliot was among the most influential poets of all time, in part because of his extraordinary skills as a critic. In *The Sacred Wood* (1920) and other volumes, he made a case for the kind of Modernism that interested him, creating a whole new vocabulary for poets and critics that included phrases and terms like "the dissociation of sensibility," "objective correlatives," and "classicism." He redrew the entire map of English and American poetry in a way that focused on Donne and the Metaphysicals, on Elizabethan dramatists like Middleton and Ford, and downgraded Milton and the eighteenth century. He presided over the Modernist moment like an archbishop, and one can hardly overestimate his influence (positive and negative) on two or three generations of poets and critics. His own poems, from "The Love Song of J. Alfred Prufrock" through the *Four Quartets*, were buried under an avalanche of exegesis and commentary. William H. Pritchard sorts through this towering and intimidating career with great skill, finding the human voice in the poetry. At the end of his chapter, he quotes a remarkably astute and prophetic comment by Randall Jarrell:

Won't the future say to us in helpless astonishment: "But did you actually believe all these things about objective correlatives, classicism, the tradition, applied to *his* poetry? Surely you must have seen that he was one of the most subjective and daemonic poets who ever lived, the victim and helpless beneficiary of his own inexorable compulsions, obsessions? . . . But for you, of course, after the first few years, his poetry existed undersea, thousands of feet below that deluge of exegesis, explication, source listing, scholarship, and criticism that overwhelmed it. And yet how bravely and personally it survived, its eyes neither coral nor mother-of-pearl but plainly human, full of human anguish!

Pritchard notes: "The voice of that future has not yet been heard; we should keep listening for it."

My chapter on Robert Frost is largely an attempt to characterize the work itself, which is curiously elusive despite its famous lucidity. Frost *is* a simple poet in many ways: the verbal surface is accessible and attractive, and there is little in the way of complex allusion; these qualities brought to Frost and his poetry an unusually large and appreciative audience, which remains in place a generation after his death. But this popularity has had its negative aspects, and Frost has long been underestimated as a major lyric and narrative poet. This remains so in spite of the efforts of such critics as Randall Jarrell, Lionel Trilling, and Richard Poirier to position him properly as a major Modernist poet. I consider Frost a poet of extraordinary force and vision whose work addresses issues such as human loneliness, mortality, and the great

Emersonian dialectic between the self and the abyss in profoundly original ways. My chapter is an attempt to define these issues and point to the places in his large oeuvre where he achieves that "momentary stay against confusion" that he considered the goal of his art.

Wallace Stevens, on the other hand, occupies the position of a genuinely difficult poet whose centrality and influence have nevertheless become increasingly obvious since his death in 1955. Helen Vendler, who writes on Stevens here, has been crucial in making this complex body of work available to readers. Stevens, in the robustly sensuous lyrics of *Harmonium* through such collections as *The Man with a Blue Guitar*, *Parts of a World*, *Transport to Summer*, and *The Auroras of Autumn*, demonstrated what Vendler calls "the importance of the metaphysical dimension in thought; of the symbolic dimension in both imagery and poetic architecture; the importance of syntax to argument; the value of fable in lyric narrative." He was also able to negotiate "the narrow no-man's-land between regular and free verse" better than any other modern poet except Eliot. Stevens, in his essays as well as in poems about poetry such as "Of Modern Poetry" and "Notes Toward a Supreme Fiction," made a case for "the immense social importance of the imagination," an argument that Vendler says has "yet to be fully absorbed."

William Carlos Williams represents another direction that Modernism took. He disliked the fact that his old friend Ezra Pound deserted the American scene and skipped off to Europe, and he relentlessly criticized what he considered the pompous allusiveness and self-conscious difficulty he saw in the poetry of Pound and Eliot, preferring to write in what he called "the American grain." Deeply influenced by Imagism, his poems are memorably concrete, and they conjure images as bright and clear as any in our poetry. As Christopher MacGowan observes in his chapter on Williams, "The temporal isolation of the image . . . allowed Williams to adopt a strategy common to much American literature." This strategy attempts to "expose and finally discount the failures of the past to fulfill the full promise of the American landscape and the American self." This aspect of Williams "reveals him as a quintessentially American exponent of Modernism, and marks his heritage with Whitman just as much as their joint interest in technical innovation." Williams's career as poet stretched from 1909 until 1962, when his magnificent last book, *Pictures from*

Brueghel, was published. For most of these years, his work received less than its due from critics. Like Stevens, however, it has only gained in influence and readership in the years since his death, and Williams's epic-length poem, *Paterson*, which was published in five books from 1946 to 1958, is considered in some detail by MacGowan and also discussed by Lynn Keller.

Hart Crane was a leading poet of the second generation of Modernist poets; his work has much in common with Pound and Eliot as well as Williams. As J. T. Barbarse puts it: "In about one generation Hart Crane has moved from the position of a reader's guilty pleasure to the James Dean of American poetry, with a legend built on a slim masterpiece, *White Buildings*, and that romancing of Modernism, *The Bridge*." As a homosexual, Crane found life at the margins of American culture difficult, if not impossible; he drowned himself in 1932 at the age of thirty-three. Nonetheless, his slim body of work has been the subject of much debate. Critics such as Yvor Winters have seen Crane as nothing more than a warmed-over Whitman in Modernist dress. *The Bridge*, in particular, owes so much to *The Waste Land* that it has been dismissed as derivative, while Crane's early work is deeply romantic, almost antimodern. On the other hand, he has been wildly praised by some of our strongest critics and fellow poets. Barbarese picks his way judiciously through this minefield in trying to ascertain Crane's consistently alluring if uncertain achievement.

The 1920s was a decade of extraordinary creativity for many American writers, including African American writers, who for the most part were not interested in the Modernist movement per se. A flowering of African American poetry known as the Harlem Renaisssance occured during this period. In his chapter on this important movement Arnold Rampersad examines the term itself, seeing it as a "metaphor for a movement that took place, with varying levels of intensity and success, in several parts of the United States and even beyond." Focusing on such poets as Claude McKay, Jean Toomer, Langston Hughes, Countee Cullen, James Weldon Johnson, Sterling A. Brown, Melvin Tolson, and Arna Bontemps, Rampersad suggests that these poets—some of whom never published a single collection of verse—"played a major role—perhaps the central role—in defining the spirit of the age." Their work was published to great effect in such journals as the *Crisis*, the *Messenger*, and *Opportunity*, and it was anthologized in James Weldon

Johnson's widely read *Book of American Negro Poetry* (1922) and *Negro Poets and Their Poems*, edited by Robert Kerlin and published the following year. The poets included in these pages "laid the foundations for the creative representation of African American social and cultural reality in the modern world," argues Rampersad. And all subsequent African American poets, including those who were part of the Black Arts movement (discussed here by William C. Cook), owe a great deal to these poets.

One of the crucial events in American poetry in the postmodern years was the emigration of W. H. Auden from England in 1939. Auden became an American citizen and he wrote a great deal of his best poetry while a resident here; in addition, his poetry was extraordinarily influential in the immediate postwar years. Theodore Roethke, Richard Wilbur, James Merrill, Richard Howard, and John Hollander can all trace crucial aspects of their work to Auden. Edward Mendelson, a critic of Auden, calls him "the most inclusive poet of the twentieth century, its most technically skilled, and its most truthful." Claude J. Summers concurs in his chapter on Auden as an American poet, suggesting that "emigration permitted Auden to reorient himself and his place in literary tradition. The break with England enabled him to abandon finally the fragmented visions of Romanticism and Modernism that he had earlier espoused for the unified assumptions of Augustanism." Furthermore, "it allowed him eventually to discard the rationalist tenets of liberal humanism for the faith of Christian existentialism." The impressive variety and scope of Auden's later poetry is treated here in detail, and Summers concludes that the goal of Auden's poetry is not visionary transport or political change (Auden once famously said that "poetry makes nothing happen") but "the affirmation of an imperfect world."

At the tail end of High Modernism were the so-called Fugitives, a group of southern poets that includes John Crowe Ransom, Allen Tate, and Robert Penn Warren. Patricia Wallace centers her chapter on Warren, who published his first poems in the 1923 and his last in 1989. The name *Fugitives* derives from a magazine by that name published at Vanderbilt University from 1922 to 1925. Though associated in their own minds with the Modernist movement (they were all admirers of Eliot), the Fugitives became the Agrarians by the time they published a collection of essays called *I'll Take My Stand* in 1930. As Wallace points out, this collection is "a problematic volume." For a start, its assumptions about race are objectionable, and "its advocacy of a return to the land and to traditional values as a cure for economic materialism was wildly off the point in 1930 for many who were hungry and unemployed." While Warren moved well beyond the attitudes expressed in *I'll Take My Stand*, many of his contemporaries did not. Ransom, who wrote a handful of the most gorgeously perfect poems in the whole of our language, suddenly stopped writing in mid-career; Tate was unable to fulfill his early promise; only Warren was left, entering a major and immensely productive phase late in life. "The whole dynamic career offers a model of ongoing creativity," Wallace argues, focusing on several of the later volumes. She points to Warren's continuing influence on younger poets.

After the great Modernist poets, the poets of the Harlem Renaissance, Auden and Warren, one enters the difficult zone of postwar and contemporary poetry. It is notoriously hard to assess one's contemporaries. Anyone who troubles to leaf through old anthologies of American verse will be stunned by how few names are recognizable. What ever became of Richard Henry Stoddard, T. W. Parsons, William Allen Butler, Alice Cary, or Joaquin Miller—each of whom once had a large following? The answer is all too obvious. Tastes shift, and what looks to one generation like "major poetry" often reads like doggerel to the next.

There is a special problem in assessing poets who belong to no recognizable "school" or movement. e. e. cummings, for instance, was immensely productive and popular for many decades in this century, and his work still has admiring readers. It is easily recognizable for its typographical oddity—a surface experimentalism that belies the highly conventional, often sentimental, romanticism of the poetry's content. Another poet difficult to categorize is Conrad Aiken, a contemporary of T. S. Eliot. He was a rigorous, even brilliant, formalist whose best work, embodied in *Preludes for Memnon* (1931), is utterly sui generis. Richard Eberhart is another anomoly: a poet whose best work was written in the late thirties and forties, he is best known for a handful of early poems, "The Groundhog," "For a Lamb," and "The Fury of Aerial Bombardment." Although his production over six decades has been enormous, his work is desperately uneven and has never attracted much in the way of sustained critical treatment. Yvor Winters and J. V. Cunningham also flourished in the immediate postwar years, advocating "discursive" poetry—poems that made an argument—but their work, too, has been hard to place, and it has largely been ignored (though Robert Pinsky, a fine contemporary poet-critic, has paid homage to Winters in his essays and poems).

One of the most prominent groups of writers of the immediate post-war decade were the Beat poets, who have maintained a large and appreciative audience of readers. As Ann Charters says: "The terms *Beat poetry* and the *San Francisco Poetry Renaisssance* refer to two different literary movments created by two loosely associated groups of writers in New York City and San Francisco who first gained a national audience for their work in the mid-1950s." Some of the more prominent members of these linked movements were Allen Ginsberg, Jack Kerouac, Gregory Corso, Lawrence Ferlinghetti, Gary Snyder, Diane DiPrima, and Michael McClure. What these poets share, in addition to a certain time frame and geographical focus, is a jazzy rebelliousness that harks back to Walt Whitman as a poetic father.

The Beat movement can be seen as a response to the restrictive atmosphere of the cold war and, more generally, the postwar emphasis on conforming to certain "traditional" values. Charters writes: "The Beats were determined to put the idealism of the American dream of individual freedom to its ultimate test." The central poetry text of this movement, treated by Keller as well as Charters, is Ginsberg's monumental *Howl* (1956), which was seized by U.S. Customs in San Francisco with the charge of obscenity. Its opening lines still echo down the corridors of the American mind:

> I saw the best minds of my generation destroyed by
> madness, starving hysterical naked,
> dragging themselves through the negro streets at
> dawn looking for an angry fix

Howl effectively reopened the vein of bardic poetry.

Two poets who are often rather misidentified as confessional poets are Theodore Roethke and John Berryman. They are both poets of ecstasy, and both owe a great deal to the traditions of American Romanticism that Emerson and Whitman set in motion. Roethke was able to absorb various streams of English and American verse, and aspects of his poetry reflect a close reading of Whitman, Yeats, Eliot, Stevens, Auden, Donne, and the Elizabethan lyricists. Yet a personal voice does emerge that is both musical and compelling. Roethke was essentially a lyricist, and—as Lea Baechler argues—an elegist. John Berryman was his exact contemporary, and he shared with Roethke an obsession with elegy. Both were poets of memory who explored the fragile mental realms of childhood with great delicacy and fervor; both were traditionalists who played with a range of conventional forms—Berryman favoring open-ended, fragmentary poems, Roethke preferring an almost grandiloquent sense of closure. The two poets are rarely studied together, but there is much to be said for this approach. "Read against each other," Baechler says, "they richly inform our own relation to loss, grief, and the work of mourning, together widening and articulating the ecstatic and terrifying territory of the 'psyche under stress.' "

Diane Wood Middlebrook's focus is on the confessional poets. She writes: "Confessional poetry was not overtly political, but it participated in the protest against Impersonality as a poetic value by reinstating an insistently autobiographical first person engaged in resistance to postwar social norms and the pressure to conform." This poetry is centered on family life, probing for the points of pressure between parents and children in particular. Among the major collections of verse that Middlebrook discusses are Robert Lowell's ground-breaking *Life Studies*, W. D. Snodgrass's *Heart's Needle*, Anne Sexton's *To Bedlam and Part Way Back* and *All My Pretty Ones*, and Sylvia Plath's *Ariel*—all books that belong to the late fifties and early sixties. Like Auden, these poets saw anxiety as the primary condition of the postwar era. But, unlike Auden, they refused to fall back upon religious faith and "the tradition." Each in his or her turn tried psychotherapy and each fell apart in different ways. What they left behind, however, was a body of work of dazzling intensity and craft. "Manifestly ordinary and accesssible," says Middlebrook, "the images of the confessional poem encode the whole culture's shame-making machinery." The influence of these poets on such contemporaries as Adrienne Rich and others is palpable and ongoing.

Indeed, this influence is studied in detail by Gregory Orr, himself a postconfessional poet, in his chapter on the "poetry of self." He sees the postconfessional mode as "a variant on the autobiographical dramatic lyric" that runs from Anne Bradstreet through Louise Glück. In a wide-ranging study he identifies three generations of postconfessionals. The first includes Randall Jarrell, Stanley Kunitz, and Elizabeth Bishop; the second, James Wright, Philip Levine, and Adrienne Rich; the third—a very contemporary group—includes Orr himself, Frank Bidart, Louise Glück, and Sharon Olds. He notes: "Using a variety of literary and psychological strategies, the youngest generation has assimilated the autobiographical encounter into the mainstream of American poetry to such an extent that, thirty years after the confessionals, it is one of the dominant modes of writing."

In a chapter called "Public Music," W. S. DiPiero argues against "the intense personalism of American poetry in recent decades, with its psychological fussiness and maniacally modest self-absorption," which he sees as "a sign of the failure of belief in the possiblitity of poetry as a truly public music." His examples of poets who still believe in this public music are George Oppen and Thomas McGrath, whom he traces back through Ezra Pound and the oral music of the Hopi Indians of Arizona. "The oral poetry of the Hopi prayers, chants, and stories," he writes, is "fused to political observance, political insofar as the social collective can continue to cohere, can keep from going crazy, only if the rituals are observed." He sees the project of Pound's *Cantos* in a similar light: "The encyclopedic didactic procedures of the *Cantos* convince me that Pound wanted his poem to be a political stabilizer as poetry had been in antiquity." And he finds the true inheritors of Pound in the ex-communist poets McGrath and Oppen, both of whom eventually saw poetry as a public space where "public music" could be heard, despite the hard truth and perhaps irreconcilable truth that a "useful poetic language, however much evolved from tradition, is essentially an idiolect, and that sets poets apart from the crowd for whom or toward whom they write."

The Harlem Renaissance, Beat poetry, and the quest for "public speech" are transmogrified in unexpected ways in the Black Arts movement of the late sixties and early seventies. The leading poet of this movement was LeRoi Jones, who later changed his name to Imamu Amiri Baraka. William C. Cook examines the work of Baraka in some detail in his essay here, looking as well at Gwendolyn Brooks, Don Lee (also called Haki R. Madhubuti), Sonia Sanchez, and Nikki Giovanni. His goal is to focus on each poet "at the moment when the contours and dimensions of that poet were being established." These poets forged a distinctly African American aesthetic, which, unlike that of the poets of the Harlem Renaisssance, did not owe much to the familiar traditions of American and English poetry. It was original and fiery, at once politically challenging and formally vexing. As Donald Gibson argues in his introduction to *Modern Black Poets* (1973), "Never before has there been any significant body of literature by black writers so closely resembling a unique black literature."

Lucy Maddox discusses Native American poetry, which (along with Chicano and Asian American poetry) has emerged as one of the richest of contemporary veins. She notes: "The cultural traditions in which Native American poetry are still grounded are the oldest indigenous traditions in North America; at the same time, Native American poetry itself is, in the strictest sense, almost entirely a twentieth-century phenomenon." While she points to the origins of this poetry in such writers as John Rollin Ridge, the mid-nineteenth-century Cherokee writer, as well as such early twentieth-century Native American poets as Emily Pauline Johnson and Lynn Riggs, she focuses on such contemporary poets as Carroll Arnett, Duane Niatum, Simon Ortiz, James Welch, Linda Hogan, Wendy Rose, Ray Young Bear, and Louise Erdrich. Maddox writes: "The particular histories to which this poetry bears eloquent witness have for too long been obscured."

An important feature of the Native American tradition is the sense of the earth as sacred ground. John Elder explores this strain in his chapter on American nature poetry. Beginning his essayistic journey with Robert Frost and concluding with Louise Erdrich (by way of Bradstreet, Whitman, Stevens, Ammons, Jeffers, Snyder, and others), he locates a "central impulse" in American poetry, a "desire to regain intimacy with the earth." He finds a pattern of "therapeutic simplification and regrounding" in this tradition, and he celebrates this "grounded circuit of separation and recovery." Elder also discusses the response of American poets to the "degradation of the natural environment." He sees the poet's task in this age of global catastrophe "as one of creative grieving," and discovers in some of our best contemporary writers "a poetry of identification with the wounded biosphere whose violation we have carried out ourselves." He concludes with a reading of a poem by Louise Erdrich in which he finds "a circuit of return, and of patient encounter with the earth."

Two final chapters focus on four contemporary poets who represent some of the divergent paths our poets have taken in recent years. As I have already suggested, the most difficult part of any survey of American poetry (or the poetry of any nation) comes when the current scene is invoked. One might have, for instance, chosen Adrienne Rich as worthy subject for extensive treatment. Certainly her work is impressive in both range and quality, and it might easily be argued that she is the central poet at work in America today. From her early, highly formal poems to the looser forms of the more recent work, Rich has contributed as much as any poet to the ongoing tradition of American poetry, that "search for a common language" she has so movingly described. And the self-consciously political nature of her work has given an urgency to her voice in all ways striking. On the other hand, one might have chosen any number of other poets who are still in mid-career: John Hollander, Sharon Olds, Linda Pastan, Nancy Willard, Galway Kinnell, Robin Morgan, Richard Howard, Robert Pack, Louise Glück, Louis Simpson, Donald Justice, Nikki Giovanni, Robert Bly, Denise Levertov, Mary Oliver, W. S. Merwin, Mark Strand, Carolyn Kizer, Marilyn Hacker, Anthony Hecht, and Anne Stevenson would all have been fine candidates for study. Because of their visibility and influence, John Ashbery and James Merrill were chosen as representatives of their generation. John Shoptaw offers a fresh reading of the work of these poets. As he notes, "Though Merrill's and Ashbery's primary poetic antecedents—Stevens, Auden, and Bishop—are nearly identical, their descendants hardly recognize each other." He explores the singular paths each has taken toward a complete, self-contained aesthetic.

The final chapter, centered on Philip Levine and Charles Wright, examines the work of two poets who have more recently "arrived" as major voices in the culture, although both have been influential among contemporary poets for the last two decades. Edward Hirsch, himself an award-winning poet, examines what he calls "the visionary poetics" of Levine and Wright. Hirsch writes, "Levine and Wright take fundamentally different stances toward human reality in their work." Levine, for instance, is a poet whose earth-centered work and concern for social justice harks back to Whitman and Williams, while Charles Wright is a mystical visionary whose ancestry includes Dickinson, Dante, Pound, and the Chinese poets of the T'ang Dynasty. What both of these poets share is a tactile sense of the endlessly evolving American attempt to find a language adequate to the vast and diverse landscape and people who inhabit these United States.

"America is a poem in our eyes," says Emerson in his prophetic and endlessly generative essay, "The Poet," which might be read as the first full attempt by one of our writers to incite a national literature into being. "The poet is the Namer or Language-maker, naming things sometimes after their appearance, sometimes after their essence, and giving to every one its own name and not another's, thereby rejoicing the intellect, which delights in detachment or boundary," Emerson continues. This call-to-the-future has modulated, most recently, into Adrienne Rich's "struggle to name the world," into Philip Levine's harsh evocation of men in Detroit working on the assembly line, into Charles Wright's passionate search for a language of redemption. The forms, the styles, proliferate as we continue to discover a national consciouness: to have it, to feel it, in order to go *through* it. Exactly where and how this nation will emerge in its postnational incarnation is something future poets and critics will have to confront. I leave it, happily, to them.

Jay Parini

The
COLUMBIA
History of
AMERICAN
POETRY

Anne Bradstreet and Edward Taylor

L IKE most literate English people American Puritans took a great
deal of pleasure in reading and writing poetry. They marked
the course of history, gave thanks to public figures, learned
their theology, examined their consciences, mourned the dead, honored
their loved ones, celebrated the creation, and translated the Bible in a
variety of poetic forms. Puritans of every occupation—schoolmasters,
housewives, ship captains, and lawyers—tried their hands at making
verse, although given the seventeenth-century preference for a literature
that combined learning with wit it is not surprising that the educated
clergyman, trained in Latin, Hebrew, and Greek, was more adept at it.

In his often quoted guide to young ministers (*Manuductio ad Min-
isterium*, 1726) the learned Boston divine Cotton Mather shuddered
at the thought of New England clergy reading the pagan Homer
("one of the greatest apostles the devil ever had in the world"); nevertheless he had to admit that Homer's example of an invocation uttered
as a "preface unto all important enterprizes" could serve as a useful
model for the seminary student, and that the Latin of Virgil, especially in his *Georgics*, "will furnish you with many things far from
despicable."

Though some have had a soul so unmusical, that they have decried all verse as
being but a mere playing and fiddling upon words; all versifying as if it were a
more unnatural thing than if we should choose dancing instead of walking, and
rhyme as if it were but a sort of moresco-dancing with bells, yet I cannot wish
you a soul that shall be wholly unpoetical.

At the same time, and with serious consequences for the kind of poetry Harvard graduates would write, Mather cautioned that while making "a little recreation of poetry in the midst of your painful studies" was a good thing, the wise student will withhold his "throat from thirst" and beware the temptation to "be always pouring on the passionate and measured pages." Above all, he warned the student reading Ovid to take care not to be sensually aroused and find himself conversing with "muses" no better "than harlots." Mather concluded his essay with an appeal for calm in the current debate between the plain and learned style, arguing that Christian gentlemen indulge one another in matters of taste and, at the same time, letting his readers know that as far as *he* was concerned, the real "excellency of a book will never lie in the saying of little," nor will it be more valuable because it shuns "erudition." Mather's own rather clumsy efforts at verse (his best poem was written following the death of seven young ministers), reminds us that the passionate amateur, full of good intentions but not totally committed to his craft, does not produce lines that breathe. Some Harvard students were content to copy lines from Shakespeare and Herrick in their diaries, and it was probably just as well. Fortunately, two Puritan poets took their art more seriously.

Both spent their formative years in England. Anne Bradstreet (c. 1612–1672) was the second of six children born to Thomas Dudley and Dorothy Yorke. We know very little about her mother, but her father's career as manager of the estate of the Earl of Lincoln and, later, as governor of Massachusetts four times and thirteen times deputy governor, is well documented. He came to America in 1630 aboard the flagship *Arbella* as one of the founders of the Massachusetts Bay Colony. His daughter and her husband, Simon Bradstreet, were with him. Together they established formidable households, with both men well trained in business and law. Simon was himself to serve as secretary to the colony and governor for ten years. Thomas Dudley was something of a poet and, for this period, unusual in his encouragement of his daughter's literary appetite. It seems fitting that she should dedicate her most ambitious literary effort (her "Quaternions," or poems on groups of four: the four elements, the four humors, the four ages of man, the four seasons of the year, and the four monarchies—the Assyrian, the Persian, the Grecian, and the Roman) to him. In her dedication she acknowledges her debt to the example of Guillaume Du Bartas (a writer now almost forgotten, but whose *Divine Weeks* as translated by Joshua Sylvester in 1641 was one of the most popular poems in seventeenth-century England) as her model, but she hopes her father will recognize his daughter's particular voice in that crowd of voices which constitutes the music of any beginning poet's work:

> I honor him, but dare not wear his wealth,
> My goods are true (though poor), I love no stealth,
> But if I did, I durst not send them you,
> Who must reward a thief, but with his due.
> I shall not need my innocence to clear,
> These ragged lines will do't, when they appear.
> On what they are, your mild aspect I crave,
> Accept my best, my worst vouchsafe a grave.
> ("To Her Most Honored Father")

When Bradstreet wrote these lines she must have done so with some future publication in mind. She shared her poems with friends and relatives and was sensitive to the fact that her reputation as wife and mother and slave to the Muses was the subject of gossip. It is characteristic of her in "The Prologue" to these poems to handle this criticism with forthrightness and a determination to proceed with her writing.

> I am obnoxious to each carping tongue
> Who says my hand a needle better fits,
> A poet's pen all scorn I should thus wrong,
> For such despite they cast on female wits:
> If what I do prove well, it won't advance,
> They'll say it's stol'n, or else it was by chance.

Bradstreet's brother-in-law, Rev. John Woodbridge, decided, without Bradstreet's permission, to let New England audiences determine this matter for themselves. On a trip to London in 1647 he brought with him a manuscript including thirteen Bradstreet poems. They were published in 1650 by Stephen Bowtell "at the sign of the Bible in Popes Head-Alley," and entitled *The Tenth Muse Lately sprung up in America*, written "By a Gentlewoman in those parts." Bradstreet's name first appears at the close of the dedicatory poem to her father. The poems have rarely been out of the public eye since. Bradstreet said the book's publication caught her by surprise and made her "blush." By the year 1666 she was anticipating a new edition:

> I cast thee by as one unfit for light,
> Thy visage was so irksome in my sight;
> Yet being mine own, at length affection would
> Thy blemishes amend, if so I could:
> I washed thy face, but more defects I saw,
> And rubbing off a spot still made a flaw.
>
> ("The Author to her Book")

No manuscript exists, but the publication by John Foster of Boston, Massachusetts, in 1678 of *Several Poems* "By a Gentlewoman in New England . . . Corrected by the Author and enlarged by an Addition of several other Poems found amongst her Papers after her Death," clearly represents our first genuine poet at her best. Most of the poems she added to *The Tenth Muse*—"Contemplations," "The Flesh and the Spirit," "Before the Birth of one of her Children," and three poems on her grandchildren, for example—are those works upon which Anne Bradstreet's present literary reputation rests. For, in contrast to the ingenious and often gnarled efforts of her male contemporaries, she speaks artfully but directly from her pages:

> If ever two were one, then surely we.
> If ever man were loved by wife, then thee;
> If ever wife was happy in a man,
> Compare with me, ye women, if you can.
> I prize thy love more than whole mines of gold
> Or all the riches of the East doth hold.
> My love is such that rivers cannot quench,
> Nor ought but love from thee, give recompense.
> Thy love is such I can no way repay,
> The heavens reward thee manifold, I pray.
> Then while we live, in love let's so persevere
> That when we live no more, we may live ever.
>
> ("To My Dear and Loving Husband")

"Contemplations" remains her best long poem. It is a work full of the wonder of the creation:

> Under the cooling shadow of a stately elm
> Close sat I by a goodly river's side,

> Where gliding streams the rocks did overwhelm,
> A lonely place, with pleasures dignified.
> I once that loved the shady woods so well,
> Now thought the rivers did the trees excel,
> And if the sun would ever shine, there would I dwell.

For all the attraction of the landscape, however, Bradstreet is no romantic. There is nothing in her poems to give Cotton Mather pause. She knows that winter always follows summer and age takes its toll of beauty. What makes the poem so pleasing is the way in which the reader, like the writer, takes the lure—only to get caught:

> Silent alone, where none or saw, or heard,
> In pathless paths I lead my wand'ring feet,
> My humble eyes to lofty skies I reared
> To sing some song, my mazed Muse thought meet.
> My great Creator I would magnify,
> That nature had thus decked liberally,
> But Ah, and Ah, again, my imbecility!

What she had forgotten is the petty reward of the temporal when viewed in eternity's perspective. Knowing the conventions of Renaissance moral verse, one might have anticipated the turn of her ending without having anticipated the power of her last lines and the striking use she makes of Biblical allusion:

> O Time the fatal wrack of mortal things,
> That draws oblivion's curtains over kings;
> Their sumptuous monuments, men know them not,
> Their names without a record are forgot,
> Their parts, their ports, their pomp's all laid in th' dust,
> Nor wit nor gold, nor buildings scape time's rust;
> But he whose name in graved in the white stone
> Shall last and shine when all of these are gone.

In 1867 John Harvard Ellis published *The Works of Anne Bradstreet in Prose and Verse*. In doing so he provided modern readers with not only Bradstreet's "Meditations when my Soul hath been refreshed with the Consolations which the world knows not," but a remarkable spiritual autobiography addressed to her "dear children":

> This Book by Any yet unread,
> I leave for you when I am dead,

> That being gone, here you may find
> What was your living mother's mind.

Puritan men and women were in the habit of keeping diaries and making notes on their spiritual histories, but those that survive are often predictable and confess nothing more alarming than disobedience to their parents. Bradstreet's is notable for her frank confession that although she has "sometimes tasted of that hidden manna that the world knows not," she has just as often been perplexed because her spiritual pilgrimage has not been one of "constant joy." Instead, there have been "times of sinkings and droopings"; she has doubted the truth of the Scriptures and wondered "whether there was a God." "I never saw any miracles to confirm me," she adds, "and those which I read of how did [I] know but they were feigned." It seems fitting that she finally settled on a poet's rather than a theologian's way of resolving her doubts.

That there is a God my reason would soon tell me by the wondrous works that I see, the vast frame of the heaven and the earth, the order of all things, night and day, summer and winter, spring and autumn, the daily providing for this great household upon the earth, the preserving and directing of all to its proper end.

Puritans were not indifferent to the things of this world. Some of the most eloquent passages about the American landscape can be found in the writings of Samuel Sewall and Jonathan Edwards. But Puritan men and women were constantly reminded of the difference between this fleeting world and the city of heavenly light:

> The city where I hope to dwell,
> There's none on earth can parallel;
> The stately walls both high and strong,
> Are made of precious jasper stone;
> The gates of pearl, both rich and clear,
> And angels are for porters there;
> The streets thereof transparent gold,
> Such as no eye did e'er behold;
> A crystal river there doth run,
> Which doth proceed from the Lamb's throne.
>   ("The Flesh and the Spirit")

Yet knowing something intellectually and living it are two quite different things. Bradstreet's poetry is attractive to us because she is so honest about her affections. Her ultimate love is for Christ—"upon this rock Christ Jesus will I build my faith, and if I perish, I perish"—but the here and now has its charms. In her delight in her marriage, in the sadness that followed the burning of her house, in the rewards of parenting, and in the heartbreaking loss of children she explores a tension between this world and the next that transcends the age in which she lived.

Edward Taylor (c. 1642–1729) was thirty years younger than Anne Bradstreet and arrived in Boston just four years before her death. Given his impressive social connections (his reputation as a Nonconforming student and teacher preceded him), he could have met the Andover poet, but it seems unlikely. He did, however, acquire a copy of *Several Poems* and added it to his remarkable library. Because Taylor's place in American literature is so assured, it is curious that so little has been discovered concerning his English years. Incomplete parish and university records have contributed to the mystery. What *is* known is that he was born in Sketchley (Burbage parish), Leicestershire County, England, during the civil wars. His father was a prosperous farmer, and years later Taylor would apply lessons learned as a boy to the soil of western Massachusetts. His familiarity with the vocabulary of the weaving trade suggests that he may have worked in a nearby shop at Hinckley. Leicestershire County was sympathetic to church dissidents and Taylor's contempt for all things Anglican was probably encouraged by the curriculum of the local schools. With obvious consequences for his poetry both early and late, he read Calvin and Augustine, learned Latin, Greek, and Hebrew, and examined exegetical texts on Job and the Canticles (or Songs of Solomon). Leicestershire schools also encouraged the study of poets like Francis Quarles and George Herbert (the least Anglican of Anglicans), and so it is that unlike Bradstreet, who modeled her music on the mellifluent measures of Sidney and Spenser, Taylor preferred the more dissonant music of the metaphysical poets, where the erudite and the colloquial, the languages of theology and farming commingled in a verse full of surprises, delighting in puns and paradoxes. Taylor would have been happy teaching in country schools just like the one he attended, but the restoration of Charles II in 1660 and difficult times for Nonconformists that followed served as an impetus to leave England and start life anew. After three years of study in Cambridge, Massachusetts, Taylor accepted a call to become the minister to the frontier town of Westfield, one hundred miles west of Harvard Yard. There he remained for the next fifty-eight years, serving as minister, physician, and public servant with great distinction.

The last of his "Preparatory Meditations" is dated 1725, the year of his retirement.

Taylor was not unknown as a poet to his contemporaries. In 1689 Cotton Mather published two stanzas of "Upon Wedlock and Death of Children," and, later, family geneologists and historians noted that he wrote verse. But it was not until Thomas H. Johnson published a sample of Taylor's work in 1937 that the world knew of the existence of a remarkable body of Puritan poetry. Johnson had been working on lives of Harvard graduates and read in John Sibley's collection of biographical sketches (1885) a brief description of Taylor's poetry. He tracked the manuscript book down and discovered it in the Yale University Library, where it had been deposited by a Taylor descendant in 1883. Johnson published a fuller selection of Taylor's work in 1939, but it was only with the publication of *The Poems of Edward Taylor*, edited by Donald E. Stanford in 1960, that the full commitment of Taylor to the act of writing poetry was revealed. The Johnson and Stanford editions of Edward Taylor did much to revise our notions of Puritans and their attitudes toward art.

Early on in Taylor criticism some mistakes were made. Family tradition perpetuated a notion that Taylor had forbidden the publication of his verse and had left instructions in his will to this effect. Furthermore, the poetry seemed too sensuous, its imagery too abundant, its tone too playful and intimate to fit the stereotype of Puritan verse. It was not uncommon to find critics hinting that Taylor was secretely Anglican in sympathy, paying too much attention to the sacrament of communion (or the Lord's Supper as the Puritans would call it) and writing too much like Donne or Crashaw not to be an anomaly. Scholarship written over the last forty years has changed all this. Taylor left no will, he died intestate, and when his relations with other Connecticut Valley ministers were explored and his sermons published, it became clear that his orthodoxy was not only unwavering, it could more accurately be described as inflexible to a fault. As to publication, the standard literary taste was dictated by London, and Taylor's poems would have seemed a hundred years behind time in 1729.

The manuscript book "Poetical Works" does not contain all of Taylor's poetry—there is a hefty four hundred and thirty-eight-page "Metrical History of Christianity," a kind of martyrology, at the Redwood Athenaeum in Newport, Rhode Island, now transcribed by Donald Stanford, for example—but it contains all of Taylor's best work. In part it is a commonplace book, and the two Latin poems with which it begins are not by Taylor but by President Charles Chauncy of Harvard, a friend of Taylor's, on the death of John Davenport, the great spiritual leader of the New Haven colony. Some of what it includes by Taylor are elegies, acrostic poems, a letter to his wife, Elizabeth Fitch, a college declamation, a poem written on the recovery of an illness in 1720, and an attack on a legendary female pope of the ninth century. All rather predictable seventeenth-century subjects for a Congregational minister. The manuscript book is fully described in Stanford. For present-day readers of American poetry there are three treasures: a group of miscellaneous lyrics, a long poem called "Gods Determinations touching his Elect: and the Elects Combat in their Conversion, and Coming up to God in Christ together with the Comfortable Effects thereof," and an almost complete group of "Preparatory Meditations before my approach to the Lords Supper. Chiefly upon the Doctrine preached upon the Day of Administration." Two hundred and seventeen meditations have survived, an extraordinary effort at sustained verse writing in any period.

It was the opening lines to "The Preface" to *Gods Determinations* that first captured the imagination of Taylor's readers, and no one who has written about him since has failed to quote them:

> Infinity, when all things it beheld
> In Nothing and of Nothing all did build,
> Upon what Base was fixt the Lath, wherein
> He turn'd this Globe, and riggalled it so trim? . . .
> Who Lac'de and Fillitted the earth so fine,
> With Rivers like green Ribbons Smaragdine? . . .
> Who Spread its Canopy? Or Curtain's Spun?
> Who in this Bowling Alley bowld the Sun?

Like Bradstreet, Taylor delights in God's creation, but the portrait here of God as craftsman, forger, architect, mason, and embroiderer, and, most fetchingly, a player in the great bowling alley of the universe, is unique. Juxtaposed to this Great Giver is ungrateful man, who disobeyed his Creator and forfeited Paradise in doing so. God, Taylor sighs,

> Gave All to nothing Man indeed, whereby
> Through nothing man all might him Glorify . . .
> But Nothing man did throw down all by Sin:

> And darkened that lightsome Gem in him.
>> That now his brightest Diamond is grown
>> Darker by far than any Coalpit stone.

Of course, for the Puritan, this is just half the tale. Paradise lost and Paradise regained is at the heart of the Christian story. It's the great subject of Michael Wigglesworth's "The Day of Doom" (1662), the most popular poem ever written in America, a work Taylor's wife knew by heart. Most famous for the fire and brimstone passages describing the soul's suffering in hell, we forget that this poem is as much about its ending as its beginning, describing the saints (for the Puritan, those believers who are saved) happy in Christ's embrace:

> For there the saints are perfect saints,
>> and holy ones indeed,
> From all the sin that dwelt within
>> their mortal bodies freed:
> Made kings and priests to God through Christ's
>> dear love's transcendency,
> There to remain, and there to reign
>> with Him eternally.

Gods Determinations dramatizes the struggle between Satan and Christ over the lost sinner, and Taylor never lets his reader forget the most extraordinary gift God gave him: the new Covenant of Faith that replaced the old Covenant of Works, broken by Adam in his disobedience. The crucifixion is Christ's cost and promise that the gates of heaven are open to those who believe in Him. Some of Taylor's finest lyric moments follow "The Souls groan to Christ for Succour," when Christ assures humanity that the powerful creature Satan would have us take him for is really "broken tootht, and muzzled sure:"

> Peace, Peace, my Honey, do not Cry,
> My Little Darling, wipe thine eye,
>> Oh Cheer, Cheer up, come see.
> Is anything too deare, my Dove,
> Is anything too good, my Love
>> To get or give for thee?

God's Determinations ends as every Puritan might have known it would, with Christ triumphant; but the idea of all the saints sharing a carriage and singing joyously on their journey toward heaven would have brought a smile to Taylor's contemporaries had they been able to read it:

> In Heaven soaring up, I dropt an Eare
> > On Earth: and Oh! sweet Melody:
> And listening, found it was the Saints who were
> > Encoacht for Heaven that sang for Joy.
> For in Christs coach they sweetly sing;
> As they to Glory ride therein.
> ("The Joy of Church Fellowship Rightly Attended")

Seventeenth-century poets working in a metaphysical tradition saw nothing incongruous about a poem dealing with salvation taking its figures from everyday events like carriage rides; neither did Puritan historians mind expending their energies reading ordinary events—none too small or insignificant—as signs of God's will. When the governor of Massachusetts saw a snake and a mouse in mortal combat, he was surprised to see the mouse emerge as victor, but his friend, Mr. Wilson, said it was a sign guaranteeing the triumph of the New England experiment, all the evidence one needed to prove that New Englanders will "overcome Satan here and dispossess him of his kingdom." This is a habit of mind going back hundreds of years, and Taylor makes ingenious use of it in watching a spider catching a fly, or a wasp chilled with cold coming to life in the sun, or thinking how much the wavering Christian looks like someone trying to avoid getting wet by running between buildings:

> Ye Flippering Soule,
> > Why dost between the Nippers dwell?
> Not stay, nor goe. Not yea, nor yet Controle.
> > Doth this doe well?
>
> Rise journy'ng when the skies fall weeping
> > showers
> Not o're nor under th' Clouds and Cloudy
> > Powers.
> > > ("Let by Rain")

In these poems Taylor employs Elizabethan song forms, and with a little patience for counting syllables and some skill at noting elision, the reader will see that this stanza has lines of 4, 8, 10, 4, 10 and 10 syllables, and this pattern is repeated in the stanzas that follow. They could have been set to music but they weren't. Taylor's "Huswifery" is the most famous of these lyrics. Taylor is thinking about the process of making cloth, and, in particular, the garment that will be a mark of salvation for the wearer. We know from his collection of sermons on the Lord's Supper that he has a passage from Matthew (22:12) in mind. This is the story of the servant who invited all to attend a wedding feast but then turned away one he had earlier urged to come: "And he saith unto him, Friend, how camest thou in hither not having a wedding garment?" For Taylor, the proper garment reflects the condition of the soul:

> Then cloath therewith mine Understanding, Will,
> Affections, Judgment, Conscience, Memory,
> My words and actions, that their shine may fill
> My wayes with glory and thee glorify.
> Then mine apparell shall display before yee
> That I am Cloathd in Holy robes for glory.

Puritans preferred the phrase *Lord's Supper* to Anglican or Roman Catholic *holy communion* because they thought of this sacrament as something to be shared. Communion could be taken by a priest in the privacy of a chapel; the Lord's Supper could not. However, they did not believe it should be shared by all. The seventeenth-century English Puritan Thomas Manton declared: "The [Biblical] word speaks to all promiscuously, as inviting; the sacraments to everyone in particular, as obliging [i.e., contractual]." New England Congregationalists, until quite late, saw this sacrament (baptism was the only other sacrament Puritan men and women celebrated) as denoting a particular mark of worthiness, to be received only by church members (not the whole congregation) who testified that they had passed beyond a mere "historical understanding" of scripture to a heartfelt "saving faith," an inner conviction of the message of Christ and a concomitant assurance of salvation. Of course, there was always the possibility of false assurance; as a result, good Puritans, as Taylor put it, lived "within doore," examining their consciences, and preparing for their monthly participation in this holiest of rites by meditating on scripture. The observation of a recent critic that Taylor's "Preparatory Meditations" are "distinctly non-Puritan," is quite wrong. We have no example of another New England writer who chose to make his poetry a spiritual diary of his response to the gift of the Lord's Supper, but neither the idea of meditation nor the language of Taylor's poetry is inconsistent with Puritan devotional practice. We will never know whether his first meditation, dated July 23, 1682, continues a method to which he had long been accustomed or represents an experimental beginning, but the fact that Taylor seems so immediately comfortable (if that's ever the word for a poetry that is always straining) with his six-line iambic pentameter stanza and its unvarying rhyme scheme suggests some earlier practice in the form. We do not have meditations for every month of the year—far from it—nor do we know exactly at what moment he wrote his poem (i.e., before or after a sermon was delivered), but we may take him at his word that his poems were written "chiefly" in response to the "Doctrine preached upon the Day of Administration" of a sacrament that was meant, as John Preston put it in 1638, to "knit the knot stronger between Christ and us."

The method of meditation that Taylor follows has a long tradition in devotional literature and always begins with the dramatization of the Biblical text, known as the "composition of place," an exercise in which the penitent tries to realize, in the most sensual way, the historical context in which the scriptural passage unfolds. What follows from this tuning up of the senses is an intellectual exercise in which the doctrinal and moral consequences of the scriptural passage are explored. This is known as an "examination of points." The final step in the meditative process is the most important one for students of Taylor's poetry, for it is the end of all meditation: colloquy, talking with God, opening the door, as Richard Baxter has put it, "between head and heart," speaking, as St. Ignatius Loyola advises, "just as one friend talks to another, or a servant to his master; now asking some favor, now blaming himself for some ill deed, now disclosing his affairs and seeking counsel in them." Taylor's "Preparatory Meditations" are hymns from the heart, outpourings in which the sinner, moved by or anticipating grace, lifts his voice in thanksgiving.

No one of the 217 surviving meditations is representative of all. Some contemplate the old Covenant of Works and the new Covenant of Faith ("Is Christ thy Advocate to plead thy Cause?"), some examine the speaker's weaknesses ("was ever Heart like mine? / A Sty of Filth, a Trough of Washing-Swill"), some contemplate Old Testament types as they are fulfilled in the New Testament by the antitype Christ ("Art thou, Lord, Abrahams Seed and Issac too?"), while some, representing many years wrestling with the Canticles, celebrate the soul's union with Christ:

> Lord! let thy Holy Spirit take my hand
>   And opening thy Graces garden doore
> Lead mee into the Same that I well fann'd
>   May by thy Holy Spirit bee all ore
>   And make my Lungs thy golden Bagpipes right
>   Filld with this precious Aire, thy praises pipe.
>   ("Meditation 129, Second Series")

These texts seem especially appropriate for meditations on a "love feast," to use Cotton Mather's phrase, and apt, too, for a Puritan who would praise God in song. Taylor knows the limits of art, but he also is aware that ours is a "fortunate" Fall, and that he is loved by a God who is generous and whose grace is free. This gives him the confidence to say:

> Unite my Soule, Lord, to thyselfe, and stamp
>   Thy holy print on my unholy heart.
> I'st nimble be when thou destroyst my cramp
>   And take thy paths when thy dost take my part.
>   If thou wilt blow this Oaten Straw of mine,
>   The sweetest piped praises shall be thine.
>   ("Meditation 44, Second Series")

The metaphysical style that so appealed to Puritan poets came into disfavor long before the seventeenth century ended, and was treated with contempt by most eighteenth-century critics. Its virtues were lost to American readers until Emerson and the New England Transcendentalists discovered the poetry of Herbert. But in a literature given to self-scrutiny it is a style bound to play a vital part, as the work of T. S. Eliot, Allen Tate, Hart Crane, John Crowe Ransom, Robert Lowell, and Amy Clampitt so brilliantly attests.

Francis Murphy

Further Reading

Bradstreet, Anne. *The Complete Works of Anne Bradstreet*. Ed. J. R. McElrath, Jr., and A. P. Robb. Boston: Twayne, 1981.

Bradstreet, Anne. *The Works of Anne Bradstreet*. Ed. Jeannine Hensley. Cambridge: Harvard University Press, 1967.

Davis, Thomas M. and Virginia L. *Edward Taylor's Minor Poetry*. New York: Twayne, 1981.

Grabo, Norman S. *Edward Taylor*. New York: Twayne, 1988.

Lewalski, Barbara Kiefer. *Protestant Poetics and the Seventeenth-Century Religious Lyric*. Princeton: Princeton University Press, 1979.

Meserole, Harrison T. *Seventeenth-Century American Poetry*. New York: Doubleday, 1968.

Morgan, Edmund S. *Visible Saints*. New York: New York University Press, 1963.

Murdock, Kenneth B. *Literature and Theology in Colonial New England*. Cambridge: Harvard University Press, 1949.

Piercy, Josephine Ketcham. *Anne Bradstreet*. New York: Twayne, 1965.

Rowe, Karen E. *Saint and Singer: Edward Taylor's Typology and the Poetics of Meditation*. New York: Cambridge University Press, 1986.

Scheick, William J. *The Will and the Word: The Poetry of Edward Taylor*. Athens: University of Georgia Press, 1974.

Stanford, Ann. *Anne Bradstreet the Worldly Puritan*. New York: B. Franklin, 1974.

Taylor, Edward. *The Poems of Edward Taylor*. Ed. Donald E. Stanford. New Haven: Yale University Press, 1960.

Wakefield, Gordon S. *Puritan Devotion*. London: Epworth Press, 1957.

White, Elizabeth Wade. *Anne Bradstreet: The Tenth Muse*. New York: Oxford University Press, 1971.

Early African American Poetry

FRICAN AMERICAN poetry began in the lyrics attached to field
hollers, ring shouts, rudimentary work songs, and songs of
familial entertainment in the early colonies of the Americas—in the North, South, and the Caribbean. These musical verses were
characterized by insistent call and and response patterns, complex
African and neo-African polyrhythms, the adaptation of European
rhyme as a means of complexifying rhythm, and the transformation and
incorporation of European harmonies into distinctive chords, which
were the forerunners of chords and lyrics that characterize the African
American lyrical poetic genres of gospel, blues, jazz, the toast, the
chanted sermon, rhythm and blues, soul, rap, and contemporary polyphonic poetry. The polyphonic poetry of such twentieth-century poets
as Derek Walcott, E. Kamau Brathwaite, June Jordan, Audre Lorde,
Robert Hayden, Ishmael Reed, Countee Cullen, Lorna Goodison,
Langston Hughes, Jay Wright, Rita Dove, Ai, and Etheridge Knight
all reconstrue African rhythmic complexity with creative and personally distinctive transformations of Euro-American, African American,
Caribbean, Latin American, and Asian styles and motifs. The designa-
tion *African American*, while an appropriate term for cultural identification, is yet another incomplete summary of a black people more accurately called the African-British-European-Native American-Asian
peoples of the Americas.

Many early accounts of contact between Europeans and Africans in
the Americas describe the facility with which Africans not only creat-

ed their own musical instruments to accompany poetry but also mastered and transformed the uses of European instruments in the development of distinctively African American accompaniment to the oral poetry of black slaves. The begrudging and racist compliments paid to these artistic slaves by their European observers cannot mask the prevalence of high skill in the composition of rhythmic oral poetry by the slaves. In one Caribbean account from the early 1660s an Englishman expresses acute astonishment when an African slave, denied the use of a European stringed instrument, makes one of better quality himself, from which he develops music to accompany oral poetry, causing the Englishman to acknowledge that the black man is human, and a genius at that.

Such descriptions are scant, and it is often difficult to filter a few reliable events from the heavy layering of racism in the perceptions of the Europeans. Unfortunately, if contemporary descriptions of their lyric poetry by the Africans themselves existed in oral or written form they are now lost to us except in the continued presence of the rhythms themselves in African American culture. In addition, for several reasons the development of polyrhythmic African American poetry is difficult to trace from colonial times to the 1920s, when scholars and others began to keep more complete records of overtly musical poetry. There was not only the problem of racial prejudice in encouraging observers to ignore poetic accomplishments in oral composition of Africans in the Americas—European and American culture as a whole belittles the oral for the sake of the written, and today not even the knowledge that the Homeric epics were composed orally is enough to convince an audience determined to believe that written texts are more intelligent and artistic than oral ones. Oral texts are persistently characterized as "folk" texts, that is to say, unaccomplished, as if human beings cease to be folk and become people once they write rather than speak their poetry.

As a result of these narrow aesthetic principles it is more convenient to describe the development of African American poetry through those written poetic works that evoke more obvious comparison with European and American poetry through formal structure, theme, and diction. Such works are numerous, although they have received little attention throughout their history. In spite of the fact that many have been published and recognized as poetry they have often been ignored by white and black critics. Unlike the orally composed poems these written poems are usually not anonymous. In form these written, self-conscious poems rely upon Euro-American construction, although they often incorporate aspects of African-influenced oral poetry, as in Maurice N. Corbett's *The Harp of Ethiopia* (1914), in which the poet sets aside the regular iambic tetrameter rhythm and uses an irregular jazz rhythm in the section entitled "The Harp Awaking." In other instances African American diction and vocabulary is blended with Euro-American poetic forms, and one poem, *De Cabin* (1915), by Fenton Johnson, uses African American dialect in regular iambic pentameter blank verse.

Nineteenth-century African American formal poems thus are a continuum of poetic experiences with irregular relationships to the oral or folk poetry of the African American people. The poems are more likely to reveal the race of the author through theme rather than word choice. The late nineteenth century was a poetic battleground in which African American poets demanded equality with whites by demonstrating equality in artistic achievement. The cultural world view then prevalent insisted that all that was best in the white world was best for all. African Americans thus attempted to prove their facility in aesthetic forms valued by whites, and neither African Americans nor whites insisted that art forms that were only black (e.g., blues, gospel, jazz) could have as high an aesthetic merit. The African American writers Frances Harper and Charles Chesnutt, for example, condemned blues poetry in their novels, although both were stalwart workers for racial equality and freedom. World War I cracked this ethnocentric world view, so that, starting in the 1920s, African American poets took full freedom in developing distinctive poetry with styles derived from Africa, African America, Europe, the Caribbean, North and South America, and even Asia.

The earliest known formal written poem by an African American is "Bars Flight" by Lucy Terry (1730–1821) in 1746. The twenty-eight-line poem recounts the fate of seven colonists attacked by Native Americans during a raid on Deerfield, Massachusetts. The poem is in irregular iambic tetrameter verse in which the author relates the particular circumstances of death or escape of her fellow villagers—Samuel Allen, singled out as the most aggressive of the colonists, is kidnapped and carried away by the raiders, John Saddler escapes across the water—and the largest number of verses are devoted to the one woman under attack, Eunice Allen.

Eunice Allen see the Indians comeing [*sic*],
And hoped to save herself by running,
And had not her petticoats stopt her,
The awful creatures had not cotched her,
And tommyhawked her on the head,
And left her on the ground for dead;

Lucy Terry was a slave of Ebenezer Wells of Deerfield, Massachusetts until 1756, when she received her freedom and married the free black, Abijah Prince. Her only poem was first published in 1895 in George Sheldon's *A History of Deerfield, Massachusetts*. She was a vigorous woman, and fought an unsuccessful court battle, going all the way to the Supreme Court, to have her son enrolled at Williams College.

Jupiter Hammon (1720?–1806?), a slave to three generations of the New York Lloyd family, was the first African American poet whose work was published in what was to become the United States. His poems: "An Evening Thought. Salvation by Christ, with Penetential Cries" (1760–61); "An Address to Miss Phillis Wheatly" (1778); "An Essay on Ten Virgins" (1779, no copy extant); "A Poem for Children, with Thoughts on Death" (with a prose piece, "A Winter Place," 1782); and "An Evening's Improvement," to which is appended "The Kind Master and the Dutiful Servant" (n.d.). Hammon's poetry reveals his strong attachment to the Wesleyan Christian revival, and, on his own behalf and that of other slaves, including Phillis Wheatley, he persistently gives thanks for having been brought into slavery for the higher purpose of becoming Christians. There is a subtle if unintentional irony in Hammon's association of Christianity with freedom. In "An Evening Thought" he writes,

Dear Jesus, by the precious Blood
    The World Redemption have:
Salvation now comes from the Lord,
    He being they captive slave.
. . . .
Ho! every one that hunger hath,
    Or pineth after me,
Salvation be thy leading Staff,
    To set the Sinner free.

Here the concepts of captivity and freedom are ambiguous enough to refer to the sinner's relationship with God as well as the slave's relationship with his master. In "The Kind Master" Hammon explicitly derives the obedience of the slave as a response to the slave's observing the master's obedience to God.

Throughout the early history of slavery in the colonies and in the United States slave owners were divided as to whether Christians could enslave other Christians, and African slaves were often denied access to Christian doctrine for fear such doctrine would eliminate them as slaves. Phillis Wheatley (1753?–1784) was certainly aware of the link between religious belief and freedom in the three versions of her poem dedicated to George Whitefield. In the earliest version (1770) of this poem, printed in broadside, Wheatley implies that Africans who become Christians must be set free.

> Take HIM, ye *Africans*, he longs for you;
> Impartial SAVIOUR, is his TITLE due;
> If you will walk in Grace's heavenly Road,
> He'll make you free, and Kings, and Priests to God.

The implication that Christianity could free African slaves evidently was highly unacceptable to Wheatley's slaveowning audience, and in a broadside printed later that year the offensive statement was changed to read:

> Take HIM, ye *Africans*, he longs for you;
> Impartial SAVIOUR is his title due;
> If you will chuse to walk in grace's road,
> You shall be sons, and kings, and priests to GOD.

In the final version of the poem, published in *Poems on Various Subjects Religious and Moral* (1773), the freedom and grace to be accorded to African Christians is replaced, certainly through the insistence of her publisher, with suffering and blood.

> "Take him, ye *Africans*, he longs for you,
> "*Impartial Saviour* is his title due:
> "Wash'd in the fountain of redeeming blood,
> "You shall be sons, and kings, and priests to God."

Wheatley's collection was the first book of poetry to be published by an African American and the second book by a woman within what would become the United States. It was published as a result of her trip to England in 1773, a visit sponsored by the Wheatley family to improve the health of Phillis, who was treated with exceptional consideration and pride by the Wheatley family. After the publication of her book Wheatley lived as a free black, although her legal manumission papers have not been found. The existence of a poetic black was so unbelievable in the colonial period that many of the colonial elders affixed their names to the title page to authenticate Wheatley's achievement in poetry.

Wheatley, greatly influenced by Alexander Pope, wrote primarily in heroic couplets, although she relied on blank verse for her poems on Harvard University, "To the University of Cambridge in New England" and "On Virtue," both of which show Wheatley's familiarity with the poetry of John Milton. Wheatley so valued the poetry of Milton that she could not be brought to sell her valuable edition of *Paradise Lost,* even when she was destitute and dying. The copy was given to Wheatley by the mayor of London during her visit there and is now in the Houghton collection of Harvard University.

Wheatley was an astonishing prodigy in the Boston Wheatley family, which had bought her as a seven year old. She mastered English and Latin, and as a teenager she translated the Niobe section of Ovid's *Metamorphoses* into English poetry. She also expressed a great desire to create an African American epic, comparing herself unfavorably to Homer, Milton, and Sir Isaac Newton in the poem "Phillis's Reply to the Answer." Perhaps the most effective statement of her desires to accomplish greatness in poetry is taken from an early poem, "To Maecenas."

> Great Maro's strain in heav'nly numbers flows,
> The Nine inspire, and all the bosom glows.
> O could I rival thine and Virgil's page,
> Or claim the Muses with the Mantuan Sage;
> Soon the same beauties should my mind adorn,
> And the same ardors in my soul should burn:
> Then should my song in bolder notes arise,
> And all my numbers pleasingly surprize;

Wheatley was to die at thirty-one, outliving all the members of the Wheatley family to which she had belonged. The Revolutionary War took its toll on slave and slaveowner alike.

George Moses Horton (1797–1880?) sought, begged, and wrote for his freedom from the North Carolinian Horton family for most of his life, but did not gain his freedom until 1865, when he followed Union troops to Philadelphia. Horton was outspoken on the wrongs of slavery, and several collections of his works were published during his lifetime. He spent his most creative period while attached to the University of North Carolina at Chapel Hill as a janitor. There he wrote many antislavery poems as well as love poems for the students for pay, and also had extensive contact with supporters interested in selling his book, *The Hope of Liberty* (1829), in order to buy his freedom. "The Art of a Poet," from *The Naked Genius* (1865), written after Horton had achieved freedom, reveals a rigorous understanding of the demands of poetry and offers a rare moment of artistic self-reflection in early African American poetry.

> True nature first inspires the man,
> But he must after learn to scan,
>   And mark well every rule;
> Gradual the climax then ascend,
> And prove the contrast in the end,
>   Between the wit and fool.
>
> A fool tho' blind, may write a verse,
> And seem from folly to emerge,
>   And rime well every line;
> One lucky, void of light, may guess
> And safely to the point may press,
>   But this does not refine.
>
> Polish mirror, clear to shine,
> And streams must run if they refine,
>   And widen as they flow;
> The diamond water lies concealed,
> Till polished it is ne'er revealed,
>   Its glory bright to show.
>
> A bard must traverse o'er the world,
> Where things concealed must rise unfurled,
>   And tread the feet of yore;
> Tho' he may sweetly harp and sing,
> But strictly prune the mental wing,
>   Before the mind can soar.

It is not known the extent to which Horton's location in the South and position as slave made it impolitic for him to speak out against his own slavery in violent terms. It is quite true that slavery in the nine-teenth century was more brutal than that of the previous century, and poets such as Charles Lewis Reason (1818–1893) and James Monroe Whitfield (dates unknown, fl. 1853) were among many who blasted a United States consciousness, morality, and politics that permitted the continued outrage of slavery. Whitfield wrote, in his poem, *America* (from *America and Other Poems*, 1853):

> America it is thee,
> Thou boasted land of liberty,—
> It is to thee I raise my song,
> Thou land of blood, and crime, and wrong.

Whitfield goes on to delineate the particular crimes of slavery, including the rape of slave women, and he accentuates the irony of African Americans who fought in the Revolutionary War "to forge fresh fetters, heavier chains for their own children." He wrote a poem in honor of the black hero, Cinque, and honored the British abolition of slavery on August 1, 1838. Ann Plato (1820?–?) also commemorates the August 1 event, but much of her remaining works are pious Christian reflections on earthly life and heavenly reward. A notable exception is "The Natives of America," a dialogic poem in which a father describes Native American life to his child. The cause and nobility of the Native Americans is lauded and the marauding, usurping Europeans are the villains. Plato lived in Hartford, Connecticut, and her collection of poetry, *Essays, Including Biographies and Miscellaneous Pieces in Prose and Poetry* (1841), was published through the help of her church.

Charles Lewis Reason (1818–1893) was a strongwilled and highly accomplished poet and teacher. Racism kept him from a high position in the Episcopal Church, and most of his working years were spent teaching in the New York public school system. Reason wrote many stirring poems against slavery as evidenced by these lines from "The Spirit Voice" (1841), where he manipulates the stanza form to present perceptions both abstract and natural.

> 'Tis thought alone, creative fervent thought!
>   Earnest in life, and in its purpose bent
> To uphold truth and right, that rich is fraught
>   With songs unceasing, and with gleamings sent
> Of sure things coming from a brighter world.

Reason's poem, "Freedom" (1846), narrates the progress of freedom from the ancient Near East, Greece, and Rome until the present, and shows the influence of, if not a direct acquaintance with, Hegel's concepts of the development of nations.

   In the decade preceding the Civil War the poets Alfred Gibbs Campbell, John Sella Martin, and Frances Ellen Watkins Harper were among those most vigorous in their condemnation of slavery and of the fugitive slave law that made it compulsory for all U.S. citizens to return fugitive slaves to their owners. Campbell (dates unknown, fl. c. 1853–1883) wrote many poems condemning the hypocrisy of Fourth of July celebrations, and was a strong supporter of women's rights and prohibition. His poem, "To a Young Mother" (in *Poems*, 1883), is remarkable for its sensitivity and avoidance of sentimentality; his antislavery poems are stark and uncompromising—"precious indeed / to Modern Moloch as the agony / of the fond mother when her child is snatched. / . . . / Or / The piercing shriek of the poor hunted slave / Torn piecemeal by his bloodhounds." ("Warning"); and he reveals an admirable capacity for intellectual openness and religious tolerance in "Cry 'Infidel.' " Campbell has full control of language, style, and emotional power in his poems, and uses blank verse, rhymed tetrameter couplets, and irregular stanza forms with ease. Perhaps his most effective poems are those of reflection, "Ode to Death," "On the Deep," and "Questionings." In the last poem he poses the supreme unanswerable question.

> If thou (as some philosophers would say),
> Art thus of God a part disintegrate,
> Imprisoned for a time in worthless clay,
> But destined still to a deific state,—
> To reabsorption in the Infinite,—
> Why thus art fettered in the murky tomb
> Of earth's soul-dungeon, where no certain light
> From Light's Eternal Source dispels the gloom?
> Is it for discipline? What need hath God
> To learn, who is Himself the Primal Fount
> Of Wisdom? To what end the weary road
> Of life's terrestrial, whence so hard to mount
> To heaven's serener clime? Is't punishment?
> Hath God then sinned? And doth God punish God?
> If thou canst fathom the Divine intent,
> Solve this dark problem, and cast light abroad?

Just prior to the Civil War John Sella Martin (1831–?) published the apocalyptic poem, "The Sentinel of Freedom," which prophesied a second coming after the United States is swept clean from the corruption of slavery. The poem has obvious connections with Milton's *Paradise Lost*, an epic that served as a model for political protest in England, the Caribbean, and the United States as early as 1705. Martin's "The Hero and the Slave: Founded on Fact" (1862) is courageous in that it castigates New England racism even as it praises the northerners for fighting the Civil War against slavery. Not many African Americans had the fortitude to argue in print with their supporters.

Both before and after the Civil War Frances Ellen Watkins Harper (1824–1911) was a popular poet, abolitionist, prohibitionist, and advocate for women's rights. Her poems on prohibition are often maudlin and sentimental, as in "The Ragged Stocking" from *Idylls of the Bible* (1900).

> Then I knelt by this little stocking
>   And sobbed out an earnest prayer,
> And arose with strength to wrestle
>   And break from the tempter's snare.

Her antislavery poetry, and especially her long epic poem, *Moses: A Story of the Nile*, is more successful in style, power, and variation of tone. *Moses*, written in irregular blank verse, retells the biblical story by making Moses a mulatto who freely chooses to return to the aid of his enslaved people. Harper's poems went through more than twenty editions in her lifetime, an astonishing testimony to her loyal audience.

After the Civil War more African American poetry focused on such unpolitical subjects as romantic love, dramatic heroes, and sentimental empassioned heroines. Eloise Bibb Thompson (1878–1927) wrote many poems in this genre, which were published in *Poems*, 1895. She spent much of her life in California, chose Italy as the setting for much of her work, and lived as a staunch Catholic throughout her life. In addition to romantic poems Thompson wrote several poems on Biblical themes, such as "Judith" and "The Expulsion of Hagar," the second theme often having special significance for African American women since Hagar was the slave concubine of Abraham, the patriarch of the Hebrews. Thompson's oeuvre also includes a tribute to Frederick Douglass.

The lyric poetry of Henrietta Cordelia Ray (1852?–1916) focused on imaginary idyllic scenes of delight and pleasure. She uses new stanzaic forms to express her approbation of nature as the fit setting of love, but often her images have prettiness without substance, as in "rose-gleam" and "aisles of space" in "Idyll."

> Down in the dell,
> A rose-gleam fell
> From azure aisles of space;
> There with a light tread
> A maiden sped,
> Sweet yearning in her face.

She wrote sonnets to her literary and political heroes, "Milton" and "Robert G. Shaw," and it is perhaps in the sonnet form that she makes her greatest creative impact. Her two published works are *Poems* (1887) and *Sonnets* (1893).

Charlotte Forten Grimké (1837–1914), best known for her extensive journals on the nineteenth century, also wrote fourteen poems encouraging abolition, admiring political daring, and giving reverence to life in the context of task and freedom. She opens "A Parting Hymn" with the following lines, which reveal her awareness of the loveliness of nature and the precarious balance of human life.

> When Winter's royal robes of white
> From hill and vale are gone
> And the glad voices of the spring
> Upon the air are borne,
> Friends who have met with us before,
> Within these walls shall meet no more.

The most important African American journalist of the latter half of the nineteenth century, Timothy Thomas Fortune (1856–1928), also wrote a volume of poetry, *Dreams of Life,* in which the poems focused on the emptiness of life, its ephemeral joys, its shortness of days. While a vigorous agitator for the right of African Americans in newspapers and journals, it seems that in his private life and reflections he brooded most over the insufficiency of life's joy to compensate for its griefs. In "We Know No More" he wrote:

> I sometimes feel that life contains
> Nothing, in all its wealth, to pay
> For half the sorrows and the pains
> That haunt our day.

The most popular and significant African American poet of the nineteenth century was Paul Laurence Dunbar (1872–1906). His popularity was so great that it is difficult to number the reprints of his many collections, the first of which was "Lyrics of Lowly Life" (1895), and often his praise has been considered excessive by those who feel that other African American poets deserve comparable attention. Dunbar's facility with all major forms of Anglo-American poetry, his gift in adapting African American dialect to these various forms, and his undeniable lyric virtuosity combine to give full justification to his high status. It is unfortunate that the American tendency to feel that "we have one already" (WHOA) has kept other poets from the attention of potential readers. However, this racist propensity of the American critical establishment should not detract from the absolute achievement of Dunbar in lyrics of both standard English and African American dialect. In his reflective poem, "Ere Sleep Comes Down to Soothe the Weary Eyes," meter, form, diction, and theme combine to amplify that human moment of self-questioning and cosmic curiosity.

> Ere sleep comes down to soothe the weary eyes,
>> Which all the day with ceaseless care have sought
> The magic gold which from the seeker flies;
>> Ere dreams put on the gown and cap of thought,
> And make the waking world a world of lies,—
>> Of lies most palpable, uncouth, forlorn,
> That say life's full of aches and tears and sighs,—
>> Oh, how with more than dreams the soul is torn,
> Ere sleep comes down to soothe the weary eyes.

Dunbar is equally effective in his dialect poems, as can be seen in "An Ante-Bellum Sermon."

> Now ole Pher'oh, down in Egypt,
>> Was de wuss man evah evah bo'n,
> An' he had de Hebrew chillun
>> Down dah wukin' in his co'n;
> 'T well de Lawd got tiahed o' his foolin',
>> An' sez he: I'll let him know—
> "Look Hyeah, Moses, go tell Pher'oh
>> Fu' to let dem chillun go."

Dunbar himself often complained that his audience, primarily white, only enjoyed his dialect poetry in what he called bad English, "a jingle in a broken tongue." Although there was certainly some racist desire to hear blacks speak "bad" English in Dunbar's audience, the power of Dunbar's dialect poetry derives not from mistakes in English but from the masterful manipulation of African and African American offbeat polyrhythms, which were a highly creative artistic innovation in the English language.

The fiery, unconventional life of Menken Adele Isaac Barclay (1839–1868) left us with perhaps the most exclamatory poetry in American letters. Barclay worked as an actress, had several husbands, lovers, and even names. Her first husband was Jewish, and Barclay herself converted to Judaism and wrote several poems on Jewish themes, including "Hear, O Israel." She lived a consciously Jewish life and received a Jewish burial at her death. Barclay saw herself as a misunderstood genius who never had the freedom to achieve her greatest artistic goals. Her works are as brilliant and fiery in diction and form as was her life, and her poetry is given to dramatic stances of repudiation, sensuousness, despair, and love. The following excerpt is from "Hear, O Israel."

> Hear, O Israel? and plead my cause against the ungodly nation!
> 'Midst the terrible conflict of Love and Peace, I departed
> from thee, my people, and spread my tent of many colors in the land of
> Egypt.
> In their crimson and fine linen I girded my white form.
> Sapphires gleamed their purple light from out the darkness of my
> hair.
> The silver folds of their temple foot-cloth was spread beneath my
> sandaled feet.
> Thus I slumbered through the daylight.
>> Slumbered 'midst the vapor of sin,
>> Slumbered 'midst the battle and din,
>> Wakened 'midst the strangle of breath,
>> Wakened 'midst the struggle of death!

Almost all of the poetry of Joseph Seaman Cotter, Sr. (1861–1949), focuses on themes of racial pride and advancement. Poems honoring Frederick Douglass, Paul Laurence Dunbar, Ralph Waldo Emerson, and Oliver Wendell Holmes express all that Cotter found best in these heroes with regard to racial equality and justice. Cotter had facility in many styles and dictions and used iambic tetrameter and the more highly respected iambic pentameter with equal ease.

In addition to the African American lyric poets of the nineteenth century, the aforementioned and other African American poets wrote epic poetry, an African American poetic genre that has been unidentified, unknown, unrecognized, and unanalyzed before. For this discussion I take epic to mean a long narrative in poetry, describing the origin, nature, or destiny of a people, race, or group, depicting a hero or heroic ideal, and incorporating the cultural ideal. Frances Harper, in her poem, *Moses: A Story of the Nile*, is one of a fellowship of nineteenth-century African American epic poets that includes James Ephraim McGirt (1874–1930), Albert Allson Whitman (1851–1901), James Madison Bell (1826–1902), George Marion McClellan (1860–1934), George Hannibal Temple (b. unknown, fl. 1900), George Reginal Margetson (1877–?), Edward Smythe Jones (1888–?), Fenton Johnson (1888–?), and Maurice N. Corbett (b. unknown, fl. 1914).

Harper's *Moses* (1889) honors the ideal of the gifted African American's return to assist the remainder of the race in achieving freedom, education, and equality. It is written in Miltonic blank verse. Since the 1700s British, Caribbean, and American poets often used Miltonic blank verse as a vehicle for demanding political change.

The ealiest African American poem in this tradition is John Boyd's *The Vision*, which was published in England in 1835. James Ephraim McGirt wrote three poems in the epic style, "Avenging the Maine," "Siege of Manila," and "Siege of Santiago." These works are primarily military in scope, and have more in common with the sixteenth-century Italian epics of Tasso and Ariosto than they have with the more pastoral epics of Dante and Milton.

Albert Allson Whitman wrote three highly self-conscious epics, *The Rape of Florida, Not a Man and Yet a Man*, and *An Idyl of the South: An Epic in Two Parts. The Rape of Florida* is almost a political treatise; it defends the Seminole Native Americans against European incursions and praises the Seminoles for their help in assisting runaway slaves. *An Idyl* and *Not a Man* deal more specifically with African American slavery and racism, with the *Idyl* giving a view of the tragic mulatto, *Not a Man* an extended poetic discussion of African American manhood.

George Marion McClellan's *The Legend of Tannhauser*, written in blank verse, is an impressive accomplishment, wedding style, diction, form, and sentiment. It is perhaps the most successful work of the genre.

In horror-stricken tones the nobles cried,
"Hear him! Hear him! So to the Venusburg
And in his blood bathe every sword." With cries
The ladies hastened from the hall, save fair
Elizabeth, who stood there shuddering
Betwixt her horror and her mighty love.

In *The Epic of Columbus' Bell* (1900) George Hannibal Temple relates the incidence by which the original bell from Columbus's ship becomes the churchbell of an African American church in New Jersey. Here the African Americans, still caught up in the prevalent world view that admires the political symbols of the nation in spite of its oppressive and racist legal systems, finds honor in preserving this palpable symbol of the coming of the Europeans to the Americas.

The comic epic is represented by George Reginal Margetson's *The Fledgling Bard and the Poetry Society* (1916), which mocks a thinly disguised Harvard University for its inability to identify true poets. Harvard University was also the subject for an epic by Edward Smythe Jones, who supposedly walked barefoot to Cambridge, Massachusetts, in order to find wisdom, knowledge, and higher education. His epic, *Harvard Square*, was written in jail, where he was placed for his efforts to achieve his goals. His production earned him a job as janitor at the university and he was allowed to listen in on classes.

In Fenton Johnson's *The Vision of Lazarus* the character travels on a Dantean journey through heaven and hell, in which Homer is found resident in a Christian heaven. Johnson's knowledge of Western literature is formidable, and although some of the scenes are a challenge to intellectual sobriety, the attributes of his other scenes are dramatic and compelling.

Maurice N. Corbett's *The Harp of Ethiopia* (1914) is the most sustained epic of this African American nineteenth-century genre. Corbett traces black accomplishment from the ancient Near East and Africa to the present, with several passages detailing the self-defense of African Americans during the Civil War. He ends the poem with prophecies of high achievements in politics and art by African Americans, and the vigor of his closing lines are effectively inspiring.

Thus we come from Lucy Terry's martial poem of communal self-defense, through the early desire to create great poetry by such writers as Phillis Wheatley and Jupiter Hammon, to arrive at the apex of nineteenth-century African American lyric and epic poetry in Paul Laurence Dunbar, Frances Ellen Watkins Harper, James McClellan, Albert Allson Whitman, H. Cordelia Ray, and Maurice N. Corbett. The immediate political requirements of the Civil War gave African American poets the freedom to write on all human themes, racism and flowers, wars and love, lynchings and childhood.

Carolivia Herron

Further Reading

Bontemps, Arna, ed. *American Negro Poetry*. New York: Hill and Wang, 1963.

Brawley, Benjamin, ed. *Early Negro American Writers: Selections with Biographical and Critical Introductions*. University of North Carolina, 1935.

Corbett, Maurice N. *The Harp of Ethiopia*. Nashville: National Baptist Publishing Board, 1914; repr. Freeport, N.Y.: Books for Libraries, 1971.

Dunbar, Paul Laurence. *The Paul Laurence Dunbar Reader*. Eds. Jay Martin and Gossie H. Hudson. New York: Dodd, Mead, 1975.

Dunbar, Paul Laurence. *The Complete Poems of Paul Laurence Dunbar*. New York: Dodd, Mead, 1980.

Harper, Frances Ellen Watkins. *Complete Poems of Frances E. W. Harper*. The Schomburg Library of Nineteenth-Century Black Women Writers. New York: Oxford University Press, 1988..

Jahn, Janheinz. *A Bibliography of Neo-African Literature from Africa, America, and the Caribbean*. London: A. Deutsch, 1965.

Loggins, Vernon. *The Negro Author: His Development in America, 1900*. New York: Kennikat, 1964.

Plato, Ann. *Essays, Including Biographies and Miscellaneous Pieces, in Prose and Poetry*. The Schomburg Library of Nineteenth-Century Black Women Writers. New York: Oxford University Press, 1988.

Porter, Dorothy B. "Early American Negro Writing." *Bibliographical Society of America Papers* (1945), 39:192–268.

—— *North American Negro Poets, 1760–1944*. Hattiesburg, Miss.: Book Farm, 1945.

Robinson, William H., ed. *Early Black American Poets: Selections with Biographical and Critical Introductions*. Dubuque: W. C. Brown, 1969.

Schomburg, Arthur A. *Bibliographical Checklist of American Negro Poetry*. New York: C. F. Heartman, 1916.

Sheldon, George. *A History of Deerfield, Massachusetts: The Times When and the People by Whom It Was Settled, Unsettled, and Resettled: With a Special Study of the Indi-*

an Wars in the Connecticut Valley, with Geneologies. Deerfield: E. A. Hall, 1895–1896.

Sherman, Joan. *Invisible Poets: Afro-Americans of the Nineteenth Century.* Urbana: University of Illinois Press, 1974, 1989.

Sherman, Joan, ed. *Collected Black Women's Poetry.* 4 vols. The Schomburg Library of Nineteenth-Century Black Women Writers. New York: Oxford University Press, 1988.

Stetson, Erlene, ed. *Black Sister: Poetry by Black American Women 1746–1980.* Bloomington: Indiana University Press, 1981.

Wagner, Jean. *Black Poets of the United States.* Trans. Kenneth Douglas. Urbana: University of Illinois Press, 1973.

Wheatley, Phillis. *The Collected Works of Phillis Wheatley.* The Schomburg Library of Nineteenth-Century Black Women Writers. New York: Oxford University Press, 1988.

Wheatley, Phillis. *The Poems of Phillis Wheatley.* Ed. Julian D. Mason, Jr. Chapel Hill: University of North Carolina Press, 1989.

White, Newman Ivey, and Walter Clinton Jackson, eds. *An Anthology of Verse by American Negroes.* Durham, N.C.: Moore, 1968.

Whitlow, Roger. *Black American Literature: A Critical History with a 1,520-Title Bibliography of Works Written By and About Black Americans.* Totowa, N.J.: Rowna and Allanheld, 1974, 1984.

Whitman, Albery Allson. *An Idyll of the South: An Epic Poem in Two Parts.* Ann Arbor: University Microfilms, 1974.

The Epic in the Nineteenth Century

THE rigid generic categories of the New Criticism have cast a long shadow upon us all, especially upon anyone now in mid-career. During the first week of an "Introduction to Literature" course I took as a freshman in 1958, students were given a list of genres with which we were expected quickly to "become familiar" (translation—"memorize"). "Epic" was tidily tucked away as the first and highest subdivision of "Narrative Poetry." A list of presumably all of the several kinds of poetry ("Narrative, Lyric, Dramatic," subclassified by stanza forms and meter) preceded similar lists for "Fiction," "Non-Fiction Prose," and "Drama." Poetry, we soon discovered, had been the first form of human literary expression and had remained the highest of literary kinds. For the truly sensitive reader, poetry was readily identifiable as a separate and special realm open to all but entered by few. Not wishing to be thought insensitive, and not yet willing to abandon all hope of entering special realms, I tried to memorize the list, but succeeded only in becoming familiar with it.

Such a list of genres, like any spreadsheet, encourages comprehensive and hierarchical thinking by denying that categories overlap. Any dunce, I was led to assume, knew poetry from prose. Never mind that the Greek word *epos* meant "narrative" and not "narrative poetry," nor that Aristotle's *Of the Art of Poetry* is concerned mostly with drama. Never mind that, as recently as 1749, Henry Fielding had founded a "new province of writing" that he had called a "comic epic poem in prose." Never mind that, among many other nineteenth-century writers, nonentities such as Scott, Cooper, Carlyle, Simms, Melville, Thackeray, Prescott, Parkman, Norris, and Kipling had all explicitly argued that the epic could and should be transformed from poetry into either historical romance or romantic history, both to be written in a poetic prose. The word *epic* was assumed to connote poetry, and poetry was not to be confused with prose.

Scholarly understanding of *epic* had reached a broad, useful, and still familiar consensus. Because of the research of Milman Parry and Albert Lord, the prefaces and translations of C. S. and C. Day Lewis, and the critical books of C. M. Bowra and Cedric Whitman, it was commonly accepted that "Primary Epic" meant the oral narrative poetry of warrior societies (Homer, Beowulf, the *Chanson de Roland*, the *Niebelungenlied*) and "Secondary Epic" meant written heroic narratives (Virgil, Dante, Milton) by authors of later, more civilized nations who wished to transform the old oral conventions into imperial and Christian contexts. Whatever followed John Milton in the way of heroic narrative, even if it were worthy of comparison to *Paradise Lost* on aesthetic grounds, was no longer an epic but something that should be discussed and taught within other generic categories.

Are such convictions now entirely of the past? You who read this essay probably assume that, at least for purposes of literary history, an epic is a poem. An epic may be short or long, joyful or despairing in tone, imagistic or narrative in structure, but most of us academics presume that we can readily select the epics from our bookshelves. The epics are thought to be those ambitious poems, from Homer to John Berryman, that celebrate some kind of heroism (be it a warrior's deed or a poet's imagination) and that convey the values and customs of a culture. If you more or less agree with such a definition, you do so in part because four fine, influential studies of "American epic" by Roy Harvey Pearce, James Miller, Michael Bernstein, and Jeffrey Walker all share these assumptions. Among academic critics the heart of the matter of American epic has been the twentieth-century long poem (Eliot, Pound, Williams, Crane, Berryman, Olson), Walt Whitman is their predecessor and poetic father, and other nineteenth-century works are either touching, ridiculous failures (Barlow's *The Columbiad*) or are simply not germane to what "the American epic" is presupposed to be.

In fairness to the reader, every writer should divulge known assumptions. When the editors of the *Columbia History of American Poetry* asked me to contribute an essay "on the American epic poem through the nineteenth century," I replied that half of my essay must concern what is ordinarily thought to be prose. I did so because I recognize no reliable and defensible distinction between prose and poetry since the mid-eighteenth century. At that time Samuel Johnson demonstrated with pitiless accuracy that there must always be a difference between poetry, which is of abiding interest, and mere verse, which is not. If, however, we define verse as the placement of words in lines of approximate metrical regularity, then the term *free verse* truly is playing tennis with the net down. On the other hand, who among us would wish to argue that long sections of *Paterson* are not poetry, simply because they have the qualities of good newspaper journalism without the bad qualities of mere verse? Robert Frost's two typically foxy raids on this problem—that all poetry is "metaphor" and that all poetry has "rhythm"—offer us no help at all; they simply claim all good literature for poetry. Are we left then with only one distinction intact: that "prose" is spaced on the page with its line lengths determined extrinsically by the margins of paper, whereas "poetry" is spaced on the page by some kind of internal standard, not necessarily rhythmic (vide Marianne Moore)? If you find this last, desperate distinction in any way useful, it's yours.

The breakdown of the distinction between prose and poetry (and therefore between epic and verse) in the early nineteenth century is not, however, a hobbyhorse of my making. It was a willful heresy that broke down Neoclassic categories and soon became the basis for new genres and for new ways of transforming old genres. We are now perhaps overly familiar with the "organicist" and vatic implications of Emerson's dictum "It is not meters, but a meter-making argument, that makes a poem," but we often forget that, by essay's end, Emerson has claimed for poetry, not only Homer, Dante, Chaucer, Spenser, and Milton, but also Plato, Pythagoras, Plutarch, Raphael, Shakespeare, Bacon, Kepler, Swedenborg, and the dictionary. As Walter Scott's widely read 1824 *Brittanica* essay on Romance shows, Scott had created in the Waverley novels a form of fiction that was meant to incorporate history, epic, and romance. The natural metaphors of an Indian comprised, for Cooper and Simms, a speech far more "poetic" than the written abstractions of the white man, be they in verse or prose. The soliloquies of Captain Ahab scan in more regular blank verse than many of the soliloquies of Milton's Satan (try it). Before, during, and after writing *The History of the Conquest of Mexico*, Prescott thought of his subject as a "magnificent epic." And Walt Whitman, that supposed exemplar of "the American epic" for the nineteenth century, contended in his 1855 preface that "the expression of the American poet . . .is to be indirect and *not* direct or descriptive or epic" (emphasis mine).

And so it goes. My point is simply that, if we wish to explore the course of "epic poetry" in nineteenth-century America, we can afford no neo-Aristotelian categories of our making. We must attend to the kinds of generic transformations authors wished to achieve and we must consider the reasons for them. Emerson, who claims to have loved bare lists of names, would surely have had scant patience with any academic list of separable and separate genres. To understand the development of "the American epic poem in the nineteenth century" we must be prepared to turn to "prose," to read carefully, and to stay loose.

Between Timothy Dwight's *The Conquest of Canaan* (1785) and Alfred Mitchell's *The Coloniad* (1858) at least nineteen epic poems were completed and published by American authors. Six would-be epics were published incomplete and five more were abandoned, probably wisely. Although epic poems continued to be written in England during the same era, the sheer amount of American heroic verse suggests an acute cultural need. Former colonials needed their own epic poem both to justify casting off the British father and to demonstrate the New Republic's cultural maturity. After the widely proclaimed failure of Barlow's *The Columbiad* (1807), the need for an American epic intensified rather than lessened. As the country entered an era of expansive nationalism, Barlow's failing was often thought to have been his outdated Deistic and international republicanism, not his lack of artistry. In the twelve to forty canto epics of Daniel Bryan (*The Mountain Muse*, 1813), Richard Emmons (*The Fredoniad*, 1827), and Walter Marshall McGill (*The Western World*, 1837), "imperium sine fine" is assumed to have been Virgil's true theme, readily transferable to America's western soil, and readily applicable against every red coat and red skin. For gargantuan dullness and unconscious ethnocentrism, such poems are truly exemplary.

During the post-Revolutionary period, however, an American determined to write heroic poetry faced admittedly insoluble problems of content and form that he (the genre in America at this time seems to have had no "she") could not quite identify. Although urgent calls for "the American epic" began to appear in periodicals immediately after the Peace of Paris in 1783, there was no agreement as to what "the American epic" should be. Was America's "epic rage" (Bishop Berkeley's prophetic term) to be concerned with the Planting of New England, the American Revolution, worldwide republicanism, or the settling of the West? If the highest national mission was religious rather than political, should not the American epic concern a universal biblical subject Milton had left untouched (vide Thomas Brockway's *The Gospel Tragedy: An Epic Poem* (1795), Elhanahan Winchester's *The Process and Empire of Christ* (1805), Johnson Pierson's *The Judead* (1844), and, of course, Dwight's *The Conquest of Canaan*). An even more vexing problem was the adapting of new subjects and new values to an old form. Because America was so grand but so recent an experiment, heroic events had not yet acquired the advantages of remote legend and would need to be made, not recalled. Americans were educated to revere the art of Homer as the first among poets, but to despise the butchery of Achilles, the glory-hunting of Hector and the deviousness of Odysseus. How then could the hero of New World Enlightenment—the peaceful, republican farmer—become the hero of a new and higher poem that was still recognizable as an epic? Were heroic couplets, councils of chieftains, visits to hell, propositions and invocations, and the whole panoply of divine machinery in any way adaptable to American heroic literature? If not, could one write an epic without them?

Not a few would-be national bards were, to be sure, blithely untroubled by such questions. With Pope's Homer at their right hand, *Paradise Lost* at their left, and Dryden's Virgil somewhere in between, they made the easy character identifications, reclothing George Washington as Aeneas, Andrew Jackson as Achilles, Lord Cornwallis or Benedict Arnold or perhaps Tecumseh as Satan, and then simply let the heroic couplets and epic conventions flow, all in the service of their country. The most spectacular public failure among the imitative poems, however, was also the most thoughtful and innovative in its purposes. In the last book of *The Columbiad*, Joel Barlow called for an end to the martial glory, religious superstition, and repressive politics of the entire epic tradition by imagining a new poet-prophet:

> For him no more, beneath their furious gods,
> Old Ocean crimsons and Olympus nods,
> Uprooted mountains sweep the dark profound
> Or Titans groan beneath the rending ground.
> No more his clangor maddens up the mind.
> To crush, to conquer, and enslave mankind,
> To build on ruin'd realms the shrine of fame,
> And load his numbers with a tyrant's name.

According to Barlow's truly radical viewpoint, fear of the unknown had led primitive peoples to create gods; worship of gods made believers servile; servility led to feudalism and priestcraft; feudalism and priest-craft have thrived by wars that maintain the power of the few over the many. Traditional epic poetry, which accepts the powers that be, has held back enlightenment by assuming that war is the essential metaphor of human existence. Only through international commerce, an international peace-keeping league, and shared advances in science and technology, could the power of the individual be released to build a new and more heroic republican order. Barlow's visionary affirmations, then ridiculed by reviewers and later shared by Walt Whitman, may contain the most practicable path for man's survival yet devised.

At least since *The Aeneid*, the tradition of epic poetry had been sustained by transformative imitation of one's predecessors. Barlow's vision of a new heroism is a New World republican's way of reshaping Milton's claim to have possessed a "higher argument" than Homer or Virgil. To envision republican heroism, however, is not the same as writing a new epic poem that convincingly affirms it. Barlow begins *The Columbiad* with lines capitalized in such a way as to be immediately recognizable as a Proposition:

> I SING the Mariner who first unfurl'd
> An eastern banner o'er the western world
> And taught mankind where future empires lay
> In these fair confines of descending day.

We are here in the domain of verse, not poetry; every line is declarative and almost every noun has its adjective. At best, such couplets convey the force of a new idea with sturdy clarity. At worst (when Barlow is elevating his diction, listing New World achievements in epic catalogues, or working through an epic simile), Barlow's medium declines into relentless bombast. The superiority of New World republicanism is proclaimed through tepid imitation of poetic conventions that are Old World and aristocratic. In approved Virgilian fashion, Barlow's invocation to the muse follows hard upon his epic's Proposition. Because his muse is Freedom rather than Urania or Athena, Barlow stakes out the defiant claim "to teach all men where all their interest lies": "Strong in thy strength I bend no suppliant knee, / Invoke no miracle, no Muse but thee." His "Freedom" however is herself a classical goddess, robed in the same frozen elevation as "Pop" Emmons's Fredonia, Edgar Poe's Psyche, New York's Statue of Liberty, or the opening icon of any film of Columbia Pictures. To throw a new garment and a new name around an old figure is to adapt but not transform it.

The choice of a proper heroic subject, though difficult enough, was not the most vexing problem in the forming of a New World epic. The very suitability of the "narrative" (*epos*) was beginning to come into question. The term could of course be conceived in traditional Aristotelian fashion as the telling of one complete heroic story made up of many incidents. Dwight's *The Conquest of Canaan*, Snowden's *The Columbiad*, Emmons's *The Fredoniad*, McGill's *The Western World*, and Alfred Mitchell's *The Coloniad* all recount wars of empire—usually one canto per battle—replete with intervening gods, single combats, and obtrusive teleology centered around American republicanism. Poets like Daniel Bryan (*The Mountain Muse*, 1813) and James K. Paulding (*The Backwoodsman*, 1819), who saw the conquest and settlement of western lands as America's heroic subject, slightly loosened traditional narrative form, imagining a sparse fictional narrative of white settlement and Indian defeat, then adding long verse discursions to achieve presumably proper length. By expanding *The Vision* of *Columbus* into *The Columbiad*, however, Barlow suggested that New World epic could no longer be narrative in the traditional sense. Barlow's subject is not the past incidents of Columbus's four voyages, but the progressive future of the entire Western world. Although *The Columbiad* recounts the achievements of many a historical hero, the poem is less a narrative than a gigantic expansion of the eighteenth-century Prospect Poem, as adapted by Barlow's generation to celebrating the Rising Glory of America.

All these models of poetic structure proved unsuccessful, perhaps inevitably so. Because American military heroism was too recent to have become legendary, recasting the Battles of Saratoga or New Orleans as New World reenactments of the glories on Troy's windy plain proved laughable to any reader with half a memory. As representative western settlers, Bryan's Daniel Boone and Paulding's Basil can have neither inner character and nor variety of daily life, because their deeds and character must somehow be heroic and ordinary simultaneously.

Barlow's structural compromise, however liberating in theory, proved unworkable on the page. Throughout the entirety of his epic, Barlow's all-knowing angel Hesper (a stand-in for Milton's Raphael) sequentially unfolds the future glories of America to an imprisoned and despairing Columbus. Heroism becomes less an individual's act than a new republican faith that can emerge in every reader; martial glory, though present in Hesper's narratives, is first subordinated and finally discredited. To become enlightened, as Columbus is always persuaded to do, becomes the essential first step toward a more democratic and scientific kind of Renaissance humanism. Such an unchanging structure promptly creates a numbing if not catatonic effect upon the reader. Barlow celebrates the progressive march of history through unrelieved use of the most static and traditional of epic conventions (the prophecy of a divine messenger). Neither Columbus nor the reader can engage the poem's important issues because Hesper is forever preparing to deliver the Deistic, republican answer to them. Any opening for individuality (Walt Whitman's "a simple separate person") or for our own imaginative response (Whitman's insistence that true poetry is "suggestiveness") is quickly foreclosed by Barlow's relentless universalizing.

Traditionalists damned *The Columbiad* for its unacceptable departures from epic form; innovators damned it for its refusal to depart from epic conventions. Those who continued to assume that the American epic had to be a long heroic narrative in verse clearly had no idea what shape "the work of genius" (Hawthorne's phrase) could successfully assume. Safety lay in ridicule. As verse epics more ponderous and traditional than Barlow's were published and fell into oblivion, the notoriety of *The Columbiad* only grew. By the 1840s Barlow's by now unread poem was assumed to contain all the failures, all the absurdities, embodied in the very notion of an American epic. Amid the trendy witticisms Barlow's poem evoked from Hawthorne, Lowell, Flint, Tuckerman, and Whipple, Poe's rather turgid judgment in "The Poetic Principle" (1849) remains both the most influential and the most dismissive: "The modern epic is, of the suppositious ancient model, but an inconsiderate and blindfold imitation. . . . The epic mania . . . has for some years past, been gradually dying out of the public mind. The day of these artistic anomalies is over."

Poe's attack on the endlessness of the modern epic and his defense of the short lyric poem are, of course, fully symbiotic critical positions. Therein, however, lies the false simplicity of his argument. In promoting his own lyric quest for Supernal Beauty, Poe greatly overreached himself. His refusal in 1849 to consider that "the modern epic" might appear in prose was, as Scott, Carlyle, Cooper, and Prescott had already demonstrated—and as Emerson well knew—as outmoded as it was rigid. Poe's notion of the "heresy of the didactic" led him not only to condemn contemporary epic imitations but also to dismiss their originals. Poe's assertion that *The Iliad* is "based in an imperfect sense of art," is almost as foolish as his conclusion that "the ultimate, aggregate, or absolute effect of even the best epic under the sun, is a nullity." We may rightly use Poe's famous essay to mark the death of the long imitative epic poem, but it demonstrates neither the nullity nor the death of epic in his own time, let alone in Homer's. Poe's poetic principle depends upon a false foreclosure.

By 1820, writers open to new ideas of heroic behavior and epic form found themselves in a choppy, open sea of literary opportunity. Scott's poems and novels had shown that the medieval lay, the gothic romance, the epic, and regional history could be mutually interwoven in the service of both prosy poetry and poetic prose. After MacPherson, Coleridge, and Scott, the illusion of oral tale telling, in verse and/or prose, began to seem the essential medium of epic. As imitative verse epics in heroic couplets or Miltonic blank verse repeatedly floundered, the possibility arose that America's great epic might be written in the once low but presently popular genre of prose fiction. The need to display epic stature through parodic imitation receded in the face of a demand for new forms that could be "original" in both meanings of the word.

The shift in media reflected shifts in values. Barlow's generation had assumed that progress lay in the spread of enlightened white civilization, a belief quite consonant with the assumption that Virgil was the most correct of poets. By the 1820s it was conceivable to reverse this assumption. Perhaps the New World's heroic subject was not the conquering of the savage by civilization, but the demise of those noble and "primitive" peoples who had embodied the qualities of the heroic age. At stake here was something far deeper than following the trends of some zeitgeist called "Romanticism." To entertain such beliefs forced writers to question the most basic literary and cultural assumptions of their upbringing. A presumably timeless hierarchy of separate literary genres had to be abandoned. The literary conventions by which epic was defined had to be reshaped into viable contemporary literary forms or dropped entirely. To protest the dispossession and victimization of Indians, Aztecs, or Incas was to undermine the notions of cultural supremacy on which the very writing of "the American Epic" supposedly rested. Such changes were as troubling as they were exhilarating. New literary forms had to be made by transforming, rather than imitating, the poems of Virgil or Milton. White authors set out to devise forms of American epic in which heroic achievement was embodied, not in what Europeans brought to the western world, but in what they had erased from it. Ironically, the search for American heroic values gained lasting literary power only when the new Indian romance both subverted the reader's assumptions about the epic genre and challenged the expansionist complacencies of the culture as a whole.

In the preface to *The Yemassee* (1835), Simms declared that "the modern Romance is the substitute which the people of the present day offer for the ancient epic." Though an attentive reader of *Rob Roy* or *The Last of the Mohicans* might have reached the same conclusion a decade earlier, Simms is bluntly advancing a proposition that he knows is still generally unaccepted. Cooper's formulation of the same argument was to be both more oblique and more informative. In his review of Lockhart's *Memoirs of the Life of Sir Walter Scott*, Cooper noted that Scott's great achievement as a writer was that "he raised the novel, as near as might be, to the dignity of the epic." To provide the proper context for reading *The Leatherstocking Tales*, Cooper ended his 1850 preface (the last words written of the whole series) with its only mention of another author:

It is the privilege of all writers of fiction, more particularly when their works aspire to the elevation of romances, to present the beau-ideal of their characters to the reader. This it is which constitutes poetry, and to suppose the red man is to be represented only in the squalid misery or in the degraded moral state that certainly more or less belongs to his condition, is, we apprehend, taking a very narrow view of an author's privileges. Such criticism would have deprived the world of even Homer.

As in Simms's formulation, the prose romance here becomes the modern domain of heroic poetry. For Simms, however, the measure of prose epic had been its success in providing "adventures among the wild and wonderful . . . crowding events in a narrow space of time." Although the Leatherstocking tales are surely not understocked with overcrowded adventures, the series as a whole confirms Cooper's claim that the character and speech of the Red Man (and of Leatherstocking, who shares Indian traits) can constitute a kind of "poetry" that is recognizably heroic.

The narratives of the first four Leatherstocking tales were clearly planned to demonstrate that the triumph of the literate, rational and technological civilization of the white man should finally be regarded as both justified and inevitable. At novel's end a capable white man is sure to marry a genteel maiden who represents the flower of civilization, while both the noble and the diabolic savage die safely away. Beneath these seemingly imposed plots, however, are counterforces that forever unravel any claim upon manifest destiny. The "Christian" white man can conquer the continent only by reverting to savage battle tactics. The reader's admiration or awe (the defining response to epic literature) is primarily directed toward a childless and preternaturally aged hero who belongs to neither red nor white culture, and who scornfully retreats from the westering civilizers he momentarily agrees to serve. In order of their writing *The Leatherstocking Tales* fittingly end, not with any picturing of the conquest of empire, but with the wilderness impassively resuming its control over Lake Glimmerglass, almost effacing all traces of the greed of Tom Hutter and the thoughtlessness of Hurry Harry March.

"The business of a writer of fiction is to approach, as near as his powers will allow, to poetry." This dictum, from Cooper's 1831 preface to *The Last of the Mohicans*, has self-consciously epic dimensions within the novel itself. Cooper's characterization of Magua, a "Prince of Darkness, brooding on his own fancied wrongs, and plotting evil," is, like Melville's Captain Ahab, inconceivable without the prototype of Milton's Satan. The moment when the natural metaphors of Magua's speech become most convincingly poetic, however, is also the moment when his own wrongs are least fancied:

The Spirit that made men . . . gave the pale faces the nature of the pigeon; wings that never tire; young, more plentiful than the leaves on the trees, and appetites to devour the earth. He gave them tongues like the false call of the wild-cat; hearts like rabbits, the cunning of the hog, (but none of the fox,) and arms longer than the legs of the moose. With his tongue, he stops the ears of Indians; his heart teaches him to pay warriors to fight his battles; his reasoning tells him how to get together the goods of the earth; and his arms enclose the land from the shores of the salt water, to the islands of the great lake. His gluttony makes him sick. God gave him enough, and yet he wants all. Such are the pale faces.

We need consider nothing in the novel beyond Cooper's magnificent account of the massacre at Fort William Henry to recognize that he assents to the historical truth of every one of Magua's poetic accusations. Magua is the victim of both a real personal wrong (Colonel Munro's whipping) and a general racial wrong (the white man's manipulation and dispossession of the red). Unlike Chingachgook and Uncas, who judge by intraracial contrasts (French vs. English, Hurons vs. Delawares), Magua's interracial thinking leads him to recognize that race war is the red man's only hope. Cooper can discredit Magua only by insisting that Magua's overriding motive is to exact an implacable personal revenge by abducting white women and then making them his concubines. Magua may, like Satan, use truth for falsehood, good for evil, but his unfancied wrongs make Uncas's quiet service of the English military seem innocently destructive to his own red race.

Cooper's reworking of epic conventions almost invariably complicates the reader's need to judge. When Chingachgook and Magua (those supposed exemplars of Cooper's "good Indian" vs. Cooper's "bad Indian"), are sent into single combat, their dust- and blood-covered bodies are described, in an epic simile, as "twisted together, like twining serpents, in pliant and subtle folds."

The last words of the novel, spoken by the aged patriarch Tamenund at the funeral obsequies of Uncas and Cora, are both more bitter and less resigned than their prototype, Priam's lament for Hector:

Go children of the Lenape. The anger of the Manito is not done. Why should Tamenund stay? The pale-faces are masters of the earth, and the time of the red-men has not yet come again. My day has been too long. In the morning I saw the sons of Unamis happy and strong; and yet, before the night has come, have I lived to see the last warrior of the wise race of the Mohicans!

If we attend to the words' meanings, and not merely to their elegiac sound, we discover that both "the anger of the Manito" and "the time of the red-man" are predicted to come again upon the white world, whether it be in worldly vengeance or in otherworldly reconciliation.

At their deepest structural level, the Leatherstocking tales are based upon the oldest convention of primary or oral epic, the semidivine pair. The Big Serpent and Hawkeye, like Gilgamesh and Enkidu, Achilles and Patroklos, Beowulf and Wiglaf, Roland and Oliver, seem to have the ability to perform anything except to escape suffering and mortality. In the Leatherstocking tales, as in all four oral epics, there is a concluding sense that the values of an heroic age have passed away with the ending of these twinned lives, leaving listener or reader saddened yet relieved to be living in a less glorious and less bloody era. Unlike all four heroic pairs, however, Chingachgook and Hawkeye represent no community and have no followers. In the oldest extant epic, Gilgamesh forms his bond with Enkidu, a dark-skinned hunter from the wilderness, and the two leave civilization to undertake adventurous tasks together. Whereas Gilgamesh finally returns to the city of Uruk to guard the walls he has built, Leatherstocking's heroism is inseparable from acts of defiance and departure. As an embodiment of the combined but unrealized potential of two cultures, Leatherstocking belongs nowhere.

Just as the popularity of *The Last of the Mohicans* was partially due to the emerging controversy over Indian Removal, so the fame of Prescott's *History of the Conquest of Mexico* (1843) reflects the debate over extraterritorial expansionism that was soon to result in the Mexican-American War. Cooper's epic heroes, as his title indicates, are vanishing, uncorrupted Indians who lament but do not openly resist Anglo-American supremacy. Although Prescott was a Conscience Whig, convinced that conflict with Mexico was a rationalization for expansion of slavery interests, he had by 1839 committed himself to shaping his history of the earlier conquest of Mexico into "an epic in prose" with Hernando Cortés as "the hero of the piece." Wedding the conventions of epic narrative to a historical fiction had allowed Cooper to be flexible, wavering, inconsistent in his judgments. By shaping his immense research into an epic history, Prescott sought—as a willed act of the historian's reason—consistently to demonstrate that the conquest of the vast Aztec empire by a few ironclad Spaniards had been a "grand drama of Western Progress," a "daring, chivalrous enterprise" full of "stupendous achievements" and exhibiting all that "extraordinary personal qualities in a hero can give."

Prescott came to his life's work, the Matter of Spain, through extensive reading and reviewing of Homer, Virgil, Dante, Ariosto, Tasso, Pulci, Ercilla, and Milton, along with much else. In his view "the poems of Homer were intended as historical compositions." The greatness of primary epic lay in the Aristotelian ability of the tale teller to convey the march of "one concentrated action, like the Ancient Drama." Oral narrative epic, always a hybrid of history and drama, was eventually transformed into medieval chivalric Romance, a genre that sacrificed concentration of action to color of poetic detail and elaboration of incident. Prescott's aim was to merge all these genres into one prose history, creating "an epic in prose, a romance of chivalry . . . which, while it combines all the picturesque features of the romantic school, is borne onward on a tide of destiny, like that which broods over the fictions of the Grecian poets."

In this last aim, if in no other, Prescott's *History* is a magnificent success—as anyone who knows the sprawl of his historical sources must attest. Perhaps because Prescott was nearly blind, he like Milton conceived a vast but shapely narrative steadily narrowing in upon acts that are simultaneously a fall and a rise: the death of Montezuma, the doomed resistance of Guatemozin, and Cortés's protracted siege of the Aztec capitol. As the barbarisms and beauties of Tenochtitlan are slowly, relentlessly leveled in book 5, Prescott earns his insistence that interest in heroic narrative depends on the epic historian's ability to sustain a Grecian sense of fatality. At the same time, however, Prescott's intended justification of Cortés collapses under the accumulated evidence of the many Spanish cruelties and treacheries that Prescott has been too scrupulous to hide. As Prescott pens the last of his panoramic word paintings—an overview of starving, defiant Aztecs standing in the rubble of their civilization—Guatemozin explicitly emerges as "the hero," while Cortés, never very convincing as a knight of chivalry, recedes back into "this remarkable man." Prescott's last attempt to provide a moral logic for "the right of conquest" remains at least as troubled as his first. The evident shift in Prescott's sympathies, his under-mining of his own purpose, may of course be ascribed to humane revul-sion against the barbarities of whites who "civilize" the savage in the name of Christ and King. But one suspects that the tradition of epic poetry was equally influential. In Prescott's closing pages, Guatemozin and the Aztecs are not sentimentalized as innocent victims of imperi-alism. They are rather viewed as heroes who, like Hector or Turnus, Beowulf or Roland, have gained glory from maintaining to the death their doomed resistance to a superior force.

A Delaware heroic poem titled *Walam Olum* ("printed record") was partially transcribed from oral delivery during the 1830s, but Cooper seems not to have known of it. Prescott's researches into Aztec accounts of the conquest stopped short of the chants and heroic laments in Nahuatle that have been preserved by Leon Portilla in *The Broken Spears*. For both Cooper and Prescott there were, of course, problems of these texts' accessibility as well as barriers caused by a non-European language and by the fragmentary nature of almost all extant heroic nar-ratives sung by defeated and preliterate peoples. To assume that these lacunae amount to disinterest, however, would be misleading. The whole European epic tradition formed a lens through which, it was thought, the heroic age should be seen. For white authors to write such narratives in various forms of prose was at least an honest use of their own literary medium. But when Longfellow raided Schoolcraft's research into Winnebago customs, fitted them into an overlay of Iro-quois mythology, blithely transformed the whole into the tripping meter of the Finnish *Kalevala*, and then offered *Hiawatha* as a coher-ent series of North American Indian legends, the result could only be poetic make-up of the most transparent kind.

To convey the epic dimensions of *Moby-Dick* in three or four pages is about as easy as defining the whale. By modifying Fielding's terminol-ogy, the question of the book's genre could be facilely settled by calling it a comic-epic-tragic-poem in prose. Closer reading shows, however, that Melville has also given us an anatomy of whaling, several oral tales, a parodic sermon or two, a romance, bad verse amidst glorious prose-poetry, a dream vision, a Shakespearean closet drama, many medita-tions, a genealogy, not a few hideous and intolerable allegories, and a mock epic as well as an epic. The power of the book clearly depends on its continuous transformation of genres as well as ideas. Because no truth is timeless or universal, no single genre can be adequate, especially if the world of mind is one's subject.

Although Georg Lukács seems not to have read Melville, both the evasive cetology chapters and the multilayered narrative of *Moby-Dick* confirm a remarkable insight from Lukács's *The Theory of the Novel* (1914):

> The novel is the epic of an age in which the extensive totality of life is no longer directly given, in which the immanence of meaning in life has become a problem, yet which still thinks in terms of totality. It would be superficial—a matter of mere artistic technicality—to look for the only and decisive genre-defining criterion in the question of whether a work is written in verse or prose.

External evidence also suggests that it was Melville's purpose to write "the American epic" in a bafflingly new genre of the sort both Lukács and Bakhtin were later to praise. Shaping his review of Hawthorne's *Mosses from an Old Manse* into a call for an heroic national literature, Melville abruptly proclaimed "we want no American Miltons." He then combined mockery of the imitative epic poem with a sly promise of better things to come:

> I was much pleased with a hot-headed Carolina cousin of mine who once said, "If there were no other American to stand-by, in literature, why, then, I would stand by Pop Emmons and his 'Fredoniad,' and till a better epic came along, swear it was not very far behind the Iliad." Take away the words, and in spirit he was sound.

Melville's nonexistent Carolina cousin fully shares the kind of pity Redburn expressed for "a neglected poem by a neglected Liverpool poet" who had written hundreds and hundreds of heroic couplets singing commercial growth along the Mersey. "This epic, from the specimen before me, is composed in the old stately style, and rolls along commanding as a coach and four." In the age of the Iron Horse or the world-roaming whaleship, the high ambition of the American epic could and should be reaffirmed. The medical cure for the epic's old stately style—hopefully not a mortal prescription—would be somehow surgically to "take away the words."

Except for a very occasional moment in the Leatherstocking tales, there had probably not been, in American heroic literature, one successful, intentionally comic passage from the time of Dwight's *The*

Conquest of Canaan through Prescott's *History of the Conquest of Mexico*. One of Melville's great achievements was to break down the long-standing division Americans had maintained between epic and mock epic. Just as Trumbull's *M'Fingal* (1785) had belonged to a dependent but supposedly separate subgenre, so Irving's *History of New York* (1809) had been a mock epic parody of current state histories that were currently claiming too much Revolutionary glory. Noah Webster's definitions of generic terms allowed no mingling of the comic and heroic. The reader of *Moby-Dick*, however, is often unsure whether Melville's adaptations of epic conventions exalt the Pequod's quest, or belittle it by contrast, or mock outmoded elements of the epic form. It is not merely by accident of a presumably changed purpose that Melville's invocation to the muse ("Bear me out in it, Thou great Democratic God!") is to be found, very much in the fashion of Lawrence Sterne, in chapter 26. Why is it that *Moby-Dick* contains so many different propositions, from the extracts of the poor devil of a sub-sub, through "this august dignity I treat of" and "the Honor and Glory of Whaling" to Melville's pretended dismissal of "other poets" in preference for the posteriority of "I celebrate a tail"? There are at least fourteen epic similes in *Moby-Dick*, many of them as suspiciously ostentatious as the elaborate three-day battle with which Melville's narrative (like Milton's war in heaven or Spenser's first book) climactically ends. Philosophical polysyllabics alternate with American slang; grandeur of language suddenly gives way to grandiloquence or obscure rant, most conspicuously so when Ishmael or Ahab claims Ahab to be the modern Prometheus. The polyglossic levels of discourse in Melville's prose contain a mingling of epic and mock-epic that reveals Melville's distrust of the very heroisms of attitude and action that continue to absorb him.

Like the 1855 *Leaves of Grass*, but in a different way, *Moby-Dick* represents a moment in literary history when generic terms retain old meanings that must be wilfully, even gleefully, broken down. Although it is useful to consider whether particular passages point toward tragedy or burlesque, grandeur or puffery, epic or mock-epic, the attempt to resolve such questions for the text as a whole leads to patent absurdity. And so it is with the character of Ahab. The armada of scholars and critics who have felt compelled to reach a judgment upon Ahab are by now revealed to have been collectively gazing into Melville's doubloon.

A fuller understanding of Ahab may still come, however, from considering the literary construction of his character and the literary contexts of his particular words. Whatever kind of "American" identity Ahab may be thought to prefigure, he is less a Nantucket whaling captain than a hero fashioned from the words of non-American poetic and dramatic models: Achilles, Prometheus, Faustus, Lear, Satan, and Manfred, to whom we should surely add Tegner's Frithiof and Carlyle's Cromwell. Ahab's birth from epic and tragic predecessors becomes readily apparent as soon as a portion of his last speech is spaced differently upon the page:

> Oh, now I feel my topmost greatness lies
> In my topmost grief. Ho, ho! From all
> Your farthest bounds, pour ye now in,
> Ye bold billows of my whole foregone life,
> And top this one piled comber of my death!
> Towards thee I roll, thou all-destroying but
> Unconquering whale; to the last I grapple with thee;
> From hell's heart I stab at thee; for hate's sake
> I spit my last breath at thee.

By association of literary idiom as well as content, Ahab's blank verse is here meant to endow him with the spirit of Milton's Satan: "the unconquerable Will, / And study of revenge, immortal hate, / And courage never to submit or yield." Just as epic poem is transformed into prose romance, however, so the literary continuity among the two defiantly rebellious hero-villains is established only to lead to a difference. Whereas Satan's "immortal hate" degenerates into lies, disguise, and a despair deserving of a "dismal universal hiss," Ahab's last speech is arguably his greatest moment. Unlike Satan, Ahab can grow in courage because his personal revenge has real cause and his metaphysical quest, however deluded, has an undeniable nobility of purpose. Instead of knowingly declaring "evil be thou my good," one-legged Ahab hopes to rid the whole world of its surely inscrutable and possibly evil God.

However much Ishmael may believe in his inner, insular Tahiti, he repeatedly exalts the power of individual resistance, even in Ahab whose quest he has condemned. Through epic simile, Ishmael aggrandizes Ahab long after Ahab has bound his crew to hunt the white whale:

> As in the hurricane that sweeps the plain,
> Men fly the neighborhood of some lone,
> Gigantic elm, whose very height and strength
> But render it so much the more unsafe,
> Because so much the more a mark for thunderbolts;
> So at these last words of Ahab's
> Many of the mariners did run from him
> In a terror of dismay.
>
> (from the chapter "The Candles")

This simile is surely an imitation (a "parody" according to Johnson's definition) of the simile Virgil used to describe Aeneas enduring Dido's wrath:

> As when, among the Alps, north winds
> will strain against each other to root out
> with blasts—now on this side, now that—a stout
> oak tree whose wood is full of years; the roar
> is shattering, the trunk is shaken, and
> high branches scatter on the ground; but it
> still grips the rocks; as steeply as it thrusts
> its crown into the upper air, so deep
> the roots it reaches down to Tartarus:
> no less than this, the hero; he is battered
> on this side and on that by assiduous words;
> he feels care in his mighty chest, and yet
> his mind cannot be moved; the tears fall, useless.
>
> (*The Aeneid* 4, tr. Allen Mandelbaum)

Once again, imitation has here become a splendid literary transformation. To Melville the destroying power of the hurricane renders Ahab all the more grand because the lone gigantic elm is the special and conspicuous mark of hostile forces. Virgil's interest is in the tenuous nature of Aeneas's resistance, the ability of the stout oak to remain firm even though its branches fall and it groans under the blast. Virgil stresses the agony of suppressing individual feeling in pursuit of a grander communal mission; Melville exalts intransigent defiance while implying its suicidal end. The reworking of a famous simile thus shifts a Roman awareness of the necessary price of Imperium into a tribute to individuality that Tocqueville would have recognized as especially American.

Moby-Dick complicates my argument that epic renderings of the heroic age enabled white American writers to give voice and stature to the very peoples being destroyed by the expansion of Euro-American culture. Admittedly, Melville pointedly shows that people of color serve only as "Squires" at the command of the ship's white "Knights," and he pens many an acerbic hit at various kinds of racial injustice. Nonetheless, racial issues are not the heart of epic conflict as they had been for Cooper and Prescott. There is more than a little smiling condescension in the portrayal of Queequeg's noble savagery. No person of color apparently has the strength of mind to resist the power of Ahab's "mighty brow." All the more reason, therefore, to note that the American Indian is at least allowed to convey Melville's last judgment through a wordless gesture. As the "federated" ship of state goes down forever, Tashtego hammers skyhawk to flag to mainmast, striking with an "etherial thrill" of both revenge and tribute.

Whitman's primacy and centrality to the tradition of the twentieth-century "personal epic" or "visionary epic" (*The Cantos*, *The Bridge*, *Paterson*, *The Dream Songs*, *The Maximus Poems*) is a far more problematic matter than we usually assume. At best, twentieth-century poets have made their several pacts with Walt Whitman, glorying in his breaking of the new wood, while insisting that he was the most pig-headed of poetic fathers. Although Pound, Crane, Williams, Berryman, and Olson all staked out varying claims to continue epic tradition in new poetic forms, Whitman himself had explicitly written in the 1855 preface that *Leaves of Grass* was "not direct or descriptive or epic." Such questions of intent and influence are vexing enough, but they pale beside an underlying problem of small audience and unaccepted form. Heroic age cultures generally cherished one preeminent epic poem because that particular heroic narrative had acquired a choric role in defining its people's identity. From Whitman's time to Berryman's, the American poet who has claimed that his own visionary power is sufficient for heroism has been discovered, promoted, supported, and read, not by the American people as a whole, but by the academy and by other writers. Instead of one continuing heroic narrative, *Leaves of Grass* and its successors offer us a gathering-up of individual lyrics, loosely and sometimes forcibly connected. More is at stake here than extending the boundaries of the word *epic* beyond useful definition. Two separable generic questions arise. Even in

1855, had prose already become the only medium sufficiently popular to satisfy the choric function of epic? Or, to phrase the issue solely in terms of poetic narrative: can any lengthy work of heroic poetry abandon tale telling and yet remain readable and memorable to the people who must finally determine its epic stature?

These are not the issues of hindsight only. Emerson's famous essay calling forth "The Poet" imagined a "genius of tyrannous eye" who would sing, not one hero and his deeds, but all America, its geography and its occupations. In his 1839 essay titled "Epic Poetry," Jones Very concluded that the very survival of epic now depended on abandoning narrative altogether:

It is in the greatness of the epic action that the poets succeeding Homer, if we except Milton, have failed; and the causes which have operated against them, will always operate with increasing force against every attempt to represent the present or future developments of the heroic character in action.

When the world is seen in terms of the self rather than the self in terms of the world, the past deed of any other person necessarily becomes secondary. And so, to Emerson, Very, and Whitman alike, Aristotelian action must now be replaced by a universal, imaginary process that originates in the democratic mind. As Very puts it, "Could intellectual power be represented with the same objectiveness as physical power, there might be as many epics now as there are great minds." For Whitman, loafing on the grass empowers everyone to experience his (or her?) heroic journey; just "shoulder your duds" and take to your own open road by imagining yourself there.

The 1855 *Leaves of Grass* proposes a defiant rejection of epic conventions rather than an adaptation of them. As Whitman planned his poem, he reminded himself, "Take no illustrations from the ancients or classics"; "What is to be done is to withdraw from precedents"; "Not the first recognition of gods or goddesses, or Greece or Rome"; "Old forms, old poems, majestic and proper in their own lands, here in this land are exiles." The very purpose of America, he wrote in *An American Primer*, is "to destroy all these [old myths and Gods] from the purposes of the earth, and to erect a new earth in their place." The greatness of the epic is the literary myth perhaps most in need of demolition. Hence "to destroy" the old poetic conventions would not transform the Old World epic (as Prescott and Melville had done) but end it forever.

Whitman's first preface describes *Leaves of Grass* as "the great psalm of the republic," not a New World epic poem. Because bardic prophecy of inner divinity is a heroism now available to all, all the poetic conventions suitable to the superior deeds of superior men must be dismissed. Instead of an elaborate proposition reworking the conventional phrase "Of——I sing," America's heroic poem is to begin with a brash seriocomic self-assertion, immediately democratized:

> I celebrate myself
> And what I assume you shall assume
> For every atom belonging to me as good belongs to you.

The fifth section of "Song of Myself" shows that the muse is neither a force of external inspiration the poet must invoke, nor the traditional standard for singing a cherished narrative. The muse is rather an ecstatic vision released at a moment of inner integration when the Self's body and soul are sexually joined. Heroic couplet and blank verse are no longer pertinent to American heroic song, in part because they are Old World forms, but, more important, because they comprise a special, elevated language. The new metric must instead replicate everyone's breath patterns, adding phrase upon phrase in alternating patterns of inspiration and respiration that sustain the illusion of "primary" oral delivery.

"Song of Myself" claims to upend what C. M. Bowra was to define as the essential purpose of epic poetry—to create awe for the hero who faces known death for the sake of honor or glory. Whitman's boast that it is "lucky to die, and I know it" is unforgettable because the word "lucky" challenges centuries of accumulated tragic response to the earthly demise of Hector and Beowulf, Adam and Jesus, and even (if we wish to update and Americanize), Leatherstocking, Guatemozin, and Ahab. Death is, at the outset, willfully ruled out of Whitman's heroic vision:

> The smallest sprout shows there is really no death
> And if there was it led forward life,
>   and does not wait at the end to arrest it,
> And ceased the moment life appeared.
> All goes onward and outward . . . and nothing collapses,
> And to die is different from what any one supposed, and luckier.

The gore of the battlefield—even the murder of the 412 Texas Rangers and the *Bon Homme Richard*'s hideous victory over the *Serapis*—only serves to show that "agonies are one of my changes of garments." Although the dead of all battles are subsumed within the two words "these irretrievable," the poem's next section suggests that, as soon as "the corpses rise . . . the gashes heal . . . the fastenings roll away," the Self's transfiguration will make any awe we still might feel for self-sacrificial death seem quite superfluous.

Sheer enjoyment of his own brag enables Whitman to write lines that may be read as either heroic or mock-heroic. To be "Walt Whitman, an American, one of the roughs, a kosmos" is to be a quantum of energy forever in process of self-transformation through his own words. Although all the Self's words are revelations, none of those revelations are permanent. As a consequence, the finality of such epic conventions as the prophecy spoken atop a high hill (vide Virgil's Anchises, Milton's Michael, Barlow's Hesper) becomes parodic in both senses. The poet leads "each man and each woman of you . . . upon a knoll" but then refuses to divulge any future at all, slyly admonishing, "Not I, not any one else can travel that road for you. / You must travel it for yourself . . . / I answer that I cannot answer, you must find out for yourself." The authority of traditional epic narrative rested in considerable degree on the "type scene" of a god's arrival—that marvelous moment when an Athena, Venus, or Raphael assumed visual shape and provided direction to human history as well as a hero's life. The arrival of Whitman's god (his own "gross" Self, of course) ends only in the balking of all whispered confidences, and the huffy proposing of questions:

> This hour I tell things in confidence.
> I might not tell everybody but I will tell you.
> Who goes there! hankering, gross, mystical, nude
> How is it I extract strength from the beef I eat?
> What is a man anyhow? What am I? and what are you?

The fact that such seeming-simple questions are unanswerable is far less important than the sheer celebration of human energy they contain. To proclaim the Self a divine animal is to replace a single hero's mortal courage with everyone's visionary daring. In 1855 Whitman celebrates that change, believing that the power of his new verse derives in great measure from demolishing the epic.

Whitman did not begin speaking of *Leaves of Grass* as an "attempt at utterance, of New World songs, and an epic of Democracy" until his 1872 preface titled "As a Strong Bird on Pinions Free." Evidence of his desire, in later life, to refashion his every accumulating volume as "an epic of Democracy" may be found everywhere. In 1867 he decided to begin each forthcoming edition of the *Leaves* with "One's Self I Sing," a new poem that, in form and content, is clearly a proposition for an epic. (Lest readers should miss the point, he also added the phrase "and sing myself" to the first line of his central poem.) In 1871 he added "As I Ponder'd in Silence" and "Song of the Exposition," both of which invoke a "Phantom" muse of war poetry and then describe the migration of this external muse from Greece to America. "Song of the Exposition" even claims, apparently seriously, that a traditionally feminine and statuesque muse can be uncovered amid such glorious democratic products as steam whistles, gasometers, and artificial fertilizers ("Smiling and pleas'd with palpable intent to stay, / She's here, installed among the kitchen ware!").

Ambitious poems like "Passage to India" and "Prayer of Columbus" now attempt, very much in Joel Barlow's fashion, to wed both the poet's heroic vision and the advances of technology to the journeyings of Columbus. A late poem like "Old Chants" positions *Leaves of Grass* at the end of a tradition beginning with the Hindu epics, proceeding through "The Iliad, Odyssey, plots, doings, wanderings of Eneas" on down to Walter Scott and Tennyson. The poet who had once written "What is to be done is to withdraw from precedents" thus insisted, at the last, upon linking his song to a whole list of epic predecessors while dutifully noting "Of many debts incalculable / Haply our New World's chiefest debt is to old poems." As early as 1867, there is pathetic evidence that Whitman's initial literary rebellion against the epic was exhausted. In his notebooks he added up the number of words in *Leaves of Grass* in order to compare his total with those of five other texts: the Bible, *The Iliad, The Aeneid, The Divine Comedy*, and *Paradise Lost*.

The writing of *Leaves of Grass* began in great heroic poetry that was not epic, and ended in bad "epic" verse that was not heroic. It may be futile, however, for me to emphasize Whitman's insight that, at least in its first edition, *Leaves of Grass* was "not epic." After all, Whitman was later to write many poems affirming America's cultural greatness; he was to combine them into a massive book; he was to describe his own life's work as "an epic of democracy." Why bother to protest such a formidable array of facts? Because it is crucial, in considering the claims upon epic advanced by later American poets, to try and determine which of these two Walt Whitmans has influenced them. Has twenti-eth-century thinking about the viability of epic poetry been shaped pri-marily by Whitman's early need to transform the genre beyond recog-nition, or by his later need to adopt the epic as the only way to lay claim to the authority of a popular bard who has truly made it new?

Antebellum forms of American epic literature were to be continued—and sometimes masterfully developed—during the closing decades of the century. For sweet mercy's sake, no more than bibliographic men-tion should be made of the five imitative epic poems published for the Columbian Quatrecentennial: John Campbell's *Republica* (1891), Henry Iliowizi's *Quest of Columbus* (1892), Samuel Jefferson's *Columbus: An Epic Poem* (1892), John Howell's *Columbus* (1893), and Franklyn Quinby's *The Columbiad* (1893—at least the fourth poem of that title). At the height of the supposed age of "Realism," that supposed "Natu-ralist" Frank Norris followed Cooper and Simms in defending the fic-tional Romance as the appropriate form of impassioned poetry for the new era. *The Octopus* and *The Pit*—with their heroic epithets, triple adjectives, repeated formulaic paragraphs, invocations of Force, and evocations of limitlessness—carry out the restorative prospectus of Norris's essay "A Neglected Epic" (1902). "The stupendous conquering of the West . . . these mysterious race movements, migrations, wars and wanderings . . . the last great event in the history of Civilization . . . has so far produced in the way of literature . . . the dime novel and nothing better!" Francis Parkman's equally vast but stylistically restrained seven-part history, *France and England in North America* (1865–1893), fully accepts Prescott's assumption that pre-Revolutionary racial and nation-al wars of empire comprise the New World's historical epic. Deter-mined to cast the three-century foreground of the French and Indian Wars into poetic prose, interesting narrative, and a properly interna-tional context, Parkman also acknowledged that Cooper's epic fiction, in particular *The Last of the Mohicans*, "has had an influence in deter-mining the course of my life and pursuits." Leslie Fiedler contends that the African American search for liberation and roots has comprised, from the era of Harriet Beecher Stowe to the era of Alex Haley, Amer-ica's "inadvertent epic."

These are all literary projects whose conceptual origins, in differing ways and with unequal results, antedate the concerns of the mid-nineteenth century. In none of them do we find that joyous blending of the heroic and the mock epic, awe and satire, oral prophecy and its own burlesque, that informs both *Moby-Dick* and "Song of Myself." Indeed, the later lives of both these writers suggest a reseparation of epic from mock-epic that very nearly precludes humor. Just as Whitman sought to present himself anew through recasting his "barbaric yawp" as an "epic of Democracy," so Melville moved away from "trying out" differing ways of celebrating a tail (tale?) toward the grimly teleological concerns of *Clarel* (1876).

Among the many possible causes for the reseparation (Realism, Darwinism, "scientific" hierarchies of race, problems of the new industrial order, etc.), the cataclysm of civil war held hideous primacy. Whatever "the American epic" had once been thought to be, the writing of it had been linked to some kind of belief in the continuing promise of the nation's republican experiment. By late 1865, it seemed evident that America had emerged intact from a war unprecedented in scale, in numbers of deaths, and in instances of courageous self-sacrifice as well as of incompetence. But it was equally apparent that, late in 1861, the United States of America had in fact ceased to exist. American writers drawn toward heroic literature were thus handed the grandest of martial subjects in an unexpected and perhaps unusable form. Instead of the conquest of other races and other imperial powers (Indians or Aztecs, French or Spanish), America's severest conflict, its bloodiest glory, had turned out to be a war among Anglo-Americans over a "peculiar institution" widely thought to have been a national disgrace. No European or American epic had yet been made of a civil war. To cast the South in the role of Satan, or the North in the role of invading Greeks, would not only impede postwar reconciliation; it would degrade the national self.

As a nurse in Union hospitals, Whitman believed that the courage of the wounded and dying men he saw surpassed all poems, "even the oldest and tearfullest . . . the old Greek mighty ones, where man contends with fate (and always yields)." By 1875, Whitman became convinced that the Civil War was "the Vertebrer of Poetry and Art, (of personal character too) for all future America (far more grand, in my opinion, to the hands capable of it, than Homer's siege of Troy)." And by the time Whitman wrote "A Backward Glance" (1888) the Civil War had assumed such centrality in his thinking about the genesis of *Leaves of Grass* that he insisted, quite erroneously, that his book could only "have emerged or been fashion'd . . . from the absolute triumph of the National Union arms."

Such anxious comparisons of the Trojan and Civil Wars show Whitman's need to demonstrate that his epic of democracy was founded on a new and higher heroism. In the "Drum-Taps" section of *Leaves of Grass*, death has become final and no longer "lucky," but no soldier can be called heroic simply because he knowingly died for battle glory or even for honor. The young men of "Vigil Strange I Kept on the Field One Night," "A Sight in the Daybreak Gray and Dim," and "The Wound Dresser" have nobly suffered an unjust, unexpected death for the sake of restoring the mystic chords of Union. Although Whitman carefully refrains from villainizing Southerners, he justifies the Civil War by seeing it as a purgative tragedy ending in national progress. As in Barlow's *Columbiad* or James Russell Lowell's once widely read "Commemoration Ode," Progress is a providential law dependent upon "the dependence of Liberty" and "the continuancy of Equality." The glory of reunion is confirmed by will of the poet, but not created by the acts of the dead. Although Whitman's "Reconciliation" is a perfectly crafted poem, it suggests that the face of the Southern enemy can somehow be washed white by the poet's kiss. Even poets as wary of martial glory as Virgil and Milton would have had difficulty seeing "Drum Taps" as the onset of a new and higher heroism. Whitman would convince us that to be the nation's wound-dresser, to bind wounds rather than to destroy evil, is to offer one's individuality to the greater service of political reconciliation.

Melville's way of giving epic dimension to civil war incurred a different kind of difficulty. Expressing the same overview as Whitman but in grimmer and more tentative terms, Melville offered, in his "Supplement" to *Battle-Pieces*, a prayer that the Civil War might prove to have been a "terrible historic tragedy" that would verify the hopes of "the bards of Progress and Humanity" by instructing "our whole beloved country through terror and pity." "The Conflict of Convictions" announces, however, that national tragedy needs to be defined through epic analogy:

> Return, return, O eager Hope,
>   And face man's latter fall.
> Events, they make the dreamers quail;
> Satan's old age is strong and hale,
> A disciplined captain, gray in skill,
> And Raphael a white enthusiast still.

As the sequence of battle pieces proceeds, the import of historical events is repeatedly uncovered by direct Miltonic reference. Slavery emerges as the new Dagon, Farragut as the new Moses, Grant as Michael, Richmond as Babylon, and so forth. Unfortunately, Melville's attempt to elevate civil war by an accumulation of such analogies ultimately works against his hope that *Battle-Pieces* will further national reconciliation. If Melville succeeds in convincing us that the South truly is Satan "gray in skill," we can only wish to dismiss the serpent with a universal hiss, rejoicing that Right has finally conquered Wrong.

In a reversal of the antebellum pattern, late nineteenth-century novelists shunned all attempt to describe warfare in heightened poetic prose. Neither John William De Forest (*Miss Ravenel's Conversion*, 1867) nor Winston Churchill (*The Crisis*, 1901) connect their Civil War fictions with the epic, even though both novelists believed in heroism. *The Red Badge of Courage* begs to be read as an ironic reversal—and an implicit attack—upon the consolatory words of the many "bards of Progress and Humanity" who had been elevating the Civil War by handy references to tragedy and epic. Perhaps the fratricide was still of too recent memory, or waving the bloody shirt was still too common, for epic fiction on the nation's cataclysm to reemerge, especially in an era when Realism was increasingly fashionable.

Nonetheless, the Civil War was to be the subject of the only twentieth-century American epic poem that has been cherished and widely read beyond the academy. Through 1957, Stephen Vincent Benét's *John Brown's Body* (1928) had sold at least 214,000 copies, only half of them in separate texts for college or secondary school use. Benét openly admired Frost and MacLeish, but remained silent about Pound and Eliot. Expatriate years in Paris during the mid-twenties (*John Brown's Body* was written in France) only made Benét more self-consciously an American. Through editing the *Yale Literary Magazine*, Benét established connections with Henry Seidel Canby, John Farrar, Thornton Wilder, and Archibald MacLeish that would help his poem win a Guggenheim, Book-of-the-Month Club publication, and the Pulitzer Prize. Benét, remained, however, very much the son of a patriotic military family that had lived both North and South. His poetic roots and populist attitudes emerged directly from Lindsay, Masters, and Sandburg. Poetry, Benét insisted in a 1941 preface to *John Brown's Body*, "is meant to be heard. It is meant for everybody, not only for the scholars. It is not a highly complicated puzzle box which you can open only with a special set of keys. . . . Poetry is open to any reader who likes the sound and the swing of rhythm, the color and fire of words." Here clearly was a scholarly bard perfectly suited to join in affirming "The People, Yes" as his nation moved reluctantly through isolationism toward a second World War. Raymond Massey read *John Brown's Body* over the national airwaves in 1939; Benét chanted his poem at West Point and across the nation's college campuses; when Benét died in 1944, he was widely mourned both as America's Union poet and as the Walt Whitman of our times.

John Brown's Body honors the Union but not war. Glorification of fratricidal carnage in the name of Freedom's heaven-protected cause is exactly what Benét's poem does not offer us. Its hero is not murderous John Brown (the "stone" and "force" of history) but Father Abraham conceived as a secular man of sorrows. The best use of soldiers' bibles has been, on rare occasion, to stop a bullet:

> There are no gods to come with a golden smoke
> Here in the mud between the York and the James
> And wrap some high-chinned hero away from death.

Attack upon the absent divinities of epic also informs the poem's satirical passages. Union congressmen with picnic lunches overlooking the first battle of Bull Run have

> Come out to see the gladiator's show
> Like Iliad gods, wrapped in the sacred cloud
> Of Florida water, wisdom and bay rum,
> Of free cigars, democracy and votes.

Benét's poem begins with a lengthy "invocation" to a fleeting, shadowy "American muse" that can be glimpsed in mountains and deserts, on plantations or bleak New England farms, in skyscrapers or even in "an immensity of wheel / Made up of wheels, oiled with inhuman sweat," but not ever, apparently, in the actual moment of combat.

The genre of so popular a poem became an immediate issue. Although Benét preferred to avoid the word epic (referring to *John Brown's Body* as "a long poem," "only a cup of silver air," and even as a "cyclorama"), Benét privately fretted that his "queer start" would make *John Brown's Body* "the most colossal flop since Barlow's *Columbiad*." Allen Tate, scornful of Benét's reverence for Lincoln, promptly declared that "the poem is not in any sense an epic . . . it is a loose episodic narrative which unfolds a number of related themes in motion-picture flashes." Three months later Harriet Monroe countered by turning the terms of Tate's denial into a way of transforming an old genre for a new age. *John Brown's Body*, she proclaimed, is "a real book, a man-size book" precisely because it is "cinema epic," brilliant flashes in ever-changing meters, "a super-journalistic epic" that frees us from all those conventions "associated too loftily with Homer and Virgil." Academics like Dudley Fitz and Robert Morss Lovett equivocated by calling the poem, respectively, "an epyllion" and "an epic in intent." Alfred Kreymborg was certain that the poetry of Benét and Hart Crane showed "renewed interest in epic forms" among American poets. Fortunately, Benét found a new way of promoting "our singing strength" at exactly the moment (Kreymborg wrongly predicted) when "one now wearies of Imagism."

Instead of arguing whether cinema could be incorporated into epic literature, reviewers in 1929 might well have considered whether "epic" cinema was not about to assume the choric function once held by heroic poetry. For the continuation of epic poetry, the abiding problem would be the mixing of kinds rather than the clash of lowbrow and highbrow. Although Benét was no Imagist, he was enough of a Modernist to be unable to resolve the problem of combining flashing images and slow narrative. The successes of his poem are the factual, vivid, and rapid images Benét recreates from history. Its insistent failures are the plodding, dull narratives made of his characters' lives. Jack Ellyat the Connecticut Abolitionist and Clay Wingate the fiery Georgia scion, Cudjo the happy Darky and Aunt Bess the loyal Mammy, Sally Dupré from Appleton Hall and Lucy Weatherby the Virginia Belle—all Benét's fictional characters are walking stereotypes with no trace of inner life. Anyone interested in their true cultural coin should spend his or her time watching *Birth of a Nation* and *Gone with the Wind*. *The Bridge* and *Paterson* may lead us to question whether Modernist poetic epic can ever reach a wide audience without satisfying the need for narrative. The disappearance of *John Brown's Body* from public view, however, suggests that a narrative verse epic will lose its impact whenever a poet fabricates characters said to embody cultural legend. William Carlos Williams's way—"a reply to Greek and Latin with the bare hands"—has at least given *Paterson* fit audience though few.

John McWilliams

Further Reading

Barlow, Joel. *The Works of Joel Barlow*. Vol. 2, *The Columbiad*. Eds. W. K. Bottorff and A. L. Ford. Gainesville, Fla.: Scholars' Facsimiles and Reprints, 1970.

Benét, Stephen Vincent. *John Brown's Body*. New York: Doubleday, Doran, 1928.

Bryan, Daniel. *The Mountain Muse*. Harrisonburg, Va.: Davidson and Bourne, 1813.

Cooper, James Fenimore. *The Last of the Mohicans*. Eds. J. A. Sappenfield and E. N. Feltskog. New York: State University of New York Press, 1983.

Emmons, Richard. *The Fredoniad*. Boston: William Emmons, 1827.

Fiedler, Leslie. *The Inadvertent Epic: From "Uncle Tom's Cabin" to "Roots."* New York: Simon and Schuster, 1979.

Lukács, Georg. *The Theory of the Novel* [1916]. Cambridge: M.I.T. Press, 1971.

McWilliams, John P., Jr. *The American Epic: Transforming a Genre, 1770–1860*. Cambridge: Cambridge University Press, 1989.

Melville, Herman. *Moby-Dick*. Eds. H. Hayford, H. Parker, and G. T. Tanselle. Evanston and Chicago: Northwestern-Newberry, 1988.

Miller, James E., Jr. *The American Quest for a Supreme Fiction: Whitman's Legacy in the Personal Epic*. Chicago: University of Chicago Press, 1979.

Paulding, James Kirke. *The Backwoodsman*. Philadelphia: M. Thomas, 1818.

Pearce, Roy Harvey. *The Continuity of American Poetry*. Princeton: Princeton University Press, 1960.

Prescott, William Hickling. *History of the Conquest of Mexico and History of the Conquest of Peru*. New York: Random House, n.d.

Simms, William Gilmore. *The Yemassee*. New York: Harper, 1835.

Walker, Jeffrey. *Bardic Ethos and the American Epic Poem*. Baton Rouge: Louisiana State University Press, 1989.

Whitman, Walt. *Leaves of Grass*. Eds. H. W. Blodgett and S. Bradley. New York: New York University Press, 1965.

Longfellow in the Aftermath of Modernism

H ENRY WADSWORTH LONGFELLOW was not merely the most popular American poet who ever lived but enjoyed a type of fame almost impossible to imagine by contemporary standards. His books not only sold well enough to make him rich; they sold so consistently that he eventually became the most popular living author in any genre in nineteenth-century America. His readers spanned every social class from laborers to royalty, from professors to politicians. A vast, appreciative audience read, reread, and memorized his poems. His work quickly became part of school curricula. It also entered the fabric of domestic and public life—to be recited in parlors and intoned at civic ceremonies. Many of his lines became so much a part of English that even a century and a half later people who have never read Longfellow quote him unawares: "Ships that pass in the night," "Footprints on the sands of time," "When she was good, she was very, very good," "The patter of little feet." Language remembers the poems its speakers love best, even if only as clichés.

Longfellow's fame was not limited to the United States. He was the first American poet to achieve an international reputation. England hailed him as the New World's first great bard. His admirers included Charles Dickens, William Gladstone, John Ruskin, and Anthony Trollope as well as the British royal family and their notoriously anti-American poet laureate, Alfred Tennyson. But Longfellow's fame went beyond the English-speaking world. His work traveled throughout Europe and Latin America in translation. When the playboy emperor of Brazil, Dom Pedro II, visited America, he asked to dine with Longfellow (and returned the hospitality by translating "King Robert of Sicily" into Portuguese). King Victor Emmanuel offered him a medal (which the poet declined). Charles Baudelaire adapted part of *The Song of Hiawatha* into the rhymed alexandrines of "Le Calumet de Paix." Franz Liszt set the "Prologue" of *The Golden Legend* to music. In England he eventually outsold Tennyson and Browning. Tennyson once bragged to a friend that he made two thousand pounds a year from poetry, then grumbled, "But Longfellow, alas, receives three thousand." Three years after his death Longfellow's bust was unveiled in the Poet's Corner of Westminister Abbey, the first and only time an American poet has received this honor.

Longfellow's popularity did not prevent him from receiving the esteem of literati; in his lifetime they generally regarded him as the most distinguished poet America had produced. Nathaniel Hawthorne, who held him just this side of idolatry, put him "at the head of our list of native poets." William Dean Howells considered him the one American poet who ranked with Tennyson and Browning. Even Edgar Allan Poe, his most outspoken critic, repeatedly referred to his "genius." His other admirers included Oliver Wendell Holmes, James Russell Lowell, John Greenleaf Whittier, Walt Whitman, and Abraham Lincoln. By late middle age he had become the public symbol of American cultural achievement. In 1881, the year before his death, his birthday was celebrated nationwide in schools with recitations and performances. "Surely," a friend told him, "no poet was ever so fully recognized in his lifetime as you."

Longfellow's fame was not merely literary. His poetry exercised a broad cultural influence that today seems more typical of movies or popular music than anything we might imagine possible for poetry. His poems became subjects for songs, choral work, operas, musicals, plays, paintings, symphonies, pageants, and eventually films. *Evangeline*, for instance, was adapted into an opera, a cantata, a tone poem, a song cycle, and even a touring musical burlesque show. Later, it became a movie three times—the last in 1929 starring Dolores del Rio, who sang two songs to celebrate Longfellow's arrival in talkies. "The Village Blacksmith" became a film at least eight times, if one counts cartoons and parodies, including John Ford's 1922 adaptation, which updated the protagonist into an auto mechanic. *The Song of Hiawatha* not only provided American artists, composers, cartoonists, and directors with a popular subject, it gave Anton Dvořák the inspiration for two movements of his "New World" symphony. It also provided the Anglo-African composer, Samuel Coleridge Taylor, with texts for three immensely popular cantatas, which until World War II were performed annually in a two-week festival at Royal Albert Hall by almost a thousand British choristers dressed as Indians. *Hiawatha's* cultural currency was so high that it was not only translated into virtually every modern European language but also into Latin. It was even recast as English prose—the way a popular movie today is "novelized" in paperback—and it eventually became a comic book. "Paul Revere's Ride" prompted too many adaptions to list, though Grant Wood's witty version underlines the poem's status as a national icon. Charles Ives's setting of "The Children's Hour" (later choreographed by Jerome Robbins for *Ives Songs*) may also have a touch of irony, but it mainly luxuriates in the poem's celebration of domesticity, for Longfellow's emotional directness appealed immensely to composers. There are over seven hundred musical settings of his work in the Bowdoin College Library.

One could go on, but I trust that by now there has been something in my catalogue of Longfellow's fame and influence to offend critics of every persuasion. Book sales and royalty figures! Patronage of kings and emperors! Comic books and movies! Dolores del Rio and red-faced English choirs! These are not valuable tokens in establishing a poet's literary merit. I offer this welter of anecdote not to argue the intrinsic worth of Longfellow's poetry, which I believe is considerable, but to make a simple point. There is something singularly odd in Longfellow's case that makes him extraordinarily difficult for contemporary critics to discuss: he is as much a part of our history as of our literature. To approach the place he occupies at the center of mid-nineteenth-century American culture a critic must cross a minefield of explosive issues: the nature of popular art, American culture's relationship to England and Europe, the social and economic assumptions of the Genteel Tradition, Christianity's place in art, the legacy of Modernism, the critical evaluation of formal and narrative poetry, the validity of didactic poetry, the literary status of poems that require no explication, the representation of females, blacks, and Native Americans by white male authors. One could go on here as well, but this catalogue is already alarmingly long. The collective lesson it holds is that to evaluate Longfellow fairly we must first recognize the historical chasm that separates his age from our own.

If Whitman and Dickinson stand at the beginning of modern American literary consciousness, Longfellow represents the culmination of an earlier tradition. To approach him postmodern readers must make the same sort of mental adjustments they do in studying Chaucer or Milton. The necessary adjustments, however, are harder to make in Longfellow's case because, paradoxically, he—and his fellow Fireside poets—still feel so familiar. They still connect so easily to parts of American public culture. But what Longfellow connects to is *popular* culture; once we bring him into the context of contemporary high culture, especially academic literary criticism, his liberal Christian humanist assumptions seem uncomfortably dated. In intellectual discourse that valorizes indeterminacy, self-referentiality, and deconstruction, Longfellow's aesthetic has more in common with that of Virgil or Ovid than with the assumptions of Beckett or Ashbery. But unlike Virgil and Ovid, who today exist almost solely as objects of academic study, Longfellow refuses to stay in the tiny cell critics have afforded him. He can still be sighted—to the scholar's embarrassment—prowling at large in the general culture.

Although he is no longer widely taught in schools, Longfellow remains the one poet the average, nonbookish American still knows by heart—not whole poems but memorable snatches. Most English-speaking Americans can quote the openings of at least five Longfellow anthology pieces, even if they don't always know the author or title: "The Village Blacksmith," "Paul Revere's Ride," *Evangeline*, "Hiawatha's Departure," and "The Arrow and the Song." What? You don't know the last one? Yes, you do—"I shot an arrow into the air, / It fell to earth, I know not where." Most people have never read these poems. They have picked them up as part of American oral culture along with proverbs, schoolyard chants, nursery rhymes, and campfire songs. Many Americans over sixty, members of a generation that did learn Longfellow in school, can quote whole swatches of poems like "Psalm of Life," "Excelsior," or "The Wreck of the Hesperus," the recitation favorites of yesteryear. Few common readers will share the scholar's surprise that Wallace Stevens's wife, Elsie, preferred Longfellow's poems to her husband's.

Almost every poet has a Longfellow anecdote. Let me tell you mine. During the nearly seventeen years I worked in business, I assiduously tried to keep my after-hours literary activity a secret, but after a decade the embarrassing news leaked out. During the next few weeks various colleagues dropped into my office to ask if I really did write poetry. When I admitted my secret vice, an odd thing happened—on four separate occasions my visitors began to recite Longfellow. It was their way of letting me know poetry was OK by them. One accountant made it halfway through "The Wreck of the Hesperus." A senior executive intoned the opening of *Evangeline* in sonorous, if exaggerated, hexameter. No one ever quoted any other author. Longfellow was the one poet they knew by heart.

If Longfellow achieved the apogee of literary fame in his lifetime, and if his reputation still persists, however diminished, among the general public, what is the current status of his reputation among literati? The answer would have dumbfounded his contemporaries: Longfellow, if he is noted at all, is now considered a minor poet of the Genteel Tradition. If he has not yet sunk to the status of an embarrassing historical footnote like Ossian or Chatterton, he stands only marginally higher among academic critics. His long poems are unread and undiscussed; he exists precariously as the author of half a dozen short lyrics found only in the thickest anthologies. He has gradually become more a name to recognize, like William Cowper or Leigh Hunt, than an author to read. He is most definitely not an author for ambitious critics to write about. Few recent books on American poetry mention Longfellow except in passing; almost none discuss him at any length. The centenary of his death was celebrated by a single volume of scholarly papers printed, significantly, not by a university press but by the U.S. Government. So little, in fact, has been written on Longfellow recently that for years Kermit Vanderbilt and later George Hendrick made the critical dearth into a sort of running gag in successive volumes of *American Literary Scholarship.* "Increasingly rare is the scholar who braves ridicule to justify the art of Longfellow's popular rhymings," Vanderbilt characteristically quipped. The current version of nineteenth-century American poetry has no place for its once preeminent figure. Contemporary taste does not esteem the genres Longfellow favored—the ballad, idyll, pastoral romance, and moral fable—nor does it highly regard the stylistic strengths his contemporaries praised—clarity, grace, musicality, masterful versification, and memorability. These are not attributes that fit easily into the traditions of Emerson, Whitman, and Dickinson. In short, the status of Longfellow's reputation among literati is a subject less suited to a critic than an elegist.

Nowhere can the decline of Longfellow's critical reputation be measured more clearly than in his representation in serious historical anthologies. (In popular anthologies like Hazel Felleman's *Best Loved Poems of the American People* his popularity continues more or less undiminished.) The three versions of *The Oxford Book of American Verse* provide an exemplary illustration. Bliss Carman's original 1927 anthology gives more space to Longfellow than any other poet, seventeen poems spread across 37 pages. F. O. Matthiessen's considerably larger 1950 *Oxford Book of American Verse,* which ran 1,132 pages to Carman's 680, prints fourteen poems occupying 39 pages. But now Emerson, Whitman, Robinson, Frost, and Stevens have more space than he does. Longfellow consequently occupies a different position in the American canon; he is not the central nineteenth-century master but instead the greatest of the Fireside poets. By the time Richard Ellmann edited *The New Oxford Book of American Verse* in 1976, Longfellow's decline was complete. He now has only eleven poems and a little over 12 pages. Thirty-five other poets have as much or more space. Even Jones Very and James Russell Lowell outrank him in the nineteenth-century canon. Overall Longfellow occupies about the same number of pages as Gary Snyder, Robert Duncan, and John Ashbery, considerably less than Denise Levertov or Galway Kinnell. How are the mighty fallen! But it is not merely the size of Longfellow's representation but its constitution that is most revealing. Ellmann includes no narrative poems in his selection (unless one considers the "Introduction" to *The Song of Hiawatha* narrative), whereas Carman and Matthiessen felt Longfellow should be represented by such narrative poems as "Paul Revere's Ride," "The Birds of Killingworth," and "The Monk of Casal-Maggiore." Ellmann reduces him to a lyric poet. Perverse as this version of Longfellow might have seemed to a nineteenth-century reader, Ellmann merely followed the current critical consensus, which downgraded most American narrative poetry, especially Longfellow's. The third edition of *The Norton Anthology of Poetry* (1970), for example, also excluded Longfellow's narratives; it reprinted only six poems—all lyrics, three of them sonnets.

If Longfellow had been "downsized" in historical anthologies, he had become invisible in most other textbooks. The format of historical anthologies forces an editor to balance his or her individual views against the consensus of the past; no once important author, however unfashionable, is easily omitted. But the general anthologist has no similar restraints. If one examines the three leading nonhistorical college poetry textbooks—X. J. Kennedy's *An Introduction to Poetry*, John F. Nims's *Western Wind: An Introduction to Poetry*, and Laurence Perrine's *Sound and Sense*, one will find not a single poem by Longfellow, only *disjecta membra*—isolated lines used to illustrate points of rhetoric and rhythm. According to William Harmon's 1990 *Concise Columbia Book of Poetry*, no poem by Longfellow currently ranks among the top one hundred most-frequently anthologized poems in English. Insofar as university-based readers are concerned, Longfellow has become a marginal figure.

Modern literary criticism on Longfellow hardly exists in the sense that it does for more overtly difficult poets like Dickinson, Stevens, or Pound. There is no substantial body of commentary on specific poems, no vital tradition of critical discourse that collectively sharpens our reading and challenges our preconceptions. The unspoken assumption, even among his advocates, has been that Longfellow's poetry requires no gloss. Consequently, many central aspects of his work have never been examined in any detail (the linguistic stylization and rhetoric of *Hiawatha*, for example) and misconceptions about his work abound. The best Longfellow scholarship often has a decidedly old-fashioned feel; it traces historical sources, clarifies textual problems, and connects biographical data to the poems. Such criticism addresses a small group of nineteenth-century specialists rather than the general readership for American poetry; it implicitly ducks the issue of Longfellow's relevance to contemporary letters. On the rare occasions Longfellow criticism has spoken eloquently to a broader audience—as in essays by Horace Gregory, Howard Nemerov, and Leslie Fiedler—his champions have usually been more concerned with the general mission of keeping him, however marginally, in the canon than with examining specific features of his work. Since Longfellow's work now largely exists in a critical vacuum, one must begin any serious examination of his work with a few basic observations about the unusual nature of his poetic development and the strange combination of circumstances that brought this multi-talented literary man into poetry.

The smooth progress of Longfellow's academic career has led his critics to miss how extraordinarily unusual his literary apprenticeship was among nineteenth-century American poets. He began writing verse in early adolescence—nothing odd there—publishing his first poem at thirteen in the local *Portland Gazette*. At Bowdoin College he applied himself seriously to writing and encountered immediate success. During his three years in college he published nearly forty poems. Certain of his literary vocation, Longfellow faced the obvious problem of how to make a living. His father, a successful lawyer from a family of lawyers and legislators, wanted his gifted son to study for the bar. Longfellow hoped to become a journalist, but struck a compromise with his affectionate parent: he would pursue a legal career if allowed a year of graduate study at Harvard to learn Italian and perfect his French.

At graduation Longfellow met with one of the many strokes of good luck that would characterize his literary career. The trustees of Bowdoin had decided to create a chair in the new field of Modern Languages. (It would become the fourth such program in the United States after William and Mary, Harvard, and the University of Virginia.) With extraordinary boldness and insight the trustees offered the future professorship to the eighteen-year-old Longfellow, whose talent and earnest application had impressed them, under the condition that he pursue graduate study in Europe. The improbable offer saved the young poet, who then knew only Greek, Latin, and a smattering of French, from his father's profession.

When the nineteen-year-old Longfellow boarded the Cadmus in May 1826 to sail for Havre, something significant happened—he stopped writing poems. The silence would last for the next eleven years. Most poets spend their twenties mastering their medium, usually by writing reams of verse that carry them from juvenilia into artistic maturity. Longfellow also dedicated this crucial decade to learning his craft, but in a different way from his American contemporaries: he studied European languages and literature, he translated an astonishing range of poetry—usually in its original meters, he wrote prose of every variety from fiction and memoir to grammar textbooks and literary criticism. When he returned to original poetry in late 1837 he had developed an unprecedented combination of skills for an American poet—a deep knowledge of European literature, a practical experience with dozens of poetic genres and forms from his work in translation, a trained critical mind, and an assured authorial voice developed by publishing a considerable amount of prose, most notably *Outre-Mer: A Pilgrimage Beyond the Sea* (1835), his autobiographical travelogue.

The factors that pushed Longfellow back into poetry have not been adequately explored by his biographers. His brother Samuel, who compiled the first, largely documentary biography in 1886, romantically assumed that the creative release came when the poet first moved into Craigie House, the elegant Cambridge manse that he would eventually own and occupy for the remaining forty-five years of his life. Herbert Gorham offers the more interesting theory that Longfellow's immersion in European literature during the previous ten years instilled in him an anxiety about the difficulty for an American artist to equal the Old World's tradition. Longfellow used the decade of scholarship to assimilate his influences, Gorham maintains, before his new situation in Cambridge unleashed his long-simmering imagination. Newton Arvin hardly examines the issue but implicitly assumes that Longfellow's less demanding and more congenial situation at Harvard allowed him time to rediscover poetry. There is truth in all of these observations, but certainly two other events sent Longfellow back to poetry—one tragic, the other mundane.

The tragic impetus was the sudden death of his first wife, Mary, during his second European sojourn in 1836. This trip had begun as a professional triumph for Longfellow. He had just accepted the Smith Chair in Modern Languages at Harvard, a position that not only gave him lighter duties and a larger salary than Bowdoin but also an escape from the intellectual isolation of Brunswick, Maine. Harvard's president, Joseph Quincy, had suggested that Longfellow return to Europe to perfect his German before assuming the chair. Eager to revisit Europe in his wife's company, Longfellow—against his father's advice—set sail. In Copenhagen, Mary, who was expecting their first child, took ill. They journeyed to Amsterdam where she miscarried and, after three week's confinement, seemed to recover. In Rotterdam she suddenly took ill again and died. Longfellow plunged into grief so profound that it pierced his customary reticence. "All day I am weary and sad," he confided to his diary, "and at night I cry myself to sleep like a child." When Longfellow arrived in Cambridge in December 1836 to begin his eighteen-year tenure at Harvard, he was a widower moving to a new city. He faced the external challenge of creating a new social identity and the internal struggle of redefining himself as a writer.

Scholarship could not bear the psychic weight of Longfellow's grief nor adequately address his need for self-definition. Almost as soon as he returned from Europe he began composing his autobiographical *Hyperion: A Romance* (1839), and within the year he had resumed writing poetry. From this time on Professor Longfellow would be primarily an imaginative writer.

The death of Longfellow's first wife has been overshadowed by the more public and horrifying death by fire of his second wife. Longfellow wrote nothing about his first wife's death beyond a few letters and journal entries, so no adequate record exists of this crucial period. "With me," he wrote in an early letter, "all deep feelings are silent ones." But seven years after Mary's death he revisited Germany and wrote the only poem that apparently alludes to his grief, "Mezzo Cammin." One of Longfellow's finest poems, the sonnet lay unpublished in his papers until after his death. (Many scholars, including the editors of the Norton anthologies, mistakenly assume that it appeared in the 1846 collection, *The Belfrey of Bruges;* the sonnet took its place there only posthumously with the publication of the *Complete Poems*). Longfellow, the most reticent of poets, seems to have considered it too personal to publish, and perhaps he also felt it was indelicate to memorialize his first wife while he courted a second, Fanny Appleton, whom he married in 1843. It is tempting to read "Mezzo Cammin" in an overtly autobiographical way, as describing Longfellow's despair at having wasted so much of his life and confessing the spiritual paralysis following Mary's death.

Mezzo Cammin

Half of my life is gone, and I have let
The years slip from me and have not fulfilled
The aspiration of my youth, to build
Some tower of song with lofty parapet.
Not indolence, nor pleasure, nor the fret
Of restless passions that would not be stilled,
But sorrow, and a care that almost killed,
Kept me from what I may accomplish yet;
Though, half-way up the hill, I see the Past
Lying beneath me with its sounds and sights, —
A city in the twilight dim and vast,
With smoking roofs, soft bells, and gleaming lights,—
And hear above me on the autumnal blast
The cataract of Death far thundering from the heights.

The sonnet borrows its title from the opening line of Dante's *Inferno*, "Nel mezzo del cammin di nostra vita," which Longfellow himself later translated as "Midway upon the journey of our life." Dante uses this metaphor to describe the age of thirty-five, the halfway point in the Bible's allotted span of human life, "three-score years and ten." The precise dating of this Italian sonnet in Longfellow's papers makes it clear he composed it at thirty-five, and the sonnet's speaker is also explicitly at the midpoint in his life and presumably, like Dante, lost in a dark wood of spiritual confusion. The first quatrain specifies the speaker's particular failure—he is an artist who has not realized his youthful ambition of lyric achievement. The second quatrain also specifies the reason for his failure; it is not indolence nor dissipation nor restlessness but a nearly fatal grief to blame. Yet already the failure is significantly qualified since his aspirations remain something the speaker "may accomplish yet." What makes this poem unusual for Longfellow is the final sestet. Rather than resolving the speaker's predicament, instead it amplifies the dilemma. The lines vividly describe how the protagonist is caught inescapably between the unrecoverable but still visible past and his distant but nonetheless inevitable death.

Few of Longfellow's poems end in such an indeterminate way. It may not have been only the poem's personal nature that led Longfellow to suppress it but also its dark and ambiguous conclusion. The sonnet, however, suggests at least two things about Longfellow in 1842 that one would not have said before his wife's death: first, he is now certain of his poetic vocation, and second, the awareness of his own mortality spurs his creative resolve.

The more mundane impetus to poetry was Longfellow's hard-earned economic security. Assuming the Smith Chair at Harvard, Longfellow had reached, at an unusually early age, the height of his profession. His years of academic toil had justified him in the eyes of his parents and the world. He now had a dependable income and was settled in a congenial spot. To a dutiful and diligent son from a middle-class family like Longfellow, these were not trivial considerations. If Longfellow eventually became the first American poet who could live off his royalties, we must not forget how economically marginal verse was in the early nineteenth century. William Cullen Bryant's *Thanatopsis and Other Poems* (1821), a volume that critics of yesteryear often cited as the first great book of American verse, earned its author $14.92 during its first five years. A charmingly symbolic sum for an American poet, but even then it wasn't much to live on. Longfellow—like Wallace Stevens and T. S. Eliot sixty years later—was essentially a bourgeois artist who needed a stable income and an orderly external routine to have the psychic freedom to create.

Whatever ambiguity existed about the young Longfellow's poetic vocation, there could be no doubt about his literary calling. When his first collection of poems, *Voices of the Night,* appeared in December 1839 the thirty-two-year-old author had already written or edited nine volumes: six small textbooks in Spanish, Italian, and French; a book of verse translation, the *Coplas de Don Jorge Manrique* (1832), which also included versions of Lope de Vega, Aldana, and Berceo; and two substantial prose works, *Outre-Mer* and *Hyperion.* He had also published a great many essays, scholarly articles, stories, and translations. Despite the demands of his academic career, Longfellow had demonstrated that he was a serious, indeed a compulsive, writer. Critics commonly fault Longfellow for not growing as a poet, as if change itself were an intrinsic sign of greatness—how many poets like Wordsworth and Swinburne or, more recently, Sexton, Lowell, and Dickey, have changed for the worse? Indeed, Longfellow's verse shows little major development across his career except for the increasing sophistication of his narrative technique and greater austerity in the late lyrics. It would, however, be more accurate to say that his early artistic growth occurred in other literary forms. The young Longfellow is found not in poetry but in *Outre-Mer, Hyperion,* and his scattered short stories. By the time he returned to poetry in his thirties—early middle age by nineteenth-century standards—he had already gone through complex, though unusual, artistic development.

Voices of the Night was one of the strangest debuts in American poetry. It contained nine new poems followed by seven poems rescued from Longfellow's teenage years. The bulk of the volume consisted of over twenty translations, including the lengthy "Coplas de Manrique," three substantial passages from Dante's *Purgatorio,* and diverse poems from Spanish, French, German, Danish, and Anglo-Saxon. The mixture of original and translated poems, the Greek epigraphs, the varied verse forms make the collection resemble an early volume of Ezra Pound more than anything typical of nineteenth-century America. The architecture of the volume (underscored by Longfellow's programmatic "Prelude") explicitly announced the return to poetry of an author who had mastered the traditions of Europe.

In *Voices of the Night* Longfellow created an influential new archetype in American culture—the poet professor. There had been versifying professors before Longfellow, but their occupation seemed incidental to their art. Longfellow's range and erudition marked a shift in the poet's cultural role from literary amateur to professional artist; poetry was no longer a pastime but an occupation requiring a lifetime of study. A century and a half later the poet professor remains one of the four common stereotypes for the American poet that permeate both high and popular culture—the others being the bohemian vagabond (Walt Whitman, Vachel Lindsay, Allen Ginsberg), the reclusive outsider (Emily Dickinson, Robinson Jeffers, Wallace Stevens), and the self-destructive fiery genius (Edgar Allan Poe, Sylvia Plath, John Berryman, Weldon Kees). Although the New Critics despised Longfellow, these poet professors were his cultural descendants.

There is another side of Longfellow's version of the poet professor that has been decisively influential. Longfellow's public persona—articulated both in his books and in his new university position—was a figure of immense literary authority, a sensibility capable of both critical and creative activity, an intelligence embracing both "the mind of Europe" and the potential of America. If the description sounds as if it were borrowed from T. S. Eliot, the resemblance is not accidental. Longfellow was the first American poet both to define his literary identity and to build its authority by systematically assimilating European literature—not just British or classical verse but, to quote Eliot, "the whole of the literature of Europe from Homer." Although Longfellow and Eliot would have charted the high points of that tradition differently, what matters is that they shifted the poet's frame of cultural reference from Anglo-American to European literature. If this turn toward European models came in part from nationalistic assertion, it also derived from a visionary sympathy for Goethe's concept of *Weltliteratur*, the dialectic by which national literatures would gradually merge into a universal concert. Longfellow's vision of the American poet's international role was central to both Pound and Eliot, and it remains a dominant force in American poetry (locked, of course, in eternal, dialectical opposition with nativism).

Although Eliot did not take his mission directly from Longfellow, he developed it in the Harvard humanities curriculum that Longfellow helped create. Pound absorbed Longfellow's vision as part of his family heritage. Although he hated to acknowledge the connection, Pound was Longfellow's grandnephew. Rejecting his illustrious forebear's aesthetics, he nonetheless wholeheartedly embraced Longfellow's notion of the poet's education, especially the importance of learning poetry in foreign languages and mastering verse technique. Pound also shared Longfellow's conviction in the continuity of American and European culture and in the artistic integrity of poetic translation. Through Eliot and Pound the American poet's destiny as heir to European culture filtered to subsequent generations. It was the role W. H. Auden assumed in his initial American phase with ambitious long culture poems like "New Year Letter" and "For the Time Being." In a more restricted way it also shaped the intellectual identity of mid-century poets like Robert Lowell, John Berryman, Kenneth Rexroth, Weldon Kees, and Randall Jarrell, who saw themselves as mediators between American and European culture. Look, for example, at Jarrell's translations of the Brothers Grimm, Goethe, Rilke, and Chekhov. One sees a similar internationalism in the next generation, among poets as dissimilar as Roberty Bly, James Wright, William Jay Smith, and Richard Wilbur—though it began to expand more noticeably beyond Eurocentric models. Although they may not have thought of their work in these terms, those poets continued a poetic tradition pioneered by Longfellow in *Voices of the Night*.

If Longfellow did not yet recognize his proper literary medium, the critics and the public did. While *Hyperion*, which had been published five months earlier, met with generally lukewarm and occasionally hostile reviews, *Voices of the Night* was an immediate success. Within weeks the first edition sold out. (There would be six printings in the first two years.) *The North American Review* claimed that Longfellow's poems— and remember there were only nine new ones plus a slight *"Envoi"*— were "among the most remarkable poetic compositions, which have ever appeared in the United States." In a letter Nathanial Hawthorne gushed, "Nothing equal to some of them was ever written in this world,—this western world, I mean." Even while criticizing the volume on other grounds, Poe, who would make a personal mission of attacking Longfellow (sometimes anonymously or pseudonymously), singled

out "Hymn to the Night" for extravagant praise. The poem, he predicted, would be "the greatest favorite with the public." Typically, Poe
sagaciously identified the book's best poem but misjudged the public's
taste. Reviewers and readers alike had already discovered their
favorite—"Psalm of Life"—which would quickly become one of the
century's most popular poems, not only in America and England but
also, in translation, as far away as Russia, Iran, and China.

A scholar could compile a small anthology of apologies for this poetic chestnut. Only four years after the poet's death his brother Samuel
wrote, "It has perhaps grown too familiar for us to read it as it was first
read." Most of Longfellow's twentieth-century defenders—Alfred
Kreymborg, Horace Gregory, Howard Nemerov, Newton Arvin, Louis
Untermeyer, and others—have taken special pains to distance themselves from those "nine jingling verses, dripping with a larger number
of clichés than any other poem in the language," that, Kreymborg
observed, "smote the heartstrings of the race." "Psalm of Life,"
Longfellow's admirers have repeatedly asserted, is not the Longfellow
they admire. Consequently, the poem has been banished from college
anthologies and "serious" selections from the poet's work, unless, as in
Cleanth Brook's and Robert Penn Warren's *Understanding Poetry* (the
locus classicus of Modernist Longfellow criticism), it was used to represent what poetry should *not* be—a sugar-coated pill offering "truth"
to readers by displaying "fine sentiments in fine language."

Surely every criticism ever aimed at "Psalm of Life" is, on some level,
true. Yet, despite repeated assassination attempts by some of the best hit
men in modern letters, this menacingly upbeat poem refuses to die.
Banished from the curriculum for nearly a century, perhaps the poem is
now just unfamiliar enough to show why it persists. As Daniel Little-
field, Jr., has demonstrated, the poem's popularity came *because* not
despite its didacticism. "Psalm of Life" draws its identity from the colonial tradition of aphorisms in such works as *The Proverbs, The New
England Primer*, and *Poor Richard's Almanack*. Kreymborg was more
correct than perhaps he knew in noting that the poem contained "a
larger number of clichés than any other poem in the language." If one
substitutes the word *aphorism* or *proverb* for *cliché* (and one person's
proverb is another's cliché), we get close to the source of the poem's
most famous mental health hazard—its extraordinary memorability. By
compressing the maximum number of sensible and uplifting proverbs

into what is probably the most mnemonically seductive meter in English, trochaic tetrameter (the measure, for example, of Blake's "The Tyger"), and rhyming every end-stopped line, Longfellow created a masterpiece of Yankee Unitarian agitprop. "Psalm of Life" fails as lyric poetry because it belongs to a different genre, inspirational didactic verse. Anglo-American Modernism banished overt didacticism from high art; indeed rejecting didactism was the first inkling of English Modernism in the 1890s. The didactic genre still exists, though in popular culture its form has shifted to prose; our contemporary equivalent is the self-help book—and poets still occasionally write them. Our "Psalm of Life" is *Iron John*.

The success of Longfellow's second verse collection, *Ballads and Other Poems* (1841), determined his literary future. While he would still occasionally undertake fiction and scholarly prose, he soon conceded to the wisdom of the marketplace. With the exception of his unsuccessful novel, *Kavanagh: A Tale* (1849), and the critical apparatus to his major translations, virtually all of his subsequent work would be in verse. *Ballads and Other Poems* also helped define Longfellow's poetic gifts both to himself and his public. If *Voices in the Night* revealed his mastery of the delicate lyric and his dexterity as a translator, the new volume revealed his other great strength—storytelling. Narrative poetry was the prime source of Longfellow's immense popularity. His superiority at creating compelling stories—clearly, movingly, and memorably—was his chief virtue in the eyes of his contemporaries and today it poses the chief obstacle to his appreciation among contemporary critics. What caused such a divergence of opinion? The answer is obvious—Modernism.

Modernism declared narrative poetry at best obsolete and at worst a contradiction in terms. By prizing compression, intensity, complexity, and ellipsis, it cultivated an often hermetic aesthetic inimical to narrative poetry. Perfecting poetry's private voice, Modernism—at least American Modernism—lost the art's public voice. In many ways what we now call Modernist poetry was a collaboration between poets and critics. If there was an unmatched explosion of poetic talent between 1910 and 1940, there was also, just slightly later, an unprecedented efflorescence of critical intelligence, which developed ways of reading the challenging new verse. Among their many accomplishments the critical champions of American Modernism established the move-ment's genealogy in nineteenth-century literature. Three unfortunate consequences of this critical enterprise, however, were a narrow recon-struction of pre-Modernist American poetry, the development of ana-lytical techniques that were useless in approaching verse narrative, and the identification of poetry with the lyric mode. Searching for the American precedents of Modernism, critics gradually narrowed the diverse traditions of pre-twentieth-century poetry to three-and-a-half major authors: Emerson, Dickinson, Whitman, and—reluctantly, for the Symbolist's sake—the critical half of Poe. Linking this purified canon to Modernism, the New Critics and their successors masterfully demonstrated the American genius for the lyric (in all its high culture varieties) and the non-narrative epic (the exploratory culture poem like *Leaves of Grass, The Cantos,* and *Paterson*). The simplified version of nineteenth-century American poetry that grew out of this critical tra-dition excludes so much interesting and enduring work that its contin-uing currency says less about what the era was actually like than how powerful Modernism still is in influencing our perceptions of the past.

No writers have suffered more from Modernism's revision of Amer-ican poetry than Longfellow and Whittier. They represent the tradi-tional aesthetic Modernism defined itself against. Consequently, they have been doubly damned. Not only have critics dismissed most of their poetry but their very poetic enterprise has been declared trivial—their chief genres marginalized, their prosody dismissed, their public voice deemed vulgar. The roots of the misunderstanding are too complex to examine fully here, but at its center are issues of genre, versification, and audience, all linked to the university's near monopoly over critical dis-course. In a critical culture where literary merit is a function of how much discourse (in classrooms or learned journals) a poetic text can generate, their expansive and lucid poems have little to offer. William Butler Yeats observed that Longfellow's popularity came because "he tells his story or idea so that one needs nothing but his verses to under-stand it." Karl Keller claimed that "Whittier has been a writer to love, not to belabor." These are lethal verdicts in today's academy. But what does a reader say about a theory of poetry that has no room for Whit-tier's "Snow-Bound" or Longfellow's *Tales of a Wayside Inn*? There is something amiss in a literary culture that serves critics to the detriment of readers.

The mistake that most of Longfellow's advocates have made over the past half century is attempting to justify his work by Modernism's standards rather than insisting it be approached—as one would other poets separated by a significant historical gap—on its own terms. The author who emerges from this doomed defense is a gifted lyric poet, perhaps—as Richard Wilbur suggests, "the best sonneteer of his century"—but he remains a decidedly minor figure next to Browning or Tennyson, Dickinson or Whitman. Once we begin to assess Longfellow on his own terms, as a master of lyric and narrative poetry, of translation and adaptation, an innovator in versification and the creator of national myths, he stands as the most versatile American poet of his century. Dickinson and Whitman surpass him in depth and intensity but no one equals his range. In his chosen field, verse narrative, he is unequalled in American poetry until E. A. Robinson and Robert Frost. His achievement in lyric poetry is less dramatic but in some ways more unusual.

Longfellow's faults as a lyric poet are too well known to belabor. His work often lacks intellectual depth. It often strays into sentimentality. His poems too often seem to begin from set conclusions rather than to discover themselves in their own imaginative process. He rarely passes up the opportunity to moralize. He is often derivative of European models. He sometimes becomes so engrossed in his metrical scheme that he loses the intensity of his poetic impulse. He rarely looks into the harsher side of reality. These are all fair criticisms, and I will add one more: Longfellow's imagination was so linear that it lacked the ability to work dialectically. His poems rarely unfold as dynamic arguments; he could not present and reconcile truly opposed points of view. This failing may partially account for the meekness that pervades so many of his poems; he could not offset his own gentle nature with a credible vision of darkness. But having catalogued Longfellow's faults, one must also point out that many of these failings are the other sides of certain virtues. The sentimentality of his worst poems comes from the same emotional directness that animates his best work. His lack of intellectual complexity is a chief strength of his popular poems and most delicate lyrics. Recognizing Longfellow's virtues amid the welter of his salient shortcomings, however, is complicated by at least two factors: he was an immensely prolific and uneven poet, most of whose work is blandly unmemorable; the cultural assumptions he made about poetry differ significantly from our own.

Longfellow's lyric poetry divides into two groups. There are the songlike poems written in a popular style, which is smooth, direct, and quick moving, and there are the crafted literary poems, which are stately, complex, and densely textured. The popular poems usually have simple syntax and they match their phrasing neatly to the line lengths. The literary poems show more complex syntax and risk stronger enjambments at the line breaks. Longfellow also differentiated the poems metrically. The popular poems usually move in stress meter, triple feet or trochees; quite often they work in a loose ballad meter with an alternating pattern of four and three stresses per line. The literary poems almost always move in rhymed iambic pentameter, a meter Longfellow used less than most major English-language poets. The popular poems often have complex, songlike stanzas with shifting line lengths and unusual rhyme schemes; they often have refrains. Longfellow, like the Elizabethan lyricists, understood that if a poet keeps the sense simple he can make the music compellingly complex. The literary poems invariably employ a standard line length and simple rhyme schemes, most often the quatrain or the sonnet. (For Longfellow, the sonnet was the quintessential high literary form.) The music, though sonorous, supports the sense rather than calls attention to itself. It is what Donald Davie might call a "chaste" style. The two types of lyric are more easily differentiated on style than subject. Longfellow dealt with serious themes in both modes, although when he wrote about overtly literary topics ("Chaucer," "Milton," "Divina Commedia") he invariably used his high style.

To illustrate the difference between Longfellow's popular and high styles, here are representative passages from two of his best-known poems, "The Tide Rises, the Tide Falls" (the popular style) and "Shakespeare" (the literary style):

> The tide rises, the tide falls,
> The twilight darkens, and the curfew calls;
> Along the sea-sands damp and brown
> The traveller hastens toward the town,
>   And the tide rises, the tide falls.

> A vision as of crowded city streets,
>   With human life in endless overflow;
>   Thunder of thoroughfares; trumpets that blow

> To battle; clamor, in obscure retreats,
> Of sailors landed from their anchored fleets;
> Tolling of bells in turrets, and below
> Voices of children, and bright flowers that throw
> O'er garden walls their intermingled sweets!

In nineteenth-century lyric poetry the chief difference between the high style and the popular style was density of effect. Popular poetry strived toward a transparent texture in which local effects were subordinated to predictable general patterns of syntax and prosody. Literary poetry compressed the effects of meter, diction, metaphor, and image to achieve a richer texture; the reader was trusted to discern the general formal patterns of sound and sense through the many changes in local textural density. These two passages display different levels of poetic effect. The popular poem allows the metrical form to determine the syntax. The literary poem revels in counterpointing the two elements; it uses line breaks to syncopate the rhythm. "The Tide Rises, the Tide Falls" neatly balances its images, placing two images or details in each line. "Shakespeare" lets the images stretch or contract irregularly; there is no set syntactic pattern framing the images. The popular poem ends each stanza with a set refrain to keep the image and the mood easily focused. "Shakespeare" tumbles forward unpredictably. The images in the popular poem usually move forward sequentially or cyclically and rarely show dialectical opposition. The images in the literary poem are more exact, unusual, and dynamic; one never knows exactly where each new image will lead.

The two styles do not represent different stages in Longfellow's career—as they did, for example, in Yeats's case. Though the high style emerged slightly later (one first sees it fully developed in *The Belfrey of Bruges* in 1845), the two styles essentially coexist through all of Longfellow's mature poetry. The poet saw both as valid literary modes. One aimed at the general audience, the other at the intelligentsia. A contemporary reader must, however, remember that in the nineteenth century the two modes were not seen in opposition; there was not yet a gulf between highbrow and lowbrow art. (It is surely not coincidental that the terms *highbrow* and *lowbrow* enter English in the second decade of the twentieth century—just as Modernism arrived in full force.) Longfellow's high style was simply a refinement of his popular mode, and the mass audience for popular poetry included the literary intelligentsia as well as common readers.

The temptation for modern critics, however, has been to assume that Longfellow's high style is naturally superior to his popular mode. His best lyric poems in the high style fit easily into contemporary notions of how genuine poetry operates. The few distinguished examples of critical analysis of specific poems—like James M. Cox's "Longfellow and His Cross of Snow"—virtually always focus on poems in the literary mode. Likewise, the handful of poems that survive in academic anthologies like "Mezzo Cammin" and "The Jewish Cemetery at Newport" (the latter surely one of the great American poems of its century), are almost inevitably products of the high style. Moreover, the fact that most of Longfellow's weakest poems are written in the popular style reinforces the scholarly prejudice toward the high style.

Although it is easier to discuss poems in the high style, since their denser verbal texture invites analysis, there is ultimately no cogent reason why Longfellow's literary poems should be categorically preferred to the best popular ones. Why should one consider "My Lost Youth" inferior to "Chaucer" because the latter has more stylistic complexity? An adequate theory of poetry leaves room to admire both. Both modes are artistically legitimate, since the test of poetry is its ability to involve and move the reader to enlightenment, consolation, or delight—not its susceptibility to critical analysis. Perhaps the real reason why the popular style appears an inferior literary medium is that its aesthetic requirements—clarity, simplicity, emotional directness, syntactic linearity, and prosodic symmetry—make it harder to write well. There is less freedom of style and subject than the high literary mode affords, and the poet faces the significant challenge of having to surprise the reader in only predictable ways. In such a transparent style every flaw and banality shows. Time is especially cruel to popular poetry; each subsequent change of attitude mercilessly exposes new imperfections.

There have probably been fewer than a dozen English-language poets who have managed to create a significant and enduring body of poetry in a popular style: Herrick, Burns, Blake, Whittier, Housman, Kipling, Stevenson, Langston Hughes, and a few others. To this select, if mostly unfashionable, company, one must add Longfellow. His many failures—and they are legion in so prolific a poet—must not blind the critic to his remarkable successes. His special gift was to bring an intense musicality and powerful atmosphere to the light texture of the popular lyric, which one sees in his best work, "My Lost Youth," "The Fire of Drift-Wood," "Snow-Flakes," "The Tide Rises, The Tide Falls," "The Ropewalk," and "Aftermath." There is even much to admire in his sentimental idylls, "The Day is Done" and "The Children's Hour," which survive a century of critical opprobrium with surprising freshness. The frank emotionalism of such poems leaves modern readers uneasy who forget the fragility of domestic happiness in an age of high infant mortality and low life expectancy. American life expectancy has doubled since Longfellow's time from approximately thirty-nine years in 1850 to seventy-five years in 1988. Medical progress has been as important as cultural trends in changing literary sensibility. (Look at how rapidly AIDS has revived a Victorian emotionalism in verse and drama.) "The Children's Hour," a poem admired by both Auden and Fiedler, was written by a man who had already watched a wife and young daughter die and would soon see his second wife suffer an excruciating death. When a literary culture loses its ability to recognize and appreciate genuine poems like "My Lost Youth" because they are too simple, it has surely traded too much of its innocence and openness for a shallow sophistication.

The issue of Longfellow's status as a major poet ultimately rests on the critical assessment of his four booklength poems—*Evangeline, A Tale of Acadie* (1847), *The Song of Hiawatha* (1855), *The Courtship of Miles Standish* (1858), and *Tales of a Wayside Inn* (1863–1873). These were the poems that earned him a preeminent position among his contemporaries, they were also the works most utterly rejected by Modernism. The long poems present a number of problems for critics, not the least of which is their proper evaluation. They are the slipperiest kind of literature to judge: they are not quite masterpieces but too good and too original to go away—like Mary Shelley's *Frankenstein* or Poe's *The Narrative of Arthur Gordon Pym*. They still command a reader's attention and linger in the memory. The poems are also troublesome for critics to discuss in a contemporary context because they bear so little relation to the subsequent tradition of longer American poems. Whereas "Song of Myself" is illuminated by the tradition it engendered, Longfellow's extended poems have little connection to twentieth-century work, not even, except tangentially, the booklength poems of Robinson and Frost. Longfellow's poems relate to earlier, mainly European traditions.

Most American long poems have been epics of self-discovery, works that consciously set out to explore and define both national and personal identities. Hence the author's autobiography eventually figures directly or indirectly in the quest. Whatever their other differences, *The Bridge, The Cantos, Paterson, A, Maximus Poems, Dream Songs, Gunslinger, The Changing Light at Sandover, History*, and *The One Day* all share the investigative dynamic of mixing personal and public mythologies. The Modernist culture epic has also been a notoriously messy genre—sprawling, discontinuous, idiosyncratic, and obscure. While each long poem has its champions, none except Whitman's, their common matrix, has been widely regarded as a success. By comparison, Longfellow's extended poems are distressingly neat and lucid: they are polished, linear, nonautobiographical narratives. Their form is not exploratory but patterned after traditional genres—pastoral romance, folk epic, and framed tales. They are neither aimed at literary intellectuals nor—with the notable exception of *Hiawatha*—obsessed with defining national or personal identity. They are conceived as serious but popular entertainments, stories meant to enlarge the reader's humanity without deconstructing his or her moral universe.

The moral element in Longfellow's extended poems cannot be minimized. Although the poems may now seem old-fashioned in form, they remain surprisingly contemporary in their concerns. *Evangeline* depicts the personal tragedies of a displaced ethnic and religious minority driven from its homeland by an imperial power. *The Song of Hiawatha*, whatever its scholarly failings, tries to present with dignity the legends and customs of Native Americans on their own terms. *The Courtship of Miles Standish*, the least interesting of the poems, critiques the harshness and brutality of military values. *Tales of a Wayside Inn*, whose very framework celebrates multiculturalism, contains stories openly concerned with environmental sensitivity, religious tolerance, political freedom, and charity. Not the least of Longfellow's influences on American culture has been political. He helped articulate the New England liberal consciousness that eventually became mainstream American public opinion. If contemporary critics are quick to point out the internal contradictions of this ideology, it still represented the most enlightened viewpoint of its era.

There is no room here for even a minimal exploration of the poems but only a few general observations. *Evangeline* is the most poetically impressive of the longer poems. It contains passages—the prologue, the burning of Grand-Pré, the journey on the Mississippi, the description of the prairies—that are both breathtakingly beautiful and, as Longinus understood the term, sublime. The story also has a magnificent narrative sweep until the end, which reveals Longfellow's central weakness as a storyteller, his sentimentality. He lacked the tragic insight necessary to carry a painful story to its inevitable conclusion; he can only resolve it in comforting terms. That *Evangeline*'s ending was, in fact, historically true does not redeem the sweet sentimentality with which the poet saturates its finale. And yet, as John Seelye has pointed out, "Evangeline does haunt us, a vague ghost adrift on the Mississippi in company with Uncle Tom and Huck Finn, those other refugee symbols of exile and disarray."

The Song of Hiawatha is probably the closest thing America will ever have to that European Romantic obsession, the national folk epic. This startlingly original poem was the work that made Longfellow the preeminently popular poet in English. It sold thirty thousand copies in its first six months in print and eventually became the most popular long American poem ever written, both at home and abroad. *Hiawatha* is also the extended poem that best displays Longfellow's two greatest gifts as a storyteller—mythmaking and narrative thrust. Like other great popular narrative artists Longfellow excelled at mythos more than logos. He could create or adapt characters that seemed to exist outside their stories. While one cannot imagine Lambert Strether outside of the particular verbal universe of *The Ambassadors*, one can easily envision Simon Legree, Count Dracula, Ebeneezer Scrooge, and Hiawatha in another medium. *Hiawatha* created a series of archetypes (some would say stereotypes) of Native American culture that have permeated the popular imagination. The most readable long narrative poem of the nineteenth century, it also displays those virtues Matthew Arnold celebrated most highly in Homer, "the rapidity of its movement, and the plainness and directness of its style." That Arnold's terms of praise sound odd to contemporary ears is one more sign of how remote our literary culture has grown from narrative poetry .

Although *The Song of Hiawatha* has received more interesting scholarly and critical attention than any other Longfellow poem, most of the analyses have been historical, biographical, anthropological, or ideological (political denunciations of *Hiawatha* have recently been the one active area of Longfellow criticism.) Consequently, the poem's specifically literary characteristics remain only half-understood. Posterity has essentially made two mutually contradictory criticisms of *Hiawatha*: first, as a narrative, its style is insufficiently naturalistic, too little, that is, like a realist novel; second, Longfellow departs too much from his mythic material and unconsciously Europeanizes his Native Americans. There is a great deal of truth in both charges, and yet they seem to miss the sheer originality of the poem, in which Longfellow tries to invent a medium in English to register the irreconcilably alien cultural material he presents. The stylistic objections to *Hiawatha*, therefore, are largely based on misconceptions of Longfellow's intentions. The most frequent criticism is of the poem's meter, the trochaic tetrameter line he borrowed from the Finnish *Kalevala*, which has seemed too artificial and formulaic to some readers. The chief advantage of this measure, however, is that it isn't naturalistic. It was an overt distancing device, as was the incorporation of dozens of Ojibway words. These devices continuously remind the listener that *Hiawatha*'s mythic universe is not our world. There are many other devices of syntax, lineation, diction, and rhetoric that give the poem its distinctive style. Although more often ridiculed than understood, the style of *Hiawatha* is in its own way as original as that of Pound's *Cantos*.

The fatal flaw of *Hiawatha* is, once again, the ending—justly notorious among scholars of Native American literature—in which Hiawatha instructs his people to accept the Black-Robes and then, like Tennyson's Ulysses, sails (or rather paddles) into the sunset. Longfellow lacked the tragic vision to recognize that there could be no humane, liberal reconciliation between Native Americans and invading Europeans. The nineteenth-century poem that *Hiawatha* most resembles (but is never compared to) is Richard Wagner's libretto for *Der Ring des Nibelungen*. Wagner also recast a disparate group of pre-Christian myths into an integrated narrative, but he understood that there can be no bloodless transition from one civilization to another: a hero and a people who do not triumph are utterly destroyed. Once *Hiawatha*'s narrative leaves mythic time for history it must face the tragic consequences of its material, but tragedy was a genre beyond Longfellow's reach—perhaps even beyond the melioristic vision of Unitarian liberalism. The first twenty cantos of *Hiawatha* achieve an oddly epic grandeur, the last two dissipate in utopian social fantasy.

Tales of a Wayside Inn makes the most convincing case for Longfellow's narrative mastery. Here, rather than tackling an epic structure, he worked in his most congenial medium, the short tale. As Newton Arvin rightly says, "No literary undertaking could have made a happier or more fruitful use of his powers . . . his storytelling genius, his sense of narrative form, his versatility, and the opulence of his literary erudition." Roughly modeled after Boccaccio's *Decameron*, Longfellow's poem consists of a series of verse tales told by a sundry group of travelers over three days at the Red Horse Inn in Sudbury, Massachusetts. The storytellers form a diverse group—a Sicilian political refugee, a Spanish Jew, a Norwegian musician, a youthful student, a broad-minded theologian, a tender-hearted poet, the Yankee landlord—and their stories draw from all of their ethnic traditions. The narrative framework is a bit rickety, but the stories themselves, which are told in an astonishing variety of metrical forms, are, despite a few weak ones, generally splendid. The best half dozen or so tales —"Paul Revere's Ride," "King Robert of Sicily," "The Cobbler of Hagenau," "Azrael," "The Monk of Casal-Maggiore," "The Legend Beautiful," and especially "The Birds of Killingworth"—rank among the best short American narrative poems ever written. *Tales of a Wayside Inn* is Longfellow at his most endearingly human. One senses here as in none of the other long poems his famous personal charm, warmth, and humor. When Howard Nemerov prepared a selected edition of Longfellow's poems in 1959, he ignored all of the other long poems to include nine selections from *Tales of a Wayside Inn*. Posterity may prove his strong preferences correct.

It is impossible to understand Longfellow as a poet without studying the translations that make up nearly half of his nondramatic verse. He was the first great poet-translator in American literature. In this respect, as in his cultural internationalism, he exercised a major, if unacknowledged, influence on twentieth-century poetry. By demonstrating how translation could nourish a poet's growth, he introduced a powerful imaginative dynamic into our tradition. Translation became a means for American poets both to perfect their craft and to assimilate the literature of other cultures. Longfellow also showed how translation allowed the American poet to demonstrate mastery over the European tradition and implicitly claim equal status to classic authors—a concept central both to Pound and Eliot and their descendants. Longfellow's commitment to translation was the practical extension of his assent to

the ideologies of internationalism and *Weltliteratur*. He stands, therefore, at the beginning of the innovative tradition of verse translation
that enlarged the possibilities of American poetry. Directly or indirectly, he is the prototype not only of Pound and Eliot but ultimately of
writers as dissimilar as Kenneth Rexroth, Robert Lowell, Richard
Wilbur, Robert Fitzgerald, W. S. Merwin, William Jay Smith, Elizabeth Bishop, John F. Nims, David Slavitt, and Robert Bly.

Longfellow also helped free translation from the monopoly of Greek
and Latin classics that had earlier formed the bulk of serious verse
translation in English. His huge body of translation consists almost
entirely of poems taken from modern languages, including work by
contemporary authors like Tegner and von Platen. If Longfellow
helped establish a new group of "modern" masters in English such as
Michaelangelo, Goethe, Gongora, Lope de Vega, and, most important,
Dante, he also dared to translate minor poets—simply because their
work interested or delighted him. When critics belittle Longfellow for
bothering with forgotten poets like Stockman, Mahlmann, Coran, and
Ducis, they forget how much easier it is to experiment with new verse
forms and genres when working with congenial but unchallenging
texts. Surely the reason that Longfellow made such an accomplished
debut as a narrative poet in *Ballads and Other Poems* was his assimilation
of the Northern European verse storytelling tradition through translating Uhland, Evald, Tegner, and various folk ballads. Likewise, his
unprecedented mastery of versification grew from his attempts to recreate foreign meters in English. If some new measure worked in a translation (such as Tegner's dactylic hexameter), Longfellow would employ
it for an original poem—a method of imaginative assimilation his grand
nephew Pound seems to have inherited.

With some notable exceptions, however, Longfellow's translations
remain more important for their influence than their abiding literary
worth. He was not the equal of Dryden, Pope, or Rossetti. His theory
of translation, which stressed "rendering literally the words of a foreign
author" while at the same time preserving "the spirit of the original,"
placed restrictions on him not usually assumed by the greatest masters
of verse translation. As Arvin observed, Longfellow's ideal for translation "was not paraphrase, and decidedly not 'imitation,' but what Dryden called 'metaphrase.' " Indeed Longfellow practiced a half-scholar-
ly/half-poetic method of translation that attempts to bring over the

original text *as poetry* into English with meticulous attention to its literal sense, diction, lineation, and precise versification. This formidable agenda placed enormous burdens on his poetic skill, but the results were frequently not only impressive but fascinatingly original. His translations of Virgil's First Eclogue done in fluent hexameter and Ovid's *Tristia* (III, x) in elegiac couplets remain remarkable. The challenge of recreating classical meters in English has obsessed poets for centuries, but no one ever managed to bring over the elegant rhythm of the Latin elegiac couplet more naturally than Longfellow:

> Should anyone there in Rome remember Ovid the exile,
>   And, without me, my name still in the city survive;
> Tell him that under stars which never set in the ocean
>   I am existing still, here in a barbarous land.

His best translations are astonishingly faithful to both the meaning and the music of the original. His versions of Goethe's intricately rhymed "Wanderer's Night-Songs," for example, show an uncanny fidelity to nearly every aspect of the German. But it was not merely technical skill that animated Longfellow's translations. He excelled at the form for the same reason he did at narrative; he possessed the "negative capability" of extinguishing his own personality in the authors he translated. He could recreate a poem in English while maintaining the strangeness of its beauty, as in this translation of Michelangelo's "Dante":

> What should be said of him cannot be said;
>   By too great splendor is his name attended;
>   To blame is easier those who him offended,
>   Than reach the faintest glory round him shed.
> This man descended to the doomed and dead
>   For our instruction; then to God ascended;
>   Heaven opened wide to him its portals splendid,
>   Who from his country's, closed against him, fled.
> Ungrateful land! To its own prejudice
>   Nurse of his fortunes; and this showeth well,
>   That the most perfect most of grief shall see.
> Among a thousand proofs let one suffice,
>   That as he exile hath no parallel,
>   Ne'er walked the earth a greater man than he.

Longfellow's greatest accomplishment as a translator was his version of *The Divine Comedy* (original edition, 1867; revised text, 1870), which reflected forty years of deep involvement with the poem. Dante's position in the English-speaking world was relatively marginal until the Romantic movement, when Coleridge, Shelley, and Byron fell under his influence. The first complete English translation of *The Divine Comedy*, Henry Cary's version, did not appear until 1814, almost five centuries after the original. Longfellow's advocacy of the poem as teacher, translator, and commentator was crucial in establishing its canonic stature in America. Not the least important part of his support was putting Dante into the center of Harvard literary studies, where, through his successors, James Russell Lowell, Charles Eliot Norton, Charles Grandgent, and George Santayana, it exercised a decisive early influence on young poets like Eliot, Stevens, and cummings. Longfellow's splendidly exact and richly annotated version remained the finest verse translation for nearly three generations, until it was superseded by the Laurence Binyon and John Ciardi versions.

If translation was an essential aspect of Longfellow's vision of the new American poet whose professionalism allowed him to participate in *Weltliteratur*, so was his dedication to prosody. Longfellow was the most versatile master of versification in American literature. His range and originality in metrics remains unprecedented. Virtually all major American poets have worked primarily in iambic, syllabic, or free verse—except Longfellow, that is, who not only used almost every traditional meter known to English but also experimented with new measures, some foreign, others original to him. He explored stress meter and mixed meters, and, as Arvin observes, his accentual poems like "The Cumberland" prefigure Hopkins's sprung rhythm. Longfellow, like George Herbert, also habitually played with stanza shapes, inventing several new forms. Sometimes he set poems of direct and simple emotion in complex and subtle stanza forms that gave them unexpected resonance, as in the intricate stanza he invented for "My Lost Youth" with its shifting line lengths and unrhymed refrain. Another of Longfellow's uncelebrated contributions to English prosody was his experimentation with the unrhymed lyric, as in "The Bells of Lynn." He also explored free verse before Whitman, as in "Tegner's Drapa" (1850) and *The Golden Legend* (1851). Longfellow's vers libre is particularly noteworthy because it eschews the Biblical prose rhythms that characterized most free verse before the fin de siècle. Here are two short passages, the first from "Tegner's Drapa," the second from the later *Christus* (1872):

> So perish the old Gods!
> But out of the sea of Time
> Rises a new land of song
> Fairer than the old.
> Over the meadows green
> Walk the young bards and sing.
>
> I am the voice of one
> Crying in the wilderness alone:
> Prepare ye the way of the Lord;
> Make his paths straight
> In the land that is desolate!

The diction is standard for Longfellow's age, and the second passage—like much early vers libre—is rhymed, but the rhythms and lineation would not be out of place in Pound's *Ripostes* half a century later. The line lengths are irregular and follow the phrasing rather than any metrical measure. The rhythm is usually rising, but Longfellow consciously disrupts the underlying iambic movement to create a looser cadence. The prosody prefigures early Modernist practices and is as innovative as anything in *Leaves of Grass*.

Today prosody is a neglected subject. Few literary critics know more than the rudiments of metrics, and, in the aftermath of the free-verse revolution, even many poets have never studied versification. The last century, however, considered prosody an essential part of literary education. Critics debated issues of versification with the vehemence our contemporaries bring to literary theory. Prosody, in fact, played an important role in Victorian literary theory. Anyone who studies the early reviews of Longfellow's books notices how much space critics devoted to discussing issues of versification. His experimentation with foreign meters, like dactylic hexameter in *Evangeline* or unrhymed trochaic tetrameter in *The Song of Hiawatha*, were hotly debated. One of his major accomplishments in the eyes of Victorian cognoscenti was his success in making classical hexameter work in English, something no other poet had ever been able to do with equal aplomb. (Even Matthew

Arnold reluctantly admired Longfellow's success with hexameter.) Surely one reason for the drop in Longfellow's reputation has been the decline of interest among both scholars and poets in formal prosody.

The early twentieth century saw two shifts in critical attitudes toward prosody, both of which prejudiced assessments of Longfellow and his fellow Fireside poets. The first was the rise of free verse. As free verse became—through a series of misconceptions, Timothy Steele has recently argued—inextricably associated with American Modernist poetry, critics revised the nineteenth-century canon to highlight poets like Whitman, who prefigured the development, or Dickinson, who ignored many prosodic conventions. As "open form" became a mainstream concept after the Beats, it mixed with nativist sentiments to declare free verse the only true American measure and condemn formal verse as a reactionary British import. This ideology dismissed Longfellow, Whittier, and their contemporaries en bloc. (Whitman's supporters have often displayed a special animus toward Longfellow, since he enjoyed a huge popularity among common readers their more obstreperously democratic poet has never approached.) But the celebration of free verse would not have been so damaging had it not combined with a second shift in attitude among the surviving defenders of formal poetry—a shift that has gone undiscussed in critical literature.

Twentieth-century American poetry has gradually developed a metrical puritanism, a conviction among both poets and critics that serious formal poetry is best written (to borrow Frost's dictum) only in regular or loose iambics. Triple and trochaic meters have gradually been relegated to light verse, classical and foreign meters regarded as technical curiosities. This metrical puritanism developed as second-generation Modernists, many of whom like Yvor Winters and Allen Tate were associated with New Criticism, tried to reconcile formal metrics with Modernism. In the process of defending traditional meter against free verse they felt it necessary to separate the meters suitable for high art from the catchy measures of popular poetry. The tightness and subtlety of iambic meters were preferred to the intrusive and looser rhythms of triple meter or the hypnotic but inflexible trochaic measures. Consequently, whereas Longfellow or Whittier, Tennyson or Browning comfortably moved between iambic and other meters, one rarely, if ever, sees a poem in triple measure or trochees by Winters, Tate, Hart Crane, J. V. Cunningham, Robert Lowell, Richard Wilbur, Anthony Hecht, or other twentieth-century American formalists. These poets looked at the overtly musical meters favored by Whittier, Longfellow, and Poe either as vulgar concessions to popular taste or artistic misjudgments. When the free-verse prejudice against metrical poetry combined with a high art bias against noniambic verse (in an environment that downgraded all narrative poetry and popular art), who was left to defend such gems as Longfellow's "Paul Revere's Ride" or Whittier's "Maud Muller" and "Barbara Frietchie"? (Pound anthologized "Barbara Frietchie" in *Confucius to Cummings*—what poet today would be bold enough to do so?) Even Matthiessen, who anthologized Longfellow's narrative poems, preferred the respectable iambic ones like "The Birds of Killingworth" and "The Monk of Casal-Maggiore." If modern criticism has created a distorted version of nineteenth-century American poetry by dismissing narrative verse and popular poetry, it has produced an equally impoverished account of the era's lyric poetry by rejecting most noniambic verse. Metrical diversity was one of the chief glories of mid-nineteenth-century poetry. By privileging iambic verse, critics not only miss some of the era's greatest poems but also obscure the commitment to popular poetry shared by most of the period's best poets.

"I am a man of fortune greeting heirs," Wallace Stevens once wrote. He might have been predicting his present place in American letters. His work generated a poetic and critical tradition that sustains his central place in the canon. Longfellow's heritage, by contrast, has few claimants. His small body of lyric poems writtten in the high style has secured him a niche in the contemporary canon, but the traditions he most richly endowed—narrative and popular poetry—were devalued by Modernism, and his contributions to translation and scholarship have been eroded by time. His direct influence on our poetry ended with Frost, though his cultural vision of internationalism continues indirectly to shape our national literary identity. Now that Modernism itself has become a historical period along with the Genteel Tradition it helped displace, a comprehensive reassessment of our poetic canon is necessary. The task is not to reject Modernism, which was our poetry's greatest period, but to correct the blindspots and biases of its critical assumptions. A reevaluation of Longfellow will be an important part of this enterprise. How will his work be revalued in the aftermath of Modernism? If he will never regain his dominant position in nineteenth-century American poetry, he will surely reemerge as a larger and more complex figure than he has recently seemed. The continuing popularity of his work—despite nearly a century of critical scorn—proves that it still has a vitality that current critical instruments are not designed to register. "Some books are undeservedly forgotten," W. H. Auden once wrote, "none are undeservedly remembered." Longfellow's vast influence on American culture paradoxically makes him both central and invisible; to reevaluate his work properly will not only require capable literary critics but unprejudiced cultural critics. He can be ignored only at the cost of misreading his century. His place in American literature brings to mind Basil Bunting's poem, "On a Fly-leaf of Pound's Cantos":

> These are the Alps. What is there to say about them?
> They don't make sense. Fatal glaciers, crags cranks
>   climb,
> jumbled boulder and weed, pasture and boulder, scree,
> *et l'on entend*, maybe, *le refrain joyeux at leger*.
> Who knows what the ice will have scraped on the rock
>   it is smoothing?
> There they are, you will have to go a long way round
> if you want to avoid them.
> It takes some getting used to. There are the Alps,
> fools! Sit down and wait for them to crumble!

This tribute to Longfellow's grandnephew applies as easily to him. If Longfellow's ultimate place in American poetry is still uncertain, one thing is sure—his best work will remain a permanent part of our literature. You will have to go a long way round if you want to ignore him.

Dana Gioia

Further Reading

Arvin, Newton. *Longfellow: His Life and Art*. Boston: Atlantic Monthly, 1963.

Dante Alighieri. *The Divine Comedy of Dante Alighieri*. 3 vols. Tr. Henry Wadsworth Longfellow. Boston and New York: Houghton Mifflin, 1904.

Longfellow, Henry Wadsworth. *The Complete Poetical Works of Henry Wadsworth Longfellow*. Boston and New York: Houghton Mifflin, 1899.

Longfellow, Henry Wadsworth. *Selected Poems*. Ed. Lawrence Buell. New York: Penguin, 1988.

The American Transcendentalist Poets

T HE practice of poetry was both tangential and central to American Transcendentalism. Tangential, in that Transcendentalism was a multiform movement, religiocentric at its core and inspired by the participants' excitement at the prospect of individual and social transformation owing to the divinity they saw inherent in or directly accessible to human nature. All but a few held the composition of verses ancillary to this goal of human transformation. Yet as late Romantics and as well-bred post-Puritan provincials thoroughly socialized into appreciation of the chaster forms of high culture, the Transcendentalists held poetry in far higher reverence than late twentieth-century culture does, prizing it as the loftiest form of artistic expression. The Hebrew prophets, the bardic and priestly poet-prophecy of other nations, Milton and Wordsworth and contemporary criticism—all these had taught the Transcendentalists to think of poetry as, in principle, the most fitting vehicle for the logos among all the literary genres. The fact that poetry had since the beginnings of the colonial period been the one and only fictive genre considered morally sound reinforced the Transcendentalists' esteem for it, as did their personal fondness for reading and writing. For they were by temperament an unusually bookish lot. Most of the men were trained to be ministers; a number of both sexes were teachers.

In short, the Transcendentalists were people of the word: eager consumers of texts and producers of discourse. For such people—from such a class and region at such a point in American history—to admire poetry and seek to write it were almost second nature.

The poetry they produced, however, has provoked nagging questions of major import. To begin: Why wasn't it better than it was? Today, Americanists credit Emerson with having ushered in an epoch in which American writing reached a standard worthy of international comparison and attained a distinctive voice of its own. Earlier coteries can be identified, such as the Connecticut Wits and the New York Knickerbockers; but the legacies of Emerson and Thoreau were much more important for the future of American letters. Yet the case for influence seems more impressive with respect to Transcendentalist thought and prose style than with respect to the movement's poetry. Transcendentalism's poetry has often seemed tame and thin by comparison to its prose: an art of cautiously bound forms, formal diction, traditional metrics that at times seem bizarrely at odds with the theory of Self-Reliance, as in Jones Very's addiction to the sonnet as the preferred vehicle for expressing the untrammeled power of the Holy Spirit. Given the Transcendentalists' admiration for poetry, why didn't they produce better results? Or was it precisely the "burden of the past," as Walter Jackson Bate conceives it, or "the anxiety of influence" in Harold Bloom's formulation, that constricted the Transcendentalists: that caused them to write more freely in essayistic prose, a form already long "naturalized" into New England culture (by reason of the sermon tradition, for example), and without the imposing cultural authority and intricate conventions of poetry, whose giants and critical interpreters were firmly associated with the old world rather than with the new. The prospect of writing a *GREAT* poem in America may have seemed as constipating to the New England Transcendentalists as the project of *GREAT* painting came to seem to their fellow Bostonian Washington Allston. Perhaps, then, it is to be expected that the Transcendentalists would have exalted poetry but succeeded at prose, that a more vigorous poetic voice would have taken another generation or so to emerge. Perhaps their true poetry was in their prose and their poetic strivings in the nominal sense can be discounted, without prejudice, as an obsolescent obligatory mannerism of a culture in the process of tranformation.

But perhaps this is to write off Transcendentalist verse too glibly—both the seriousness and the quality of that effort. Possibly we have missed something, judged their poetry by the wrong criteria? The continuity between Emerson's poetry and that of Dickinson, who seems to have read Emerson's verse with at least a degree of interest (to the point that one of her few published poems was mistaken for his work) suggests, for example, that a cavalier attitude toward the poetry of Transcendentalism is precipitous. If Dickinson could have found something useful here, if Robert Frost was serious when he praised Emerson's "Uriel" as the "best western poem yet," if the dean of Indo-Anglian poets, Nissim Ezekiel, is sincere in his professed respect for Emerson's poetry, then perhaps we should take the poems of at least Emerson seriously. Indeed, one may dare to go a good deal further than this. But before any sort of case can be made for their work, we need first to recall who the Transcendentalist poets were.

On the strength of the quality and influence of his two published volumes—*Poems* (1845) and *May-Day and Other Pieces* (1867)—Ralph Waldo Emerson (1803–82) must certainly be reckoned Transcendentalism's leading poet. Emerson authored a good half of the titles that would appear on most readers' short lists of the strongest poems of the movement. But Emerson was less committed to the medium of verse than three younger figures whose work he supported and helped to publish. William Ellery Channing the younger (1817–1901), who composed a half-dozen uneven volumes (assembled in Walter Harding's 1967 edition of his *Collected Poems*), was thought by the other Concord Transcendentalists, if not by the movement at large, to be the group's most dedicated poet. Channing was the only Transcendentalist poet whose style truly evolved—from shorter lyrics to longer narrative and dramatic poems. But he was a poet of striking passages rather than of whole poems. Christopher Pearse Cranch (1813–92), better known for his cartoon of Emerson's transparent eyeball, was a painter and poet of lesser seriousness but greater consistency than Channing who published three volumes that include several of Transcendentalism's most articulate lyrics: *Poems* (1844), *The Bird and the Bell* (1875), and *Ariel and Caliban* (1887). More narrowly but more profoundly gifted than either, at least in the earlier years of his career, was Jones Very (1813–80), who specialized in visionary religious sonnets that came closer than the work of any of his other Transcendentalist colleagues to realizing the ideal of poetry as inspiration. Very's works remained largely unpublished during his life, except for a small selection of *Essays and Poems* collected by Emerson (1839). James Freeman Clarke's edition of Very's *Poems and*

Essays (1886) and William Irving Bartlett's publication of additional Very manuscript poems in *Emerson's "Brave Saint"* (1942) rounded out his canon.

Like Very, but in a far more secularized mold, Henry Thoreau (1817–62) started his career as an aspiring poet, versifying extensively in his twenties and undertaking the most ambitious program of reading in classical and English poets of any Transcendentalist, until after the Walden experience he turned almost exclusively to prose. His *Collected Poems* were edited in 1943 by Carl Bode. By contrast, Bronson Alcott (1799–1888) blossomed as a poet in old age, producing two slim volumes: *New Connecticut* (1881), a reminiscence of boyhood, and *Sonnets and Canzonets* (1882). Other Transcendentalists who wrote goodly amounts of poetry included Margaret Fuller (1810–50), Ellen Hooper (1812–48), her sister Caroline Sturgis Tappan (1818–88), and the Transcendentalist ministers William H. Furness, Charles T. Brooks, Theodore Parker, Samuel Johnson, and Samuel Longfellow. Fuller and Hooper were the most gifted among these. Fuller's poetry was represented in her *Papers on Literature and Art* (1846); Hooper's collected poetry was printed in an unpublished edition of "Poems" (n.d.), the one known copy of which is owned by the Boston Public Library.

Of the several dozen strongest poems that stand out amid this body of perhaps three thousand—mostly short lyrics and never more than a hundred lines or so—a good half are by Emerson; works by Thoreau, Very, Cranch, and Channing make up the bulk of the rest. An additional several dozen poems contain striking passages of some length. In the discussion that follows, I have managed to make at least brief reference to many, though hardly all, of my own favorites, quoting them in part or whole. Many of the rest can be found in two judicious anthologies edited by Perry Miller, *The Transcendentalists* (1950) and *The American Transcendentalists* (1957).

To identify the Transcendentalist poets and state one's preferences are easy tasks. Simply call the roll of people associated with the movement who wrote poems, then talk about the texts that interest you. To define the internal coherence of the field is much harder, at least once one tries to move from doctrine to form; for the stylistic peculiarites of the poetry written by the Transcendentalists are less idiosyncratic than those of Whitman, Dickinson, or most of the major British Romantic poets. Often Transcendentalist poems seem to recycle eminent precursors: George Herbert (Emerson's "Grace"), John Milton (Emerson's "Woodnotes," the title allusion to Shakespeare taken from "L'Allegro"), Wordsworth (Channing's *The Wanderer*), Shelley (Cranch's *Satan*). The chief strands of stylistic influence were Romanticism and the Renaissance, with secondary infusions from Neoclassic, classical Greek, Sanskrit, and archaic European models (bardic poetry and sagas). Since most Transcendentalists wrote poetry with the left hand, as it were, and since on principle they prized ideas and experience more highly than form, it is not surprising that their poetry was a heterogeneous assemblage of more or less traditional short lyric and mid-length narrative genres. As we look more closely, however, patterns begin to emerge.

The most fundamental of these is a persistent striving for the arresting compressed statement.

> Thy beauty fades, and with it too my love
> (Very)

> Great God, I ask thee for no meaner pelf
> Than that I may not disappoint myself
> (Thoreau)

> The issues of the general soul
> Are mirrored in its round abode
> (Channing)

> The passive master lent his hand
> To the vast soul that o'er him planned
> (Emerson, couplet from "The Problem"
> inscribed on his gravestone)

> the white phantom of an ancient maid
> Doing its shopping on a pistareen
> Or the lame parson's sulky, time-worn trap,
> Sahara's sermon creaking in the wheel
> (Channing)

> I slept, and dreamed that life was beauty
> I woke, and found that life was duty
> (Hooper)

Sweet is the pleasure
Itself cannot spoil!
Is not true leisure
One with true toil?
(John Sullivan Dwight)

Guard thee from the powers of evil;
Who cannot trust, vows to the devil.
Walk thy slow and spell-bound way;
Keep on thy mask, or shun the day—
Let go my hand upon the way.
(Margaret Fuller)

Heart to heart was never known;
    Mind with mind did never meet;
We are columns left alone
    Of a temple once complete.
(Cranch)

I hear not with the ear,—the heart doth tell
Its secret deeds to me untold before
(Very)

Virtue palters; Right is hence;
Freedom praised, but hid;
Funeral eloquence
Rattles the coffin-lid.
(Emerson)

When thou approachest to the One,
Self from thyself thou first must free,
Thy cloak duplicity cast clean aside,
And in thy Being's being be.
(Alcott)

This kind of thing easily becomes facile (Dwight) or overstrained (Alcott). But when it works, the poem administers an electrical jolt. The jolt can serve many purposes: prophetic rage (Very), satirical stiletto-dig (Channing), visionary enthusiasm (the Emerson couplet), elegiac wistfulness (Cranch). Transcendentalist poems often strike one as a kind of bardic or homiletic wisdom literature.

The Transcendentalists' taste for the aphoristic moment was whetted by their reading interests: in biblical proverb, Latin epigram, Celtic and Anglo-Saxon laconics, Metaphysical emblem poetry, and the closed couplet of seventeenth- and eighteenth-century verse, perhaps especially the related genres of epithet, epitaph, and inscription. Such models appealed to them for reasons of principle as well as taste. They believed that the peaks, the quintessences, of experience count for more than temporal sequence. Furthermore, as amateur metaphysicians reading the book of nature from a loosely pantheistic standpoint, they sought to find the universe in the grain of sand: to push through to the ultimate truth-statement about an image or event. Epigrammaticism registers all this insofar as it seems to stand for a perfect encapsulated conceptual distillation of the object. The epigram's impersonality also appealed to the Transcendentalists. Epigram converts the mood of the moment into prophetic truth, converts subjective voice into oracle. This depersonalization reflects the Emersonian conviction, shared by most of the circle, that what justifies the self is its universality. Finally, the epigrammatic series, or the longer poem comprised of striking discrete epithets or propositional statements or allegorized images, reflects the Emersonian corollary that truth never stands still but must be stabbed, thrust, or jabbed at perpetually. "The quality of the imagination," as he put it, "is to flow, and not to freeze."

What I have called the impersonality of Transcendentalist poetic utterance requires special attention here, given the importance to the movement of the underlying principle (self beomes Self to the extent that it is universal rather than personal), but more particularly its wide importance as a problematic that helps to define the structure and voice of the poems to issue from the movement. A number of the strong Transcendentalist poems are about the problem of rehabilitating the self (with a small *s*) by converting it into Self so as to achieve the state of impersonality of which the poem's speaker sometimes serves as model, sometimes as antimodel. Let us look at two examples.

> 'Tis to yourself I speak; you cannot know
> Him whom I call in speaking such an one,
> For thou beneath the earth liest buried low,
> Which he alone as living walks upon;
> Thou mayst at times have heard him speak to you,
> And often wished perchance that you were he;

And I must ever wish that it were true,
For then thou couldst hold fellowship with me;
But now thou hear'st us talk as strangers, met
Above the room wherein thou liest abed;
A word perhaps loud spoken thou mayst get,
Or hear our feet when heavily they tread;
But he who speaks, or him who's spoken to,
Must both remain as strangers still to you.

(Very, "Yourself")

If the red slayer think he slays,
  Or if the slain think he is slain,
They know not well the subtle ways
  I keep, and pass, and turn again.

Far or forgot to me is near;
  Shadow and sunlight are the same;
The vanished gods to me appear;
  And one to me are shame and fame.

They reckon ill who leave me out;
  When me they fly, I am the wings;
I am the doubter and the doubt,
  And I the hymn the Brahmin sings.

The strong gods pine for my abode,
  And pine in vain the sacred Seven;
But thou, meek lover of the good!
  Find me, and turn thy back on heaven.

(Emerson, "Brahma")

  In both poems, an enlightened being speaks prescriptively but enigmatically to one lying in the darkness of alienation from his more authentic self, a self implicitly conceived as spirit or essence. The riddlesomeness befits the listener's benighted condition, perhaps. The rhetorical strategy in each case is to try to tease or shock the reader into enlightenment: Emerson by the argument that Brahma the world-soul is omnipresent, but inaccessible to the "meek lover of the good" who compulsively dualizes; Very by the doubletalk of insisting (with some justice?) that the sick reader can't follow the conversation that the speaker is holding with the reader's inner self (paradoxically portrayed here as the more public and exterior of the two selves) from whom he is separated by his sickbed. Both poems' speakers critique the speciousness of personality as we ordinarily think of it, and point to a transpersonal form of self-realization that is arrived at by coming to terms with a more universal form of being that lies more deeply within the self than the mundane ego fathoms. Very intensifies the paradox of inner = universal by representing the superficial self as "buried" in its sickbed, while the true inner self communicates with the spirit.

Very's evangelical voice makes his mode of impersonality more parochial, also more "lyric," than Emerson's exoticization of the impersonal through the mask of "Brahma." This is an exemplary difference. Looking in Very's direction, we descry a series of poems in which a more or less determinate speaker aspires to a state of transpersonality; in Emerson's direction, we find a group of authoritative-sounding voices who seem to function as temporary loci of the universal. Two short Thoreau poems will illustrate this.

> Light-winged Smoke, Icarian bird,
> Melting thy pinions in thy upward flight,
> Lark without song, and messenger of dawn,
> Circling above the hamlets as thy nest;
> Or else, departing dream, and shadowy form
> Of midnight vision, gathering up thy skirts;
> By night star-veiling, and by day
> Darkening the light and blotting out the sun;
> Go thou my incense upward from this hearth,
> And ask the gods to pardon this clear flame.
>
> ("Smoke")

> Here lies the body of this world,
> Whose soul alas to hell is hurled.
> This golden youth long since was past,
> Its silver manhood went as fast,
> And iron age drew on at last;
> 'Tis vain its character to tell,
> The several fates which it befell,
> What year it died, when 'twill arise,
> We only know that here it lies.
>
> ("Epitaph on the World")

In the first poem, printed in *Walden*, the speaker revises mythology by mythologizing himself (with smoke as his proxy) as an upward-soaring Icarus of godlike pretense. In the second, a poem that could almost have been by Jonson or Prior or Pope (take your choice, depending upon whether you hear the tone as solemn, mocking, or borderline), he coolly surveys the fate of the world from a godlike height. In the one poem the speaker performs an action; in the other the speaker is nothing more more than a voice. In each, however, the ritualistic quality of the prosody (following from the genres of invocation and epitaph) conspires with other elements to push the poem toward the condition of speakerlessness.

But the eclipse of the speaker in Transcendentalist poetry, these Thoreau poems show, is really after all less a matter of transcending individuality than of reluctance to create a lyric voice to begin with. Consider Bronson Alcott's decision to write his *New Connecticut* in the third person and replay autobiographical detail similarly to Whitman in the first part of "There Was a Child Went Forth," as if to illustrate the adventures of a typical "farmer's boy" and "pedler" (the two autobiographical chapters presented here). With the exception of Channing the Transcendentalists rarely showed any sustained interest in experimenting more than fitfully with a semiautobiographical persona like those of Wordsworth, Whitman, and Dickinson. Alcott, for example, records what clearly seem to be autobiographical details with an almost total absence of subjective feeling:

> Of letters mindful, emulous of lore,
> Not willingly let he occasion slip
> To chalk upon his mother's cleanly floor
> His earliest essays at rude penmanship.

Even Transcendentalist poetry that adheres less doggedly to pre-Romantic models, as Thoreau does to invocation and epitaph or Alcott does to Neoclassical bucolics (cf. Robert Bloomfield, *The Farmer's Boy*), often hesitates to develop an interiorized speaker. The Emerson poem closest to the greater romantic lyric, "Musketaquid," illustrates this hesitancy. In it a determinate speaker pictures himself disporting within a determinate nurturing landscape, but there is no localized moment, no unique event, no temporality to the poem. The speaker bathes, breathes, follows, finds—but in no case engages in any specific action:

what's recorded is a series of characteristic gestures, rather, to the end of celebrating the nurturance of what emerges as a quite generic vision of the rural landscape as home ("meadows bottomless," "broad orchards resonant with bees," etc.). Likewise, Margaret Fuller's "Thoughts," seems to promise a particularized experience (the subtitle reads, "On Sunday Morning, when Prevented by a Snow Storm from Going to Church") of a localized ex cathedra lyric meditation, but the poem develops as a series of generalized ideas, "Ours is the faith of Reason," "There is a blessing in a day like this," etc. Fuller's finest poem, "Meditations," another mid-length sequence of religious musings set against a naturescape more fully realized, and featuring a speaker that is more dramatized, again imagines the subjective experience in summarizing, almost paradigmatic terms ("To-day, for the first time, I felt the Deity, / And uttered prayer on hearing thunder").

More often than not the development of the subjective mood in Transcendentalist poetry expresses loss or lack of self-integration. In Emerson's "Days" the speaker's position of distinct self-defined separateness is the measure of his inadequacy and vulnerability:

> Daughters of Time, the hypocritic Days,
> Muffled and dumb like barefoot dervishes,
> And marching single in an endless file,
> Bring diadems and fagots in their hands.
> To each they offer gifts after his will,
> Bread, kingdoms, stars, and sky that holds them all.
> I, in my pleached garden, watched the pomp,
> Forgot my morning wishes, hastily
> Took a few herbs and apples, and the Day
> Turned and departed silent. I, too late,
> Under her solemn fillet saw the scorn.

One insufficiently grasped reason why this poem has consistently impressed readers is its terse enactment of the Blakean myth of the fall into individuality. The first six lines, spoken to all appearances by no determinate speaker, present the tableau of the days and its meaning with a confidence that belies the subtone of wonderment and mysteriousness. With the ensuing shift from archetypal image to personal anecdote, the subtone takes over the poem to produce a mood of frustration, regret, and self-dissatisfaction. The vision of the inadequacy of the self to command the resources of the day, in other words, is "enacted" by a speakerly "lapse" from the authoritative impersonality to vulnerable subjectiveness.

This studied anticlimacticism is not unique in the Emerson canon, although "Days" is the most striking example of it. At the end of "Hamatreya" the force of the Earth-Song's retort to the complacent propertarian farmers ("Earth endures / Stars abide . . . / But where are old men?") is signaled by a sudden subjective shift:

> When I heard the Earth-song
> I was no longer brave;
> My avarice cooled
> Like lust in the chill of the grave.

Awakening to mortality correlates with awakening to subjectivity. A similar thing happens in "Uriel." This poem starts with a bardic assertiveness ("It fell in the ancient periods / Which the brooding soul surveys") that is maintained through the narrative of Uriel's confusion-producing defiance of orthodoxy. But then Uriel is shown as lapsing into "a sad self-knowledge, withering." He becomes a diminished being, a bit like Milton's Satan as *Paradise Lost* unfolds, although even at the end he maintains a certain archangelic ironic hauteur. Given this pattern in "Days," "Hamatreya," and "Uriel," it is not surprising that Emerson could finish "Threnody," his elegy to his young son, only by imagining Waldo's individuality merged with the infinite as part of an orderly cosmic process.

Emerson's early poem, "Each and All," provides an oblique commentary upon this notion of the risks of subjectivity. Its theme is the necessary interdependence of the animate parts that go to make up a world: "All are needed by each one; / Nothing is good or fair alone." This is initially presented in a voice befitting the doctrine, the voice of the impersonal epigrammatist who speaks the aforesaid couplet. Then, however, follow three anecdotes, the first two seemingly autobiographical, of disappointment at the results of taking individual items out of their contextual ensembles: a wild bird put in a cage, seashells fetched from the shore, a bride who seems to lose her magic when taken from "the virgin train" where the bridegroom first longingly espied her. The contemplation of these disillusions the speaker ("Then I said, 'I covet truth; / Beauty is unripe childhood's cheat' "). But then, in another reversal, he becomes newly aware of *his* context—outdoors on a beautiful summer day—and his alienation fades as he merges into the all: "Beauty through my senses stole; / I yielded myself to the perfect whole." By means of this sequence the poem strongly suggests that the self-centeredness of the perceiving ego is the price of individuation. Individuation is the problem, not the solution; the solution is for personality to be absorbed back into the all, so that the speaker returns as it were to the state of healthful impersonality maintained in the first part of the poem. Seeing this we understand the full satirical purport of the three exempla, such as the weirdly misogynous-seeming anecdote of the bridegroom's disillusion immediately after marriage. The point is that the man's behavior is perversely appropriative, and that this perversity is of the same genre as the speaker's petulantly egocentric rejection of the enchantment of the world as a mere show of appearances. Reviewing the poem as a whole, we perceive, further, that the author never really allowed the pathology of subjectiveness to do much more than begin to assert itself, inasmuch as the I-mood is really an illustrative device to substantialize an argument rather than an indulgence of subjective lyricism. Hence the indifference of ascribing the three individual anecdotes to "my" experience (bird and shells) or "another"'s (bride).

If Emerson is the Transcendentalist poet in whom a critique of subjectiveness is most adroitly developed and deployed at the stylistic level, it is Ellery Channing who dwells most obsessively upon the correlation between subjectivity and inadequacy. Channing's poems using a generic or impersonal speaker radiate an easy grace and cheerfulness of spirit, ranging from the mellow to the jaunty, distinct from the characteristic voices of the rest of the Transcendentalist cohort:

> He came and waved a little silver wand,
> He dropped the veil that hid a statue fair,
> He drew a circle with that pearly hand,
> His grace confined that beauty in the air;—
> Those limbs so gentle, now at rest from flight,
> Those quiet eyes now musing on the night.

This little personification of "Moonlight" shows a relaxed, nonprogrammatic command over visual nuances refreshing to encounter amid the documents of Transcendentalist striving. As Channing verges toward confessional, however, his tone loses its composure and becomes rattled, defensive, and self-pitying. The retrogression can be measured by considering as a series his four most ambitious narrative poems: "Wachusett" (1856), a topographical ramble in couplets reminiscent of Neoclassical locodescriptivism; *Near Home* (1858) and *The Wanderer* (1871), two works in which the speaker juxtaposes himself at length to a series of more-or-less idealized figures more-or-less modeled on Thoreau; and *Eliot* (1885), a long remorseful Byronic wallow featuring a Channing-like protagonist who feels himself deserted and abandoned by those he now realizes he cared for. "Wachusett," the best of Channing's longer works, maintains a kind of crisp assurance by endowing the speaker with the diagnostic omniscience traditional to this genre:

> Baptist, and Methodist, and Orthodox,
> And even Unitarian, creed that shocks
> Established church-folk; they are one to me,
> Who in the different creeds the same things see,
> But I love dearly to look down at them,
> In rocky landscapes like Jerusalem.

But as Channing's voice gets more reflexive its brittleness surfaces as a felt problem:

> fancy the dull man wandering round
> As I, vexing the sly world with questions,
> Heard his queries solved and plainly answered:
> . . . .
> Conceive I held all, clearly explicate,
> Here in my hand: might I so front the wood?
> Should it not flout and leer? cast grinning outlooks?

It is not hard to imagine the voices of these two passages issuing from the same person, but in the latter the awareness of vulnerability that arises from the mood of query rather than pronouncement totally destroys the speaker's confidence and causes him to turn the satire of the first passage against himself. This is a plight that Jones Very, by contrast, does not fall into, because he almost never lets his speaker be vulnerable.

The closest Very comes to this is in his more tender poems of pious assurance, like "The Presence":

> I sit within my room, and joy to find
> That Thou who always lov'st, art with me here,
> That I am never left by Thee behind,
> But by thyself Thou keep'st me ever near;

The fire burns brighter when with Thee I look,
And seems a kinder servant sent to me;
With gladder heart I read thy holy book,
Because thou art the eyes by which I see;
This aged chair, that table, watch and door
Around in ready service ever wait;
Nor can I ask of Thee a menial more
To fill the measure of my large estate,
For Thou thyself, with all a father's care,
Where'er I turn, art ever with me there.

This poem expresses a feeling that Thoreau once pointed out is surprisingly rare in English poetry: genuine, spontaneous affection for God. To a degree, Very resembles George Herbert here. But only to a degree: for there is no hesitancy, no insecurity about the speaker's claim of closeness to God: no possibility of slippage, of falling into perversity, or of God declining to show favor. The sonnet renders what to all appearances is a permanent state of grace, but to the extent that it depicts as indefinite continuation what is in the real world a transient peak experience it transforms the speaker into a superhuman being quite unlike Herbert's personae. In this Very follows the Transcendentalist preference for defining the self in terms of its loftiest possibilities. In a quieter way Christopher Cranch—Transcendentalism's next-most-prolific sonneteer—does the same in "The Garden":

Naught know we but the heart of summer here.
On the tree-shadowed velvet lawn I lie,
And dream up through the close leaves to the sky,
And weave Arcadian visions in a sphere
Of peace. The steaming heat broods all around,
But only lends a quiet to the hours.
The aromatic life of countless flowers,
The singing of a hundred birds, the sound
Of rustling leaves, go pulsing through the green
Of opening vistas in the garden walks.
Dear Summer, on thy balmy breast I lean,
And care not how the moralist toils or talks;
Repose and Beauty preach a gospel too,
Deep as that sterner creed the Apostles knew.

Cranch's trappings are more typically Transcendentalist than Very: not the evangelical piety of the prayer closet but the natural piety of the orchard. Yet the mood and place are basically the same. Here, too, perfect peace, perfect calm, perfect security. Here, too, the security of the enclosed setting completely responsive to the speaker's needs. Like Very's furniture, the presences in Cranch's garden "around in ready service ever wait" to minister to the speaker. The secularization of bliss in Cranch's poem combines with the greater degree of metrical informality (the degree of enjambment, for instance) to provide the illusion of a rather quotidian, personalized speaker figure compared to Very's persona, who at first seems an artifact of dogma by comparison. Yet Cranch's Adamic "I" is no less an allegorical contrivance, no less a figure or exemplar of the awakened consciousness, only awakened in this case into the realm of Arcadia rather than into the realm of the Apostles.

To achieve this allegorical-uplifting effect one needn't present the speaker in a state of perfect security or bliss. This is clear from Thoreau's most polished poem, "Sic Vita." Here are the first two of its seven stanzas.

> I am a parcel of vain strivings tied
>   By a chance bond together,
>   Dangling this way and that, their links
>   Were made so loose and wide,
>   Methinks,
>   For milder weather.
>
> A bunch of violets without their roots,
>   And sorrel intermixed,
>   Encircled by a wisp of straw
>   Once coiled about their shoots,
>   The law
>   By which I'm fixed.

Written to accompany a gift of flowers, this poem—like Herbert's "The Altar" or "The Flower"—represents graphically the image it describes, in this case a loosely assembled bouquet. This visual pun, the device of the extended metaphor of ego as bouquet, the rhetorical mode of assertive statement, make the poem speak, however, in a voice that's opposite the state of passivity and ephemeralness to which the persona confesses. This was a method Emerson had mastered before him, as in "Grace," which a fellow Transcendentalist mistook for Herbert's work.

> How much, preventing God, how much I owe
> To the defences thou hast round me set;
> Example, custom, fear, occasion slow,—
> These scorned bondmen were my parapet.
> I dare not peep over this parapet
> To gauge with glance the roaring gulf below,
> The depths of sin to which I had descended,
> Had not these me against myself defended.

Those scorned bondmen were the speaker's parapet in more ways than he perhaps intended. They did not simply provide him with the internalized restraints on conduct to which he directly refers. In the person's capacity as speaker they provided him with a rhetorical parapet of allegorization by which to defend against having to dip into the experience of sin even at the fantasy level. They provided an apparatus that would restrain subjectivity, indeed would altogether alleviate the need to present a speaker in the predicament of feeling tempted, by transposing a hypothetical narrative into a configuration and a sensibility supposed to be fragile into a state of prayerful resolve, the crisis safely past: a state in which the "me" is nowhere near becoming an individual. Perhaps the greatest defense that the scorned bondmen provide is that they keep the speaker safely generic: grammatically an I, effectively an everyman.

The moral conservatism of Emerson's "Grace," anomalous among his better poems, contrasts diametrically with Ellen Hooper's stunning untitled poem on a similar subject.

> Better a sin which purposed wrong to none
> Than this still wintry coldness at the heart,
> A penance might be borne for evil done
> And tears of grief and love might ease the smart.
> But this self-satisfied and cold respect
> To virtue which must be its own reward,
> Heaven keep us through this danger still alive,
> Lead us not into greatness, heart-abhorred—
>
> Oh God, who framed this stern New-England land,
> Its clear cold waters, and its clear, cold soul,
> Thou givest tropic climes and youthful hearts
> Thou weighest spirits and dost all control—
> Teach me to wait for all—to bear the fault

That most I hate because it is my own.
And if I fail through foul conceit of good,
Let me sin deep so I may cast no stone.

This is one of the neglected gems of Transcendentalist poetics: moving eloquently and surefootedly from the opening declaration to the remarkable affirmation of willingness, in effect, to be damned in order to escape from the Sahara of smugness. It is such a poem as Hester Prynne might have written—had she been a poet—after her seven years of alienation. In direct contrast to "Grace" the speaker here identifies the bondmen Emerson praises as the cause of a state worse than sin and invokes God to help her fight free of their restraints. Better the deep sin than self-repression in the parapet of respectability. The speaker's vehemence, and the striking paradoxes of the "foul conceit of good" (which recalls the "meek lover of the good" in Emerson's "Brahma") and of imagining God as a possible accessory to mortal sin (which goes well beyond anything in Emerson, even the "devil's child" passage in "Self-Reliance")—these elements at first create the impression of a more subjective speaker than that of "Grace." But not altogether so. The sentiment is more idiosyncratic, yes, but the experience is not made more subjective. "Sin" remains abstract, the speaker's inner state a tissue of abstractions—"wintry coldness," "self-satisfied and cold respect." Just as "Grace" leaves unsaid the experience that the parapet kept from happening, so this poem leaves unsaid the experience that might happen if the speaker were to leap from it. In each poem, the ceremonial of invocation turns the "I" effectively into a "we."

The genericization of the nominally subjective speaker in Transcendentalist poetry is related to its interest in what superficially looks like Victorian dramatic monologue. Emerson especially favors this form, in such poems as "Alphonso of Castile," "Mithridates," "Étienne de la Boece," "Merlin," "Saadi," "The Nun's Aspiration," and "Brahma." These poems I call "superficially" like Victorian dramatic monologue because Emerson makes little attempt to record the internal fluctuations of mood or the stylistic variance between cases that Browning introduced into *Men and Women*. This should not be held against him, as a sign that he tried and failed to do what Browning and Tennyson did better. For their psychological and linguistic realism was of very little interest to Emerson, who, significantly, favored the highly stylized *Idylls of the King* over all the other works of these two poets. Alphonso, Mithridates, and the rest are not, for Emerson, individual consciousnesses but conceptual positions. To move from one to another is to vary the attitude (e.g., Brahma's Olympian elusiveness vs. Merlin's vehemence) but not the level of abstraction.

A good way to verify and calibrate this point is to look at the shifts of speaker that occur occasionally, very occasionally, within Transcendentalist poems. Rarely are these shifts registered by major stylistic shifts. The case of Emerson's "Hamatreya" is less typical than his "Merlin's Song." "Hamatreya" makes a modest attempt to use vernacular for his farmers ("This suits me for a pasture; that's my park") and oracular language for the Earth-song ("But the heritors? / Fled like the flood's foam"). In "Merlin's Song," on the other hand, Emerson moves from outer to inner speaker without a hitch:

> Hear what British Merlin sung,
> Of keenest eye and truest tongue.
> Say not, the chiefs who first arrive
> Usurp the seats for which all strive

Even more striking is the seeming identity of the voices of sphinx, poet, and persona in "The Sphinx," given the debate structure of the poem and the technical difference of estate between mythological figure and mundane narrator.

This monoglossia holds true also for the movement's most ambitious dramatic poem, Cranch's *Satan: A Libretto* (1874; later republished under the title of "Ormuzd and Ahriman"). Cranch here converts the tradition of romantic Satanism into the most probing exploration of the philosophy of evil in Transcendentalist poetry. Satan is the text's main theologian, and the message he announces to a rather confused chorus of spirits, predictably enough, is that he is not what he is thought to be: "I / Am but the picture mortal eyes behold." The traditional Christian view of sacred history as hinging upon a holy war between God and Satan is a dualistic fiction perpetrated by mortals unwilling to see the monistic principle of love as the one supersensible force. This is essentially a mythologization in the garb of *Prometheus Unbound* of Emerson's doctrine of "Compensation"—that polarity is omnipresent in the phenomenal world but nonexistent in the noumenal realm of the soul's inmost nature.

> Naught evil, though it were the Prince of evil,
> Hath being in itself. For God alone
> Existeth in Himself, and good, which lives

> As sunshine lives, born of the Parent Sun.
> I am the shadow of that Sun,
> Opposite, not opposing, only seen
> Upon the underside.
> . . . .
> I symbolize the wild and deep
> And unregenerated wastes of life,
> Dark with transmitted tendencies of race,
> And blind mischance . . .

As in Shelley, Cranch's beautiful idealisms of moral excellence are differentiated prosodically (Satan and the Archangel Raphael speak in blank verse, the spirits generally in rhymed tetrameter) but not linguistically or in respect to degree of reflexiveness or interiorization. Through them doctrinal attitudes are ventriloquized and attached to names and shadowy figures as positions, not personalities, engage in debate.

Transcendentalist poetry is therefore by and large not a poetry of particularized experience interested in psychological complication but a poetry of attitudes expressed by turns in aphoristic statements, tableaux of images, narratives and monologues of typic figures, whether they call themselves "I" or Xenophanes. The Wordsworth of "Tintern Abbey" was less interesting to the Transcendentalists than the Wordsworth of the Immortality Ode; the Milton of the great autobiographic asides in *Paradise Lost* or the sonnet on his blindness was less interesting to them than the Milton of "Il Penseroso." The preceding analysis has followed the standard practice of featuring Emerson's poetry more conspicuously than that of the rest of the Transcendentalist group, in agreement with the usual estimate of its relative quality and impact, but not the customary approach of treating the poets one by one; for the commonality of their thematic-stylistic repertoire, through serendipity and cross-fertilization, seems to require presenting their work as an ensemble, at least at the points disussed. On these points the group seems fairly unified.

In those fundamental respects the poetry of Transcendentalism seems as closely akin to Neoclassical and Metaphysical poetry as to the "poetry of experience" of the Romantics and Victorians, more akin to Dickinson than to Whitman, more akin to the Fireside poets (Bryant, Longfellow, Lowell, Holmes, Whittier) than either to Dickinson or to

Whitman. Where the Transcendentalists—Emerson and Thoreau, at least—more closely anticipate their two great American successors is in their degree of prosodic experiment: the roughening and breaking and shifting of meters.

> Go, blindworm, go,
> Behold the famous States
> Harrying Mexico
> With rifle and with knife!
> (Emerson, "Ode: Inscribed to W. H. Channing")

> Conscience is instinct bred in the house,
> Feeling and Thinking propagate the sin
> By an unnatural breeding in and in.
> I say, Turn it out doors,
> Into the moors.
>   (Thoreau, "Conscience")

Emerson's prophetic rage deforms the baseline iambic trimeter almost beyond recognition. Thoreau starts out with a loose dactyl-trochee form that gets increasingly doggerelized and clipped, starting in line three—a metrical reflection of his protest against the forms of a socially rather than naturally produced conscience. Thoreau is careful to act out his deviationism at the linguistic level as well: breaking one's meter correlates with vernacularizing one's syntax and language.

In Emerson's numerous prose reflections and poems about poesis (a favorite topic for Cranch and Channing also), something like a theory of prosodic deviance emerges. On the one hand, Emerson fancifully imagines prosody as sanctioned by the nature of things: he traces rhythm to pulse-beat, rhyme to the principle of polarity:

> The rhyme of the poet
> Modulates the king's affairs;
> Balance-loving Nature
> Made all things in pairs.
>   ("Merlin," part 2)

Yet, Emerson stresses,

> The kingly bard
> Must smite the chords rudely and hard,

> As with hammer or with mace;
> That they may render back
> Artful thunder . . .
>   ("Merlin," part 1)

The passage enacts what it would describe, as does the ode to Channing, which, along with "Bacchus," is Emerson's most impressive act of metrical deformation: the first a thunderous jeremiad, the latter an exuberant piece of metrical inebriation from which Dickinson might have derived "I taste a liquor never brewed."

Such Emersonian and Thoreauvian experiments might be seen as anticipating Whitmanian free verse and Dickinsonian off-rhyme (cf. Emerson's "go"/"Mexico"—as well as the wonderful half-rhymes throughout the first stanza of "Threnody," as Emerson moves from the heights of "desire" to the sonorous depths of "mourn.") To take these liberties as protests against "rules" of poetic form is to credit them, up to a point justly, as serious expressions of the Transcendentalist program of disrupting orthodoxy at every level and as symptoms and harbingers of the antiformalism often claimed to be one of the most distinctive marks of the American poetic tradition from Whitman and Dickinson to the present.

This argument, however, requires severe qualification in several respects that force us to a different view of Transcendentalist and perhaps even also American poetics than is commonly espoused. First, Transcendentalist, Whitmanian, and Dickinsonian prosodic disruptions were all only part of a state of prosodic ferment that started in the early Romantic era with the revival of popular forms like balladry and (in Blake) fourteeners and that reached an unprecedented height in the mid-nineteenth century in the work of Poe (cf. his pride in the novelty of the meter of "The Raven"), Browning (who deliberately wrote craggy, clotted blank verse), Longfellow (his revival of hexameter, his quixotic experiment with trochees in *Hiawatha*), and the virtuosity of Tennyson and Swinburne. Second, it is not clear that history will show antiformalism to be the primary thrust of *either* Transcendentalism *or* American poetics generally. To put this more explicitly: Whitmanian openness may prove to have been less pervasive in American poetry than the more restrained experimentation represented by the Transcendentalists' lover's quarrels with bound forms and, in the next generation, by the poetry of Emily Dickinson. Robinson, Frost, much of

Pound and Eliot and Stevens; Dunbar and McKay and Countee Cullen; John Crowe Ransom, Elizabeth Bishop, Robert Francis, Sylvia Plath, Gwendolyn Brooks, Richard Wilbur—their prosody can be referred back, in most cases by analogy rather than genealogy of course, to the aesthetic of liberty-within-restraint represented by Transcendentalism's subjection of bound forms to pressure and deformation. In varying degrees much of their work also recalls Transcendentalism's sublimation of the subjectified persona and narrative-descriptive amplification to a rhetoric of cerebral rather than visceral intensity committed to filtering represented experience through the lens of philosophic or moral reflection.

This diagnosis puts what is often disparagingly thought of as the conservatism of Transcendentalist *and* American poetry in its proper light. A Whitman-centered account of American poetics makes the contrast between Anglo and American poetics pleasantly dramatic at the expense of the truth, the truth finally even of Whitman himself. More accurate than an autochthonous myth of American poetic history that winds up dancing around a selective version of Whitman, fathered by an even more selective version of Emerson, would be a myth of American poesis as part of a transatlantic Anglophone community almost as interlinked in the nineteenth century as in the High Modernist era, a narrative in which the splitting out of the Transcendentalist group quickly seems artificial except insofar as it helps one to concentrate on how Transcendentalist poems reflect the play of certain ideas more or less peculiar to the movement. Yet I must also immediately amend that statement, because to take the first steps toward the critical revision I propose it is imperative to focus one's intellectual energies more intensively on Transcendentalist poetry for awhile, in order to convince oneself that the best of it does indeed deserve a place on the literary-historical map once again being redrawn as the millennium approaches: that it gains, not loses, in interest when seen as more a traditional than a proto-Whitmanian artifact, and that its conservatism is as important a key as its iconoclasm to understanding what it tells us about the history—and the achievement—of American poetry as a whole.

Lawrence Buell

Further Reading

Buell, Lawerence. *Literary Transendentalism: Style and Vision in the American Renaissance.* Ithaca: Cornell University Press, 1973.

Hennessy, Helen. "The Dial: Its Poetry and Poetic Criticism." *New England Quarterly* (1958), 31:66–87.

Miller, Perry, ed. *The American Transcendentalists: Their Prose and Poetry.* Garden City, N.Y.: Doubleday, 1957.

——— *The Transcendentalists: An Anthology.* Cambridge: Harvard University Press, 1950.

Stauffer, Donald Barlow. "The Transcendentalists." In Donald Barlow Stauffer, ed., *A Short History of American Poetry*, pp. 93–114. New York: Dutton, 1974.

Yoder, R. A. *Emerson and the Orphic Poet in America.* Berkeley: University of California Press, 1978.

Emily Dickinson

EMILY DICKINSON was born on December 10, 1830, in Amherst, Massachusetts; she had an older brother, Austin (b. April 1828) and a younger sister, Lavinia (b. February 1833). Her father and grandfather were successful lawyers and politicians; both were active in the affairs of Amherst College, which, along with two other men, her grandfather had founded. The Dickinsons were a closely knit family, and all three children were lifelong residents of Amherst. When Austin married (in 1855), he and his wife lived next door to the parental home; neither Lavinia nor Emily married.

The one major trauma in Dickinson's life was severe eye trouble: she suffered several episodes of blindness in the early 1860s, and in 1864 and 1865 she made two long visits to Boston to be treated by an eye surgeon. Although she had been vivacious and socially active in her young womanhood, in the 1860s she became increasingly reluctant to engage in a social life that entailed going into public, perhaps because of this visual disability. Very few facts are known about her private life, which appears to have been relatively quiet.

Dickinson seems to have begun writing seriously in about 1848, and there was nothing in the least secretive about it: she enjoyed a local reputation for great wit, and many of her poems were read by family and friends. Moreover, in April 1862 she initiated a correspondence with Thomas Wentworth Higginson, a highly respected Boston man of letters, and the poet regularly included her work in the correspondence, which continued until her death in May 1886. Nonetheless, only about fourteen poems were published during her lifetime.

After Emily's death her sister Lavinia discovered 1776 poems among the papers. Lavinia took about half of these to Austin's close friend, Mabel Loomis Todd; and together with Higginson, Mrs. Todd published a slender selection in 1890 (with major editorial revisions to "regularize" them). During the course of the next more than half-century a steady stream of Emily Dickinson's poetry "leaked" out to the public; however, it was often so thoroughly mutilated by the editorial process that readers could make no clear assessment of the poet's work.

Finally, in 1951–1955 a reliable variorum edition of the *Complete Poems* was published by Thomas Johnson, and only then did "Emily Dickinson" make her entrance into the world.

The poet Lydia Sigourney, whose creative years coincided with Emily Dickinson's, was both celebrated and rewarded in her day. In his essay, "Autobiography in the American Renaissance," Lawrence Buell reminds us that it was Sigourney who produced "the first full-dress autobiography written by an American author of either sex whose primary vocation was creative writing," and he goes on to observe that

the record is altogether a striking mixture of literary modesty and self-advertisement, dramatizing the offsetting point that personal literary aspirations mustn't come first but also asserting that they have given her life its ultimate direction. Or to put the matter another way, Sigourney accepts society's proposition that literary professionalism is tolerable only when it does not "interfere with the discharge of womanly duty"; she structures [the account of] her life accordingly, so that the literary achievement comes after and (she argues) as an outgrowth of a domesticity that she refuses to see as other than fully satisfying.

To some, Sigourney's constructions of "the woman as author" may seem coy or disingenuous; however, Sigourney herself saw them as necessary defensive maneuvers in a society that read her work voraciously, but had little or no tolerance for the notion that a *woman* might take the profession of writing *seriously*.

Consider the reception of Fanny Fern's female bildungsroman, *Ruth Hall*, in 1854. Although the novel was effusively domestic, it nonetheless portrayed the antifeminist bias of the public world in frankly indignant terms; as a consequence, it was excoriated by critics who called it "unnatural," "irreverent," and "unfeminine." Thus if everyday experience in mid-nineteenth-century America had not taught the woman who would be an author the wisdom of remaining an entirely private person and the danger of revealing her commitment to vocation, the reception of this scandalous, but immensely popular piece of fiction produced a public demonstration of that lesson in Emily Dickinson's twenty-fourth year. Consider, now, Dickinson's ambivalent attitude toward publication. Consider her ultimate decision not to accept the professional role of "author" during her lifetime. For decades, critics (most of them male) have judged these to be proofs of eccentricity. Considered in the contemporary context, however, does it not seem more an evidence of prudence and of the determination to enjoy aesthetic autonomy—to be the unchallenged "eye/I" that scrutinizes and defines, and not the mere object of gaze?

Walt Whitman was her fraternal twin in many ways: he defied the moral pieties of the day; he radically subverted the accepted patterns of rhythm, rhyme, and linguistic usage. But because he was a man who had worked in the newspaper and printing business—a man who was well acquainted with the marketing principles of the publishing world—from the very beginning of his career Whitman took immense care to construct a public image of "The Poet." He crafted a voice for the preface to the first edition of *Leaves of Grass* that promises to speak (without restraint) for *all* the people; he included a frontispiece engraving of himself in working clothes, hand on hip, facing the reader with (apparently) nothing whatsoever to hide. And as time went on, he organized a prodigous proliferation of photographic images—"Walt Whitman," who became (convincingly) the "good gray poet." This entire campaign, which need not have been false merely because it was self-conscious, imposed powerful limitations upon the reader's constructive imagination, and, as a consequence, we are inclined to read Whitman's poetry with *his* image of "The Poet" in mind.

The same cannot be said for Dickinson. Poetically she was a comparable rebel: her work defied the moral truisms of mid-Victorian America; it violated the accepted practices of versification even more boldly than Whitman's work; and what was probably most deviant, it had been authored by a serious female poet in an age when women were not supposed to take writing seriously in any way. Ironically, posterity stood in need of some comprehensive construction of "The Poet" from Emily Dickinson even more than it did from the assiduously inventive Mr. Whitman; however, the mores of the historical moment imposed all but insuperable impediments to a woman author's providing such a construction (as the example of Lydia Sigourney demonstrates). Thus, Emily Dickinson wrote no prose essay of any sort about "The Poet"; and as for pictures, only one stilted daguerreotype of the adolescent Emilie Dickinson remains. To put the matter succinctly: Dickinson left us the work (a concatenation of brilliant, sometimes cryptic poetry), but she utterly declined to bequeath her version of "The Poet."

And so, Dickinson's posthumous readers have constructed their own accounts of "The Poet."

In 1890, in a preface to the first published selection of her poems, Thomas Wentworth Higginson laid out the essential elements of the standard scenario: he defined Dickinson's work as a pure "expression of the writer's own mind . . . verses . . . like poetry torn up by the roots, with rain and dew and earth still clinging to them." This original construction of "Emily Dickinson, 'the poet,' " served not to clarify the work, but to hint at the possibility of a tantalizing mystery. Indeed, the problem of understanding this poetry has been compounded by a number of "mystifying" factors. First, until the Thomas Johnson variorum edition of the *Complete Poems* (1951–1955), Dickinson's work was published in bits and pieces—sporadically and in corrupted form. Second, Dickinson commands an astonishing range of tone, attitude, voice, and subject—all the while speaking as "I" (what Michel Foucault has termed the "first person" of the "second self," an "author-function" that it would be false to identify with the real author). Third, the poems are dense and powerful; they would be difficult under the best of circumstances. Fourth, like Whitman, in her strongest poems Dickinson sometimes uses such radically subversive tactics that they disrupt the cohesive properties of language itself (which was her intent). Finally, the entire corpus is so large that merely becoming conversant with every part of it is a prodigious task.

Confronted with an alluring enigma of such proportions, many readers have begun by accepting the central notions of Higginson's construction. They have presumed that Dickinson's work was in some fundamental way spontaneous (an emanation of "natural" genius rather than the product of meticulous, self-conscious, highly literate craftsmanship); and they have held, almost as an article of faith, that the poems are essentially, even exclusively personal (that is, morbidly *self*-focused—the versified responses to some particular series of events in the poet's life). Finally, building upon such premises, these readers have supposed that the best way to understand the *poetry* was first to construct "The *Poet.*" The result has been a dizzying array of "possible 'Poets' ": Dickinson in the throes of insanity (sometimes hysteria; sometimes depression); Dickinson the disappointed lover (the genders of the beloved object have varied according to fashion); Dickinson the would-be suicide; Dickinson the survivor of an abortion, the victim of Porphyria, of lupus, etc., etc. American authors have sometimes done rather peculiar things that are a matter of historical fact (Hawthorne lived reclusively in his mother's attic for eight years), but in most cases we have been willing to make some distinction between the work and the person who wrote it. Not so with Emily Dickinson. In her case, we have developed fanciful constructions of "The Poet" *first*, and then we have deployed them in an attempt to understand the poetry.

In his suggestive essay, "What is an Author," Michel Foucault explains how this construction of "The Author" can shape our understanding of a text. Those "aspects of an individual, which we designate as an author . . . are *projections*, in terms always more or less psychological, of *our [own] way of handling texts.*" Thus the "author-function" inheres in the *reader* (and not intrinsically in the author—although she or he may undertake to influence it, as Whitman did): in extreme cases, it may become the dominant component of the reading process and may be used to explain "the presence of certain events within a text, as well as their transformations, distortions . . . and modifications." Such has often been the case with the readers of Emily Dickinson's poetry.

At the outset of this discussion of Dickinson's work, then, let me enumerate the assumptions about "The Poet" that inform it.

1. Emily Dickinson was highly intelligent, probably more intelligent than most of her readers.
2. She suffered from severe eye trouble, and by 1860 or 1861, she had become reluctant to leave the familiarity of her home and its grounds. Subsequent to several operations on her eyes (in 1864 and 1865 when she was in her mid-thirties and had already written the greater part of her poetry), her reticence seems to have become absolute. Until her final years, these were her only major illnesses: she suffered from no serious mental illness save this home-boundedness in her later years.
3. Her poetry is "about" no particular series of *personal* crises, not "about" Emily Dickinson: instead, it speaks generally—addressing the *human-*condition, not her individual personal situation. Dickinson's notion of the human condition was, of course, influenced by her personal situation; in this respect, she is like all other poets.

4. Coming from a family of sophisticated lawyers and politicians (both her father and grandfather served many terms in the Massachusetts Legislature; her father served one term in the United States House of Representatives), she had a firm grasp of political realities. The immense power of men in America did not escape her notice.

5. Having received a superb classical education and being naturally inclined to supplement it widely, she knew the standard literary texts thoroughly; in addition, she knew the Bible virtually by heart.

6. She was a *serious, systematic poet*: for her, writing poetry was a vocation that demanded discipline, the freedom for intense concentration, and craftsmanship.

7. She was ambitious (a trait that is most candidly expressed in her letters).

8. She was fiercely proud and independent—unwilling to conflate vocation with celebrity, unwilling to tailor her work to placate either the demands of latter-day Puritanism or the exigencies of the Victorian marketplace in America.

9. Nonetheless (like the major *male* poets of her day), she construed herself as working intimately and intrinsically within the context of a literary heritage: poem after poem is matched against the work of other poets—God (in the Bible), Emerson, Wordsworth, Tennyson, Poe, Milton, Pope, Dante, Shakespeare, to cite a few.

10. She could perceive with ruthless clarity that this literary heritage had no natural place in it for a *woman* poet of her power and ambition.

11. Thus she used the art of poetry subversively: she created a distinctive *female* voice of great power, and one use to which she put it was the undermining of comfortable stereotypes and social pieties that falsified women's *actual* experiences. (It is this *subversive* intention that is similar to Whitman's.)

12. One component of Dickinson's "modernism" can be defined by employing Myra Jehlen's distinction between "meaning" and "knowledge." " 'Meaning,' as it replaced 'knowledge,' was a linguistic entity that was fully and stably apprehensible, because its components were wholly contained in the account itself. 'Knowledge,' on the other hand, was relational, and referred back continuously to a reality it never entirely comprehended and that thus, in any given account of things, always remained insurgent. One could say, in short, that knowledge is history while meaning is text." It follows, then, that no artist can alter our *understanding of history* without first laying hold of language, repossessing it, and altering its meanings to conform to "reality." If the game is "history" (or its handmaiden, "literature,"), the nonnegotiable preliminary struggle is over "language."

Repossessing the linguistic and artistic forms of the patriarchy became the focus of Dickinson's art.
13. I've saved the best for last. She had a superb, mischievous, radically inventive sense of humor.

This is a long literal-minded list. Perhaps it could be summarized in this way: Emily Dickinson was a great poet who happened to be a woman.

In his essay, "Myth and the Production of History," Richard Slotkin observes that "myth does not argue its ideology, it exemplifies it." In Slotkin's terms, Emily Dickinson's work may be said to inscribe a new *myth* (and perhaps that is part of her great appeal)—that the power of a " 'Woman' Poet" must be defined by the encompassing power of "*Poet.*" She did not bother to argue that women should write strong poetry; instead, she devised ways to create strong poetry as a *woman poet*—repeatedly renegotiating forms and conventions that had long been established as singularly male. She invented these new strategies, virtually ex nihilo. Understood in this way, her accomplishments are nothing short of astonishing.

For example, suppose that you are Emily Dickinson, and you want to write love poetry. You are serious and immensely gifted, and you have virtually no appropriately gendered exemplars: in this genre, the traditional speaker is male, and the accepted role for women is as the *passive* recipient or the *objectified* focus of praise and (perhaps) passion. Dickinson could, of course, look to the work of Elizabeth Barrett Browning; under the circumstances, it would be surprising if there were no echoes. Thus one noteworthy fact about Dickinson's love poetry is that it does not bear a greater resemblance to *Sonnets from the Portuguese*: both Dickinson and E. B. Browning express passion; however, there is a textual density and complexity in Dickinson's work that much exceeds E. B. Browning's—perhaps because Dickinson so boldly (and often humorously) subverts the traditions that have failed to offer women an active voice.

One typical form for love poetry is the blazon—verse that catalogues the beauties of the beloved. Dickinson would have become acquainted with it from the work of Shakespeare and Campion; twentieth-century readers might know it from a poem like Frost's "The Silken Tent" (that is, as a form, it has not yet gone out of fashion—although it is still an implacably male-dominated form). If Dickinson wanted to use it, how then could she proceed? Should she praise her beloved's brawny limbs and bearded cheeks? Should she boast that no other woman could buy herself such a pretty piece of pulchritude? Put this way, the task sounds both silly and perhaps impossible; however, unless Dickinson could *get around* such problems, she had to forego the form entirely. Her witty solution (Johnson 339) is a reconfigured blazon that retains the praise for a woman, but articulates it in the *woman's* own voice and on her own terms.

The lovers are parted, and the woman thinks of her "Absentee" beloved:

> I tend my flowers for thee—
> Bright Absentee!

And she becomes sexually aroused:

> My Fuchsia's Coral Seams
> Rip—while the Sower—dreams—
> Geraniums—tint—and spot—
> Low Daisies—dot—
> My Cactus—splits her Beard
> To show her throat— . . .

> A Hyacinth—I hid—
> Puts out a Ruffled Head—
> And odors fall
> From flasks—so small—
> You marvel how they held—

Every man is personally aware of the fact that sexual excitement will cause an erection; for this reason, phallic imagery finds its way into love poetry. Every woman is personally aware of the fact that sexual excitement will cause the vulva to become engorged, the clitoris to become erect, and secretions to suffuse the genitalia. It is this *female* process that Dickinson's poem elaborates with such eloquent, metaphorical wit. True to the blazon convention, Dickinson's speaker praises a woman (herself!): but she dislodges the praise from its usual, merely superficial level in order to exalt a more fundamental "feminine" capacity. The "flasks," which configure both uterus and vagina, may seem "small"; however, during pregancy and birth, they have the capacity to contain a baby! Thus the poem celebrates both passion and the possibilities for procreation that this passion signals.

No longer the possession of a male lover and the object of his scrutiny, the female speaker of this poem is boldly self-possessed—pleased with the many dimensions of her sexuality and well-equipped to articulate their value. There is even a subtle "political" statement here: an intimation that often the blazon becomes a fatuous form of love poetry that deals so imperfectly with the *complexities of an actual woman* it can hardly be said to express *real* love at all. The best-known blazons of the Elizabethan era were those that had been put to music. Thomas Campion's "There is a Garden" is one such poem, and it has survived to have centuries of adolescents ridicule it for its fruit-and-vegetable delineation of the "feminine."

> There is a garden in her face
> Where roses and white lilies grow . . .
> There cherries grow which none may buy
> Till cherry-ripe themselves do cry.

Perhaps the humor of Dickinson's intertextual "response"—to Campion's poem in particular and more generally to a tradition of love poetry that disempowers women—constitutes the last laugh.

There are a number of consistent themes in Dickinson's love poetry; however, none is more pervasive than the insistence that the two lovers be *equal*. Well aware that women had been cast into a subordinate role for thousands of years (and by innumerable forms of social and religious convention), Dickinson would sometimes open a poem with some form of this traditional configuration:

> Forever at His side to walk—
> The smaller of the two!
> Brain of His Brain—
> Blood of His Blood—

Only suddenly to overturn it:

> Two Lives—One Being—now—
>
> Forever of His Fate to taste—
> If grief—the largest part—
> If joy—to put my piece away
> For that beloved Heart—
>
> All life—to know each other—

A junior colleague brought this poem (Johnson 246) to me, saying, "I would like to teach this, but I am puzzled by its tonalities. On the one hand it seems to attack the male's tendency to dominate; but on the other, it seems a rather tender expression of affection." Together we concluded that the poem rejected *not men*, but all the conventions that have defined the relationship between sexes in such distorted and demeaning ways.

The poem announces its ultimate goal in the first word: neither man nor woman shall hold power over the other; they walk *together*. Yet at first, the woman's "smaller" stature threatens to suggest an inevitably subordinate role. Fully to appreciate the power with which Dickinson claims a different destiny for women, readers must realize that the language of her verse appeals to an earlier poetic invocation of that precise moment in the ancient past when "love" is said to have begun, Eve and Adam in Eden catching sight of each other for the very first time, rapt with wonder and eloquently innocent.

Just before the Fall, Eve speaks ingenuously to Adam of this first meeting: "What could I doe, / But follow strait, invisibly thus led? / Til I espi'ed thee, fair indeed and tall, . . . back I turn'd, / Thou following cryd'st aloud, Return fair Eve, / Whom fli'st thou? whom thou fli'st, of him thou art, / His flesh, his bone; to give thee being I lent / Out of my side to thee, neerest my heart / Substantial Life, to have thee by my side / Hencefore an individual solace dear; / Part of my Soul I seek thee, and thee claim / My other half" (*Paradise Lost* 4:475–488). Dickinson's poetic "opponent" here is Milton, whose work she echoes in order to italicize their *different* views of the appropriate relationship between the sexes. Adam and Eve began in loving equality, yet Milton's poem justifies the Christian tradition of male dominance by claiming that it was precisely this parity that led humanity into perdition. Thus our first parents were exiled from Paradise, and the woman was commanded to submit to the rule of the man forever after. "Children thou shalt bring / In sorrow forth, and to thy Husband's will / Thine shall submit, he over thee shall rule" (*PL* 10:194–196; see also Genesis 3:16).

If a *male* poet were to work intertextually against Milton's *Paradise Lost*, he might do so in the spirit of combative admiration—attempting to prove that he could best Milton at his own game. Emily Dickinson has something quite different in mind: she does not want to play this kind of combative "male" game; thus, she does not choose to match her manipulation of blank verse against Milton's. Instead, she uses her poetry to repudiate the world view that Milton had defended, arguing that woman ought *not* subordinate herself to man. When passion is generous, Dickinson's verse asserts, Edenic equality can persist even after the Fall. *True* lovers can create a new "Paradise." Thus although the first two lines of this poem acknowledge the lovers' disparity, in the three lines that follow, those feelings that unite them also dispel all discrepancies between them—"Brain" and "Blood" perfectly matched—and equality is affirmed.

Paradise Lost and Genesis are not the only prior texts whose cadences and notions inform this apparently slender, but surprisingly complex argument for equality in love. Stanza two moves from the Old Testament to a reverberation from the New: Jesus avowed, "Verily I say unto you, There be some standing here, which shall not taste of death" (Matthew 16:28). Christ's promise had been predicated upon Christian faith; Dickinson's redaction of this promise ("Forever of His fate to taste—") ties immortality to the power of the lovers' feelings for each other. And yet, almost immediately, with a kind of rapid glissando, Dickinson moves from this Biblical intonation to the domestic experience of everyday men and women. A wife who is quite confident in her autonomy and parity with her mate may still *choose* to share her husband's grief, may even choose to bear "the largest part"; and if there is "joy," she may even decide to put her portion aside for him, like a dainty piece of pastry, an affectionate surprise for her "beloved Heart—."

Other things are at work in this poem as well. Dickinson had a comprehensive, sophisticated education at the Amherst Academy: the school's curriculum was especially strong in math and science, and no distinction was made between the education of boys and girls. The poet's understanding of math extended even to the calculus, and her delight with mathematical puzzles can often be found in the poetry (she is especially fond of ratios). In this poem she plays delicately with notions of finity and infinity, equality and inequality; however, her "solution" is consistent. The *absolute symmetry* of love between peers.

Thus several things combine to make Dickinson's poetry inaccessible. One is the flexibility of tone along with the complexity and density that characterizes virtually all of her best work. The poems, so short and so seemingly transparent, are simply difficult according to the standards that scholars generally apply. The problem is not that Dickinson is weird or undisciplined in some exotic or clinical way; the problem is that, like John Donne, she is very demanding of her reader. The difference is that most readers of Donne's poetry are willing to credit the self-conscious operation of genius and talent, while many readers of Dickinson's poetry cling to some notion of an intensely personal, spontaneous form of writing in her case.

In truth, however, there *is* a second problem that compounds the first. Far from being aesthetically "eccentric," Dickinson deliberately set herself to work *within* her literary heritage: her verse contains resonances of the Bible, Shakespeare, Milton, Wordsworth, Tennyson, and Poe—to name just a few. Yet painfully aware of the limitations that a male-centered heritage had imposed upon women who wished to be poets, she almost always deploys her echoes of this heritage "against the grain." She is, at one and the same time, canonical and *anti*canonical, and this extraordinary and unexpected combination has contributed in large measure to our difficulty in "placing" her. One cannot simply ignore the male-authored, male-focused poetical tradition that preceded her; one cannot comfortably read her work within that tradition, either, because her poems sustain a vital attitude of strenuous *contradiction*—not arguing feminism, but enacting it. Under these circumstances it would be surprising if we did not find Emily Dickinson's poetry difficult.

It helps a great deal to understand the attitudes that explicitly shaped her particular "moment" in American history.

Although Emily Dickinson did not begin the systematic process of making fair copies of her work until she was almost thirty, her letters indicate that she had already begun to write seriously during her late adolescence—in 1848 when she was about eighteen. It was a time when American authors had begun to theorize about the process of writing poetry.

Two years earlier, in 1846, Edgar Allan Poe had published his essay, "The Philosophy of Composition," in *Graham's Magazine*, and even the most cursory glance at the American poetry that was generally published in the late 1840s will demonstrate the pervasive influence of Poe's theories and practices. Gothic fiction raged throughout the monthly magazines, and lugubrious poetry about death filled not only the pages of periodicals but the columns of newspapers as well. Although many serious poets scorned Poe's work (Emerson called him "the jingle-man"), few failed to have some opinion of him in the late 1840s. More-over, Poe had made a striking pronouncement about the connection between women and art; and the prescriptive force of this statement continues even today to exert tremendous power over the configuration of American culture. Poe declared that "the death of a beautiful woman is, unquestionably, the most poetical topic in the world—and equally is it beyond doubt that the lips best suited for such a topic are those of a bereaved lover."

If you are Emily Dickinson—that is, if you are a *woman* who is also a *poet*—such a prescription presents immediate and obvious problems.

The assumption that men have a preemptive right to speak about women was deeply ingrained in virtually all the traditions that Dick-inson was forced to work with; however, Poe's *unique* construction of the "passive, silent woman" takes this notion to its ultimate extremi-ty. The woman is literally dead. How, then, to empower her? It is one mark of genius that Dickinson was able to fashion some of her most masterful poems in response to this challenge—poems in which the speaker (often explicitly gendered female) has already died. In general Dickinson's tactic is to transform Poe's notion from an extremity of female passivity to an ultimate form of feminine hero-ism in which the speaker explores the experiential "reality" of death itself.

Sometimes the timbre of Dickinson's poems about death have an air of bravura: " 'Tis so appalling—it exhilarates— / So over Horror, it half Captivates— / . . . Looking at Death, is Dying— / Just let go the Breath— / And not the pillow at your Cheek / So Slumbereth—." Here, Poe's trope of the male lover looking at a dead woman becomes transformed into a woman poet who has the courage to "look" square-ly at death itself—probing to discover the meaning of that final moment that awaits us all, and then imposing aesthetic structures upon her insights. The result is a unique form of empowerment: "It sets the Fright at liberty— / And Terror's free— / Gay, Ghastly, Holiday!" (Johnson 281). At other times, Dickinson combines this extraordinary notion of the speaking dead with the matter-of-fact tones of everyday speech: " 'Twas just this time, last year, I died. / I know I heard the Corn, / When I was carried by the Farms—" (Johnson 445). In both cases Dickinson has transformed Poe's beautified picture of death into an examination of the terrifying actuality that awaits us all.

Modern readers are apt to comment upon the frequency with which Dickinson returns to this subject of death—"How morbid," people say. Perhaps. But if Dickinson was morbid, so was everyone else in her culture. Poe's aestheticizing of death (along with the proliferation of Gothic fiction and poetry) reflects a pervasive real-world concern: in mid-nineteenth-century America death rates were high. It was a truism that men had three wives (two of them having predeceased the spouse); infant mortality was so common that parents often gave several of their children the same name so that at least one "John" or "Lavinia" might survive to adulthood; rapid urbanization had intensified the threat of certain diseases—cholera, typhoid, and tuberculosis.

Poe and the Gothic tradition were one response to society's anxiety about death. Another came from the pulpit: mid-nineteenth century sermons took death as their almost constant subject. Somewhat later in the century, preachers would embrace a doctrine of consolation: God would be figured as a loving parent—almost motherly—who had prepared a home in heaven for us all, and ministers would tell the members of their congregation that they need not be apprehensive. However, stern traces of Puritanism still tinctured the religious discourse of Dickinson's young womanhood, and members of the Amherst congregation were regularly exhorted with blood-stirring urgency to reflect upon the imminence of their own demise. Repeatedly, then, in attempting to comprehend Dickinson's work, a reader must return to the fundamental tenets of Protestant Christianity, for her poetry echoes the Bible more often than any other single work or author.

In part this preoccupation with the doctrines of her day reflected a more general concern with the essential questions of human existence they addressed. In a letter to Higginson she once said, "To live is so startling, it leaves but little room for other occupations." And to her friend Mrs. Holland she wrote, "All this and more, though *is* there more? More than Love and Death? Then tell me its name." The religious thought and language of the culture was important to her poetry because it comprised the semiotic system that her society employed to discuss the mysteries of life and death. If she wished to contemplate these, what other language was there to employ?

In part, however, conventional Christianity—especially the latter-day Puritanism of Dickinson's New England—represented for Dickinson an ultimate expression of patriarchal power. Rebelling against its rule, upbraiding a "Father" in Heaven who required absolute "faith" from his followers, but gave no discernible response, became a way of attacking the very essence of unjust authority, especially male authority.

> Of Course—I prayed—
> And did God Care?
> He cared as much as on the Air
> A Bird—had stamped her foot—
> And cried "Give Me"—
> My Reason—Life—
> I had not had—but for Yourself—
> 'Twere better Charity
> To leave me in the Atom's Tomb—
> Merry, and Nought, and gay, and numb—
> Than this smart Misery.
>
> (Johnson 376)

The most striking feature of the verse is its attitude of indignation, a reaction to Divine indifference that hints at full-scale revolution. Yet there is a cunning strategy of camouflage at work as well. Rebellion has been so skillfully clothed in the cadences of a pert schoolgirl's language that unwary readers may miss the poem's complexity. The speaker is "smart" enough to demand her rights from the omnipotent Father (although she is "smarting" from the pain of his callous behavior). What is more, the speaker's bitter rebuke, " 'Twere better Charity / To leave me in the Atom's Tomb—" is but the modern reformulation of an ancient complaint, "Let the day perish wherein I was born" (Job 3:3), and the function of this subtle echo is to suggest that although several millennia have passed, the pattern of Divine authority has remained fundamentally unchanged. Perhaps Milton could believe that the consequence of tasting the fruit of knowledge was a "fortunate fall"; however, Dickinson succinctly dismisses it as no more than "smart Misery."

It is true that the stern doctrines of New England Protestantism offered hope for a life after death; yet in Dickinson's estimation, the trope that was used for this "salvation" revealed some of the most repellent features of God's power, for the invitation to accept "faith" had been issued in the context of a courtship with a macabre, sexual component. It was promised that those who had faith would be carried to Heaven by the "Bridegroom" Christ. "Blessed are they which are called unto the marriage supper of the Lamb" (Revelation 19:9). Nor did it escape Dickinson's notice that the perverse prurience of Poe's notions were essentially similar to this Christian idea of Christ's "love" for a "bride" which promised a reunion that must be "consummated" through death. Thus the poem that is, perhaps, the apotheosis of that distinctive Dickinsonian voice, "the speaking dead," offers an astonishing combination: this conventional promise of Christianity suffused with the tonalities of the Gothic tradition.

> Because I could not stop for Death—
> He kindly stopped for me—
> The Carriage held but just Ourselves—
> And Immortality.
>
> We slowly drove—He knew no haste
> And I had put away
> My labor and my leisure too,
> For His Civility—
>
> We passed the School, where Children strove
> At Recess—in the Ring—
> We passed the Fields of Gazing Grain—
> We passed the Setting Sun—
>
> Or rather—He passed Us—
> The Dews drew quivering and chill—
> For only Gossamer, my Gown—
> My Tippet—only Tulle— . . .
>
> Since then—'tis Centuries—and yet
> Feels shorter than the Day
> I first surmised the Horses Heads
> Were toward Eternity—
>
> (Johnson 712)

The speaker is a beautiful woman (already dead!), and like some spectral Cinderella, she is dressed to go to a ball: "For only Gossamer, my Gown— / My Tippet—only Tulle—." Her escort recalls both the lover of Poe's configuration and the "Bridegroom" that had been promised in the Bible: "We slowly drove—He knew no haste / And I had put away / My labor and my leisure too, / For His Civility—." Their "Carriage" hovers in some surrealistic state that is exterior to both time and place: they are no longer earth-bound, not quite dead (or at least still possessed of consciousness), but they have not yet achieved the celebration that awaits them, the "marriage supper of the Lamb."

Yet the ultimate implication of this work turns precisely upon the *poet's* capacity to explode the finite temporal boundaries that generally define our existence, for there is a third member of the party—also exterior to time and location—and that is "Immortality." *True* immortality, the verse suggests, comes neither from the confabulations of a male lover nor from God's intangible Heaven. Irrefutable "Immortality" resides in the work of art itself, the creation of an empowered woman poet that continues to captivate readers more than one hundred years after her death. And this much-read, often-cited poem stands as patent proof upon the page of its own argument!

Poe was not the only American theorist of poetry who exerted wide influence during Emily Dickinson's years of apprenticeship. In 1844 (Dickinson's fourteenth year), Emerson had published his widely read, highly respected essay "The Poet," the essay that would inform Whitman's construction of his own public persona—"the poet, a man of the people." In many ways, Emerson's definition of "the poet" was also ideally suited to Dickinson, for Emerson believed that the existential commonalities of everyday life were the most appropriate subject for poetry. "O poet!" he wrote, "a new nobility is conferred in groves and pasture, and not in castles, or by the sword-blade, any longer."

Yet Emerson's evocations of the "poet" are consistently, even relentlessly masculine:

The poet is representative. He stands among partial men for the complete man, and apprises us not of his wealth, but of the commonwealth. The young man reveres men of genius, because, to speak truly, they are more himself than he is. . . . [The poet] unlocks our chains, and admits us to a new scene. . . . Every verse or sentence, possessing this virtue, will take care of its own immortality. The religions of the world are the ejaculations of a few imaginative men.

"The poet" works, then, by a sublime form of seminal effusion (for although the word "ejaculation" had a delicate ambiguity in nineteenth-century usage, the implication of masculine sexuality was never entirely absent). "The poet need not have schooling: he might be a farmer, a fisherman, a statesman, even an insurance salesman." Such a definition *seems* inclusive; Emerson intended it to be "American." However, the one thing that he casually omitted was a feminine possibility: the notion that "the poet" might also be a wife, a daughter, a seamstress, a housewife seems not to have occurred to Emerson; or if it did, he chose not to record the fact in this pronouncement.

It is not surprising that Emerson took delight in Whitman's work—that their relationship was almost one of literary father and son. When Emerson received a copy of the first edition of *Leaves of Grass* as a gift from the author (whom he had never met), he wrote Whitman a now-famous letter of profound appreciation: "I find incomparable things said incomparably well," he said in part; "I find the courage of treatment which so delights us, and which large perception only can inspire. I greet you at the beginning of a great career." It is the kind of letter that most young poets only dream of receiving, an *imprimatur* from America's leading man of letters. Best of all, it offered support for Whitman's radical experiments in verse and encouragement to break new artistic ground. Whitman, well aware of its value, reprinted Emerson's letter for all the world to see in the 1856 edition of *Leaves of Grass.*

So far as we know, Dickinson never sent her work to Emerson for comment. She did, of course, send it to Higginson, who when confronted by *her* boldly innovative verses, seems primarily to have confessed his bafflement. But then it is unlikely that *anyone* would have written a letter to Dickinson like the letter Emerson wrote to Whitman—because she was a woman. True, there were a few women who managed to support themselves by writing verse; however, readers and critics alike expected such women to write predictably and certainly *not* to exhibit the "courage of treatment" that would produce radically new forms of verse. What is more, there was a world of difference between making a living and embarking upon a career. Women were grudging permitted to make a living, but the aspiration for career was thought unnatural in a female; and in the rare case when a "career" did evolve for a woman, as it did for Lydia Sigourney, even the woman herself was inclined to become apologetic for her success.

It is understandable, then, that Higginson could not realize that the voice in much of Dickinson's poetry was meant to be "representative"—standing "among partial [human beings] for the complete [human being]." Or that it said "incomparable things incomparably well." Instead, like many a modern reader, he was misled by the intensely engaging illusion of personal immediacy and urgency ("I" is the most frequently used word in her poetry)—misled, perhaps, by the power of the verse itself. Thus with apparently some anxiety for the author's emotional welfare, after he had read only about eight of her poems, Higginson wrote Dickinson to say that he thought she needed friends; and after he had read perhaps half a dozen more, he evidently made such pressing inquiries about the "voice" he had encountered that the poet felt compelled to dissect her method for him in a rather flat-footed, literal manner. "When I state myself as the Representative of the Verse," she wrote, "it does not mean—me—but a *supposed person*." In 1862, the notion of a "Representative" speaker alluded pointedly to Emerson.

In "The Poet," Emerson had explained what it meant to be "representative": "All men live by truth, and stand in need of expression. . . . We study to utter our painful secret. . . . We need an interpreter. . . . [and it is 'the poet' who writes] what will and must be spoken." Most people cannot give voice or shape to their most intimate feelings and fears, and the "Emersonian" component of Emily Dickinson's mission as an artist set out to address this problem—to say the things her readers might say if they, too, had been given the gift of words. Dickinson's unique innovation in responding to Emerson's injunction that "the poet" ought to be "representative" was to write as a woman in an explicitly domestic realm, but to do so with *power*. It is in such an environment, she might have argued, that the intrinsic similarities among people can *best* be seen. However much we may seem to differ from each other, our most secret joys and fears are remarkably alike. Thus while in public our lives may appear very different, one from another, in private—in the intimate recesses of the domestic world—our hopes and fears are very similar. Paradoxically, then, a woman poet might even prove to be the best "representative man."

Dickinson is able to exploit this issue of gender in a wide variety of ways. Sometimes, the sexual identity of Dickinson's speaker is entirely suppressed—as in the hauntingly beautiful poem that begins, "Safe in their Alabaster Chambers—" (Johnson 216); sometimes, as in the poem that begins "Of Course—I prayed—," there is no more than an *intimation* of the feminine; and sometimes, as in "Because I could not stop for Death—," the speaker's feminine identity is rather fully elaborated.

However, a number of the most elegantly subtle applications of the feminine can be found in verses that do not identify the speaker by gender, but nonetheless juxtapose imagery from an explicitly domestic world against the forces of death and decay.

> The Bustle in a House
> The Morning after Death
> Is solemnest of industries
> Enacted upon Earth—
>
> The Sweeping up the Heart
> And putting Love away
> We shall not want to use again
> Until Eternity
>
> (Johnson 1078)

At first glance the reader might suppose the sexual identity of this speaker to be essentially immaterial and the poem's message to be a very general one: after death, the quotidian business of life must go on.

However, this is *only one part* of the poem's meaning. The death of a loved one necessitates a particular kind of "Bustle in a House," a series of tasks to be performed, generally by women. Gruesome work, like preparing the body for interment; tedious work, like unpacking drawers and closets to apportion the belongings of a now extinguished "self": a thoughtful, melancholy process that both recalls the past and provokes speculation about an afterlife. Thus as befits the occasion, this poem offers an opinion about eternity; however, a reader must understand the routines of housework to appreciate it. This "Sweeping up the Heart" is a form of cleaning, to be sure, a domestic obligation that becomes an emotional purgative as well. The speaker's deep insight is that this is no daily chore of dusting off and throwing out. Instead, it is *seasonal* work with *cyclical* implications, the careful folding up and putting aside of summer or winter clothes we shall not "want to use again" until a new year has begun. Jesus had said, "A little while, and ye shall not see me: and again, a little while, and ye shall see me, because I go to the Father" (John 16:16); and it is this explicit promise of a reunion in heaven that the domestic imagery of the poem recollects.

Repeatedly, Emily Dickinson construes the housewife as a soldier who "mans" the front lines in our engagement with the forces of destruction. Sometimes (as in the poem above) the ruminations of this housewife-poet are filled with hope; more often, however, she sees herself fighting the one battle that we are all doomed, ultimately, to lose.

> All but Death, can be Adjusted—
> Dynasties repaired—
> Systems—settled in their Sockets—
> Citadels—dissolved—
>
> Wastes of Lives—resown with Colors
> By Succeeding Springs—
> Death—unto itself—Exception—
> Is exempt from Change—
>
>   (Johnson 749)

Domestic imagery suffuses this verse in ways that seem at first to suggest a positive reading: an "adjustment" might be work for a seamstress but it could also be a homeopathic remedy; and "repairing" minor wounds and "resetting" dislocated joints were both medical procedures that were generally managed without a doctor's assistance in the mid-nineteenth century. Thus by the time we encounter the notion of "Citadels" that can be "dissolved" like sugar in water, we are apt to suppose that if only the compassionate values of home and hearth could applied to the public world, the ills of life would be eradicated (a fond fantasy of Victorian America).

However, this illusion is dispelled in the second stanza. Persephone-like, the speaker joins the spring in "resowing," bringing forth new life and repairing (resewing) the fabric of human experience. Inevitably, however, all her victories will be swallowed up in Death—"itself . . . / exempt from Change—."

Who sees the sly work of time more minutely or consistently than the housewife? The "Cuticle of Dust" that appears around the drinking glass overnight, the "Borer in the Axis" of the apple. Who comprehends more circumstantially that "Crumbling is not an instant's Act," and that "Delapidation" may happen incrementally, but that it also continues unremittingly? It is, perhaps, a *woman's* particular privilege to understand that cobwebs in the parlor are but the visible sign of an ineradicable "Cobweb on the Soul" (all quotes here are from Johnson 997).

It is not surprising, then, that many of the poems that give voice to despair most forcefully and poignantly are strung together with this stabilizing imagery from the domestic world.

> I felt a Cleaving in my Mind—
> As if my Brain had split—
> I tried to match it—Seam by Seam—
> But could not make them fit.

> The thought behind, I strove to join
> Unto the thought before—
> But Sequence ravelled out of Sound
> Like Balls—upon a Floor.
>
> (Johnson 937)

The unifying tropes here deal with sewing and knitting, the woman's craft of joining things together in an orderly, artful manner and of maintaining order. These metaphors function specifically to steady the almost hysterical tone of the verse by firmly affixing it to the tangible, reassuringly familiar processes of the home. Such an aesthetic maneuver permits Dickinson's *poem* to be a coherent success, even though the speaker herself confesses failure: her story (that is, her "yarn") entirely unravels "Like Balls—upon a Floor."

Like Frost's female speaker in "The Hill Wife," the housewife-poets in Dickinson's work understand that an insatiable wilderness is only biding its time, impatiently waiting to retake the world. Nowhere is this stark vision more clearly articulated than in the elegy that begins "How many times these low feet staggered—." Here, the care-worn woman has laid aside her thimble for the last time, and the voracious engines of dissolution have already begun to work: "Buzz the dull flies—on the chamber window— / Brave—shines the sun through the freckled pane— / Fearlesss—the cobweb swings from the ceiling—" (Johnson 187).

Carried to its logical conclusion, this is a vision of chaos and dissolution; however, the verses that give voice to this vision are always masterfully crafted to be entirely coherent. Consider, for example, a poem in which Dickinson contests the age-old theological argument "from 'Design,' " an argument claiming that the existence of a highly structured, orderly universe necessarily implies the existence of a benevolent architect, God. The verse itself *enacts* the counterargument by subverting the grammatical structures that impart order and "design" to language; its carefully modulated disjunctions, then, become a coherently aesthetic reflection of cosmic disorder.

> Four Trees—upon a solitary Acre—
> Without Design
> Or Order, or Apparent Action—
> Maintain—
>
> (Johnson 742)

This stanza mimics sentence form, but its transitive verb requires an object to be complete. Because no object is supplied, the grammatical utterance breaks down—mutilated—having failed to make connection. Like the Divinity.

Most often Dickinson's poetry pulls in one way or another against the various patterns that impart *conventional* order to poetry—sometimes strenuously. This habit of resistance, so characteristic that it even lends a distinctive *visual* element to the inscription of Emily Dickinson's poems upon the page, has two origins. First, as we have seen, no one had prepared a place for a *woman* poet of original genius—traditional verse forms had evolved almost exclusively for a male voice—and those men of letters whose constructions of "The Poet" dominated the American mid-nineteenth century wrote with a brazen certainty that this *poet* would be a *he*, a certainty so deep it did not require defense. Inevitably, then, if a *woman* wished to write "incomparably well," to have that "courage of treatment" for which Emerson praised Whitman, she was constrained to fly in the face of convention. Second, Emily Dickinson espoused an openly rebellious attitude toward God and toward the various forms of male authority that He epitomized as "Burglar! Banker—Father!" (Johnson 49). Discovering aesthetically effective strategies to "break the rules" was her poetic mode of defying this authority—an intrinsic expression of both power and play, and a deeply satisfying way to assert her own unassailable autonomy.

Consider something so apparently trivial as Dickinson's habit of employing dashes instead of other, more usual marks of punctuation. For generations there have been readers who want to discover a "grand scheme" that can decode the unruly verse and subdue it to regulation, and it is just such rule-bound limitation that Dickinson is seeking to elude. Thus her dashes consistently subvert the tidy logical relationships that commas and semicolons and the like would impose. The subversion is generally gentle (and exquisitely modulated); it never makes the verse incoherent. Instead, it is just jarring enough to keep the reader unsettled. Sometimes the dashes do little more than control the pace of a poem. For example:

> This—is the land—the Sunset washes—
> These—are the Banks of the Yellow Sea—
> (Johnson 266)

The underlying metaphor of a boat upon rolling water is affirmed here by dashes, which make the verse seem to rock back and forth.

Sometimes, however, Dickinson makes much more profound use of this device as in the poem that begins "I felt a Funeral, in my Brain." This verse gives an excruciating account of the experience of death; its speaker is pulled forward irresistably toward some ultimate unknown; and the force of time, which moves the speaker inescapably toward this confrontation, is given grammatical representation by a thumping, accelerating use of parataxis—one thing after another in dreadful progression—And ... And ... And." Yet the conclusion of the verse is suspended in superb uncertainty, and it is a masterful manipulation of dashes in the last line that makes the superb uncertainty of this conclusion possible. "And I dropped down, and down— / And hit a World, at every plunge, / And Finished knowing—then—" (Johnson 280). "Then" what? Is "then" a finality: "And finished knowing then."? Or is "then" merely an unfinished transition to some unknowable state of consciousness: "And finished knowing. Then— . . ."? It is disturbing not to know. It is meant to be.

Even more unsettling than her use of dashes, however, is Dickinson's capacity to exploit the many ontological properties of language. In *On the Margins of Discourse* Barbara Herrnstein Smith has written about the *representational* possibilities of words themselves and thus of literary texts.

As a general class, literary artworks may be conceived of as *depictions* or representations, rather than instances, of natural discourse. . . . Thus lyric poems typically *represent* personal utterances, or, to use Goodman's picturesquely unidiomatic terms, such poems are *pictures* of utterance.

In any given lyric poem, then, any given word may do at least two things simultaneously: it may have a referential function, pointing mimetically toward some supposed object; at the same time, it may become *an object itself*—a single sign that constitutes an aesthetic configuration or a puzzle in miniature. Consider the following particular example. The poet begins:

> All I may, if small,
> Do it not display
> Larger for the Totalness—

'Tis Economy
To Bestow a World
And withhold a Star—
Utmost, is Munificence—
Less, tho larger, poor.
                    (Johnson 819)

The first-level meaning of this poem asserts that despite the speaker's meager resources, she is willing to give everything; she then inquires whether *everything* (even if it is not very much) does not constitute a rather great sacrifice. When the second level is considered—that is, when the words are taken as *objects in themselves*—the configuration of the inscription becomes an impish word game, a paradox that affirms the first meaning while asserting the speaker's ultimate and uniquely unimpeachable power as poet. The *coup* turns upon the fact that the *word* "small" contains the *word* "all."

God, Who has everything in the real world of referential words and palpable objects, has given a great deal; however, He has also withheld a great deal, and so He still retains much. In the real world of referential words and palpable objects, the speaker has very little, and if she gives "all" away, she will have nothing left. However, in the "*inscribed*" reality of this lyric poem, the artist has created a context in which a paradox can exist. Dickinson has constructed a speaker who is "small," and who *gives* everything; nonetheless, the same speaker will also continue to *retain* everything, for the word *small* will continue to *contain all* so long as language exists. Moreover, the bold paradox will remain audaciously alive so long as the inscription of the verse remains to be read.

There are certain words whose inscribed properties were especially appealing to Dickinson: small/all is a frequent location for linguistic games; eye/I (and every word with a long I *sound*) was a multifaceted pun that Dickinson employed to assert "self." The word "noon" was replete with possibility: it is "no" face-to-face; it is a palindrome of a word, the same whether read forwards or backwards; it is a word with "nothing" in it (actually "twice nothing," two zeroes); yet it might be construed as a word with infinity in it (∞). Clearly, much of the immensely unsettling power of Dickinson's verse derives from her skill in juggling these ontological possibilities and from her habit of exploiting the many possibilities for meaning in the words she employed. Thus if lyric poems can "represent personal utterances," Dickinson forces her reader into a constant state of uncertainty about whether it is the "representational" component of individual words themselves that is in play or the capacity of language to mimic "personal utterances" by naming things in the real world.

It is not surprising, then, that so many readers have found Emily Dickinson's poetry "difficult" or "cryptic." Literally, it *is* cryptic: it is full of internal puzzles. What is more, it is an assertion of aesthetic power, a form of linguistic competition.

Confronted with such extraordinary intelligence, such sophistication, such talent, such audacity—what reader would not want to know more about "Emily Dickinson" of Amherst? And since genius is always surprising (and genius that flourishes in solitude is doubly surprising), it is no wonder, perhaps, that readers are not altogether prepared to credit Dickinson's self-consciousness, and that we are inclined instead to cling to outlandish notions of spontaneous writing. Finally, since many of Dickinson's poetic inventions are tinged with anger and an air of challenge—since they *do* leave a reader unsettled and unnerved, and since they are often *meant* to do just that—it is not in the least surprising that readers and scholars have had a powerfully defensive reaction to them. Thus they construct an "Emily Dickinson" whose difficulties are the manifestation of some infirmity or impairment: "The Poet" was sick or suffering from emotional distress; therefore, her verse is hysterical and occasionally unfathomable. If we can't understand Dickinson's work, it is *her* problem.

All of this is understandable; however, it robs us of the best gift of all: the range and complexity of the poetry itself. If we are to have "Emily Dickinson" at all, perhaps we must take her entirely on her own terms:

> I reckon—when I count at all—
> First—Poets—Then the Sun—
> (Johnson 569)

The poetry was all she left; it appears to be all she *wished* to leave.

Cynthia Griffin Wolff

Futher Reading

Dickinson, Emily. *The Complete Poems of Emily Dickinson.* Ed. Thomas H. Johnson. Boston: Little, Brown, 1960.

——— *The Manuscript Books of Emily Dickinson.* Ed. Ralph Franklin. 2 vols. Cambridge: Harvard University Press, Belknap Press, 1981.

——— *The Poems of Emily Dickinson.* 3 vols. Ed. Thomas H. Johnson. Cambridge: Harvard University Press, 1951, 1955.

Eberwein, Jane Donahue. *Dickinson: Strategies of Limitation.* Amherst: University of Massachuetts Press, 1985.

Loeffelholz, Mary. *Dickinson and the Boundaries of Feminist Theory.* Urbana: University of Illinois Press, 1991.

Pollack, Vivian. *Dickinson: The Anxiety of Gender.* Ithaca: Cornell University Press, 1984.

Wolff, Cynthia Griffin. *Emily Dickinson.* New York: Knopf, 1986.

Walt Whitman's Revisionary Democracy

WALT WHITMAN has emerged, over time and through successive generations of criticism, as the central poet of our literature. Indeed, American poetry may be read as a series of reactions to Whitman, typified by Ezra Pound in his poem "A Pact"—

> I make a pact with you, Walt Whitman—
> I have detested you long enough,
> I come to you as a grown child
> Who has had a pig-headed father;
> I am old enough now to make friends.

It was Whitman, Pound says, who "broke the new wood." And indeed, Whitman wrote a kind of poetry like nothing under the sun, and he left behind in *Leaves of Grass*—the title he gave to his collected poems—a body of work that we may never fully absorb.

The originality of Whitman's literary accomplishment contrasts sharply with the modesty of his origins. Walt Whitman was born in the farm community of West Hills, Long Island, on May 31, 1819, the second eldest of Louisa Van Velsor's and Walter Whitman's eight surviving children. His ancestors included Dutch and Quaker farmers who had settled in the Long Island countryside. Whitman's idyllic childhood there was disrupted during the 1823 real estate boom when the family moved to Brooklyn and his father began a second career in building and selling houses. Although he boasted of his progressive stance on political matters and numbered Tom Paine among his acquaintances, Whitman's father was a short-tempered, tight-fisted man who played the petty tyrant at home and quarreled frequently with his literary son. Whitman consequently looked to his mother for affection. But his fondest memory of those early years was not concerned with either parent but with General Lafayette's visit to Brooklyn. In a greeting that would become significant for Whitman's later understanding of his poetic vocation, the aged hero from the Revolutionary era traversed the barrier separating the generations and, lifting the five-year-old Whitman from out of a Brooklyn crowd, embraced him.

Whitman attended Brooklyn public schools for six years, beginning about 1825, although he ended his formal education at the age of eleven to become an office boy in a law firm. Whitman's reading projects during this period included Walter Scott's romances, the writings of Count Volney, Robert Dale Owen, Frances Wright, and Thomas Paine, all collected in his father's library. Whitman's adolescent years were also distinctive for the variety of his employments. At twelve, he wrote sentimental fillers for the *Long Island Patriot*, a weekly whose editor shared the political views of Whitman's father. After the family moved back to West Hills in 1834, Whitman stayed in Brooklyn, published pieces for the *New York Mirror*, and began the training as a journeyman printer he would complete in 1835. After the two great fires of 1835 crippled the printing industry, Whitman rejoined his family, now in Hempstead, Long Island, and for the next five years, alternated teaching in small-town schools with printing for local newspapers. In the wake of a well-publicized controversy over his unorthodox teaching methods, Whitman initiated a series of other interests. He began his own newspaper, the weekly *Long Islander*, in 1838, and became active that year as well in local debating societies, reading groups, and political organizations. In early 1840 he started work on a highly conventional series of poetic sketches he published in the Long Island *Democrat*.

Between 1842 and 1845 the New York printing industry enjoyed something of a renaissance with forty more newspapers entering the marketplace. In 1842 Whitman became editor of the New York *Aurora*, and over the next twelve years he developed a political rhetoric compatible with the publishing market's demands.

Eighteen forty-two was a significant year for Whitman's later development. In March he heard Emerson deliver a lecture on poetry in

Manhattan that included a passage that Whitman would later invoke as his poetic credo:

The poets are thus liberating gods. The ancient British bards had for the title of their order, "Those who are free throughout the world." They are free, and they make free. An imaginative book renders us much more service at first, by stimulating us through its tropes, than afterward, when we arrive at the precise sense of the author. I think nothing is of any value in books excepting the transcendental and extraordinary. If a man is enflamed and carried away by his thought . . . let me read his paper and you may have all the arguments and history and criticism.

After hearing Emerson on poetry, Whitman aspired to remake himself in Emerson's image of the poet. But the poetry he produced in that year was slack, and predictably sentimental, lacking the promise of *Leaves of Grass*. His deepest intuitions were not recorded in a poem but derived from his reflections on the consequences of an editorial he wrote for the *Aurora* on April 12, 1842, when the resentment he had directed against the Irish Catholics resulted in a "no-popery" mob attacking St. Patrick's Cathedral. In the retraction he prepared for the next day's edition, Whitman expressed resolves that would later become part of the 1855 preface. "We go for the largest liberty—the widest extension of the immunities of the people, as well as the blessings of our government."

After the editor of the *Aurora* fired him in mid-May for what he referred to as Whitman's "laziness," within the year Whitman became, in rapid succession, the editor of a rival daily, the *Evening Tatler*, the author of a temperance novel, *Franklin Evans; or the Inebriate*, and the regular contributor of poetry and short fiction to such literary periodicals as the *Democratic Review, Aristidean, American Review, New Mirror*, and *Rover*. Over the next eight years, Whitman wrote theater columns, book reviews, and political editorials for a number of newspapers, including the prestigious *Brooklyn Daily Eagle*. During this period, Whitman's political views were comparably volatile. When he began writing for the *Eagle*, Whitman endorsed the expansionist views of the paper's owner, Isaac Van Anden. But by 1848 Whitman had become a Free Soil Democrat, opposed to the annexation of more slave territory. Following the publication, on January 3, 1848, of an editorial in which he expressed these views, Van Anden fired Whitman. This event proved once again fortuitous for the opportunity it afforded Whitman to travel to New Orleans on the first of the two prolonged trips away from New York in his lifetime. The editorial position he secured for himself at the *New Orleans Daily Crescent* lasted from March 5 until May 25, when arguments with that paper's owners led to the termination of Whitman's services.

Whitman returned to New York by way of the Mississippi, the Great Lakes, and the Hudson River. But his visit to the South had not changed his opposition to slavery. In 1848 he became the founding editor of a Free Soil paper, the *Freeman*, in whose editorial pages he was preoccupied with a troubling political contradiction. Because Whitman believed in the free labor of the working men and women of Brooklyn, he was persuaded for a short time that abolitionism, in its opposition to Negro slavery, indirectly justified wage slavery. Opposed to slavery in every form, Whitman now believed that partisan politics had compromised the principle of liberty.

Over the next five years he wrote experimental poetry; became a delegate to the Buffalo Free Soil Convention; attended plays and operas; learned carpentry; spoke at political rallies; began a regimen in self-education including readings in world-religions, natural history, Emerson, and Egyptology; cultivated friendships in the Brooklyn artists' as well as Manhattan laborers' communities; and declaimed verses from Homer, Shakespeare, and the Bible along deserted stretches of Coney Island beaches. Gay Wilson Allen has described this "long foreground" prior to the publication of *Leaves of Grass* succinctly.

The most important period in the life of Walt Whitman, the poet, was the years between 1850 and 1855. Outwardly it was undramatic and judged in terms of worldly success it was a failure. But intellectually and spiritually these were the most exciting and adventurous years that Whitman had experienced, for during this half-decade he wrote and printed the first edition of his *Leaves of Grass* and thereby created a new epoch not only in American but also in world literature.

Affording no indication of that epoch-making literary event, Whitman's previous occupations were nevertheless the basis for the wide range of his metaphors and his inclusive sense of audience. The self of which Whitman sang in the volume's central poem—"Song of Myself"—derived characteristics from the full itinerary of his personae—teacher, editor, dandy, stroller, ward leader, compositor, delegate, orator, carpenter, politician, house-builder. It emerged as a composite and adhesive rather than exclusive identity.

Indeed the entire volume, whose preface was comprised of a collage of passages from the newspaper editorials he had written over the preceding fifteen years, might be described as a compendium of the lessons Whitman had learned in his other vocations. The theater had taught him to understand writing as a performance before an audience learning how to respond. From the printer Whitman had discovered that words on the page should be construed as if as changeable as the readers to whom they were addressed; from the mass daily the value of a public medium available to everyday events; from Emerson how to immerse daily events in a transcendental mood; from the politician social responsibility; from the poet absolute responsiveness; from the carpenter pride in work; from General Lafayette the value of a transhistorical salutation; from the stroller how to become absorbed in passing scenes; from the orator how to absorb the interest of others.

Whitman's connections in the printing trade facilitated the publication of *Leaves of Grass* on July 4, 1855, when James and Thomas Rome requested Whitman's assistance in setting type for the eighty-five pages of poetry and ten of prose, bound in the slim, handsome green cloth folio with gold leaf ornament. Before his death on March 26, 1892, Whitman would see *Leaves of Grass* through eight other editions, with material added and deleted to suit the needs of the times.

The contradictory features represented in the portrait of Walt Whitman that accompanied the 1855 volume of *Leaves of Grass* made it clear the poems were not addressed solely to a literary clientele but to working-class men and women. Through this literary reflection of their image Whitman encouraged understanding of the working class's participation in the national experiment as his poetry's true subject. Outfitted in clothes of the laboring class, Whitman projected a figure whose bearing—bearded, unbuttoned, relaxed, looking directly at the reader—derived from the poetry. On page 29 of the quarto that portrait was identified as "Walt Whitman, an American, one of the roughs, a kosmos, Disorderly, fleshy and sensual . . . eating, drinking and breeding, No sentimentalist . . . no stander above men and women or apart from them." In quite literally embodying poetry's value for working men and women, Whitman hoped to animate their desire to read his book of poems as if it were necessary to their continued vitality.

In his traveling back and forth between two separate groups of friends—the bohemian artist and the working-class communities—

Whitman silently aspired to mediate between these factions. He wanted to make it manifest in his poetry that literature was as interested in the working class as they should be in it. As enjambed lines in "Song of Myself" brought representatives of the working-class elbow to elbow with the literary elite, Whitman introduced the two groups to one another and invited both to envision their lives as improvised out of a common submerged self. In 1855 the fear of impending civil war heightened awareness of social factions and aroused his anxiety over what might be called a salutation scarcity. Whitman's premonition that political divisiveness would result in the failure to return greetings inspired him to understand *Leaves of Grass* as a prolonged salutation to the United States reading public. That greeting is proffered most famously in "I celebrate myself and sing myself and what I assume you shall assume." But Whitman indicates the intended vast range of social acknowledgment in the following lines from "Song of the Answerer":

> He says indifferently and alike, *How are you my friend?* to the President at his levee,
> And he says *Good-day my brother*, to Cudge that hoes in the sugar field;
> And both understand him and know that his speech is right.

As had Lafayette for him, Whitman provided his readers with the spectacle of a citizen who greeted the United States as if it were his own invention. A question from the 1855 preface, "Does this acknowledge liberty with audible and absolute acknowledgement?" assigns a political function to this expansive speech act. The audible manifestation of absolute acknowledgement, a return of greeting, *realizes* liberty and thereby renders an individual's demand for freedom commensurate with the more inclusive social demand for equality.

In its status as a permanent salutation Whitman's poetry responded to the more general social anxiety over the break-up of the Union he expressed in the 1855 preface. The relation between the poetry and the 1855 preface possesses consequently the structure of a fulfilled wish. Because the central political terms, "liberty," "equality," "absolute acknowledgement," recorded in the prose preface were provocative rather than descriptive and lacked referents in Europe's political history, Whitman aspired to construct "democratic vistas" for these incitements to a shared political life, spaces wherein these unprecedented political terms might acquire social value.

In declaring "The United States are themselves the greatest poem," Whitman associated the cultivation of adequate responsiveness to his poetry with a political education in how to actualize the nation's founding terms.

Their Presidents shall not be their common referee so much as their poets shall. Of all mankind the great poet is the equable man. . . . Nothing out of its place is good and nothing in its place is bad. He bestows on every object or quality its fit proportions neither more nor less. He is the arbiter of the diverse and he is the key. He is the equalizer of his age and land.

Understood as the "greatest poem," however, the United States realized wishes that were not homegrown but originated with European desires for political betterment and social renewal. Whitman became the "equalizer of his age and land" because he indicated how the United States' geography was constructed out of Europe's hope for a better world. When re-viewed in the light of *Leaves of Grass*, the United States emerged as Europe's afterlife. The land Americans already have, Whitman concludes, is the one Europeans once wanted.

America does not repel the past or what it has produced under its forms or amid other politics or the ideas of castes or the old religions . . . is not so impatient as has been supposed that the slough still sticks to opinions and manners and literature while the life which served its requirements has passed into the new life of the new forms.

Whitman's assertion in the 1855 preface to *Leaves of Grass* that the poet rather than the president was the nation's "common referee" responded as well to political aspirations much closer to home. In naming three of Whitman's brothers—Andrew Jackson, Thomas Jefferson, and George Washington—after United States presidents, Whitman's father had conflated patriotic with paternal sentiments. In his verse Whitman extended into the national community the role he played as mediator between his brothers and their parents. Following the death of his father shortly after the publication of *Leaves of Grass*, on July 11, 1855, the roles of national bard and substitute parent merged.

As I argued in *Visionary Compacts*, the "Children of Adam" sequence he would add to the 1860 edition expanded Whitman's kinship group to include the entire U.S. population, past and future, women and men "en-masse," and he identified what he called the "body electric" as the democratic equivalent of what European monarchs called the "king's second body." In associating the properties of permanence, immutability, and transferability with the office rather than the body of the monarch, the king's second body rendered the institution immortal. In proposing the "body electric" as the political instrument ensuring the nation against the death of democracy, Whitman borrowed metaphors from physics to explain its dynamics. Once switched on the body electric rendered kinetic the individual's "potential" for multiple associations, thereby enabling each citizen's access to a network of associations. As with his other political fictions, Whitman's *Leaves of Grass* became the experimental field upon which he demonstrated the possible social effect of the poetic construct.

When placed in that field of force the "body electric" replaced carefully parsed sentences with speech floods: streams of words capable of immersing individual parts of speech in a more inclusive linguistic process. As these powerful flows built up momentum they induced the individual parts of speech in Whitman's sentences to discharge their individual differences into energies capable of attracting other syntactic units. Listen to the linguistic energies in the following passage as they materialize democracy's "body electric":

> The pure contralto sings in the organloft,
> The carpenter dresses his plank . . . the tongue of his foreplane
>   whistles its wild ascending lisp,
> The married and unmarried children ride home
>   to their Thanksgiving dinner,
> The pilot seizes the king-pin, he heaves down with a strong arm,
> The mate stands braced in the whale boat, lance and harpoon are ready,
> The duck-shooter walks by silent and cautious stretches,
> The deacons are ordained with crossedhands at the altar,
> The spinning girl retreats and advances to the hum of the big wheel
>
> ("Song of Myself")

The separate phrases in this prolonged sentence do not represent but *associate* individuals. They draw single, separate persons, otherwise silently passing each other by, into a larger social movement. As these persons and the parts of speech with which they are associated gather mass, they do not remain separated. The kinetic energy flooding through successive social figure binds them together. As it transmutes individual potential into this social motion, the passage spills out a multiplicity of possible selves, involving each individual in a more inclusive identity. Whitman believed this model of democratic kinship necessary to supplant Europe's ancestral lineages. In place of successive generations of blood relatives, the individuals associated in this passage undergo instantaneous evolution. Each figure finds in the ensemble a revelation of the possible materializations of his or her own body. After each figure understands these other shapes as potential ancestors and descendants, Whitman declares representatively for the body electric: "There was never more inception than there is now. Nor any more youth or age than there is now; And will never be any more perfection than there is now" ("Song of Myself").

In catalogues like this one gathering masses do not impede the development of individual citizens but accelerate their "evolution." Unlike geneticists, who understood this process as the result of thousands of years of evolution, Whitman believed each individual needed only to "merge in the general run [of a social movement] and await his development." Represented as involved in each other's evolution, every member of the body electric becomes kin. What differentiates this mass demonstration from related family gatherings, however, is the "equality" Whitman assigns to each "developing" figure. Whereas Whitman does not call attention to the differences among individuals, he nevertheless indicates their necessity for the development of all humankind. Because each individual contributes to this collective biological process, no single individual, when construed from the perspective of the inclusive process, can be described as superior or inferior. What Whitman calls the "perfection" of the human form depends equally upon each of the parts materializing that perfection. When Whitman asserted that "there will never be any more perfection than there is now," he referred to the full run of the human form represented in this passage for a gloss. The "human catalogues" in the poetry thereby proved Whitman's belief in the democratic masses' power to develop potentialities for humankind that he had recorded in the prose preface:

To these [the masses] respond perfections not only in the committees that were supposed to stand for the rest but in the rest themselves just the same. These understand the law of perfection in masses and floods . . . that its finish is to each for itself and onward from itself . . . that it is profuse and impartial.

In thereby correlating poetic innovations with such political doctrines as the "man en-masse," "social ensemble," and the "body electric,"

Whitman insisted on their interdependence. Other formal experiments such as the abandonment of uniform stanzaic patterns and the virtual elimination of rhyme lacked immediate social referents. While the repetition of lines and phrases resembled the "thought rhythm" of the King James Bible, Whitman's elevation of the verse line into the basic rhythmical unit constituted a purely formal innovation. In disregarding meter altogether Whitman originated a form of free verse without precedent in literary history.

Whitman claimed that his variable musical effects were influenced most profoundly by the aria and recitative passages, what he called the superb "vocalism" of the Italian opera. Because Whitman understood it to be a poetic faculty lying dormant within each of his readers, he recommended particular exercises for their cultivation of vocal range:

What vocalism most needs in these States, not only in the few choicer words and phrases, but in our whole talk, is ease, sonorous strength, breadth and openness. Boys and girls should practice daily in free, loud reading—in the open air, if possible [. . .] let your organ swell loudly without screaming—don't specify each syllable or word, but let them flow—feel the sentiment of what you read or say, and follow where it leads.

Whitman proposed the following lines from the 1855 "Song of Myself" as a sample of how to practice this advice:

> A tenor large and fresh as the creation fills me,
> The orbic flex of his mouth is pouring and filling me full.
>
> I hear the trained soprano . . . she convulses me like the
>   climax of my love-grip;
> The orchestra whirls me wider than Uranus flies.
> It wrenches unnamable ardors from my breast.

Whitman did not confine his demonstration of such unheard-of vocal power to individual lines but extended it to include the entirety of *Leaves of Grass*. As the soprano's aria had exalted Whitman, so would Whitman exalt those readers whose identities were to be understood subsequently as in need of Whitman's poetry. As their interlocutor Whitman addressed the "answerer" in each of his readers. But he did not intend as a consequence of this conversation that his readers identify with any single argumentative position or social doctrine. If we understand notions such as the "body electric" as resources for improvisation rather than fixed doctrines, it is clear Whitman never in fact recommended any specific doctrines to his readers. He "embodied" instead the energetic exchanges, the give-and-take productive of them. Had he espoused specific political or religious doctrines Whitman would have affirmed a separate rather than electric identity and a foundationalist rather than pragmatic attitude. To promote the latter Whitman invented for himself a malleable position within what he called an everchanging "colloquy" with his readers. Reducible neither to self nor to other and not exactly the equivalent of intersubjectivity, what we might call Whitman's intersubject resulted in a never ending conversation.

I have discussed Whitman's theory of poetry in "Poetics of Pure Possibility," from which the following observations are drawn. When Whitman declares, in "Song of Myself," "And what I assume, you shall assume," the "you" does not refer to a reader with an identity entirely separable from the activity of reading the poem: the "you" is instead virtually anticipated by the speaker before he can speak a word. Or, as Whitman puts it, in "A Song of the Rolling Earth," "those are not the words, the substantial words . . . they are in you." Throughout Whitman's poetry the reader's "you" supplements "I" as the "latency" remaining unspoken in every utterance. Consequently, neither "I" nor "you" alone can be said to constitute the speaking voice, but only the profound relation between them that the poetry animates. When impersonated by this resonant voice the speaker represented in the poetry alternately anticipates a reader's responses yet changes places with the reader, producing a voice that by turns questions, exhorts, commands, swears, soothes, deceives, screams, cozens, doubts, echoes, recriminates, and often downright gabs. Whitman explains the resultant fusion of voices succinctly in "Song of Myself": "It is you talking just as much as myself, I act as the tongue of you, / Tied in your mouth, in mine it begins to be loosen'd." By alternately impersonating both sides of an implicit dialogue, then, Whitman's voice undergoes constant modulations, startling enough in their effects to be his voice's equivalent of the transformative power of metaphor.

The power of this modulation, however, can be attributed neither to the speaker nor to the "answerer" but only to the voice resulting from their fusion. From their voices, there "proceeds another eternally curious of the harmony of things" (preface to the 1855 edition of *Leaves of Grass*). Depending upon the intensity of its register, Whitman describes the sound of this fusing voice variously as a "hum," "lull," "drift," and even "a barbaric yawp," and he claims to prefer this sound, which we could call the unspoken resonance of his words, to the individual words themselves: "The words of my book nothing, the drift of it everything" ("Shut Not Your Doors"). As the outward form of the invisible and "unlaunch'd" poem that can never be written or *confirmed* into print, the printed words reveal only the "shreds" or the "debris" of an inexpressible, ever-elusive power of vocality, the "barbaric yawp" that precedes yet *under*writes audible voices. Whitman's poems do not propose themselves to be images or a precise rendition of emotions but the confluence of "dumb voices." Like echoes that sink into consciousness in the silences between speech, the resultant "lulls" are less sounds in themselves than resoundings of already spoken words that paradoxically precede individual utterances and re-sound through them.

To actualize such an *inter*locutive voice Whitman developed various innovations in poetic form. He abandoned the passive and active voice for one in an intransitive mood and capable of declaring, "I sing myself and celebrate myself." In this singular construction the "I" refers to an agent neither totally separated from its activity of singing, as it would be in the active voice, nor wholly acted upon, as it would in the passive. Whitman's "I" occupies what linguists call the middle voice, by which they refer to a verbal performance whose speaker is inside the process of which he presumes to be the agent, who effects something that is simultaneously effected in him.

Since Whitman's persona is different with each new poem, it cannot be ascribed to the empirical identity, Walt Whitman. The sheer intensity of the songs transfigures Whitman's empirical ego into what he calls in "That Shadow, My Likeness" a "likeness" of his true self, capable of appearing only within the interlocutive process effected in "caroling these songs."

> That shadow my likeness that goes to and fro seeking a livelihood, chattering, chaffering.
> How often I find myself standing and looking at it where it flits,
> How often I question and doubt whether that is really me,
> But among my lovers and caroling these songs,
> I never doubt whether that is really me.
> ("That Shadow My Likeness")

The correlation the speaker adduces between caroling and being among lovers is a topic I shall take up shortly. For now it is important to realize that when Whitman wrote "I sing myself" he literally meant that his singing brought a self into being.

Put starkly Whitman believed he had turned himself into the consciousness of singing—but a consciousness of a peculiar kind. Since Whitman's voice engenders the confluence of self and other, it partakes of all the sensual delight inherent in such fusion. When Whitman incarnates the voice of *inter*locution, it is not as a disembodied voice but as a "body electric," covered with "instant conductors all over"—not merely a speaking voice but a fully sensualized, listening, smelling, seeing, tasting, touching one, longing for renewed relations with others. Perhaps, since only the sexual urge approaches the intensity of the consequent desire for union, in passages such as this one Whitman uses sexuality as the appropriate metaphor for that desire.

> I believe in you my soul . . . . the other I am must not abase
>   itself to you,
> And you must not be abased to the other.
> Loafe with me on the grass . . . . loose the stop from your throat,
> Not words, not music or rhyme I want . . . . not custom or lecture,
>   not even the best,
> Only the lull I like, the hum of your valved voice.
> I mind how we lay in June, such a transparent summer morning;
> You settled your head athwart my hips and gently turned over upon me,
> And parted the shirt from my bosom-bone, and plunged your tongue
>   to my barestript heart,
> and reached till you felt my beard, and reached till you held my feet.
>
> Swiftly arose and spread around me the peace and joy and knowledge
>   that pass all the art and argument of the earth;
> And I know that the hand of God is the elderhand of my own,
> And I know that the spirit of God is the eldest brother of my own,
> And that all the men ever born are also my brothers . . . . and the
>   women my sisters and lovers,
> And that a kelson of the creation is love;
> And limitless are leaves stiff or drooping in the fields,
> And brown ants in the little wells beneath them,
> And mossy scabs of the wormfence, and heaped stones, and elder
>   and mullen and pokeweed.

In these lines Whitman's self becomes intercorporeal with that of the "you"—each self experiencing itself as the interiority of the other. Both the sexual and interlocutive selves can here be said to incarnate a give-

and-take intense enough to render the giver indistinguishable from the taker. That is to say, the sexual self, like Whitman's intersubject, incarnates the fusing relation between persons rather than any individual identity. Consequently, when Whitman speaks from out of that "body electric," he treats all his relationships in the world as ones in which he touchingly ventures "the verge of myself, then the outlet again."

But sexuality indicates only one of Whitman's metaphors for the intersubjects. Through an even more telling strategy, the "I"—and this is especially true when it is associated with multiple predications—seems surrounded, even *spoken*, by natural processes.

> If I worship any particular thing it shall be some of the
>   spread of my body;
> Translucent mould of me it shall be you,
> Shaded ledges and rests, firm masculine coulter, it shall be you,
> Whatever goes to the tilth of me it shall be you,
> You my rich blood, your milky stream pale strippings of my life;
> Breast that presses against other breasts it shall be you,
> My brain it shall be your occult convolutions,
> Root of washed sweet-flag, timorous pond-snipe, nest of guarded
>   duplicate eggs, it shall be you,
> Mixed tussled hay of head and beard and brawn it shall be you,
> Trickling sap of maple, fibre of manly wheat, it shall be you;
> Sun so generous it shall be you,
> Vapors lighting and shading my face it shall be you,
> You sweaty brooks and dews it shall be you,
> Winds whose soft-tickling genitals rub against me it shall be you,
> Broad muscular fields, branches of liveoak, loving lounger in my
>   winding paths, it shall be you,
> Hands I have taken, face I have kissed, mortal I have ever touched
>   it shall be you.

While the subject in these lines is immersed in such confluent activities it does not dominate, but as if it is itself no less fluid the "I" merges with them. In *Leaves of Grass* Whitman not only liquefies himself but manages to melt and occasionally evaporate the most resistant objects into a merging flow. This observation supplies still another key for understanding Whitman's famous catalogue constructions, for in these, too, objective scenes surround Whitman, but without any one scene assuming visual priority, and without the group disarticulated to a sequence of scenes. These resonate, flowing into, even echoing one another, displace the priority of the gaze, and render themselves finally *indistinguishable from spoken words*. Through this remarkable technique Whitman effects a profound confusion of the senses, for in the catalogues he manages so to intertwine the acts of speaking and seeing that he seems to *speak seeing*.

As the "similitudes" of the interlocutive voice designating in Whitman's verse the original relation for all creation, the speaker, reader, and individual poems—in fact, all of the subjects and all objects of *Leaves of Grass*—flow into the "hum" of a "valvéd voice." Throughout the poetry Whitman's "I" as "you" partakes of the rapid transformation of this unspoken voice, until the speaker evaporates into its unspeakably thin air, "I depart as air, I shake my white locks at the runaway sun, I effuse my flesh in eddies and drift it in lacy jags."

Despite Whitman's spectacular expectations, the public response to *Leaves of Grass* was initially mixed. The most adulatory reviews were written by Whitman himself and published anonymously in the *United States Review* and the *Brooklyn Daily Times*. In his review for *Putnam's Monthly* Charles Eliot Norton described *Leaves of Grass* as a "curious and lawless collection of poems . . . neither in rhyme or in blank verse, but in a sort of excited prose broken into lines without any attempt at measure or regularity." But after reading the complimentary volume Whitman had sent him in Concord, Ralph Waldo Emerson responded with an enthusiasm seemingly greater than Whitman's. "I am not blind to the worth of the wonderful gift of *Leaves of Grass*," Emerson began his letter of July 21, 1855. He continued, "I find it the most extraordinary piece of art and wisdom that America has yet contributed."

The section of the letter on which Whitman focused his attention began with the sentence "I greet you at the beginning of a great career, which yet must have had a long foreground somewhere, for such a start." By way of this sentence Emerson, speaking for himself, returned the greeting Whitman had extended to the universe, thereby acknowledging Whitman's poetic achievement. Whereas Emerson sent this as a private letter, Whitman, without asking Emerson's permission, turned it into a public advertisement. He had copies of the letter printed up, then bound them up in copies of *Leaves of Grass* he sent to prominent authors and book review editors. In October he let Horace Greeley publish the letter in his *Tribune*, and stamped "I Greet You at the Beginning of A Great Career, R.W. Emerson" in gold print on the spine of the 1856 second edition of *Leaves of Grass*.

The usage to which Whitman put Emerson's private letter is significant as an indication of his public persona. In the lecture on the poet Whitman heard in 1842 Emerson had called for an American bard. In "Song of Myself" Whitman announced himself as the incarnation of that persona, and in Emerson's letter he found confirmation in that identity.

What Emerson's lecture had not called for, however, was Whitman's intense and explicit account of sexuality. The 1856 edition included his response to Emerson's letter, which outlined their differences of opinion and included the following rationale for his celebration of sexuality:

Infidelism usurps most with foetid, polite face, among the rest infidelism about sex. By silence or obedience to the pens of savans, poets, historians, biographers, and the rest, have long connived at the filthy law, and books enslaved to it, that what makes the manhood of a man, that sex, womanhood, maternity, desires, lusty animations, organs, acts, are unmentionable and to be ashamed of, to be driven to skulk out of literature with whatever belongs to them. This filthy law has to be repealed—it stands in the way of great reforms. Of women just as much as men, it is the interest that there should not be infidelism about sex, but perfect faith. Women in These States approach the day of that organic equality with man, without which, I see, men cannot have organic equality among themselves. . . . I say that the body of a man or woman, the main matter is so far quite unexpressed in poems; but that the body is to be expressed, and sex is. Of bards for These States, if it come to a question, it is whether they shall celebrate in poems the eternal decency of the amativeness of Nature, the motherhood of all, or whether they shall be the bards of the fashionable delusion of the inherent nastiness of sex; and of the feeble and querulous modesty of deprivation.

Emerson's letter and Whitman's response replaced the 1855 preface in a second edition whose central theme became the exaltation of America's spiritual and physical progress. Despite Emerson's pleas in the 1860 edition, Whitman did not delete but elaborated his celebration of sexuality into the "Enfants d'Adam" (later called "Children of Adam") and "Calamus" sequences (unabashedly erotic poems of loving comradeship between men). In so doing, Whitman made clear his intention, not to give up, but to pursue his differences with Emerson on the matter of sexuality into new poems and new contexts throughout the remainder of his career.

In his exchange of letters with Emerson Whitman proposed the celebration of sexuality as a release of the blockages impeding democratic processes. In urging acceptance of suppressed bodily urges Whitman intended to restore health to the body politic. But these themes had application as well to Whitman's own family experience. Whitman's politically progressive father was notoriously repressive about sexual matters. This attitude had disastrous consequences for several members of Whitman's family: his older brother, Jessie, the victim of tertiary syphilis, was committed to an insane asylum; Andrew married a prostitute who neglected their children after he died of tuberculosis during the Civil War; Edward was born feebleminded; his sister Hannah suffered from sexual frustration throughout her marriage; his sister Mary endured decades of physical and mental abuse from her alcoholic husband, Ansel Van Nostrand.

Perhaps it was partly to free himself from this constrictive family narrative that Whitman inaugurated a program of unrestrained sexual gratification. But the "Calamus" poems also presented Whitman with an opportunity to exempt his father posthumously from guilt over his children's failures, and to discriminate his imaginative allegiance with Emerson from his bond with his father:

> I throw myself upon your breast my father,
> I cling to you so that you cannot unloose me,
> I hold you so firm, till you answer me something.

> Kiss me, my father,
> Touch me with your lips, as I touch those I love,
> Breathe to me, while I hold you close, the secret of the
>   wondrous murmuring I envy,
> For I fear I shall become crazed if I cannot emulate it, and
>   utter myself as well as it.

In a highly persuasive reading of these lines from the 1860 edition Harold Bloom explains how their homoerotic theme enabled Whitman to separate himself from Emerson (who rejected the theme) and recover his own identity through a posthumous extension of male comradeship to his actual father:

As the covenant with Emerson that begat the poetic self ebbs, so the rejected covenant with the actual father is accepted and made whole. Emersonian self-reliance freed Whitman from the totalizing afflictions of the family romance. Now the consequences of the poetic analogue of the family romance allowed Whitman a reconciliation he never found while his father was alive. Imaginative loss quite literally is transformed into experiential gain.

Because repressed sexuality had replaced working-class life during this period as Whitman's representative theme, his persona underwent a related shift. At the base of its spine, the 1860 edition portrayed a butterfly on an outstretched finger; in place of the 1855 portrait of Whitman the working-class poet, the frontispiece engraving now represented a figure, wearing a foppish windsor tie and a sporting Byronic collar beneath a shock of wavy hair and flowing white beard. While the 1860 edition sold better than had the previous two (John Burroughs reported that between four and five thousand were sold eventually), Thayer and Elldredge, the publishers of the 1860 edition, went bankrupt in 1861, and Whitman, who had depended on them for his livelihood, lost the royalties they owed him. To supplement his income he wrote a series of historical sketches about Brooklyn for the *Brooklyn Standard.* Despite the relative popularity of the third edition Whitman's social standing did not improve. When Emerson tried to make him a member of the elite Saturday Club in Boston, its other prominent members, Longfellow, Lowell, and Holmes, all rejected him.

In the prose and poetry he wrote during this period Whitman transformed these social exclusions into indirect affirmations of the unprecedented social order that awaited formation out of the unique resources of his prophetic poetry. Reinventing himself as if in response to the specific needs of this period in the nation's history, Whitman became the "poet-comrade." The scenario to which he consigned this social form entailed an imaginative erotic bond extended across the generations to readers whose longing for Whitman's physical presence resulted from their reading the poetry:

> The bards of ages hence, when you refer to me, mind not so much my
>   poems,
> Nor speak of me that I prophesied the states, and led them the way of
>   their glories,
> But come, I will take you down underneath this impassive exterior—
>   I will tell you what to say to me:
> Publish my name and hang up my picture as that of the
>   tenderest lover,

The friend, the lover's portrait, of whom his friend, his lover,
   was fondest . . .
Whose happiest days were far away, through field, in woods, on hills,
   he and another, wandering hand in hand, they twain, apart from
other men,
Who oft as he sauntered the streets, curved with his arm the shoulders
   of his friend—while the arm of his friend rested upon him also.

                       ("Recorders Ages Hence")

The "adhesiveness" binding Whitman across time to this lover took precedence over ordinary amativeness. In his homoerotic bond with such comrade lovers, Whitman acknowledged the value of heterosexual intercourse, but as the dynamic necessary to effect the generational differences upon which his poetry depended for its "immortality."

In 1862, however, news of an injury Whitman's younger brother, George, had sustained in the Battle of Fredericksburg led him to Washington, D.C., and still another change in persona. While he found that George was relatively healthy, the sight of the other wounded men, some with their limbs amputated, others blinded or in various stages of morbidity awakened in Whitman a profound sympathy. In these young soldiers he found the loving comrades his poetry had only envisioned. He believed their need for compassionate attention was directly addressed to the poet who had declared agonies to be "one of my changes of garments . . . I am the man, I suffered, I was there."

Whitman stayed in Washington throughout the war, alternating writing a collection of poems that would be published in 1865 as *Drum-Taps*, with writing letters, distributing reading matter, tobacco or condiments, and consoling the wounded. In becoming the "Wound Dresser" for the young men who often depended upon him alone for comfort and community, Whitman realized the deepest urge he had suppressed in *Leaves of Grass*: to become the mediator between the living and the dead. In keeping vigil as the wounded died Whitman bore witness to the central mystery of creative life—its double capacity to bring death to the living and life to the unborn. As the conduit for both generative and degenerative forces Whitman imagined himself the site through which these different energies traversed and flooded into one another. In an effort to describe the regenerative figure who emerged at this intersection, Whitman proposed an enigma: "Could we imagine such a thing— let us suggest that before a manchild or womanchild was born it should be suggested that a human being could be born." Tenney Nathanson, in his excellent commentary on this enigma, pursued it into the mysterious center of Whitman's creative project. "Sexual difference ought to be a mere accident, a secondary or surface quality," Nathanson explains, "and the undifferentiated identity it replaces should be recoverable." Neither "manchild" nor "womanchild," this visionary human being not yet marked by sexual difference is apparently unaffected by that process of generation out of which it presumably emerges. Complete in itself, it seems self-sufficient and virtually self-created. The poet who achieves rebirth by announcing this presence in the poems incarnates his visionary ambitions. During the war years the dying, whose wounds he dressed and to whose mortality he bore witness, seemed visionary presences, apparitions in need of Whitman's poetry for the continuation of their present lives as well as the record of their experiences.

In performing this service during the war years Whitman associated *Leaves of Grass* with the central nation-making event. The war was, Whitman explained, his poetry in action. The elegies Whitman wrote following Lincoln's assassination associated his project with the Central Man of the nation's political mythology. Deploying the images descriptive of his own beginnings from "Out of the Cradle Endlessly Rocking," that is, the lilac bush, hermit thrush, evening star as likewise appropriate for the nation's collective task of mourning Lincoln's death, Whitman effectively identified his own poetic taste with Lincoln's martyrdom. Throughout "When Lilacs Last in the Dooryard Bloom'd," Whitman turned Lincoln's martyrdom into a synecdoche for all the nation's dead. When Whitman presumed the right to recollect Lincoln, whose sacrifice had secured the nation's immortality, from within his poetry he tacitly associated *Leaves of Grass* with the national memory. He thereby encouraged his readers to recollect *Leaves of Grass* along with the Civil War, and to understand their own lives as the renewal of both the Civil War dead and Whitman's poetry.

> I cease from my song for thee,
> From my gaze on thee in the west, fronting the west, communing
>   with thee,
> O comrade lustrous with silver face in the night.
> Yet each to keep and all, retrievements out of the night,
> The song, the wondrous chant of the gray-brown bird,
> And the tallying chant, the echo arous'd in my soul,
> With the lustrous and drooping star with the countenance full
>   of woe,

With the holders holding my hand nearing the call of the bird,
Comrades mine and I in the midst, and their memory ever to keep
   for the dead I loved so well.
For the sweetest, wisest soul of all my days and lands and this for his
   dear sake,
Lilac and star and bird twined with the chant of my soul
There in the fragrant pines and the cedars dusk and dim.

Partly as a result of his friend William D. O'Connor's publication of *The Good Gray Poet* in January of 1866, Whitman's persona as the incarnation of the National Memory was more successful than had been the previous three. O'Connor's hagiographical efforts on Whitman's behalf were directed against James Harlan, who, after reading the 1860 edition, had fired Whitman from his post in the Department of the Interior. Whitman, who had a hand in the preparation of the O'Connor portrait, was subsequently assigned to another governmental post, and over the next twenty-six years energetically engaged in remaking himself after the image of the Good Gray Poet.

Favorable responses in Europe and the United States attended this reinvention. In February 1868 William Rossetti published his selected edition of *Poems of Walt Whitman*. A. C. Swinburne compared Whitman favorably with William Blake, as did the wife of Blake's biographer, Anne Gilchrist (who later proposed marriage). In the United States Whitman's poetry received progressively better reviews, and Richard Bucke, the philosopher of cosmic consciousness, and John Burroughs, the naturalist, became literary allies. Moreover, one of the fantasies he had recorded in his "Calamus" poems, of a transgenerational homoerotic friendship, was quite literally realized—in Whitman's relationship with Peter Doyle. Whitman had first met Doyle when serving as the "Wound Dresser" for Confederate soldiers, and remained intimate with him throughout the remainder of his life, writing letters of parental advice as well as comradely (and erotic) affection.

In 1871 he published a philosophical essay entitled *Democratic Vistas* in which he further refined his understanding of democracy, consolidating it into a philosophical stance remarkably similar to William James's and John Dewey's pragmatism. Two years later a paralytic stroke forced him to leave Washington, D.C., and move in with his brother George in Camden, New Jersey. His mother's death, four months later, deepened a depression from which he did not fully emerge until 1876, with the overwhelmingly favorable public reaction to an article (which appeared in the January 26 edition of *Camden West Jersey Press*) entitled "Walt Whitman's Actual American Position" (and probably written by Whitman himself). The essay lamented the nation's neglect of its true bard, and following its publication in England, Edmund Gosse, Alfred Lord Tennyson, George Saintsbury, and Lord Houghton added their names to the growing list of Whitman's admirers.

Whitman began publishing again in 1876 with the so-called sixth (really a reprinting of the 1871 fifth) edition of *Leaves of Grass*. From 1876 until his death Whitman did all he could to consolidate his reputation. To his everlasting credit, those efforts did not include censorship of any of his earlier views. In fact, when Whitman added "To a Common Prostitute" to the 1881 edition, the district attorney of Boston declared the edition obscene.

Throughout the last decade of the poet's life Horace Traubel helped him collect his prose and poetry in what would be called the "deathbed edition." But most of Whitman's poems from this period concerned his difficulty in separating himself from his poetic "fancy." In the poems he collected under the title "November Boughs," Whitman completed an identification of cosmic seasonal cycles with *Leaves of Grass* and the rhythms of his own life, and thereby permanently imprinted himself as well as his poetry within the repetitive motions of nature.

But if Whitman had trouble separating his life from his poetry, he left his readers the more difficult task of properly inheriting the poetry. The difficulty pertains to Whitman's unprecedented claim for the timeliness of his poems, which he often described uncannily not merely as his own past taking the place of his readers' present but of his readers' future becoming present during Whitman's activity of writing. The following lines from "Full of Life Now" record as the first of Whitman's claims the fact that he depends on the reading activity for continued life:

> When you read these lines I that was visible am become invisible
> Where it is you, compact, visible realizing my poems, seeking me.

The following lines from "Crossing Brooklyn Ferry" record the more astonishing claim that Whitman's poetry has transformed his present into a bridge spanning past and future, capable of absorbing the reader's future within his past:

It avails not, time nor place—distance avails not,
I am with you, you men and women of a generation, or ever so many
    generations hence,
Just as you feel when you look in the river and sky, so I felt . . .
Who knows, for all the distance, but I am as good as looking at you now.

The crossing effected in these lines between the writing and reading of
the poem precipitates an understanding of Whitman as at once earlier
and in need of this subsequent activity of reading to be renewed, yet also
later than the reader's activity, which consequently seems somehow
anterior to Whitman's presence. "Consider, you who peruse me,
whether I may not in unknown ways be looking upon you." The effect
of such lines is the haunting sense that Whitman has recollected the
reader from his past and transmuted the prophetic memory at work in
his poetry into the power to act upon the reader's historical present—as
if it were a suppression of Whitman's re-visionary democracy.

The resulting difficulty of adequate response was not confined to
Whitman's descendants. In an essay on Whitman's work his contemporary John Burroughs observed that

Whitman completes no poems, apart and separate from himself. . . . His lines
are pulsation, thrills, waves of force, indefinite dynamics, formless, constantly
emanating from the living centre, and they carry the quality of the author's personal presence with them in a way that is unprecedented in literature.

I have already proposed that Whitman understood his presence in the
poems as indissociable from the United States' ongoing experiment in
democracy. As that process changed, Whitman reinvented his persona
to answer different needs. During Whitman's own lifetime his persona
originated from the radical contradiction between the everyday lived
experiences of Brooklyn's working class and the nation's democratic
ideals, and it ended up as the National Memory personified in the Good
Gray Poet. Whitman did not understand this changeable persona to be
coincident with his personal biography but with the nation's history, and
he expected each generation to reinvent him out of its own needs. Writing for widely different audiences in the 1920s, Hart Crane and
Langston Hughes found in Whitman's poetry the inspiration for a
renaissance. In the 1950s Allen Ginsberg resisted the academy's efforts
to suppress the sexually liberatory aspects of Whitman's poetry in the
name of a formalist agenda. More recently, such poets and critics as
Marge Piercy and Michael Moon who understand U.S. nationalism as

itself a constraint on democratic processes have discovered a Whitman answerable to the needs of the feminist and gay rights movements. That each of these Whitmans has emerged in that permanently transitional space between an already articulated and an as yet unrealized democracy constitutes the abiding value of Whitman's presence to a political experiment which, like the poet, is forever undergoing dramatic revision.

Donald Pease

Further Reading

Allen, Gay Wilson. T*he Solitary Singer: A Critical Biography of Walt Whitman.* New York: Macmillan, 1955.

Anderson, Quentin. *The Imperial Self: An Essay in American Literary and Cultural History.* New York: Vintage, 1972.

Bloom, Harold. *Agon: Towards a Theory of Revisionism.* New York: Oxford University Press, 1982.

Burroughs, John. *Notes on Walt Whitman as Poet and Person.* New York: American News, 1867.

Chase, Richard. *Walt Whitman Reconsidered.* New York: William Sloane, 1955.

Erkkila, Betsy. *Whitman the Political Poet.* New York: Oxford University Press, 1989.

Mathiessen, F. O. *American Renaissance: Art and Expression in the Age of Emerson and Whitman.* New York: Oxford University Press, 1941.

Miller, James E., Jr. *A Critical Guide to "Leaves of Grass."* Chicago: University of Chicago Press, 1959.

Moon, Michael. *Disseminating Whitman: Revision and Corporealty in "Leaves of Grass."* Cambridge: Harvard University Press, 1992.

Nathanson, Tenney. *Whitman's Presence: Body, Voice, and Writing in "Leaves of Grass."* New York: New York University Press, 1992.

Pease, Donald E. *Visionary Compacts: American Renaissance Writings in Cultural Context.* Madison: University of Wisconsin Press, 1987.

———— "Blake, Crane, Whitman, and Modernism: A Poetics of Pure Possibility." PMLA (1981), 96:64–85.

Rubin, Joseph Jay. *The Historic Whitman.* University Park: Pennsylvania State University Press, 1973.

Zweig, Paul. Walt *Whitman: The Making of the Poet.* New York: Basic Books, 1984.

Edgar Allan Poe

POE (1809–1949), who had been orphaned and then disinherited, remained impoverished, even destitute, for most of his life. In a confessional preface to *The Raven and Other Poems* (1845), his most substantial volume, he expressed his belief that serious poetry would always be unsalable in the materialistic society of America. He explained that financial pressures had turned him toward fiction and criticism and prevented him from pursuing a career as a professional poet. "Events not to be controlled have prevented me from making, at any time, any serious effort in what, under happier circumstances, would have been the field of my choice."

Poe was an extremely precocious poet. During his adolescence his Richmond schoolmaster Joseph Clarke had called him a born artist who wrote genuine poetry while other boys cranked out mechanical verse. When Poe was eleven years old his foster father, John Allan, showed Clarke a manuscript volume of his poems, which the ambitious boy wanted to have published. But Clarke, thinking this would flatter Poe's inordinate vanity, advised against publication and the project was dropped. Poe published three volumes—in 1827, 1829, and 1831—by the time he was twenty-two. He then remained comparatively silent for the next fourteen years, and wrote only one or two major poems annually during the last three years of his life.

When Poe came to maturity William Cullen Bryant and John Greenleaf Whittier were the leading American poets. He had nothing to learn from them and turned for nourishment to the English Romantic poets. He was strongly influenced by the aesthetic theories of Coleridge, identified with the rebellious persona of Byron, and was inspired by the epic poetry of Shelley and the lyrics of Keats.

Poe, with characteristic critical acuity, particularly admired two of his English contemporaries. He declared of Elizabeth Barrett (who had not yet married Robert Browning), "her poetic inspiration is the highest—we can conceive nothing more august. Her sense of Art is pure in itself." He was even more enthusiastic about the mournful lyricism, the poetical excitement, the pure idealism, and the ethereal beauty of Alfred Tennyson. Poe revered this "magnificent genius" and exclaimed: "I consider Tennyson not only the greatest Poet in England, at present, but the greatest one, in many senses, that England, or any other Country, ever produced."

Poe first expressed his theory of poetry in the "Letter to B_____," his first prose work, which was addressed to his publisher Elam Bliss and included as a preface to his *Poems* of 1831. This "Letter" contained high praise for Coleridge, who had a profound impact on Poe's poetic imagination, his critical principles, and his speculative mind. After praising Coleridge's mind and learning, Poe breathlessly extolled his explosive imaginative force. "Of Coleridge I cannot speak but with reverence. His towering intellect! his gigantic power! . . . In reading his poetry, I tremble, like one who stands upon a volcano, conscious, from the very darkness bursting from the crater, of the fire and the light that are weltering below."

In the "Letter to B_____" Poe lifted a sentence, without acknowledgment, from chapter 14 of Coleridge's *Biographia Literaria* (1817). Coleridge wrote:

A poem is that species of composition, which is opposed to works of science, by proposing for its *immediate* object pleasure, not truth,

and Poe repeated:

A poem, in my opinion, is opposed to a work of science by having, for its *immediate* object, pleasure, not truth.

Floyd Stovall, who called Coleridge "the guiding spirit of Poe's entire intellectual life," has effectively summarized his extensive debt to the English poet. Like Coleridge, Poe believed that poetry gives pleasure by being indefinite, music is an essential element in poetry, beauty is the sole province of the poem, poetic beauty has the quality of strangeness, the poem must have unity of effect, the true poem must be brief, passion and poetry are discordant, and the tone of the poem should be melancholy.

Poe's major poetic themes include victimization, power and powerlessness, confrontations with mysterious presences, extreme states of being, dehumanization and its cure, the relation of body and soul, memory of and mourning for the dead, the need for spiritual transcendence and affirmation. Poe's beliefs that the dead are not entirely dead to consciousness, his hope that love could transcend death, and his apprehension of beauty beyond the grave were inspired by the early deaths of his mother, of Jane Stanard (the idealized mother of a school friend), and of Frances Allan (his foster mother). These three losses—in infancy, adolescence, and young manhood—were the most profound emotional experiences of Poe's early life. In "The Philosophy of Composition" he expressed a crucial aesthetic principle by categorically stating, "The death of a beautiful woman is, unquestionably, the most poetical topic in the world." He particularly admired and imitated the disembodied women in Tennyson's poems and affirmed, "He excels most in his female portraitures; but while delicate and graceful they are indefinite; while airy and spiritual, are intangible."

Poe had been writing poems while a student at the University of Virginia and while working at his foster father's countinghouse in 1826, and continued to do so while serving as a common soldier in 1827. He had gradually accumulated a thin manuscript, and may have left Richmond for Boston, after quarreling with the overbearing John Allan, because it was a literary and publishing center. His first work, *Tamerlane and Other Poems*, was paid for by Poe and published anonymously "By a Bostonian." Brought out by a young printer, Calvin Thomas of 70 Washington Street, in July 1827, when Poe was only eighteen years old, the forty-page pamphlet received no attention and fell stillborn from the press. Fifty copies were printed, of which only twelve have survived, making it the rarest and most valuable of American first editions. In the preface Poe apologized for the quality of his verse and magnified its merit by emphasizing his precocity. He claimed, with considerable exaggeration, that "the greater part of the Poems which compose this little volume, were written in the year 1821–22, when the author had not completed his fourteenth year." In the advertisement to his second volume of poetry he explained the indifferent reception of the first and suggested that malignant forces had stifled his talent. The title poem, Poe said, "was printed for publication in Boston, in the year 1827, but suppressed through circumstances of a private nature."

The epigraph to *Tamerlane* from William Cowper's "Tirocinium"—

Young heads are giddy, and young hearts are warm,
And make mistakes for manhood to reform—

excused himself and appealed to John Allan to forgive the youthful excesses that had led to their estrangement and to Poe's flight from home. It also began the confessional mode of many of his later poems, and employed his characteristic method of simultaneous concealment and revelation.

The historical Tamerlane was born near Samarkand, in remote and exotic central Asia, about forty years after Kubla Khan. This cruel Tartar warrior rose from humble origins —"A cottager, I mark'd a throne / Of half the world as all my own"—to become the conqueror of Persians, Russians, Indians, Arabs, Turks, Chinese, and to create an empire that extended from the Black Sea to the interior of Cathay. Though Tamerlane had been the subject of a play by Christopher Marlowe in 1590, Poe followed the "oriental" tradition of exotic settings and characters made famous in the eighteenth and early nineteenth centuries by Montesquieu's *Persian Letters*, Voltaire's *Zadig*, Johnson's *Rasselas*, Beckford's *Vathek*, Byron's *The Giaour*, and Moore's *Lalla Rookh*. Poe, who knew virtually nothing about the real Tamerlane but felt free to write about him, apologized for his ignorance and begged "the reader's pardon for making Tamerlane, a Tartar of the fourteenth century, speak in the same language as a Boston gentleman of the nineteenth; but of the Tartar mythology we have little information."

Tamerlane is meant to be an allegory of Poe's poetic ambition and disappointed love for his teenage Richmond sweetheart, Elmira Royster. Poe's love for Elmira had, surprisingly, already been the subject of a prose sketch, "The Pirate" (1827), by his older brother Henry, and a play, *Merlin* (1827), by his friend Lambert Wilmer. In Poe's poem the dying pagan conqueror absurdly confesses to a Christian friar on his deathbed that his overweening ambition and conquest of the world have deprived him of human love:

How was it that Ambition crept,
  Unseen amid the revels there,
Till growing bold, he laughed and leapt
  In the tangles of Love's very hair?

In May 1829, the month after his discharge from the army, the distinguished Philadelphia publishers, Carey, Lea & Carey, offered to bring out Poe's second volume of poetry if—following the current practice with unknown authors—Poe would insure them against loss by paying one hundred dollars for the cost of publication. Poe, who of course did not have the money, appealed to John Allan to underwrite the book and rather speciously argued that one hundred dollars "must be the limit of any loss, supposing not a single copy of the work to be sold.—It is more than probable that the work will be profitable [though Carey, Lea & Carey did not seem to think so] & that I may gain instead of lose, even in a pecuniary way." The pragmatic Allan, though once willing to publish Poe's schoolboy verses, knew a bad deal when he saw one. Predictably, he censured Poe's foolish request and refused any aid.

In December 1829, after further negotiations, Poe's seventy-two page *Al Aaraaf, Tamerlane and Minor Poems* was finally published in Baltimore by a less prestigious firm, Hatch & Dunning, in an edition of 250 copies. Floyd Stovall has noted that

the predominant moods of the 1827 volume as a whole are those of wounded pride and resentment for the wrongs, real or imagined, that he had suffered, and the dominant tone of the 1829 volume is one of disillusionment with the world and escape into some more congenial realm of dream or of the imagination.

The 264-line title poem was suffused with a fashionable Romantic melancholy and with a melodious incoherence—reminiscent of the fuzziest passages in Shelley's *Prometheus Unbound* (1820)—that made it extremely difficult, if not impossible, to understand. Poe's explanation did not clarify matters. He told his potential publisher, Isaac Lea, that the title of the poem came from a Limbo described in chapter 7 of the *Koran*,

from the Al Aaraaf of the Arabians, a medium between Heaven & Hell, where men suffer no punishment, but yet do not attain that tranquil & even happiness which they suppose to be the characteristic of heavenly enjoyment. . . . I have placed this "Al Aaraaf" in the celebrated star discovered by [the Danish astronomer] Tycho Brahe which appeared and disappeared so suddenly. . . . Even after death, those who make choice of the star as their residence do not enjoy immortality—but, after a second life of high excitement, sink into for-getfulness & death. . . . The poem commences with a sonnet (illegitimate) à la mode de Byron in his "Prisoner of Chillon." But this is a digression.

Poe's use of Tycho Brahe's discovery on November 11, 1572, of the star he called Al Aaraaf may have been influenced by the way Keats had used the discovery in 1781 of the planet Uranus (which he compared to the excitement he felt when first reading Homer in English) in his son-net "On First Looking into Chapman's Homer" (1816). Poe complet-ed only two of the projected four parts of his longest poem (which few readers have wished any longer) and seemed to suggest, in the vaguest possible way, that one might avoid earthly sin through devotion to higher beauty. The best part of the poem is the lyrical apostrophe to the goddess of harmony, whose name he borrowed from one of the Sirens and later used as the title of one of his best stories:

> Ligeia! Ligeia!
>   My beautiful one!
> Whose harshest idea
>   Will to melody run,
> O! is it thy will
>   On the breezes to toss?
> Or, capriciously still
>   Like the lone Albatross,
> Incumbent on night
>   (As she is on the air)
> To keep watch with delight
>   On the harmony there?

The failure of Poe's longest poem undoubtedly influenced his belief, later expressed in "The Poetic Principle," that a poem, to be effective, must be short.

The most accomplished poem in Poe's second volume was his "Son-net—To Science," a romantic protest against scientific rationalism, which destroys the mythology that nourishes and sustains the creative imagination:

> Why preyest thou thus upon the poet's heart,
>   Vulture, whose wings are dull realities? . . .
> Hast thou not dragged Diana from her car?
>   and driven the Hamadryad from the wood
> To seek a shelter in some happier star?

This theme had been similarly expressed in William Blake's antirationalist poem, "Mock on, Mock on, Voltaire, Rousseau" (1803).

> The Atoms of Democritus
> And Newton's Particles of Light
> Are sands upon the Red Sea shore,
> Where Israel's tents do shine so bright.

Between his second and third volumes of poetry Poe wrote an important autobiographical poem, "Alone" (1829). Originally inscribed in a lady's album, it was not published until 1875. Poe had been orphaned at the age of two, taken in but not adopted by his foster parents, and kept in a dubious and insecure social position. His transatlantic voyages and five years of education in England during his childhood, his artistic temperament and nascent poetic powers made him feel—and actually be—an exceptional, isolated individual. In "Alone," an introspective and analytical poem about his youth, he emphasized the difference between his feelings and those of others, and his pessimistic tendency to see, "When the rest of Heaven was blue / . . . a demon in my view:

> From childhood's hour I have not been
> As others were—I have not seen
> As others saw—I could not bring
> My passions from a common spring—
> From the same source I have not taken
> My sorrow—I could not awaken
> My heart to joy at the same tone—
> And all I lov'd—*I* lov'd alone.

After being bought out of the army Poe became an unlikely cadet at West Point. While there he began to construct his Byronic persona and—quickly losing interest in military matters—concentrated his efforts in publishing his third volume of poetry. Poe amused his classmates at West Point, as he had done at the University of Virginia, with his own verse. One friend, perceiving a new aspect of Poe's character, after he had decided to leave the Academy, mentioned that "he would often write some of the most forcible and vicious doggerel. . . . I have never seen a man whose hatred was so intense." The only surviving example of Poe's West Point verse is a tame squib—rather than biting satire—on the martinet Lieutenant Joseph Locke who taught military tactics and, as inspector, was responsible for reporting all infractions of the rules. Mentioning the eminent philosopher who shared the officer's surname, Poe wrote:

> John Locke was a notable name;
>> Joe Locke is a greater; in short,
> The former was well known to fame,
>> But the latter's well known "to report."

Eager to see Poe's scandalous satires in print, most of the cadets subscribed seventy-five cents each to underwrite publication. This sum was deducted from their official accounts by the treasurer of the Academy, who in April 1831 sent Poe a check for $170. Poe's heavily revised and considerably augmented third volume, *Poems*, was brought out by Elam Bliss in New York the following month in an edition of about five hundred copies. In gratitude it was dedicated to the "United States Corps of Cadets." But this volume was received by them "with a general expression of disgust." The puny, miserably produced booklet, bound in green boards and badly printed on coarse paper, "contained not one of the squibs and satires upon which his reputation at the Academy had been built up."

Poe had published half his poems by 1831. But he had earned nothing from his verse, and the following year began writing stories out of financial necessity. He had made considerable poetic progress—not only in new, but also in revised poems—from 1827 to 1831, as he struggled to free himself from dependence on John Allan and achieve artistic as well as personal maturity. His best poems from the early years, in addition to "Sonnet—To Science," are "Israfel," "The Sleeper," "The Valley of Unrest," "The City in the Sea," and the first "To Helen" (all 1831).

Israfel, according to the *Koran* and Poe's note to that poem, is an angel "whose heart-strings are a lute, and who has the sweetest voice of all God's creatures." In this mysteriously incantatory poem Poe, aspiring to the heights of poetic inspiration, suggests that it would be much more difficult for the melodiously named Israfel, if burdened by mortal constraints, to sing joyously of earthly sorrows. Conversely, mortal poets would sing more beautifully if they enjoyed Israfel's celestial state:

If I could dwell
Where Israfel
  Hath dwelt, and he where I,
He might not sing so wildly well
  A mortal melody,
While a bolder note than this might swell
From my lyre within the sky.

Poe found in Romantic poetry an artistic correlative for his own unhappy life. He believed the most beautiful poetry came from the deepest feelings (the "heart-strings"), but that it was difficult to write in a philistine world that constrained and ignored the poet's art.

"The Sleeper," "The Valley of Unrest," and "The City in the Sea" form a distinct thematic group and represent a self-conscious dramatization of doom. "The Sleeper" is Poe's first expression of his characteristic portrayal of the twilight state between life and death. The grieving lover wishes a peaceful sleep for the beautiful dead woman, and morbidly prays, "Soft may the worms about her creep!" But he also fears that her rest will be disturbed. In "The Valley of Unrest" the imaginary landscape reflects human sadness as nature weeps for the man's loss of innocence. The restlessness of the sad valley is evoked by the magnificently melancholy descriptions of its trees:

Ah, by no wind are stirred those trees
That palpitate like the chill seas
Around the misty Hebrides!,

and of its flowers:

They weep:—from off their delicate stems
Perennial tears descend in gems.

"The City in the Sea"—inspired by accounts in Flavius Josephus's *History of the Jewish Wars* (written in the first century A.D.) of the wicked biblical city of Gomorrah, which lay buried, decomposing, and sinking beneath the hideously serene waters of the Dead Sea—portrays Poe's ghastly apocalyptic vision.

But light from out the lurid sea
Streams up the turrets silently—. . .
Up many and many a marvellous shrine
Whose wreathed friezes intertwine

> The viol, the violet, and the vine. . . .
> While from a proud tower in the town
> Death looks gigantically down.

During schooldays in Richmond Poe, for the first time, had "lov'd alone." He had met Jane Stanard, the mother of his friend Robert, and had given her all the affectionate devotion of a son. Whenever he was unhappy at home he sought her sympathy, and always found comfort and consolation. Deeply despondent when Jane died insane at the age of twenty-eight in April 1824, he often visited her grave with her son.

Jane Stanard, "the first, purely ideal love of my soul," inspired Poe's most beautiful elegiac love lyric. Changing Jane to the more poetic "Helen" and addressing her with his favorite woman's name (variants of which appear in the later "To Helen," in "Eleonora," and in "Lenore"), he compares, in sensual rhythm, her sustaining loveliness, which symbolizes a visionary classical ideal, to ancient triremes that carry an exhausted but victorious Greek warrior home from the fragrant coast of Asia Minor. The poem contains, at the end of the second stanza, two of Poe's finest and most famous lines; and it portrays the older, maternal, unattainable Jane, as he gazed at her from afar, as the statuesque soul who embodies Hellenic perfection:

> Helen, thy beauty is to me
>   Like those Nicéan barks of yore,
> That gently, o'er a perfumed sea,
>   The weary, way-worn wanderer bore
>   To his own native shore.
>
> On desperate seas long wont to roam,
>   Thy hyacinth hair, thy classic face,
> Thy Naiad airs have brought me home
>   To the glory that was Greece,
> And the grandeur that was Rome.
>
> Lo! in yon brilliant window-niche
>   How statue-like I see thee stand,
>   The agate lamp within thy hand!
> Ah, Psyche, from the regions which
>   Are Holy-Land!

Poe had brought out accomplished volumes of verse when he was eighteen and twenty years old. But his *Poems* of 1831, an extremely impressive achievement for a young man of twenty-two, was the best book written, so far, by an American poet.

As Poe entered manhood the unbearable tensions in his divided personality led him to perversely self-destructive behavior, to conflict with authority and to sometimes morbid despair. He would communicate this dark mood to his correspondents in an attempt to elicit their pity and sympathy, and kindly friends would offer encouragement and try to coax him out of his melancholy. But Poe's deep-rooted gloom went far beyond the characteristic melancholy of Byron and Coleridge, and could not, despite encouragement from friends, be readily dismissed. After searching his soul he recorded one of his most personal and profound beliefs. "To be *thoroughly* conversant with man's heart, is to take our final lesson in the iron-clasped volume of Despair." There is no escape to the dream-world in "To One in Paradise" (1834), where—as in "Alone"—ineradicable grief overshadows the present and blights the future:

> Ah, dream too bright to last!
> Ah, starry Hope! that didst arise
> But to be overcast!
> A voice from out the Future cries,
> "On! on!"—but o'er the Past
> (Dim gulf!) my spirit hovering lies
> Mute, motionless, aghast!

In December 1835 Poe celebrated his appointment as editor of the *Southern Literary Messenger* in Richmond by publishing in that journal scenes from his unfinished closet drama *Politian*. Though it was named after an Italian poet and imitated the hackneyed and tedious conventions of Jacobean tragedy, the play in verse was actually based on the notorious incident that had taken place in Frankfort, Kentucky, in 1825. Colonel Solomon Sharp, a politician, had seduced Ann Cook, who bore him a child. When the child died, he broke his promise and refused to marry her. Jereboam Beauchamp, an attorney, though much younger than Ann, sought her hand. She finally agreed to marry him if he promised to kill Sharp before the wedding. Beauchamp challenged him to a duel, but Sharp, being in the wrong, refused to fight. At 2 A.M. on November 7 Beauchamp called Sharp to the door of his house and stabbed him in the heart. After a trial Beauchamp was condemned to death and Ann acquitted of complicity in the crime. Both attempted suicide. Ann died, Beauchamp survived and was hanged on July 7, 1826. This story of revenge also inspired Thomas Holley Chivers's *Conrad and Eudora* (1834) and William Gilmore Simms's *Beauchamp* (1842) as well as Robert Penn Warren's *World Enough and Time* (1950). When reviewing Simms's novel Poe wrote: "No more thrilling, no more romantic tragedy did ever the brain of a poet conceive than was the tragedy of Sharp and Beauchamp."

Unfortunately, Poe know no more about Renaissance Italy than he did about Central Asia at the time of Tamerlane. The wooden hero, archaic style, and melodramatic plot of *Politian* did not do justice to this tragic story. There was a vast, fatal chasm between his theory and practice, and this play did precisely what he would warn against in his own dramatic criticism. "The first thing necessary," Poe later wrote, "is to burn and bury the 'old models,' and to forget, as quickly as possible, that ever a play had been penned. . . . A closet-drama [not meant to be performed on stage] is an anomaly—a paradox—a mere figure of speech. . . . The proof of the *dramatism* is the capacity for representation."

In the play Poe names the characters after historical figures. But he conflates the Italian poet Angelo Poliziano with the English Earl of Leicester (a contemporary of Shakespeare). Leicester, who is visiting Rome, represents Beauchamp. Baldassare Castiglione (the real author of *The Book of the Courtier*) is Sharp. Both men are rivals for the love of Lalage. The pointless repetition of banalities in one brief excerpt suggests the astonishing awfulness of this play:

> *Di Broglio*: I've news for you both. Politian is expected
> Hourly in Rome—Politian, Earl of Leicester!
> We'll have him at the wedding. 'Tis his first visit
> To the imperial city.
> *Alessandra*: What! Politian
> Of Britain, Earl of Leicester?
> *Di Broglio*: The same, my love.
> We'll have him at the wedding.

It is not surprising that a literary friend, after reading the play, advised Poe to abandon tragedy and write farces in the manner of French vaudevilles.

Financial necessity forced Poe to concentrate on fiction, criticism, and editorial jobs from 1835 to 1845. The success of his *Tales* in June

1845 encouraged Wiley & Putnam to bring out his fourth and final volume, *The Raven and Other Poems*, in a similar format in November. This edition, dedicated to Elizabeth Barrett, contained twelve (out of thirty) poems—including "The Haunted Palace," "Dream-Land," and "The Raven"—that he had written since the youthful volume of 1831, and several others that had been extensively revised.

Poe's brief preface was curiously confessional and defensive. He deprecated his own work (as if to forestall hostile critics) and wrote: "I think nothing in this volume of much value to the public, or very creditable to myself." He also justified reprinting his eleven youthful poems—including "Tamerlane" and "Al Aaraaf"—in order to prove the originality of his poetry:

Private reasons—some of which have reference to the sin of plagiarism, and others to the date of Tennyson's first poems—have induced me, after some hesitation, to re-publish these, the crude companions of my earliest boyhood. They are printed *verbatim*—without alteration from the original edition—the date of which is too remote to be judiciously acknowledged.

"The Haunted Palace" first appeared in Poe's finest story, "The Fall of the House of Usher" (1839), and expresses the themes of the story in poetic form. The narrator of this tale arrives for a visit at the urgent request of his boyhood friend Roderick Usher, and is "ushered" into a strange chamber to greet his host. The weirdly eccentric Usher is an irreclaimable eater of opium, which intensifies experience at the same time that it allows him to escape from reality, and suffers excruciatingly "from a morbid acuteness of the senses." After Usher's twin sister Madeline passes through the chamber like an apparition, the narrator learns that she is gradually wasting away with a mysterious disease.

A decadent but singularly talented hermit, Usher improvises long musical dirges, paints phantasmagoric conceptions of long sealed tunnels bathed with ghastly and inappropriate rays, and writes an allegorical poem, "The Haunted Palace," in which a "hideous throng" of "evil things" prophesy his doom. Poe explained that "by the Haunted Palace I mean to imply a mind haunted by phantoms—a disordered brain." To the narrator the poem suggests that Usher is gradually losing his mind:

> And travellers, now, within that valley,
>> Through the encrimsoned windows see
> Vast forms that move fantastically
>> To a discordant melody,
> While, like a ghastly rapid river,
>> Through the pale door
> A hideous throng rush out forever
>> And laugh—but smile no more.

The poet-critic A. E. Housman admired the sensual music of this poem, but felt the allegory in the first four stanzas—before the mood changes to suggest desolation and destruction—was too insistently schematic:

The Haunted Palace is one of Poe's best poems so long as we are content to swim in the sensations it evokes and only vaguely to apprehend the allegory. We are roused to discomfort, at least I am, when we begin to perceive how exact in detail the allegory is; when it dawns upon us that the fair palace door is Roderick Usher's mouth, the pearl and ruby his teeth and lips, the yellow banners his hair, the ramparts plumed and pallid his forehead, and when we are reduced to hoping, for it is no more than a hope, that the wingéd odours have no connexion with hair-oil.

After Usher has recited the premonitory poem, Madeline apparently dies and is prematurely entombed in the family vault. But when she manages to escape and clasps Roderick in a vengeful death-embrace, he finally succumbs to the terrors he had anticipated throughout the story and expressed in the poem. As the narrator flees the house during a violent storm, its fissure widens and he hears the final death cry of Madeline, "My brain reeled as I saw the mighty walls rushing asunder—there was a long tumultuous shouting sound like the voice of a thousand waters—and the deep and dark tarn at my feet closed sullenly and silently over the fragments of the '*House of Usher.*'"

Poe's preoccupation with unnatural and irrational states of consciousness that free the mind from the constraints of reason and allow it to enter the realms of imagination inevitably attracted him to dreams and the unconscious. "Dream-Land" (1844)—a land of death and of nightmare—explores unknown areas of the human mind as the dreamer awakens and describes his vision:

> By a route obscure and lonely,
> Haunted by ill angels only,
> Where an Eidolon [phantom], named Night,
> On a black throne reigns upright,
> I have reached these lands but newly
> From an ultimate dim Thule—
> From a wild weird clime that lieth, sublime,
> Out of Space—out of Time.

In this hypnotic poem the traveler-narrator has escaped from the agonizing time and space of the real world into the disintegrating phantasmagoric landscapes where he encounters spectral "Memories of the Past." But this mysterious though strangely soothing land hides its mournful meaning from him. His sad soul can behold it, like St. Paul in I Corinthians 13:12, only through a darkened glass that obscures his perception but diminishes his pain.

Although Poe's works are unique in the literature of his time, they have striking affinities with two painters who were his contemporaries. Poe and Francisco Goya (1746–1828) both helped define the origins of the modern temper in literature and in art. The nightmares of flying demons in "The Sleep of Reason Produces Monsters" (*Caprichos*, no. 43) foreshadow the morbid opium dreams in "The Fall of the House of Usher" and the monstrous nightmares in "Dream-Land":

> By the dismal tarns and pools
>   Where dwell the Ghouls,—
> By each spot the most unholy—
> In each nook most melancholy,—
> There the traveller meets aghast
> Sheeted Memories of the Past.

Poe's connection with the English visionary painter John Martin (1789–1854) is even more remarkable. In June 1841 Poe wrote a charming fantasy, "The Island of the Fay," to accompany an engraving, by his Philadelphia friend John Sartain, after a painting by John Martin. But his closest affinities are with Martin's gigantic, apocalyptic paintings (as Poe wrote in "Dream-Land") of

> Mountains toppling evermore
> Into seas without a shore;
> Seas that restlessly aspire,
> Surging, unto skies of fire.

Like John Martin, Poe portrays—in works like "The City in the Sea" and *The Narrative of Arthur Gordon Pym*—ancient cities overwhelmed and devastated by cataclysmic floods; fantastic, menacing, fire-swept, blood-soaked landscapes; demonic figures, claustrophobic caverns, eerie turreted castles hanging on the edge of jagged mountains; and monstrous boulders thundering down to the depths of desolate valleys.

Poe had dedicated *The Raven* to Elizabeth Barrett, praised her poetic inspiration and pure art, and wrote that "with the exception of Tennyson's 'Locksley Hall,' I have never read a poem combining so much of the fiercest passion with so much of the most delicate imagination, as [her poem] 'Lady Geraldine's Courtship.' " And he indicated his high opinion of this work by imitating its complicated rhyme and rhythm in "The Raven." In "Lady Geraldine's Courtship" Barrett wrote: "With a murmurous stir uncertain, in the air a purple curtain," and Poe echoed this with: "And the silken, sad, uncertain rustling of each purple curtain."

When "The Raven" appeared as the title poem of Poe's book he prefaced the volume with a gracious tribute, dedicating the volume to her "With the most Enthusiastic Admiration and with the most Sincere Esteem." Acknowledging this tribute in April 1846, Barrett described the unnerving effect "The Raven" had had in England and cunningly praised the rhythm that Poe had stolen from her own poem:

Your "Raven" has produced a sensation, a "fit horror," here in England. Some of my friends are taken by the fear of it and some by the music. I hear of persons haunted by the "Nevermore," and one acquaintance of mine who has the misfortune of possessing a "bust of Pallas" never can bear to look at it in the twilight. I think you would like to be told our great poet, Mr. Browning . . . was struck much by the rhythm of that poem.

Barrett could not quite explain its powerful impact and the conflicting emotions the poem had inspired, and told Browning: "There is poetry in the man, though, now & then seen between the great gaps of bathos. *Politian* will make you laugh—as the 'Raven' made *me* laugh, though with something in it which accounts for the hold it took upon people."

Poe's symbolic raven—which follows the Romantic tradition of Coleridge's albatross, Shelley's skylark, and Keats' nightingale—was influenced not only by Barrett's "Lady Geraldine's Courtship" but also by Grip, the raven, "the embodied spirit of evil," in Dickens's *Barnaby*

Rudge (1841). In one scene of that early novel, which describes the destructive events that took place in London in 1780,

Barnaby has been arrested and imprisoned for his part in the Gordon Riots. Grip, the raven, remains faithful to his master. They sit and brood in the semi-darkness of the cell, and the sunlight filters through the narrow window, casting the shadow of the bars upon the floor, and Grip's shadow, too, when he chooses to sit upon the window ledge. The whole atmosphere of the prison is somber and chilled. The flames of the fiercely burning city sometimes reflect in Grip's eyes.

Poe had pondered for several years the mournful sound of the long *o* in the key word, "Nevermore," as well as the foreboding central symbol in the poem. He wrote "Lenore" in 1831; he named one kind of benign quiet "no more" in "Silence" (1840); he used the word "evermore" in "The Conqueror Worm" (1843); and "nothing more," "evermore," and "word Lenore" finally evolve into "Nevermore" in "The Raven." Poe explained the dramatic action of the poem in "The Philosophy of Composition" (1846):

A raven, having learned by rote the single word "Nevermore," and having escaped from the custody of its owner, is driven at midnight, through the violence of a storm, to seek admission at a window from which a light still gleams—the chamber-window of a student, occupied half in poring over a volume, half in dreaming of a beloved mistress deceased.

An incantatory first-person narrative with cunning internal rhyme, "The Raven" portrays the monomaniacal obsession of a melancholy man who (like Roderick Usher) is hovering on the edge of madness. The marble bust of Pallas on which the bird perches represents intellectual wisdom; the plumed, ill-omened raven stands for intuitive truth. As grief dominates hope, the deranged speaker demands a comforting answer that the monodic bird—"emblematical [Poe said] of *Mournful and Never-ending Remembrance*"—cannot provide. All his questions are answered negatively, all consolation refused. As his self-torturing anguish intensifies, the hopeless suffering narrator is forced to realize that there will be no reunion, after death, with the lost Lenore:

"Prophet!" said I, "thing of evil!—prophet still, if bird or devil!
By that heaven that bends above us—by that God we both adore—
Tell this soul with sorrow laden if, within the distant Aidenn,
It shall clasp a sainted maiden whom the angels name Lenore—

Clasp a rare and radiant maiden whom the angels name Lenore."
Quoth the Raven "Nevermore."

In his fascinating, highly original, but not strictly accurate essay, "The Philosophy of Composition," Poe gave an idealized and rationalized account of how he conceived, composed, and completed his most famous poem. After considering the length, effect to be conveyed, tone, refrain, and character of the crucial, oft-repeated word, he chose "Nevermore" and a nonreasoning creature that was capable of speech, combining "a lover lamenting his deceased mistress and a Raven continuously repeating the word 'Nevermore.' " Ignoring his debt to Elizabeth Barrett, Poe claimed that "nothing ever remotely approaching this [stanzaic] combination has ever been attempted." He then explained the masochistic impulse of the narrator, who questions the raven "half in superstition and half in that species of despair which delights in self-torture. . . . He experiences a phrenzied pleasure in so modeling his questions as to receive from the *expected* 'Nevermore' the most delicious because the most intolerable of sorrow."

Poe was delighted with this poem. When he met the Kentucky poet William Ross Wallace on the streets of New York, he expressed his naive and egoistical enthusiasm.

"Wallace," said Poe, "I have just written the greatest poem that ever was written."
"Have you?" said Wallace. "That is a fine achievement."
"Would you like to hear it?" said Poe.
"Most certainly," said Wallace.
Thereupon Poe began to read the soon-to-be-famous verses in his best way—which . . . was always an impressive and captivating way. When he had finished it he turned to Wallace for his approval of them—when Wallace said: "Poe—they are fine; uncommonly fine."
"Fine?" said Poe, contemptuously. "Is that all you can say for this poem? I tell you it's the greatest poem that was ever written."

"The Raven," which told a concrete, dramatic story, was an immediate sensation, and Poe awoke—like Byron after the publication of *Childe Harold's Pilgrimage*—to find himself famous. Surpassing the popularity of any previous American poem, "The Raven" was reprinted throughout the country and inspired a great number of imitations and parodies. Poe frequently appeared, throughout 1845, as a literary lion in fashionable salons. Poe had written this celebrated poem, he frankly told a friend, to achieve popularity, and had surpassed his wildest expectations: " 'The Raven' has had a great 'run'—but I wrote it for the express purpose of running—just as I did [my story] 'The Gold-Bug.' The bird beat the bug, though, all hollow."

An extremely effective orator, Poe had a soft, mellow voice and a slight Southern accent. He dressed, as always, in mournful raven black and would often be asked to read his famous poem. Adjusting the atmosphere to suit the mood of his work, "he would turn down the lamps till the room was almost dark," one listener recalled, "then standing in the center of the apartment he would recite those wonderful lines in the most melodious of voices. . . . So marvelous was his power as a reader that the auditors would be afraid to draw breath lest the enchanted spell be broken." Elmira Royster Shelton, the Richmond sweetheart who met Poe again at the end of his life, remembered that his recitals could terrify as well as bewitch his audience: "When Edgar read 'The Raven,' he became so wildly excited that he frightened me, and when I remonstrated with him he replied he could not help it—that it set his brain on fire."

Despite his self-deprecating preface and the hostility his severe literary criticism had aroused, *The Raven* received many favorable reviews. His former employer, Nathaniel Willis, called Poe "unquestionably, a man of genius" and urged him to abandon destructive criticism and concentrate on his poetry. Poe's sometime friend, Thomas Dunn English, agreed that Poe's "power to conceive and execute the [poetic] effect, betokens the highest genius," and pronounced him "the first poet of his school." The South Carolina novelist William Gilmore Simms, despite having suffered rough handling in Poe's reviews, expressed his high opinion of Poe's imaginative powers and characterized him as "a fantastic and a mystic—a man of dreamy mood and wandering fancies." Noting the difficulty of Poe's work, Simms said "his scheme of poem requires that his reader shall surrender himself to influences of pure imagination." And the Transcendentalist Margaret Fuller, in an unusually fair-minded review, wrote that Poe's poems "breathe a passionate sadness, relieved sometimes by touches very lovely and tender."

After the publication of *The Raven* Poe seemed to have difficulty composing, and wrote only one or two important poems each year during the final lustrum of his life. A Richmond friend recorded that "Mr.

Poe seems to have been incapable of writing poetry with sustained effort. Impulsive, erratic, he would soon weary of the task and lay aside the sketchy outlines of his poem, to be filled up, touched and retouched."

Many of the poems written during his last years were addressed to specific women—Fanny Osgood, Marie Louise Shew, Helen Whitman, and Annie Richmond. They inspired his romantic feelings and he courted them, assiduously but disastrously, after the death of his wife Virginia from tuberculosis in January 1847. These women were attracted to Poe's creative genius, his prestige and power in the world of letters, his notorious character, and tragic demeanor. As Lady Caroline Lamb said of the reckless Byron, "He was mad, bad, and dangerous to know."

Poe met the first of these ladies, Fanny Osgood, in March 1845. A sentimental Massachusetts poetess of slight talent but great charm, two years younger than Poe and in delicate health, Fanny was a lively, kindly, and attractive woman with two children. "In character she is ardent and sensitive," Poe wrote, with considerable warmth, "a worshipper of beauty; universally admired, respected, and beloved. In person she is about the medium height and slender; complexion usually pale; hair black and glossy; eyes a clear, luminous grey, large, and with great capacity for expression." They soon established a sympathetic rapport, and Poe felt she was the only friend who really understood him.

Poe enhanced and etherealized his courtship by writing three rather slight and self-consciously literary poems to Fanny. Like many other writers, Poe extracted the maximum benefit from each of his poems. The utterly conventional, all-purpose, and continuously recycled "To F____S O____D" was originally written in 1834 for his cousin Elizabeth Herring, addressed the following year to Eliza White (the daughter of the publisher of the *Southern Literary Messenger*) and finally touched up to praise Fanny's virtues: fidelity, gentleness, grace, and beauty. In a similar fashion the cost-efficient "To F_____" was originally addressed in 1835 "To Mary" and retitled ten years later. In this poem—whose lines, "And thus thy memory is to me / Like some enchanted far-off isle," echo the famous opening lines of "To Helen"—the dreams and memory (rather than the reality) of Fanny grant him peace and solace, and allow him to escape from a troubled, stormy world. The third poem, "A Valentine," written on February 14, 1846, was the only one composed expressly for Fanny. In these verses Poe says that her name (revealed by reading the first letter of the first line, the second letter of the second line, and so on), often uttered by poets, is a "synonym for Truth."

Marie Louise Shew—who had devotedly nursed both Virginia and Poe—became, after the death of his wife, an object of Poe's affections. Unlike Fanny Osgood, Mrs. Shew—then married to and later divorced from a New York water cure physician—was an unsophisticated lady with no interest in literature. Plain-looking, kind-hearted, and deeply religious, she generously devoted her life to nursing the poor and the suffering.

Imitating the pattern of his courtship with Fanny, Poe began by writing valentine poems to Marie Louise, and followed them with passionate letters. In his description of an ideal landscape in his story "The Domain of Arnheim" (1847), Poe also paid tribute to Marie Louise by writing of "the sympathy of a woman, not unwomanly, whose loveliness and love enveloped his existence in the purple atmosphere of Paradise." "To M. L. S_____" (February 1847) conventionally praised her soft words, seraphic glance, fervent devotion, and angelic spirit, and expressed gratitude "for the resurrection of deep-buried faith / In Truth—in Virtue—in Humanity." "To [Marie Louise]," published exactly a year later, described the difficulty of expressing his love for her in "unthought-like thoughts that are the souls of thought"; and echoed the words and images of Keats's sonnet "When I Have Fears" in his homage to her:

> for 'tis not feeling,
> This standing motionless upon the golden
> Threshold of the wide-open gate of dreams,
> Gazing, entranced, adown the gorgeous vista,
> And thrilling as I see . . .
> Amid empurpled vapors, far away
> To where the prospect terminates—*thee only*.

While Poe was visiting her home in May 1847 Marie Louise briefly assumed the role of Muse and, when inspiration was flagging, helped him complete the first draft of "The Bells":

He came in and said, "Marie Louise, I have to write a poem. I have no feeling, no sentiment, no inspiration—." I answered we will have supper and I will help you. So after tea had been served in a conservatory with windows open, near a church—I playfully said, here is paper. A Bell (very jolly and sharp) rang at the corner of the street. He said "I so dislike the noise of bells tonight. I cannot write. I have no subject. I am exhausted." So I took his pen and wrote "The Bells. By E. A. Poe," and I mimicked his style, and wrote "the Bells, the little silver Bells, &c. &c." he finishing each line.

"The Bells" (1849), once a popular favorite at public recitations, is a somewhat mechanical, onomatopoeic, forced *tour-de-force*, in which the four resonant stanzas describe both the positive and negative sensations suggested by the various sounds of bells. The silver sledge bells tinkle merrily

> In the icy air of night!
> While the stars that over sprinkle
> All the Heavens, seem to twinkle
> With a crystalline delight.

The melodious golden wedding bells foretell a world of happiness and harmony. The brazen "alarum" bells inspire terror as they clang and clash to announce the danger of a frantic fire:

> In the startled ear of Night
> How they scream out their affright!
> Too much horrified to speak,
> They can only shriek, shriek.

Finally, the climactic, solemn tolling of iron bells, influenced by some unknown demonic power, suggests the groaning and sobbing of mourners in a funeral:

> In the silence of the night
> How we shiver with affright
> At the melancholy meaning of the tone!

Poe's third lady, Helen Whitman, was a poetical widow living in Providence. Romantic in temperament and interested in spiritualism, she shaded her eyes with a fan and existed in the same crepuscular light that pervaded Poe's stories. She clothed her fragile beauty in silken draperies, lace scarves, floating veils, and trailing shawls. And, like one of Poe's fictional invalids, frequently sniffed strong-smelling ether as a stimulant for her weak heart.

Poe's romance with Helen began, as with Fanny, with a sentimental poetic flirtation. After she published "To Edgar A. Poe," the first of sixteen effusive poems addressed to him, he responded with his appropriately vague and ethereal "To Helen." This conventional poem opens with his recollection of the first time he saw (but did not speak to) her, when he was visiting Providence in July 1845 with Fanny Osgood. Helen, on that fateful midnight, was dressed in white and taking a breath of air in her enchanted rose garden:

> Their odorous souls in an ecstatic death—
> Fell on the upturn'd faces of these roses
> That smiled and died in this parterre, enchanted
> By thee, and by the poetry of thy presence.

The divine light in Helen's eyes inspired Poe with the hope of future love; and he wishes "*to be saved* by their bright light, / And purified in their electric fire."

Annie Richmond was a kind and simple lady, more like Marie Louise Shew than Fanny or Helen. Living in Lowell, Massachusetts, she was happily married to a prosperous paper manufacturer and had one daughter. Though she lacked intellectual and literary interests, Poe and Annie's strong mutual attraction (tolerated by her husband) quickly developed into a passionate but platonic romance. Poe seemed to love her more deeply than any of the women he was involved with at the end of his life.

As usual, Poe wrote a story and poems about Annie, and sent her intensely emotional love letters. In "Landor's Cottage" (1849), a description of an ideal house in a charming setting and complement to "The Domain of Arnheim," Annie makes a cameo appearance as Marie Louise had done in the earlier story. Poe emphasizes their immediate and intuitive sympathy as well as her grace, enthusiasm, romantic expression, and gleaming eyes.

Poe's idealized portrait of Annie in the story was followed in March 1849 by his long love-offering, "For Annie." This was the best as well as the most tender and melodious poem that Poe had written to a woman since he had composed the first "To Helen" for Jane Stanard in 1831. "For Annie" describes Poe's recovery from his suicide attempt with an overdose of laudanum the previous November and alludes to the "holy promise" he had extracted from Annie: "that, under all circumstances, you will come to me on my bed of death." It opens with a dramatic, throbbing rhythm that expresses Poe's gratitude for recovery from his dangerous illness:

> Thank heaven! the crisis—
>   The danger is past,
> And the lingering illness
>   Is over at last—
> And the fever called "Living"
>   Is conquered at last. . . .
>
>
> The sickness—the nausea—
>   The pitiless pain—
> Have ceased, with the fever
>   That maddened my brain.

Freed at last from the torments of passion, his tantalized spirit, in a deathlike but fully conscious state, finds repose amidst the myrtle, rose, rosemary, pansies, and rue that symbolize—in the contemporary. "language-of-flowers" books—love, beauty, fidelity, thought, and grace.

Halfway through the poem the focus shifts to the true and beautiful Annie, whom he sees in a dream that suggests their maternal-filial relations. Annie now protects him and shields him from harm:

> She tenderly kissed me,
>   She fondly caressed,
> And then I fell gently
>   To sleep on her breast.

The final stanza, which ends on an unusually positive note, provides a gentle contrast to the suffering suggested in the opening one. Poe attributes his recovery to the devoted care, loyalty, and love that are expressed in the luminous eyes of the kind but passive Annie:

> But my heart it is brighter
>   Than all of the many
> Stars in the sky,
>   For it sparkles with Annie—
> It glows with the light
>   Of the love of my Annie.

T. S. Eliot rightly observed of Poe's memorable rhythm: "Only after you find that it goes on throbbing in your head, do you begin to suspect that perhaps you will never forget it."

Poe, an unreliable and drunken suitor, never managed to marry any of the women he courted toward the end of his life—though he was briefly engaged to two of them. He continued to live with his devoted aunt and mother-in-law, Maria Clemm, and to remain faithful, in his pathological fashion, to the memory of his dead wife. Poe's deeply felt though somewhat morbid and sentimental sonnet, "To My Mother" (1849), is dedicated, not to his real mother Eliza Poe or to his foster mother Frances Allan—who were never entirely satisfactory—but to Maria Clemm. She was also bound to him as the mother of his wife and he addresses her with the passion of a lover:

> Because I felt that, in the Heavens above,
>   The angels, whispering to one another,
> Can find, among the burning terms of love,
>   None so devotional as that of "Mother,"
> Therefore by that dear name I long have called you—
>   You who are more than mother unto me. . . .
> My mother—my own mother, who died early,
>   Was but the mother of myself; but you
> Are mother to the one I love so dearly,
>   And thus are dearer than the mother I knew.

The greatest poem of Poe's last years was "Ulalume" (December 1848), whose title suggests ululation, or wailing. Inspired by the death of Virginia, this tortured tribute was an appropriate memorial to his wife. When Poe read this work aloud to guests before publication, "he remarked that he feared that it might not be intelligible to us, as it was scarcely clear to himself." But its meaning is not quite as obscure as he suggested. The poem concerns the conflict between the soul (symbolized by Psyche), who urges him to remain loyal to the memory of his dead wife, and sensual love (represented by Astarte, the Phoenician moon goddess associated with Venus), who suggests the possibility of a new love.

The rhythmic and hypnotic opening stanza describes the late season and spectral setting (reminiscent of the opening paragraph of "The Fall of the House of Usher"). It alludes to the French operatic composer Daniel François Auber and to Robert Weir—Poe's former teacher—who taught drawing at West Point for more than forty years:

The skies they were ashen and sober;
  The leaves they were crispéd and sere—
  The leaves they were withering and sere:
It was night, in the lonesome October
  Of my most immemorial year:
It was hard by the dim lake of Auber,
  In the misty mid region of Weir:—
It was down by the dank tarn of Auber,
  In the ghoul-haunted woodland of Weir.

Roaming, restless, and alone, in this fantastic landscape, which he compares to Mount Yaanek (or Erebus), a recently discovered volcano in Antarctica, the narrator engages in serious discourse with his Soul. As the night advances he describes—in exquisitely delicate lines—a new moon and associates it with Astarte:

At the end of our path a liquescent
  And nebulous lustre was born,
Out of which a miraculous crescent
  Arose with a duplicate horn.

Then, remembering the satanic torments of "the worm [who] never dies" in Isaiah 66:24, he seeks in the flickering stars the forgetful "Lethean peace of the skies." Though Psyche warns him against those stars, he replies that they are merely part of a dream that promises "Hope and Beauty" and poses no danger to him. After pacifying Psyche he reaches the door of a tomb, which, she tells him, " 'Tis the vault of thy lost Ulalume!" Suddenly, he realizes that he has unconsciously returned to the grave of his beloved on the first anniversary of her death. *She* has shaped his vision of the weird landscape that contains her "dread burden." Realizing that he is still tormented by an inextinguishable grief, he knows he will always remain in her thrall:

Then my heart it grew ashen and sober
  As the leaves that were crispéd and sere—
  As the leaves that were withering and sere—
And I cried— "It was surely October,
  On *this* very night of last year,
  That I journeyed—I journeyed down here!—
  That I brought a dread burden down here—
  On this night, of all nights in the year,

> Ah, what demon has tempted me here?
> Well, I know now, this dim lake of Auber—
>   This misty mid region of Weir:—
> Well I know, now, this dank tarn of Auber—
>   This ghoul-haunted woodland of Weir."

In May 1849 Poe completed his last poem, "Annabel Lee." Though early poems—like "Tamerlane" and "Al Aaraaf"—were allegorical, his later works, especially those about women, became increasingly autobiographical. His favorite theme, grieving for the death of a beautiful woman, had been the subject of "Lenore," "The Sleeper," "To One in Paradise," "The Raven," and "Ulalume," and recurred in "Annabel Lee." But in the last poem, as in the story "Eleonora," young love transcends death and survives in spiritual union.

This mournful dirge on ideal love achieves its effects through subtle variations and balladlike repetition. The slightly archaic, fairy-tale opening describes the idyllic setting:

> It was many and many a year ago
>   In a kingdom by the sea
> That a maiden there lived whom you may know
>   By the name of Annabel Lee;—
> And this maiden she lived with no other thought
>   Than to love and be loved by me.

But even the angels became jealous of this innocent child-love. They sent down a chilling wind that carried Annabel away and "shut her up in a sepulchre / In this kingdom by the sea." Their souls remained linked, however, and the narrator continues to dream of Annabel and to feel her presence in his life. At night he demonstrates his morbid devotion to her memory by sleeping next to her grave:

> And so, all the night-tide, I lie down by the side
> Of my darling—my darling—my life and my bride,
>   In her sepulchre there by the sea—
>   In her tomb by the sounding sea.

Annie Richmond, whose name resembled the heroine's, was the first to see the manuscript of "Annabel Lee." Sarah Anna Lewis (whose poems Poe had been bribed to review), Helen Whitman, and Elmira Shelton (whom he would soon court in Richmond) each believed that *she* was the subject of the poem. But Fanny Osgood was surely right in thinking that this poem—like "The Raven" and "Ulalume"—was really about Virginia Poe. Virginia was the only one of these women he had loved when she was a child, who had loved him exclusively, who had been his bride, who had shivered during a fatal illness and who had died.

The posthumous publication of Poe's last poem was unusually complex. To make certain that it would appear in print, Poe gave a copy to his literary executor, Rufus Griswold, sold the manuscript to the Richmond editor John Thompson to repay a five-dollar debt, and also sold it for publication to *Sartain's Union Magazine*. After Poe's unexpected death, Griswold and Thompson both jumped the gun: the former included it in his obituary of October 9, 1849, the latter in the November issue of his *Southern Literary Messenger*. It did not appear in *Sartain's* until January 1850.

In December 1848, just before his break with Helen Whitman, Poe published in the *Southern Literary Messenger* his most important aesthetic statement, "The Poetic Principle," which he read at his impressive public lecture in Providence that month. Poe defined poetry as "The Rhythmical Creation of Beauty" and illustrated his ideas with excerpts from some of his favorite authors: Moore, Hood, Byron, Shelley, and Tennyson, as well as from Bryant and Longfellow.

Arguing strongly against "epic mania" and prolixity in poetry, Poe declared that

a long poem does not exist. I maintain that the phrase, "a long poem," is simply a flat contradiction in terms. . . .

That degree of excitement which would entitle a poem to be so called at all, cannot be sustained throughout a composition of any great length. After the lapse of half an hour, at the very utmost, it flags—fails—a revulsion ensues— and then the poem is, in effect, and in fact, no longer such . . . [because it has lost] that vital requisite in all works of Art, Unity.

Long works like *Paradise Lost*, Poe maintained, were "merely a series of minor poems." This theory explained the failure of his only long poem, "Al Aaraaf," and his inability to finish any of his other long works: *Politian*, *The Narrative of Arthur Gordon Pym*, and *The Journal of Julius Rodman*.

Poe also criticized poetry written for didactic or moral purposes and expressed his belief in "pure" poetry: "There neither exists nor *can* exist any work more thoroughly dignified—more supremely noble than this very poem—this poem *per se*—this poem which is a poem and nothing more—this poem written solely for the poem's sake." Poe's ideas on brevity, originality, and unity of effect, his emphasis on music, sound, and rhythm, his belief in suggestiveness, strangeness, and melancholy, surely constitute, as Edmund Wilson has observed, "the most remarkable body of criticism ever produced in the United States."

Poe's personal and poetic reputation suffered terribly because of Rufus Griswold's malignant obituary of 1849 and memoir of 1850. It did not begin to recover in America until 1875, when Sara Sigourney Rice organized the memorial ceremony by soliciting statements about Poe's work from eminent writers in America and abroad. She then included these letters in her volume of reminiscences and speeches. Words of praise arrived not only from Bryant, Whittier, Longfellow, and Holmes, but also from Tennyson and Swinburne. Rice's volume was the first opportunity for Americans to see how highly Poe was regarded in Europe.

Tennyson, whose work Poe had admired, reciprocated his feelings and generously called him "the most original genius that America has produced," one "not unworthy to stand beside Catullus, the most melodious of the Latins, and Heine, the most tuneful of the Germans." Swinburne took care to emphasize the best part of Poe's uneven work and praised "the special quality of his strong and delicate genius, so sure of aim and faultless of touch in all the better and finer part of work he has left us."

The English poets who followed Swinburne in the Decadent, Aesthetic, and *fin-de-siècle* tradition—Dowson and Wilde—emphasized the beauty of Poe's lyrics and (unlike Emerson and Whitman) were not concerned with the deliberate absence of "moral principle." Dowson said the euphonious "The viol, the violet, and the vine" from "The City in the Sea" was his favorite line of poetry. Wilde also praised Poe as "this marvellous lord of rhythmic expression."

The Pre-Raphaelite Brotherhood, a group of painters who first came together in 1848, included Poe in their list of "immortals," which, they said, constituted "the whole of their creed." They kept his reputation alive in the dark days between his death and the memorial ceremony in 1875. The poet and painter Rossetti, who dominated the group, mentioned near the end of his life that one of his major poems, "The

Blessed Damozel" (1847), written when he was only eighteen, had been influenced by Poe's "The Raven": "I saw that Poe had done the utmost it was possible to do with the grief of the lover on earth, and so I determined to reverse this condition, and give utterance to the yearning of the loved one in heaven."

Poe was also important to Victorian authors as a theorist of poetry. Walter Pater, whose aesthetic ideas influenced many late nineteenth-century writers, took over Poe's concept, expressed in his early "Letter to B_____," that music—which produced pleasurable sensations and stirred men's deepest feelings—intensified the effect of poetry. Poe believed that "music is an *essential*, since the comprehension of sweet sound is our most indefinite conception. Music, when combined with a pleasurable idea, is poetry." Following Poe's emphasis, Pater exalted music as the most abstract and therefore the purest art. In *Appreciations* (1889) he called music "the ideal of all art whatever, precisely because in music it is impossible to distinguish the form from the substance, the subject from the expression."

It took one hundred years for Poe's poetic reputation to be fully established in America. In 1949 Eliot, overcoming his initial reservations, admitted that "by trying to look at Poe through the eyes of Baudelaire, Mallarmé and Valéry, I became more thoroughly convinced of his importance, of the importance of his *work* as a whole." Eliot's essay was followed by praise from three leading poets of the next generation. "Our Cousin, Mr. Poe," 1949, by Allen Tate (who, like Baudelaire, had the same domelike forehead as Poe), the favorable introduction to Poe's works in 1950 by W. H. Auden (who had by then settled in America), and "The House of Poe," 1959, by Richard Wilbur (who would write a brilliant series of essays about him).

Poe's sometime employer George Graham said that "literature to him was religion; and he, its high-priest." It was this aspect of Poe that most appealed to the French. He was the catalyst who inspired the high art of Symbolist poetry, which (like most of Poe's verse) did not narrate events but described psychological states. Like Poe in "The Poetic Principle," the French Symbolists believed that poetry should create beauty and be "written solely for the poem's sake." It should convey a sense of mystery, and suggest a superior—even divine—reality.

Poe was praised by the Goncourt brothers, by Stéphane Mallarmé and Paul Valéry, by Paul Claudel and André Gide. He also had a profound influence on Charles Baudelaire's *My Heart Laid Bare* and on poems like

"To She Who Is Too Gay," "The Living Flame," "Spleen," "Voyage to Cythera," and "The Seven Old Men," in *The Flowers of Evil* (1857), as well as on Arthur Rimbaud's use of synesthesia in his sonnet "Vowels" (1871) and the "unveiling of mysteries" in *A Season in Hell* (1873).

Neither Poe's mannered Latinate style nor his highly idiosyncratic content became a *direct* model for subsequent poetry (as Pound said: "no one who has tried to write like Poe . . . has done anything good"). Yet his extensive influence on later writers has been quite out of proportion to the extremely uneven quality of his hundred poems. Though Poe has always appealed to popular taste, his originality and imagination have also had a considerable impact on the most advanced thinkers and more serious writers. Poe has overcome his notorious personal reputation (which today makes him interesting rather than repulsive), survived the vicissitudes of taste during the last hundred and fifty years, and remains our contemporary because he has always appealed to basic human feelings and expressed universal themes common to all people in all languages: dreams, love, loss; grief, mourning, alienation; terror and insanity, disease and death.

Jeffrey Meyers

Further Reading

Auden, W. H. "Edgar Allan Poe." In Edward Mendelson, ed., *Forewords and Afterwords*, pp. 209–220. New York: Random House, 1974.

Davidson, Edward. *Poe: A Critical Study*. Cambridge: Harvard University Press, 1957.

Eliot, T. S. "From Poe to Valéry." In T. S. Eliot, *To Criticize the Critic*, pp. 27–42. New York: Harcourt Brace, 1965.

Hoffman, Daniel. *Poe Poe Poe Poe Poe Poe Poe*. Garden City, N.Y.: Doubleday, 1972.

Mabbott, Thomas Ollive, ed. *The Poems of Edgar Allan Poe*. Cambridge: Harvard University Press, 1969.

Meyers, Jeffrey. *Edgar Allan Poe: His Life and Legacy*. New York: Scribner's, 1992.

Stovall, Floyd. *Edgar Poe the Poet*. Charlottesville: University of Virginia Press, 1969.

Tate, Allan. "The Poetry of Edgar Allan Poe" [1968]. In Allan Tate, *Memories and Essays*, pp. 115–127. London: Carcanet, 1976.

Wilbur, Richard. "Introduction." In Richard Wilbur, *Poe*, pp. 7–39. New York: Dell, 1959.

Wilbur, Richard. "Poe." In Perry Miller, ed., *Major Writers of America*, pp. 369–398. New York: Harcourt Brace, 1962.

Lowell, Teasdale, Wylie, Millay, and Bogan

Passionate expression of emotion, revelation of personal sensibility, apparent delicacy overlaying sensuality and self-assertion, musicality created by diction and cadence, a vigorous grace of form: these qualities are characteristic of much work by a succession of American women poets. This tradition reached a peak in the second and third decades of the twentieth century, when such poets as Sara Teasdale (1884–1933), Elinor Wylie (1885–1928), and Edna St. Vincent Millay (1892–1950) enjoyed popular favor, flourishing careers, and critical praise.

The reasons for the broad appeal of their musical and moving poems are apparent on first reading. The fascinating complexities beneath polished surfaces are not. Through the 1940s American students continued to read poems by these women; some of their work maintained a quiet popularity in the years that followed. Yet by mid-century all three—like other successful female poets of their era—had fallen into critical disregard.

A new assessment of such disregard, and of the poetry itself, has begun. Understanding the value of these poets' work, and the reasons behind the changing estimations of that value, restores to us a fuller picture of a vital era in American poetry. It can also offer us a new avenue into work by other American poets, including not only Amy Lowell (1874–1925) and Louise Bogan (1897–1970) but also such neglected writers as Adelaide Crapsey (1878–1914), Anne Spencer (1882–1975), Georgia Douglas Johnson (1886–1966), Genevieve

Taggard (1894–1948), Eunice Tietjens (1884–1944), and H.D. (Hilda Doolittle, 1886–1961).

For half a century Teasdale, Wylie, and Millay have generally been ignored or treated as embarrassing mistakes in vulgar taste. Lowell is often presented as an interesting, somewhat comic, figure in literary sociology, but hardly someone to be taken seriously as a poet. Bogan earned respect for her work as a critic as well as prizes for her poetry, yet all too frequently she too has been passed over or short-changed or praised in terms that distort her poetic achievement.

What has caused this? A study of anthologies of twentieth-century verse suggests that the changes in critical appraisal do have some correlation with the gender of the poets—and of those who do the selecting. Important anthologies edited by women and published in multiple editions from the mid-teens to the mid-thirties (such as Margery Gordon and Marie B. King's *Verse of Our Day*, or Harriet Monroe and Alice Crobin Henderson's *The New Poetry*, or Jesse Belle Rittenhouse's three collections of "modern verse") contain much greater ratios of female poets to male than do present-day anthologies, edited by men, that cover the same period.

But gender alone does not explain the situation. Some poetry by women was accorded a place in the canon. The marvelously dry, and ostensibly self-deprecatory, syllabic verse of Marianne Moore (1887–1972) evidently did not threaten critics in the antifeminist period in American literary scholarship that took hold during the thirties and gained strength after World War II. Even Louise Bogan, whose work derived creative energy from her complex (and sometimes inhibiting) relationship with the female lyrical tradition, was rather one-sidedly praised by her friend Theodore Roethke for freedom from the "embroidering," "lyric . . . posturing," "lamenting the lot of the woman," and "caterwauling" of other women poets. An appearance of neutered chastity, of restraint in language and content was, it seems, acceptable in ways that stirring self-expression and musicality were not.

Consciously avant-garde female poets of the early twentieth century have been neglected too, but for different reasons than more lyrical writers. In the poetry of Gertrude Stein (1874–1946), Mina Loy (1882–1966), and Laura Riding Jackson (1901–1991) the reader finds difficult experimental language, conspicuous erudition, and profound displays of intellectual force. Loy explored epistemological, metaphysical, and aesthetic issues, rejecting traditional concepts of femininity through a rigorous and unsentimental analysis of female experience and consciousness in patriarchial culture; Stein and Riding Jackson did the same through brilliant complexities of thought and linguistic innovation. Their avant-garde qualities deprived the three of a broad popular audience, but at least they could not belittled in terms suggesting a shallow girlishness.

Yet just as the sly subversions and covert sexuality of Moore's poetry have recently been brought to light, so the value of Stein's, Loy's, and Riding Jackson's work is overcoming critical evasion and sloth. No longer can the poetry of early twentieth-century American women be limited to one or two representatives accorded a quiet niche within an androcentric hierarchy, *if* the work seems inhibited rather than passionate, *if* it does not boldly claim a place in the grand traditions of English lyric or philosophical verse, *if* it eschews heightened sound and assertive rhythms, and *if* it does not call attention to such disruptive phenomena as female artistic creativity and female desire. Recent critical and biographical studies such as Jean Gould's and Richard Benvenuto's on Lowell, William Drake's and Carol Schoen's on Teasdale, Judith Farr's on Wylie, and a growing body of work on Millay and Bogan reveal the increasing interest in some of these women and their work.

The foundations for the current reassessment were, in fact, laid in 1923, just as the golden years were drawing toward an end. In her essay "Two Generations in American Poetry," Amy Lowell tells us that from the late nineteenth century through the first decade of the next American readers of poetry found themselves in "a world of sweet appreciation . . . of caged warblers, which species of gentle music-makers solaced it monthly from the pages of the 'Century' or the 'Atlantic Monthly.' " Then, as life in the United States changed, a poetic revolt began. ("Prosperity is the mother of art," writes the pragmatic Lowell, "no matter how odd such an idea may seem.")

So far, the story is a familiar one, though other critics have found more of interest than Lowell did in such turn-of-the-century lyric poets as Lizette Woodworth Reese (1856–1935) and Louise Imogen Guiney (1861–1920). But observe how Lowell describes the work of the new generation, the generation of Carl Sandburg, Robert Frost, H.D. and other Imagists, Edgar Lee Masters, and (though she does not mention him by name) of Ezra Pound: "this new poetry, whether written by men or women, was in essence masculine, virile, very much alive. Where the nineties had warbled, it was prone to shout."

Observe, too, how she describes the literary generation that followed, a breathtaking ten years later. Of the younger poets, the ones "doing the better work" she calls the Lyrists. She praises their skill in versification, and declares expression of emotion to be their "chief stock in trade." The best of them, she tells us, are Elinor Wylie and Edna St. Vincent Millay: "It is, indeed, a feminine movement, and remains such even in the work of its men."

Readers today may find themselves troubled by Lowell's unexamined images of shouting, virile masculinity and musical, emotional femininity, even though the poet-critic was quick to describe Wylie as "one of the most intellectual" of American poets. Yet in understanding the poets and the poetry of the United States from the mid-1910s through the 1930s—as in understanding the history of their changing critical reception—considerations of sexual difference and gender politics are inescapable. Recent scholars, including Sandra M. Gilbert and Susan Gubar, Emily Stipes Watts, Cheryl Walker, Elaine Showalter, William Drake, Jean Gould, Alicia Suskin Ostriker, Gillian Hanscombe and Virginia L. Smyers, and Bonnie Kime Scott have followed Lowell's lead in investigating the various powerful effects of gender on the lives and art of literary women of that era.

One such effect may indeed be "warmth of feeling" or "poetic intensity." In 1951 Louise Bogan stated in her history of twentieth-century American poetry that the line of this quality "moves on unbroken" from the nineteenth century to the twentieth, in the poetry of women. And despite the disdain she had professed in 1935 for the work of "female songbirds" and her "own lyric side," Bogan here shows the shift in attitudes that was to continue through her later years. She argues that restoration of emotional energy to American poetry was grounded in "womanly attributes," was made possible through the liberating social changes effected by feminists, and was "accomplished almost entirely by women poets through methods which proved to be as strong as they seemed delicate."

Those strong and delicately realized methods of their craft, that "poetic intensity," the "line of feeling" running through the work of Lowell, Teasdale, Wylie, Millay, and Bogan herself, commends them to us. They (as well as H.D. and their other poetic sisters and daughters) have had to come to terms with—to don or drape anew—the mantle of their nineteenth-century heritage of female lyricism. Most often, they have done so to very good effect.

Eclectic and wide-ranging in her art, Amy Lowell is usually discussed in terms other than her relationship to the female lyrical tradition. But, in fact, she wrote beautifully of personal passions, and her work is a record of stimulating and successful experimentation with the music of finely wrought words.

Despite the self-doubts engendered in her as a girl who did not fit the standard image of female beauty, when she came into her own in her thirties Lowell took herself quite seriously as an artist and as a professional. She was also generous in her support of other writers, male as well as female, writing in new voices and new modes. In a successful power stuggle with Ezra Pound she advocated a collaborative—rather than his authoritarian—approach to the editing of the second Imagist anthology. In all of this she drew on the nineteenth-century tradition of professional women writers, on a conventionally masculine assertiveness, and on the conventionally feminine ability to connect with others. This same range of traits is evident when she places herself in literary history.

In her long poem "The Sisters," Lowell constructs for herself a literary ancestry that makes evident the complex relationships of women writers in her day to their foremothers. The poem begins by explaining the relative scarcity of women poets: it is a result of the great demands of motherhood and the other "every-day concerns" of women's lives. Here the poet breaks with the many Victorian writers who celebrated female self-sacrifice and a circumscribed domesticity.

Naming Sappho, Elizabeth Barrett Browning, and Emily Dickinson as her "older sisters," Lowell explores their greatness, the differences among them, and "how extraordinarily unlike / Each is to me." Perhaps, in the way of poets, she protests her uniqueness a bit too much, but this is hardly surprising in a time when "we women who write poetry" were considered "a queer lot." The nineteenth-century female lyricists are left out altogether, and Barrett Browning is chided for her failure to write "beyond the movement of pentameters." Dickinson is most highly praised, especially for her "range of mind." But when Lowell commends Sappho for her impassioned amatory poems and "her love-liness of words," the younger writer praises the very qualities that dis-tinguished those of her contemporaries she dubbed the Lyrists.

Lowell's covert affinities with other earlier literary women are made clearer in her perceptive and subversive book-length poem, *A Critical Fable*, published anonymously in 1922. In this witty, antimisogynist description of the contemporary poetic scene (which sent the American literary world into a buzz of curiosity, outrage, and sly delight), she again gives Dickinson top marks, citing her as the one nineteenth-cen-tury American poet—male or female—she can "sincerely admire." But the poem's narrator remains open to a variety of poetic styles, assuring us that current literary taste gives "no prominence / To rhyme or the lack of it."

Here, Lowell jocularly describes herself and her work as "electrical . . . prismatic . . . outrageous . . . erratic / And jarring to some, but to others ecstatic," an innovator and champion of the bold new genera-tion. Yet she admits "there's always a heart / Hid away in her poems for the seeking; impassioned, / Beneath silver surfaces cunningly fash-ioned." Recognizing this is essential to a complete picture of this poet of many voices and modes.

Those carefully made poems of Lowell's express her belief in the fun-damental relationship of poetry and music, a belief that, despite the for-mal innovations of much of her poetry, clearly links her to the lyrical tradition. In 1919 she gave a lecture at Harvard (famous in part for being the first ever given by a woman at that proud institution) entitled "Some Musical Analogies in Modern Poetry." The preface to Lowell's breakthrough second book, *Sword Blades and Poppy Seed* (1914), advo-cates an alternative name for vers libre: "unrhymed cadence," a term that draws deliberately on musicology's vocabulary for expressive rhyth-mic phrasing. "Merely chopping prose lines into lengths does not pro-duce cadence," Lowell writes; "it is constructed upon mathematical and absolute laws of balance and time." This position not only defended free verse against those who criticized it as impoverished or anarchistic, it also allowed her to publish poems in the new mode alongside sonnets and other metrical poems with varied rhyme schemes—as well as experiments in "polyphonic prose," the intense interweaving of vowels, consonants, and accentual patterns that she liked to compare to the many voices of an orchestra.

The groundwork for her careful attention to effects of sound must have been laid by the formal poetry of the nineteenth-century "music-makers" Lowell heard as a child. She grew up listening to the much-admired light verse of her famous cousin James Russell Lowell, and to what her father chose to read aloud: the songlike poems written (often by women) for children, and selections from Longfellow or Frances Ridley Havergal's *Morning Bells*. (Amy Lowell's biographer, S. Foster Damon, describes this anthology as "abominable"—presumably because it contained the sentimental rhymed and metrical verse so popular at the time.)

In a 1917 essay entitled "Poetry as Spoken Art" we learn something of why Lowell did so well at public readings of her work: "Poetry is as much an art to be heard as is music," she writes, and gives very good advice on how to read all kinds of poems aloud. The essay describes the essential linkage of sound and feeling that every lyric poem enacts. It is the "musical quality" of poetry "which differentiates it from prose, and it is this musical quality which bears in it the stress of emotion without which no true poetry can exist."

The last six poems in Lowell's Pulitzer Prize-winning book *What's O'Clock* (which she completed shortly before her death in 1925), exemplify how Lowell found in the sonnet a form still vital, still capable of containing and shaping that "stress of emotion." The sequence is addressed to Eleonora Duse, the acclaimed actress who more than twenty years before had set young Amy afire with the idea of making art from words; it explores themes of beauty's endurance and power to inspire. As suits passionate poems written to this demanding form, metaphors of molding, carving, mirroring, stamping, and lenses made of "twisted glass" mingle with those evoking the heat and dazzle of intense responses to the actress and her art. The second poem of the six announces its musical nature by declaring itself "a letter or a poem—the words are set / To either tune." It then describes the poet (or, in a brilliant ambiguity, the poem itself) as a drop of sealing wax "impressed" with "a fret of workmanship." The result is "like melted ice"—frozen, "precise/ And brittle"; nonetheless, the sonnet suggests, having been so formed, it may show images of great, even divine, power. And of course, such well-made poems enabled the poet to express quite openly her feelings for the one she so admired.

Despite the emotional repression advocated by the androcentric Modernist aesthetic, Lowell's work demonstrates that her self-description in "A Critical Fable" is indeed accurate. One indication is her many striking images of sexuality. Some of these are not gender-marked, or include a phrase, such as "supple-limbed youth" in "White and Green" (1914), that steers the reader toward assuming heterosexual desire. One of her best-known poems, the free-verse dramatic monologue "Patterns" (1916) presents female sexuality as "softness . . . pink and silver" hidden away, waiting to be released by a "heavy-booted," stumbling male lover. Like earlier female writers of the so-called Erotic school such as Ella Wheeler Wilcox (1850–1919), Lowell here objects to the suppression of womanly desire: "passion / Wars against the stiff brocade," against "each button, hook, and lace" of the persona's proper attire.

The poet sometimes—as in the relatively early poems "Clear, with Light Variable Winds," "The Basket," and "The Shadow"—adopted a male point of view when celebrating an idealized female beauty. Over time Lowell increasingly used explicit images of lesbian eroticism; many of her love poems were inspired by her longtime companion, Ada Dwyer Russell. For example, in "Aubade" (written in 1913, about a year and a half after Lowell met Russell, and published after Russell began sharing her home in 1914), the poet writes:

> As I would free the white almond from the green husk
> So would I strip your trappings off,
> Beloved.
> And fingering the smooth and polished kernel
> I should see that in my hands glittered a gem beyond
>   counting.

The 1919 *Pictures of the Floating World* is rich with such images. "The Weather-Cock Points South" describes parting the "leaves" of the beloved, "The smaller ones, / Pleasant to the touch, veined with purple; / The glazed inner leaves," until "you stood up like a white flower." In "A Decade," Lowell writes: "When you came, you were like red wine and honey, / And the taste of you burnt my mouth with its sweetness."

Lowell broke with the previous century by writing, as in these examples, both more far more explicitly and in the Imagist mode. But at the same time she was carrying on the feminine tradition of ardent love poems. The same held true when she helped enrich twentieth-century

American poetry by drawing on the literary heritage of China and Japan. *Fir-Flower Tablets*, the 1921 anthology of renditions of Chinese verse that Lowell produced in conjunction with her old schoolmate, Florence Wheelock Ayscough, acknowledges a distant foremother: its title translates the name of the fine sheets of paper made by the most successful woman poet of Chinese poetry's golden age, Xue Tao, whose best-known work includes superlative amatory verse. Lowell's search for new forms led her to write English haiku. But despite its title and its debt to Japanese models, the late sequence "Twenty-Four Hokku on a Modern Theme" reminds the reader once again of poems by nineteenth-century American women, as its lucid images mingle sorrow, self-abnegation, and self-pity with moving declarations of adoration.

The variety of form, tone, and voice within the full range of Amy Lowell's work makes her impossible to pigeonhole with a single convenient label such as Imagist. She strove to learn from many poets and to forge a new aesthetic for a new age. She also strove to write each poem in whatever manner best suited it; often that manner was rooted in the lyrical and passionate poetry of the immediate past.

Sara Teasdale is sometimes taken to be Amy Lowell's opposite: an unrebellious daughter to nineteenth-century poets in the traditional feminine mode, a sentimental songbird warbling on in the new century. Indeed, in "A Critical Fable," Lowell underlines the negative implications of that metaphor, describing Teasdale as "a little green linnet / Hung up in a cage," and faults her for a range limited to one tone, "the reflex amatorial." Yet Lowell is quick to observe that Teasdale's "poetry succeeds, in spite of fragility, / Because of her very remarkable agility." This "dainty erotic" is characterized as a skillful seducer of her audience, who reveals to the careful reader "a primitive passion so nicely refined," then slips away, thus preserving her essential autonomy. Although Lowell pokes at bit of fun at "Our love-poet, *par excellence*," she also places Teasdale squarely in a line of descent from Lowell's own poetic foremothers, Sappho and Elizabeth Barrett Browning—only "Our Sara is bolder" than the latter, "and feels quite at ease / As herself."

If Lowell's relationship to the female lyric tradition is stronger than most of her critics would have us see, Teasdale's is more complex. Teasdale's work is charged with a deceptive air of spontaneity; it shines with a deceptively clear gloss. But—as her notebooks and letters reveal—the art and effort were in fact considerable. And the poems themselves remind us that the caged bird's song is not always a simple one.

Teasdale achieved striking, subtle effects from metrical variations and from the use of varied line-length. But in the early years of her poetic maturity she tuned her ear to the cadences of vers libre, and learned from the new way of writing a great deal about word choice and the power of the image. From then on she occasionally chose to use a musically adept free verse.

Whatever the form, her lyrics focused on the expression—and examination—of human feeling. In a 1919 essay she states, "The poem is written to free the poet from an emotional burden." Teasdale lived and wrote in a time of enormous social change, and her poetry draws into question notions of the previous era about what was proper in women's lives—especially, emotional lives—and women's art.

In her own life, deftly though she managed it, that questioning was costly. Her biographers show that it was also unconscious or quickly repressed, as Teasdale clung to appearances of the old order in the day of the New Woman. At age twenty-four, living in her parents' home, she professed impatience with women who chose self-realization over self-sacrifice, off-handedly citing the heroine of Ibsen's *A Doll's House*. But even in her earliest collection of poems, Teasdale writes to an exalted ideal lover, "I bid you awake at dawn and discover / I have gone my way and left you free." For all that this departure is said to be a "gift" that breaks the speaker's heart, the slam of the door as Nora leaves the doll's house in search of her own freedom seems to echo—contradictory and poignant—between these lines.

Certainly Teasdale's description of the changing times into which the nineteenth-century British poet Christina Rossetti had been born tells us something about both women: "Such changes are a strain on the individual called upon to undergo them. We cannot live through one of the crucial acts of the drama of civilization without paying for the privilege." Teasdale's often painful relations with men—her tendency toward love relationships unrequited on one side or the other, and her evasive marriage—show something of how she paid.

Teasdale defended sincere, direct self-expression as essential to true poetry—and hid herself behind a variety of complex, conflicting speakers who suggest a complex, conflicted self. "The finest utterance of women's hopes has been on love," she wrote in the introduction for *The Answering Voice* (1917; revised edition, 1928), her anthology of love poems by women. Again and again the speaker of her poems is "crying after love" ("Spring Night," 1915), in lyrics that appear intensely personal. Teasdale's first two books in particular (*Sonnets to Duse and Other Poems*, published privately in 1907, and *Helen of Troy and Other Poems*, 1911) contain many brief, skillful expressions of love-longing. Sometimes a poem appears to accept the limitations assigned to women, as in "The Wanderer":

> But what to me are north and south,
>   And what the lure of many lands,
>   Since you have leaned to catch my hands
> And lay a kiss upon my mouth.

But often passion remains unrealized: "Loves come to-night to all the rest / But not to me." ("But Not to Me").

Even the early poems, however, reveal underlying tensions between sexuality and the chastity required by Victorian morality. The very female image of the "velvet rose" in "A Maiden" evokes an intense, frustrated physical desire:

> And since I am a maiden
>   My love will never know
> That I could kiss him with a mouth
>   More red than roses blow.

The poem "Union Square" points out the cost of traditional feminine modesty, causing a sensation when *Helen of Troy* was published. Though the poem's speaker claims to feel it is "well" that the man she loves "never leaned to hear / The words my heart was calling," she cries out with envy of the streetwalkers who are able (in a naively glorified picture of a sex-worker's life) to "ask for love," as she may not.

A sharp irony is also at work in "The Kiss," with its interrogation of the same romanticized notions she appears to express uncritically elsewhere. After the speaker receives the kiss she hoped for, she becomes "like a stricken bird / That cannot reach the south." What causes this wounding that prevents fulfillment? "His kiss was not so wonderful / as all the dreams I had," we are told—and are left to wonder whether the hurt comes from the lover's inadequacy or from the idealization of romantic love as a woman's one source of happiness. Indeed, the poem leaves open the question of whether the "dreams" were dreams of a romance no real man could live up to or other dreams (like those of

"The Wanderer," who in fact had "loved the green, bright north, / And . . . the cold, sweet sea") that must now be given up.

Many poems in *Rivers to the Sea* (1915) posit the conflict between romance and self quite distinctly. "I Am Not Yours" is sometimes read as an example of the desire women were expected to have, to be "lost" in love. In fact, the poem quite subversively asserts an individuality that continues despite that well-learned longing: "Yet I am I, who long to be / Lost as a light is lost in light."

The title of another poem casts the struggle in disguised terms, "New Love and Old." But the true tension emerges at the end, when the love now set aside is asked, "Shall I be faithless to myself / Or to you?" The answer to this dilemma could be almost flippant, in a tone more usually associated with Millay, or even Dorothy Parker (1893–1967); in "Song," a lover is given distinct demands:

> You must love me gladly
>   Soul and body too,
> Or else find a new love,
>   And good-bye to you.

Sometimes, in a more conventional manner, the resolution to the conflict between vulnerability and independence lies in death, as in the beautiful lyric, "I Shall Not Care."

Teasdale's career was to explore this crucial tension many times, moving more and more often to the side of the self. "The Crystal Gazer" (in *Dark of the Moon*, 1926) expresses the intent to "take my scattered selves and make them one." And the first poem in the same book, "On the Sussex Downs," locates the source of poetic creativity quite clearly: "It was not you, though you were near. . . . It was myself that sang in me."

The final section of *Flame and Shadow* (1920) is titled "Songs for Myself." Although its first poem, "The Tree," begins, "Oh to be free of myself," and although those following pick up the growing themes of age, disillusionment, and mortality, "Song Making" tells us that the poet "had to take my own cries / And thread them into a song"—even though "the debt is terrible / That must be paid." Teasdale never stopped making a personal and passionate art, however painful the process.

One alternative to the "terrible" price of self-awareness achieved through self-expression is silence, an alternative many women have chosen. Teasdale examines this cultural expectation in a number of poems. In "From the Sea" (1915), a woman addresses a man she adores, saying, "praise me for this, / That in some strange way I was strong enough / To keep my love unuttered." Yet her first knowledge of her unattainable beloved came from the speaking-out of poetry: "all my singing had prefigured you." "Night Song at Amalfi" (1915) more distinctly undermines the ideal of feminine reticence:

> Oh, I could give him weeping,
>   Or I could give him song—
> But how can I give silence
>   My whole life long?

"What Do I Care" (1920) seems, however, to repudiate the effort to assert individuality through the lyrical expression of emotion. Yet it does not choose self-effacement; it speaks of the greater strength of the mind, which is "a flint and a fire . . . proud and strong," while the poet's songs are only "a fragrance" and "do not show me at all": the last line states, "It is my heart that makes my songs, not I." But of course, in a rich and thought-provoking paradox, all this is set forth in the form of a song.

The idea of silence did attract Teasdale. She wrote (in "Those Who Love," 1926) of romantic heroines like Guinevere and Iseult, "Those who love the most, / Do not talk of their love." Even her Sappho asserts (in Teasdale's 1915 poem "Sappho") that she seeks at her life's end autonomy in a rest from making poetry: "I will not be a reed to hold the sound / Of whatsoever breath the gods may blow, / Turning my torment into music for them." Again, the reader discovers a paradox, for of course this refusal is expressed in seven pages of powerful blank verse. And what the world knows of Sappho it knows from her poetry. An earlier poem to the Greek poet's daughter, "Cleis" (1911), reminds us that Cleis, too, was preserved in a poem. Teasdale knew the same would be true of her; "Refuge" (1917) is but one of many houses "made of shining words, to be / My fragile immortality."

Teasdale continued to consider, in poetry, the value of keeping still. By 1926, when *Dark of the Moon* was published, Teasdale could write, "I have less need now than when I was young / To share myself with every comer / Or shape my thoughts into words with my tongue" ("The Solitary"). In her last book, *Strange Victory* (1933), Teasdale was to assert in one poem ("Age") that silence is appropriate to "the sad wisdom of age."

Teasdale's poetry ultimately subverted nineteenth-century ideas of feminine fulfillment in romantic love. The young dreamer of the early poems came to learn that "the heart asks more than life can give" ("Moonlight," 1920). A few years later she advised, "Take love when love is given, / But never think to find it / A sure escape from sorrow" ("Day's Ending," 1926). Yet in the book she finished shortly before her death, *Strange Victory*, Teasdale indicates that some sort of comfort is possible. "Last Prelude" suggests that the longed-for release from painful separateness that romantic love did not provide could come in the upward rush of "melody," in poetic inspiration. And in "Secret Treasure" the poet declares the value both of lyrical art and of autonomy within the mind, telling us that even when no poems took shape in actual words, she found "unencumbered loveliness" in "a hidden music in my brain."

Elinor Wylie, like Teasdale, found a balm in the making of art and in the life of the mind. She too was well aware of the dangers to a woman in her society who expressed her passions, in life as well as poetry. And she too carried on nineteenth-century traditions of feminine lyricism; her strong, supple verse made skillful use of rhyme and metrical variation as it dealt with emotions made problematic by pressures toward silence and inhibition.

But unlike her contemporary, Wylie broke the rules of conventional propriety. She left her mentally ill first husband (and her young son) to live with Horace Wylie, the married man who would become her second husband only after years of social censure. Her relationship with the writer William Rose Benét was openly acknowledged well before she divorced Horace and married Benét. In the last two years of her life Wylie devoted much of her emotional—and artistic—energy to a married Englishman who avoided a sexual involvement. Her poem "Silver Bells and Cockle Shells," first published fifteen years after her death in *Last Poems of Elinor Wylie* (1943), asks whether she fled from each of the three marriages for love of flight itself, or because each time there was "something" she had to "flee to find."

Wylie valued self-fulfillment over the dictates of society, but she knew the cost of doing so. Her first book of poems (*Incidental Numbers*, privately printed in 1911) includes a poem on "Eve in Heaven" dated four months after Elinor and Horace ran off together. Shunned by angels, scorned by saints, and decried by the damned for her sin of sexual love, Eve does not flinch but smiles. She pities the Virgin Mary who "was never there . . . poor soul!"

Wylie wrote of hard-won strength. In "Let No Charitable Hope" (*Black Armour*, 1923), we are told:

> I was, being human, born alone;
> I am, being woman, hard beset;
> I live by squeezing from a stone
> The little nourishment I get.

Solitary and beleaguered by restrictions placed upon her gender, this speaker takes what she needs from life. The poem closes with another wry and fearless smile.

On the verge of adulthood, however, Wylie chose to conform. The loving memoir written by her younger sister, Nancy Hoyt, tells us that in her late teens the poet "was passionately interested in her school work," preferring study to parties and flirtation; her teachers "wished her to become a college graduate, or even a lady professor." Instead, young Elinor entered the round of dances and dressmakers prescribed for a debutante. In doing so, she chose a strategy that was to become the subject and the manner of much of her art: she chose the protection of artifice, and hid her true self away. Nancy Hoyt reports that the glittering dresses Wylie favored later were, to her, "coats of mail, armor against the world when she would put them on."

Beautiful constructs and artful facades made fine hiding-places for this vulnerable female poet. "You would shoot nightingales," Wylie wrote to Benét before their marriage. "Only of course they are clever about hiding" (from an unpublished letter cited by William Drake in *The First Wave*). In a late poem "To a Lady's Countenance" (*Angels and Earthly Creatures*, 1929), Wylie writes of a face as coolly alluring as her own, calling it a "silly mask." Wylie was famous for her elegant beauty—and frowned upon for the pride she took in it. Yet the countenance, "arranged with coquetry and grace," is said to be a "veil concealing sorrow's face."

Despite the eagerly circulated stories about Wylie's love of the spotlight, she was quite capable of criticizing herself. A poem first published anonymously in the *New Yorker* ("Portrait in Black Paint, with a Very Sparing Use of Whitewash") pokes fun at her own pretensions, including the "false impression that she's pretty." Light though the poem is, it appears heartfelt when it articulates the conflict between developing an appealing appearance and developing the intellect: "Her mind might bloom, she might reform the world / In those lost hours while her hair is curled." As the English novelist Edith Oliver remembered Wylie, "She loved beauty . . . created it;—in her person and her surroundings, as well as her writing. It was, in a sense, the passion of her life."

Or perhaps Wylie found protection from passion in a chill, polished presence. "Firth of Forth," a ballad left unfinished at her death, describes a brave and regal woman, whose posture and auburn hair suggest Wylie's own:

> O she was fair, or fair enough,
> Her body was straight as a new-cut lance;
> Her heart was armoured by the stuff
> That's iron to mischance.

Feeling is dangerous: Wylie does not excise it from her work, as androcentric Modernist poetic orthodoxy would have had her do, but she proclaims that truth. "From the Wall" advises, "Woman, be steel against loving, enfold and defend you, / . . . Lock up your heart like a jewel . . . / be iron, be stone." The poem, first published in 1943, was written during the time she was leaving her second husband for William Benét; Benét described it as "bitterly realistic."

As Cheryl Walker has pointed out, eighteenth- and nineteenth-century American women often expressed in their poetry a sense that sex was something brutish, to be transcended in favor of the purer passions of artistic sensibility. Wylie responded similarly to the vulnerability accompanying sexual love. Her first commercially published book, *Nets to Catch the Wind* (1921), begins with a poem on "Beauty": it is "neither good nor bad, / But innocent and wild!" Yet she casts her own celebration of beauty in terms of conflicts over womanly erotic feeling expressed by other women poets; beauty is depicted as female, it "consumes her like a curse" to be called "wicked" (as Wylie was), and "too much" love kills her "who had / the hard heart" of a prepubescent child.

Wylie's physical experiences with men evidently were of a "violence of lust." In another posthumously published poem, "The Persian Kitten" lies down between two lovers in bed, enforcing restraint as it separates them "like a sword." *Trivial Breath* (1928) includes a "Confession of Faith": as the speaker lies "alone / By the beloved one," she tries to "erect defence / Against love's violence"; a lover cannot be a friend. In

"The Puritan's Ballad," a woman tells how she feared the inhuman and "dreadful" strength of a young man's arms, and how when the couple yielded to desire, "We were no longer friend and friend, / But only lover and lover." The solution offered a few pages later is to "retreat" emotionally from physical love: the poem "Where, O Where?" ends, "each night I hide / In your bed, at your side." Yet Wylie evidently took no pride in whatever led her (in the words of the first of the three "Subversive Sonnets" published after her death) "to keep myself unto myself/ To lock the door," declaring her refusal of her lovers not "holy chastity" but "mere . . . old-maidishness."

The body, then, was for Wylie a source of unhappiness. *Black Armour* opens with a poem, "Full Moon," in which the self is a spirit caged inside the body, and feels "the clean bones crying in the flesh." A few pages later, "Epitaph" describes a woman made more beautiful "in coldest crucibles of pain," something about which Wylie's intense headaches taught her a great deal. This woman is purified, made more beautiful and—interestingly—"more desired" by her agonies, but her end lies in the grave. Wylie's popular "Hymn to Earth" (1929) uses elevated language, refined thought, and powerful images to make new the old knowledge that the body is "clay" and "dust." "Chimera Sleeping" in the same volume reminds us, however, that "beauty's pure pathetic shape" is born of mortality; it is "the honey breath / Issuing from the jaws of death." This strange creature of the imagination, the chimera, with its "cold transparent flesh," has both gained and lost in its refinement away from "fear and grief" and "love."

Wylie often sought a solution to the problems attendant upon life in the body by attempting to move beyond the realm of the senses. Her poems tell us she is a "Puritan" who favors "Bare hills, cold silver . . . /. . . skies . . . snowy gray / . . . And sleepy winter" ("Wild Peaches"). Images of coldness and colorlessness pervade her work, including such well-known lyrics as "Velvet Shoes" and "Silver Filigree" (all 1921). A poem that appeared in *Poetry* magazine seven months before she died reminds us of the social pressures that encouraged this self-presentation. Addressing "The Heart Upon the Sleeve," the poet says, "They take you for . . . a stain / Of vanity and pride," when in fact her sleeve also bears "invisible" drops of tearlike "transparent blood": to lose the red of passion is to be protected by disguise.

It is not only a negative view of sexuality that links Wylie to the association of love and anguish in the work of nineteenth-century female lyricists. Her great sonnet sequence "One Person" (in *Angels and Earthly Creatures*) beautifully explores—as Teasdale also did—the emotions surrounding a love that must remain unexpressed. The sequence praises the man Wylie loved late in her life, using the self-deprecatory posture traditional both to the sonnets of the Renaissance and to the love poems of later women.

Yet Wylie's art and thought are grounded in something more profound than an unawakened sexuality or an unexamined parroting of conventional feminine attitudes toward romance. Just as she learned from—and grew beyond—the turn-of-the-century Aestheticist movement, so she expresses in the "One Person" sequence the philosophical culmination of her long concern with the body's painful failures and the possibility of intellectual and spiritual communion. The poems exemplify what Louise Bogan was to call (in a 1947 essay) "Wylie's ability to fuse thought and passion into the most admirable and complex forms." They acknowledge the limitations set as much by time or her own psyche as by her beloved's refusal to enter into an adulterous affair. Sonnet 6 tells him:

> I have believed me obdurante and blind
> To those sharp ecstasies the pulses give:
> The clever body five times sensitive
> I never have discovered to be kind
> As the poor soul . . .

In fact, the sestet goes on to declare that the "miracle" of the speaker's love is ultimately beyond the ken of soul and body both.

The resolution of many tensions—eros and transcendence, sad frustration and triumphant contentment, mortality and love that outlasts death—comes in the splendid final poem. It speaks of a desire beyond denial or the grievous knowledge of human "doom," ending "let us . . . touch each other's hands, and turn / Upon a bed of juniper and fern" (Sonnet 18). In the mingling of sharp fragrant evergreens and feathery short-lived ferns, the spiritual and the sensuous conjoin; the poet achieves an acceptance of physicality, at least in the realm of the imagination.

This delicate, powerful coming-to-terms is not unprecedented in Wylie's work. It is the body that makes language, and so makes the poetry through which spirit and feeling can be articulated:

The only engine which can fabricate
Language from spirit is the heart of each:
Industrious blood has braided into speech
The airy filiments of love and hate.
            ("A Red Carpet for Shelley, II" 1928)

She who devoted herself to creating art as "pure" and "far removed" from earth as the moon reminds us in "To a Book" (1928) that the "roots" of poetry are nonetheless sunk in "this inferior substance" that gave it birth—flesh not only mortal but undeniably female: "you are mine, and I was worthy / To suckle you, as very woman."

In the end the poet must be true to herself and her own "nature." The "Love Song" that follows the sonnet sequence in *Angels and Earthly Creatures* asserts this: she bids farewell to her beloved and to her "weeping," proclaiming, "I set that archangel / The depths of heaven above you." This exalted figure can only be the long-dead man Wylie identified with and greatly loved: Percy Bysshe Shelley. Figures based on Shelley are central to two of her four novels, and to a fifth, left uncompleted at her death. The scholarly side repressed in Wylie's youth reemerged when she reached maturity and undertook a serious, wideranging study of Shelley's life and works. In this disembodied Romantic poet Wylie found a passion that did not endanger her autonomy but gave her inspiration and sustained her lyric strength

Wylie's early death was a great personal loss for Edna St. Vincent Millay, one that inspired moving elegiac poems. A gifted female lyricist had been "shaken from the bough, and the pure song half-way through" ("Over the Hollow Land," 1939). Like Wylie, Millay made poetry for the modern age in new renditions of time-honored modes and dared to conduct her personal life by her own rules. After the League of American Penwomen rejected Wylie on the grounds of immoral behavior, Millay wrote to them, "I too am eligible for your disesteem. Strike me too from your lists, and permit me, I beg you, to share with Elinor Wylie a brilliant exile from your fusty province." The disdain for pettymindedness, the proud commitment to her ideals, the generosity of spirit, and the well-honed edge of her words: these are characteristic of Millay.

For Louise Bogan in 1939 Millay's characteristics included "magnanimity of nature" and "a strange mixture of maturity and unresolved youth," including "childish fears of death and . . . charming rebellions against facts." The negative critique, of course, reveals as much about Bogan as about her subject; it is also representative of Millay's fall from high critical regard as a brilliant lyricist with thoroughly modern attitudes toward life and love. Bogan's final assessment, in 1951, is equally telling. Just before praising Wylie's "mature emotional richness," she chides Millay for excessive emotionality. But Bogan ungrudgingly acknowledges Millay's outstanding gift for writing in the lyrical manner of John Keats, praising her best work for cutting "into the center of complicated emotion."

Artful tapestries emerge from these knots of feeling sliced open by Millay's words, as text after text is woven from them and the reader discovers how each poem is made more complex by the varied stances and voices of the others. In assembling a shifting succession of poetic speakers Millay became something more than the literary or emotional quick-change artist some have seen her as. There may be safety, even freedom, for an imperiled self protected by many masks, or the reader may be led to recognize the fluidity of a psychological subject constructed of just such verbal guises.

The high tradition of the English sonnet gave Millay, in the words of one of her most famous poems, a "golden vessel of great song" into which passion could be poured, preserving it within a single shape, and making it possible to take in (1923). This tradition provided her with a gleaming—if not always fashionable—vocabulary of images, syntax, and diction; the poet also used contemporary colloquialisms, enriching her work with deft counterpoints of classicism and modernity in language as in content.

"I can make / Of ten small words a rope to hang the world!" Millay wrote in an early long poem ("Interim," written before the spring of 1912 and published in her first book, *Renascence and Other Poems*, in 1917). This exercise in dramatic blank verse covertly celebrates the young woman's entry into the male-dominated realm of poetry, even as it notes poetry's limitations. It also recognizes a disruptive potential in feeling, asking, "O little words, how can you run so straight / Across the page, beneath the weight you bear?"

The generative tension between restraint and self-expression, so powerful in the work of other nineteenth-and twentieth-century female poets, concerned Millay throughout her life. "I will put Chaos into fourteen lines," she wrote in a poem that appears in the posthumous collection, *Mine the Harvest* (1954). But enjambment undercuts any simplistic concept of mastering energy through artistic form: "and let him thence escape / If he be lucky." This hint that excessive restraint diminishes vitality is underlined when the forced mingling of Chaos and Order is described as a "pious rape" of Chaos by the poet; there is something "not yet understood" in the passion that the form claims to control.

Formal verse is one of many means of self-protection to be found among the methods of Millay's art. As Jane Stanbrough has pointed out (in an essay in *Shakespeare's Sisters*), the poet's frequent images of suffocation, confinement, and victimization—often expressed in gender-specific terms—reveal the risks and damages to women in patriarchal society. Light-hearted celebrations of independence in such famous poems as "Thursday" ("I loved you Wednesday,—yes—but what / Is that to me?," 1920) tell only a part of the tale.

Millay's use of the sonnet links her to a long tradition of masculine views of women and romantic love. She could make capable use of male personae, just as she often wrote of love in the terms of sorrow and longing articulated by nineteenth-century American women. She also (as in the sonnet beginning "Love is not blind," 1923) wrote of love for a female figure from the viewpoint of an "I" not gender-marked; Anne Cheney's 1975 biography discusses Millay's transition in her twenties from a lesbian (or bisexual) orientation to a heterosexual one. It is the variety of perspectives, tones, and moods that allows Millay's poetry to voice complexities of sensibility no single attitude or poetic idiom could catch.

Millay wrote many poems debunking sentimental concepts of women and love. Like the sexual activity of her Greenwich Village days, this allowed her to shatter the code of feminine decorum that caught up Teasdale and Wylie. Some readers see this as a successful defiance, others as an enactment of male-identified values similar to her use of a masculine nickname—"Vincent"—and pronouns; Millay was not the only woman of the Jazz Age to express her new freedoms through her sexuality or by equating autonomy with conventionally masculine traits.

Emily Stipes Watts links Millay's blithe air of sophistication to earlier women such as Frances Sargent Locke Osgood (1811–1850), a successful poet who wrote lines like: "My task must be now, to endure him! / Heighho! but I've caught him at last!" It is not far from Osgood's poem to Millay's "Daphne" (1920), which concludes, "to heel, Apollo!" or from there to such audacious sonnets as "I shall forget you presently, my dear" (1920) or the one ending "I find this frenzy insufficient reason / For conversation when we meet again" (1923).

The situation, however, is hardly one of simple hedonism. The last poem mentioned begins, "I, being born a woman and distressed / by all the needs and notions of my kind," subtly reminding us that desire consists of socially constructed "notions" as well as physiological "needs"; it portrays the body's erotic responses as "the poor treason / Of my stout blood against my staggering brain."

The well-known sonnet sequence *Fatal Interview* (1931) offers many examples of the striking originality of Millay's adept enunciations of conventional—and unconventional—feminine attitudes toward love. "Women have loved before as I love now," number 26 begins. The speaker compares herself to Helen of Troy, Isolde, and other "Heedless and willful" women who gave themselves up to love, despite the price, but she claims that "of all alive / I only in such utter, ancient way / Do suffer love." The old way had a tragic grandeur, she says, but it was self-destructive; women's emotional lives have changed.

Inspired by her affair with the younger poet George Dillon, the sequence treats the nineteenth-century female lyricists' theme of forbidden love. Millay and her husband Eugene Boissevain maintained an ideal of openness to sexual relationships outside marriage, but the second sonnet sets forth powerfully mixed feelings. Desire is as compelling here, and as dangerous to the female speaker, as in any high-pitched amatory poem. Yet she knows "the wound will heal, the fever will abate"—and knows, too, what she's learned from living with a new sexual ethic, that "the scar of this encounter like a sword / Will lie between me and my troubled lord." The reader is left to decide which is swordlike (phallic, painful, distancing), the aftereffects of an extramarital involvement or the lovers' encounter itself.

Millay's realistic views of female experience acknowledged the force of romantic love even as she resisted that "bitter crust." The close of one sonnet from *The Harp-Weaver* (1923) blends a defiant pride with the time-worn idea of painful thralldom to the beloved: "But if I suffer, it is my own affair." A free-verse poem in the same volume firmly if reassuringly asserts the speaker's need for independent action. On her way to "The Concert," she explains:

> Why may you not come with me?—
> You are too much my lover.
> You would put yourself
> Between me and song.

On her return from a disembodied and solitary immersion in the music she will be "a little taller / Than when I went."

Another aspect of this realism was Millay's conscious commitment to feminism and her pleasure in the successes of the suffrage movement and other women poets. Responding to a declaration by the poets Arthur Davison Ficke and Witter Byner that the Transcendentalist vision of her award-winning poem "Renascence" had to be the work of a "brawny male" and not a "sweet young thing," the slightly built twenty-year-old wrote them a letter asking, "Is it that you consider brain and brawn so inseparable?—I have thought otherwise." The arch tone of such early letters modulates to an amused understanding of gender roles in a witty sonnet ("Oh, oh, you will be sorry for that word!" 1923) that responds to a man's condescension with scorn for one so easily manipulated. Since he will not acknowledge their intellectual equality, the speaker will play the role of the coquette, "sweet and crafty, soft and sly"—until she walks out on him. She will act as women have been supposed to, but in fact that acting, and her intellect, put her in control.

Biographers attribute Millay's awareness, and her assurance, to the loving, gynocentric world in which her independent-minded divorced mother raised Edna and her two younger sisters. "You brought me up in the tradition of poetry," Millay wrote her "Dearly Beloved" mother in 1921, "and everything I did you encouraged"; in a posthumously published untitled poem, the poet—worn down by illness, persistent pain, chemical dependency, and grief for the dead—praised Cora Buzzelle Millay's courage as "Rock from New England quarried," and told of her own need for her mother's legacy.

In later years Millay often turned from musical self-expression to write more overtly political poetry—for example, poems for the executed anarchists Nicola Sacco and Bartolomeo Vanzetti, sonnets on the Japanese invasion of Manchuria and the Spanish Civil War, a long closet drama called *Conversation at Midnight* (1937) analyzing economic, political, ethical, and religious questions, and, as World War II developed, much work aimed at molding opinion in the United States, some of which was read over the radio as part of the war effort. Her growing focus on social issues and her increasing expressions of anguish in the face of human flaws, like her expanding poetic exploration of the natural world, have frustrated readers who are charmed—or profoundly moved—by the poems on which Millay established her early reputation. Some critiques of her later work's weakness are deserved, but they arise in part from the breaking of expectations based on Millay's captivating and finely crafted love poems—or on her gender.

Yet Millay's skillful construction of her tapestries of feeling places poems from every decade of her life among the finest in the language. In 1912 an unknown young woman created a literary sensation with "Renascence," expressing a mystical experience in terms derived from the feminine singers of the previous era: "My anguished spirit, like a bird, / Beating against my lips I heard." In 1923 she became the first woman to receive the Pulitzer Prize for poetry. By 1941 she had become the renowned public poet, despite increasing negative responses from the critics, writing, in a high-flown occasional "Invocation to the Muses" unpublished in her lifetime,

> If I address thee in archaic style . . .
> It is that for a little while
> The heart must, oh, indeed must from this angry and
>   outrageous present
> Itself withdraw.

Through all the changes, however, Millay remained the woman who wrote in "The Dragonfly" (1923), "Men behold me . . . Walled in an iron house of silky singing." But the unformed pupa hidden behind lyrical bulwarks transforms within its self-made chrysalis to emerge with "brazen wing," to rise above the seed-filled touch-me-nots and pink flowers of the procreative realm, "Free of these and making a song of them."

Millay's 1920 poem "The Singing-Woman from the Wood's Edge" takes a spirited look at her culture's view of the woman poet as a hybrid oddity. This female music-maker is cheerfully contemptuous of her father, a repressive patriarchal priest who did at least teach her the high language of psalms and classical learning; she sides with her mother, an unrestrained, sensuous creature of nature and weaver of magic webs. The singing-woman cannot imagine herself as anything but what she is, "a prophet and a liar"—in other words, a poet in the mainstream of the Western tradition.

For Louise Bogan, the resolution of what her society defined as a dissonant combination, "woman" and "poet," was not so easy. Her strategies for psychological survival and aesthetic success included a discriminating use of restrictions in the form and content of her poetry. She found in intellectual and verbal rigor a way to assert her artistic gifts, one that conveys a transformed version of the inhibition often required of female poets. The results included compelling, tightly disciplined poems on the disturbing topic of womanly emotionality—metrical and free-verse lyrics that display an unsurpassed sense of the music of the English language.

Biographers point out that Bogan's observations of her parents' turbulent relationships and her mother's extramarital affairs must have taught her early on to distrust unrestrained emotions. Yet young Louise also associated her mother with beauty, talent, and vitality. As late as 1962, in a lecture that carries forward her growing pride in the artistic achievements of women, Bogan counsels that women writers "must not lie . . . whine . . . attitudinize . . . theatricalize . . . nor coarsen their truths." She particularly denounced both "the role of the *femme fatale*" and "little girlishness."

Bogan's striving for a controlled impersonality—untainted by stock feminine poses or sentimental excess—was, of course, grounded in more than the circumstances of her childhood, two difficult marriages, or the painful love affairs of her early twenties. It was a carefully developed aesthetic position, an aspect of male Modernist doctrine that she assimilated and bent to her own purposes. Although the volume of Bogan's work was reduced by her self-imposed limitations, her critical principles enabled her to make enduring art.

Born almost a quarter-century after Lowell, Bogan reached maturity not with, but slightly after, a major feminist efflorescence in politics and literature. In the fall of 1923, when her first volume of poetry appeared, she was featured in *Vanity Fair* as one of the youngest "Distinguished American Women Poets Who Have Made the Lyric Verse Written by Women in America More Interesting Than That of Men." But her association there with Lowell, Millay, Teasdale, Wylie, and other literary woman was a far more positive thing than it came to be for critics in subsequent decades.

The reassertion of dominance by male Modernists (and their critical followers) analyzed by Gilbert and Gubar in *No Man's Land* had much to do with the revolt against the self-expressive poetry of the female lyricists. A similar anxiety may have brought about Bogan's insistence on women's limitations. Perhaps she described herself when she said in 1962, "The blows dealt women by social and religious change were real, and in certain times and places definitely maiming." Her next sentence seems to pick its way through territory mined with psychological peril, asserting that woman is "not the opposite or the 'equal' (or the rival) of man, but man's complement." And women's art, she felt, must accord with what she saw as women's nature.

As Bogan's place in the canon of modern poetry grows more secure, it is important not to forget the effect upon her work of the female lyricist tradition about which she felt such ambivalence. When musical verse with the appearance at least of direct and simple self-expression went out of style during the 1930s, she dissociated herself (in the words of a 1938 essay quoted by Jaqueline Ridgeway) from its potential excesses of "bathos" and "limpness" of form even as she reminded her readers of the "high tension" at work in the best such poems. She also hinted at the role of gender in fashion's swing, noting the "ridicule" and "contempt" being directed toward "Female lyric grief."

In her late teens Bogan read Teasdale, Guiney, Reese, and other women skilled at expressing feeling tempered by highly polished forms—and learned much from them. Yet she needed to differentiate herself. The poem "My Voice Not Being Proud," in her first book (*Body of this Death*, 1923), claims a poetic voice not "like a strong woman's, that cries / Imperiously aloud." The intricate rhyme scheme of the poem reins in every end-word but the headstrong "cries." In fact, however, the voice is certainly strong, and quietly proud.

Like Teasdale and Millay, moreover, Bogan develops the heritage of nineteenth-century women's poetry by voicing a critique of romantic love. In "Knowledge" (1923) she echoes the previous era's association of love and death in terms of present-day disillusionment: "passion warms little / of flesh in the mould." "The Changed Woman" (1923) "relearns" the nineteenth-century lesson that ardor brings wounds—and the twentieth-century lesson that "the wound heals over." But, we're told, this woman will ultimately yield again to the "unwise, heady" and seductive force "ever denied and driven"; readers are invited to reexamine the title with all the skepticism of the new age. "Girl's Song" (1929) similarly unites with the familiar theme of springtime love-sorrow, a modern worldly awareness that "another maiden" will fall for the faithless lover.

Bogan's poetry makes clear the price for women of the old myths of romance—and the new myths of her own Greenwich Village experiments in free love. She expresses compassion for those who have lived by both versions of vulnerability to the passions, even as she wryly reproves their foolishness. "Chanson Un Peu Naive" (1923) releases a radiant scattershot of ironies, aimed at the female experience of sex, at those who intend to escape the near-death it brings (physically, in orgasm or childbirth, as well as emotionally, in betrayal), at those who believe lovers' lies even while they utter them, at those like the young Millay who make the "pretty boast" of liberation, at those who fail to recognize that pain's warning signal may make it one's truest friend, and at those—including of course herself—who fashion poetry from all this.

Nevertheless, formal verse seemed necessary to Bogan to handle risky emotions. A 1948 letter states that the "burden of feeling" (the phrase echoes Teasdale's 1919 essay) is best taken up *"instantly"* by a practiced poetic technique (Bogan's emphasis). In "Single Sonnet" (*Sleeping Fury*, 1937) the poet calls on the "heroic mold" of the poem's structure to "take up, as it were lead or gold / The burden." Feeling is described as a "dreadful mass" that cannot be lifted from its torpor without "Staunch meter"; Ridgeway notes that the typescript of the poem indicates it was written at Cromwell Hall, the sanitarium where Bogan received treatment in 1931.

Bogan's early poem, "Sub Contra" (1923), expresses the tension between upwelling emotion and its containment in poetry. The title suggests that a lyric begins in resonant tones almost beneath the threshold of hearing, building from delicate tremors to "one note rage can understand." The poet invokes sounds rooted in the heart, which rouse the mind—as well as craft, which brings what is "riven" into the harmony of a chord. The poem, however, snaps shut with a warning against excess control. The final rhymed iambic tetrameter couplet plays off against the previous loosely cadenced stresses and subtle echoings (the preceding rhymes have run *abcdefcedbaf*) as it calls for freedom from rigidity—"for every passion's sake."

Thus Bogan carries on her argument against the overwrought thrill her poetic mothers were accused of *and* against the neurotic deadening of sensibility of the backlash. The formal poem without "life" provided by feeling is a lackluster thing, like an artificial "Homunculus" (1937). The homunculus-poem, not engendered in ardent procreation but constructed in a learned alchemist's fleshless flask, "lacks . . . Some kernel of hot endeavor," a hazardous but essential source of bodily—perhaps specifically female—energy. In her pivotal 1947 essay "The Heart and the Lyre" Bogan wrote of the "impoverishment" that would result from an abandonment by women of emotionality "because of contemporary pressures or mistaken self-consciousness." Written after years of analysis and introspection, one of Bogan's rare last poems ("Little Lobelia's Song," 1968) was to recognize a further danger of repression: how speechless rage at abandonment sours into sleeplessness, depression, and tears.

Dangerous though it may seem, then, Bogan joins her foremothers in declaring passion essential to poetry. And she too found an empowerment in the making of verbal music. The title of her "Song for a Slight Voice" (*Dark Summer*, 1929) alludes ironically to the notion of an unassertive songstress, but the speaker warns:

> If ever I render back your heart
> So long to me delight and plunder,
> It will be bound with the firm strings
> That men have built the viol under.

Clearly, the singer, and the energetic rhythms of her song, have considerable ability to control.

Music, born of the emotions and needed as protection from the hurt they can bring, is in Bogan's view something as greatly to be desired as sexual release. "Musician" (*Poems and New Poems*, 1941) uses the rhyme scheme of a modified Shakespearean sonnet on short lines individually modulated to embody meaning through rhythm. An erotic yearning charges the descriptions of the music-maker's hands. But the much-desired plucking of strings—like the relief of poetic inspiration—has been long delayed. In light of the artistic silences of Bogan's later years these warnings seem prophetic.

Studies by Elizabeth Frank and Gloria Bowles, among others, have recently joined the volumes edited by Martha Collins and Ruth Limmer in elucidating Bogan's life and work. Many aspects of her art have received critical notice—her remarkable use of myth, her compelling explorations of the unconscious, her deep concern with mutability and the human condition, her relation to the Romantic as well as the Symbolist and High Modernist aesthetics. Yet no one aspect seems more essential to our understanding of that art than its grounding in the body: the body that pulses, hears, and sings. "The Alchemist" (1923) speaks of how flesh "still / Passionate" and oddly "unmysterious," outlasts all efforts of will and mind to refine it away. "You may have all things from me," a woman says to a lover in "Fifteenth Farewell" (1923), "save my breath." The first of these two intricately crafted Petrarchan sonnets finds in that "slight life in my throat ... / ... Close to my plunging blood," the inbreathing and outflow from which the lyric poem is born. This very physical thing is stronger than heart's pain or the rift between emotions and intellect, the divided "breast and mind."

Bogan seemed intensely aware that her body was a female one. Frustrated when her work was treated by critics in round-up reviews of recent books by women, she struggled with assimilated misogynist attitudes of her times. In a letter written two months before her fortieth birthday the only woman she lists among the nine examples of "oddly assorted authors" she read in her formative years is the British lyric poet Alice Meynell (1847–1922), although in fact there were a number of others. She describes "what I did and what I felt" then as "*sui generis.*" Yet unique though she was, she came to know her parentage—her mothers and her fathers both. Bogan spoke human truths that transcend the channels formed by gender, but she spoke with a profound awareness of gender's molding force on the experience and the expression of those truths.

Jeanne Larsen

Further Reading

Bogan, Louise. *Achievement in American Poetry, 1900–1950.* Chicago: Henry Regnery, 1951.

——— *The Blue Estuaries: Poems, 1923–1968.* New York: Farrar, Straus and Giroux, 1968.

Drake, William. *The First Wave: Women Poets in America, 1915–1945*. New York: Macmillan, 1987.

Lowell, Amy. *Complete Poetical Works of Amy Lowell*. Boston: Houghton Mifflin, 1955.

Millay, Edna St. Vincent. *Collected Poems*. Ed. Norma Millay. New York: Harper and Row, 1956.

Teasdale, Sara. *The Collected Poems of Sara Teasdale*. New York: Macmillan, 1937.

Walker, Cheryl. *Masks Outrageous and Austere: Culture, Psyche, and Persona in Modern American Women Poets*. Bloomington: Indiana University Press, 1991.

———— *The Nightingale's Burden: Women Poets and American Culture Before 1900*. Bloomington: Indiana University Press, 1982.

Watts, Emily Stipes. *The Poetry of American Women from 1632 to 1945*. Austin: University of Texas Press, 1977.

Wylie, Elinor. *Collected Poems of Elinor Wylie*. New York: Knopf, 1932.

———— *Last Poems of Elinor Wylie*. New York: Knopf, 1943.

Women Poets and the Emergence of Modernisn

"I ALWAYS wanted to be historical," Gertrude Stein said, and she always was. She was at the center of the avant-garde art and literary worlds in Paris in the first half of the twentieth century, a friend of Pablo Picasso and Henri Matisse as well as Ernest Hemingway and Sherwood Anderson. Nonetheless, she has not figured prominently in the literary history of poetic Modernism, nor have other women Modernists such as H.D. and Marianne Moore who were equally active in the literary circles of London and New York where they lived. Although these women poets were productive writers, often friends and even editors and reviewers of the so-called High Modernists who have come to dominate accounts of the movement, they themselves have been largely neglected figures in the conventional literary histories, for a variety of reasons.

Chief among the reasons for this exclusion has been the critically generated misperception that Modernism did not develop from the work of the women poets. Stein's radical experimentation has remained unassimilated to the movement, divided, as it has been conventionally, into the two strands of Imagism and Symbolism. Her poetry, growing out of her scientific training and her interest in experimental painting as well as her own experience, ranged in new and different directions toward both exactitude and nonreferentiality, maintaining a constant interest in experimentation. In contrast to the marginal status of Stein, H.D. has been granted such a central position in the short-lived Imagist movement that the full range of her interests has been easily discounted, and her development even within Imagism has been traced largely through the limited view of its first publicist, Ezra Pound. Finally, Marianne Moore's syllabic verse has appeared to be merely idiosyncratic and without any acknowledged influences, although recent examinations of the works of Elizabeth Bishop and Sylvia Plath have begun to correct that impression and to argue for her significance to these poets, at least.

Another reason for excluding these women from literary history, again both effect and cause, is the fact that, until recently, their work was not readily accessible. Much of Stein's poetry was published posthumously in an expensive edition. Marianne Moore's constant revision of her poetry has made it difficult to establish her texts. However, with the publication of the *Selected Writings of Gertrude Stein* (1962), *The Yale Gertrude Stein* (1980), *H.D.: Collected Poems: 1912–1944* (1983), and *The Complete Poems of Marianne Moore* (1967), the work of these poets is now more easily obtainable, although even now their complete works are available only in archives.

Behind these acknowledged reasons for overlooking women poets in the history of Modernism is a blindness to the experience in and of their poetry. When their contemporary poets, Ezra Pound, T. S. Eliot, William Carlos Williams, Wallace Stevens, praised their work, they recognized it not for its unique and different properties but for the ways in which it most resembled their own work. Thus, for example, Marianne Moore was valued by Richard Aldington as an Imagist; by Pound for her "logopoeia," by Stevens for her new romanticism, by Eliot for her classicism, and by Williams for cleaning up the language. In all these valuations Moore is made to seem a disciple rather than an original genius. More recently, literary historians such as David Perkins, M. L. Rosenthal, and Albert Gelpi have followed the same strategy, including the women Modernists only as they fit into an understanding of the movement dominated by the men.

Simply inserting these women poets into the movement, although it will provide a broader conception of Modernism than we now have, will not offer a better understanding of their work unless they are considered not as adjuncts to the men but as original experimental writers on their own terms. They are distinctly different from the men, who were themselves experimenting against the sentimentality of Victorian poetry. These women shared this antipathy to sentimentality but did not often share the positions of their male contemporaries, whose experimental forms often masked conservative—even reactionary—attitudes toward women, society, and politics, and whose interests in myth and history excluded women. The women were in some ways more radical in their literary experiments as well as their social and political views.

In this double rebellion, then, and writing in a tradition with no easily identifiable immediate female predecessors, these women were both extremely free from restraints to experimentation and at the same time susceptible to a strange inhibition of expression. Stein and H.D. felt restricted at first from the full expression of their erotic experience. Although they wrote some of the most original love poetry of their generation, they worked toward it tentatively, first writing in a language coded to conceal their subject and in a hermetic style. Moore's reticence had other sources in her temperament, her upbringing, and her experience. She too began to write in elaborate formal structures that restrained rather than released expression. The surface difficulty of the texts of these three poets, unlike the difficulties of their male contemporaries, derives from both the boldness of their experimentation and their hesitant search for a way to express their own way of seeing. Theirs was a doubled experimental writing—experimenting within an experimental movement.

Nonetheless, Gertrude Stein's early "portraits" (1912), H.D.'s early prose poem, *Notes on Thought and Vision* (1919), and Marianne Moore's second volume of poetry, *Observations* (1924), all indicate the importance of their roles as spectators, looking from the position of the woman, and the extent to which they wanted to differentiate their way of seeing from that of all others. The positions from which they look are quite different from each other, and yet they are united in their interests in an experimental writing that derives from a new way of seeing, a new opening of the perceiving subject.

A closer examination of these three writers will indicate how fully their ways of looking are figured in the metaphor of childbirth and maternity. Although only H.D. was actually a mother (and an indifferent one at that), these women poets all found that they could use the woman's unique experience of procreation as a metaphor for not just literary creation but their ways of looking. The female body, as a place of growth and of both separation *and* attachment, provides the literal figure for Stein's early portraits, for H.D.'s vision, and for Moore's observations. The metaphor is not new; both men and women poets, from Philip Sidney and Anne Bradstreet to the present day, have used it. What is surprising is the use these women poets could find for the metaphor in a period when the female body was either negated or appropriated as other, abject, defiled.

Gertrude Stein wrote, "The literature of a hundred years ago is perfectly easy to see, because the sediment of ugliness has settled down and you get the solemnity of its beauty. But to a person of my temperament, it is much more amusing when it has the vitality of the struggle." Although it has now been almost a hundred years since Stein began to write, she has still not found her place in the literary history of the Modernist movement in American poetry. She has had to wait for the development of a fully responsive criticism. If in poststructuralism and French feminist theory Stein's work has now found that critical response, neither of these approaches attempts to place the work in literary history. As a result, Stein might still be amused by the ongoing struggle to locate her in the emergence of Modernism.

Only recently has the importance of her poetry been acknowledged and the work of exploring its radical experimentation with new modes of signification begun. Such explorations, emphasizing the poetry's lesbian themes and polysemous language, have considered it necessarily antipatriarchal and thus different from the writings of her male contemporaries. Stein herself would have disagreed with this view, of course; she looked upon her own work as at the center of experimental writing in her own time. And it was.

Her first appearance in a periodical should have alone established her historical importance because it came in the special issue of *Camera Work* (1912) put out by Alfred Stieglitz as an immediate response to the critical rejection of Cubism that followed its introduction to the American scene in the 1911 issue of his journal. Stieglitz printed Stein's two portraits of Matisse and Picasso along with representative paintings and sculptures by these artists and argued in an editorial that Stein's "articles themselves, and not either the subjects with which they deal or the illustrations that accompany them, are the true *raison d'être* of this special issue." Before the famous Armory Show of 1913, then, Stein had been established as a major innovator, and *Camera Work* continued to publish her as it persisted in presenting Cubism to the American public. Again, in a special issue of 1913, *Camera Work* featured Stein's

"Portrait of Mabel Dodge at the Villa Curona" as well as Picasso's portrait of Stein, connecting these visual and verbal experimentations with nonrepresentational art.

As Stein's work began to appear in the little magazines published before World War I, she became the subject of interpretive debate. Her importance in American literary circles can be measured by the essay, "How to Read Gertrude Stein," by Carl Van Vechten, printed in *Trend* (1914). This essay argues for her nonreferential art, claiming that everyone tries to make sense out of Stein just as everyone wants to make photographs of Picabia's drawings. But, Van Vechten claims, the essential aim of their art is their attempt to get away from such sense. Thus, very early in the Modernist revolution Stein's art was celebrated for its difference, its liberation from the "sense" of a reading that would dominate its playfulness, and, although Van Vechten did not specify it, for what we would now identify as its feminist element.

This feminist aspect of her work, its release from a dominating "sense," again unidentified as such, was what William Carlos Williams also wanted to praise when he pointed to its subversive tendency. Asked to contribute a manifesto and essay to the newly established *Pagany* in 1929, Williams named his work first, "Manifesto: in the form of a criticism of the works of Gertrude Stein." Later published in two pieces as "Manifesto" and "The Work of Gertrude Stein," in its first draft this essay claimed that Stein was the most modern of the Modernists. If he omitted this accolade from the essay that was finally published, he retained his praise of Stein, claiming that, like her friends the painters, she recognized that the purpose of art is form itself, the resolution of its own strategies in organizing materials. Williams hailed Stein's work along with Dada and surrealism as art that saves the mind from doctrinaire formulas and encourages the free play of language.

This early recognition of Stein's importance rested largely on her prose, which formed the bulk of her published work: *Three Lives* (1909), *Tender Buttons* (1914), *Geography and Plays* (1922), *The Making of Americans* (1925). Although she was writing poetry during this period (and *Tender Buttons* is itself a prose poem), most of her poetry was not published until after her death, in *Bee Time Vine and Other Pieces (1913–1927)* (1953), *Painted Lace and Other Pieces (1914–1937)* (1955), and *Stanzas in Meditation and Other Poems (1929–1933)* (1956).

However, this distinction of genre is not entirely accurate, and even here Stein is more experimental than this commentary has allowed. Her work is not easily separated into genres; she worked to overthrow the conventions of genre, to mix prose and poetry, and to question the idea of a continuous work. What is printed in the form of prose, *Tender Buttons*, for example, may have none of the narrative, grammatical, or syntactical continuity that typifies prose. Furthermore, the continuity of a long prose piece can be interrupted by an abrupt change in style, as in the case of *Tender Buttons*, where the third and final section, "Rooms," was composed almost certainly in 1911, before the first two sections completed in 1913, and represents an earlier style of writing. Even this minor shift of chronology is important because Stein moved rapidly through changes of style, and an arbitrary rearrangement of her writing in a single volume would confuse a sense of her development. She was relentless in her experimentations, claiming that once she found it could be done, she lost interest in it.

Stein's revolutionary fervor bypassed genre and chronology to concentrate on words alone, and her work has been divided effectively, not into books or genres but into verbal and syntactic styles. After *Three Lives* Stein began to work in what she has called the "insistent" style of repetitive and incantatory words, exemplified in her portrait of Picasso mentioned above as the first of her experimental works to be published. That portrait concludes:

This one was one having always something being coming out of him, something having completely a real meaning. This one was one whom some were following. This one was one who was working. This one was one who was working and he was one needing this thing needing to be working so as to be one having some way of being one having some way of working.

The "insistent" style of gerunds here is an effort to capture the rhythm of the personality or, as she claimed in *The Autobiography of Alice B. Toklas*, exactitude in the description of an inner and outer reality. This style is underpinned by the metaphor of childbearing for the creative act. "Having . . . something . . . coming out of him," Picasso is identified with an instinctual and generative power rather than a rational one. Again, in a notebook entry, she claims that her brother, Leo Stein, did his work with his brains but that she and Picasso created from an inner propulsion that they did not control. She saw herself and Picasso as important because both of them could release the power in themselves and others by listening, observing, and describing.

To do this she experimented tirelessly, never listening nor looking from the same position. She went through constant changes in writing "portraits," moving from her early repetitive gerundive style to a style that played with nonreferentiality—in which words were used as things, not to point to something beyond themselves but to be equivalent to it. The change can be seen in the "Portrait of Constance Fletcher," done around 1911, which starts with the gerunds of the insistent style and again with the metaphor of gestation: "She was filling in all her living to be a full one, she was thinking and feeling in all her living in being a full one." Then the portrait shifts to "If they move in the shoe there is everything to do." Of this style, Stein writes, "This has not any meaning." Its culmination in *Tender Buttons* severs language from referentiality and marks Stein as a precursor of the postmodern questioning of representation, the subject, sequential narration, and logical meaning.

In the period when Stein wrote *Tender Buttons* she was engaged in creating an imagery of the female body, focusing on details of the female anatomy and beginning to consider her own work as a writing of the body in what has been called an uncanny anticipation of the theoretical formulations of Luce Irigaray and Julia Kristeva some fifty years later. In *Tender Buttons*, for example, she uses frequent images of the color red, suggesting menstruation and defloration as well as stains, bleedings, and secretions. Also, she makes the connection between menstrual or uterine images and her own writing in "A Petticoat," where she lists, "A white light, a disgrace, an ink spot, a rosy charm," placing the "ink spot" of writing next to the rosy spot on her petticoat.

From 1914 to 1919 Stein began to write plays, using speech fragments or "voices," and working with commonplace, even banal phrases that are quite different from the "lively words" of her earlier nonreferential period. For example, "White Wines" begins, "Cunning very cunning and cheap, at that rate a sale is a place to use type writing. Shall we go home." Later, in "Lifting Belly" (1915–1917), Stein's interest in ordinary speech rhythms creates a simple conversation between two lovers. The conversation in this style has a referential meaning that much of Stein's experimental writing seems designed to deny. Its interest is in its subject, the erotic experience of two women lovers, the wit of its language (Stein was living in a town outside Belley when she wrote it, for example), and the playfulness of its tone. But, like earlier experiments, "Lifting Belly" is also marked by verbal excess and the play in language, indications again of an interest in the text's surface pleasure and what has come to be called *jouissance*.

In the 1920s Stein moved away from this experiment to concentrate on another aspect of the surface of the text, the melody of words, as a way of investigating the possibilities of sound itself. She claimed that she liked to set a sentence for herself as a tuning fork and metronome and write to that time and tune. In "Sonnets That Please," from *Bee Time Vine*, she used the melody of the nursery rhyme: "I see the luck / And the luck sees me / I see the lucky one be lucky. / I see the love / And the loves sees me." She could also echo the rhythm and tone of more serious poetry, as in *Stanzas in Meditation*, part 2, stanza 1: "Full well I know that she is there / Much as she will she can be there / But which I know which I know when / Which is my way to be there then." But *Stanzas* retains the playfulness that characterizes much of Stein's work, opening with "I caught a bird which made a ball" and continuing through 164 stanzas to conclude in the penultimate stanza with "Thank you for hurrying through."

From her experimentation with melody and her efforts to play with the music of poetry, Stein moved in the late twenties and early thirties to reinvent for herself some of the structures of literary order she had abandoned earlier. In "A Description of the Fifteenth of November: A Portrait of T. S. Eliot," she writes a parody of pompous literary language, mixing sense and nonsense: "On the fifteenth of November we have been told that she will go either here or there and in company with some one who will attempt to be of aid in any difficulty that may be pronounced as at all likely to occur." But even here, repetition, the recurring motif of the fifteenth of November, holds together this collection of entirely arbitrary material.

She appeared to be interested in this period in continuity and cumulative significance, organizing her work around successions of single words. "Patriarchal Poetry" (1927) keeps the title phrase as a refrain throughout the text in order to display the banality of the poetic tradition that Stein wanted to overthrow. The long poem contains variations of rhythm and purpose. Repetitive phrases constitute some lines, such as "Patriarchal poetry reasonably. / Patriarchal poetry administratedly. / Patriarchal poetry with them too." At other points she uses straightforward statement—"Patriarchal poetry makes no mistake makes no mistake in estimating the value to be placed upon the best and most arranged of considerations of this." Here, clearly, she has abandoned the play on words in order to convey quite directly her negative judgment and subversive intent.

In the late twenties and early thirties Stein wrote in a variety of styles, composing short works and the lengthy *A Novel of Thank You* and two of her most experimental works, *Four Saints in Three Acts* and *Lucy Church Amiably*. But these works belong to conventional genres of drama and prose narrative in which she worked in the thirties and forties. With the publication of *The Autobiography of Alice B. Toklas* in 1933 Stein achieved the kind of popular reputation she had sought, and, in that decade, at least, her work, became, if not less experimental, at least more willing to negotiate with the conventional. She returned later in her career to experiments in prose that anticipated the *nouveau roman*.

The immediately recognized importance of Gertrude Stein's writing in the emerging stages of Modernist poetry was her willingness to detach words from referential meaning and employ them as painters used paint or musicians used sound. Stieglitz linked her work to the analytical Cubism of her friend Picasso. Williams compared the music of her work to that of Bach, arguing for its abstract design. And Sherwood Anderson compared her to American women of the old sort, scorning factory-made foods in her "word kitchen." Like Stieglitz and Williams, Anderson too felt she would be understood better at some future time when her audience would catch up to her experiments.

In her own lifetime, of course, she did become better known, but not for her experimental writing. Until recently, she remained a writer's writer. In a late interview she reported being asked how she managed to get so much publicity. She answered that it was because she had such a small audience. She advised artists to begin with a small audience that really believes in their work because such an audience will make a big noise whereas a big audience does not make a noise at all. This perception of her position is both true and untrue. She had a small and influential audience among her contemporaries; but the publicity she attracted (and courted) came not from that audience so much as from her acquaintance with influential painters and writers and her willingness to publicize it. Still, it is the small audience interested in experimental writing that can be credited with renewed exploration of her work.

What they value in Stein's work is her willingness to attempt an extreme revolution in the use of words. For example, if she shared with Williams an interest in the abstract design of an arrangement of words, she was willing to detach those words from referentiality more fully than he was. His "so much depends / upon / / a red wheel / barrow" is not so thoroughly cut off from referentiality as her "One or Two. I've Finished": "There / Why / There / Why / There / Able / Idle."

This fearlessness in experimenting with words manifests itself also in her willingness to break with narrative continuity, established genres, and the linear logic that supports them. As a result, she was free to explore new ways in which her experience might be incorporated in a text. Moreover, her prolonged search for a way of expressing her own erotic experience and her love relationships allowed for the widest range of experimental writing, from the early hermetic style that encoded her subject in *The Making of Americans* to the more open repetitive expression of "Lifting Belly." In this endeavor she brought into literary language a range of experience not much explored by other Modernists. Perhaps only Hart Crane among the male Modernists wrote anything approaching this kind of poetry, although, as we shall see, at this time H.D. was developing her own hermetic rendering of love poetry.

Stein's contribution to Modernist experimentation is deeply dependent upon everything that patriarchal categories devalue: women's erotic experience, the material of language, the play of irrational process in narrative, the surface pleasure of the text. *Tender Buttons* (1911–1913) is a discovery of an aspect of language and experience that, as one critic has argued, exposes the sacrificial enterprise of male culture and envisions a means of subversion that anticipates an important strand in later Modernism. Stein's formal experimentation started from her study with William James and her commitment to the experimentation of pragmatism. And it derived also from her questioning of authority in her private life. In breaking free both formally and thematically from the linear logic of patriarchal language, Stein was able to uncover the hidden erotic pleasure of everyday life and the language that expresses it. Her emphasis on the signifier in its play of rhythm, repetition, sound association, and intonation, marks her as a precursor of the feminist theorists writing in the late twentieth century.

If Gertrude Stein's appearance in *Camera Work* in 1912 indicated her importance in the emerging Modernist movement, H.D. was also catapulted to a place of prominence in the pre-World War I literary revolution by the poems signed "H.D. *Imagiste*" in the January 1913 issue of *Poetry*, which were followed two months later by the essay and manifesto on Imagism written by Ezra Pound and F. S. Flint. In literary history she was to be for years to come the embodiment of Imagism and the restrictive poetics enunciated in Pound and Flint's manifesto:

1. Direct treatment of the "thing," whether subjective or objective.
2. To use absolutely no word that [does] not contribute to the presentation.
3. As regarding rhythm: to compose in sequence of the musical phrase, not in sequence of a metronome.

If the three poems by H.D. that Ezra Pound sent to *Poetry* were better representations of this Imagist program than those by Pound and her husband, Richard Aldington, published at the same time in *Poetry*, it was because H.D. had already perfected the style that Pound claims to have discovered. For her it was a way of restraining and encoding emotions that threatened to overcome her. She gave Pound the credit for discovering her, reporting that she showed him her poems, and he advised her to cut a line here, shorten a line there, and offered to send them to Harriet Monroe. But her first poems in *Poetry* suggest that she was already an accomplished poet before Pound intervened to get her poems published. Developing along her own lines, she must have realized even then that, as she commented years later, "Ezra would have destroyed me and the center they call 'Air and Crystal' of my poetry."

Nonetheless, in the early years of the Modernist movement, she published regularly and actively engaged in the literary life of London. Her poems appeared in *Des Imagistes: An Anthology* (1914), and she assisted in collecting and selecting poems for the 1915, 1916, 1917 volumes of *Some Imagist Poets: An Anthology*. For one year, 1916–1917, she substituted for her husband, Richard Aldington, as literary editor of the *Egoist*, and was herself succeeded by T. S. Eliot. In 1915 she won the Guarantors' Prize from *Poetry* for "The Wind Sleepers," "Storm," "Pool," "The Garden," and "Moonrise," and in 1917 she won the Vers Libre Prize from the *Little Review* for "Sea Poppies." *Sea Garden*, her first volume of poetry, was published in 1916. Additional volumes of poetry appeared: *Hymen* (1921), *Heliodora and Other Poems* (1924), *Col-*

lected Poems of H.D. (1925), and *Red Roses for Bronze* (1931). After, there was a long hiatus in her published works, and she did not begin to publish poetry again until the first volume of *Trilogy*, *The Walls Do Not Fall*, appeared in 1944.

It is a strange history and perhaps best explained by her beginnings in Imagism, which have been misleading in establishing her poetic interests. Despite Pound's program, when H.D. came to write her own poetics, in a manuscript written in 1919 but not published until 1982 as *Notes on Thought and Vision*, she moved beyond the restrictive tenets of Imagism to found her art on a much more elaborate and personally responsive idea of vision. In this short text she describes an experience that occurred during a healing visit to the Scilly Isles in 1919, three months after she miraculously survived the birth of her daughter during a bout of influenza. Her poetics developed as intimately connected with both her experience of giving birth and the maternal affection and love that she received at the time from her friend Bryher. Although she never published this text, it contains germs of ideas about creativity that would inform her later work.

For H.D. creative vision was not "the direct treatment of the thing" but a view into the "overmind," which she described as "a cap of consciousness over my head . . . like water, transparent, fluid yet with definite body, contained in a definite space. It is like a closed sea-plant, jelly-fish or anemone." Although she admitted that those jellyfish states of consciousness are of two kinds, "vision of the womb and vision of the brain," and that before the birth of her child such states seemed to come definitely from the brain, she claimed that most dreams are visions of the womb. The womb or body is itself the most creative, as H.D. concluded, "The oyster makes the pearl in fact. So the body, with all its emotions and fears and pain in time casts off the spirit, a concentrated essence, not itself, but made, in a sense, created by itself."

Here, again, the metaphor of birth serves to explain this woman writer's conception of creativity. By contrast, commenting perhaps on the published list of Imagist Don'ts, H.D. claimed, "The new schools of destructive art theorists are on the wrong track." Her theory was constructive rather than destructive, and she indicated what the right track would be in terms of maternal creativity: "Memory is the mother, begetter of all drama, idea, music, science or song." Through such memory, she had access to the "overworld consciousness" that is revolutionary and life-giving, as she argued, "Two or three people, with healthy bodies and the right sort of receiving brains, could turn the whole tide of human thought, could direct lightning flashes of electric power to slash across and destroy the world of dead, murky thought" and bring the whole force of the power of beauty and overworld consciousness back into the world.

Notes on Thought and Vision owes an obvious debt to the body consciousness of D. H. Lawrence, whom H.D. knew, and to another friend, Havelock Ellis, whose work on sexuality interested her; but its emphasis on the womb and on creativity as begetting distinguishes her work from theirs. Its style, too, is unique. Unlike Pound and Eliot, who wrote their critical essays in the continuous prose of logical argument and with the authority of reformers, H.D. created an experimental text that is organized in the form of the montage, which she, like Stein, took from the cinema and modern art. Although she has an important and prophetic message about the need for a creative and constructive vision for her own age, she writes a text that is composed of random and fragmentary "notes" rather than of a continuous and coherent argument.

If in writing criticism H.D. was unwilling to govern the text from an authoritative point of view, in her poetry she was even more open and receptive or more willing to be infiltrated and perhaps hidden entirely within another identity. In this state, she could identify with the god of crossroads, in "Hermes of the Ways": "But more than the many-foamed ways / Of the sea, / I know him / of the triple path-ways, / Hermes, / who awaits." "Dubious, / facing three ways," Hermes is a crossroads figure, split and yet optimistically waiting. In this sense, he resembles, as does H.D., Stein's portrait writer, open to others, and the image of the mother, receptive and waiting.

Responsive to others, she was also willing to reinterpret them and connect their stories with her own, rewriting the role of women in myth by allowing Eurydice and Artemis, for example, to tell their stories of defiance. "Eurydice" begins in regret with the statement, "So you have swept me back," but she goes on to discover the power of her own position and concludes, "At least I have the flowers of myself, / and my thoughts, no god / can take that." Artemis, speaking in "Orion Dead," claims, "I am poisoned with the rage of song."

Not just the woman rising against her own victimization but the woman silenced and thus offering a mute indictment of her society was

H.D.'s subject. She moved outside the process of male myth-making to comment on its silencing of women in "Helen." In this early poem, taking as her subject Helen of Troy, the literary embodiment of female beauty and sexual passion, H.D. rewrote the traditional story of Helen, to claim, "All Greece hates / the still eyes in the white face" "could love indeed the maid, / only if she were laid, / white ash amid funereal cypresses." For H.D. the male idealization of women was dangerous and life-denying. This figure of Helen remained in H.D.'s imagination until she finally reworked her story completely in *Helen in Egypt*, written in 1952–1955. But even early in her career, she set herself deliberately against conventional beauty, claiming, of the "Sheltered Garden," "I have had enough. / I gasp for breath . . . for this beauty, / beauty without strength, / chokes out life." And the poem concludes: "O to blot out this garden / to forget, to find a new beauty / In some terrible / wind-tortured place."

Beneath the Greek myths and history of her early poems, H.D. suppressed a personal struggle that was more openly revealed in the largely unpublished autobiographical fiction of the twenties and thirties. However, three poems that she cut to publish as expansions of fragments from Sappho in *Heliodora* (1924) are in their complete form personal revelations of her desertion by her husband. "Amaranth" (published as "Fragment 41": " . . . *thou flittest to Andromeda*") concludes with a section omitted from the *Heliodora* version in which the abandoned woman says to her lover, "How I hate you for this," and the goddess, speaking to the betraying lover, warns, "*Turn if you will from her path*" "*but you will find / no peace in the end / save in her presence.*" "Eros" (published as "Fragment 40": *Love . . . bitter-sweet*") admits in both versions "to sing love / love must first shatter us." Finally, in "Envy" ("Fragment 68": " . . . *even in the house of Hades*"), the deserted lover envies her beloved "your chance of death" in war. She confesses her frigidity, again in a passage omitted from the first published version. Her beloved was, she writes, "more male than the sun-god, / more hot, more intense," while she was "unspeakably indifferent."

In contrast to these unhappy love poems is a group of poems in *Hymen* that link a restored sense of integrity with either chastity or lesbian love. "White World," "Prayer," "Song," "Evadne," "The Islands," "At Baia," "Fragment 113." "The whole white world is ours . . . delight / waits till our spirits tire / of forest, grove and bush." Here she identified whiteness with creation divorced from procreation. In "Demeter" procreation or motherhood is a passionate if deeply conflicted state. Demeter says, "I am greatest and least." Although Demeter can boast, "Strong are the hands of Love," when she is confronted with the question, *"What of her — / mistress of Death?,"* she can only reply, "Ah, strong were the arms that took / (ah, evil the heart and graceless)." But she concludes by avowing her own superior maternal love, claiming that death's "kiss was less passionate!"

The poems in *Hymen* (1921) and *Heliodora* (1924) indicate a mind in conflict, removed from the "overmind" of *Notes on Thought and Vision* yet searching for that presence in her life. For example, "Fragment 113": "'*Neither honey nor bee for me,*' " advises against passion that is "old desire," "old pain," "not honey, not the deep / plunge of soft belly / and the clinging of the gold-edged / pollen-dusted feet." Rather, the poem argues for "heat, more passionate / Of bone and the white shell / and fiery tempered steel." Again, in "Fragment 36": "*I know not what to do: my mind is divided,*" another free working of Sappho, the choice she must make is: "Is song's gift best? / is love's gift loveliest?" "I know not what to do" is the repeated refrain amid "strain upon strain." At the borderline again, the speaker says, "so my mind hesitates / above the passion / quivering yet to break, / so my mind hesitates / above my mind, / listening to song's delight."

Red Rose for Bronze (1931), the last volume of poetry published before *Trilogy*, some thirteen years later, does not reveal any deepening of her resources. The lines thin out until they appear to be merely nervous repetitions of words: "stroke, / stroke, / stroke" or "this / this / or this, / or this thing" in the title poem. Although a number of lines in poems start with "I say," in fact the voice is muted, the speaking subject passive and suffering. Even the translations take on this mood. The defiance of the earlier speakers, the violence of the imagery, the turmoil of the passion—all are restrained in this volume. By 1931 the experimentation in poetic expression of H.D.'s early work appeared to have run its course.

In the 1930s she wrote far less regularly than she had in the previous two decades and published very little. She wrote short stories, some poems intended for a short volume that she projected as "A Dead Priestess Speaks," and she translated and published Euripides' *Ion* with her own commentary (1937). But the accomplishments of her early poetry that established her as a presence in the emerging Modernist movement appeared to be over. She may, as it seems, have lost her sense of direction, or she may have succumbed to the difficulties of suppressing or encoding her emotional alliances in language that she felt was required even by the avant-garde audience to which she appealed. Clearly the difficulties of speaking as a woman engaged her imagination deeply, but although she was in correspondence with other women writers she lacked the community of interests that the male Modernists could generate among their friends. It was not until the violence of World War II jolted her that she was able to find her voice and to create the woman-centered poetry that the experiences recorded in *Notes on Thought and Vision* promised. Her reputation rests now on this work of her later period and, like Stein, on work that remained largely unpublished in her own lifetime.

In the emergence of Modernism, as its history is conventionally written, H.D. has been an important figure because of her role in the short-lived Imagist movement. Yet even within that movement H.D. was writing poems that may have been spare in language, concrete in imagery, and sharply focused, but were also engaged in refracting complicated and conflicting emotions, erotic experience, and creative anxiety. More important than her brief appearance as "H.D. *Imagiste*," was her effort to write about a woman's erotic experience and to suggest, with whatever contradictions, the presence of a celebratory "overmind consciousness." Like Gertrude Stein's, her work was distinguished by its exploration of female eroticism. Moreover, her revision of myth, her engagement with the violence of war as well as with the misogyny of her generation, mark her as an astute social and political critic and identify the range of her interests beyond Imagism.

The reasons why she should have stopped her experiments in poetry and have lost her sense of direction are probably not fully recoverable. She suggested in notes made during her sessions with Freud in 1933 that unlike other poets she knew she was not interested in a poem once it was written. "There is a feeling that it is only a *part* of myself there," she said, and went on to explain that perhaps this is "partly due to the fact that I lost the early companions of my first writing-period in London, you might say of my 'success,' small and rather specialized as it was."

One early companion that she did not lose was Marianne Moore, whose first volume of poetry she and Bryher brought out in 1921 without Moore's knowledge, collecting the poems she had published in little magazines and printing them in a twenty-four-page booklet, *Poems*, at the Egoist Press. Although Moore had been reluctant to publish a book and expressed astonishment when this book was sent to her, she found it "remarkably innocuous." She and H.D. provided encouragement and support for each other from the beginning, reviewing each other's works, publishing or helping each other get published, and corresponding over a lifetime. They had been students at Bryn Mawr together, although H.D. left without graduating and remembered Moore only as the "mediaeval lady . . . in a green dress" at the Bryn Mawr May Fête. They established contact when Moore sent some poems to the *Egoist*, then edited by H.D.'s husband, Richard Aldington.

Writing in the *Egoist* in 1916 H.D. called Moore the "perfect technician," who wrote with the assurance of her craft and with the perfect artist's despair of ever finding an appreciative audience. H.D. argued, "She is fighting in her country a battle against squalor and commercialism. We are all fighting the same battle." Their bond, H.D. acknowledged, is in "our devotion to the beautiful English language."

In turn, reviewing H.D.'s *Hymen* in *Broom* (1923), Moore was more pointed in her praise of the "magic and compressed energy of the author's imagination." She admired her "faithfulness to fact." But most arresting is Moore's comment on the woman writer:

Talk of weapons and the tendency to match one's intellectual and emotional vigor with the violence of nature, give a martial, an apparently masculine tone to such writing as H.D.'s, the more so that women are regarded as belonging necessarily to either of two classes—that of the intellectual freelance or that of the eternally sleeping beauty. . . . There is, however, a connection between weapons and beauty. Cowardice and beauty are at swords' points and in H.D.'s work, suggested by the absence of subterfuge, cowardice and the ambition to dominate by brute force, we have heroics which do not confuse transcendence with domination and which in their indestructibleness, are the core of tranquillity and of intellectual equilibrium

The pointedness of this comment, which might come as a surprise from a woman much praised by her male colleagues, indicates the intensity of Moore's need for the encouragement as well as the example that H.D. provided her.

Moore's publishing career started in 1915 when a group of her poems appeared in the *Egoist* and in the April and May issues of *Poet-*

ry, two of the most important little magazines of the day. Of the first seven poems that appeared in these two magazines, only the antiwar poem, "To Military Progress," survived among her collected work. Although some of her early poems were more explicitly Biblical than her work was to remain (for example, such poems as "Appellate Jurisdiction," a commentary on St. Paul's discussion of sin and redemption in his epistle to the Romans, or "That Harp You Play So Well," a poem contrasting David the psalmist with King David), she stated early the moral stance that she was to maintain throughout her career.

She moved quickly to different subjects, encouraged no doubt by a remarkable visit to New York City in 1915 where she became acquainted with major figures in the avant-garde literary world. She met Alfred Kreymborg, who accepted some of her work for *Others* and introduced her to Alfred Stieglitz's photographs. She then met Stieglitz, who showed her paintings by Picasso, Picabia, Marsden Hartley, and gave her copies of *Camera Work*. In addition, she met Guido Bruno, editor of *Bruno's Weekly*, among other short-lived avant-garde publications. He too published Moore's poems as well as an article by Richard Aldington praising her work.

This busy one-week trip to New York City brought her to the attention of important writers and editors, and she was quick to take advantage of the opportunities they offered both in publishing and in revising her work. In fact, her precocious development suggests that she needed only encouragement and the right outlets to inspire the experimental writing that would win her an important place among the early Modernists.

Between 1915, when she first started publishing, and 1924, when her second volume of poetry, *Observations,* appeared and later won the *Dial* award, Marianne Moore's writing developed rapidly, and she established herself both as a poet and a critic. Like Stein and like H.D., first presented as a Cubist and an Imagist, respectively, in the emerging years of the Modernist movement, Moore gained a special kind of attention when Harriet Monroe published a "Symposium" on her first volume, *Poems* (1921), in *Poetry*. A debate on the book's merits, written by Monroe with quotations from others, the "Symposium" argument centered on whether Moore was a poet. H.D., Bryher, and the critic Yvor Winters argued that she was, and Winters claimed that, with the exception of Wallace Stevens, she was the best poet in the country. On the other side, Marion Strobel, an associate editor of *Poetry*, complained that Moore, despite her intelligence, had not learned to write simply. And Pearl Andelson, identified as "another poet-critic," asserted that her poems were "hybrids of a flagrantly prose origin." Her male contemporaries among the poets expressed their praise of her work elsewhere: Pound, in the *Little Review*, acclaimed her as a distinctly American poet; Eliot, reviewing *Poems* in the *Dial*, cited her quite new rhythm, her peculiar jargon, and "an almost primitive simplicity of phrase" as her great achievements; and Williams, in the *Dial*, called her poetry "a true modern crystallization, the fine essence of today."

Although Moore was acclaimed from the beginning as an experimenter, the peculiar nature of her experimentation may not at first appear to have any affinity with the experimental writing of Stein and H.D. Her interest in the elaborate structures of syllabic verse seems quite different from the word portraits of Stein and the free verse of H.D. Nonetheless, her tireless revision of the precisely fixed form of her poems marks an interest in the fluidity of form that is close to their interests. Firm though she could be in her moral convictions, Moore remained nonetheless tentative when it came to form, both the forms on which she gazed and those which she created. She never fixed firmly the body of her work, leaving *The Complete Poems* quite incomplete, with omissions that may not be accidents but can often be casualties. Publishing various versions of poems throughout her lifetime, she seemed never quite satisfied with the distinctive forms she had been at such pains to elaborate.

Like Stein and H.D., Marianne Moore had to work toward a form that would suit her purposes. The first stage of her writing, from 1915 to the publication of *Poems* in 1921, was marked by experiments in stylized language. Using the already unusual syllabic form that she had converted to her own purposes, varying the length of the lines and including internal rhymes, she would experiment still further by converting published poems from syllabic to free verse or from free verse back to syllabic, as, for example, "When I Buy Pictures," which started in a syllabic version but was first published in free verse, or "Poetry," which went from syllabic to free to syllabic verse. Far from tinkering, Moore was experimenting with form, retaining an element of open form even as she wrote in closed formal structures. Like Stein's unwillingness to be dominated by referential meaning and H.D.'s receptivity to the voices of varied speakers, Moore's revisionary habits indicate an unwillingness to be fixed even in the intricate forms that attracted her.

Unlike Walt Whitman, who was also a tireless reviser, Moore worked not with open forms but with very complicated and elaborate structures. When she revised, she could not simply add to her form as Whitman so often did. Subtracting rather than adding was her characteristic strategy, as if she felt she could move toward what she calls, in "To a Snail," " 'the first grace of style' . . . 'compression' " by successive, if shorter, versions of her poems. Although she settled early on a permanent and stylized presentation of her own bodily image, encased in a black cape and tricorn hat, she could never fix firmly the body of her own work.

Her revisionary strategies are an indication of her attitude toward the body as changeable and malleable, a surface to be adorned and concealed by infinite variations of style, an attitude she transferred to the subjects of her poems. Late in her life when she was asked about the source of her poetry, Moore quoted George Grosz's explanation of art, "Endless curiosity, observation, research, and a great amount of joy in the thing." If the endless curiosity kept her at revision, the joy she mentioned connects Moore with Stein and H.D. as celebratory seers. It allows her to be what she called an "imaginary possessor" both of the pictures she looked at and of those she created. Like Stein and H.D. when she looked, Moore opened herself to the other, not to appropriate it or triumph over it but to appreciate it, aware, as she wrote, in "The Labors of Hercules," that "one detects creative power by its capacity to conquer one's detachment." Besides, she queried, in "Critics and Connoisseurs," "What is / there in being able / to say that one has dominated the stream in an attitude of self-defense."

Moore's openness is distinguished from Stein's mixture of inside and outside as well as from H.D.'s visionary consciousness by its relentless tentativeness and its conviction that "To have misapprehended the matter is to have confessed that one has not looked far enough," as she wrote in "England." Combined with this willingness to look far enough is a reluctance to be too familiar, to imagine that the other is fully understood, to settle firmly on a final view.

Moore's interest in looking drew her to consider other skilled observers such as the "Old Tiger," which she addressed in an early poem with sympathetic attachment: "you to whom a no / is never a no, loving to succeed where all others have failed, so / constituted that opposition is pastime and struggle is meat, you / / see more than I see but even I / see too much." She discovered in the old tiger a model for the poet with an "eye which is characteristic / of all accurate observers." Unlike the "cultured, the profusely lettered" (one might even say the literary establishment), the tiger, "scorning to / push," knows "that it is not necessary to live in order to be / alive."

This watchfulness and patience between the eye and its object (the habits of the poet no less than the predator) were exactly what Moore found absent from T. S. Eliot, in work such as "Portrait of a Lady." In an early review of *Prufrock and Other Observations* in *Poetry* (April 12, 1918), Moore attacked the "ungallantry, the youthful cruelty, of the substance of the 'Portrait.' " Clearly, she preferred the tiger's habits of observation to this particular poet's. It is the eye of the accurate observer that she herself trained on objects and on her own poetry, discovering often that she herself had not quite accurately organized her form. Attentive to the body of the work, her diligence is evident in a poem like "The Fish," which she revised to indicate how the illusions of poetic form can coincide with the poem's play on optical illusions. The first version is organized in this way:

The Fish

Wade through black jade.
Of the crow blue mussel-shells, one
Keeps adjusting the ash-heaps;
Opening and shutting itself like

An injured fan.

The revised version is organized more fluidly:

The Fish

wade
through black jade
   Of the crow-blue mussel-shells, one keeps
   adjusting the ash-heaps;
   opening and shutting itself like

an
injured fan.

The change in the shape of the body of the text has made a difference to its reading. A poem that opens with the optical illusion of fish wading through jade and "barnacles which encrust the side / of the wave" will be aware of the optical illusion or interpretive difference between the two distinct lineations of the poem above. The eye sees and the ear hears the rhyme in the second version, arresting the reading in a consideration of this paradox, preparing it for the final paradox of the sea: "All / external / marks of abuse are present on this / defiant edifice."

External marks are what Moore studied in detail. The china swan with "swart blind look askance / and gondoliering legs" or the "Camellia Sabina" with its "pale / stripe that looks as if on a mushroom the / sliver from a beet-root carved into a rose were laid" or "The firs" [which] "stand in a procession, each with an emerald turkey-foot at the top"—these examples elaborate the ways in which she was attentive to the surface as an infinitely variable phenomenon.

Her sensitivity to detail might suggest an interest only in surfaces, but she had a clear sense of the limits of detail and an awareness that not all external marks could be so clearly seen. In "An Octopus," for example, which moves through eight pages toward the compliment that "Relentless accuracy is the nature of this octopus / with its capacity for fact," Moore was more interested in capaciousness than in accuracy. Over and over, she insisted that there is no way to accurately measure the twenty-eight ice fields she detailed. At the start, the "octopus" is described as "deceptively reserved and flat"; "Completing a circle" around it, she claimed, "you have been deceived into thinking you have progressed."

The "octopus" is unapproachable, a place where all our observational skills are unreliable and even water is "immune to force of gravity in the perspective of the peaks." Spotted ponies, "hard to discern," fungi "magnified in profile," inhabit a landscape that is tricky, changeable, and impossible to accurately fix in view. She pictured the octopus-glacier " 'creeping slowly as with meditated stealth, / its arms seeming to approach from all directions.' "

Here is no " 'deliberate wide-eyed wistfulness' " in the description of nature but rather a constant iteration of the impossibility of "relentless accuracy" in seeing and capturing anything in language, although she refused to resolve " 'complexities which still will be complexities / as long as the world lasts.' " "An Octopus" is a view of the inscrutability of nature imagined by a woman and as a woman. The glacier is "of unimagined delicacy," "it hovers forward 'spider fashion / on its arms' misleadingly like lace." It is "distinguished by a beauty / of which 'the visitor dare never fully speak at home,'" "odd oracles of cool official sarcasm," which nonetheless differ from the wisdom of those " 'emotionally sensitive' " whose hearts are hard.

Hovering forward with arms approaching from all sides, this imagined glacier would appear to be the very image of the engulfing mother, yet unlike Whitman's old crone out of the sea this feminized landscape is imagined not so much as personally threatening but as stalwartly resistant. Its mysteries are those of "doing hard things," of endurance, of unimaginable resistance to the poet's imaginative grasp. They are mysteries appreciated and confirmed here by this woman poet who imitated them.

"An Octopus" is certainly the most menacing maternal image among these three poets. Unlike Stein's "having something coming out" of herself and H.D.'s vision of the womb the hovering many-armed octopus-glacier seems as ominous as it might be delicate, beautiful, and durable. Yet Moore's maternal image is embodied in the "unegoistic action of the glaciers," where this remarkably unegoistic poet could locate the interaction that forms the bond between nature and poet, reality and language, in terms that serve also to describe the interaction between mother and child. The poet was not afraid of this natural landscape, even when she was aware of its powerful and often inscrutable presence.

Observation, with its attendant skills of separation *and* attachment, forms the basis of Moore's experiments. It manifests itself also in her efforts to discover how poetry differs from prose in an age when, as Moore wrote in "So far as the future is concerned" (1915), "rhyme is outmoded." Later revised as "The Past is the Present," she quoted Habakkuk's "exact words, 'Hebrew poetry is prose / with a sort of heightened consciousness.' Ecstasy affords / The occasion and expediency determines the form." Here, Moore was trying to identify with revolutionary poets like Pound and at the same time to indicate her distance from them by allying herself with the moral and prophetic strain of Habakkuk that was quite distinct from the Greek and Chinese sources of Pound's own early poetry.

This position, both inside and outside the developing Modernist movement, is best expressed in "Poetry" (1919), which opens with the famous admission: "I, too, dislike it." As if agreeing with the detractors who saw Modernist poetry as simply difficult, Moore went on to claim that "we / do not admire what / we cannot understand." She then catalogued subjects that the Modernists might use for poetry—although the genteel tradition would have relegated them to prose—the bat, the elephant, a wild horse, a tireless wolf, the critic, even the baseball fan, statistician, and " 'business documents and / school-books.' " Moore's conclusion that "all these phenomena are important" aligned her with the Modernists, until the poem turns again against her contemporaries, claiming that we shall not have poetry until poets can be " 'literalists of the imagination.' " In the meantime, she claimed, if you demand "the raw material of poetry in / all its rawness" and the "genuine," "you are interested in poetry." She could not reconcile the opposition here between content and form, between the possibilities of poetry and its realization either in her own work or in that of her contemporaries. This poem about poetry was never to quite satisfy her, and she spent a lifetime recasting it, first cutting it to a shorter free-verse form, for *Observations* (1925), then returning it to its original form with minor variations in the *Selected Poems* (1935), and then, in the *Complete Poems* (1967), cutting it to only part of the first three lines, relegating the longer version to a footnote.

This ceaseless revision of her work led her to move away from the syllabic form she had developed early on to a kind of free verse with embedded rhymes. She began in 1921 by converting into this freer verse form poems she had already written in syllabic verse, such as "When I Buy Pictures," "Picking and Choosing," and "England," as well as "Poetry," and she continued to write in free verse until 1925, just before she became editor of the *Dial* and stopped writing poetry until 1932. The incentive for this experimentation in form may have been her closer connection with a community of poets and with the *Dial*, or it may have been inspired by Pound's suggestions for revision of the syllabic version of "A Graveyard," which Moore redid in free verse and published as "A Grave" in the *Dial* in 1921. Her experiments in free verse may also have come from her efforts, if not to simplify her poetry, then to free it from exaggerated intricacies of form, realizing that "Truth is no Apollo / Belvedere, no formal thing," as she wrote in the final stanza, breaking the syllabic form of "In the Days of Prismatic Color." Free verse allowed her to accommodate prose more freely, and her poems began openly to include quoted passages identified by quotation marks. The magnificent poems of her free-verse period, including "Marriage" and "An Octopus," are some of her most celebrated and difficult as well.

Moore's lifelong interest in observation made her a superb editor even if it meant that she stopped writing poetry when she took up editing the *Dial* from 1925 to 1929. The magazine had a circulation of eighteen thousand and it published the best writers of the day. Its editor was, then, in a position of considerable power, and Moore used that power to great effect. She published Crane's "To Brooklyn Bridge," Pound's Canto 22, William Butler Yeats's "Among School Children," and poems by Williams, Louis Zukofsky, and Stanley Kunitz, among others. She also wrote the monthly "Comments" on subjects of her own choosing, which were not unlike the subjects of her poetry. And she continued to contribute book reviews, agreeing to consider only those writers for whom she felt some sympathy, such as Eliot (*Sacred Wood*), e. e. cummings, Stevens, Williams, Stein. In her editorial work she played an important part in the development of Modernism. By the time she returned to writing poetry in 1932 both she and the Modernist movement were established. Her return in the next decade to the syllabic verse that she had developed at the beginning of her career marked once again her independence.

Stein, H.D., and Moore—these three women Modernists—went to extremes in their early experimental poetry: Stein followed her friends among the painters to the limits of nonreferentiality, where language could not proceed, and consequently never attracted a wide audience; H.D., so overwhelmed by visionary experience and a private life of conflicted emotions that she exhausted her creative impulse, fell silent in mid-career, and did not resume writing until the shock of the Second World War drove her to produce her major long poems; and Marianne Moore made such a great effort to distinguish her characteristic style of presentation from that of others that she seemed to be at times merely idiosyncratic even as she could not settle on a final form for her work. Perhaps these extreme solutions and the poetic silences they occasioned are cause and effect; they may indicate an insistence on independence that was ultimately too exhausting. But the length of their careers, the variety of their experiments, the development of their own styles are indications that Stein, H.D., and Moore were among the most tenacious and experimental writers of their day, working from a wholly different and more revolutionary attitude toward poetic authority than the High Modernists.

Early on these women wrote out of a radical impulse in the first stages of the emerging Modernist movement. By the time that Modernism had arrived at the point where it could be identified with one great founder, such as Pound, it had concentrated its energies on the task of the long poem, which included history in an effort to conserve and memorialize rather than create and disrupt. From the very beginning the women Modernists all expressed their resistance to this codification and to an identification with their own generation of male poets. Stein claimed that "she did not understand why since the writing was so clear and natural they mocked at and were enraged by her work," but, of course, she did everything she could to distance herself from such figures as Pound, whom she called a village explainer, and Eliot, whom she parodied. H.D. set her poetics against the "new schools of destructive art theorists," among whom she must have numbered her friend Pound. Moore, generally more agreeable, nonetheless exercised her independence, not only in her reviews but in her energetic editing of poems such as Hart Crane's "The Wine Menagerie," which she accepted for the *Dial* and radically changed.

In contrast to what they regarded as negative and destructive attitudes these women poets were anxious to establish a poetics based on generativity, revision, and a curiosity that confirmed otherness. In their work the lyric "I" dissolves in an interactive process that allows a participatory celebration even of such a thing as a glacier's obduracy, in Moore's "The Octopus," or a "dubious" crossroads god, in H.D.'s "Hermes of the Ways," or the painter's "having always something being coming out" in Stein's portrait of Picasso. Because they were considered marginal figures even by their friends among the male Modernists, these women were free to experiment long after their male contemporaries were moved to consolidate and conserve their positions. Moreover, the relentlessly experimental writing of these women poets was not limited by the misogyny, reactionary politics, and conservative impulse that held back their male counterparts. They have waited almost a century for the readers that they have today because they were at least that far ahead of their times.

Margaret Dickie

Further Reading

Costello, Bonnie. *Marianne Moore: Imaginary Possessions.* Cambridge: Harvard University Press. 1981.

DeKoven, Marianne. *A Different Language: Gertrude Stein's Experimental Writing.* Madison: University of Wisconsin Press, 1983.

Friedman, Susan Stanford. *Penelope's Web: Gender, Modernity, H.D.'s Fiction.* Cambridge: Cambridge University Press, 1990.

———— *Psyche Reborn: The Emergence of H.D.* Bloomington: Indiana University Press, 1981.

Friedman, Susan Stanford, and Rachel Blau DuPlessis. eds. *Signets: Reading H.D.* Madison: University of Wisconsin Press, 1990.

H.D. *H.D.: Collected Poems, 1912–1944.* Ed. Louis L. Martz. New York: New Directions, 1983.

Hollenberg, Donna Krolik. *H.D.: The Poetics of Childbirth and Creativity.* Boston: Northeastern University Press, 1991.

Holley, Margaret. *The Poetry of Marianne Moore: A Study in Voice and Value.* Cambridge: Cambridge University Press, 1987.

Moore, Marianne. *The Complete Poems of Marianne Moore.* New York: Macmillan, 1967.

Neuman, Shirley, and Ira B. Nadel, eds. *Gertrude Stein and the Making of Literature.* Boston: Northeastern University Press, 1988.

Ruddick, Lisa. *Reading Gertrude Stein: Body, Text, Gnosis.* Ithaca: Cornell University Press, 1990.

Slatin, John. *The Savage's Romance: The Poetry of Marianne Moore.* State Park: Pennsylvania State University Press, 1986.

Stapleton, Laurence. *Marianne Moore: The Poet's Advance.* Princeton: Princeton University Press, 1978.

Stein, Gertrude. *Selected Writings of Gertrude Stein.* Ed. Carl Van Vechten. New York: Modern Library, 1962.

———— *The Yale Gertrude Stein.* Selections, with an introduction by Richard Kostelanetz. New Haven: Yale University Press, 1980.

Steiner, Wendy. *Exact Resemblance to Exact Resemblance: The Literary Portraiture of Gertrude Stein.* New Haven: Yale University Press, 1978.

Robert Frost and the Poetry of Survival

Robert Frost (1874–1963) was among the great poets of this century—or any century. Only T. S. Eliot and Wallace Stevens, in his own lifetime, could be thought of as challenging voices. Nevertheless, as original as Frost was in his own extraordinary ways, his work can be read as a culmination of the tradition of plain-spoken poetry in which the natural world is mined for metaphors of spirit: a tradition mostly associated in English poetry with William Wordsworth, who at the beginning of the nineteenth century defined a poet as simply "a man speaking to men."

Frost was a competitive man, as his biographer Lawrance Thompson has shown. Two of his main rivals at the start of his career were Edwin Arlington Robinson (1869–1935) and Carl Sandburg (1878–1967). Robinson was a poet of considerable gifts whose dramatic lyrics are still underestimated by critics. As Roy Harvey Pearce has written in *The Continuity of American Poetry* (1961): "Robinson at his best transformed the characteristically egocentric nineteenth-century poem into a vehicle to express the exhaustion and failure of its primary impulse." Robinson showed that to renew the old-fashioned Romantic lyric, poets would have to come to terms with nature as it had been affected by the industrial revolution. They would have to deal with a mechanized, impoverished, soiled, even burnt-out world. In a beautiful poem called "Walt Whitman," Robinson wrote, "The master-songs are ended, and the man / That sang them is a name." No more the mere celebration of man, nature, and machine that Whitman created in *Leaves of Grass*.

Robinson pioneered an American version of the dramatic monologue that had been popular in England throughout the century. He conjured a small New England town called Tilbury Town, which he peopled with such types as Richard Cory, Charles Carville, Minniver Cheevy, Luke Havergal, Aunt Imogen, and Eben Flood. He characterized New England, in his poem "New England," as a place "where the wind is always north-north-east / And children learn to walk on frozen toes." And his acerbic, depressive New Englanders seem always on the brink of survival. Some, such as poor Richard Cory, "a gentleman from sole to crown," do not survive: Richard Cory, "one calm summer night, / Went home and put a bullet through his head."

Frost was asked to write an introduction to a book of Robinson's poetry shortly after the poet's death. In a letter to a friend at the time of this request, he wrote of Robinson: "How utterly romantic the enervated old soak is. The way he thinks of poets in the Browningese of "Ben Jonson"! The way he thinks of cucolding lovers and cucold husband in "Tristram"! Literary conventions! I feel as if I had been somewhere on hot air like a fire-balloon. Not with him altogther. I haven't more than half read him since "The Town Down the River." I simply couldn't lend a whole ear to all that Arthurian twaddle twiddled over after the Victorians." For all this vitriol Frost nevertheless learned a good deal from Robinson, a debt he would never acknowledge.

Sandburg, too, had an influence on Frost. An almost exact contemporary, he "made it" before Frost, reciting his Whitmanlike poems in celebration of America across the country: "Chicago," "The People, Yes," "Grass," and others. Like Vachel Lindsay, whom he resembles in spirit, Sandburg sought a popular audience and developed a homey persona that played well in public—as Frost would later do himself. Sandburg learned a great deal, as Frost had, from Amy Lowell, H.D., and Ezra Pound, the Imagists, and his famous poem "Fog" became a model of sorts for a "modern" poem, as he describes it rolling in

> on little cat feet.
>
> It sits looking
> over the harbor and city
> on silent haunches
> and then moves on.

Sandburg wrote that poetry is "a series of explanations of life, fading off into horizons too swift for explanations." This marries well with

Frost's famous definition of poetry as "a momentary stay against confusion." Sandburg is always blither, more simple-minded, and "softer" than Frost. And in many ways Frost invented himself in contrast to a man like Sandburg, whose easy liberalism and identification with "the common man" struck him as false. Frost is the loner, the individualist, and his poetry is a poetry of survival.

Frost's accomplishments as a poet were hard won. A New Englander who spent some time in San Francisco as a child, he struggled for recognition for two decades after dropping out of Dartmouth and Harvard and marrying his hometown sweetheart, Elinor Miriam White. (Elinor and Robert had been tied for valedictory honors in their senior class at Lawrence High School, in Massachusetts.) Frost stumbled from job to job, farming in Derry and Franconia, New Hampshire, teaching school, loafing. He loved listening to his country neighbors, paying attention to what he called "their tones of speech." It was this tone that he would capture and transform in some of his best poems.

In 1912 at the age of thirty-eight Frost quit his job of teaching at Pinkerton Academy, a rural prep school in New Hampshire, and sailed to Britain with his wife and young children. He had pretty much in hand the poems of *A Boy's Will*, his first book, which takes its title from a poem by Longfellow. In fact, by this time he already had completed much of his second book, *North of Boston*. The Frosts settled in a little English village called Beaconsfield, and Frost set out to meet everyone who was important in poetry circles in Britain, such as Ezra Pound. He also met a young poet called Edward Thomas, who would have a profound influence on his work. Frost's rural subjects fit in nicely with the Georgian school of poets who were just gaining a wide audience in Britain, and Frost found a publisher rather swiftly. David Nutt brought out *A Boy's Will* in 1913.

Frost, as always, understood exactly what he was doing. He was writing pastoral verse—poems on rural subjects written for a well-educated "city" audience—much as Horace and Virgil had done in ancient Rome. In *The Pastoral Art of Robert Frost* (1960) John F. Lynen writes with savvy about what "pastoralism" means in Frost:

Frost, like the writers of old pastoral, draws upon our feeling that the rural world is representative of human life in general. By working from this nodal idea he is able to develop in his poems a very broad range of reference without ever seeming to depart from particular mattters of fact. He says nothing of other places and other times—he gives us only the minute particulars of his own immediate experience; yet . . . the things described seem everywhere to point beyond the rural world. The effect is to create a remarkable depth of reference.

Frost, then, is not a naive chronicler of farm life in rural New England. He is a poet fully aware of every influence, from the ancient writers of Greek and Roman eclogues through the Romantics right up to his immediate contemporaries. Furthermore, he was a "Modernist" in his own way, which is why Ezra Pound—the ringmaster of literary Modernism—found him interesting.

Shortly after the publication of *A Boy's Will* in England, Frost wrote a memorable letter to his friend John T. Bartlett. In it he put forth a theory of poetry that he called "the sound of sense." "I am possibly the only person going who works on any but a worn out theory (principle I had better say) of versification. You see the great successses in recent poetry have been made on the assumption that the music of words was a matter of harmonized vowels and consonants. Both Swinburne and Tennyson arrived largely at effects in assonation. But they were on the wrong track or at any rate on a short track. They went the length of it." He separated himself from these writers, who represented the reigning orthodoxy. "I alone of English writers have set myself to make music out of what I may call the sound of sense."

The idea behind Frost's "sound of sense" theory is fascinating. "The best place to get the abstract sound of sense is from voices behind a door that cuts off the words," Frost explains. "It is the abstract vitality of our speech." In other words, the specific denotation of the words, what we usually think of as "content," is less important than the way the language moves something akin to the "mind's ear."

Frost expanded in this same letter on how the "sound of sense" relates to poetic meter. "If one is to be a poet he must learn to get cadences by skillfully breaking the sounds of sense with all their irregularity of accent across the regular beat of the metre." The metrical line is fixed, unnatural: a set number of strong accents or "beats." Ordinary speech fits irregularity into the abstract pattern of the meter. But the poetry in a line (another way of describing the "sound of sense") is the product of the difference between the abstract metrical line and the natural flow of speech.

The obsession with ordinary speech and its relation to poetry is partly what makes Robert Frost a modern poet. There is nothing of the elevation of poetic style found in many Victorian poets in his work, nothing self-consciously "poetic." The poetry resides in the plain sense of things, the articulation of moments of clarity and poise, the accumulation of what might be called "wisdom" in the residuals of meaning that have accrued by the end of the poem.

Another aspect of Frost's theory—one he would hold for life—is his understanding of symbolism and how it functions in a poem. Frost liked to call himself a Synecdochist. "If I must be classified as a poet," he wrote in another letter, "I might be called a Synecdochist, for I prefer the Synecdoche in poetry—that figure of speech in which we use a part for the whole." A symbol is always synechochal, which is to say that an image is meant to represent something larger than itself. The metaphorical aspects of the image are nonspecific, which gives them an aura of suggestiveness.

The poem "Mowing"—from *A Boy's Will*—is a good example of Frost's technique:

> There was never a sound beside the wood but one,
> And that was my long scythe whispering to the ground.
> What was it it whispered? I knew not well myself;
> Perhaps it was something about the heat of the sun,
> Something, perhaps, about the lack of sound—
> And that was why it whispered and did not speak.
> It was no dream of the gift of idle hours,
> Or easy gold at the hand of fay or elf:
> Anything more than the truth would have seemed too weak
> To the earnest love that laid the swale in rows,
> Not without feeble-pointed spikes of flowers
> (Pale orchises), and scared a bright green snake.
> The fact is the sweetest dream that labor knows.
> My long scythe whispered and left the hay to make.

Frost liked to write about working—physical labor—and he found in physical labor a synecdochal image: the "mowing" of the poem "stands in" for larger motions of the mind and spirit. That this is not just a poem about mowing hay should be obvious from the first line. Why was there "never" a sound beside the wood but one? Frost is separating this mowing from any purely physical act; the mowing is a mental action that isolates the poet (a favorite theme in Frost's work overall). The poet—and here "mowing" is analogous to writing poems—is thoroughly absorbed in the work that is productive of meaning. As if to reinforce the connection, the scythe is said to be "whispering." What does it whisper? Frost, in the Romantic tradition, does not place too much emphasis on the conscious aspects of literary production. A poet's meanings are "accidental." Thus, the mower says "I knew not well myself" what meaning was produced by his motion.

In typical Frostian fashion the speaker goes on to muse about possibilities: perhaps it was this or that. One sees a gradual unfolding of thought as image leads to image, as revelation produces revelation. As Lawrance Thompson notes in his early study of Frost called *Fire and Ice: The Art and Thought of Robert Frost* (1942):

The central theme is built around this blending of the earnest love which derives satisfaction from the activities of the immediate moment. The extensions of the imagery suggest a much deeper emotional perception than that derived from a mere statement of the essential meaning. Objects and sounds, the grass, the woods, the mower, sunlight, the snake, the flowers—all these combine to accentuate the intense pleasure within the mower himself.

Clearly, the physical act of mowing is only part of the story.

Frost adored paradox, and the surface simplicity of his poems is often undermined by currents of paradoxical meaning that undercut the central, surface motion of the poem. In effect, the poems "deconstruct" themselves. In "Mowing" there is the surface meaning that concerns the act of haying. The satisfaction of the work is contrasted with the "dream of the gift of idle hours," the feeling of relief that the work is accomplished and the feeling that one might have gained something: gold, a job done. The poet of the surface quickly interjects his belief that "anything but the truth would have seemed too weak," thus celebrating the work itself as the goal. To extend the analogy to, say, poetry: the goal is the writing of the poem, not the resulting reputation of the poem or poet. Indeed, with an aphoristic compression worthy of Ralph Waldo Emerson, Frost's great precursor, Frost says: "The fact is the sweetest dream that labor knows." Nevertheless, the last line subverts this. "My long scythe whispered and left the hay to make."

The last line is pregnant with possibilities. "Left the hay to make" is a Symbolist's ideal moment: an image that ramifies in many ways, that carries beyond its immediate denotation. To leave the hay "to make" is to let it ripen in the sun. The result of the work—the nourishment of cattle, for instance—comes later: months later, perhaps, as the cows in the winter barn munch on the hay. But one can hardly avoid other echoes; "Make hay while the sun shines" is only one (and plays into the sexual metaphor implicit in "Mowing," where the analogy to making love is obvious enough). Perhaps the poet's work is an avoidance of seizing the moment elsewhere? That a man's complete meaning is derived alone, at work, without women, is a consistent theme in Frost and one that could be explored at length in all of his work. But, most telling, the last line of "Mowing" suggests that meaning is not at hand, that the goodness of the work is an afterecho, something that follows indeterminately. This undermines the poem's central theme, which is that the "fact" is the best thing. (Although, even here, one should stop to wonder why a fact is the sweetest *dream* that labor knows.)

There is almost no poem by Frost that does not yield to long and careful reconsideration. His work resists easy interpretation; indeed, it often seems that Frost designed the poems to fool the innocent reader into taking the "easy gold" of a quick interpretation. Almost invariably, these quick readings are wrong. Frost is plainly the most deceptive poet in the history of our literature. He himself once said in a letter that "any poem is most valuable for its ulterior meaning."

The quest for "ulteriority" is all part of the Frostian world. On the surface one finds the sentimentalized view of New England embodied in familiar images: dry stone walls, woodlots, lonely farmhouses, woods full of snow, fields of flowers, good-hearted country people. But only a very superficial reading stops there. An early poem like "Storm Fear" is typical of the Frostian view of man against nature:

> When the wind works against us in the dark,
> And pelts with snow
> The lower chamber window on the east,
> And whispers with a sort of stifled bark,
> The beast,
> 'Come out! Come out!'—
> It costs no inward struggle not to go,
> Ah, no!
> I count our strength,

Two and a child,
Those of us not asleep subdued to mark
How the cold creeps as the fire dies at length,—
How drifts are piled,
Dooryard and road ungraded,
Till even the comforting barn grows far away,
And my heart owns a doubt
Whether 'tis in us to arise with day
And save ourselves unaided.

Frost's personae in his poems are often afraid of the natural world. There is none of the mystical urge to unite with nature one sometimes finds in Romantic poets. The nature of New England is inhospitable, something to be "got through." Frost—and his surrogates in his poems—want to stand apart from nature; the emphasis, always, is upon survival, the effort to "save ourselves unaided."

Frost's second book of poems, *North of Boston*, which followed a year after *A Boy's Will*, is perhaps his most brilliantly sustained collection. It contains half a dozen of his most famous poems: "Mending Wall," "The Death of a Hired Man," "Home Burial," "A Servant to Servants," "After Apple-Picking," and "The Wood-Pile." This last poem, one not often recognized as one of Frost's very best, is a remarkable example of the Symbolist work of his early period. It is about a man who is "out walking in a frozen swamp one grey day"—a typical situation in a Frost poem. The poet-as-loner is a frequent image, one that derives from the Romantic tradition (one thinks especially of Wordsworth here, who in a poem such as "Resolution and Independence" walks out in the countryside in search of instruction of a spiritual kind). The speaker in Frost's poem stumbles upon a cord of wood in the middle of a symbolic Nowhere: "a cord of maple, cut and split / And piled—and measured, four by four by eight." What was it doing out there, beyond the reach of human activity? There was no house in sight for it to warm, no other signs of humanity. It was just left there to "warm the frozen swamp as best it could / With the slow smokeless burning of decay."

Again, one searches Frost for "ulteriority," for the synecdochal meaning of the poem. What does the woodpile "stand for" in addition to its most literal, and important, level of meaning? It would be misguided not to recognize that, most crucially, this is a poem about a woodpile. One can almost hear Frost smirking at the critic who would too quickly leap to grab at metaphorical rings of interpretation. Nevertheless, the woodpile is clearly an object of human labor, the product of careful craftsmanship and sustained attention. It is, of course, very like a poem: something constructed for the sheer love of doing it, left by itself to "warm the frozen swamp as best it could." The natural world, left to its own devices, is pointless in Frost's deeply humanistic view of reality; indeed, one may well take William Blake's line as a gloss on all of Frost's poetry: "Without man, nature is barren."

In *North of Boston* Frost also began to experiment with the dramatic poem—the monologue or dialogue poem. An old couple, Mary and Warren, discuss the fact that "Silas is back" in "The Death of the Hired Man." Silas, an old hired man who has left Warren's employment, has come home to die. Frost catches the regional cant of these voices with eerie perfection:

> "Where did you say he'd been?
>
> "He didn't say. I dragged him to the house,
> And gave him tea and tried to make him smoke.
> I tried to make him talk about his travels.
> Nothing would do: he just kept nodding off."
>
> "What did he say? Did he say anything?"
>
> "But little."
>
>   "Anything? Mary, confess
> He said he'd come to ditch the meadow for me."
>
> "Warren!"
>
>   "But did he? I just want to know."
>
> "Of course he did. What would you have him say?
> Surely you wouldn't grudge the poor old man
> Some humble way to save his self-respect.
> He added, if you really care to know,
> He meant to clear the upper pasture, too."

On and on Mary and Warren struggle to come to terms with the fact that "Silas is back." The final turn, of course, is that Silas is dead and the wrangling is all for nought. Frost had an astonishing gift for drama—indeed, he is one of our best dramatic poets. And "The Death of the Hired Man" remains among his most memorable efforts, as does

"Home Burial," a poem about a young couple trying to come to terms with the death of a child.

Anyone who imagines that Frost romanticizes country people and farm life has not read his poems carefully. The world conjured in these poems is not idyllic. Death, exhaustion, illness, marital bitterness, cold, and moral bankruptcy are close at hand. Frost's poems are built upon darkness, and the world he sees is one where sublimity, as in Wordsworth, is fostered by both beauty and terror in equal proportions.

A poem in *Mountain Interval* (1916), Frost's third volume, called " 'Out, Out—' " is among his strongest, darkest, and most exemplary poems about country people. Its opening is memorable in every way:

> The buzz saw snarled and rattled in the yard
> And made dust and dropped stove-length sticks of wood,
> Sweet-scented stuff when the breeze drew across it,
> And from there those that lifted eyes could count
> Five mountain ranges one behind the other
> Under the sunset far into Vermont.

Frost's easy command of the blank verse line is breathtaking. The poem opens with an idyllic version of rustic country life, but it soon takes a turn into some of the darkest regions of this poet's emotional territory. The boy who is the subject of the poem is cutting wood with the buzz saw when his sister calls him in to supper. He turns quickly, and the saw cuts off his hand. The economy of the way Frost expresses himself here adds to the dislocation one feels:

> At the word, the saw,
> As if to prove saws knew what supper meant,
> Leaped out at the boy's hand, or seemed to leap—
> He must have given the hand. However it was,
> Neither refused the meeting.

In that "However it was" one locates a dark whimsicality that is part of the Frostian tone.

The narrative continues with succinct power. A doctor is called, and soon the doctor "put him in the dark of ether." But there is really nothing that can be done for the poor boy:

> He lay and puffed his lips out with his breath.
> And then—the watcher at his pulse took fright.

No one believed. They listened at his heart.
Little—less—nothing!—and that ended it.
No more to build on there. And they, since they
Were not the one dead, turned to their affairs.

The seeming callousness of those last lines are part of the Frostian effect. A casual reading might well give the reader the impression that Frost is portraying these people as pragmatic to a point of inhumanity. But the total meaning of the poem, framed by the title's quotation from *Macbeth*, goes beyond mere callousness. Frost invokes the tradition of tragedy, where "life is but a walking candle." It is as if these rude country folk understand the larger point and in some way transcend their humble circumstances in what William Pritchard calls the "weird, unforgettable bluntness" of the poem. They are deeply enthralled to the labor-value of the boy. His hand is gone, so there was "No more to build on there." The buzz saw, snarling and rattling, is a product of the mechanical revolution that has in effect ruined the lives of these people. It implies a world beyond the farm, an economic system that has diminished the world as a whole.

Mountain Interval also contains "The Oven Bird," one of Frost's unforgettable sonnets. Like "Mowing," it is a poem implicitly about the act of writing, about a bird who "knows in singing not to sing," which is to say that he must abandon the worn-out poetical diction and rhetorical conventions of his predecessors and offer a new kind of song. "The question that he frames in all but words / Is what to make of a diminished thing." The last two lines resonate with implications. What poet now writing is not faced with this dilemma? The world as we find it, much as the world Frost found, is sadly diminished, and the poet's job in the twentieth century has been what to make of this world, how to respond to its indignities, its savage and vengeful self-absorption, its greed, its abandonment of common decency and justice.

Perhaps the most haunting poem in *Mountain Interval* is "An Old Man's Winter Night," a poem about an old man dying in the wintry climate of New England and alone: "All out-of-doors looked darkly in at him / Through the thin frost, almost in separate stars." The poem meditates implicitly on the human condition as a whole, though it remains neatly, even maniacally, focused on the single old man here who "stood with barrels round him—at a loss." The old man is somehow made to bear the weight of all human loneliness, even though "a light he was to no one but himself / Where now he sat, concerned with he knew what, / A quiet light, and then not even that." The man's inner light, as it were, goes out as he sleeps; there is nothing left but the glimmer in the woodstove and the pale moonlight. The poem ends with a handful of deeply haunting lines:

> One aged man—one man—can't keep a house,
> A farm, a countryside, or if he can,
> It's thus he does it of a winter's night.

The word "keep" is central here, as elsewhere in Frost, carrying a freight of ambiguous meanings. The word's original denotation, in the Anglo-Saxon, is "to hold, to seize." By implication, a person's duty in life is to bear witness (as in the title of a late volume by Frost, *A Witness Tree*), to maintain a vigil. Frost's poet is a hermit who nonetheless lets his light shine, keeps the faith, holds steady against the chaos of the universe.

Critics such as Lionel Trilling and Randall Jarrell have stressed the darkness in Frost, his sense of the spiritual blight, and they were right to do so. But there is a side of Frost that might be called "twilight." It emerges in poems like "After Apple-Picking," "Hyla Brook," "The Sound of Trees," and in so many of the later poems. Frost is always the poet of survival, and survival for him entails the act of cognition itself. "After Apple-Picking" is, according to Reuben Brower and other critics, one of Frost's finest moments. It is a deeply strange poem, to be sure. It begins:

> My long two-pointed ladder's sticking through a tree
> Toward heaven still,
> And there's a barrel that I didn't fill
> Beside it, and there may be two or three
> Apples I didn't pick upon some bough.
> But I am done with apple-picking now.

Again, one must look beyond the surface of a Frost poem to make any real sense of it. First, the poem is not about the work of apple-picking but about the feelings that follow from it. "I am drowsing off," the speaker says in the monologue. And the poem begins to conjure a peculiar dream state, a twilight in which the poem moves between the real world and the dream world, between life and art. "I am overtired / Of the great harvest I myself desired," says Frost. Here is the exhaustion of composition, with its unbearable desire for something that can never be accomplished, since poetry is always a search for something beyond reach, a quest for a simulacrum of heaven, a place where the absolute is attainable and where all contrarieties are reconciled. Frost, still a young poet, displays an almost overwhelming burden of possibilities: "There were ten thousand thousand fruit to touch, / Cherish in hand, lift down, and not let fall." The last line quoted is heart-breakingly beautiful, the syntax imitating and embodying the action it mimics, with the asymmetry of the last phrase ("and not let fall") made wonderfully strange by its lack of parallelism.

Mountain Interval also contains the famous "Birches." In a fine book called *Robert Frost and New England*, John Kemp identifies this poem as the place where a different kind of Frost poem has its origins. These are the poems—and there are more and more of them as Frost's career unfolds—where the poet speaks as farmer-sage, as a homespun philosopher. The poem as a form of wisdom literature has an honorable tradition, of course, and Frost at his best does this kind of thing very well. "Good fences make good neighbors" is a line spoken by a farmer in "Mending Wall" that typifies his approach to poetry. In "Birches" there is no farmer speaking but Frost himself as farmer when he presents a totalizing statement in the last line of the poem, "One could do worse than be a swinger of birches." The calculated understatement here in some ways undercuts the poem, which is mostly a splendid monologue. Indeed, there are incomparable passages in "Birches," as in this image of the girls in the following lines:

> You may see their trunks arching in the woods
> Years afterwards, trailing their leaves on the ground
> Like girls on hands and knees that throw their hair
> Before them over their heads to dry in the sun.

The symbolic motion of the poem, too, is controlled with consummate artistry. The poem is about boys climbing birches (the sexual implications of this, as in "Mowing" and "Putting in the Seed," are wonderful to contemplate) to subdue them, to ride them to the ground. Indeed, the poem moves toward a remarkable statement: "Earth's the right place for love: / I don't know where it's likely to go better." These lines, according to James M. Cox in a strong essay called "Robert Frost and the End of the New England Line," are "Frost's greatest lines—lines which reveal the grace and loss and gain of all Frost's life and language."

I think one may take Frost at face value in many of his wise utterances, as in the above instance. But Frost is dangerously canny, and—as such—he often means less than he says or, occasionally, the opposite of what he says. A crucial example is found in "The Road Not Taken," which ends with the often-quoted lines:

> Two roads diverged in a wood, and I—
> I took the one less traveled by,
> And that has made all the difference.

A less than rigorous look at the poem may lead one to believe that Frost's "moral" is embodied in those lines; the poem is taken as a call to independence, preaching originality and Emersonian self-reliance. But the poem deconstructs its conclusion stanza by stanza. The poem's first three stanzas follow:

> Two roads diverged in a yellow wood,
> And sorry I could not travel both
> And be one traveler, long I stood
> And looked down one as far as I could
> To where it bent in the undergrowth
>
> Then took the other, as just as fair,
> And having perhaps the better claim,
> Because it was grassy and wanted wear;
> Though as for that the passing there
> Had worn them really about the same,
>
> And both that morning equally lay
> In leaves no step had trodden black.
> Oh, I kept the first for another day!
> Yet knowing how way leads onto way,
> I doubted if I should ever come back.

The poem, in fact, stresses that there is no difference, or little difference, between the two roads offered—it is all in the mind. The second stanza claims that "the other" is "just as fair." The same stanza concludes that this same path is worn "really about the same" as the first road, presumably the more well-traveled road. Indeed, by the third stanza the point is confirmed: "And both that morning equally lay / In leaves no step had trodden black." What more evidence does a reader need? So what is the "one less traveled by" that makes "all the difference" to the speaker? The clue to the meaning of this poem lies in the two lines that open the final stanza: "I shall be telling this with a sigh / Somewhere ages and ages hence."

The poet will be telling his grandchildren, say, that he "took the road less traveled by" and that it "made all the difference." But he will be lying. The poem is, perhaps, about the tendency in this poet and, by extension, the tendency in all of us to romanticize our past, to lay claim to the "road less traveled," to glorify "the road not taken." But, indeed, the road not taken is *not taken* yet. The title itself embraces the dazzling and tantalizing ambiguity of this poem, which is infinitely more complex than first meets the eye. One should read this poem as a warning. Frost is saying: Don't take me literally.

Frost's fourth book, *New Hampshire* (1923), contains a number of Frost's best-known lyrics: "Fire and Ice," "Dust of Snow," "The Aim Was Song," "Nothing Gold Can Stay," "Stopping by Woods on a Snowy Evening," "For Once, Then, Something," and "The Need of Being Versed in Country Things." Frost's penchant for the brief lyric with an aphoristic bite is sharpened to a point of fire in many of these poems, which marry beautifully with W. H. Auden's chief requirement for poetry—that it be "memorable language." One never forgets a poem like "Dust of Snow":

> The way a crow
> Shook down on me
> The dust of snow
> From a hemlock tree
>
> Has given my heart
> A change of mood
> And saved some part
> Of a day I rued.

Here, Frost ties in with so many other Modernist writers in savoring the moment of sudden illumination, what Joyce called an "epiphany." But in Frostian fashion there is something underplayed as well; a mere change of mood is all that is celebrated, a shift in feelings. The poem also, by implication, presents a rather gloomy image of the poet as solitary depressive as he wanders in the wintry landscape rueing the day.

New Hampshire much more than *Mountain Interval* marks a beginning of the persona of Frost as philosopher of the common man, a persona that would eventually smother the poet. The long title poem "New Hampshire" is not, for instance, one of Frost's finer moments. Frost claims here to have "written several books against the world in general." He mentions having recently visited New York, where he gets involved in "converse with a New York alec / About the new school of the pseudo-phallic." Here is the onset of a frustrating Frostian stance: Frost as Reactionary. There is no doubt that Frost identified with political conservatism; what he takes aim at in his poems is anti-New. He hates anything that smacks of Freudianism. He hates Marxism. He is the New England equivalent of a Southern Agrarian, preferring small farming communities to large industrial cities. He hates the modern world, with its machines, its pace, its lack of values, its tendencies toward collective behavior. He is always the Emersonian or Thoreauvian Romantic, the individualist, falling back upon a stance of self-reliance. One mostly applauds these views, except when Frost gets cute, as he does increasingly in poems from "New Hampshire" on.

Frost would from now on alternate masks. He could still write in his powerful "realistic" mode, and many of his very best poems in this style lay ahead of him, including "Spring Pools," "Acquainted with the Night," "Design," "Provide, Provide," "The Silken Tent," "The Subverted Flower," "The Most of It," "Directive," "The Gift Outright," and "Choose Something Like a Star." But, increasingly, the books contained chatty, even verbose, presentations such as "The Lesson for the Day" and "Build Soil." The latter, for instance, rambles on in this vein:

> Is socialism needed, do you think?

> We have it now. For socialism is
> An element in any government.
> There's no such thing as socialism pure—
> Except as an abstraction of the mind.
> There's only democratic socialism,
> Monarchic socialism—oligarchic,
> The last being what they seem to have in Russia.

This is Frost giving vent to hot professorial wind.

In 1920 Frost quit a teaching job at Amherst College to begin, as he wrote to his friend Wilbur Cross, "hurling fistfulls [of poems] right and left." He claimed to have "kicked himself free from care and intellectuality." He had recently won a Pulitzer Prize—the first of four he would receive in his liftetime—and was ready to dig in. The oddity is, of course, that Frost's digging in did not result necessarily in better poems.

There was something self-satisfied in Frost that, in his lesser poems, hurt him. One sees this attitude reflected in a telling letter to a poet-friend, Kimball Flaccus:

You wish the world better than it is, more poetical. You are that kind of poet. I would rate as the other kind. I wouldn't give a cent to see the world, the United States or even New York made better. I want them left just as they are for me to make poetical on paper. I don't ask anything done to them that I won't do to them myself. I'm a mere selfish artist most of the time. I have no quarrel with the material. The grief will be if I can't transmute it into poems. I don't want the world made safer for poetry or easier. To hell with it. That is its own lookout. Let it stew in its own materialism. No, not to Hell with it. Let it hold its position while I do it in art. My whole anxiety is for myself as a performer. Am I any good? That's what I'd like to know and all I need to know.

This attitude hurt Frost terribly in the long run. But there were marvelous reprieves from this selfishness, and Frost would time and again find himself engaged with the world in the generous way that is essential for the production of great poetry.

West-Running Brook appeared in 1928. It opens with "Spring Pools," one of Frost's most powerful and enigmatic lyrics.

> These pools that, though in forests, still reflect
> The total sky almost without defect,
> And like the flowers beside them, chill and shiver,
> Will like the flowers beside them soon be gone,
> And yet not out by any brook or river,
> But up by roots and bring dark foliage on.

As with so many of Frost's poems, the natural world is a source of metaphor, and metaphorical thinking is for Frost the most refined level of thought. As Margaret Edwards notes in an essay called "Pan's Song Revised" that was included in the first volume of *Frost: Centennial Essays* (1974), this poem regards nature as a cycle wherein the "purpose of destruction—in this case the absorption of the pools—is creation." Edwards continues, "The water will 'bring dark foliage on.' The pools make summer possible. And yet there is that note of regret for what the inevitable process will 'blot out and drink up and sweep away.'"

West-Running Brook also contains "Tree at My Window," a poem that meditates on the traditional Romantic conflict between subject and object, posed here as an opposition between "inner weather" and "outer weather." The poet, in classical fashion, addresses the tree:

> Tree at my window, window tree,
> My sash is lowered when night comes on;
> But let there never be curtain drawn
> Between you and me.

He goes on to contemplate this "thing next most diffuse to cloud" and says that not all the rattling of the leaves-as-tongues "could be profound." But he identifies with the tree, reaching for a reconciliation of subject and object through imaginative sympathy:

> But, tree, I have seen you taken and tossed,
> And if you have seen me when I slept,
> You have seen me when I was taken and swept
> And all but lost.

The poem moves toward an ingenious resolution in the final stanza:

> That day she put our heads together,
> Fate had her imagination about her,
> Your head so much concerned with outer,
> Mine with inner weather.

Thus, the human mind is mirrored by the natural world, and the natural world is, conversely, mirrored; the concern with "weather"—which one might identify with "mood" or "spirit"—connects the two worlds, draws them into the same cognitive sphere.

The demarcation of "inner" and "outer" worlds is discussed in lively terms by Frank Lentricchia in "Robert Frost and Modern Literary Theory" (in the *Centennial Essays* volume):

Something in Frost wants to distinguish landscapes, to mark off "inner" from "outer," subject from object, human from nonhuman; perhaps it is because Frost feels so strongly that the outer landscape is not congenial to the self: the sash, at night, must be lowered, we must stay enclosed for our own good. All of which is to say that this poem, like so many poems by Frost, is grounded in a tough realist's view of things. Yet Frost gives us no unnavigable gulf between subject and object. The sash must be lowered, of course, but the curtain must never be drawn across the window. Thus, between self and not-self Frost places a transparency which allows for an interaction of sorts, as enclosed self and weathered tree take creative looks at one another.

The tree is like a person, in that it dreams and drifts in sleep; the speaker, treelike, is "taken and swept / And all but lost." So we get a complex sense of the relations between interior and exterior landscapes, with consciousness as "weather" serving as a kind of mediating space. (Lentricchia notes that John Dewey, like William James before him, believed that selfhood exists only as something potential until it is, in Dewey's words, "both formed and brought to consciousness through interaction with an environment.")

A Further Range appeared in 1936. As the title suggests, Frost was attempting to look beyond what he had done already in poetry. Unfortunately, the collection is weighted down with poems that, in retrospect, seem chatty and slight. Frost was by now on the college reading circuit in a busy way, moving from college town to college town and reciting his poems to large and appreciative audiences. He was rapidly becoming the quintessential American bard, and audiences looked to him for "delight" as much as "wisdom." Poems such as "Departmental" and "A Record Stride" are burdened with a fatal cuteness. The latter, for instance, ends with a sophomoric few lines:

> And I ask all to try to forgive me
> For being as over-elated
> As if I had measured the country
> And got the United States stated.

It is hard to forgive Frost for this kind of poetry.

Nevertheless, *A Further Range* contains "Design," arguably one of the best sonnets ever written by an American poet. It is a frightening poem, one that confronts the dire possibility that the universe is not only godless but that God is evil. In keeping with the Imagist tendencies in modern poetry, Frost centers the poem on a picture:

> I found a dimpled spider, fat and white,
> On a white heal-all, holding up a moth
> Like a white piece of rigid satin cloth—
> Assorted characters of death and blight
> . . . .
> . . . .
> A snow-drop spider, a flower like a froth,
> And dead wings carried like a paper kite.

The white spider—already a freak of nature—has landed on a white flower with a white moth in its grip. None of these three elements is normally white, which gives each of them an abstract eeriness. The fact that these elements are "mixed ready to begin the morning right, / Like the ingredients of a witches' broth—" is deeply ironic: indeed, the language parodies the language of breakfast cereal ads. What we get here is an image that combines death and blight. There is nothing life-enhancing about anything in this piece of nature.

In the sestet of the sonnet, where issues raised in the octet are traditionally resolved, Frost simply offers three haunting and unanswerable questions:

> What had that flower to do with being white,
> The wayside blue and innocent heal-all?
> What brought the kindred spider to that height,
> Then steered the white moth thither in the night?
> What but design of darkness to appall?—
> If design govern in a thing so small.

The poem is in many ways the key to Frost's universe, a poem so perfect in its execution that one cannot imagine a word placed otherwise. Frost's tone is deftly controlled throughout, with the poet's serious point balanced nicely by the parodic language of the first stanza. Ever aware of the linguistic roots of words, Frost is inwardly winking when he uses the word "rigid" to modify "satin cloth." Likewise, at the end, he is certainly aware (as a former Latin teacher) that the word "appall" means "to make white" in its root sense. And Frost is delighting in the way he can wring an unexpected turn of meaning from the Classical argument from design.

That Frost was intimately familiar with English and American poetry is never in doubt: his work is full of quiet echoes of his predecessors. In "Design," for instance, one hears, a mock-echo of William Cullen Bryant's classic "To a Waterfowl," in which Bryant meditates on the argument from design and writes of God as "He who, from zone to zone / Guides through the boundless sky thy certain flight." One also sees in this poem a careful working out of some ideas raised by William James, the pragmatist, as Richard Poirier argues in *Robert Frost: The Work of Knowing* (1977).

A Witness Tree appeared during the Second World War, in 1942, when Frost was sixty-eight. It is the last of his books where the strong lyric gift of the earlier books remains present in any substantial way. The book opens with "The Silken Tent," a seamlessly perfect sonnet composed of one sentence. The subject and verb of the sentence are completed after the first two words are uttered: "She is." The poem is a conceit, with the "she" compared to a silken tent in many different ways. The poem unfolds with a sureness and directness that takes away one's breath, especially as the sonnet moves into its concluding motion, in which we learn that "she" is bound by the cords that hold the tent in place but "loosely bound / By countless silken ties of love and thought / To everything on earth the compass round." And it is "only by one's going slightly taut / In the capriciousness of summer air" that any sense of bondage is made apparent.

The high standard of "The Silken Tent" is maintained in a dozen more of the lyrics in *A Witness Tree*. One of the lesser known of these is "Come In," a poem that might be considered archetypally Frostian in that the protagonist wanders out by himself in the woods or countryside, often at night, and encounters something along the way that gives him pause to meditate. There is usually a piece of Yankee wisdom at the end. "Come In" fits this pattern nicely. The poet encounters a thrush—a very Romantic thing to do! The thrush is frequently identified, of course, with poetry. Yet the poet-wanderer of "Come In" doesn't want to come in, or to be taken in by the poetry of the thrush:

> But no, I was out for stars:
> I would not come in.
> I meant not even if asked,
> And I hadn't been.

A few pages later one encounters "The Most of It," which is equal to anything else in Frost. In this poem the poet-wanderer "thought he kept the universe alone." Again, Frost uses the word "keep" in a special way; here, it has the haunting sense of "being responsible for." His reason for thinking himself so responsible is the Blakean one. "Without man, nature is barren." Frost's nature is indeed cold, and it often seems to lack the humanization that William Blake demanded. Frost's hero calls out across the lake, hoping for "counter-love" and "original response." But what he gets instead is the sound of a great buck that leaped out of the woods and swam across the water toward him:

> Pushing the crumpled water up ahead,
> And landed pouring like a waterfall,
> And stumbled through the rocks with horny tread,
> And forced the underbrush—and that was all.

The force of "The Most of It" resides in the ferocity of the vision of nature embodied in the crudely powerful buck. Here is raw energy without human purpose.

"The Subverted Flower," which comes soon after, deconstructs "human" nature in the same brutal terms, this time embodied in the sexual urge of an adolescent boy who is reduced by his drives to a dog who froths at the mouth and seems to "bark outright." The poem is a little drama, with boy and girl confronting each other in a ritual dance of sorts out in a field. The setting is lush:

> She was standing to the waist
> In goldenrod and brake,
> Her shining hair displaced.

He is standing with a flower in his hand: the flower being a thinly disguised phallus. Indeed, "he flicked and flung the flower." And he gets caught as the girl's mother approaches and is horrified by the crude sight that she is forced to witness.

The girl is frothing at the mouth, too, as the poem is brought to a compelling halt, with the three-beat meter pounding like a bass drum as the melody of the lyric plays lightly over the drumming triple beat:

> And oh, for one so young
> The bitter words she spit
> Like some tenacious bit
> That will not leave the tongue.
> She plucked her lips for it,
> And still the horror clung.
> Her mother wiped the foam
> From her chin, picked up the comb
> And drew her backward home.

With the noble exception of "The Gift Outright," an unusual and unusually panoramic Frost poem, *A Witness Tree* falls away in the second half of the collection. While most poets would be delighted to have written poems such as "Time Out," "The Lost Follower," or "The Rabbit Hunter"—to mention a few of the more interesting poems that may be found here—the compact fury of Frost's best work is missing.

Frost wrote two long dramatic poems in the mid-forties: *A Masque of Reason* (1945) and *A Masque of Mercy* (1947). The former is a witty digression on the theme of Job, while the latter's focus is Jonah. In each

case the orginal Biblical story is replayed in a contemporary setting. But
there is little real drama in these masques, which are digressive and
pseudophilosophical in the manner of "West-Running Brook." Nevertheless, they are relatively unknown and deserve a wider readership
than they have thus far gotten.

In 1947 *Steeple Bush* was published. Reviewing this collection in the
New York Times Book Review, Randall Jarrell said that "most of the
poems merely remind you, by their persistence in the mannerisms of
what was genius, that they are the productions of someone who once,
and somewhere else, was a great poet." This is sadly true, although Jarrell wisely excepted a poem called "Directive," which is Frost's attempt
to write what M. H. Abrams once identified as "the greater Romantic
lyric." It is one of Frost's finest moments, a poem of huge imaginative
pressure that opens with some of this poet's most compelling lines:

> Back out of all this now too much for us,
> Back in a time made simple by the loss
> Of detail, burned, dissolved, and broken off
> Like graveyard marble sculpture in the weather,

And continues, building on these specific details:

> There is a house that is no more a house
> Upon a farm that is no more a farm
> And in a town that is no more a town.

"Directive" is both an elegy for a world lost in time and a program for
the future. It is Frost's version of Wordsworth's "Tintern Abbey," and
like that poem it begins with a journey backward to place where one
once had inspiration. Frost, at the tail end of his poetic career, senses his
own flagging powers. The focus is gone. The poet's language, once
capable of being fired to a fever pitch, has cooled. But here the poet
blows on the coals, which now break upon themselves and burn bright-
ly one last time. The poet returns to a child's playhouse by a stream,
where he finds a mock version of the Holy Grail. But here, in childhood, was the source of inspiration. Here in the woods by the stream
was the origin of all poetry:

> A brook that was the water of the house,
> Cold as a spring as yet so near its source,
> Too lofty and original to rage.

These lines provide a marvelous gloss upon Frost's entire corpus. His verse was always too "lofty and original to rage." The poet finds here, briefly, that momentary stay against confusion that has always meant so much to him, these Wordsworthian "spots of time" where time dissolves.

Except for the Keatsian "Choose Something Like A Star," there are few other places in *Steeple Bush* where one can easily rest for long. And there is very little to commend *In the Clearing*, which appeared in March of 1962. But Frost was, after all, almost ninety by the time this last book appeared.

Looking over the entire career of Robert Frost, one sees a breathtaking vista. Poem after poem breaks ground in places where one might never have thought a house of stanzas (a "stanza" is, literally, a room or floor) could be erected, and Frost builds and builds. His work is full of permanent settlements. His language and tone, his angles of vision, are a huge part of American literature and consciousness. And he has provided inspiration for contemporary poets as diverse as Richard Wilbur, Donald Hall, Robert Pack, Peter Davison, and Seamus Heaney. One is tempted, with Frost, to conclude by repeating his own great lines ending "Directive": "Here are your waters and your watering place. / Drink and be whole again beyond confusion."

Jay Parini

Further Reading

Frost, Robert. *The Poetry of Robert Frost.*, Ed. Edwin Connery Latham. New York: Henry Holt, 1969.

Poirier, Richard. *Robert Frost: The Work of Knowing.* New York: Oxford, 1977.

Pritchard, William H. *Robert Frost: A Literary Life Reconsidered.* New York: Oxford, 1984.

Thompson, Lawrance, and R. H. Winnick. *Robert Frost, A Biography.* New York: Holt, Rhinehart and Winston, 1981.

Ezra Pound's Imagist Aesthetics:
Lustra to *Mauberley*

T HE letters page of the *American Book Review* from November-December 1987 staged a nasty but epitomizing confrontation over Ezra Pound: Sister Bernetta Quinn, an apologist, defended the *Cantos* from the "irresponsible attack" of Paul Oppenheimer, who had ripped Pound in the previous issue; Oppenheimer, in his turn, savaged Quinn and the *Cantos'* "pervasive bigotry," "vapid ideas of economics and history," and "frequently poor writing." The opposition of aesthetic and moral realities says all there is to say about how much of Ezra Pound's reputation is still in dispute. Nearly fifty years after the Bollingen Committee awarded its prize to the *Pisan Cantos* people cannot make up their minds whether Pound is the man Eliot named "the better craftsman" or the man Wyndham Lewis once called "a man of impeccable taste and no vision." Pound's reputation goes on swinging between extremes of admiration and contempt, attracting biographers and others, amazed by how much of such a controversial life, through historical innocence or insensitivity, can be peeled away from its poetry.

Whether through merit or controversy, Pound has stayed in print. The collected shorter poems, *Personae* (1926), went through several editions and at least seven impressions before arriving in Baechler and Litz's truly satisfactory, recent, and much revised *Personae: The Shorter Poems of Ezra Pound* (New Directions, 1990), which contains not only an index and an accurate table of contents but detailed appendixes as well. Despite a respectable complement of published dissertations like

George Kearns's *Guide to Ezra Pound's Selected Cantos* (Rutgers University Press, 1980) and scholarly escorts like Edwards' and Vasse's alphabetical *Annotated Index to the Cantos of Ezra Pound: Cantos I–LXXXIV* (University of California Press, 1971), the editorial condition of the 815 pages of my 1986 reprint suggests, to someone if not of good will then at least paying attention, that what the *Cantos* need principally (and after ten printings) is a good copyeditor. Pound's letters contain some of the greatest prose written in the century and the best introduction to his work. They are often difficult but endlessly entertaining, give a capsule history of twentieth-century art, and ought to be required in all creative writing programs.

By some estimations the criticism may outlast the poetry. It was first collected by T. S. Eliot in the early fifties when Eliot edited and introduced *Literary Essays of Ezra Pound*, drawing from four earlier books—*Pavannes and Divisions* (1918), *Instigations* (1920), *Make It New* (1934), and *Polite Essays* (1937)—and noting the existence of much fugitive material, some "rescued from the files of periodicals" by the faithful James Laughlin, owner and publisher of New Directions. Eliot was limited by space and wholly excluded excerpts from two other major prose works: *Guide to Kulchur* (1938)—which has been more or less continuously in print and reappeared in 1970 with a brief preface by Pound, then two years away from death—and the earnestly undergraduate but still readable *The Spirit of Romance* (New Directions, 1968). A book Eliot neither mentioned nor excerpted, *Gaudier-Brzeska: A Memoir* (New Directions, 1979), is central to Imagism or Pound's art criticism. William Cookson undertook to supplement Eliot's selection and to "show the unity of Ezra Pound's vision" with *Ezra Pound: Selected Prose, 1909–1965* (New Directions, 1973), which contains writing on politics, religion and money along with some jejune aesthetic reflection that Eliot ignored, such as "I Gather the Limbs of Osiris" (1911–12). After the music and art criticism, both of which have found their way into collections, Pound's *Translations* (New Directions, 1953), *Confucius* (New Directions, 1951), and *The Confucian Odes* (New Directions, 1959) are probably indispensable to any knowledge of the man Eliot called "the inventor of Chinese poetry for our time." Finally, Pound the biographical project has, over the decades, attracted several biographies whose interest stops with their subtitles. We've seen Pound the "difficult individual," the "last rower," and most abysmally, "the solitary volcano," but none can claim the exhausting objectivity of

Humphrey Carpenter's *A Serious Character: The Life of Ezra Pound* (Houghton Mifflin, 1988), which ranks easily with Charles Olson's moving record of conversations with Pound at St. Elizabeth's, Earl Stock's not unbearable *Life of Ezra Pound* (Avon, 1970), and Hugh Kenner's critical masterwork, *The Pound Era* (University of California Press, 1972).

Pound is too enormous to surround in no matter how encyclopaedic an essay, so I limit myself to early and middle Pound, from *Lustra* through *Hugh Selwyn Mauberley*. I concede the objective validity of the moral issues: Pound's political excesses have blocked access to his poetry (and criticism) for so long and for so many that it is not unfair to wonder whether the former has not permanently ended passion for the latter. Two major assumptions, moreover, precede me. The first is the core insight of *The Pound Era*: "Pound's work, say from *Lustra* to the last *Cantos*, is the longest working-out in any art of premises like those of Cubism." I would put an even finer point on this: Pound, early or late, was an Imagist. The two-line "In a Station of the Metro," which appeared first in *Poetry* in 1912 and in a slightly different form in *Lustra*, is the formula that embodies the premises behind longer and more complex works—the works of Pound's own maturity, *Mauberley* and *The Cantos*, and work influenced by Pound, from Eliot's *The Waste Land* and Zukofsky's *A* to Olsen's *Maximus* poems, Ginsberg's *The Fall of America*, and Ammons's *A Tape for the Turn of the Year*. A second assumption: Imagism, no matter how congenial attempts to discredit it, was the first serious attempt to rethink poetry's discursive directions since Wordsworth. What happened to Imagism after Amy Lowell transformed it into "Amygism" is of historical interest only, but its theoretical implications, especially on poetry as a spoken medium, are not. As Pound himself said, "The great writers need no debunking," and Pound remains one of the great American writers of the English language. To take seriously him and his brainchild, Imagism, is to unpack the visionary background of twentieth-century art and understand why it is so hard, why it seemed so new, and why so many of its practitioners were so pessimistic about its future.

The distance Pound covered between *Ripostes* (1912) and *Lustra* (1915) is a measure of what he set out to escape—Romanticism principally and Symbolism secondly—and the poetic methodology that he would invent and call Imagism. After an education in broad cultural realities—modern technology, Cubism, oriental poetry—the "doctrine of the Image" reemerges as the ideogrammic method of the thirties. But Imagism itself is preceded by a cocooning, as it were, from which, if his prose alone is any indication, Pound brought two senses of himself. The first, that he was charged with a pedagogical mission, is, depending on your view of Pound's poetry, either its glory or calamity. The second, that a "scientific" understanding of the art of poetry is indispensable to its production or consumption, issues in an instrumentalist approach to everything, especially art. While the instrumentalist theme never disappears from Pound's poetry or criticism, it is, and especially early in the century, the demonic twin of American poetic theories, from Eliot's early criticism to Williams's description of a poem as a "machine made out of words." Both senses, one of the poet's role and the other of his philosophy, appear in "I Gather the Limbs of Osiris" (1911–12). "The artist seeks out the luminous detail and presents it. He does not comment. His work remains the permanent basis of psychology and metaphysics." Throughout the essay he distances himself from "Scholarship," meaning institutional learning, by retreating to similar revisionary formulations—capitalizing *Luminous Detail* in the second paragraph, for instance. His debt to Shelley's *Defense*, to Coleridge, to French Symbolism is undeniable. He is a Shelleyan legislator ("As for myself, I have tried to clear up a certain messy place in the history of literature"—he was barely twenty-six when he wrote this), a Socratic dialectician charged with cleaning up public taste by requiring poets and readerships to know things, and at times a doctor ("If a book reveal to us something of which we were unconscious, it feeds us with its energy; if it reveal to us nothing . . . it draws energy from us"). In a section called "On Technique" he seems to find his range: "Let us imagine that words are like great hollow cones of steel of different dullness and acuteness. . . . Let us imagine them charged with a force like electricity, or, rather, radiating a force from their apexes— some radiating, some sucking in." The thing runs on for another one hundred or so words and makes us wish he would explain his explanation, especially since he ultimately places the passage under erasure ("This peculiar energy which fills the cones is the power of tradition, and the control of it is the 'Technique of content,' which nothing short of genius understands"). Only his enthusiasm forgives the silliness of the analogy. By comparison, the one Eliot fetched out eight years later to explain how poetry is like science—"I invite you to consider . . . the action which takes place when a bit of finely filiated platinum is introduced into a chamber containing oxygen and sulphur dioxide"—is almost tame. Not silly, however, is how much Pound needed a metaphor of precisely this instrumentalist character to mediate the recidivistic post-Symbolist-late-Romantic rhetoric quickening his own.

Symbolism worried Pound. Verlaine and Baudelaire he lumped together, claiming that neither "is the least use, pedagogically, I mean. They beget imitation and one can learn nothing from them." The Symbolist "dealt with 'association,'" "degraded the symbol to the status of a word," conferred on his symbols "a fixed value." Yeats, whose presence drew Pound to England in 1906 and whom Pound, late in 1913, served as amanuensis and collaborator, was also suspect. A "transparent lamp around a spiritual flame," Yeats called the symbol, itself the manifest content of what emanates from *Anima Mundi*. "O Rose, red rose, proud rose of all my days" is a pointer to no real rose at all but to an abstraction that stands for Ireland, Intellectual Beauty, whatever Yeats wishes. As late as the *Pisan Cantos* (1948), Pound identified visionary Symbolism with spiritual evil:

> Le Paradis n'est pas artificiel
> and Uncle William dawdling around Notre Dame
> in search of whatever
>
>   paused to admire the symbol
> with Notre Dame standing inside it
>
>   (Canto 83)

The French sentence is an allusion to Baudelaire's *Les Paradis Artificiels*, a memoir of hash-and-opium addiction indebted to DeQuincy: the clear line-of-sight is from Baudelaire, who represents by implication the late-Romantic and Symbolist traditions, to Yeats, who represents even later variants of both. A *paradis artificiel* is a rhetorical necessity imposed on the world by those who cannot live in it and derives from a *goût de l'infini*, a taste for infinity (as Baudelaire titles the first chapter). The world of Verlaine's *Claire de Lune,* say, or of Yeats's "Byzantium" are just such artificial paradises, toy or substitute worlds. A symbol, Pound believed, is potentially evil because it fixes an existential value in a word and replaces a physical with an intellectual (or mystical) value; the Symbolist then proceeds—and the analogy with charging money at interest, or usury, certainly would not have escaped Pound—to circulate the substitution term as poetic currency. "The imagiste's images," on the other hand, "have a variable significance, like the signs a, b, and x in algebra," Pound said. The resilience of the image was its ability to resist capture by whatever rhetoric a greedy politician or an incompetent poet might dream up to exploit it.

There is no getting around this last point: Pound was obsessed with the exploitation of language. His faith in the poet as public servant, a major persona in *Lustra*, stands behind his denunciation in *Gaudier-Brzeska: A Memoir* (1915–16) of "the periodic sentence and the flowing paragraph" as behind the fall of Renaissance Italy. "For when words cease to cling close to things, kingdoms fall, empires wane and diminish. Rome went because it was no longer the fashion to hit the nail on the head. They desired orators." The image was itself an *instrument* of vision, a lens, as well as an expression of that organic property of human consciousness to which Coleridge gave the name Imagination. Like a scientist, the Imagist learned from history and used it; unlike the scientist, he dealt in emotions. "I see," said the unidentified Russian to Pound, "you wish to give people new eyes, not to make them see some new particular thing." The vision of this new artist-as-scientist gained focus through the image, which resisted reduction to the monadic simplicity of the symbol, whether a placard word, a political slogan, or a poetic term.

One needs to keep Pound's moral fervor in mind in reading *Lustra* for another reason: his obsession with historical memory, memory as written record. He seems at times to regard human history as a faintly imbecilic curator constantly misplacing or destroying the productions of human genius, and only kept in line by poets. One of the "lessons of history," he says in the 1929 "How To Read," again playing Shelley's Unacknowledged Legislator, is that "maintaining the very cleanliness of the tools, the health of the very matter of thought itself" is the poet's job.

The individual cannot think and communicate his thought, the governor and legislator cannot act effectively or frame his laws, without words, and the solidity and validity of these words is in the care of the damned and despised *litterati*. When their work goes rotten . . . order goes to pot.

Durability, he adds, depends on *utility*, and utility measures your closeness to tradition. Thus, while aligning yourself with tradition guaranteed nothing, in the long run it was less dangerous than the Symbolists' "systematic derangements of the senses," which replace traditional means with a hermetic vocabulary of sensation, impressions, and feeling "deprived of intellect, and out drunk on its 'lone, saying it is the 'that which is beyond the intelligence.'" Tradition could at least tell you what needed to be done. Tradition, moreover, according to Pound's understanding of it, is essentially historical memory embodied in books and cultural monuments that no personal apocalypse can touch. Pound before *Lustra* had matured a recognition of how much Symbolist aesthetic had yielded *legitimately* to tradition—or historical memory: he was never blind to the formal beauty of works of genius, like those of Baudelaire, Rimbaud (whom he translated), and Yeats; *Lustra* gave him the opportunity to find out how much of that formal yield tradition would permit him to carry over the threshold of *Lustra* and into the practice of Imagism and the extroverted art of his maturity.

From the opening page it is clear that *Lustra* is a book with a mission. What it is Pound suggests in the definition of *lustrum* he adds below the dedication: "an offering for the sins of the whole people, made by the censors at the expiration of their five years of office." The poems are ritual sacrifices made by a public official about to leave office; *Lustra* is therefore a public service and a uniquely public book. Satirically brooding over morality, society, and poetry's power to change things, the poems either laugh at their audience or ask their audience to laugh at itself; they are usually framed as envoys directed to twit this or that vested interest and to bring some reforming sense to British taste. The self-conscious "Tenzone" opens the book, and it is typical. Pound's readership is likened to "a timorous wench" fleeing from him, "a centaur / (or a centurion)," and preyed on by pimping critics:

> Will they be touched with the verisimilitudes?
>   Their virgin stupidity is untemptable.
> I beg you, my friendly critics,
> Do not set about to procure me an audience.

This mob of blameless virgin consciousnesses fleeing the "touch" of his songs or of Pound himself is the reading public toward which Pound strikes a typical pose ("I mate with my free kind upon the crags"). The poems possess a kind of adolescent masculinity—a description not absurdly applied to the contents of a book whose author so often addresses its parts as if they were male children—and a masculinity not entirely uncomplicated by learned ironies. The distich "touched with the verisimilitudes" alludes obliquely to Horace (3:3), for instance. Pound is also opening a personal referential domain in *Lustra*: in his correspondence he had a habit of comparing intellectual to sexual penetration. The plenum of sexual power, or so Pound apparently believed, was a kind of IQ. As he wrote in a postscript to his translation of Remy de Gourmont's *The Natural Philosophy of Love* (1921), "The brain itself, is, in origin and development, only a sort of great clot of genital fluid held in suspense or reserve." Successful entrance into another consciousness is, therefore, a kind of sexual victory, a measure of the strength of intellect over stupidity. This in a way explains the genealogy of the crag-denizen of the ending—a classical centaur, Tennyson's eagle and Nietzsche's Zarathustra—all paradigms of predatory, isolated, vigilant masculinity. Occasionally the irony is less esoteric: "The Condolence," which Pound writes to console himself, anticipates the charge of voyeurism, so often leveled at Whitman:

> We are compared to that sort of person
> Who wanders about announcing his sex
> As if he had just discovered it

Coopting the charge takes the bite out of it, but the attitude, retrograde or not ("the female is ductile"), never disappears from his work ("The female is a chaos, the male / is a fixed point of stupidity," he says in a later canto).

In "The Garden," not incidentally one of the great lyrics of the twentieth century, the attitude actually matures. A young girl is passing a railing in Kensington Gardens:

> Like a skein of loose silk blown against a wall
> She walks by the railing of a path in Kensington Gardens,
> And she is dying piece-meal
>   of a sort of emotional anaemia.

Of several such poems where Pound describes an encounter this is the most finished and most suggestively titled. He presents the objects of physical and poetic vision by a subtle "super-positioning," to use the word he uses to explain how Imagism works. "The 'one-image poem' is a form of super-position, that is to say, it is one idea set on top of another," so he sets Kensington on Paradise to prove the poet-physician's diagnosis ("emotional anaemia"). In the five-line "Shop Girl," which appears later in the book—

> For a moment she rested against me
> Like a swallow half blown to the wall.
> And they talk of Swinburne's women,
> And the shepherdess meeting with Guido.
> And the harlots of Baudelaire.

—he reproduces this figurative vehicle—fragile sensuality buffeted by wind—but there is a subtle difference. The shop girl is a swallow to whom an ephemeral sensuality clings; the young girl in Kensington is a "skein of loose silk," not even a creature but a *thing* upon whom the world's impact is not tragic, but inevitable:

> And round about there is a rabble
> Of the filthy, sturdy, unkillable infants of the very poor.
> They shall inherit the earth.

This backhanding of the Sermon on the Mount ("Blessed are the meek, for they shall inherit the earth") looks easy, but one wonders what lesser competence might have done with the idea. A more hypotactic approach—"who shall inherit the earth," say, or "The meek shall inherit the earth"—would have produced either studied preciosity or mere pretension. But Pound's triumph is in raising the poem from the level where it is merely self-regarding, the spot where most of Imagism's officially anthologized poetry languished, to permanent seriousness. A sentimental morality has produced a biological cul de sac of exquisite breed and excessive delicacy, no Eve but an enigmatic mock-up; everything about her is fastidious and overdetermined by a religion reduced to aphorisms. Moreover, this is no Eden, so why should what is sturdy and unkillable *not* inherit the earth?

> In her is the end of breeding.
> Her boredom is exquisite and excessive.
> She would like some one to speak to her,
> And is almost afraid that I
>   will commit that indiscretion.

The prosody, end-stopped for two lines before casually and ironically rolling to a stop, reacts to the "end" of breeding. London's street rats collaborate in fulfilling the prophecy precisely because what they surround reproduces itself only if forced to. Breeding is an impasse to precisely the eugenic miracle it proposed. Given the book's alignment of sexuality and intelligence, moreover, the contact that the alien Pound represents is more than sexual: he offers to "touch with verisimilitude" the cultivated pococurantism of the well-bred whose choice is either dilutation or annihilation.

Pound's on-again, off-again love affair with British society—which, after all, produced his wife—is driven by an obsession with civilization and "order" not unanticipated in a suburban boy who once attended a military academy. "The Garden" telescopes that obsession successfully and gathers a series of similar savagings in its range. An exhausted moral system has also produced "Les Millwin," their "mauve and greenish souls" lying "like so many unused boas" in the balcony at the Russian ballet, their eyes—note the adjective—"aenemic"; "The Bellaires" ("The good Bellaires / Do not understand the conduct of this world's affairs"); the horse-faced lady, of "Simulacra," who recites Swinburne as Pound passes; the svelte woman who rests her unslippered feet on a restaurant table napkin ("Black Slippers: Bellotti"); the predatory relations swarming the corpse in "The Social Order"; the "little Aurelia" given in marriage to the "palsied contact" of Phidippus ("Society"); and the woman who casually sizes up Pound in "The Encounter":

> All the while they were talking the new morality
> Her eyes explored me.
> And when I arose to go
> Her fingers were like the tissue
> Of a Japanese paper napkin.

These brief satires are a continuing, coherent reflection on twentieth-century morality; their subjects are spiritually related, all victims of the same "botched civilization" that Pound attacks in *Mauberley*, although in *Mauberly* the provocation is the slaughter and "wastage as never before" of World War I. From *Lustra* on, Pound is telling essentially the same story, spinning the same fable about the consequences of a morality that substitutes the symbol for the real thing, studied weakness and incubated sexuality for classical strength, and most disastrously for the artist, mystical pleasures for physical ones.

It would be going too far to assert that in his frank love of sensuality Pound ignores the consequences. *Mauberley*'s creator was not, like his creation, "an hedonist." One day, in "The Tea Shop" the waitress "is not so beautiful as she was, / The August has worn against her. / She does not get up the stairs so eagerly." The poem trips over its own logic:

> Yes, she also will turn middle-aged,
> And the glow of youth that she spread about us
>   as she brought us our muffins
> Will be spread about us no longer.
>   She also will turn middle-aged.

The gently introjected future has some of the psychological sadness of Whitman's narrative of the twenty-nine bathers in *Song of Myself* and some of the bitterness of Baudelaire's "Les Fenêtres." But Baudelaire is too often a people collector bent on voyeuristic reductions of life to "legends" while Pound comes closer to Whitman's compassion. The iteration of line 5 gently turns the poem from satire to elegy without getting stuck in sentimental *ubi sunt* reveries. The girl is, after all, the waitress who "brought us our muffins." Yet which of us will not, like her, "turn middle-aged"? This mere sketch demonstrates a mature balance of sensuous wisdom and moral realism that bears out the book's title.

Discussions of Ezra Pound and his influences can come down to checklists of his reading—to material sources—and attract those with scholarly passions more archaeological than, say, biological. A convenantal understanding seems to be at work: Pound is the sum of the cultural details identified in the footnotes to the poems, outside of which the man himself hardly existed. This overstates the critical preoccupation of Poundians, but only a little. A line like Pound's "They shall inherit the earth" is a *source*, that is, is writing reduced to the material level of print, where a line or a phrase points self-consciously "backward" to its antecedent(s) and, in a sense, gives itself away. Critics like Harold Bloom have attacked both Eliot and Pound not so much for pointing backward but for having done so with such demanding self-consciousness that "familiarity with the text" means being familiar with the whole textual "family" it belongs to, and returning the prodigal—*Mauberley, The Waste Land*—to that make-believe network of extended literary relationships called *tradition*, which is merely another version of Freud's "family romance." For *source* Bloom has *influence*, which points, not to the bare thinghood of the antecedent ("Blessed are the meek, for they shall inherit the earth"), but to the dialectic of renewal or disaster that happens when two poets (Matthew 5:5; Pound, "The Garden") creatively, which is to say antagonistically, encounter each other. Kenner's position is the outgrowth of Eliot's powerful cautionary fable, clearly among the most influential essays of the century, "Tradition and the Individual Talent" (1919), which promotes impersonality, a respect for tradition, and radical indifference to—even disrespect for—"originality." Eliot is himself repeating Matthew Arnold's evangelizing for an unbroken canon of values, a tradition to which each generation's work is laboriously and unabashedly mortgaged.

Modernism is arguably the godchild of Arnold and daughter of Eliot, with Pound as midwife, so it is important to understand how poetry comes to be made according to the early Eliot. The process is strikingly like the production of scholarship—a continuous and cumulative hieratic undertaking, with "disinterested" critics acting as an oversight committee conducting traffic flow. But an antithetical criticism views such a reverential stance as hogwash. Poets do *not* collaborate like initiates lining up for the laying on of hands. The assumption that the production of poetry somehow involves *cooperation* with the very tradition that is out to get the poet leads to a sentimental confusion of the manifest content of the *given poem* with its latent content, which is what it *refers to,* and which is always prior, greater, "better." It is acceptable to superimpose the Garden of Paradise and the Kensington Gardens only so long as the priority of the former is respected and the result is irony, which preserves the distinctions between locations; it is not acceptable to assume that the poet wants to overcome the irony and—as though suddenly recognizing, like a child uncovering its eyes, his own *originality*, a quality of poetic genius that Eliot refused to countenance—redo the Fall or send up the Sermon on the Mount.

On the face of it, *Lustra* is no place for antithetical critics. Much of the poetry gives itself up immediately, like "Amities," with its epigraph from Yeats, its French allusion, and a six-line coda in Pound's own Latin that bittersweetly renounces some of Pound's older, less vital professional friendships. The funny "Epitaphs" to Fu I and Li Po (who "also died drunk. / He tried to embrace a moon / In the yellow river"), "Our Contemporaries," a send-up of the recently deceased Rupert Brooke that got Pound into minor trouble with Harriet Monroe, and "The Three Poets," a Catullan satire of poets, are glibly referential and show no signs of struggle. Slightly more vicious is "Tempora," where "The Dryad" who stands in Pound's yard, "With plaintive, querulous crying," calls not the name of Tammuz, the god she serves, but "May my poems be printed this week? / The god Pan is afraid to ask you, / May my poems be printed this week?" The "Dryad," a coinage reserved for his letters to Dorothy Shakespear, whom he was courting, enciphers H.D., endlessly tortured by a life-long crush on Ezra and by her vulgar love of art, or at least getting published. Like the young girl in "The Garden," she is ruined by a refinement uneducated in the sort of self-conscious irony that Pound in "Epilogues" directs against his own poems, which he dismisses as a "seven days' wonder."

There is, more hopefully, "The Lake Isle," one of Pound's several attempts to exorcise Yeats, either through straight parody or mocking tributes like "Au Jardin," from *Ripostes*, a satire of Yeats's "The Cap and Bells." In "The Lake Isle" Pound asks the gods to send him, not to Inn-isfree, but to "a little tobacco-shop," with shiny scales, neat shelves, and "whores dropping in for a word or two in passing, / For a flip word, and to tidy their hair a bit." Pound gets Yeats right down to phrasing, and the closing is memorable:

> O God, O Venus, O Mercury, patron of thieves,
> Lend me a little tobacco-shop,
>> or install me in any profession,
> Save this damn'd profession of writing,
>> where one needs one's brains all the time.

But here Pound is merely having fun with Yeats's horror at being relat-ed through his mother to the purse-proud Butlers. The poem's turn toward Yeats is nowhere as complex as, say, the turn of Stevens's "Anec-dote of the Jar" away from Keats's "Grecian Urn." The other influences advertise themselves openly, in epigraphs (Lope de Vega), titles ("After Ch'u Yuan," whose opening line is another Yeatsian echo, "I will get me to the wood"), internal quotations (*"Lugete, Veneres! Lugete, Cupidi-nesque!"*), and outright translations (Catullus's "To Formianus' Young Lady Friend," Bertran de Born's "Dompna Pois De Me No'us Cal"). But in most cases a good raking-out with Ruthven's *Annotated Guide* shows influences to be *sources* after all and suggests a connection, though to a lesser extent than with *Ripostes*, with an autograph book. This is precisely the procedure that critics usually adopt in reading Pound: winding their way, usually in Kenner's wake, through Pound's work to disclose the author of the inscription, at times to reenact the poetry's cultural complexity while tacitly admitting to its psychological aridity. Psychological complexity can mean many things, though always it is where or when one's sense of mortality is touched by the poet's sense of her own—the heavenly hurt that Dickinson says scars us with "internal difference / Where the meanings are." If this turns the point around to mean that cultural complexity is psychological complexity in Ezra Pound, the judgment that concludes Kenner's *The Pound Era* ("Thought is a labyrinth") is not unintentionally ironic but accidentally profound. In *Lustra* the poetry begins making a full about-face, turning the often weakly rendered subjective energies of *Ripostes* outward, toward social satire and cultural criticism. There is of course nothing inherently unpoetic about this volte face. Whether Ezra Pound wanted to be solved out of his work by replacing him or his thought with the labyrinthine culture behind it is not the same as asking, without irony, whether Pound's obsession with written history—or his obsession with memory as written record—so utterly displaces subjective interests from *Mauberley* and the *Cantos* as to make those poems, at least for some, unreadable.

The negotiation of influence in *Lustra* is a crucial threshold beyond which Pound will tend, if I may put it in this blunted way, more and more to substitute objective for subjective interests, historical for human complexities—the image and luminous detail for the lived occasion, or as he says in *Mauberley*, the "Classics in paraphrase" for the lesser "mendacities" of an era of uncontrolled introversion. It is with this understanding that readers must regard "A Pact"—a nine-line poem of relative inconsequence to critics except as an index of what *not* to look for in Pound—i.e., a sense of the importance of Whitman. Donald Davie, in *Ezra Pound* (Viking, 1975), dismisses both Whitman and Blake with a rousing post-Watergate reminder that American democratic traditions were "framed on neoclassical models by assiduous Grecians like Jefferson and Adams," illogically implying that any embrace of Whitman (or Blake) is a rejection of assiduous Grecians and European influence. Early in his career Pound did see Whitman just that simplistically :

[Whitman] is America. His crudity is an exceeding great stench, but it *is* America. He is the hollow place in the rock that echoes with his time. He *does* "chant the crucial stage" and he is the "voice triumphant." He is disgusting. He is an exceedingly nauseating pill, but he accomplishes his mission.

Yet this essay of 1909, "What I Feel About Walt Whitman," withholds as much as it gives. Moses, as someone versed in the Bible once reminded me, was guaranteed the nearest glimpse any man has ever had of the Creator and hid himself in a hollow place in the rock to witness the passage of Yahweh: Whitman is the hollow wherein the voice that is great within us echoes and Pound-Moses hides. What is on Pound's mind is the issue of poetic succession, a real worry by 1915 and "A Pact." Its famous opening—

> I make a pact with you, Walt Whitman—
> I have detested you long enough.
> I come to you as a grown child
> Who has had a pig-headed father.

—carries over the note of specious exasperation from 1909. But the poem makes an interesting and unanticipated tonal shift:

> I am old enough now to make friends.
> It was you that broke the new wood,
> Now is a time for carving.
> We have one sap and one root—
> Let there be commerce between us.

The very clarity of the verse may obscure what is also going on. The breaking of the "new wood" must refer to the revolution that is Whitman's prosody, a revolution, Pound says in a letter of 1931, that "the Concord school" missed, failing "to see the forest for the trees." The man who insists on "breaking the pentameter" is therefore gesturing to the father of free verse, but the gesture is initially antithetical: "pig-headedness" stands for Whitman's lack of refinement, whereas Pound is "a Walt Whitman who has learned to wear a collar and a dress shirt," as he says in that same essay. All of this explains the poet's *detestation* but not *why* it has been surrendered. The answer can be found in the immediate textual logistics. Eleven poems precede "A Pact," among them "Tenzone," an apology for his own power, "The Garden," his demystification of the Fall, and the three poems titled "Salutation," "Salutation The Second," and "Commission," each of which contains instructions to poems setting out like children from their parent. "Commission," which comes before "A Pact," opens,

> Go, my songs, to the lonely and the unsatisfied,
> Go also to the nerve-wracked, go to the enslaved-by-convention,

Bear to them my contempt for their oppressors.
Go as a great wave of cool water,
Bear my contempt of oppressors,

and ends, "Go out and defy opinion, / Go against this vegetable bondage of the blood. / Be against all sorts of mortmain." This is a prosody, a litany of directives, educated in Whitman's lists; this audience is also the audience Whitman targets. The paternal pose that Pound himself strikes toward his poems leads to his alarmed recognition that his own detestation of the father is, in its way, conventional. Hence that last line, with its redefinition of the father-son relationship as a business deal: Walt the Forebear vanishes into Whitman the Forerunner. The prodigal returns only after he has dispatched his own children.

Whitman arrived early and stayed late. In the *Pisan Cantos*, Pound, having found Whitman "in a cheap edition" in a latrine, aligns him with tradition through echoes of section 2 of *Song of Myself*

hast 'ou swum in a sea of air strip
        through an aeon of nothingness
when the raft broke and the waters went over me . . .

—which he re-echoes in the Libretto to Canto 81:

Hast 'ou fashioned so airy a mood
        To draw up leaf from the root?
Hast 'ou found   a cloud   so light
        As seemed neither mist nor shade?
                    (Canto 81, 105–8)

Whitman's humility before the natural world brought home to him the absurdity of those who "feed on the specters in books," and the irony was hardly lost on Pound, sixty-years old, broken in health and his books reduced to left-behinds, that it is Whitman who rescues him "from the gates of death":

Have you reckon'd a thousand acres much? have you reckon'd
        the earth much?
Have you practis'd so long to learn to read?
Have you felt so proud to get at the meaning of poems?
                    (*Song of Myself*, 2:29–31)

Canto 82 completes the cycle of antithetical completion and recognizes in Whitman another poet-outcast, another Villon, En Bertrans, Dante, another Pound:

> "Fvy! in Tdaenmarck efen dh' beasantz gnow him,"
>   meaning Whitman, exotic, still suspect
>   four miles from Camden
>   "O troubled reflection
>   "O Throat, O throbbing heart"

The broken English, which introduces a quotation from "Out of the Cradle Endlessly Rocking," belongs to Richard Reithmuller, author of *Walt Whitman and the Germans* (1906) and instructor of German at the University of Pennsylvania. "Four miles from Camden" would place you near Penn, in downtown Philadelphia, where Whitman is still "exotic, suspect," and still considered a bizarre choice to name a bridge after. The surface of Pound's *Cantos* and all of his work after *Lustra*, so over-wrought with allusions raw and refined, is a not at all superficial expression of his insistence on a poetry of double accomplishments: a poetry possessed of the integrity of good history and driven by the passion of memory that precedes great understanding. Rarely is that surface more pitted than when it meets Whitman, who really does seem more than historical memory, scholarship, or intellectual passion can comprehend. The work of preservation that Pound carried on occupied the surface of his art; this privileged relationship to Whitman is an important and violent breaking of the surface.

Imagism is essentially an elliptical approach to poetic design, substituting juxtapositional for connected meanings. In *Lustra* Pound invents Imagism, with the most fully foregrounded example of the habit realized in "In A Station of the Metro," as he aligns the "apparition" of "faces in the crowd" with "petals on a wet, black bough." The point of any "poem of this sort," he says in 1918, "to record the precise instant when a thing outward and objective transforms itself, or darts into a thing inward and subjective," implies a critical distance between subjective and objective interests; poets measure, define, and apportion these distances by introducing, reducing, or maintaining them. To exercise the Imagist habit is to see two things outside the hierarchy of normal perception:

> With clouds over Taishan-Chocorua
>   when the blackberry ripens
> and now the new moon faces Taishan
>   (Canto 83)

Right through the *Cantos* one can find small and large examples of what Pound has matured from conscious strategy to a mental habit of perceiving the world doubled—Japan's Mt. Taishan superimposed on New Hampshire's Mt. Chocorua, for example. Imagism was conceived as a philosophy of perception, an absolute way of looking at the world.

It was also a fairly characteristic modern rescue operation to free poetic subjectivity from both its enemies (science) and its friends (French Symbolism, Romanticism). Eliot's assertion of an objective correlative (in the 1919 essay "Hamlet") in emphasizing the existence of an objective, hard, here-and-now world to which poetic imagination is responsible attempts the same thing. Here is Eliot:

> The only way of expressing emotion in the form of art is by finding an "objective correlative"; in other words, a set of objects, a situation, a chain of events which shall be the formula of that *particular* emotion; such that when the external facts, which must terminate in sensory experience, are given, the emotion is immediately evoked.

All this about "objects," a "formula," and "external facts" is revealingly mechanical; yet Eliot, like Pound, wants to square the traditional subjective interests with a new objectivity. Pound's radical departure from Eliot is that the image *simultaneously* foregrounds the subjective and objective directions—an arrow with two heads, what Kenner calls a *vector*—which occupy imagination as phenomenological equals. There is a world of difference in their terminological directions, between what in Eliot is "evoked" and what in Pound "*darts inward.*" Eliot seemed almost pathologically disinclined to approve the *poet*'s subjectivity; even in his most generous discussions Eliot made subjectivity the property of the *poem*, teased out ("evoked") not by readers so much as by the poem's magnetic attraction to (or deflection from: it may fail to work) tradition. Hence the endlessly interesting platinum wire analogy that he invites us to consider in 1919's "Tradition and the Individual Talent," and his assertion that "the more perfect the artist, the more completely separate in him will be the man who suffers and the mind which creates." Poets are *catalysts*; poetic compounds are emotions.

For all his instrumentalism, Pound was indifferent to or comfortable with the faint fideism of "the Imagist *faith*" (my italics) and its 1913 list of "tenets":

I. Direct treatment of the "thing," whether subjective or objective.
II. To use absolutely no word that does not contribute to the presentation.

III. As regarding rhythm: to compose in sequence of the musical phrase, not in sequence of the metronome.

Years ago, Frank Kermode (*The Romantic Image*, 1957) pointed out how Pound's noisiest scientific formulations of poetic strategies or poetic power—"As the abstract mathematician is to science so is the poet to the world's consciousness," from "The Wisdom of Poetry" (1912) is typical—inevitably fall prey to their unacknowledged context of production. You could compile a small book of extracts demonstrating how distracted Pound was by his need to conduct the imagination through the fields that science had claimed and to get it past his own Romantic nostalgia for the summer dream beneath the tamarind tree. Whence the Imagist protocols, which join ancient poetic wisdom to Ben Franklin's approach to personal self-improvement. Imagism was that détente, so typically American, between poetry and science, at once a "conscious aesthetic to fill the place of Rimbaud's intuitions," in Kermode's words, and what Kenner memorably termed "specifications for technical hygiene." Both the philosophy and the precept derive from the same excited source.

No matter how magical the properties of the "Image," its acquisition, proposed by Pound in typically instrumentalist, do-it-yourself fashion, looks easy. This, of course, leads to a final, bittersweet irony. What prompts Pound's claim, in *Gaudier-Brzeska*, that "Imagisme is not symbolism" is a contempt for the Symbolists' "mushy technique," which in turn is motivated by an even deeper disgust with what Pound terms, rightly, Symbolist "rhetoric":

Ibycus and Liu Ch'e presented the "Image." Dante is a great poet by reason of this faculty, and Milton is a wind-bag because of his lack of it. The "image" is the furthest possible remove from rhetoric. Rhetoric is the art of dressing up some unimportant matter so as to fool the audience for the time being.

What Pound could not have foreseen, and what would issue from the hand of Amy Lowell in a year or so, was precisely an Imagist rhetoric, where the "tenets" of Imagist theory became identified with the do's-and-dont's of Imagist practice, and where Imagism, now "Amygism," began supporting a small canon of Imagist anthologies. By then Pound had already kissed off both the movement and its sometime expressions. The change was swift. In August of 1914, less than eighteen months after the formulation of an Imagist Doctrine, Pound uncomfortably curtsies to Amy Lowell's planned Imagiste anthology. "I should like the name 'Imagisme' to retain some sort of a meaning. It stands, or I should like it to stand for hard light, clear edges." No "democratized committee" can be trusted with it. But in October Lowell broke his heart with the ad for her book, *Sword Blades and Poppy Seed*:

Of the poets who to-day are doing the interesting and original work, there is no more striking and unique figure than Amy Lowell. The foremost member of the "Imagists"—a group of poets that includes William Butler Yeats, Ezra Pound, Ford Madox Hueffer—she has won wide recognition for her writing in new and free forms.

Pound's response is a two-sentence post-card: "Congratulations. Why not include Thomas Hardy?" Later that month, he breaks with "official" Imagism and writes to Lowell,

I don't suppose any one will sue you for libel; it is too expensive. If your publishers "of good standing" tried to advertise cement or soap in this manner they would certainly be sued. However we salute their venality. Blessed are they who have enterprise, for theirs is the magazine public.

In that (out-of-print) scholarly curiosity, William Platt's *The Imagist Poem: Modern Poetry in Miniature* (Dutton, 1963), Imagism lives on, represented by those who did not do the movement a disservice (Pound, H.D., Moore, T. E. Hulme, Eliot, Lawrence, Stevens, cummings, Pound) and by those who did. Lowell's poems, when not simply horrible ("If I could catch the green lantern of the firefly / I could see to write you a letter," from "The Lover"), were simply, at times intensely, inane. For example, in "Wind and Silver" she writes of the "greatly shining, / . . . Autumn moon" floating "in the thin sky,"

> And the fish-ponds shake their backs and
>   flash their dragon scales
> As she passes over them.

Without regarding what the theory of the image implied apart from what official Imagism produced, the theory's crucial implications and attendant problems are indistinguishable from a host of differently problematic, essentially unimportant poems.

Two extracts from Pound's prose introduce the problem. One is a letter to e. e. cummings of April 6, 1933, where the subject is the appearance of a line of print on a page: "The normal or average eye sees a certain width without heaving from side to side. May be hygienic for it to exercise its wobble, but I dunno that the orfer [*sic*] shd. sacrifice himself on that altar." After noting how much of a typical line he can see at once, Pound then adds,

But I don't see the rest of the line until I look specially at it. Multiply that 40 times per page for 400 pages. . . . Mebbe there is wide-angle eyes. But chew gotter count on a cert. no. ov yr. readers being at least as dumb as I am. Even in Bitch and Bugle I found it difficult to read the stuff consecutively.

The second extract is an aphorism from *The A. B. C. of Reading*:

Rhythm is a form cut into TIME, as a design is determined SPACE.

The letter reveals an unusual attention to the appearance of printed words in a magazine like *Hound & Horn* ("Bitch and Bugle"), where one has to contend with the confinements of margins. Pound's decision to attend to the look, rather than to the sound, of the line he quotes gains support from the metaphor of "wide-angle eyes": one instrument of vision (the human eye) is defined by way of an analogy with another one (optical lens).

The aphorism relating time and space, moreover, expresses the same instrumentalist theme the letter voices, only with more sophistication. Poetic rhythm is homologized with graphic design through an analogy that opposes time to space. Yet what is slightly extraordinary about Pound's view is the conception of language that drives it: linguistic material carries a specific spatial component; poetic materials, that is to say, are precisely *materials*. Words, like marble or metal, have extension and weight; their physical placement or semiotic design is as accountable for their semantic value, what they come to mean, as what they always, or already, mean in the mind of the author ("orfer"). Meaning gets displaced across a "certain width" the eye "wobbles" over. Just to bedevil Pound the instrumentalist, I propose this counter-statement:

Allegories are things that Relate to Moral Virtues [.] Moral Virtues do not Exist[;] they are allegories & dissimulations [.] But Time & Space are Real Beings [,] a Male & a Female [.] Time is a Man [,] Space is a Woman [,] & her Masculine Portion is Death [.]

Blake would say that Pound, like Joshua Reynolds, is a mere materialist who errs in thinking of pictorial viewing space as the accidental by-product of whatever occupies it, as some *thing* a painter governs and exploits through rationings of canvas or paper, either of which piece of material *is* space. The Imagist, he would say, is a bookkeeper who generalizes about the relation of a thing in one column of his ledger to something on the other through appeal to freestanding categorical headings ("Time": "Space"). Blake would find such ledgerdemain brutal—each item immobilized in its proper class, human agency buried in a syntactical network of passive voicings (rhythm "*is cut*", design "*is determined*"). The connecting agency is either remote, impersonal, marginalized, or displaced by the revisionary logic of the objective correlative and the doctrine of the image. The Blakean advances time and space as "Real Beings" (compare the logic of capitalization informing both poets' spellings of *time* and *space*) that interact sexually. The instrumentalist displaces the emphasis from himself or intervening (creative or critical) agencies to the *materials*.

The consequences of Modernism's overall departure from Romanticism are all around us, but I want to emphasize this one of Pound the Imagist particularly: he tended to express relationships *between things* in terms of primarily visual connections *between words*, much in the same way that the members of a sculptural group are connected by the viewer. He goes on to regard words as *currency* in the sense of possessed of *material* weight, and, committing the Blakean sin of viewing the eye as an instrument one sees *with* rather than *through*, he spreads his language across the page as though language were sensation, to reproduce a mental effect or "image." If Pound's self-conscious sensitivity to the semiology of poetry seems the mere sweet nothings of Pound scholarship, the fact is that many later movements not only inherit the sensitivity but in some cases (Objectivists, Beats, Black Mountain poets, concretists, Language poets) pass it on. Charles Olson's *Maximus*, clearly preoccupied with Imagist technical discoveries, is a thoroughly learned, occasionally great poem, but it is owned by the *Cantos* the way Wigglesworth's absurd *The Day of Doom* seems owned by *Paradise Lost*. Olsen's preoccupation with the physicality of language, which he learned from Pound, leads to a kind of gnomic doting over it, and while the ambition is epical, the poetry is sometimes minimalist babble, or plain bad e. e. cummings. The playful seriousness Ammons brings to writing a "long skinny poem" on a roll of adding machine tape is the outgrowth of a lapsed Poundian's understanding of history as the history of literary technique, of "substance running / through shapes of itself,

/itself the running." A self-consciousness about his own marginality in the medium is part of the poet's success. Clarence Major's *Surfaces and Masks* is a more recent derivative:

> Smells of fried fish
>   and grilled steaks
> at outdoor table
>   across from Piazzale Frari.
> Italian lessons, anybody?

Inherent in the stepping-down the rungs of prosody to touch the thing is the desire our century learned from Pound, the desire to record, to experience the technique itself. "To Pound," says the critic Massimo Baciagalupo of this problematic preoccupation, "a full correspondence between reality and discourse is possible; this elementary mimetic hypothesis he never questions overtly," and as a result

[Reality] is barred from the *Cantos*, not because it is "vile," as Mallarmé would have said, but because the page is the sole actuality, Pound's world is all told in his lines, it is all present, explicit, equally lit. . . . In other words Pound's poetry is primarily *matter*.

Pound occasionally and fondly quoted an axiom central to the Medieval nominalist: *nomina sunt consequentia rerum*, names are the outcomes of things. The implications for poetry's *cognitive* value of so wholesale an acceptance of this philosophically difficult position are that there are no connections between poetry and the "real" world: all poetic speech is therefore a kind of idiolect.

This disjointedness effects, moreover, a break in the relations between Imagist discursive strategies and the way communication "really" happens. This break produces a second result and one that appears so often to be the *cause* of the difficulty encountered in reading all modern poetry: discursive material, the connective tissue of narrative, gets absorbed, *overt* links between or among perceptions are suppressed, historical gestures are compressed into allusions, precedent contexts are buried in titles, blank spaces (which are after all part of a text's physical design) or footnotes—viz., *The Waste Land*. Even Hemingway, whose "experimental" period begins and ends with *In Our Time* (or *in our time*), buried the details of Catherine and Frederic's lovemaking in the spaces between the narration (*seriatim*) and concealed the fact that Catherine is giving Frederic a pre-op enema by leaving stage directions out of the dialogue (chapter 16, *A Farewell to Arms*). Examples abound. The point is that the aesthetic vision behind the examples is the Imagist one, which is at bottom driven by a view of words as *external things* that stand for, do the work of, the *external things* they name. That this vision reflects a radical alertness on the part of the writer to private technology (the typewriter), movies, Cubism, the phonograph, and vaudeville is an interest, but not a decisive one. The twentieth-century's lusting for a visual prosody does not arrive with Imagism: Mallarmé (*Un Coup De Dés*) and Apollinaire (*Calligrammes*), to take two proximate examples, had already experimented with what Renato Poggioli once called *visible lyricism*. The question of concern is how far one can share in this awareness and evaluate it in light of tradition, or of the past. One wants to know how to read poetry impregnated with concerns so "untraditional" and connected so tenuously with the whole concept of reading.

Which, of course, is exactly the question Pound's letter to cummings raises in its advancing of a visual hygiene of the printed word. The question is posed more dramatically by Imagism's enabling text, "In a Station of the Metro," which appeared in the April 1913 issue of *Poetry* and in a slightly different form in *Lustra*. In the original version Pound spaces the words apart and stops the first line with a colon: "The apparition   of these faces   in   the   crowd." "In the 'Metro' hokku," he writes to Harriet Monroe, "I was careful, I think, to indicate spaces between the rhythmic units, and I want them observed." His directive is stark in its implications: the spaces between phrases are recovered as units of sound, the eye having first been persuaded that each (spatiotemporal) unit reposes in isolation from those surrounding it. The eye, in other words, and not the ear, governs meaning. But what is this poem supposed to *sound* like? The metrical habits we learn in school help us to assimilate poetry to familiar anticipatory patterns that yield means of enjoying or at least of analyzing what's new. Yet this two-line poem—decisively not haiku—comes without directions. Instead, it has a physical design that distracts from what one normally expects of poems—recurrent patterns of sound. Scanning the first line is useless because it yields either a line of dactylic trimeter (if the scansionist is ready to elide the first two words and swallow the last syllable of *apparition*) or some bizarre enforcement of the pentameter (if he is tone-deaf). Accepting either, moreover, what about

Petals   on a wet, black bough,

a line clearly less dactylic than spondaic? Making the point this way (to borrow a phrase of Pound's) is like dragging your own heroic corpse around the walls. Each case cancels the next because the poem deliberately sets out to "break the pentameter" and disable the scansion routines learned in Latin class. Conventional strategies are useless because they are blind to a poem's physical shape—how do we scan the spaces?—yet the unconventional one demanded of us here is somehow too precious. Is it creditable to give a *sonic* value to the *spaces between the sounds* without defining the   pause's duration?   The "pause" can be in fact either one of vision or of hearing, Kenner's "perceptual units" and "speakable units" or Pound's "rhythmic units" at the same time.

What, moreover, about that hinted off-rhyme (*crowd / bough*)? And last, what about the tendency of the typology to blur syntactical assignments? After all, the most confounding element, the one that finally defeats traditional analysis, is that the poem has no verb. The action that takes place between the seeing of the crowd and the seeing of the petals is *unpredicated* in the two senses of the term. No one element *performs* in both lines to bind them: as with Pound's aphorism, agency (human or nonhuman) is suppressed. Nor can any element in the strict sense be *inferred* from the sight of the crowd to the petals: what is there about *apparition* to suggest "petals" rather than, say, "raindrops" or "ghosts"? There is no unific Blakean imagination at work: on one side of the ledger are the crowding "faces," on the other the "petals." What follows the colon is a configuration of objects physically and psychologically independent of what comes before. Not only is it difficult to describe what goes on but it is almost impossible to decide what the precise nature of *description* has come to involve. The destination or direction of what Philip Wheelwright, compelled by this poem to neologize, termed its "semantic motions," is equivocal: the critic cannot say what the poem says because speech and ordinary telling seem to be but a part of its operations.

I mount this polemical analysis only to demonstrate the scale of real vexation that this two-line poem has provoked since it appeared. Aside from the wars undertaken by critics foxed in their attempts to find a place for it in the *materia* of tradition or the taxonomies of metaphor (the card includes Northrop Frye, Hugh Kenner, Philip Wheelright, Terrance Hawkes, and Aristotle: nobody's happy with "one-image poem"), there is the problem that the poem is obviously about something, though about what, none is dead sure. Kenner saw a classical *topos* in the juxtaposed interior (train station) and exterior (petalled bough), a vague fingerprinting of Persephone's chthonian and ouranean natures. Davie rises to another level of ingenuity with the idea that the two lines deliberately transpose technical strategies, making the poem be about its own technique. Distressingly, however, Pound had none of the devices of poetry, speech, rhythm, or measure in view when he experienced his "metro-emotion." Or so he admits in the passage in *Gaudier-Brzeska* that has become Modernist homiletic, where he recounts his reaction to getting off the Paris train one day in 1912 and stepping into the steamy crowd of "beautiful" faces. "I do not mean that I found words, but there came an equation [...] *not in speech, but in little splotches of colour"* (my italics). The emotion, he goes on to explain, required over a year to discover its proper verbal shape. To describe the shaping dynamic, he fetched out the term "super-position," again from graphic art. To risk putting too fine a point on it, this slide show of visionary *mattes* had no literary precedent and apparently translated so directly from inspiration into visual form one wonders what "reading," here anyway, amounts to.

The question posed by Imagist practice, apart from the theory, is how authentic a contribution to traditional poetic strategies it is. The Imagist looks for arrangements, for controlled environments of words that represent with physical immediacy his or her meaning rather than interpretive proxies. So discontinuities of perception spill into typographical arrangement; a square of asterisks visually alludes to a neon sign (Williams's "The Attic Which Is Desire"), shape alone asserts that a poem is a poem (Williams's "Poem"), or that it looks like what it is about (Moore's "The Fish"). The extreme implication of such designs is that each word is each perception: to rearrange the signs is to rearrange the things they stand for. It was this implication that prompted George Whalley (*Poetic Process*, 1967), to complain, apropos of all visual models, "I should like to abandon the term 'image' altogether." To the extent to which we understand poems as "linguistic events," Whalley says,

the element of "meaning" must enter; and since utterances can only convey meaning as they unfold themselves in time, the element of time must enter. . . .

Criticism, aesthetics, and poetics can profitably recognize that poetry is no more accessible than music, and that Poetic cannot operate unless the ear is engaged.

Imagist poetics, moreover, at work in poems as different in scale and success as *Mauberley* and *The Waste Land* run counter to what instinct tells us is central to the operations of literary art, and of poetry especially. "Linguistic events," as Whalley remarks, "are not themselves sensory": poetry speaks through measures of sensuous time and marks mental "events" in oral memory. "I made it out of a mouthful of air" means that historical memory is not burdened but *released* by speech, in speech. A visual prosody runs in the opposite direction, and transfers the debt that consciousness paid to memory to shaping and spacing, to footnotes, allusions, headnotes, epigraphs, and the sprawl of signs. The poem is a "linguistic event" at maintenance level—that of the page. Recent attempts to reduce poems like Williams's "The Red Wheelbarrow" to a prosodic core of "two undistinguished lines of blank verse"—

> so much depends upon a red wheel barrow
> glazed with rain water beside the white chickens—

misses both Williams's point, which is not the narrowly aesthetic one advanced by the New Aesthetes, and even their own. What is at issue is not the state of the art or romancing it back to metrical health, but the state of culture, which is the *status* of human thought, suddenly thrown into doubt once memory shrinks into what it remembers, becomes the physical "burden of the line," and is disengaged from time. The question remains whether Imagism is capable of discovering in *subsequent* history something that sustains its most striking innovations.

Between *Lustra* and the *Cantos*, Pound's *Mauberley* (1920) appears as his last attempt to craft a statement of ambition, and Pound's attention is divided interestingly between the technical and the thematic. *Mauberley* is so decisively an outgrowth of Pound's experience as the craftsman of *Lustra* that it may both productively and accurately be considered, despite the distance of a half-dozen years or so, as the immediate outcome of Imagist discipline. Pound was tired of London and everything connected with it and would soon leave for Paris;

Mauberley is also a leave-taking. A dozen years later Pound recollected how he and Eliot, disgusted with the old formalism of the Georgians and the new formalism of the Imagists, "at a particular date in a particular room,"

decided that the dilutation of *vers libre*, Amygism, Lee Masterism, general floppiness had gone too far and that some counter-current must be set going. . . . Remedy prescribed "Émaux et Camées" (or the Bay State Hymn Book). Rhyme and regular strophes.

He was always as interested in the arguments he conducts with the world as in those he conducts with himself, and so produced a poem that would concentrate his pedagogic passions ("an endeavour to communicate with a blockheaded epoch") in a novel technical way ("an attempt to condense the James novel").

Pound's approach to the autobiographical novel-in-verse captured his settled affection for the sculptural energies of Gautier's poetry in Imagism's major insights about juxtapositional narrative. The prosodic result is a DeChirico grouping of some fairly old-fashioned *vers de société* around an unnamed thematic center. The indispensable guide to the poem, John Espey's *Ezra Pound's Mauberley* (University of California Press, 1974), demonstrates the extent to which Pound was born-again by reaquaintance with Théophile Gautier's *Émaux et Camées*, the Greek of Bion, and Robert Browning, the poet who in the long run may be Pound's truest Penelope. Structurally, the poem, which is in two parts, is a complicated intersecting or superimposing of two visions, or versions, of Pound himself. Pound as Pound apparently narrates part 1, titled "E.P. Ode Pour L'Election De Son Sepulchre," the tomb assigned either to Pound or to the persona, Mauberley, who is killed off at the conclusion of the second part (titled simply "Mauberley"). Each major division embraces a series of disconnected portraits of literary personalities—Espey identifies them—and over the whole there broods a disembodied cultural voice, a maskless prefiguration of the Eliot-Tiresias of *The Waste Land*.

Mauberley extends *Lustra*'s moral preoccupations, with the difference that the prosodic vehicles are different and that Pound, seizing the opportunity for narrative, tends to type his "characters." It is as though "My Last Duchess" had been written by someone more interested in interior decoration that in dialogue, attention turned from the drama of life and death to the paintings we see going in and to Claus of Innsbruck's bronze seahorse, which we pass on the way out. Pound goes further in condensing characteristic gestures of voice or personal details than one would imagine possible in a *typical* narrative. The two-quatrain sketch that begins

> "Conservatrix of Milésien"
> Habits of mind and feeling,
> Possibly. But in Ealing,
> With the most bank-clerkly of Englishmen?
>
> (1:11)

is, in a sense, a version of the fate of the girl in "The Garden." All her breeding reduced to trained instincts, "those her grandmother / Told her would fit her station," she ends up in a conventional suburban situation with a bank clerk. Pound is still puzzling through the consequences of healthy sexuality oversocialized and overpoliced by conscience. That two of the first line's three words are not in English notches one crucial difference from "The Garden," and the glib framing of these conversational rhythms notches another. If not transcripts, these poems are miraculous eavesdroppings into Pound's educated vernacular, with all its polyglot short-hand and ventriloquism. Like the conventional Imagist poem, *Mauberley* demands a reader with a literary intelligence active enough to supply not only the missing external transitions but the internal references as well. The sections specifically, on the other hand, are formally familiar, their thematic concerns, like those of the *Lustra* poems, social and moral, and their overall effect aphoristic:

> All things are a flowing,
> Sage Heracleitus says;
> But a tawdry cheapness
> Shall outlast our days.

Pound left out the footnotes when his poem first appeared; what results is the first of Modernism's long poems that is nearly unreadable without them, or a concurrent education in social trivia. This point is worth emphasizing: *Mauberley* is a portent, not just of the character but the degree of technical difficulty readers will encounter in later Modernist epics. The result, in Espey's words, is that "any critic's evaluation of

Mauberley is in all probability a miniature of his evaluation of the *Cantos*, with the single qualification that though the strengths remain constant, the flaws are magnified in the larger work."

The problem of immediate and postponed reference is easily epitomized. Take a famous example from the first part, section 3. Through seven quatrains Pound moves, balancing his disgust for the present against unqualified praise of the past. A "tea-gown" is compared to the prized muslin of ancient Cos, a "pianola" to Sappho's "barbitos," Christ to Dionysus, "Faun's flesh" to the now mechanically pressed communion wafer, and Pisistratus to our elected "knave or eunuch," all of which ironic pairings merely lead up to the astonishing final quatrain:

> O bright Apollo,
> τίν' ἀνδρα, τίν' ἥρωα, τίνα θεόν,
> What god, man, or hero
> Shall I place a tin wreath upon!

The Greek of line 2, from Pindar's *Second Olympian Ode*, is silently translated by Pound in line 3: six words compress Pindar's poem and all that Pindar represents into Pound's. For those who can transliterate it, the Greek—*tin andra, tin' heroa, tina theon*—sets up a brilliant pun. In one allusion Pound condenses an entire tradition, asserting the disproportion, comically reminding you, if you get it, that Pindar's poem is a prayer that upon transliteration is absurdly lost in its modern "equivalents" (*tin*). The effect is like watching a sleepwalker wake up in a busy intersection; the past cannot survive unwarped transition into our modernity; Pound wants not only to make the point but, a good Imagist, to *dramatize* it. The result is radical irony, where each element comments on without communicating anything to the other. The gross foregrounding of the allusion brings history into the "plot" of *Mauberley*; those adding moustaches to the *Mona Lisa* or bringing live horses on stage already knew the technique. The problematical difference associated with *Mauberley* and its successors is that one cannot get the joke unless one knows Greek. Human indifference appears to rise, moreover, in proportion to the scale of difficulty. In the latest edition of Ellman and O'Clair's Norton anthology all the key Greek words are *misspelled*, with the correct letter *gnu* (here and elsewhere) replaced by the look-alike *upsilon*. Pound would have loved the irony.

Another issue, of at least equal importance to the study of how sources are brought to bear in Pound's work, is why, and the answer in general has to do with Pound's desire to open the referential textual dimension so that the poet literally carries on his education in public. The larger structures are related by approximation instead of thematic interpenetration; allusion squeezes discursive asides into bursts of meaning. The juxtapositional insight of Imagist poetry, or so one might think of it, is nothing more than the extension of the allusive habit from the level of the line to the stanza. At times, as in the instance of Pindar, whose meaning is teased into another context, the effect is startling. The technique is in evidence everywhere in Eliot's *The Waste Land*, a fact that should surprise no one, given that its editor was an Imagist who had already experimented with elliptical strategies in *Mauberley*. In both poems allusions carry internal as well as external vectors. Part 1, section 1 of *Mauberley* begins, "For three years, out of key with his time, / He strove to resuscitate the dead art / Of poetry"; section 2, part 2 ("Mauberley") opens an internal dimension by backhanding the opening of part 1: "For three years, diabolus in the scale, / He drank ambrosia, / All passes, ANANGKE prevails." The shared syntactical contours are alive to the difference between the overlapped figures—"E. P.," whom we may as well identify with the author himself, and his Shelleyan antitype, "Mauberley," who discontentedly dissipated his spiritual treasure while Pound strove to raise the dead. True accuracy concedes subtle differences, of course: Eliot solves the issue of thematic interpenetration by encircling his poem with Tiresias, his *persona*; *The Waste Land* is at bottom a dramatic monologue whose original title ("He Do the Police in Different Voices"), odious or not, is still its most decisive gloss.

Mauberley, though, is a bit harder to characterize. A Bert-and-Ernie correlation of *The Waste Land* and *Mauberley* would notch obvious differences: in genre (dramatic and narrative), point-of-view, prosody (Eliot's vers libristic and Pound's formalist), illocutionary setting (Eliot includes footnotes, Pound does not), and so forth. But the decisive difference is thematic and tonal, and an opportunity to boldface that difference is in the apparent coincidence that both poems contain an allusion to the *same line* of Dante: "Siena mi fe'; disfecemi Maremma." In Dante's original the lines are spoken by Pia de Tolmei, whose husband, the Duke of Siena, murdered her in their castle: "Sienna," her hometown, "made me, and Maremma," her husband's, "unmade me." Eliot's translation of the line is less that than traduction—"Highbury bore me. Richmond and Kew / Undid me" (293–94, "The Fire Sermon")—to which he adds a simple pointer to "*Purgatorio* 5:133," of which Eliot's distich is a pastiche. Pound gives us no note and uses the line as the title of the second of the four portraits that comprise section 5 of part 1 of *Mauberley*:

> Among the pickled foetuses and bottled bones,
> Engaged in perfecting the catalogue,
> I found the last scion of the
> Senatorial families of Strasbourg, Monsieur Verog.

Scholarship reveals that the model for Verog is Victor Plarr (1863–1929), friend of Yeats, fellow Rhymer, and biographer of Lionel Johnson. The poem fills four quatrains with Verog's reminiscences and concludes with a bittersweet *salut*—

> M. Verog, out of step with the decade,
> Detached from his contemporaries,
> Neglected by the young,
> Because of these reveries,

which suggests to whoever, unassisted by notes, has unearthed Dante's presence in the poem, that Plarr/Verog was "seduced" from Strasbourg to England and "unmade" by the change but decent enough in the end. One turns from Pound's to Eliot's poem with undisguised shock:

> "Trams and dusty trees.
> Highbury bore me. Richmond and Kew
> Undid me. By Richmond I raised my knees
> Supine on the floor of a narrow canoe."

The voice, Tiresias's, conflates all the female voices—Marie ("Marie, hold on tight"), Madame Sosostris, Mrs. Porter, Lil, Cleopatra, the typist home at tea-time, and even Vivien Eliot ("My nerves are bad tonight. Yes, bad. Stay with me."). But Eliot's deployment of Dante is so different from Pound's we may see in it an index of radical creative displacement. Like Pound's use of Pindar, Eliot's englishing of Dante produces a brilliant pun ("*Undid* me"), but unlike Pound, Eliot positions Dante in such a way that Dante's Pia is absorbed into Eliot's proxy and stages the ironic confrontation of past and present without surrendering Eliot's lasting obsession in *The Waste Land* with the rootlessness of human desire, which explains the violated character of modern sexual pleasure. By simple contrast Pound permits the line's resonances to continue in both directions, neither containing nor excluding any and thereby highlighting Pound's lasting obsession, the tragic obliteration of historical memory. His technique points outward, always toward the readership with which he could never break off arguing.

For all of its satirical compression and experimental enthusiasm, *Lustra* ends on a note of earnest nostalgia for the past. "Provincia Deserta" is one of those strange poems where Pound nearly discloses the subjective interests he spent his career retrofitting as technical goals. He ruminates over a walking tour he made through Provence in 1913, but given the satirical beat of the rest of the book his earnestness seems misplaced. The poem, about walking and looking at what is and is no longer there, moves by an unusual logic of predication. Line after line begins with "I have walked" or "I have seen" or a similar expression. The tone in fact is *formulaic*, a series of declarations with an eerie likeness to the visionary syntax of Enoch's Gospel or Rimbaud's *Le Bateau Ivre* where the rhetorical emphasis is evenly divided between subject and object, Seer and what he sees at once. So each line names something observed or heard, but, unusually for Pound, each leaves the reader's attention suspended. Is it "the stream full of lilies" or the fact that Pound "peered down" into it that is important? The goal of all this irresolution is not immediately clear. A sentimental journey? Filler? There is in fact something sentimental about all of it, especially the ending:

> So ends that story.
> That age is gone;
> Pieire de Maensac is gone.
> I have walked over these roads;
> I have thought of them living.

In a book where the poems are told to "go" here or there as though they were children, *walking* is a word alive with suggestiveness, and a prosody that steps line by line down the world is imitating right down to tone Pound's own careful ritual of rediscovery in Provence. More to the point is that this book dramatizes Pound's discovery of his own poetic fatherings and by that much feels suddenly prepared to be "let in," admitted to the tradition whose best sights and sounds he has prayerfully repeated. These are not places but shrines; *I have walked*, he says, roads that are both the country roads of Provence and the paths of traditional *virtù*, and all along *I have thought* of them "as living." Now then, we might imagine him thinking (though not saying aloud), now that I have done this, I would be made part of it. *Let me in.*

If there is a tragic aspect to the Imagist project, it is its neurotic fixation upon historical continuity and the concurrent anxiety over a history emptied of meaning, a province deserted by what gave it meaning in the first place. History was to the Modernist the opportunity that Nature was to the Romantic, a chance to wrest the personal from the impersonal. None seized it with greater passion than Pound or the American poetry that succeeded him. American poetry *primarily*: Modernism is a provocation to thinking of authenticity, intentionality, historicity, and chronological personality, and the provocation issues from an American preoccupation with historical legitimacy. (A standalone category of Modern British Poetry is, outside of course catalogues and period designations, simply unimaginable.) To think of tradition the way Nick Carraway thought of personality, "as a series of unbroken gestures," was a blessing reserved for those whose ethnocentric sleeps were undisturbed by the nightmare of rootlessness and immigration that at some point intercepts the work of every American poet in this century. It still does. The American contribution, a self-consciousness about origins and history's design, produced an impossible goal: the recording of objective history, history *as it was*, in poetry, which of all media of human expression is the most overdetermined by subjectivity. Personal intention and traditional authenticity, doubled into a unified obsession over what Pound called either integrity or sincerity, bedeviled his work. At the same time, and like every other twentieth-century writer who has followed Shelley's lead, Pound worried about the *cognitive* value of art, about the kind of information a poem might expedite to a public that he envisioned, and with terrible urgency, seducing to his side.

J. T. Barbarese

Further Reading

Baciagalupo, Massimo. *The Forméd Trace: The Later Poetry of Ezra Pound.* New York: Columbia University Press, 1980

Bernstein, Michael André. *The Tale of the Tribe: Ezra Pound and the Modern Verse Epic.* Princeton: Princeton University Press, 1980.

Bloom, Harold, ed. *Ezra Pound.* New York: Chelsea House.

Carpenter, Humphrey. *A Serious Character: The Life of Ezra Pound.* Boston: Houghton Mifflin, 1988.

Kenner, Hugh. *The Pound Era.* Berkeley: University of California Press, 1971.

——— *The Poetry of Ezra Pound.* Lincoln: University of Nebraska Press, 1985.

Pound, Ezra. *A. B. C. of Reading.* New York: New Directions, 1960.

——— *The Cantos of Ezra Pound.* New York: New Directions, 1970.

——— *Ezra Pound: Selected Prose, 1909–1965.* Ed., with an introduction by William Cookson. New York: New Directions, 1973.

——— *Gaudier-Brzeska: A Memoir.* Rev. ed. New York: New Directions, 1970.

——— *The Letters of Ezra Pound: 1907–1941.* Ed. D. D. Paige. New York: Harcourt, Brace, and World, 1950.

——— *Literary Essays of Ezra Pound.* Ed., with an introduction by T. S. Eliot. New York: New Directions, 1968.

——— *Personae: The Shorter Poems of Ezra Pound.* Rev. ed. Ed. Lea Baechler and A. Walton Litz. New York: New Directions, 1990.

T. S. Eliot

F OR his graduation exercises at Smith Academy, in St. Louis, Thomas Stearns Eliot composed and recited a poem of fourteen rhymed stanzas in which appropriately lofty and inspiring sentiments were uttered about youth, age, the road of life, sons departing the school to which they would return—changed but still loyal; most grandly, about the modern world:

> Great duties call—the twentieth century
> More grandly dowered than those which came before,
> Summons—who knows what time may hold in store.

Five years or so later, having graduated from Harvard and having read some French poets, notably Jules Laforgue, Eliot was writing lines like the following:

> Wipe your hand across your mouth, and laugh;
> The worlds revolve like ancient men and women
> Gathering fuel in vacant lots.

From an expansive, large-souled looker into the future and what it held for mankind's great destiny, he had become an imagistic ironist, still making grand and mysterious gestures ("The worlds revolve like ancient men and women / Gathering fuel") but now in an unillusioned manner. It was the "modern" note, that note which initially strikes a reader picking up Eliot's poetry.

Or so it struck this reader when as an undergraduate I read to myself and read aloud the opening lines of "The Love Song of J. Alfred

Prufrock": "Let us go then, you and I, / When the evening is spread out against the sky / Like a patient etherised upon a table." "You and I"—who are we and what sort of relationship is this? "When the evening is spread out against the sky"—when exactly does that occur and how can one tell? "Like a patient etherised upon a table"—how is the evening "like" an etherised patient and what does such a likeness portend? In fact I didn't ask these questions, didn't pause and shake my head in dismay over them but instead read on, either pretending the difficulties were only temporary and would be resolved or electing to hear what the poet would say next, what new strange collocation of details would puzzle and excite. Sure enough, within a few lines occurs the infamous couplet—"In the room the women come and go, / Talking of Michelangelo"—utterly memorable, but what did it mean? That whatever sort of women they are in whatever sort of room, coming and going, they are, all of them, talking of Michelangelo. But what are they saying and what does it have to do with the "sawdust restaurants with oyster shells" just preceding or the patient etherised upon a table with which we began? Is it an unworthy thing to do, to talk of Michelangelo—horribly superficial perhaps? But we are told nothing of how the talk is conducted, in what accents or at what level of perception; no more than with the sawdust restaurants and its oyster shells are we given clear signals on how to regard the talking women. But we remember the couplet in which they appear.

Or so thinks one of the "we" who learned to read poetry during the age of Eliot, an age that began in the early 1920s, when "Prufrock" and *The Waste Land* and a number of influential critical essays had given him a reputation as the significant poet-critic of his time. That significance only widened until his death in 1965, even though after *Four Quartets* (1943) he had ceased almost entirely to write poetry. To a college student in the 1950s Eliot's name was magic, the source of profound wisdom about the chaos of modern civilization and the difficulties—the impossibilities—of successful communication between human beings. Even as we struggled in our lives, sometimes with pretty good results, to know and love some other people, Eliot's work was there as a great looming warning, a grim shaking of the head at the vanity and fragility of human wishes and aspirations. "Between the idea and the reality . . . Falls the shadow," he told us in *The Hollow Men*, and the words reverberated. And while his poetry was revered as a source of

disenchanted wisdom about life, his critical and historical pronouncements in *The Sacred Wood* and *Selected Essays*, his valuations and comparisons of writers past and present, were deployed in countless undergraduate and graduate English papers. Notions of tradition, or the dissociated sensibility that had overtaken English poetry in the
seventeenth century, or the "objective correlative" that Shakespeare in
Hamlet was unable to discover—these Eliotic formulations were
invoked by way of giving authority to whatever argument we were
attempting to make. Less important to us were the late attempts at
social and religious polemic—the books about culture (*Notes Towards
the Definition of Culture*) and religion (*The Idea of a Christian Society*)
where Eliot spelled out, with maximum qualification and circumspec-
tion, his exclusionary notions of life in a world he said was "worm-eaten
with liberalism." Nor, despite the popular success of *The Cocktail Party*,
did the plays command our lively attention. It was the small body of
poems and a selection of essays from a much wider spread of prose writings, that constituted his powerful appeal.

The question is whether the appeal is still felt by teachers and students in the last decade of this century. (I am assuming there does not
exist a younger nonacademic reading public for Eliot's writings.) His
death coincided with a time when American poets were becoming more
responsive to William Carlos Williams's experiments in the American
grain than to the "classical" values Eliot espoused and the by then too-
familiar poems that had made his reputation. And as Wallace Stevens's
body of work became increasingly influential, as—under the critical
authority of Harold Bloom and Helen Vendler—his status as our most
important poet was asserted, Eliot's reputation enjoyed no comparable
enriching. In fact there was a perceptible decline in the capacity of his
poetry to make a difference in people's lives. His centennial was celebrated in 1988, and the novelist Cynthia Ozick, writing in the *New
Yorker* the following year, put the matter in a way that was accurate in
its estimation of how the winds have been blowing, though it was also
excessive and melodramatic in its overall tone.

In the early seventies, it was still possible to uncover, here and there, a tenacious English Department offering a vestigial graduate seminar given over to
the study of Eliot. But by the close of the eighties only "The Love Song of J.
Alfred Prufrock" appears to have survived the indifference of the schools—as
two or three pages in the anthologies, a fleeting assignment for high-school

seniors and college freshmen. "Prufrock," and "Prufrock" alone, is what the latest generations know (barely know); not "The Hollow Men," not "La Figlia che Piange," not "Ash-Wednesday"—not even "The Waste Land." Never "Four Quartets." And the mammoth prophetic presence of T. S. Eliot himself—that immortal, sovereign rock—the latest generation do not know at all.

Having herself been one of the generation that eagerly discovered Eliot, Ozick feels saddened by the loss, but she is also unhappy at the reactionary nature of Eliot's political and social attitudes, and she ends her essay by informing us solemnly that it is our "unsparing obligation to dismiss the reactionary Eliot," even as we will probably miss forever "the golden cape of our youth, the power and prestige of high art."

Ozick's conclusion is put forth in a more self-important tone than Eliot used about himself (he once told an audience that since he had a reputation for "affecting pedantic precision" he should not like to lose it). But even more misguided is her attempt to make Eliot less disagreeable to the liberal conscience by telling us we must "dismiss" his reactionary opinions. Surely the business of a good reader consists in something other than condemning qualities in a writer that don't square with certifiably correct morals and politics. If we are uneasy about some or all of Eliot's references to Jews—about, say, his pronouncement in *After Strange Gods* (1934) that since a traditional society needs to be homogeneous, "reasons of race and religion combine to make any large number of free-thinking Jews undesirable"—we should analyze and judge the remark by putting it in relation to comparable assertions and ideas in Eliot's prose and verse. Dismissing it is no more called for than embracing it, and the same may be said of controversial and disturbing moments in the writings of (among others) Milton, Tolstoy, and D. H. Lawrence. It may even be the case that a great writer's power is commensurate with his power to offend.

But I am less interested in quarreling with Ozick than in qualifying her assumption that "the latest generation" doesn't at all know Eliot's poetry. Without asking which poet it is the latest generation knows *well*, it can be said that over the years and right up through a just completed semester numbers of students have read Eliot with me in courses called Modern Poetry, Modern British Poetry, and Modern American Poetry, and these students have found him no less difficult or less interesting than they find Yeats or Stevens, Robert Lowell or Elizabeth Bishop. Ozick's reading of the world-cultural poetry barometer that registers who's high and who's low must be corrected by the insistence that at least at one college—and I suspect at many more—Eliot is alive and well, his poems, and to some extent his criticism, seriously and satisfyingly engaged with by members of the latest generation.

My attempt in the following pages is to speak not as an impartial, objective observer of the poetry scene, as this century nears its termination, but rather as a critic and teacher who values and is moved by Eliot's work as a whole and who finds parts of it to be of supreme literary quality. While I don't mean to tag certain poems as exclusively the ones in which that quality can be found, I shall mainly focus on three of them from different stages in Eliot's career—"The Love Song of J. Alfred Prufrock," *The Waste Land*, and *Four Quartets*—and on the criticism he wrote in the years roughly from 1917 to 1922.

"Prufrock," with the help of Ezra Pound, was first published in *Poetry* in 1915, but it was written in 1910–11, the year Eliot spent abroad, mainly in Paris. It is often pointed out that, as with "Portrait of a Lady," written during the same period, its milieu is Boston. Yet "Prufrock" is the sort of poem that refuses to be located in one topographical cityscape or another, and, in fact, Eliot's biographer, Peter Ackroyd, terms the "yellow fog" in the poem a St. Louis one. Its landscape is, for want of a better word, psychological, and in perhaps the poem's moment of greatest feeling its protagonist wonders if "it would have been worth it, after all" to have made some large annunciation to the woman, the "she" who lolls and entertains him amidst marmalade and cups of tea. "After" (a key reiterated word in the poem) these and many other pieces of worldly furniture are enumerated, Prufrock suddenly exclaims,

> It is impossible to say just what I mean!
> But as if a magic lantern threw the nerves in patterns on a screen.

To say "just" what you mean would be presumably to move beyond the excitements and inadequacies of metaphor into the realm of truth, where words mean precisely what they say—a world exactly contrary to the poetic one Eliot creates.

It is as if we were to look at a series of nerve patterns and as if somehow these constituted not a composite visual shape but a musical performance, indeed a love song. "Prufrock" has no plot, no narrative with a beginning, middle, and end; its characters aren't characters but nervous ghosts who mysteriously appear and disappear as elusively as the yellow fog that slides along its street. In the course of various formulations, or half-formulations, the "I," who tells us he has "known" just about everything, decides that he doesn't dare disturb the universe, that he shouldn't "presume" to begin to do anything, that probably he "should have been a pair of ragged claws," that he is not a prophet (even if he's seen his own slightly balding head brought in on a platter), that he really can't manage to pass as either a Lazarus or a Hamlet figure, that he's "almost" (but not quite?) ridiculous, almost (capitalized) "the Fool." Finally, that the mermaids won't sing to him whether he eats a peach and wears white flannel trousers or whether he doesn't. What I'm suggesting by this cavalier assembling of the "facts" about J. Alfred Prufrock is that there aren't any facts, that the "content" of the poem is really a hoax—or rather an occasion for a voice to make haunting music.

To hear that music one must read the poem aloud to a friend, to a class of students, or declaim it silently to the listener within. I can think of no single piece of writing more wholly dependent for its effect on the "performance" that R. P. Blackmur once said was the only way to know literature "afresh"—"in reading and seeing and hearing what is actually in it at this place and this time." For example, one of the important ways Eliot exercises a hold on our ears is to make sequences out of repetitions that don't quite repeat, as in the three quietly lengthening verse paragraphs (from six lines to seven to eight) in the middle of the poem, beginning with "For I have known them all already, known them all." Recall the closing questions in each unit: "So how should I presume?" And how should I presume?" "And how should I begin" (that last one preceded by "And should I then presume?"). Or recall the echoing "And would it have been worth it, after all, / Would it have been worth while," and the copresence, but in varying patterns, of other echoes echoing: " 'I am Lazarus, come from the dead, / Come back to tell you all, I shall tell you all'"; "That is not what I meant at all. / That is not it, at all.'" What in a reading aloud is heard as ingeniously melodic, subtly compelling, refuses to be carried over into the sentences of a quoting critic at his typewriter.

A contemporary English critic, Barbara Everett, once wrote that the voice in "Prufrock" (it makes more sense to say *in* "Prufrock" the poem rather than *of* Prufrock the character) manages to hold us through its spellbinder's charm. This spell, though, is very much an aural one, depending less upon any sense or point about life that is made—beyond the general declaration of weary futility, of having come too late and missed out on everything—than on the seductive drawn-out repetitions, the music of consonantal and vowel echoings. Indeed the theme of weary futility is contradicted by the vitality of the verbal, aural performance. An example from the first of two tercets about the mermaids that end the poem:

> I have seen them riding seaward on the waves
> Combing the white hair of the waves blown back
> When the wind blows the water white and black.

This is really not so much a vision as it is something heard, from "seen" to "seaward," from "waves" to "white" to "waves" to "when" to "wind" to "water" to "white," from "blown back" to "blows . . . black"—an auditory tour de force, surely. For all Eliot's explicitly acknowledged debt in "Prufrock" and the other early poems to Laforgue ("My early vers libre, of course, was started under the endeavor to practice the same form as Laforgue. This meant merely rhyming lines of irregular length, with the rhymes coming in irregular places"), it is the English Tennyson of "The Lotos Eaters" these lines recall:

> but evermore
> Most weary seemed the sea, weary the oar,
> Weary the wandering fields of barren foam.

And rather than asking exactly what the mermaids are doing out there (aside from "combing"), we experience the doing as an effect registered memorably by someone who has "lingered in the chambers of the sea" as Eliot did in the echo chambers of this poem. The astonishing thing about "Prufrock" is, of course, how it has continued to speak to the most unlikely readers. Or maybe there is no such thing as an unlikely reader: writing about teaching literature in a community college Clara Clairborne Park remembers one of her students telling her, "I must have read that poem fifty times . . . I *am* J. Alfred Prufrock." Of such is the power of "a piece of rhythmical grumbling"—Eliot's own phrase about *The Waste Land*, but even more applicable to "Prufrock"—to cast a spell over the responsive ear.

In "The Frontiers of Criticism," Eliot's 1956 lecture delivered to fourteen thousand people gathered in the baseball stadium at the University of

Minnesota, he said, in a typically self-deprecatory disclaimer, "I fail to see any critical movement which can be said to derive from myself." Perhaps the disclaimer is not so much self-deprecatory as a proud fending off of those who come after Eliot the true original: how could you think (we might conceive him saying) that *I* can be held responsible for this or that critical procedure or movement? In fact, for all the academic recycling of Eliotic terms that occurred in the 1940s and 1950s, Eliot's critical convictions and principles do not take kindly to being passed along. We may speak of some critic as a Poundian or Leavisite or a follower of Yvor Winters (Wintersian?) but never as an Eliotian or even a follower of Eliot. This has to do with the absence in Eliot of a systematic critical method ("the only method is to be very intelligent," he said in his preface to *The Sacred Wood*) or a prescribed method for conducting literary analysis, which we find, to one degree or another, in Pound and Leavis and Winters. As for Eliot's much-used terms, which have had such a strong, even notorious life, they have by now all been thoroughly and adversely criticized; no critic today would use "dissociation of sensibility" or "objective correlative" without the most elaborate qualification.

Still, Eliot remains the major poet-critic of our century, taking a rightful place in the line from Ben Jonson to Dryden, Samuel Johnson, Coleridge, and Matthew Arnold. The last-named was felt by Eliot as his immediate predecessor, whose work, while it deserved much respect, had also to be firmly placed in perspective. So in introducing his first volume of criticism, *The Sacred Wood*, Eliot saluted Arnold's plea for a criticism that would complement and make more self-aware the work of poets. He agrees with Arnold that this work had not been sufficiently done for the Romantics, nor, by implication, for the poets who were currently writing in English one hundred years later. But he wishes also that Arnold had been more of a practical critic; that he had, in Eliot's examples, taken it upon himself to compare Thackeray with Flaubert, or analyzed Dickens and compared him with George Eliot and Stendhal. Instead Arnold spent too much of his time "attacking the uncritical" and concerned himself more with matters of culture, society, and religion than with literary ones. About which Eliot remarks, adducing his contemporaries H. G. Wells and G. K. Chesterton, "The temptation, to any man who is interested in ideas and primarily in literature, is to put literature into the corner until he cleaned up the whole country first." So his judgment was that Arnold was more a "propagandist for criticism" than a critic.

Eliot didn't begin by attempting to clean up the whole country; in fact it was not until after his assuming editorship of the *Criterion* in 1922—and especially after his conversion to Anglo-Catholicism in 1927—that his interest shifted from the comparison and analysis of individual writers and literary works to (in words from his preface to the second, 1928, edition of *The Sacred Wood*) "the relation of poetry to the spiritual and social life of its time and of other times." His most productive, most brilliant years as a "pure" critic of literature were the ones in which his creative work flowered—from the publication of *Prufrock and Other Observations* in 1917 to *The Waste Land* in 1922. After that, although he wrote a number of fine essays about particular writers (perhaps most notably about Dante, Samuel Johnson, Byron, Tennyson, and Yeats), those for which he is most strongly remembered had their birth within a fairly small range of years. (A list of them would include essays on Marlowe, Jonson, *Hamlet*, Philip Massinger, the Metaphysicals, Marvell, Dryden, Blake, and Swinburne.)

Often in the briefest of compasses, Eliot can make a brilliant redirection of our sense of a writer. For example, the Swinburne essay is only six pages long, but these are pages in which, as Eliot says approvingly about Aristotle in "The Perfect Critic," he is "swiftly operating the analysis of sensation to the point of principle and definition." In a series of lightninglike comparisons of lines from Swinburne's verse with lines from that of Thomas Campion, Shakespeare, and Shelley, Eliot establishes his point about how Swinburne's genius was to identify meaning and sound, to present "emotion" that is "never particular, never in direct line of vision, never focussed"—emotion reinforced by "expansion." A moment from these comparisons may suggest Eliot's typical operation in his essays and reviews. He is about to compare Swinburne with Shakespeare, then with Wordsworth:

It is, in fact, the word that gives him the thrill, not the object. When you take to pieces any verse of Swinburne, you find always that the object was not there—only the word. Compare

> Snowdrops that plead for pardon
> And pine for fright

with the daffodils that come before the swallow dares. The snowdrop of Swinburne disappears, the daffodil of Shakespeare remains. The swallow of Shakespeare remains in the verse of *Macbeth*; the bird of Wordsworth

Breaking the silence of the seas

remains; the swallow of "Itylus" disappears.

This is dazzling, virtually sleight-of-hand. Fully to register these comparisons a reader would have to remember Swinburne's "Before the Mirror" (whence the snowdrops), then lines from act 4 of *The Winter's Tale* about the daffodils, then think of the "temple-haunting martlet" (the "swallow" in *Macbeth* that Duncan invokes as he prepares to enter Macbeth's castle), then Wordsworth's nightingale in "The Solitary Reaper," and finally the evanescence of Swinburne's swallow ("Swallow, my sister, O sister swallow"). Whether anyone is able or likely to do all this even as he or she ponders the convincingness of Eliot's comparisons, is doubtful. More likely we may just nod agreement, impressed by the breezy authority with which the critic proceeds to his conclusion that in Swinburne's verse "the meaning is merely the hallucination of meaning, because language, uprooted, has adapted itself to an independent life of atmospheric nourishment."

Eliot's practical criticism, as instanced in the particularly telescoped example of it, is seldom or never a matter of patient analysis of a poem but rather of provocative assertion and invitations to compare one poem or series of lines with another. It is invigorating to read him partly because the twists of his discourse (not typically a soberly conducted "argument") have the surprise and originality of poetry itself. He likes to strew difficulties in the paths of his readers and himself—anything to make things other than cut and dried. In the following sentences from a never-reprinted *Athenaeum* review of 1919, "The Education of Taste," he sets out the difficulties that lie in the way of the practicing critic who must make decisions about how to operate:

To communicate impressions is difficult; to communicate a coordinated system of impressions is more difficult; to theorize demands vast ingenuity, and to avoid theorizing requires vast honesty.

The neat movement here from theorizing to the avoidance of theorizing, then the capping reference to "generality" in which earlier terms like impression and honesty are brought back, has the force of true wit, Oscar Wilde crossed by Matthew Arnold. And Eliot is especially vigilant toward well-known literary terms a naive, insufficiently disillusioned poet or critic might rely on—terms like "technique." In prefacing the second edition of *The Sacred Wood* he takes us around the mulberry bush by beginning with a definition of poetry that—like Swift's definition of good prose as "proper words in proper places"—says everything and not much of anything in particular. Poetry, Eliot writes, consists of "excellent words in excellent arrangement and excellent metre." But what more can be said?

That is what is called the technique of verse. But we observe that we cannot define even the technique of verse; we cannot say at what point "technique" begins or where it ends; and if we add to it a "technique of feeling," that glib phrase will carry us only a little farther. We can only say that a poem, in some sense, has its own life.

In other words there is no shortcut, indeed no road through to certainty in literary matters. We can only say that "in some sense" a poem has its own life; or we can say, in Eliot's echo of Bishop Butler, that in considering poetry "we must consider it primarily as poetry and not another thing." Or, in that same playful preface to *The Sacred Wood*, we may agree that poetry is "a superior amusement." Is that a sufficient definition? Not at all:

I do not mean an amusement for superior people. I call it an amusement, an amusement *pour distraire les honnêtes gens*, not because that is a true definition, but because if you call it anything else you are likely to call it something still more false. If we think of the nature of amusement, then poetry is not amusing; but if we think of anything else that poetry may seem to be, we are led into far greater difficulties.

Such sidestepping and ducking has its perils, and in his later prose Eliot would succumb to them, as in the often lugubrious fussings of *Notes Towards the Definition of Culture*. But they also tease and refresh our minds in salutary ways.

Eliot performed similar services with regard to words like *tradition, rhetoric, satire*—perhaps most important—*wit*, the promotion of which quality into a major one for great poetry may be his most forceful contribution to literary criticism. In "Andrew Marvell" (1921) he made a memorable attempt to define—even as he deprecated the possibility of clearly defining it—that quality of wit which distinguished Marvell's work and which over the course of subsequent centuries had been nearly absent from English poetry. Eliot's account claims that the seventeenth century took the "high" style developed in Marlowe and Jonson and separated it out into qualities of wit and magniloquence. While allowing that the terms are fluid, and that the style of Marvell, Cowley, Milton and others often showed these qualities blended, he attempts to distinguish Caroline wit from what followed it:

The wit of the Caroline poets is not the wit of Shakespeare, and it is not the wit of Dryden, the great master of contempt, or of Pope, the great master of hatred, or of Swift, the great master of disgust. What is meant is some quality which is common to the songs in *Comus* and Cowley's Anacreontics and Marvell's Horatian Ode. It is more than a technical accomplishment, or the vocabulary and syntax of an epoch; it is, what we have designated tentatively as wit, a tough reasonableness beneath the slight lyric grace. You cannot find it in Shelley or Keats or Wordsworth; you cannot find more than an echo of it in Landor, still less in Tennyson or Browning; and among contemporaries Mr. Yeats is an Irishman and Mr. Hardy is a modern Englishman—that is to say, Mr. Hardy is without it and Mr. Yeats is outside of the tradition altogether.

It can be found, he goes on to add, in Laforgue and Gautier, two poets Eliot had managed to make use of in his own work during the decade that had just concluded.

Such an account is itself a specimen of wit, right down to the lyric grace of naming those three great masters of contempt, hatred, and disgust, and the tough reasonableness—or so it pretends to be—of excluding both Hardy and Yeats from any consideration in these terms. Like most exciting passages in Eliot's criticism, we read and silently correct its overstatements: we *can* find wit in some of Keats, even in Shelley occasionally; we know that the dismissal of Yeats and Hardy is too sweeping, unfair. But as Eliot's friend Wyndham Lewis reminds us, satire is always unfair, and Eliot's early criticism is never far from a satiric—or at least a mischievously subversive—perspective on things. "Someone said: 'The dead writers are remote from us because we *know* so much more than they did.' Precisely, and they are that which we know." These sentences from "Tradition and the Individual Talent" might be turned upon Eliot's own criticism insofar as its formulations have entered the bloodstream of later generations of readers who were helped to become critics by having to move beyond the Eliot criticism that they knew.

With the publication of the first volume of Eliot's letters, reaching to the end of 1922, we have a rich particular sense of what we knew only in outline before: that his marriage to Vivien Haigh-Wood in 1915 became progressively more painful and that both his health and hers worsened. In his case a "breakdown" occurred in 1921 when he took rest cures, first in Margate, then in Lausanne, Switzerland, even as he was finishing *The Waste Land*. Epistolary Eliot was able at times to take a sardonically humorous perspective on his problems, saying that he felt himself to be "living in one of Dostoyevsky's novels, you see, not in one of Jane Austen's," or assuring a correspondent that his health wasn't all that bad: "My teeth are falling to pieces, I have to wear spectacles to read, and from time to time I am contorted with rheumatism—otherwise I am pretty well." Meanwhile Vivien was writing his mother about the deplorable condition of "Tom's" wardrobe ("his old underwear is still thick and in *fair* condition, but it needs *incessant darning*. Darning alone takes me hours out of the week"), especially his lack of pyjamas: "He is still worse provided with pyjamas than anything. . . . He is very rough with his pyjamas, and shirts—tears them unmercifully."

It is of interest then to contemplate this hapless creature (as Eliot and his wife present him to others) carrying out brilliantly various public roles in the years 1917–1921: working efficiently in the colonial and foreign department of Lloyd's Bank, teaching night school and extension courses in English literature, turning out enormous amounts of journalism for the *Egoist* and *Athenaeum*, and (in his spare time, one might say) assembling a second volume of verse, *Poems 1920*, consisting, most importantly, of "Gerontion." "Gerontion" is Eliot's bleakest, chilliest, most inaccessible poem, virtually "unreadable" by the procedures we use to read more conventional works. It is Eliot at his most complicatedly and concentratedly allusive as well as his most elusive. What are we to make of a monologue (if it is that) which in seeming to draw itself together near the end proffers the following sentiment—"I would meet you upon this honestly"—in which there is no credible "I," in which the "you" doesn't exist, and in which the adverb "honestly" can't be credited as accurately modifying any credible verb? The referential currency of such a line is about equal to that possessed by the figures—no more than names, really—who momentarily surface in the poem, then just as mysteriously disappear, as Hakagawa bows among the Titians, as Madame de Tornquist shifts the candles, and as Fräulein von Kulp turns in the hall, one hand on the door. Gerontion, whoever "he" may be, puts it thus: "Vacant shuttles weave the wind." The weaving and unweaving of verbal patterns in Eliot's most relentlessly verbal poem has the effect, so it seems to this reader, of rendering the large windy portents about Christianity and history less rather than more intelligible. As always in Eliot, the poem has wonderfully memorable lines, especially those from the section about history that begins "After such knowledge, what forgiveness?" But they don't contribute to a meditation that sustains itself in moral content as well as in rhetorical flourish. "Whenever a character in Shakespeare makes a direct appeal to us," Eliot wrote in " 'Rhetoric' and Poetic Drama," "we are either the victims of our own sentiment, or we are in the presence of a vicious rhetoric." That he was aware of this assertion in relation to "Gerontion" and that he set out to have the poem's speaker expose himself as fraudulent, is conceivable, yet doubtful. We should remember that he seriously considered using the poem as prologue to *The Waste Land*, desisting only when Pound told him he must not.

I should prefer to think that the harassed Eliot—caught in a painful marriage, overworked, plagued by bad teeth and eyesight, contorted by rheumatism, pajamas falling to pieces, living in, as it were, a novel by Dostoyevsky—cheered himself up by seeing himself in the dramatic light of a poem, as he said Othello was really cheering himself up in his speech before he stabs himself:

He is endeavouring to escape reality, he has ceased to think about Desdemona, and he is thinking about himself. . . . Othello succeeds in turning himself into a pathetic figure, by adopting an *aesthetic* rather than a moral attitude, dramatizing himself against his environment. He takes in the spectator, but the human motive is primarily to take in himself.

The question is perhaps whether either Gerontion or "Gerontion" succeeds in taking *us* in, without the five acts of tortuous dramatic development Shakespeare subjects Othello to and that makes his final end so moving. My answer is that brilliant as the poem is it lacks the humor and humanity of "Prufrock." And for all its evocation of aridity, of "Thoughts of a dry brain in a dry season," it fails to take us in, to take hold of us the way Eliot was about to do in *The Waste Land*.

But how does *The Waste Land* "take hold"? Not so many years ago it seemed important to try to loosen the poem from the interpretive structures critics had attached to it; there was so much "scaffolding"—to use

Cleanth Brooks's word about what his own influential essay on the poem provided—that it was all but impossible to see the object the scaffolding surrounded. Now, much of that surrounding material has fallen away or has become so inert that it's simply no longer of interest. Few critics these days deal with the poem by applying the Fisher King legend, Jessie Weston's *From Ritual to Romance*, or Frazer's *The Golden Bough*. It was of course Eliot himself in his introductory note who attached these books and legends to the poem, but the notes to *The Waste Land* are a kind of playful poetry themselves. It is Eliot's superior amusement, for example, to remind us that the hermit-thrush in "What the Thunder Said" is "*Turdus aonalaschkae pallasii*," that he's heard it in Quebec Province, and that "its 'water-dripping song' is justly celebrated." Eliot's notes, if not taken too seriously, are harmless and sometimes amusing. But other sorts of notes or glosses adhering to the poem, whether they exist in, say, *The Norton Anthology of Modern Poetry* or in the mind of an individual reader, can be more insidious, more inhibiting to creative, responsive reading. I am thinking of a gloss such as Norton gives to the Baudelaire allusion at the end of part 1, "The Burial of the Dead": "*You: hypocrite lecteur!—mon semblable,—mon frere!*" After identifying the source, the editor says that "with this line Baudelaire and Eliot assault the reader and draw him accusingly into the same plight as themselves." The problem with this assertion is, of course, that after reading the footnote no sensible reader is going to feel the least bit assaulted. It's just one more allusion to store untroubled in the mind and then read on. Or consider the moment when the narrator, regarding the morning crowd flowing over London Bridge, suddenly recognizes someone named Stetson and addresses him as "You who were with me in the ships at Mylae!" The anthology note identifies Mylae as a battle in the first Punic War between Rome and Carthage, then says that "it merges with the First World War, in which the speaker and Stetson fought; both wars are seen as pointless and futile." This is an example of an editorial anxiety to fill in the blanks which the poem so carefully does *not* fill in: we are told neither that these figures fought in the First World War nor that the war was pointless. (And if—as Eliot's own note claims—all the poem's "characters" merge into Tiresias, it's hard to see how, being blind, he could have fought in any war.)

Samuel Johnson's wisdom about notes should be remembered, when in his editorial preface to Shakespeare he wrote, "Particular passages are cleared by notes, but the general effect of the work is weakened. The mind is refrigerated by interruption; the thoughts are diverted from the principle subject." A poem such as *The Waste Land* as much as a Shakespeare play suffers when the reading of it is constantly interrupted by a recurrence to notes or their equivalent. What we need to work at instead is keeping the poem moving, paying attention to the sequence; above all, listening to the voices—for it is voices in motion that make up the poem's substance. Again, Johnson's advice to the reader of Shakespeare is wholly appropriate to reading Eliot:

Let him read on through brightness and obscurity, through integrity and corruption; let him preserve his comprehension of the dialogue and his interest in the fable. And when the pleasures of novelty have ceased, let him attempt exactness, and read the commentators.

Another way of putting it is Wyndham Lewis's way, when, decades ago, he said about Joyce's *Ulysses*, recently published, "No one who looks *at* it will ever want to look *behind* it." Lewis was paying grudging tribute to the incredibly rich surface Joyce's book presents to the reader. And Eliot himself, in his essay of 1923, *"Ulysses*: Order and Myth," said that Joyce had given him "all the surprise, delight, and terror that I can require." We may presume that these qualities emanated from looking at and listening to the surface of *Ulysses*, rather than from probing the depths of Joyce's thought or discovering deep meanings supposedly hidden in his book. During the time he wrote *The Waste Land* Eliot was preoccupied with what he called, in his 1919 essay on Ben Jonson, "poetry of the surface." Many of the things he admired in Jonson's dramatic art he named in terms that could equally well apply to the art of *The Waste Land*: "simplified characters," a "flat distortion" in the drawing, "an art of caricature," "a brutality, a lack of sentiment, a polished surface, a handling of large bold designs in brilliant colours"—one could go on. "We cannot call a man's work superficial when it is the creation of a world; a man cannot be accused of dealing superficially with the world which he himself has created; the superficies *is* the world," wrote Eliot, summing it all up by calling Jonson's drama "a titanic show." The phrase would not be amiss as a collective name for the different "shows" of which *The Waste Land* is composed, whether as conducted at Madame Sosostris's or on London Bridge, or round behind the gashouse, or in the typist's flat.

The challenge lies in saying something relevant and appropriate to these surfaces without saying too much, without foisting a burden of "meaning" on the poem (as do explanatory footnotes, often) that makes it merely portentous. Consider the marvelous and scary utterances of the "neurasthenic" woman, as she is sometimes referred to, in the first section of part 2, "A Game of Chess." "Under the brush, her hair / Spread out in fiery points / Glowed into words, then would be savagely still," as she implores the faceless narrator to "Speak to me," to "Think." Vivien Eliot, who must have been in her husband's mind when he wrote these lines, was reduced to a single marginal response to those words as they appeared in *The Waste Land* manuscript—"Wonderful!" There was no more that needed to be said, and a similar enthusiastic exclamation might be made to the woman in the pub (in the second half of "A Game of Chess"), as she runs on about what she told Lil about how to treat her husband Albert who has been in the army and wants a good time: "And if you don't give it him, there's others will, I said. / Oh is there, she said. Something o' that, I said." Neither of these women should be understood as representing or embodying some large important symbolic value—some truth about modern civilization. For if we insist on making the characters representative of something "more," something deeper, we run the risk of missing out on surface intensities, memorable accents and associations—what Lil's friend and critic, referring to the hot gammon Lil and Albert served her, calls "the beauty of it hot." Shakespeare comes to mind again and the critical habit of treating his plays (particularly the last ones) as symbolic utterances, large spiritual meanings about ultimate things. Yet the surface of these plays is so much more active, complex, and just plain interesting than what supposedly lies behind it, that to translate language and events into other terms is simply to dilute and enfeeble them.

Blackmur's name for what Eliot gave us in *The Waste Land* was "sensual metaphysics." In a provocative comment from his Library of Congress lectures (*Anni Mirabiles*, 1921–1925) he confronted the surreal nightmare passage in part 5, "What the Thunder Said," in which "a woman drew her long black hair out tight," in which the towers turn upside down and the bats crawl downward "down a blackened wall," and voices sing "out of empty cisterns and exhausted wells":

The exegetes tell us, and it is true, that we are in Chapel Perilous and the Perilous Cemetery is no doubt near at hand, and it may be as one of the exegetes says that we hear something like the voice of John the Baptist in the last line. But for myself, I muse and merge and ache and find myself feeling with the very senses of my thought greetings and cries from all the senses that are.

Testimony such as this risks being no more than a fancier version of the professor in the classroom assuring his students of how deeply he is moved by a passage. But we can risk it, in the interests of opening up rather than shutting down the poem.

The most challenging of recent reconsiderations of *The Waste Land* is to be found in Christopher Ricks's *T. S. Eliot and Prejudice*, which doesn't address the poem as a whole but selects the openings of part 1 and part 5 with a view to demonstrating how Eliot's poetry is a principled refusal to strike and maintain clear, dramatic postures—the unmistakable postures of sentence sounds that Robert Frost said poetry should provide. As Ricks shows, in patient detail, Eliot's openings—"April is the cruelest month" and "After the torchlight red on sweaty faces"—are memorable ones, but the sequences these lines initiate are anything but clearly marked: "The force of this opening [he is speaking of the "April" one] is in its combination of unmistakable directness with all these lurking possibilities of mistaking its direction." For all their differences of vocabulary and emphasis both Blackmur and Ricks prefer to respond to the volatile surface intensities of language rather than the stable meanings some critics have presumed to lie underneath them. My own experience in teaching the poem is that if you read it aloud and ask what people hear in it—anywhere in the five parts—the variety of responses, most of them cogent and relevant, will prove *The Waste Land* to be a work eminently hospitable to divergent ways of reading it, and full of—in Ricks's phrase—"lurking possibilities of mistaking its direction." These qualities make the poem still vibrant after seven decades of interpretation; my procedure here has been, accordingly, not to offer another one but to consider the question of and the necessity for "interpretation."

On the other hand, if it is true—as Henry James insisted it was in "The Art of Fiction"—that "art lives upon discussion, upon experiment, upon curiosity, upon variety of attempt, upon the exchange of views and the comparison of standpoints," then *Four Quartets* may be the least vibrant poem in Eliot's oeuvre, justifying Cynthia Ozick's statement that the latest generation "never" reads it. Even with the publication in 1978 of

Helen Gardner's fine study of the poem's composition, the relative absence of exchange of views, of lively argument about the poem's status, has persisted. Commentators are agreed, for the most part, that the *Quartets* are a mixture of very private and very public poetry, and that as a result its texture is extremely uneven. The question is whether such unevenness is a fault in the poem or the source of its power and beauty.

Donald Davie's way of distinguishing, broadly, the two kinds of characteristic poetry in the *Quartets* is to call one "the sonorous opulence of Mallarmé," the other a "prosaicism so homespun as to be, from time to time, positively 'prosey' or 'prosing.'" And he adds that Eliot's famous remark about how "the poetry does not matter" is directed at the second, prosaic pole. But the statement about poetry not mattering occurs in the second section of "East Coker," part 2, after the Mallarméan opalescence of "What is the late November doing / With the disturbance of the spring." That lyric having concluded itself, there is a blank space after which a voice intones:

> That was a way of putting it—not very satisfactory;
> A periphrastic study in a worn-out poetical fashion.

And we are told that "one" is still left with the "intolerable wrestle / With words and meanings," also that "the poetry does not matter." It is an extravagant thing for a poet who has spent his life wrestling with words and meanings to say, and it surely has just as much reference—perhaps more—to the "poetical" Mallarmé-like passages in the poem as to the prosaic ones it might be seen as rationalizing or justifying. At the same time the claim about poetry not mattering shouldn't be taken too solemnly, as commentators sometimes do when they compare Eliot's work to the late Beethoven quartets, which also, it is said, try to get "beyond" music (as Eliot would get beyond poetry). In fact the differences between listening to Beethoven and reading Eliot are a lot more apparent and significant than the similarities. Let us say rather that they may be compared only to the extent that, despite the innovative, unconventional gestures these artists make in tonality and rhetoric, each remains intractably committed to his medium—Beethoven to music, Eliot to words.

Ten years after he completed "Little Gidding" Eliot published "The Three Voices of Poetry," an essay that contains a number of interesting formulations about the creative act, the most relevant to our purposes being one he uses to distinguish two of these voices—the first and most important of which is that of the poet when he is primarily not attempting "to communicate with anything at all." Eliot draws on Gottfried Benn's lecture "*Probleme der Lyrik*," but prefers to use the term "meditative verse" rather than "lyric" for this first voice. It (the first voice) originates from something germinating in the poet for which he must find words; it is nothing so definite as an idea, not even an emotion—it is what Eliot calls an "obscure impulse," and he says the following about the poet's relation to that impulse;

> He does not know what he has to say until he has said it, and in the effort to say it he is not concerned with making other people understand anything. He is not concerned, at this stage, with other people at all: only with finding the right words or, anyhow the least wrong words. . . . He is going to all that trouble, not in order to communicate with anyone, but to gain relief from acute discomfort.

The Waste Land, we remember, was in Eliot's term just a piece of rhythmical grumbling in which various obscure impulses causing active discomfort (a nervous collapse, say) eventually found their way into an order of right—or at least the least wrong—words.

It may be objected that Four Quartets is not The Waste Land and that its impulse is less an impulse than an idea expressed by Eliot in a number of ways over the postwasteland years: that we lived in a society worm-eaten with liberalism, that the modern world was no longer capable of entertaining the "higher dream," as Dante had, that "the world is trying the experiment of attempting to form a civilized but non-Christian mentality—an experiment which will fail but only after which failure can the world be saved from suicide." In other words, Four Quartets seems to have issued from an Eliot, or a part of him, very much concerned with making other people understand that something terribly wrong had happened to the world, and that the poet's task was to warn them of what had happened and to inspire them with the possibilities of another kind of happening.

My contention is that if *Four Quartets* were such a poem, concerned with giving poetic expression to the sentiments Eliot had been expressing—sometimes harshly, even intemperately— in his prose, it would be much less of a poem than it is. His own distinction still holds: that prose may legitimately concern itself with ideals, while poetry can only deal with actuality. Eliot's sense of "actuality" was subtler and more complex than his social polemics could suggest. What is most moving about the *Quartets* is the way they try to talk sense about ideas and ideals, addressing us in the second voice (the poet "talking to other people"), entertaining a formulation, apologizing for it ("That was a way of putting it, not very satisfactory"), faltering and losing confidence in the usefulness of what they are trying to do; then pausing perhaps and, gathering impetus, beginning again but in a different key, moving out somewhere beyond us, no longer occupied with our needs and interests since they have something more intimate and private in sight. For adequate demonstration of such movement one needs to read aloud an extended passage; here I simply draw attention to the fifth section of "East Coker," which begins, wearily, with a confession to us that twenty years have been largely wasted ("the years of *L'entre deux guerres*") and the struggle to use words brings inevitable failure, that each "raid on the inarticulate" is also a deterioration, that the burden of the past is immense and overwhelming, that "conditions" (wartime England in 1940) seem "unpropitious" for any attempt at recovery. But (grimly) "for us, there is only the trying. The rest is not our business."

Then, after a space, the voice resumes, still addressing us, evidently, but with rather more "poetic" inclinations, speaking intensely about a "lifetime burning in every moment" or "old stones that cannot be deciphered," and of the respective "times"—under starlight, under lamplight—in which we spend our evenings. After mention of the second evening comes a parenthetical phrase ("The evening with the photograph album"), signaling to my ears the moment when the second voice turns into something else (you cannot speak a parenthesis to an audience) and the lines no longer are organized by an order of punctuation:

> Old men ought to be explorers
> Here and there does not matter
> We must be still and still moving
> Into another intensity

Then a glimpsed "union" changing into "communion," as through the cry of wave and wind, through "the vast waters / Of the petrel and the porpoise," the poetry explores, in associative monologue, its subject— the subject of the four poems taken together—continuously winding and unwinding itself. F. R. Leavis once named that subject, with special reference to the beginning of "Burnt Norton," "a radical inquiry into the nature and methods of his exploration." Let us say rather, "of exploration," by way of noting the poem's reach beyond the merely personal. And what it explores is not merely the conditions of spiritual and religious possibilities but other matters of intimate and ultimate concern as well, which presented themselves to a man and poet very much in the "middle way" (Eliot was fifty-five when he published "Little Gidding"). The poem was an attempt to ascertain what things mattered and how much they mattered: questions of present, past, and future time, the writing of poetry, the love of worldly and unworldly things, stillness and speech, one's origins, one's ancestors, one's childhood, the meaning of history, of servitude, of freedom, the circumstances of a nation at war. What it has to "say" about these matters is not to be extracted from its poetry, which turns out to matter very much. When a saying is extracted and contemplated in its "translated" form the result is unmemorable, but within the poem, from time to time, memorable things happen. In the language of the "dead master" in "Little Gidding" who comes to admonish the "I" about the gifts of old age:

> So I find words I never thought to speak
> In streets I never thought I should revisit
> When I left my body on a distant shore.

In the spring of 1933, during a nine-month stay in the United States (he had determined to separate permanently from his wife), Eliot visited the University of Virginia to deliver some lectures later published as *After Strange Gods*. In their reflections on orthodoxy (the subtitle was "A Primer of Modern Heresy") the lectures figure as Eliot's most controversial prose utterances. But early in the first lecture there is an extraordinary passage in which he describes his impressions of the New World on arriving from England the previous fall:

My local feelings were stirred very sadly by my first view of New England, on arriving from Montreal, and journeying all one day through the beautiful desolate country of Vermont. Those hills had once, I suppose, been covered with primaeval forest; the forest was razed to make sheep pastures for the English settlers; now the sheep are gone, and most of the descendants of the settlers; and a new forest appeared blazing with the melancholy glory of October maple and beech and birch scattered among the evergreens; and after the processions of scarlet and gold and purple wilderness you descend to the sordor of the half-dead mill towns of southern New Hampshire and Massachusetts.

He goes on to say that the "happiest" lands are those in which the long struggle between man and the environment had brought about a successful accommodation between landscape and "numerous generations of one race," and he concluded that "those New England mountains seemed to me to give evidence of a human success so meagre and transitory as to be more desperate than the desert." He would go on to speak to his Virginia audience about the importance of tradition, and in the preface to the published volume would characterize their university as "one of the older, smaller and most gracious of American educational institutions, one of those in which some vestiges of a traditional education seem to survive."

I need not dwell upon what certainly appears to be a bit of wishful thinking, if not just outright flattery, on Eliot's part, nor will I further consider the context of the previously referred to remark about how free-thinking Jews are undesirable in a traditional society. When called to the bar of judgment Eliot will probably be willing to negotiate with and revise his terms; at any rate he never reprinted the lectures. But non-negotiable, as I hear it, is the description of his stirred local feelings as he ventured through New England, observing and being saddened by the transitoriness of human success. It is the most authentic of Eliotic notes, and—for all the differences between early and late work—is there in the poems from the beginning of "Preludes," with its withered leaves and lonely cab horses, right down to the end of "Little Gidding," with its children in the apple-tree, "Quick, now, here, now, always—." Three decades ago, in "Fifty Years of American Poetry," Randall Jarrell surveyed our poets from the first half of this century. When he came to Eliot, Jarrell decided it was appropriate to speak, not from his own voice in the present, but from the point of view he imagined the future would take about this writer:

Won't the future say to us in helpless astonishment: "But did you actually believe that all these things about objective correlatives, classicism, the tradition, applied to *his* poetry? Surely you must have seen that he was one of the most subjective and daemonic poets who ever lived, the victim and helpless beneficiary of his own inexorable compulsions, obsessions? . . . But for you, of course, after the first few years, his poetry existed undersea, thousands of feet below that deluge of exegesis, explication, source listing, scholarship, and criticism that overwhelmed it. And yet how bravely and personally it survived, its eyes neither coral nor mother-of-pearl but plainly human, full of human anguish!

The voice of that future has not yet been heard; we should keep listening for it.

William H. Pritchard

Further Reading

Ackroyd, Peter. *T. S. Eliot: A Life*. New York: Simon and Schuster, 1984

Eliot, T. S. *Collected Poems: 1909–1962*. New York: Harcourt-Brace, 1963.

———— *Selected Essays: 1917–1932*. New York: Harcourt-Brace, 1932.

Kenner, Hugh. *T. S. Eliot: The Invisible Poet*. New York: McDowell-Obolensky, 1959.

Kermode, Frank, ed. *Selected Prose of T. S. Eliot*. Harcourt-Brace, 1975.

Ricks, Christopher. *T. S. Eliot and Prejudice*. Berkeley: University of California Press, 1988.

Gardner, Helen. *The Composition of Four Quartets*. London: Faber, 1978.

Marianne Moore and Elizabeth Bishop

"A S FAR AS I know," Elizabeth Bishop wrote in "As We Like It," her 1948 essay on the older American poet who was by then her close friend and correspondent, "Miss Moore is The World's Greatest Living Observer." Much literary criticism and classroom instruction since has linked these two women poets as great observers and describers of nature and natural creatures. This chapter, which might better bear the paradoxical title, "Decoupling Marianne Moore and Elizabeth Bishop," will chafe against the task of treating them together once again. It will resist easy linkage and will attempt to bring into relief some of the sharp distinctions between Moore's and Bishop's separate poetic accomplishments.

There are, of course, useful comparisons to be made as well as anecdotes about the two friends to tell, but to consider Moore and Bishop always together as some special subspecies of female American poet is, after all, to persist in a kind of marginalization. It is to overlook their individual poetic personalities and their other important literary affiliations (or what Moore called "consanguinities") as well as their respective influences on younger American poets. Moore's and Bishop's differences—in such crucial matters as descriptive or nature writing, literary influence, religious or meditative sensibility, relation to the visual arts, and attitude toward sexuality as poetic subject and poetic strategy—hinge upon the question that Marianne Moore's 1924 landmark book, *Observations*, poses: the question of what and how to observe.

Before the twenty-three-year-old Elizabeth Bishop met the then forty-seven-year-old Marianne Moore outside the reading room of the New York Public Library on a Saturday afternoon in the spring of 1934, she had poured over many of Moore's magazine publications and had gone to some trouble to locate and read *Observations*. It was Moore's most important single volume to date (her *Selected Poems* would appear just a year later in 1935). The selection and arrangement of that remarkable, out-of-print book are not preserved in the misleadingly entitled *Complete Poems of Marianne Moore* (1981). Here is part of the first poem in the edition that the young Bishop opened, entitled "To an Intra-Mural Rat," about one man who reminded her of those

> Once met, to be forgot again
>   Or merely resurrected
> In a parenthesis of wit
> That found them hastening through it
>   Too brisk to be inspected.

This rhymed and syllabically arranged epigram, one of Moore's slighter works, still arrests attention with its syntactical high gloss. Its tartness still surprises. Although the archly elegant grammar is somewhat difficult to follow—and it is part of Moore's satiric strategy here to create a realm of supraconversational refinement that establishes the regal speaker's superiority over her subject—the tone is plain enough. We are overhearing the poet clearly, if politely, in a voice that may remind us of Moore's Bryn Mawr (biology major's) education, calling some man a rat.

As he is an "intra-mural rat," he must take part in some competitive activity within the bounds of a school or institution. Since the author (who had enthusiastically climbed a lamppost at a suffragette demonstration) is an ambitious writer near the beginning of her career, we may imagine that the offending rat-man belongs to some literary equivalent of an "old-boy's club." Ironically, the self-important male lacks individuality; he is like "many men" and confined within the woman writer's mere "parenthesis of wit." The words "hastening" and "brisk" evoke the rapid movement of similar vermin as well as self-reflexively pointing up the swiftness of the single sentence that records the poet's peremptory response. "To An Intra-Mural Rat" implies, then, that the subject scrambles about with a mindless ambition, not taking the time to look into his own soul, to inspect himself. It suggests also that the speaker *could* inspect her subject *if* she so wished—if she found him worth prolonged attention.

It is impossible for us to open *Observations*—or for the youthful Elizabeth Bishop to have done so—without confronting a highly individual writer whose barbed wit and capacity for cool, laboratory-like appraisal command respect, and who is intent upon inserting herself into an early Modernist male-dominated dialogue. This initial impression is reinforced by subsequent poems in the book, which address themselves to explicitly or implicitly male personages, to some praised or satirized "you" (e.g., "To a Prize Bird," "To a Strategist," "To Military Progress," "To a Steam Roller"). To Elizabeth Bishop, an aspiring writer about to graduate from Vassar, the boldness of this older woman writer's dialogic self-assertion as well as her descriptive virtuosity and undeniable formal accomplishment must have been exhilarating. In her memoir of Marianne Moore, "Efforts of Affection" (composed in the early 1970s and first published posthumously in *Vanity Fair* in 1983), Bishop remembers Moore's book as an "eye-opener."

We can in retrospect see Marianne Moore's *Observations* as of comparable moment in the history of Modernist publication as T. S. Eliot's 1917 *Prufrock and Other Observations*, Wallace Stevens's 1923 *Harmonium*, or William Carlos Williams's 1923 *Spring and All*. It marked the then thirty-seven-year-old Moore's real American literary debut—the earlier 1921 *Poems*, a mere twenty-four pages, having been arranged and published in England at the Egoist Press by her friends H.D. and Bryher. In the nearly one hundred pages of her 1924 collection Moore implicitly asks and answers the question, What physical and moral subjects shall I inspect? What, precisely, is worth my prolonged and painstaking scrutiny?

The book that begins, as we have seen, with the brisk dismissal of one subject—a smug, conformist male—gradually reveals the answer to the question of preferred subject matter in poems that Elizabeth Bishop singled out for mention in her memoir.

Poems like "An Octopus," about a glacier, or "Peter," about a cat, or "Marriage," about marriage, struck me, as they still do, as miracles of language and construction. Why had no one ever written about things in this clear and dazzling way before?

All three works noted by Bishop are from the second half of *Observations*, and far from the miniature of "To An Intra-Mural Rat," "An Octopus," and "Marriage" are Moore's most extended and ambitious poems. Although two of the three works cited describe in loving detail natural phenomena (a glacier, a cat), they are also, as Bishop certainly recognized, about much more. What else are Moore's fastidious "nature" poems concerned with, and why do they appear in a book that also anatomizes the social institution of marriage? To answer these questions is to close in on the striking differences between Marianne Moore's and Elizabeth Bishop's approaches to descriptive or nature writing.

The Norton-anthologized "Peter," briefest and most accessible of the three poems mentioned, is about the cat "Peter" himself, the fiercely individualistic poet herself (the cat, then, who caught the "intra-mural rat"), and about the undeniable appeal of all forms—however discommoding their outcome, let the chips fall where they may—of honest and exuberant self-expression,

> It is clear that he can see the virtue of naturalness,
> that he does not regard the published fact as a surrender.
> . . . .
> an animal with claws should have an opportunity to use them.
> The eel-like extension of trunk into tail is not an accident.
> To leap, to lengthen out, divide the air, to purloin, to pursue.
> To tell the hen: fly over the fence, go in the wrong way
> in your perturbation—this is life;
> to do less would be nothing but dishonesty.

A key, and very unBishop-like, term in this buoyant defense of uninhibited individualism is "virtue." Whatever her ostensible subject, Marianne Moore is always delineating virtues and vices. Her poems— or "imaginary gardens with real toads in them" (see Moore's "Poetry")—resemble the productions of eighteenth-century satirists as well as Robert Herrick's seventeenth-century poetic garden *Hesperides* in that they are loci for both praise and blame. As the word "surrender" in the passage above alerts us, Marianne Moore's stance is combative: she consistently views her life, particularly her life in literature, as a war zone. In traditional Christian terms—and Marianne Moore was the sister of one Presbyterian minister and the granddaughter of another—that struggle is defined as spiritual, taking place within the individual soul. This Christian viewpoint is upheld in Moore's World War II poem "In Distrust of Merits," where she writes, "There never was a war that was / not inward"; many of Moore's descriptive poems proffer emblems of such hard-won Christian virtues as humility, hope, and fortitude. But Moore's combativeness is social as well as spiritual, outward as well as inward. She is (to call up yet another literary precursor) like Spenser's maiden-warrior Britomart in her fierce opposition to human vices in general, and to male obtuseness, vanity, and brutality in particular.

Here are some relevant, and irreverent, lines from the two additional poems that Bishop singled out in "Efforts of Affection." From "Marriage," on the figure of the husband:

> There is in him a state of mind
> by force of which,
> perceiving what it was not
> intended that he should,
> "he experiences a solemn joy
> in seeing that he has become an idol."

And from "An Octopus," describing the glacier-topped, perilous, and yet life-supporting Mount Rainier:

> Inimical to "bristling, puny, swearing men
> equipped with saws and axes,"
> this treacherous glass mountain
> admires gentians, ladyslippers, harebells

In these isolated passages from two poems that actually began (during Moore's note-taking stage) as one poem, the writer bristles back at "bristling" prideful males. She registers her indignation by means, it is worth noting, of quotation from two male authors—Anatole France and Clifton Johnson, respectively—as Moore tells us in the footnotes she assiduously supplies. Of course, the two capacious poems are more wide-ranging in their subject matter and, on the whole, more balanced in their outlook than these excerpts make them appear. Certainly the female figure in "Marriage," who "loves herself so much, she cannot see herself enough," is not, like Caesar's wife, above suspicion. Nevertheless, Moore's satiric impulse and feminist determination permeate *Observations*, as when this part-Irish redhead replies to what she says "men say" in "Sojourn in the Whale," a poem that is on the surface about the enduring "feminine temperament" of beleaguered Ireland but is *au fond* about Marianne Moore herself:

> "Compelled by experience, she
>
> will turn back; water seeks its own level": and you
>> have smiled. "Water in motion is far
>> from level." You have seen it when obstacles happened
>>> to bar
> the path—rise automatically.

The young woman who composed these lines, who incorporated the acidic remarks cited previously in her two longest poems, and who placed "To an Intra-Mural Rat" at the beginning of her career-establishing collection did not mind if she occasionally affronted. She had, as we know, a ready answer for critics who might object to her as too caustic or even "catty": "As for the disposition invariably to affront, / an animal with claws should have an opportunity to use them."

The energy that propels Moore's poetic project is, I have been suggesting, at once ethical and retributive. We probably will never know, although it is a fascinating question, just how much this career-driving energy derived from and was sustained by Moore's religious, omnipresent, and critically voluble mother. Mary Warner Moore raised her two children alone after John Milton Moore was institutionalized following a mental breakdown before Marianne was born. Moore lived with her mother continuously until Mrs. Moore died in 1947, when Marianne was sixty. Casting about for some useful and absorbing project after her mother's death, Moore committed herself to translating—as it turned out, not very successfully—the *Fables* of La Fontaine. In her old age she became an increasingly popular public figure in her famous tricorne hat and cape, a sort of declawed and adorable poetic mascot (even appearing on Johnny Carson's *Tonight Show*). Although she went on writing until her death in 1972, practically all of Moore's best work was completed before 1947, written while she enjoyed the company, the refined and by all accounts nearly Johnsonian conversation, and the peculiarly moral brand of criticism of her devout single parent.

Of course, Moore's descriptive poems—whatever their ethical or retributive function—do demonstrate her affectionate respect for the natural world as well as her passion for accurately presenting that world's most minute details. This respect and this passion we see everywhere in lines that compare creatures or objects to other natural creatures or objects, offering up a rich and strange display of nonhuman "otherness": "his prune shaped head and alligator eyes" ("Peter"); "This elephant skin / which I inhabit, fibred over like the shell of the cocoanut" ("Black Earth"); "Of the crow-blue mussel shells, one keeps / adjusting the ash heaps; opening and shutting itself like / an / injured fan" ("The Fish").

But Marianne Moore, so much more than an entertaining and eccentric menagerist, is a weightier writer than many have acknowledged. As Bishop put it early on, in her 1948 essay on Moore's poetry, "Although the tone is frequently light or ironic the total effect is of such ritualistic solemnity that I feel in reading her one should constantly bear in mind the secondary and frequently sombre meaning of the title of her first book: *Observations.*"

Moore's title does invite association with religious rites or observances. At the same time, it cannily calls to mind laboratory dissection and inspection—thus holding out the promise of poetic contents scientific, dispassionate, and resolutely Modern. The title may also have been chosen to suggest Yankee self-reliance and a spirit of democracy: any literate American can jot down a few observations, or a few arresting quotations, Moore appears to say. In fact, this baseball-aficionado, a loyal fan of the Brooklyn Dodgers, repeatedly promoted the notion that what she did was nothing effete or so very out of reach. (About poetry Moore famously remarked in the poem of that title, "I, too, dislike it"; she referred to her longest poem, "Marriage," as just "a little anthology of statements that took my fancy"; and she expressed her preference [in "England"] for "plain American which cats and dogs can read!") Finally, the richly connotative word "observations" recalls Moore's satiric remarks and sketches—her talent, often at aristocratic odds with her democratic allegiances, for skillful *social* dissection.

"Mother; manners; morals," Elizabeth Bishop muses in her "Efforts of Affection," freely associating on Marianne Moore's double initial: "manners *as* morals? Or is it morals *as* manners?" At a time of life when she was reaping the rewards of her own creative labors, the mature Bishop fondly (and just a touch superciliously) reflects back on her relation with her poetic "mother." In specific Bishop may here be recalling instances of the older writer's prudishness—as when in October of 1940 Moore had objected to Bishop's use of the term "water-closet" in the poem "Roosters." But Bishop is also, with her Alice-in-Wonder-land-like wordplay on "manners" and "morals," pointing to a more general and important aesthetic difference.

If Marianne Moore's poetic personality may be described as ethical, combative, and retributive, then behind Elizabeth Bishop's body of work we sense a more vulnerable spirit, at once elegiac and yearning. This, I think, at least partly accounts for Moore's enduring and mutually supportive relationship with Ezra Pound (since Pound, however disastrously misguided at times, was always ethically driven), and it suggests an additional reason for Bishop's closeness to Robert Lowell, an elegiac writer if there ever was one. The same distinction in poetic voice or personality may also be why critics—particularly male critics—have tended to write about Moore with mixed awe and irritation, while Bishop seems consistently to have elicited a tone of protective affection. T. S. Eliot, for instance, praised Moore sincerely but somewhat oddly, saying that she was "too good to be appreciated anywhere," while a more recent male critic has referred to Moore's "fortresslike" nature. A popular adjective for Bishop, in contrast, has been "poignant"; the same critic (Robert Pinsky) who used the word "fortresslike" for Moore has in Bishop's case adopted more easygoing and affectionate adjectives: "amusing," "genial," and "sad." It is not that these terms, often shrewdly deployed in their critical contexts, are wrong—but that they interestingly suggest familial parallels. The two very different critical tonalities that Moore and Bishop have elicited would seem to register something like response to a formidable and judgmental mother versus response to a talented but emotionally frail sister. When, for example, Robert Lowell compared Bishop's poetry to Moore's, he found the younger woman's writing "softer, dreamier, more human, and more personal."

Of Lowell's comparative adjectives, I find "dreamier" the most telling. Elizabeth Bishop's father died when she was an infant; and her mother, having suffered a series of mental breakdowns, was permanently institutionalized by the time Elizabeth was five. Bishop's poetry, unsurprisingly, is full of longings and losses. It yearns for some (always finally unattainable) resting place, even as it aches nostalgically for the stable childhood home that in her case never really existed. Many poems take on the quality of daydreams. Some actually purport to record dreams (e.g., "The Weed," "The Unbeliever," "Crusoe in England"). And variations on the word "dream" show up no fewer than thirty-seven times in *The Complete Poems*. It is no wonder that in the 1930s the young Bishop was enamored of French surrealist writing. She seems always to have been fascinated by what occurs in the liminal state between consciousness and unconsciousness, waking and sleeping. This fascination with nonrational states and blurred boundaries turns up in "The Moose" and "Five Flights Up" from her final book, *Geography III*, as well as in much earlier poems from *North & South*, such as "Love Lies Sleeping," "Roosters," or "Sleeping Standing Up," which begins with these lines:

> As we lie down to sleep the world turns half away
> through ninety dark degrees;
> the bureau lies on the wall
> And thoughts that were recumbent in the day
> rise as the others fall,
> stand up and make a forest of thick-set trees.

This rhymed and mostly iambic stanza, which sounds almost like a lullaby, possesses a grave and childlike quality, a sort of logical illogic: dreams or late-night thoughts become trees that stand up when the daytime, conscious thoughts / trees fall down. Bishop's half-humorous, half-ominous physicalizing of the relentless—and, as the verb "stand up" suggests, almost sexually potent—unconscious is the sort of move Marianne Moore had in mind when she said that Bishop had a talent for "exteriorizing of the interior." On an imaginary chart that would line up poets from "most conscious" to "least conscious," Marianne Moore, carrying her tiny notebooks with their cross-referenced indexes, would be near the opposite end from Elizabeth Bishop, who approached the task of poetic composition far less rationally. Bishop preferred (to borrow a phrase from her 1978 elegy for Robert Lowell, "North Haven") "drifting, in a dreamy sort of way."

For Elizabeth Bishop "drifting," both mentally and physically, was a mode of being. Her descriptive writing records the observations not of a stay-at-home library researcher (like Marianne Moore) but rather of an inveterate traveler. Perhaps this difference in preferred creative environment or positioning has to do with the creatrix behind the scenes in each case. (As Bishop put it in her indirectly autobiographical poem, "Crusoe in England": "Home-made, home-made! But aren't we all?") Where the mother was, there we find the daughter. In Moore's case that would be always the same apartment, with its precisely placed clutter of interesting *objets* and its carefully lemon-oiled furniture. In Bishop's case, that location would be nowhere at all—since her institution-alized mother was never with her, never present. And so the daughter of the absent mother is always on the move, sending postcards and exotic gifts (rattlesnake fangs, a paper nautilus, a pickled coral snake, Cuban tree snails) to her mentor or poetic "mother" back in Brooklyn.

The poems themselves take place on the move. The speaker of Bish-op's most anthologized poem, "The Fish" (*North & South*), is literally drifting at sea in her "little rented boat" when she (the speaker is indis-tinguishable from the poet herself) hooks a "battered and venerable / and homely" fish:

> . . . Here and there
> his brown skin hung in strips
> like ancient wallpaper,
> and its pattern of darker brown
> was like wallpaper:
> shapes like full-blown roses
> stained and lost through age.

In "The Moose," one of the great poems from Bishop's last book, details of passing scenery are faithfully recorded by a bus passenger (again, we assume, Bishop herself) on her way to Boston from Nova Scotia as she witnesses the "shifting, salty, thin" fog that "comes closing in."

> Its cold, round crystals
> form and slide and settle
> in the white hen's feathers,
> in gray glazed cabbages,
> on the cabbage roses
> and lupins like apostles

The description in both cases shows a Moore-like respect for nonhu-man "otherness" in all of its particularity. But this poet demonstrates lit-tle interest in moral abstraction (the possibility, capitalized upon by Marianne Moore, for linking physical details to Christian virtues such as humility or fortitude). Solitary and somewhat melancholy, Bishop instead is grateful for some passing visual distraction.

Marianne Moore possesses a scientist's interest in natural phenome-na as well as a moralist's appreciation for nature as emblematic oppor-tunity. But for Elizabeth Bishop nature takes on a more dramatic and psychological character: it is for her a presence that leads not only (as it always must for the projective human mind) back to personal preoccupations but also refreshingly away from the tangle of her own too-familiar thoughts. In the above-cited passage from "The Moose" the fog may be said to evoke or "exteriorize" the bus traveler's internal, dreamlike state (and the poem moves suggestively from fog and twilight to darkness). But the fog is, as important, just an interesting phenomenon of the coastal weather outside the bus. The fog-covered "lupins like apostles" may nostalgically recall Bishop's churchgoing early childhood in Nova Scotia—yet they remain, as the modest simile reminds us, real flowers, independent of personal associations. The writing here, in other words, moves back and forth from outside to inside, in Bishop's characteristic "dreamy sort of way." The seemingly haphazard rhyming ("thin" / "in"; "crystals" / "apostles") helps to conjure up an atmosphere in which past and present, exterior and interior intermingle, unexpectedly chiming with or echoing one another. When the poem concludes, after a female moose on the highway has momentarily halted the bus, it is as if the traveler has glimpsed something inside as well as outside herself: a temporary answer to her craving for a home and mother in this female creature that is "homely as a house." The moose also comes as a reassuring reminder—arriving mysteriously, from the darkness—of a natural world outside that is free of the heavy weight of human history.

Like so many of Bishop's "questions of travel" (to borrow the evocative title of her third book of poetry), "The Moose" is a poem of questioning and quest. Here, as elsewhere, the poet-questor drifts toward some psychological as well as geographical destination—only to meet with another question, or questions: "Why, why do we feel / (we all feel) this sweet / sensation of joy?" ("The Moose"); "But how could Arthur go, / clutching his tiny lily, / with his eyes shut up so tight / and the roads deep in snow?" ("First Death in Nova Scotia"); "Should we have stayed at home, / wherever that may be?" ("Questions of Travel").

Even when the poems do not end in the interrogative they resist definitive answers or conclusions. For example, one of Bishop's most stately and ambitious productions, "At the Fishhouses," ends inconclusively with the observation that "our knowledge is historical, flowing, and flown." Hers remains a world of self-forgetful, exquisite attentiveness to natural detail in the midst of deep uncertainty and spiritual restlessness.

A fascination with dreams or dream imagery, a spiritually questing nature, and a marked preference for the interrogative mode. These general qualities I have been pointing to in Elizabeth Bishop's writing we find also in her most important literary precursor, the seventeenth-century Anglican minister and metaphysical poet, George Herbert.

Marianne Moore, too, as we will see, struck source-gold in the rich mine of the English Renaissance. This is another link between the two modern women poets—but one that calls also for decoupling. Moore and Bishop were attracted to very different literary models for reasons that may be explained partly by their own remarkably divergent family experiences. In their separate procedures of Modernist self-fashioning, Moore and Bishop put their respective Renaissance models to very different use.

When she was fourteen Bishop found a volume of Herbert (whom she had never read) in a secondhand bookshop in Provincetown. Many years later, in a talk she gave on "Influences" for the Academy of American Poets, she recounted the event: "I read some of his things there in the bookshop and liked them so much I bought the book. . . . Herbert has always been one of my favorite poets, if not my favorite."

Throughout her life, George Herbert remained for Bishop an almost palpable presence. She recorded, in her early twenties, a marvelous dream in which he appeared in "a beautiful dark red satin coat" (like a *bishop*?) and promised to be "useful" to her. Bishop habitually brought along her copy of Herbert when she traveled, and was particularly pleased and grateful when she received the gift of Robert (Cal) Lowell's family edition of Herbert. When Cal—who, like herself, had a drinking problem—was going through an especially difficult time in the late 1950s she wrote to him from Brazil, recommending George Herbert's translation of an Italian "Treatise on Temperance & Sobriety." Herbert, then, seems to have been for Bishop at once a literary and psychological resource: a wellspring, over the years, of poetic techniques and topics ("The Weed" in her first book is a self-avowed "imitation" of Herbert's almost surrealistic dream-allegory, "Love Unknown") as well as a kind of friend whom she included in other friendships and to whom she was in the habit of turning for comfort.

From earliest childhood, when she went to both Presbyterian and Baptist churches in the small Nova Scotian town of Great Village with her maternal grandparents, Bishop was a lover of Protestant hymns. In her short, often roughly three-beat lines we see the influence of hymn meter as well as of Herbert's hymnlike verses, with their mixed meters and short lines. Herbert's poems reassured, with what Bishop called "homely images and their solidity." They appealed to her combined religious and domestic yearnings and were associated in her mind with childlike wonder and innocence. Bishop said that she was particularly attracted to Herbert's simple demeanor and "naturalness of tone," and she adopted for her own purposes his childlike persona and predilection for Anglo-Saxon monosyllables. Here, for example, is George Herbert's humorous parody of himself in a melancholy mood: "I reade, and sigh, and wish I were a tree" ("Affliction I"). And here is Bishop in the persona of Robinson Crusoe, in a similarly self-pitying and self-mocking frame of mind: "The sun set in the sea; the same odd sun / rose from the sea, / and there was one of it and one of me" ("Crusoe in England").

If the tone and monosyllabic tendencies of each poet are often alike, the contexts out of which Herbert and Bishop write differ, of course, dramatically. The seventeenth-century pastor of Bemerton presents himself in his poems as the sometimes querulous "Child" of a "Lord" against whose absolute power he is wont to chafe (as in "The Collar"). But no matter how often the child in Herbert's world complains or rebels, he can never be absented from his omniscient, omnipresent, and loving lord. Herbert's troubled speaker comes to realize over and over throughout *The Temple* that he is always, already, at home. While Bishop, like Herbert, seeks a home, she never finds one. If she, too, writes a poetry of spiritual struggle, in her skeptical and secular world—unlike Herbert's orthodox Christian one—that struggle has no resolution beyond the provisional constructs of her art.

Marianne Moore, as I have said, was not like Elizabeth Bishop an "unbeliever" (see Bishop's poem "The Unbeliever")—and Moore had her own deep and religiously engaged interests in seventeenth-century literature. Born into a devout Presbyterian family, Moore attended church throughout her life and conferred about ideas for sermons with her minister brother, John Warner. Her spiritual sensibility, like Bishop's (like everyone's), was closely related to her family experience. In Moore's case, we have a close-knit, single-parent household bonded in Christian practice—while in Bishop's case we find a near-orphan's skeptical and nostalgic relation to Christianity. If Bishop's personal constellation of religious associations met an answering—and "useful"—echo in the poetry of George Herbert, Marianne Moore would be enabled by a strikingly different literary-cum-spiritual model.

While at Bryn Mawr (1905–1909) Moore took a year-long course in seventeenth-century English prose, a subject that attracted her both aesthetically and morally. (The note "relig," in tiny handwriting, appears in the margins of her class notes next to particularly stirring passages.) Of all the Renaissance prose writers she studied Sir Thomas Browne seems to have been closest to her heart. Moore repeatedly cites him as a kind of ethical and stylistic standard during her years as editor of the *Dial* in the 1920s, and features of Browne's prose show up strikingly in her poetry.

Browne drew on early Renaissance bestiaries in compiling his *Pseudodoxia Epidemica*, with its entries "Of Snayles," "Of the Elephant," "Of the Basilisk," and so forth—while Moore's literary table of contents includes "To a Snail," "Elephants," "The Plumet Basilisk," and so on. Like her literary "father," Moore engages in naturalistic investigation for its own sake as well as in the expectation that the "Book of Nature" will yield moral instruction. As Browne puts it in his *Religio Medici* (*A Doctor's Religion*):

The wisedome of God receives small honour from those vulgar heads, that rudely stare about, and with a grosse rusticity admire his works; those highly magnifie him, whose judicious enquiry into his acts, and deliberate research of his creatures, return the duty of a devout and learned admirer.

"Deliberate research": the phrase must have had enormous appeal for this biology major and nascent writer—seeking at once to hold on to the fortifying family religious tradition and to strike out in crisply objective poetic directions, to "modernize" herself. (And this, we should remember, was Moore's independent project: Pound's famous Imagist credo, "A Few Don'ts," first appeared in *Poetry* in 1913, four years after Moore's formative Bryn Mawr period.)

Sir Thomas Browne's stylistic practices as well as his subject matter lent themselves to Moore's paradoxically traditional brand of Modernism. She adopted his classical allusiveness, dense assonance and consonance, Latinity, and interesting obliquity:

Antiquity held too light thoughts from Objects of mortality, while some drew provocatives of mirth from Anatomies, and Juglers shewed tricks with Skeletons.   (Browne, *Hydriotaphia, Urn-Burial*)

> . . . Though Mars is excessive
> in being preventive,
> heroes need not write an ordinall of attributes to enumerate
> what they hate.
>
> (Moore, "Armor's Undermining Modesty")

Most telling, I think, is that something very like Browne's brief ethical crystallizations, what we might call his penchant for the trenchant, resurfaces in Moore's poetics. Compare these separate phrases of Browne's and Moore's:

> The heart of man is the place the Devils dwell in
> thus is Man that great and true Amphibium
> the way to be immortal is to die daily
> there is a general beauty in the works of God
>
> (Sir Thomas Browne)

> Love / is the only fortress / strong enough to trust to
> Contractility is a virtue / as modesty is a virtue
> The power of the visible / is the invisible
> Beauty is everlasting / and dust is for a time
>
> (Marianne Moore)

All these statements use the present tense of the stative verb "to be"; all point not to variable particulars but to permanent and ethical precepts. (And yet, as Moore said, "Too stern an intellectual emphasis upon this quality or that detracts from one's enjoyment." It is worth noting in passing that both Moore and her seventeenth-century predecessor provide genuinely *funny* moments, although these suffer from the surgery of citation. As Moore writes, almost with a sidelong smile, in "The Pangolin": "Among animals, one has a sense of humor. / Humor saves a few steps, it saves years.")

We can see, then, that Moore's and Bishop's primary models are tonally and stylistically poles apart. The great baroque prose of Sir Thomas Browne does not inventory the same range included in the great meditative poetry of George Herbert. But both are, it should be noted, English Renaissance males. This is of course not anomalous in the saga of American Modernism, which includes Ezra Pound's call for "a renaissance, or awakening" in letters, as well as T. S. Eliot's 1921 essay praising the seventeenth-century Metaphysicals. But in this historical context neither Moore nor Bishop was a slavish imitator—each having discovered her important precursor independently, at an early age. Each aligned herself with a non-Eliotic Renaissance model (not Donne, not a Jacobean playwright), each thus taking her individual place in this widespread twentieth-century revaluation and suggesting to her literary descendants alternative avenues to explore or ores to mine.

If we look for the late twentieth-century descendants of Marianne Moore we are likely to spot poets who have adopted not so much the clear-eyed satire and ethical urgency that reside at the heart of Moore's work as the surface decoration, so to speak, of her poetic "house." Lesser poets have imitated the syllabic meter and fancy stanzaic shapes that may—if divorced from their original Modernist function—come to seem like so much Victorian gingerbread. The display of quotation and vocabulary that in Moore's original managed to subvert "poetic" expectation, in feebler copies can seem fussy, like geegaws in an overfurnished library. What was Modern reverts, ironically, to quaintness. What was fresh in one context becomes fusty in another.

Moore has more importantly affected American poetry in ways that are, perhaps, more difficult to see. Rightly overlooking mediocre imitators, Harold Bloom for one claims as Moore's poetic progeny such original and nonservile students of her work as Richard Wilbur, May Swenson, and Bishop herself. Moore made respectable the allusive-descriptive poem in American letters. And she must, through the sheer exuberance of her early Modernist example, have emboldened untold other women to write. It is a pity that she is not read more, both in and out of classrooms and workshops. No one's poetry can teach a young writer more about how to take up a subject—a place, an institution, a person, animal or object—and then to consider it from a number of possible physical and moral angles. No one shows us how to ask with more intelligence and more thoroughness, "Just what is this thing that I am looking at?"

In contrast, given Elizabeth Bishop's popularity among now powerfully ensconced critics and poets as well as her recent pervasiveness as a workshop model, the self-proclaimed "heirs" of Bishop are now legion. The more gifted of her poetic children—and, by this time, grandchildren—have found ways to adopt for their individual purposes her proclivity for "exteriorizing of the interior." I am thinking of such divergent writers as Frank Bidart and Elizabeth Spires. Some of her weaker imitators seem to have decided that a general ambiance of urbane melancholy, a handful of travel journal exoticisms, and a sort of fey, interrogative tic will suffice. Writerly responses to Bishop, as to Marianne Moore, range from surface to depth—from an aesthetic version of yuppie acquisitiveness to genuine understanding and affection.

In crucial matters, including descriptive or nature writing, literary influences, and religious or meditative sensibility, Moore's and Bishop's differences, as I have argued, are pronounced—their distinctions hinging upon the two poets' individual responses to the question of what, and how, to observe. Continuing absorption with this issue of observation led each of them to take more than a passing or dilettante's interest in the visual arts. Each, in fact, repeatedly said she'd like to have been a painter—unsurprising, perhaps, given the richly descriptive nature of their writings. That Moore and Bishop were drawn to very different visual artists, and that their respective writings resemble different kinds of art works, should also arrive as no surprise.

In 1916 Marianne Moore and her mother moved from Carlisle, Pennsylvania, to Chatham, New Jersey, where Marianne's older brother had accepted a post as minister of the Ogden Memorial Presbyterian Church. This meant that the twenty-nine-year-old poet could regularly take train trips into Greenwich Village to meet other writers and visit galleries, including the famous Stieglitz ("291") gallery at 291 Fifth Avenue. Then, in 1918, with John Warner abroad as a navy chaplain, Mrs. Moore and Marianne moved to an apartment at St. Luke's Place in the Village. Here they remained until 1929, when they made their final move, to Brooklyn.

This must have been an extremely exciting time for the young poet, who met such artists as Charles Demuth and Georgia O'Keeffe, and, among influential art critics, Paul Rosenfeld and Henry McBride. The latter two became her colleagues at the *Dial*, a magazine of the arts that reviewed important exhibitions and printed photographs of works by (among others) Rousseau, Marin, O'Keeffe, Brancusi, Picasso, de Chirico, Cocteau, and Seurat. We have at the end of this century nothing like the New York City of the teens and twenties, when the arts were "making it new" in a welter of creative verve and reciprocity. "Over here," Moore wrote to Ezra Pound in 1919, "it strikes me that there is more evidence of power among painters and sculptors than among writers." In those contemporary fine arts Moore, who had independently "modernized" herself, found a powerful source of aesthetic invigoration and affirmation.

Sometimes Moore's literary practices even resemble well-known strategies of Cubist painters. (She carefully saved, it is worth noting, several early reviews of Cubist art.) Like Braque or Picasso or Gris, Moore wishes to present her subjects from many juxtaposed angles. First fragmenting a given subject (a cat called "Peter," for example) into its component parts, she then rearranges those parts into a new, multi-perspectival and more abstract whole. Her found quotations, too: like elements of collage—like Cubist bits of actual newsprint from *Le Jour*—their reassembly on the page calls into question the facile distinction between museum artifacts and the disposable products of every day. Even Moore's practice of syllabic composition makes for deliberately disorienting effects, similar to those of Cubist art. It is the verbal rather than the visual line, though, that is broken unexpectedly. Through dissections of syntax and odd positionings we are forced to think and see freshly—as here, in a passage describing a scarred cliff, from "The Fish":

> All
> external
>   marks of abuse are present on this
>   defiant edifice—
>   all the physical features of
>
> ac-
> cident . . .

But Moore's engagement with the visual arts exceeds the limits of the Modern. In her poetic gallery we find Egyptian, Roman and Chinese art, as well as Giotto, da Vinci, and El Greco. Perhaps the most important pre-Modern artist for her was the German engraver and painter Albrecht Dürer (1471–1528), whose work she mentions in several poems and in praise of whom she composed a 1928 "Comment" for the *Dial*. Evidently, Moore, who herself sketched numerous creatures, some charmingly, often from museum models or book illustrations (e.g., jerboas, a pterodactyl, a tiger salamander, a baby opossum, a giant anteater), was taken with the linear exactitudes of Dürer, who also often came by his knowledge of exotic landscapes or creatures second hand (e.g., lions or his famous rhinoceros).

Moore was drawn as well to the quiet religious qualities of Dürer's graphics, as she tells us in the *Dial* in her inimitable fashion: "There is danger of extravagance in denoting as sacrosanct or devout, an art so robust as to include in it that which is neither, but Dürer's separately perfect media do somehow suggest the virtues which St. Jerome enumerates as constituting the 'hous of cryst.'" Like the German artist, Moore sought, in contemplation of concrete particulars, general truths; for her, "the power of the visible / is the invisible." What Moore celebrates in Dürer is his "capacity for newness inclusive of oldness," a bricolage typical of her brand of Modernism, so paradoxically traditional and radical.

Elizabeth Bishop, who drew sketches and watercolors of places where she'd lived or visited, valued the arts, not Moore's way, for their capacity to communicate general and spiritual truths, but rather for their evocation of specific human experiences in individual locales. Her own art urgently wishes to remember, to collect, to *keep*: a treasured house, a childhood event, a romantic love, a natural object or creature, a scenic view. This obsession with keeping may be compared to Wordsworth's poetry of recollection (especially since Bishop once called herself "a minor female Wordsworth"), but it parallels, too, the visual obsession of painters, particularly realist artists.

Although Bishop hung abstract paintings as well as photographs and travel mementos on the walls of her various houses and apartments, what she especially relished was naive realism. During her years in the late 1930s in Florida, for example, she was drawn to the work of the Cuban folk artist, Gregorio Valdes, whom she commissioned to paint a large picture of the house in which she was living. Later, when the frail old painter died, she wrote a combined memoir and tribute:

The first painting I saw by Gregorio Valdes was in the window of a barbershop on Duval Street, the main street of Key West. The shop is in a block of cheap liquor stores, shoeshine parlors and poolrooms, all under a long wooden awning shading the sidewalk. The picture leaned against a cardboard advertisement for Eagle Whiskey, among other window decorations of red-and-green crepe-paper rosettes and streamers left over from Christmas and the announcement of an operetta at the Cuban school—all covered with dust and fly spots and littered with termites' wings.

Bishop here honors the painstaking efforts of this folk artist by meticulously "painting" the scene of her first encounter with a Valdes painting. Valdes's naive presentation in the barbershop was, as Bishop recounts with almost childlike wonder, "a view, a real View," of a road lined on either side by seven palm trees, with a tiny man on a donkey in the middle of the road, "and far away on the right the white speck of a thatched Cuban cabin."

This incident in Key West may remind us of Bishop's much earlier discovery of George Herbert in the Provincetown bookshop. To be sure, Herbert and Valdes practiced different arts in different eras, with dissimilar sophistication, but in Bishop they struck a common chord. In both cases some deep need associated with childhood and domesticity has been answered.

By asking Valdes to paint a large picture of her house, Bishop in a way is asking him to perform an act of magic. Once commemorated in paint, perhaps her house will become more than just another temporary, if charming, abode. Perhaps the picture, being large, will sympathetically make the dream of "home" seem immediate and attainable (unlike, then, the distant "white speck," or phantom, of the Cuban cabin in that first-seen Valdes painting). It is as though Bishop were asking a fellow recorder of life's passing surfaces to create for her not just a painting but a Platonic Idea: "A house, a real House" (something not unlike the "proto-dream-house" in one of her best poems, "The End of March").

Of course, Bishop knows that the painted replica, like her actual Key West abode, can never be more than an unsatisfactory mock-up of her dream (just as she realizes, poignantly, that the house in "The End of March" is "perfect! But—impossible"). And, to end this little story, here is Bishop's account—rueful, oneiromantic, and playful—of finding Valdes's delivered painting, propped against a wall on her veranda:

As I came home that evening I saw it there from a long way off down the street—a fair-sized copy of the house, in green and white, leaning against its green-and-white prototype. In the gray twilight they seemed to blur together and I had the feeling that if I came closer I would be able to see another miniature copy of the house leaning on the porch of the painted house, and so on—like the Old Dutch Cleanser advertisements.

In another of her prose pieces, a funny and delightful account of the time she spent working in 1934 as a correspondence-course instructor for the "U.S.A. School of Writing," Bishop contrasts what she calls " 'primitive' writing" with primitive painting. She cannot abide the "slipshodiness and haste" of the former, with its "lack of detail." But Bishop clearly cherishes the primitive painter who "loves detail and lingers over it and emphasizes it at the expense of the picture as a whole." Primitive painting retains—in its naive way, highlights—what Bishop sees as the essential element of verbal as well as visual art: patient and faithful rendering of the bright bits and pieces of life.

It is her valuing of assiduous mimesis that leads Bishop to celebrate even her great-uncle's earnest but undistinguished oil paintings, in two poems that are self-mockingly but unreformedly obsessed with memory. "Large Bad Picture" (from *North & South*) begins with the rather Wordsworthian enjambed pentameter line, "Remembering the Strait of Belle Isle or." (Here, I am recalling Wordsworth's famous opening: "Five years have passed, five summers, with the length.") And "Poem" (from *Geography III*) seems to recollect that recollector of emotions in tranquillity with yet another pentameter: "life and the memory of it so compressed." These two poems we find positioned in Bishop's first and last books, respectively, as if to underscore the twofold analogy. Her poetry is like primitive painting (if more sophisticated and self-conscious); it is like Wordsworth's poetry (if less consoling and grandiloquent). For Bishop, there is "One Art," and its muse, or mother, is *Memoria*.

Mothers *as* muses? Or is it muses *as* mothers? The issue of the creatrix behind each poet, a topic that surfaced briefly elsewhere, will occupy this chapter's final paragraphs. But first I want to make a few summary remarks— also under the rubric of gender and engendering—about Moore's and Bishop's strikingly different relations to sexuality as poetic subject and poetic strategy.

Marianne Moore remained unmarried and, evidently, sexually chaste. Elizabeth Bishop's most long-lasting relationship was with her Brazilian companion, Lota de Macedo Soares. Since both poets eschewed or eluded traditional heterosexual relationships, it has been easy for readers to link them together as impersonal, and generally asexual, descriptive writers. But sex is energy, and easy conflation of the two poets obscures the peculiarly intense and differently sublimated energy of each.

Although Moore's satiric jibes in *Observations* can be seen as obsessed with sexual difference and discordance, her subject matter is not what most people would call "sexual"—which is to say that she does not write romantic-erotic poetry. "Some," said Marianne Moore, "are not interested in sex pathology." Wisely, she does not write about what she has not experienced. The closest she gets to sexual celebration is in this somewhat precious and uncharacteristically fin-de-siècle passage from "Marriage":

> Below the incandescent stars
> below the incandescent fruit,
> the strange experience of beauty;
> its existence is too much;
> it tears one to pieces

Moore's attempted acknowledgment here of the power of sexuality—requisite, after all, in a poem that purports to inventory the institution of "Marriage"—betrays her discomfort. The lines shy away from actual human bodies, referring instead to "stars" and "fruit." One senses Moore's anxiety and embarrassment as she tries on for this occasion the ill-fitting hand-me-down of the Romantic poet's "pleasurable pain."

Moore—like many poets, perhaps even most—writes sexier lines when she is not writing about sex. In her work we find this essential commodity, paradoxically, in its absence—in the tense, erotic charge of the language itself rather than in any steamy scene the language portrays:

> . . . with the sweet sea air coming into your house
> on a fine day, from water etched
>   with waves as formal as the scales
> on a fish.

Saying these lines aloud—pronouncing the almost too-pretty long *e*'s and feeling the way "etched" comes between two *f*s and adds up, in some satisfying way, to "fresh," a near homonym for "fish"—you don't have to be told that Moore is a sensual writer. And yet this is hardly heavy sensuality: a chenin blanc rather than a late harvest riesling. Neither is this a poetry of interpersonal intimacy, the only intimacy here being that of the poet with her own five unjaded senses and her typewriter. If we want to read poetry of intersubjective rather than intrasubjective passion, we had better look elsewhere—not to this astonishing American original who averred that "innate sensuality is a mildew."

Elizabeth Bishop's great subject, in contradistinction, is intersubjectivity. What engages her is relationship, whether with another natural creature (e.g., a fish or a moose), a friend, a family member, or a lover. Often these entities are paradoxically absent presences, but absence or distance in Bishop's poetry only sharpens the yearning for relationship.

And Bishop is undeniably a love poet. That she has not generally been regarded as such is the result of two related facts: her lesbianism and her practice—so consistent that one might almost call it a policy— of poetic indirection. The one must be understood, at least partly, as defensive response to the other, since Bishop evidently felt, or could at times feel, her sexual dispensation as the "difference that kills, / or intimidates, much / of all our small shadowy / life" ("Song for the Rainy Season"). There are specific tropes, in fact—*inversion*, and what I have called *thirdness* (the trope of the third thing, or *tertium quid*, outside the categories of two)—that recur obsessively throughout Bishop's oeuvre. These recurrent tropes evoke—indirectly, as was her policy—the transformative power along with the pleasure and anxiety she associated with her sexual state.

Marianne Moore understood, if she did not approve, the romantic impulse in Bishop's work. After all, she had sponsored and agreed to "introduce" two of Bishop's early poems in a 1935 anthology called *Trial Balances*—one of those two being (in Bishop's words) a group of "two or three feeble pastiches of late seventeenth-century poetry called "Valentines":

> Love with his gilded bow and crystal arrows
>   Has slain us all,
> Has pierced the English sparrows
> Who languish for each other in the dust,
> While from their bosoms, puffed with hopeless lust,
>   The red drops fall.

Moore's accompanying remarks in *Trial Balances* proffer a withering kindness: "Miss Bishop's sparrows are not revolting, merely disaffecting." Much later, when Bishop showed Moore her elegant and haunting lyric of unfulfilled desire, "Insomnia," Moore (who was a warmhearted supporter of Bishop all her life) called it "a cheap love poem."

Moore and Bishop, then, are clearly divided over the use of sexual or romantic subject matter. Both poets, though, do use in their work (even as they sometimes call into question) strategies that have been seen as typically "feminine." A list of these would include reticence or modesty, a tendency to digression or apparent meandering, and self-forgetful attentiveness to others. But in each writer's work these general strategies appear for different reasons and to different effect.

Marianne Moore, like all Modernists, was reacting against what Ezra Pound called the "sentimentalistic, mannerish" nineteenth century. As a woman writer she was also particularly anxious to distinguish herself from nineteenth-century "poetesses," within whose works (according to all major male Modernists) that century's smarmy sins were writ most large. That Moore could distance herself from the disreputable emotionality of her immediate female predecessors through the adoption of "feminine" reticence is, of course, ironic. Ironic, too, is Moore's deployment of the supposedly feminine predisposition for digression. By making room for multifarious and obliquely related quotations and allusions, she still "masculinizes" and modernizes her poetry—rendering it impersonal, learned, and interestingly "experimental." As a final twist, by attending in an unegoistic way to small creatures and objects, Moore revises a typically female role: through self-forgetful attentiveness she arrives at descriptions every whit as scientific and un-"sentimentalistic" as Pound himself could wish.

Bishop's battle is not so much with the pale specters of nineteenth-century "poetesses" as it is with male Romantic poets—and with herself. She owns a different personal agenda within a different literary-historical context. She is a nature poet who nevertheless critiques the Romantic poet's appropriation of nature; a feminist who adopts in her most autobiographical poems male personae; a love poet who conceals as well as reveals her passion. Bishop's use of typically "feminine" writing strategies, unlike Moore's, would seem to stem at least in part from a divided and uneasy nature. She felt a need for sexual disguise as well as a related desire to escape at times into the salutary "otherness" of the natural world. Unsurprisingly, then, it is in a translation—a service of attention to another's work, allowing for the greatest reticence of self-expression—that Bishop perhaps most unabashedly expresses her own attitude. Here is Elizabeth as Carlos Drummond de Andrade, in the last stanza of "Don't Kill Yourself," from the Portuguese:

> In the meantime you go on your way
> vertical, melancholy.
> You're the palm tree, you're the cry
> nobody heard in the theatre
> and all the lights went out.
> Love in the dark, no, love
> in the daylight, is always sad

That "cry / nobody heard in the theatre" poignantly recalls the beginning of "In the Village," Bishop's autobiographical short story about her mother's last visit home (to Bishop's grandparents' house) before final institutionalization:

A scream, the echo of a scream, hangs over that Nova Scotian village. No one hears it; it hangs there forever, a slight stain in those pure blue skies. . . . The scream hangs like that, unheard, in memory—in the past, in the present, and those years between.

To the memory of the mother's demented scream are added other, more reassuring sounds: the bells of cows, chiming softly; the "beautiful pure" clang of a blacksmith's hammer—bright fragments from the surfaces of life. Still, Bishop's despairing repetition of one verb here, "hangs," reminds us that what she carries with her always is this inaudible screaming, this absent presence, this frightening but necessarily yearned-for mother. Bishop's inheritance, as her synaesthetic, understated phrasing suggests, has included a permanent "slight stain" to blot her happiness, an indissoluble suspicion that she herself may be stained or tainted: somehow, at base, wrong.

How different was the experience of this lonely and anxious child—whose "mother tongue" was a scream followed by silence—how different that was from the experience of the much-hovered-over child of that ex-English teacher and enthusiastic phrasemaker, Mary Warner Moore. (If there is a synonym for "mother" it can only be "language.") Language, in the often impoverished Moore household, lent gentility and special intimacy to life: words were exchanged, hoarded, treasured; spoken sentences were long and periodic.

In "Efforts of Affection," Bishop rather wistfully recounts being told by Mrs. Moore how a little cast-iron horse (then ensconced in the Moores' bathroom) had occasioned one of the toddler Marianne's charming verbal exclamations. Marianne had dressed the horse up in some lace at her Auntie Bee's house and had been scolded for it by her mother: "But the infant Marianne, the intrepid artist, replied, 'Pretty looks, Ma! Pretty looks!'" Enviable and amazing this must have seemed to Bishop: over the years this mother had kept tucked away, to be brought out on special occasions, the anecdote of her infant daughter's turn of phrase.

The close-knit family of three wrote letters when absences afforded, exchanging interesting or uplifting quotations, describing and solidifying for one another their experiences in words. They even gave pet names to one another: "Rat" for Marianne, "Badger" or "Weaz" ("Weasel") for John Warner, and "Bunny," "Mole," or "Bear" for Mrs. Moore. Of most immediate importance for Moore's poetry, Marianne kept "conversation notebooks" in which she hoarded nuggets of her mother's speech for future occasions. Lamentably, the conversation notebook of 1921–1928 has been lost, but several of Mrs. Moore's high-minded aphorisms from the 1935–1941 notebooks inform Moore's poems of the period (particularly, "In Distrust of Merits"): "The dust of the earth that walks so arrogantly"; "War—there is one answer—the warfare within"; "Faith is an affectionate thing—a patient thing."

In the terrains of language and of physical locale, then, we see Marianne Moore positioning herself in ongoing, affectionate, and erudite conversation, attempting—evidently without resentment—to please, impress, and amuse the mother always with her, observing too, over her shoulder. Elizabeth Bishop, in contrast, has to try to fill the linguistic vacuum bequeathed her by mapping her observed islands of experience—"their flora, / their fauna, their geography"—to make them somehow more substantial, more real. As Bishop reminds herself in her villanelle, "One Art": "It's evident / the art of losing's not too hard to master / though it may look like (*Write* it!) like disaster."

This is perhaps the most elemental difference between these two gifted American women. Because their distinctions are so many, it is time that each poet had a chapter of her own.

Jeredith Merrin

Further Reading

Bishop, Elizabeth. *Elizabeth Bishop: The Collected Prose*. Ed. Robert Giroux. Farrar, Straus and Giroux, 1984.

——— *Elizabeth Bishop: The Complete Poems, 1927–1979*. New York: Farrar, Straus and Giroux, 1983.

Costello, Bonnie. *Elizabeth Bishop: Questions of Mastery*. Cambridge: Harvard University Press, 1991.

——— *Marianne Moore: Imaginary Posssessions*. Cambridge: Harvard University Press, 1981.

Goldensohn, Lorrie. *Elizabeth Bishop: The Biography of a Poetry*. New York: Columbia University Press, 1992.

Kalstone, David. *Becoming a Poet: Elizabeth Bishop with Marianne Moore and Robert Lowell*. New York: Farrar, Straus and Giroux, 1989.

——— *Five Temperaments: Elizabeth Bishop, Robert Lowell, James Merrill, Adrienne Rich, John Ashbery*. New York: Oxford University Press, 1977.

May-Lombardi, Marilyn, ed. *Elizabeth Bishop: The Geography of Gender*. Charlottesville: University Press of Virginia, 1993.

Merrin, Jeredith. "Elizabeth Bishop: Gaiety, Gayness, and Change." In Marilyn May-Lombardi, ed., *Elizabeth Bishop: The Geography of Gender*. Charlottesville: University Press of Virginia, 1993.

——— *An Enabling Humility: Marianne Moore, Elizabeth Bishop, and the Uses of Tradition*. New Brunswick, N.J.: Rutgers University Press, 1990.

Millier, Brett C. *Elizabeth Bishop: Life and the Memory of It*. Berkeley: University of California Press, 1993.

Moore, Marianne. *The Complete Poems of Marianne Moore*. New York: Macmillan/Viking, 1981.

——— *The Complete Prose of Marianne Moore*. Ed. Patricia C. Willis. New York: Viking, 1986.

Stapleton, Laurence. *Marianne Moore: The Poet's Advance*. Princeton: Princeton University Press, 1978.

Wallace Stevens

WALLACE STEVENS (1879–1955) lived a life that was large-ly uneventful by ordinary standards. He was born in Reading, Pennsylvania, the second of five children, three of whom would become lawyers like their father, Garrett Barcalow Stevens (himself the son of a farmer). Not much is known of Stevens's mother, Margaretha Catharine Zeller, the daughter of a shoemaker, who became, before her marriage, a teacher in the Reading schools; Stevens recalled her reading chapters of the Bible aloud, and playing the piano and singing. He said of her "I am more like my mother than my father." Stevens's father, though at first a successful businessman, eventually saw his businesses (a bicycle factory and a steel plant) fail, and the decline in his fortunes caused a nervous breakdown in 1901 from which he emerged a depleted man. Wallace Stevens, after com-pleting the classical course at Reading Boys' High School (where he won prizes), spent three years at Harvard as a special student. There, he met the half-Spanish/half-American poet and philosopher George Santayana (then teaching philosophy at Harvard); they exchanged poems, and Santayana became a lifelong model for Stevens of the pos-sible cultural continuities between Europe and America. At Harvard Stevens studied English, German, and French literature as well as medieval and Renaissance art—all interests he was to keep up during his life. He was elected president of *The Harvard Advocate* (the under-graduate literary magazine), to which he had contributed several poems.

"I am going to New York, I think, to try my hand at journalism," he wrote in his diary just before leaving Cambridge; his father could not afford to pay for a fourth year in college, and Stevens was unwilling as yet to enter law school. But after a year of working as a reporter for the New York *Tribune*, Stevens yielded (shocked, in part, by the depressing sights he saw in his assignments), and entered New York Law School; in 1904 he was admitted to the New York State Bar. In the same year he met, and began to court, a beautiful but uneducated young woman from Reading named Elsie Moll. Stevens's father bitterly disapproved of the match, and he and his son broke off relations (the son no longer staying in his father's house on visits to Reading); neither of Stevens's parents attended his wedding to Elsie in 1909, and he and his father never spoke again, though after his father's death in 1911 Stevens visited his mother periodically till she died in 1912. In 1924 the Stevenses' one child, a daughter named Holly, was born; Holly Stevens became the eventual editor of her father's journals and letters. The Stevenses' marriage seems to have been an increasingly incompatible one; Holly Stevens believes her mother "suffered from a persecution complex." The Stevenses did not entertain, and Elsie Stevens became a virtual recluse.

From 1904 to 1916 Stevens practiced law in New York; in 1916 he moved to Connecticut and joined the young Hartford Accident and Indemnity Company, for which he worked as a surety lawyer (becoming eventually a vice president) until he died in 1955. Though he did not cease to write poetry, and think about it, his first years as a lawyer, and even his early years with the Hartford, when he was frequently on the road investigating surety claims, were ones of relatively scant output. During that period he had literary acquaintances in New York City (among them, Marianne Moore and Alfred Kreymborg) and published poems in journals, but it was not until he was almost forty-four that his first (and now famous) volume, *Harmonium*, was published by Knopf (1923). A second, expanded edition was published in 1930; there followed the successive trade volumes from Knopf, each of them marking a clear departure from what had gone before:

Ideas of Order (1935)
The Man with the Blue Guitar (1937)
Parts of a World (1942)
Transport to Summer (1947)
The Auroras of Autumn (1950)

In 1954 Knopf issued the *Collected Poems* (which included a group of poems, entitled *The Rock*, written since the publication of *The Auroras of Autumn*). The *Collected Poems* was awarded the National Book Award and the Pulitzer Prize in 1955, shortly before Stevens died of cancer. Stevens's daughter, who visited the hospital daily during his final ten-day stay, "vigorously denies" that he was converted to Roman Catholicism on his deathbed. (The Roman Catholic hospital chaplain reported in 1976—more than twenty years after Stevens's death—that he had baptized Stevens, yet he could point to no record of the baptism, nor any contemporary testimony to it, though Roman Catholic priests are required to record all baptisms.) Stevens had not been a member of any church during his adult life.

Though Stevens's lectures and essays on poetry had been collected in 1951 in *The Necessary Angel*, after his death uncollected poems and essays still remained, which were issued together, edited by Samuel French Morse, under the title *Opus Posthumous* (1957; revised, amplified, and reedited in 1989 by Milton Bates). *Letters*, selected and edited by Holly Stevens, appeared in 1966; his youthful journal, edited with a commentary by Holly Stevens, came out in 1977 as *Souvenirs and Prophecies: The Young Wallace Stevens*; and Stevens's commonplace book, *Sur Plusieurs Beaux Sujects*, edited by Milton Bates, appeared in 1989. The Huntington Library in California now owns most of the Stevens papers, including his voluminous genealogical correspondence, as he attempted in later life, with professional help, to trace his Dutch ancestry.

Stevens is, in one sense, a very European poet. His poetry is intimately in touch with Latin ancestors (especially Virgil and Lucretius), with Dante (from whom he derived his tercets), with French Modernist poets (especially Baudelaire, Valéry, and Laforgue), and with British predecessors (notably Shakespeare, Wordsworth, Keats, Browning, Tennyson, Pater, and Yeats). His connection with these writers is obvious in many of his themes but also strongly visible in his style, in, for instance, his constant recourse to Latin etymologies and to French vocabulary and syntax, his inventive recreation of the English pentameter, his rhapsodic rhetoric, and his lifelong modifications of European and English sonnet form. Stevens was bold enough to claim, in his *pensées* collected under the Erasmian title "Adagia," that "French and English constitute a single language." He subscribed to

French periodicals and bought (sight unseen, from a Parisian dealer) French paintings.

And yet Stevens is, in both theme and style, a conspicuously and even outrageously American poet. Unlike his expatriate contemporaries Eliot and Pound; unlike Williams, born of foreign parents and schooled in Switzerland; unlike even Frost, who had to go to England to find poetic company and early publication, Stevens never went to Europe at all. The necessary Americanness of American poetry was a constant preoccupation to Stevens, from the early "The Paltry Nude Starts on a Spring Voyage" (1923) to the very late "The River of Rivers in Connecticut" (1955). Stevens interrogates the adequacy of America to poetry and of poetry to America more often than any of his contemporaries except Williams, and spent more time walking the American countryside and recording it than the other Modernists. Any comprehensive account of Stevens has to represent him as a Euro-American poet interested in both the exotic and the native.

Stylistically, Stevens excels in vastly different styles, whether in short forms (the aphorism, the anecdote, the riddle, the enigma) or in very long ones (the meditation, the topographical poem, the didactic poem). In this stylistic and formal variety he resembles Wordsworth, whose lyrical ballads ("The Idiot Boy") so little resemble his *Prelude* that it is sometimes difficult to believe they are both works of the same hand. The novice reader of *Harmonium* can scarcely conceive of "Bantams in Pine Woods" and "Sunday Morning" as poems by one author; and although Stevens's style was to become more homogeneous with the years, one finds even in *The Rock* distinct stylistic moments, ranging from the rapturous ("Night and its midnight-minting fragrances") to the worldly ("St. Armorer's was once an immense success"), from the philosophical ("It is as if being was to be observed") to the realistic ("The steeple at Farmington / Stands glistening"), from the blunt ("A scrawny cry from outside / Seemed like a sound in his mind") to the naive ("Ariel was glad he had written his poems"). To read Stevens is to be trained by him to read all his styles and all his genres.

Stevens is ranked high by his readers (and by his increasingly numerous commentators) for several different reasons. Though nothing in his thought (which derives from William James, Santayana, Bergson, and

Nietzsche, among others) is philosophically original, no modern poet has been better at reproducing in verse the way a meditative mind moves—inching forward, doubling back over its tracks, qualifying its original assertions, unfolding the ambiguity and self-deception of its own phrases, querying its own results, mocking its own certainties. This seductive mimicry of the thought process gives Stevens's long poems part of their enduring appeal. Stevens's firm positing of the constructive powers of the imagination ("The only marvelous bishops of heaven have always been those that made it seem like heaven") countered by an equally corrosive skepticism ("And yet what good were yesterday's devotions?" ["Montrachet-Le-Jardin"]) make him attractive to historians of ideas in poetry, for whom he serves as an exemplar of the Modernist American questioning that destroys (or at least deconstructs) the shakily balanced articles of Whitman's and Emerson's philosophic optimism. (Stevens's own optimism is based on the renewing quality of destruction itself.)

Many readers find Stevens's (often deadpan) comedy irresistible. In life Stevens was often thought "sarcastic" by some of his colleagues, who found his tendency to instant metaphorical caricature more than they could take; a sympathetic colleague, Wilson Taylor, records Stevens's referring to a fellow lawyer as "having a smile that was like the silver plate on a coffin." Stevens's other characteristic habit, especially in correspondence, was to affirm almost at once the opposite of what he had just written; once he had made a statement or advanced a proposition its converse seemed to him equally true. To some readers this has seemed like teasing, or wanton insouciance. In poetry these same qualities—frequent and brilliant metaphor, frequent and unsettling self-contradiction—engender the comedy of his work. He is rarely without self-irony, and his self-metaphors—as the giant in "The Plot Against the Giant," as the comic pilgrim Crispin of his early poetic autobiography "The Comedian as the Letter C," as "Professor Eucalyptus" in "An Ordinary Evening in New Haven," as "Canon Aspirin" in "Notes Toward a Supreme Fiction," and so on—mock such aspects of himself as his large size (he may have suffered from acromegaly), his restlessness, his academic tendency to the didactic, and his religious yearnings. The comedy of his work resides also in its linguistic brio, its affinity for nonsense, and its gaiety ("Poetry is the gaiety (joy) of language," he says in the "Adagia").

Others read Stevens as a poet of the earth and its seasons; the seasons and the weather became for Stevens (who followed Keats in this respect) all-purpose equivalents for the transcribing of emotion. His poems on spring (such as "Not Ideas About the Thing But the Thing Itself"), on summer (especially the long poem "Credences of Summer"), on autumn ("The Auroras of Autumn" matching exactly its summer twin), and on winter (of which the most famous is "The Snow Man") are themselves a compendium of American weather; and from the beginning he is intent to revise the Keatsian agricultural pastoral of lambs and robins and wheat into an American poetry of deer, quail, and berries in the wilderness:

> Deer walk upon our mountains, and the quail
> Whistle about us their spontaneous cries;
> Sweet berries ripen in the wilderness.
> ("Sunday Morning")

Stevens's wide poetic landscape extends from the sun, the morning star, and the moon through the aurora borealis to Mount Chocorua; from the harvest fields in Pennsylvania to the Swatara river there; from "Hartford in a Purple Light" to "The River of Rivers in Connecticut." As he said, he was a poet of "Local Objects"—"those few things / For which a fresh name always occurred, as if / He wanted to make them, keep them from perishing." (As the last quotation shows, he preferred to write about himself in the reticence of the third person.)

Still others read Stevens as a religious poet in search of a "supreme fiction" to replace the idea of God present in his Presbyterian upbringing. "The death of one god is the death of all," he says in his "Adagia," and after abandoning his original Christian faith Stevens came to see that, like all myths, it had been invented by the human imagination through poesis (which for Stevens meant all our creative and constituting fictions and systems, whether of religion, law, social order, or domestic arrangements). "This happy creature," Stevens says of the poet, "—It is he that invented the Gods. It is he that put into their mouths the only words they have ever spoken." Since "Christianity is an exhausted culture," it follows that "it is the belief and not the god that counts," and that "the final belief is to believe in a fiction, which you know to be a fiction, there being nothing else. The exquisite truth is to know that it is a fiction and that you believe in it willingly." These axioms, and others like them, are rephrased in the poems: "Poetry / / Exceeding music must take the place / Of empty heaven and its hymns," he wrote in "The Man with the Blue Guitar"; and he was to pursue this Arnoldian and Paterian project down through the late essay "Two or Three Ideas":

To see the gods dispelled in mid-air and dissolve like clouds is one of the great human experiences. . . . It was their annihilation, not ours, and yet it left us feeling that in a measure we, too, had been annihilated. . . . At the same time, no man ever muttered a petition in his heart for the restoration of those unreal shapes. There was always in every man the increasingly human self, . . . all there was or so it seemed; and whether it was so or merely seemed so still left it for him to resolve life and the world in his own terms.

Until recently Stevens was usually described as an apolitical poet, remote from the social realities of his era. In part this opinion arose because Stevens himself omitted from his *Collected Poems* his single most socially oriented poem, a long sequence called "Owl's Clover" (representing history, the owl of Minerva, flying among its "posies," the clover). This poem, composed during the Depression, meditates on the value of art in a time of destitution, and the inevitable extinction of all cultures over time. The notion of Stevens as a poet unconcerned with social reality also gained currency because Stevens was rarely a journalistically topical poet; he seldom wrote directly about first-order events. Lately critics have been uncovering Stevens the poet of society, who wrote not only about World War I ("Lettres d'un Soldat") and the Depression ("Mozart, 1935"), about the Italian invasion of Ethiopia ("Owl's Clover") and World War II ("Examination of the Hero in Time of War"), about racial division in America ("The Sick Man") and American religious inheritance ("The Old Lutheran Bells at Home"), but who also wrote of gender difference (Canon Aspirin and his sister), of troubled relations between the sexes (in a good deal of the earlier poetry), of cultural desuetude ("Notes Toward a Supreme Fiction," "Description Without Place"), of totalitarian aesthetics ("Owl's Clover"), of relativism of cultural value ("The Man on the Dump"), and so on. Stevens wrestled directly and continually in the twenties and thirties with the journalistic and academic pressure on poets to write poems commenting openly on social and political issues. In this respect Stevens's position places him between Eliot (who turned away from the role of engaged poet toward the role of the Christian observer allying himself with monarchy and classicism) and overtly political poets like Pound and Auden, writing directly on political themes. Though Stevens's poetry became less topical, understandably, as he aged, he never abandoned his interest in the pressure exerted by fact—current reality—on the poetic imagination, and the counterpressure of the imagination pressing back:

The poetry of a work of the imagination constantly illustrates the fundamental and endless struggle with fact. It goes on everywhere, even in the periods that we call peace. But in war, the desire to move in the direction of fact as we want it to be and to move quickly is overwhelming. Nothing will ever appease this desire except a consciousness of fact as everyone is at least satisfied to have it be. (*Opus Posthumous*, p. 242)

Since this latter happy condition is never likely to occur, the imagination, against the unhappiness and dissatisfaction of every day, continues to counter with its representations of a possible perfection:

> There is still
> The impossible possible philosophers' man,
> The man who has had the time to think enough,
> The central man, the human globe, responsive
> As a mirror with a voice, the man of glass,
> Who in a million diamonds sums us up.
>   ("Asides on the Oboe")

Of course one can understand representations of perfection only if one understands the negative of which they are the positive. In that sense even Stevens's most idealistic moments can be read as a critique of his culture.

Stevens's idealism received its most acute wound neither from political chagrin, nor from religious disbelief, nor from cultural relativism, but from erotic disappointment. The most powerful confirmation of his youthful tendency to idealize was his falling in love with Elsie Moll, to whom, during the five years of their engagement, he wrote copious letters of devotion and infatuation, and for whose sake he broke off relations with his father. A good part of his poetry treats the disillusion that followed his marriage, first in such explicit poems as "Le Monocle de Mon Oncle," "Red Loves Kit," "Good Man, Bad Woman," and "The Woman Who Blamed Life on a Spaniard," and later in poems more abstracted from the immediate situation, such as "World Without

Peculiarity" and the first section of "The Rock." It was disillusion that first made Stevens see interior emotional conviction as a form of madness; the disappearance of what one was sure was real (and had publicly confirmed by the act of marriage) made all mental reality suspect. Stevens did not reattempt romantic love. Instead he scrutinized, relentlessly, the reality he had once obscured by willful erotic blindness, until he could say, at seventy, in the poem "The Rock," that the biological imperative alone could account for two young people rushing from their respective childhood homes to embrace passionately at the boundary of marriage, their meeting

> An invention, an embrace between one desperate clod
> And another in a fantastic consciousness,
> In a queer assertion of humanity:
>
> A theorem proposed between the two—
> Two figures in a nature of the sun,
> In the sun's design of its own happiness.

Although the Stevensian themes that I have been sketching—intellectual, pastoral, religious, topical, nativist, erotic—have perhaps drawn most of Stevens's readers to his work, readers are equally drawn (whether they realize it or not), by his exceedingly original voice, conveyed through his many experiments in language. Some of those experiments are startling, as when the clichéd "Arab moon" becomes "An Arabian in my room, / With his damned hoobla-hoobla-hoobla-how, / Inscribes a primitive astronomy" ("Notes"). Other experiments are rhythmical, and funny, like the address to the rooster in "Bantams in Pine Woods": "Chieftain Iffucan of Azcan with caftan / Of tan with henna hackles, halt!" But Stevens has serious voices as well as comic ones, and his serious voices experiment chiefly with etymology, syntax, and registers of diction, so that Latinate and French-derived and Anglo-Saxon words cohabit self-consciously rather than at random, the rhapsodic is astringently cut with the gnomic, and the commonplace and the sublime and the banal all rub shoulders in the verse.

Because Stevens is so many-sided, and has attracted such different sorts of readers, he is variously represented by different commentators. A deconstructionist critic will be interested in Stevens's anticipation of contemporary attention to absences, negatives, gaps, contradictions, and ambiguities; a theorist may look at the tendency of Stevens's poetry to allegorize its own moves and place Stevens's essays on poetics in the line of Coleridge and Shelley; an Americanist will focus on Stevens's inheritance from Emerson, Poe, Whitman, Dickinson, William James, and Santayana; a genre critic will see Stevens as a link in the history of lyric written in English, whether in England, America, or elsewhere; a historian of Modernism will focus on Stevens as a representative of the twenties through the fifties (where Stevens is interestingly hard to place, as he is successively Imagist, nativist, neoromantic, minimalist, and so on); a contemporary critic might want to see him as the precursor of, e.g., Ashbery. In what follows I will be chiefly concerned with Stevens's lyric poetry—the work by which, after all, he is remembered—rather than with Stevens as a philosopher, historian of his society, or theorist.

The first thing to say about Stevens's poetry is that it appeared late (1923) and flowered even later (the nineteen-forties, from his sixtieth year on, was the period of his greatest productivity). Stevens had the extreme good luck to write powerfully and freshly until a few months before his death. Perhaps because the bulk of his work was written in middle and old age, the typical Stevens poem is not mimetic: that is, it does not relate a recognizable event of everyday human life. Normally, in reading lyric poetry, we look for a first-order mimetic story—"I wandered lonely as a cloud . . . / Till all at once I saw a crowd, / A host of golden daffodils." Stevens rarely adopts this mode of lyric, perhaps because it so immediately recalls all the greater Romantic poems ("My heart aches," etc.) Instead, the typical Stevens poem will pitch its beginning in what is already a symbolic or parabolic mode: a bantam rooster (an "inchling") will encounter in its path a much larger cock-rooster (a "ten-foot poet") and will confront him with the plucky but terrified rage of a minor artistic beginner coming up against a major "universal" chieftain of the tribe of poets. The bantam-sentry stands his ground on his own turf, his pine woods, and cries out to his impressive threatener,

> Chieftain Iffucan of Azcan in caftan
> Of tan with henna hackles, halt!
> Damned universal cock, as if the sun
> Was blackamoor to bear your blazing tail.
>
> Fat! Fat! Fat! Fat! I am the personal.
> Your world is you. I am my world.
> ("Bantams in Pine Woods")

This shout of confrontation pits the lyric poem (regarded in nineteenth-century America as an effeminate genre suitable rather for poetesses than for men) against the epic poem—that genre of "masculine" scope, of heroism, of characters larger than life-size. Why would Stevens choose to represent the challenge of the lyric to the epic as a quarrel between a bantam and a full-size rooster? Such a tactic can mislead even experienced readers; one academic critic has seen this poem as voiced by a bantam rooster meeting the actual man Stevens in the woods: " 'Fat! Fat!' he says to Stevens, who indeed had a bulky figure," concludes this critic. To the contrary, Stevens identifies with the bantam—one of his characteristically self-deprecating self-portraits—trying to make his masculine stand on lyric, personal, ground. Stevens found the literal banal and boring; for him a poem became a poem only by finding a symbolic figure for its predicament. "Every poem is a poem within a poem: the poem of the idea within the poem of the words" ("Adagia"). The poem of the idea is the symbol representing the idea, as the confrontation of bantam and cockrooster is here the symbol of the idea of lyric confronting epic. Having found the poem of the idea, Stevens has to find the poem of the words (here, the absurd rage-diction of the puny bantam). Every Stevens poem thus presents a double problem of decoding; since the poem-of-the-words is appropriate to the *poem* of the idea (bantam-vs.-cock), one decodes the language to find out what is going on between this bantam and this cock. Then one has to decide what is the *idea* of which bantam-vs.-cock is the poem. Since the cock is a ten-foot poet and the bantam is an inchling, we have to think about big poets and little ones, which translates reasonably enough into the conventional hierarchy of genres, in which epic traditionally dominated over lyric.

Another example. In a first-person, first-order Romantic lyric a poet might say (did say), "I die, I faint, I fail!" Such a poem would convey directly, as a personal experience, terminal exhaustion, silence, and chill, and might of course illustrate its feelings with simile or metaphor. Stevens will transfer such personal feelings onto a second-order symbolic landscape of broken vegetation, in which a metaphor acts as reality:

> In this bleak air the broken stalks
> Have arms without hands. They have trunks
>
> Without legs, or for that, without heads.

"Bad is final in this light," the poem asserts. Affixed to this second-order, symbolic narrative is a third-order title, one that symbolizes, or sums up, the already symbolic story of the vegetation. The summary-title is a quotation (probably itself a Southern dialect aphorism) from one of Stevens's friends, Judge Arthur Powell of Atlanta: "No Possum, No Sop, No Taters"—the epitome of a deprived time. The "low" diction of the third-order title is itself different from the wintry intelligence of the poem's narrative diction, and neither one gives us the putative first-order mimetic diction ("I feel broken; I feel mutilated; I feel even decapitated") that we can intuit behind the second-order vegetation-narrative.

A survey of Stevens's titles, even in his first book, reveals how many of them are of this third-order sort, serving as a summary or epitome of the concerns, literary or thematic, of the poems they head: "Earthy Anecdote," "Domination of Black," "Le Monocle de Mon Oncle," "Metaphors of a Magnifico," "Cy Est Pourtraicte, Madame Ste Ursule, et les Unze Mille Vierges," "Fabliau of Florida." *Explanation, theory, paraphrase, anatomy*—such "literary" words keep turning up in Stevens's titles. This suggests that for Stevens titles were a form of caption, seizing the whole in one glance. The titles are often genre analyses of the poem that follows them—this is an anecdote, this is a tale, this is a soliloquy. Once Stevens had translated feeling into the poem of the feeling ("the fiction that results from feeling," as he called it in "Notes"), he could invent a diction for his poem and write its actual lines. But then, when he was done, he subjected the whole to an intellectual (and often ironic) appraisal, which generated a literary evaluation of it and prompted its title.

This procedure has, understandably enough, been found off-putting by some readers. They see first the title, with its literary allusion or its obliquity of reference, and think that since the title is devoid of "human interest" (unlike "The Solitary Reaper," or "Upon Going to Bed," or even "The Nymph Complaining for the Death of Her Faun") the poem itself is likely to lack human reference as well. Next readers encounter a strange narrative about bantam roosters or the northern lights, often not even phrased in the first-person singular. Worse, they may meet, skipping the title and starting directly with the poem, a creature from some wholly unknown fable: "In Hydaspia, by Howzen, / Lived a lady, Lady Lowzen, / For whom what is was other things." And, looking back to the title for help, readers in this instance find that the title is "Oak Leaves Are Hands"—no help at all.

The reader trained on first-order mimetic lyric is at first at a loss in many of Stevens' poems. One way to become at home in Stevens's world is to read his easier discursive poems, "The Idea of Order at Key West," for instance, which sufficiently resembles its Romantic predecessors like "The Solitary Reaper," "The World Is Too Much with Us," and "Kubla Khan" to make the inexperienced reader feel at ease. Another way to become at home in Stevens's world is simply to immerse oneself within it, since, as he himself said, "Each poem proves another and the whole" ("A Primitive Like an Orb"). Stevens's rule of thumb in writing was that "the poem must resist the intelligence / Almost successfully" ("Man Carrying Thing"). In the "almost" lies his concession.

Stevens's riddles of purport press his reader to notice the language of the poem, since it seems at first an obstacle to, rather than a means of, import. The poem then becomes—as any poem not dulled by over-familiarity should—a friction of language into iridescence, redeeming communication from the bland transparency of its everyday, information-retailing behavior. The modern reader reads, in a practical sense, almost exclusively for information-retrieval; Stevens's aim is to retrain that reader into a consciousness of the surface of language, that "visible core" (as Ashbery calls it) which by its manner suggests its depths.

At the heart of many of Stevens's poems are harsh and unpalatable experiences revealed only gradually through his intense stylization. The famous poem, "The Emperor of Ice-Cream," resisted explication for some decades, perhaps because no one took the trouble to deduce its implicit narrative from its stylized plot. (The Russian formalist distinction between "story" and "plot" is often useful for this and other Stevens poems.) The basic "story" of "The Emperor" is that of a person who goes to the house of a neighbor, a poor old woman, who has died; the person is to help "lay out" (arrange for decent viewing) the corpse in the bedroom, while other neighbors are sending over home-grown flowers, and yet others are preparing food, including ice cream, for the wake.

Stevens "plots" this story into two equal stanzas: one for the kitchen where the ice cream is being made, one for the bedroom where the corpse awaits decent covering. He "plots" it further by structuring the poem as a series of commands from an unknown master of ceremonies, directing—in a diction of extreme oddness—the neighbors in their funeral duties: "Call the roller of big cigars, / The muscular one, and bid him whip / In kitchen cups concupiscent curds. / . . . / / Take from the dresser . . . / . . . that sheet / . . . / And spread it so as to cover her face." Both the symbolic kitchen stanza (life as concupiscence) and the symbolic bedroom stanza (death as final) end with the same third-order refrain echoed by the title: "The only emperor is the emperor of ice-cream." Faced with life (however slovenly and appetitive) in the kitchen and death (with its protruding horny feet) on the bed, one must, however unwillingly, acquiesce in the reign of life.

We cannot know what personal events prompted this 1922 poem, apparently set in Key West (so the poet Elizabeth Bishop conjectured, who knew Key West, where Cubans worked at the machines in cigar factories, where blacks always had ice cream at funerals), but it derives resonance from Stevens's mother's death ten years earlier. What is certain is that it represents symbolically, with the Procrustean bed of its two rooms, the bitter moment of choosing life over death, at a time when life seems particularly lonely, self-serving, lustful, and sordid. Art is exposed as too scanty in its powers to cover up death; the embroidered sheet (a figure for the embellished page), if it is pulled up to cover the dead woman's face, reveals her "horny feet," which show "how cold she is, and dumb." In choosing to "let the lamp affix its beam," as in a morgue, and in acquiescing to the command, "Let be be finale of seem," Stevens makes his momentous choice for reality over appearance.

Besides their symbolism on the level of narrative imagery—bantams, broken vegetation, ice cream—most of Stevens's poems have a symbolic structural architecture of the sort necessitating the two rooms ("stanzas") in "The Emperor of Ice-Cream." The symbolic architecture is not always constructed solely by stanzas. Often another of Stevens's structural means is a variation in the length of the sentences composing the poem. Here is one typical sentence pattern, that of the poem "Somnambulisma," an eighteen-line poem of six tercets. The poem affirms that human beings come to feel at home in the indifferent physical universe because poets (singer-scholars) acculturate them over the long periods of human history, giving them successive descriptions and systemizations of that universe. At first each poetic effort seems ineffectual, personal, doomed to incompleteness and insufficiency, but then Stevens sees that the whole of the cultural domestication of the universe is greater than the sum of its parts. In keeping with his democratic aims for art, he concludes that the poet-scholar gives to human beings, as cultural clothing, not "regalia" suitable to Europe but "personalia" suitable to America:

> On an old shore, the vulgar ocean rolls
> Noiselessly, noiselessly, resembling a thin bird,
> That thinks of settling, yet never settles, on a nest.
>
> The wings keep spreading and yet are never wings.
> The claws keep scratching on the shale, the shallow shale,
> The sounding shallow, until by water washed away.
>
> The generations of the bird are all
> By water washed away. They follow after.
> They follow, follow, follow, in water washed away.
>
> Without this bird that never settles, without
> Its generations that follow in their universe,
> The ocean, falling and falling on the hollow shore
>
> Would be a geography of the dead: not of that land
> To which they may have gone, but of the place in which
> They lived, in which they lacked a pervasive being,
>
> In which no scholar, separately dwelling,
> Poured forth the fine fins, the gawky beaks, the personalia,
> Which, as a man feeling everything, were his.

The table below shows the number of lines occupied by each of the seven sentences of the poem and represents each tercet by a roman numeral:

I. 3 lines   (the tercet = the sentence: the norm)

II. 1 line   (the two sentences make up one tercet;
    2 lines   the tercet is still intact, end-stopped)

III. 1 1/2 lines   (the three sentences make up one tercet;
     1/2 line   the middle sentence is the shortest in
     1 line   the poem; the tercet, end-stopped, is still intact)

IV–VI.   9 lines   (this sentence, the final one, occupies the whole
                           second half of the poem, spreading over three tercets,
                           which wash successively into each other)

This structure effectively divides the poem into two parts—one nine-line part of many pauses, one nine-line part of no pausing. A look at the first part shows three "feeble efforts" by the bird, which comprise a second overlaid structure on top of the structure of end-stopped versus nonend-stopped tercets. In this second structure a three-line effort subsides into one line, a two-line effort declines into a line and a half and then a half-line, and the final line in part 1 stops dead. This depressing series of feeble efforts is "corrected" by the expansive exaltations of the nine-line sentence of part 2. The whole double pattern—of end-stopped versus nonend-stopped tercets and of apparently unsuccessful attempts versus a re-reading of those attempts as cumulatively successful (however partial each one)—enacts, on the structural level, the import of the plot on the narrative level.

Stevens also "plots" his poems at the level of the syntax within each individual sentence, a syntax that is lavish in its use of dependent clauses, appositives, and changes of tense and mood—all of them means by which the narrative of the poem is incrementally advanced, bit by bit. Stevens depends as well on a reader's knowledge of etymology, since much of his wordplay depends on Latin roots (so that a root such as *quaerere*, to seek, is present for him in all his uses of its variants, including *inquire*, *quest*, *exquisite*, *perquisites*, etc.) Stevens's frequent use, in his discursive mode, of compound Latinate words (*trans-parent*, *a-spect*, *e-voke*, *re-store*, *ex-temporize*, *in-tricate*), demands that the reader give full force to both halves of the etymology, as in the case of the word *traverse*, the operative word in the close of "An Ordinary Evening in New Haven":

> It is not in the premise that reality
> Is a solid. It may be a shade that traverses
> A dust, a force that traverses a shade.

Since Stevens liked to pun on words containing the syllable *verse*, such as *universe*, he expected the reader to notice that the dynamic word here, *tra-verse*, standing for the energy we used to call that of the soul, contains the word for the poet's medium, "the world in a verse" ("Arrival at the Waldorf"). What is the shade (ghost) that traverses a dust (*pulvis es, homo*) but the soul? What is the force that traverses that shade after death but its lingering spirit? One feels Stevens's triumph in finding the word *traverse—trans-vertere,* "to turn its way across, to plough a U-turned furrow"—recalling, as it does, the Latin origin in the act of ploughing of the very word for composition in metered lines, *verse,* and recalling as well his early "blasphemous" American poem "Ploughing on Sunday":

> Remus, blow your horn!
> I'm ploughing on Sunday,
> Ploughing North America.
> Blow your horn!

In Stevens's first book, *Harmonium,* "Ploughing on Sunday," with its "primitive" language, was one of Stevens's first consciously American poems. Blasphemy of the inherited Protestant pieties was one way for poets to be American, not English. "Some keep the Sabbath going to Church—" (wrote Emily Dickinson in her own blasphemous poem on Sunday morning) "I keep it, staying at Home." Stevens's "high" *Harmonium* poem on the same subject, "Sunday Morning," adopts a female persona, who repudiates churchgoing in favor of staying home in her peignoir, having a late breakfast of "coffee and oranges" accompanied by her cockatoo. (The lady probably derives from Monet's "Woman with a Parrot" in the Metropolitan Museum—Monet's woman is wearing a peignoir, and has a parrot on a perch with orange peels at the bottom; to clinch the identification, she is wearing a monocle on a cord around her neck, linking her to "Le Monocle de Mon Oncle." Stevens was often inspired by paintings: "The Man with the Blue Guitar" was prompted by a painting by Picasso, as the poem tells us, and no doubt other poems will gradually be linked to paintings Stevens saw; in the Armory Show of 1913 there was a Hopper, now at the Carnegie Institute in Pittsburgh, that may have inspired "Sailing After Lunch.") In revising his 1915 feminine Wordsworthian and Keatsian "Sunday Morning" into his 1919 masculine and nativist "Ploughing on Sunday," Stevens acts out his own divided poetic loyalties. Much of *Harmonium* can be seen as a quarrel between English euphony and American dissonance, European *richesse* (Botticelli's *The Birth of Venus* in the Uffizi) and American insufficiency ("The Paltry Nude Starts on a Spring Voyage"). The

American "paltry nude" would like to be as splendid as the Renaissance Venus, but we have to take her as she is. She starts on a spring voyage, yes,

> But not on a shell, she starts,
> Archaic, for the sea.
> But on the first-found weed
> . . . .
>
> She too is discontent
> And would have purple stuff upon her arms

Eventually, Stevens believed, "the goldener nude of a later day" would become visible, when America would have its own Renaissance, finer than Florence's.

Stevens's Americanness is the burden of his 1922 manifesto in *Harmonium*, the comic spiritual autobiography in blank verse called "The Comedian as the Letter C." In it his French protagonist Crispin quits Bordeaux (land of the troubadours, the originators of modern lyric), tries out the Mexican tropics, but ends up in North America, believing in regional literature ("The man in Georgia waking among pines / Should be pine-spokesman"), and settling down with a wife "and daughters with curls." This satiric Browningesque narrative style (derived from "Sordello") never reappears in Stevens, but just as we can find almost all of the later Keats in *Endymion*, so we can see in "The Comedian" the seedbed for much of the later Stevens.

In the thirties, when Stevens confronted the extreme social conditions of a demoralized American capitalism, and felt the powerful pressure of socialist imperatives in literature, he published in succession *Ideas of Order* (1935, in a limited edition), *Owl's Clover* (1936, another limited edition), and *The Man with the Blue Guitar* (1937). These, and *Parts of a World* (1942, but at least a third of it composed in the thirties), are the volumes most preoccupied with the social function of poetry. He said of the first part of "Owl's Clover," "The subject I had in mind was the effect of the depression on the interest in art. . . . If I dropped into a gallery, I found that I had no interest in what I saw. The air was charged with anxieties and tensions." Setting a "noble" marble statue representing winged horses rising into the air (his symbol for Euro-American art) against a poor woman, old, dressed in black (his symbol for destitution), Stevens confronted the apparent uselessness of fine art to those suffering from the Depression. He pursues the question into the mass art of Russian Socialist Realism ("Concerto for Airplane and Pianoforte") and then into the cultural limits of Western art: "But could the statue stand in Africa?" The question is finally referred to Necessity itself, which governs aesthetic production as it governs everything else in the universe; to it, all cultural production is the same, equally favored: "The voice / In the jungle is a voice in Fontainebleau." Ananke, the Greek tragic god of Necessity, determines cultural survival: "He, only, caused the statue to be made / And he shall fix the place where it will stand."

Stevens's later long poems have neither the autobiographical (if allegorical) narrative base of "The Comedian" nor the topical base of "Owl's Clover." Instead, as their titles suggest, they are long meditations. "The Man with the Blue Guitar," because it is suggested by a Picasso painting, adopts a folk persona and a "primitive" ballad form of tetrameter couplets. In its dialogue between the guitarist and his audience it confronts the inevitable stylization of art with ordinary perceptions of reality:

> They said, "You have a blue guitar,
> You do not play things as they are."
>
> The man replied, "Things as they are
> Are changed upon the blue guitar."

As Stevens rings the changes on this theme through his thirty-three "takes" on the subject, he is continuing the aspectual method of writing he had first proposed in his famous piece of Imagist chinoiserie, "Thirteen Ways of Looking at a Blackbird." Every "way of looking" is another reality—or, as the "Adagia" have it, "Things seen are things as seen." The later long sequences of the forties—"Notes Toward a Supreme Fiction," "Esthétique du Mal," "Credences of Summer," "The Auroras of Autumn," and "An Ordinary Evening in New Haven"—ranging in length from ten to thirty-one linked cantos, are all aspectual poems, considering, respectively, belief ("Notes"); evil and pain, both physical and spiritual (the mid-war "Esthétique"); the cycles of physical fertility ("Summer"); the eventual destruction of all cultures ("Auroras"); and, finally, "not grim reality but reality grimly seen" ("An Ordinary Evening"). It should be recalled, when reading these sequences as when reading Eliot's *Four Quartets*, that they were conceived and written during the cultural obliteration and human carnage of World War II. Stevens's inveterate belief in the necessary transformation of the mimetic into the symbolic should not blind readers to the profound engagement of his poetry, especially in the long sequences, with social and cultural suffering.

Stevens once wrote (in the essay "Three Academic Pieces") that poetry works by structural analogy: "The accuracy of accurate letters is an accuracy with respect to the *structure* of reality" (italics mine)—not a transcription of the events of reality, not a journalistic fidelity to fact, but a symbolic *analogy* to the basic shapes of reality. Stevens's poetry reproduces, in *his* structures (X-rays of reality), what he perceives to be *reality*'s underlying structures—as we saw in "The Emperor of Ice-Cream," with its two symbolic rooms, or in "Somnambulisma," with its initially flagging efforts soaring into rejuvenating possibility. The long poems, too, enact through their aspectual circumnavigation of a topic those rises and falls of feeling that we know from the greater Romantic lyric. But where the Romantic lyric aims generally at some resolution of its convulsion of doubt or fear, Stevens aims at a circular open-endedness, a dynamic interplay of polar opposites. A poem moves from its "ever-early candor" to its "late plural" ("Notes") and then turns back to candor again. It needs both Alpha and Omega: "Alpha continues to begin. / Omega is refreshed at every end" ("Ordinary Evening," VI). For this reason Stevens's poems need Alpha-passages of "primitive" or "nonsensical" or "poor" vocabulary and also Omega-passages of Latinate, celebratory, highly evolved, hierophantic language. He aims "to compound the imagination's Latin with / The lingua franca et jocundissima" ("Notes"); it is of course typical of Stevens' humor that he should express the imagination's Latin in English and the common lingua franca in Latin (thereby enacting linguistically his aim to "compound"—make a composite—of them).

The long poems of the forties (with the partial exception of "Esthétique du Mal," which has some lyric sections) are all written in the blank-verse line that Stevens perfected over his career, and which the contemporary poet Donald Justice has analyzed and praised as a line genuinely responsive to American speech rhythms. Internal rhymes often connect successive lines of this blank verse, and it is densely patterned by passages of parallel syntax. Stevens's pentameter could often accurately be called a trochaic rather than an iambic pentameter, since its rhythms are so frequently falling ones:

> The last leaf that is going to fall has fallen.
> The robins are là-bas, the squirrels in tree-caves
> Huddle together in the knowledge of squirrels.

In fact, the falling rhythms are often dactylic:

> These are the edgings and inchings of final form,
> The swarming activities of the formulae
> Of statement.

This second passage suggests how Stevens's "pentameters," unlike those of his more regular predecessors in England and America, often contain tetrameter fragments, speeding up the discursiveness of the poem, giving it a spoken irregularity, while retaining a metrical rhythm. These keep the poem from the monotony he dreaded, from a one-tone-ness of mere didactic instruction.

The long sequences are also enlivened by their frequent changes of lyric subgenre. Though "The Auroras of Autumn," for example, is, taken as a whole, a lyric meditation on time's destructions, its subgenres include definition (I and VI), valediction (II–IV), narration (V, IX), metaphysical query (VII), meditation (VIII), and exhortation (X). The long poems are also vivified by a memorable series of allegorical personae—to name only some of those found in "Notes Toward a Supreme Fiction," Ozymandias and his spouse Nanzia Nunzio, Canon Aspirin, "an Arabian in my room," "the MacCullough," major man, the old seraph, the great statue of the General Du Puy, the planter who loved his island, the blue woman, a fallen head of a Central American divinity, the "great captain and the maiden Bawda," and so on.

Stevens's long apprenticeship to the weather and the turning year underlies his late paired seasonal poems "Credences of Summer" and "The Auroras of Autumn." Stevens liked the cusps of seasons, times like "the earliest ending of winter," moments when "the last leaves that are going to fall have fallen." Such asymptotic rises and declensions represented for him "the swarming activities of the formulae of statement, / Directly and indirectly getting at" reality. Since each formulation is an approximation, one can never capture reality itself in language: it remains "the vital, arrogant, fatal, dominant X," the algebraic "unknown" ("The Motive for Metaphor").

Stevens's last years, during which he wrote the poems grouped under the title *The Rock* in the *Collected Poems* (and others printed in *Opus Posthumous*) produced a sublime poetry of inception, newness, and freshness. Although there are poems about decay and death, there are, equally, poems about the astonishing yearly self-renewal of the earth, about man's eye as the "silent rhapsodist" of the planets ("The Rock"). Stevens perceives that at the very "antipodes of poetry" one becomes "a child again," and hears "the cricket of summer forming itself out of ice" ("A Discovery of Thought"). The famous final soliloquy of his muse, the "interior paramour," declares that "God and the imagination are one," but prefaces that declaration with the rhetorical phrase, "We say," rendering the assertion a human locution rather than "the" truth. Stevens had in fact long ago emancipated himself from the definite article attached to the word "truth": "It was when I said, / 'There is no such thing as the truth,' / That the grapes seemed fatter, / The fox ran out of his hole" ("On the Road Home"). Stevens's conviction that "*the* truth" did not exist as such made him discover as his ideal form a sequence of improvisations, repetitions, variations, and anecdotes, each an aspectual part of a truth. Any ideologue was, for him, like the Russian revolutionary Konstantinov—"the lunatic of one idea / In a world of ideas, who would have all the people / Live, work, suffer and die in that idea / In a world of ideas" ("Esthétique du Mal"). In resisting the pressure toward ideological verse in the twenties and thirties, he found his own aspectual genius.

Stevens's reputation has grown steadily since his death in 1955, and his influence can be seen in the work of many subsequent American poets—among them A. R. Ammons, John Ashbery, Charles Wright, Mark Strand, and Jorie Graham. What poets have learned from Stevens is the importance of the metaphysical dimension in thought, and of symbolic construction in both imagery and poetic architecture; the importance of syntax to argument; and the value of fable in lyric narrative. The narrow no-man's-land between regular and free verse has been explored more fully by Stevens than by any other Modernist poet except Eliot, and writers retaining a musical connection with British prosody, while conscious of its necessary hybridization with American idiom and intonation, find a pattern for study in Stevens.

Stevens's remarks on the theory of poetry, in such poems as "Of Modern Poetry" and "Notes Toward a Supreme Fiction" and also in his essays, have yet to be fully absorbed. Their assertion of the immense social importance of the imagination is not yet ratified in American culture. For Stevens "the imagination" is the name we give to the human capacity to create new systems—philosophical, political, aesthetic, and domestic. The expressions of these systems (in texts, law codes, art works, kinship structures, etc.) are a measure of the generative fecundity of the imagination. Stevens was acutely conscious of deficiencies in his own life (cf. "The Dwarf") and in the life of his society, of the poverty of our erotic imagination (our "paltry" Venus), of the primitive ambition of our art (a gray and bare stoneware jar in lieu of Keats's ornamented marble urn), of our economic failures ("Mozart, 1935"), and of the unbridged gap between the races, black and white. His "sick man" (in the late poem of that title in *Opus Posthumous*), hears "in the South, bands of thousands of black men, / Playing mouth organs in the night," and, equally, "Here in the North . . . voices of men, / Voices in chorus, singing without words." Both musical groups are wordless; each has its own harmony. It is up to the sick man to wait for the "unison of the music of the drifting bands / And the dissolving chorals," and in the meantime to imagine "the words of winter in which these two will come together." The sick man will die, like Moses, in the wilderness, Stevens implies by the title of this poem of his seventieth year, but he will die "choosing out of himself, out of everything within him / . . . / The peaceful, blissful words, well-tuned, well-sung, well-spoken," words of a poetry that will hail and heal. The tuning is for the black bands, the singing is for the white chorus, the speaking is for the aging poet—the words will make the three one. It is a utopian poem, written by a man who is sick with the sickness of his racially divided country.

In a response to a 1946 questionnaire sent to him by the *Yale Literary Magazine*, Stevens wrote:

If people are to become dependent on poetry for any of the fundamental satisfactions, poetry must have an increasing intellectual scope and power. This is a time for the highest poetry. We never understood the world less than we do now nor, as we understand it, liked it less. We never wanted to understand it more nor needed to like it more. These are the intense compulsions that challenge the poet as the appreciatory creator of values and beliefs.

(*Opus Posthumous*, p. 311)

Stevens's own self-elegy, tacitly expressed in his elegy for Santayana, "To an Old Philosopher in Rome," is based on Waller's great poem of old age, "Of the Last Verses in the Book," which closes with these memorable images:

> The soul's dark cottage, battered and decayed,
> Lets in new light through chinks that time has made;
> Stronger by weakness, wiser men become,
> As they draw near to their eternal home.
> Leaving the old, both worlds at once they view,
> That stand upon the threshold of the new.

Stevens shows Santayana "On the threshold of heaven . . . / / The threshold, Rome, and that more merciful Rome / Beyond, the two alike in the make of the mind." Santayana's symbol is the light of a single candle—"A light on the candle tearing against the wick / To join a hovering excellence, to escape / From fire and be part only of that of which / / Fire is the symbol: the celestial possible." Stevens, whether in his earliest hope to plough North America with verses or in his late hope, as the sick man, to join the divided races with new words, remains a poet of that celestial possible—many-faceted, irreducible, perennial.

Helen Vendler

Further Reading

Bates, Milton. *Wallace Stevens: A Mythology of Self.* Berkeley: University of California Press, 1985.

Bloom, Harold. *Wallace Stevens: The Poems of Our Climate.* Ithaca: Cornell University Press, 1977.

Brazeau, Peter. *Parts of a World: Wallace Stevens Remembered.* New York: Random House, 1983.

Cook, Eleanor. *Poetry, Word-Play, and Word-War in Wallace Stevens.* Princeton: Princeton University Press, 1988.

Doggett, Frank, and Buttell, Robert, eds. *Wallace Stevens: A Celebration.* Princeton: Princeton University Press, 1980.

Leggett, B. J. *Wallace Stevens and Poetic Theory.* Chapel Hill: University of North Carolina Press, 1987.

Stevens, Holly. *Souvenirs and Prophecies: The Young Wallace Stevens.* New York: Knopf, 1977.

Stevens, Wallace. *Collected Poems.* New York: Knopf, 1955.

———— *Letters.* Ed. Holly Stevens. New York: Knopf, 1966.

———— *The Necessary Angel.* New York: Vintage, 1942.

———— *Opus Posthumous.* Ed. Milton J. Bates. New York: Knopf, 1989.

Vendler, Helen. *On Extended Wings: Wallace Stevens' Longer Poems.* Cambridge: Harvard University Press, 1969.

———— *Wallace Stevens: Words Chosen Out of Desire.* Knoxville: University of Tennessee Press, 1984; repr. Cambridge: Harvard University Press, 1988.

William Carlos Williams

WILLIAM CARLOS WILLIAMS'S career as a published poet stretched from his first book of poems in 1909 until his final collection, *Pictures from Brueghel*, in 1962. For most of those years he felt that his achievement, and his ideas on the necessary course for American poetry in the twentieth century, languished in neglect. At the same time, he saw T. S. Eliot, a figure against whom he came to define many of his own poetic concerns, winning fame, followers, and the most prestigious national and international awards. In the last dozen years of his life, however, Williams not only received widespread recognition for his work, he became something of a mentor to a number of the most important American poets of the 1950s. These poets looked to him as part of their own search for alternatives to the prevailing mode of a complex, highly allusive poetics, as Williams had also looked for an alternative to what he saw as Eliot's legacy. His friends and correspondents included Charles Olson, Robert Creeley, Robert Lowell, Allen Ginsberg, and Denise Levertov, all of whom responded in their own ways to what they learned from Williams the man and Williams the poet.

In some ways Williams was very much a small-town figure. He was born, grew up, and died in Rutherford, New Jersey, a small suburban town a twenty minutes' bus ride from New York City. His marriage of more than fifty years was to a local girl, Florence (the Flossie of a number of poems). Rutherford and the surrounding towns supply many of the subjects for Williams's verse and prose (he published four novels, a number of plays, and many essays, in addition to his poetry). The near-by city of Paterson provided the focus and the title of his five-book long poem. A full-time pediatrician for forty years, Williams's medical practice took him into the homes of the local people, from the poor Italian immigrants of nearby Guinea Hill, to the comfortable middle-class homeowners of Rutherford, and into the hospitals of the nearby cities.

Yet the background to Williams's career in poetry was no more provincial than his medical training (he studied in Leipzig in 1909–1910). While attending the University of Pennsylvania from 1902–1906 for his medical degree, Williams formed close friendships with Ezra Pound, H.D., and Charles Demuth. Pound proved a vital early contact, for once he had moved to London he sent Williams useful advice and details of the latest literary journals and subsequently arranged for the publication of Williams's early work. When Williams visited London in 1910 he met Yeats through his friend. Pound's international reach also served to introduce Williams to some of the early Modernist poets in New York. Williams then began many years of using Rutherford's proximity to the city to travel in frequently, keeping up with the latest developments within the writing and painting communities.

This duality within Williams's biography feeds importantly into his work. In the world of Williams's poetry the technical innovations and the insistence upon change and renewal fuse with the constants, of nature and its cycles and of the promise of America—buried, ignored, but ever a potential force. Also a constant presence in Williams's work are the energies of love and sexual attraction. Marriage, for Williams, is the stable presence, always demanding renewal, even if through illicit sexual encounters. The poet who lived and died in the same town expressed a fervent commitment to the local—to the clear presentation of what was under his nose and in front of his eyes. Stanza form was not to be dictated by tradition or by rules inherited from other cultures but was to be shaped by engagement with the object. The language of the poem should be direct—what Williams came to argue was the language and rhythm of American speech. But this commitment to the local was to be made with no concession to provincial standards. The poetry of America must express the condition of the country, and thus would lack the polish and completeness of poetry written in the European tradition, but this poetry should match the international standards of Modernist achievement. Thus, although Williams set himself against the international school of Eliot and Pound—Americans he felt wrote about rootlessness and searched an alien past because of their failure to write about and live within their own culture— he kept up with the latest books and journals coming out of the European centers, published a number of his own books in Europe and his poems in European magazines, visited Europe again in 1924 for six months, and translated a French surrealist novel and some major French poets.

The resulting tension, which gives a characteristic energy to Williams's poetry, is illustrated in the difficulty he had in entitling his third book of poems. He was torn, he told Marianne Moore in a 1917 letter, between the Spanish title "Al Que Quiere!" (To Him Who Wants It) and "The Pleasures of Democracy"—between the uncompromising demands upon the audience made by the Modernist and the desire to be a poet of the people. He wanted both titles, but settled for the former.

Twelve years before that third book, according to Williams's *Autobiography* (1951), the poetry he was writing while at college was of two kinds: poetry influenced by Keats and poetry influenced by Whitman. This division between the work of tradition and that of the iconoclast foreshadows Williams's later sense of the choices open to the contemporary American poet, but his earliest extant pieces show him writing verses strongly influenced by the English poet.

In 1909 Williams gathered together some of his shorter poems and published his first book, *Poems*, printed, as were his next four titles, at his own expense. The poems strike a tone of late Romantic weariness and a yearning for release from what the poetic voice sees as the vulgar industrial world, thus mirroring many of the magazine poems of the day. In "The Uses of Poetry," the only poem from the volume Williams allowed to be republished in his lifetime, the poet describes his "fond anticipation of a day" when he can read "poesy" to a "lady . . . / The while we glide by many a leafy bay." As this poem has it, through reading poetry "the door of sense" is closed and imagination takes flight away from the present world of "anguish." "The Uses of Poetry" is characterized by everything the later Williams would spurn. A sonnet, it uses archaic poetic diction, inversion, and rhyme, and argues that poetry aids the mind to escape the pressures of the present moment and the contemporary world.

Williams proudly sent a copy of his book to Pound in London, who bluntly replied that the poems were derivative and out-of-date. Pound's letter included one of the many reading lists that Williams was to receive from his friend over the years (one of which, forty years later, he would reproduce in *Paterson*). By 1949 Williams would feel that Pound could also learn something from him. In 1909, however, he was glad of his friend's advice and even took it a little too much to heart. The poems in his next book, *The Tempers* (1913), copy the style and tone of some of Pound's own experiments.

Williams did not reprint any of the 1909 *Poems* in his own collected volumes, and made clear that he did not ever want them reprinted. The editors of Williams's *Collected Poems* (which appeared in two volumes, in 1986 and 1988) confined themselves to including three, "The Uses of Poetry," and two that Reed Whittemore quoted in his 1975 biography *William Carlos Williams: Poet from Jersey*. (Ironically, this most derivative of Williams's publications is the rarest book in the Williams's canon, a fire having destroyed many of the unsold copies about ten years after publication. Only about a dozen of the books are known to exist.)

In 1912 Pound arranged the first magazine publication of Williams's poetry, in London, where a year later *The Tempers* appeared. In contrast to the earlier book, the poems contain a greater diversity of rhythm, some passionate emotion comes into the address to the ever-present "lady," and the poet often takes up the world-weary tone of Pound's exiled troubadors. If the modern world is still inadequate for poetry, the poet at least writes his lament from within it, and does not seek the escape yearned for in "The Uses of Poetry." But within the book a few poems reveal the characteristic voice that Williams would go on to develop. "Mezzo Forte" records a moment of exasperation with a cat, and "Hic Jacet" is a poem written out of Williams's medical experience, noticing (although with a rather heavy irony) the prosperous condition of the coroner's "merry little children." Williams also included translations of some Spanish ballads, the Spanish—maternal—side of his heritage always serving for Williams as a resource against the potential oppression of the English tradition, which he sometimes associates with his English-born father.

A measure of Williams's development over the next twenty years—but also of the continuity of his interests—can be seen in a comparison of the *Tempers'* translation of the Spanish ballad "Poplars of the meadow" with that in his 1936 book, *Adam & Eve & the City*. For example, toward the end of the ballad, where the 1913 version has:

> Since you are ware of my absence.
> God, wilt Thou give me patience
> Here while suffer I ye,

The 1936 version is more focused and economical, and the diction more contemporary:

> When you discover my absence.
> May God give me patience
> Here in my misery,

The differences between the two versions stem from Williams's immediate and sustained interest in the ideas of Imagism proposed by Pound in 1912 and 1913. But before Williams began what amounted to a career-long exploration of some of its implications, he published in the London journal the *Egoist* a long poem titled "The Wanderer: A Rococo Study," which revealed the disparity, at this time, between his ambitions and his ability to execute them. A poem of almost two hundred and fifty lines, "The Wanderer" presents the concerns that were becoming central to Williams's poetics. Taking up a position "at the prow" of the Manhattan ferry, the narrator asks himself: "How shall I be a mirror to this modernity?" Pushed to address this question by an aged muse figure (whom Williams later said he modeled on his grandmother), the narrator at first seeks the kinds of fanciful flights yearned for in "The Uses of Poetry." But the muse, who is presented in deliberately unidealist terms, forces him to look carefully at what he sees before him—including the hungry families waiting out the Paterson strike of 1913. The poet now recognizes that he must commit himself to the close recording of the contemporary and the local, as it is, and not strained through conceits that pretend a beauty where there is none. The muse figure conducts a mysterious ritual by the local river, "the filthy Passaic," in which the poet's old self floats off downstream and the new self becomes a "wanderer," somewhat like Thoreau, in his own locality, now open to the new and the actual.

"The Wanderer" is hardly the revolutionary poem its themes proclaim. Its narrator's position on a ferry is not its only borrowing from

Whitman, and the poem contains some of the poetic diction and inversions of Williams's earlier verse. Williams tried revising it in 1917 for *Al Que Quiere!* but the poem remains more important as a manifesto than as an achievement. Yet "The Wanderer" is a crucial work in Williams's career, as he recognized in putting the poem first in his 1951 *Collected Earlier Poems.* Williams also often claimed the poem as the forerunner of *Paterson,* and quotes from it in the last, summary, pages of *Paterson V.*

Williams's poetry took a new direction in response to the discussions of Imagism, his exposure to these ideas was one of a number of important influences upon him in the years immediately following *The Tempers.* Chief among these new contacts was another connection supplied by Pound. Williams became a frequent visitor to the Grantwood, New Jersey, artists' colony, which included among its group Alfred Kreymborg and Man Ray. Subsequently, Williams came to know a number of the avant-garde European artists working in New York to escape the war across the Atlantic.

A number of the strategies of Imagism, although early abandoned by Pound, appealed to Williams as a way to declare independence from European conventions of style and to bring the American scene and the American voice into his work. The three famous principles each had their appeal: direct treatment of the "thing," no superfluous language, and a demand for variety of rhythms. The "thing" could be the American scene or object; the approach and presentation was key, not the intrinsic poetic worth of the object treated. The contemporary American scene offered as rich a source of material as the time-honored landscape of Europe. This principle was reinforced by Pound's insistence that the natural object should be the adequate symbol. The coroner's children of "Hic Jacet" deserved their place in a poem as much as the classical deities who pepper many of the poems in *The Tempers.*

The demand for economical language and a discarding of conventional rhythms could be claimed as the presentation of American directness and could justify poems written without a bow to the traditions of genre. Whereas for Pound Imagism was a declaration of independence from what he felt were the rhetorical and emotional excesses of Victorian verse, for Williams and some other American poets it was a declaration of independence from the European tradition. In fact,

Williams's own version of Imagism initially contains a high degree of emotional content. His next book, *Al Que Quiere!*, for example, frequently exhorts his "townspeople" on the virtues of the commonplace in a style in which exclamation points do the work that a crisp, inventive presentation of the object will achieve a few years later.

An associated aspect of the Imagist strategy reinforced Williams's developing concerns—its claims for the temporal independence of the image, and the poem. Pound argued that "an image is that which presents an intellectual and emotional complex in an instant of time," further distancing the demands of history and tradition from the poem. Williams wrote two longer poems in these years, "History" and "March," which self-consciously recognize and present the achievements of past civilizations but end with a demand that the poet create a new record from the American scene and moment. In "History" the setting is the Metropolitan Museum of Art in New York, and in "March" Williams's own memory of visiting in Europe the Assyrian sculptures and the frescoes of Fra Angelico. The continuities of love and violence, death and faith, shape the thematic connections within each poem, but the importance of the present need is finally emphasized. Whether that need is faced courageously, with every acknowledgment of the destructive energies necessary for its expression, or is diffused through a nostalgic return to the past that represses the claims of the present, becomes a central dialectic within Williams's important historical essays in his *In the American Grain* (1925), and in his treatment of history in *Paterson*.

The temporal isolation of the image also allowed Williams to adopt a strategy common to much American literature, to both expose and finally to discount the failures of the past to fulfill the promise of the American landscape and the American self. This aspect of Williams's concerns reveals him as a quintessentially American exponent of Modernism, and marks his heritage with Whitman just as much as their joint interest in technical innovation. (A number of critics have explored the relationship, and Williams has also been discussed in the context of Emerson, and of the American poetic tradition generally.) Consistently in Williams's work an oppressive ideology, a despair born of failure to meet expectations, the power of death itself, can be thrown off as the key first step to the process of renewal—with every recognition that the subsequent achievement will itself in turn have to be thrown off.

In his characteristic work, which begins with the poetry of *Al Que Quiere!* Williams's poetry is often concerned with beginnings, but this is accompanied by a recognition of the deeply rooted continuities that for Williams lie beyond the restrictive cultural connections with European tradition that he wishes to break. The often anthologized "Tract," while focused upon a funeral and exhorting greater simplicity and concreteness within the ritual, is finally about preparation, a way to bring renewal out of loss, and is also a recognition of a commonality. Many poems redefine traditional themes in contemporary terms. A number of poems are titled "Pastoral," others describe dawn or a morning ritual, and still others explore the potential richness of a sexual encounter. The opening prose of *Spring and All* (1923), a book that combines prose and poetry, imagines the destruction of a world trapped by conventions, and creates through the imagination a climate within which its poems can "enter the new world naked," and the "black eyed susan" that is the focus of its final poem take root and bloom. The newness of the imagined world is one with the cycles of nature.

This fundamental continuity, however, is only realized after a break from the superficial connections supplied by what for Williams is a too prevalent, desperate adherence to convention. Thus he always emphasizes the danger inherent in breaking the moment from its temporal flow, the break necessary to allow the moment its full expression within the poem. In *Paterson* the spectacular Passaic Falls that are at the center of the poem are both the place of discovery and also the place of greatest danger—the "rock's / lip," where the waters gather and "leap to the conclusion and / fall, fall in air! as if / floating, relieved of their weight, / split apart." On the level of technique the same emphasis appears in Williams's use of line and stanza breaks. The word "edge" is a key one in Williams's poetics. The edge of the line, like the place of discovery that is the edge of the Falls, breaks up expectations of the relationship of syntax and idea to the individual line, and to stanza form, as the poem moves down the page.

By the time of his 1918 essay "Prologue to *Kora in Hell*," which introduced a book of prose improvisations, Williams had started to find his own voice and to distance himself from Pound and from a number of other Modernist poets. The improvisations themselves are a series of prose pieces Williams apparently wrote daily during the flu epidemic of 1917, coming home exhausted and writing whatever came into his head. According to Williams's own account of writing *Kora in Hell*, he arranged the improvisations in a loose order, and then wrote some commentaries upon them by way of attempted clarification—although some of the "clarifications" are as dense and obscure as the passages they comment on.

Discussing the improvisations in *Spring and All* (1923), Williams conceded "their fault is their dislocation of sense, often complete," but, as a number of critics have pointed out, the greater loosening of syntax that Williams allowed himself in these prose pieces led to the poetry of his following books, *Sour Grapes* and *Spring and All*, having a new daring in their line breaks and linguistic juxtapositions. The method also allowed him to practice his aesthetic of writing without a preconceived form and under a pressure that demanded full attention only to the act of self-expression, without the intervention of expected norms of mediation. In the 1928 prose and poetry sequence "The Descent of Winter," for a later example, Williams presents the work as the notes of a diary, for a similar purpose, and in general a Williams poem strives for an effect of spontaneity as part of its poetics of immediacy. The improvisations stand as his first full experiment with the possibilities of the strategy.

In the extended prose "Prologue" that introduces the improvisations, Williams sets himself against the international school then emerging in the poetry of Pound and Eliot, with its emphasis on the place of tradition and the past in fully engaging the present. In his witty and forceful essay, Williams declares that Eliot's poetry "is the latest touch from the literary cuisine, it adds to the pleasant outlook from the club window." He terms Pound "the best enemy United States verse has," and characterizes both as "men content with the connotations of their masters." He imagines "an international congress of poets" in Paris, and wonders what the Frenchmen present would make of United States verse if Pound rose and read Eliot's "La Figlia Che Piange" as representative American poetry.

In the essay Williams carves out his own position in the debate about the direction for Modernist poetry. Quoting from letters he has received from the poets themselves, Williams disagrees with Wallace Stevens, asserting that multiple points of view within a poem can more clearly bring out unseen characteristics of an object. He takes issue with H.D.'s claim that there is something "sacred" about the creative impulse, and argues with Pound on the importance of the local in poetry. Williams agrees that no valuable alternative is offered by the Chicago school of such poets as Carl Sandburg and Edgar Lee Masters, but he presents as undertaking important original work such painters as Marcel Duchamp and Wassily Kandinsky as well as his old friend Charles Demuth. Among writers, Williams singles out for praise his associates Alfred Kreymborg and Maxwell Bodenheim, writers whom very few would put above T. S. Eliot today. But whatever the essay's shortcomings as literary criticism, the "Prologue" remains central to an understanding of Williams's position and the poetics he developed from it.

As Williams's discussion of painters in the "Prologue" indicates, as he started to find his own voice his poetry came to have an increasingly visual orientation. A Williams poem often became one that had to be seen on the page, as well as read, a characteristic that Williams could particularly exploit by composing most of his poems directly onto the typewriter. Some of this visual impetus reflects the pictorial aspects of Imagism, although some critics have suggested that Williams's diagnostic methods as a doctor would also have contributed to the appeal.

Equally crucial to the increasing emphasis upon the visual in Williams's work was the achievement of the Modernist painters in finding a vocabulary of revolt against the kind of conventions that Williams wanted to take on. Pound had recognized in his Imagist manifestoes that poetry was behind painting in its discovery of a contemporary form and language. Among the European artists in New York for the duration of the war, Williams found a general spirit of iconoclasm, and, as the "Prologue" indicates, he was particularly interested in the work of Marcel Duchamp.

Duchamp challenged some fundamental assumptions about the relationship of an artist to a work of art, and in the "Prologue" Williams argues for the importance of Duchamp's ideas. He notes that Duchamp at one point declared that his composition for that day would be the first thing he saw upon entering a hardware store. Bringing back a snow shovel (Williams remembers it as a pick-ax) Duchamp hung it in his studio as his work *In Advance of the Broken Arm*. The strategy matches Williams's attempt to engage the object world without preconceptions and to incorporate the world of objects—transformed by the creative will of the artist, a force that Williams came to term "imagination"—into his work. *Paterson* would include such objects as the drilling record of an artesian well, letters sent to the poet, and extracts from New Jersey histories and newspapers.

Williams also recounts Duchamp taking a full-size photograph of his famous painting *Nude Descending a Staircase*, touching it up with a little paint, and declaring it a new composition. Such an action parallels Williams's emphasis upon technique being the important part of a poem's meaning, and offered reading experience, rather than what the poem is "about." And Duchamp's action also, as with the snow shovel example, returns the authority of compositional decisions to the artist, and away from the conventional expectations of an audience.

What critics have come to call the "visual text" of a Williams poem appears in his work in a number of ways. In Williams's more reflective, memory-oriented poetry of the 1950s, the poems are structured around a triadic line spaced across the page from left to right. The three-step line visually reflects the descent into the self and the store of experience being reencountered that is the theme of the poems. At other times, most often in the 1930s, Williams makes the title of a poem also function as the first line, a visual effect that has to be seen on the page.

Sometimes Williams incorporates the language and appearance of signs into his poems. In the 1923 poem "Rapid Transit," from *Spring and All*, some of the poem's language is apparently taken from a highway campaign and a subway poster, among other sources:

> Careful Crossing Campaign
> Cross Crossings Cautiously

> THE HORSES   black
>   &
> PRANCED   white

> Outings in New York City

In this extract, what set of verbal relationships are to be given priority in a reading, those running downwards or across? The relationships are as much visual as semantic, and Williams builds the cross-cutting tensions of the two into the poem. The device further demonstrates the way that this poetics of immediacy must finally be multidirectional, the fullness of its engagement with and exploration of the moment not compromised by a linearity associated with the temporal. "I ascend" Williams writes in another poem from *Spring and All*, "and at the same time / I descend."

The multidirectionality and nonlinguistic reach of Williams's use of signs are part of his attempt to, as Kenneth Burke noticed in an early review, dissolve the space between subject and object. (Williams titled a poetry journal he coedited in the early 1920s *Contact*.) In "The Attic Which is Desire:" Williams reproduces the commercial sign he can see from the attic study in which he is writing his poem:

```
        *       *       *
        *       S       *
        *       O       *
        *       D       *
        *       A       *
        *       *       *
```

In "April" the objects are even further removed from the linguistic, the poem incorporating a skull and crossbones and two arrows, signs encountered at a hospital. One page of *Paterson*, in Book III, where thematically a flood is occurring, consists of fragments of sentences from many sources—overheard speech, books, Williams's own verse—each moving in a different direction across and up and down the page.

Williams wants the object world to enter the poem with a minimum degree of mediation from language or from the structure of the poem itself—although he is always aware that a poem is a linguistic construction. The attempt of the poem to minimize this meditation is another of the creative tensions within a Williams poem. In a 1931 essay on Marianne Moore, which, like much of Williams's criticism, is most helpful for revealing his own concerns, Williams praises his friend for "wiping soiled words or cutting them clean out, removing the aureoles that have been pasted about them or taking them bodily from greasy contexts." Thus, in one well-known example, a poem from *Spring and All* later titled "The Rose," Williams examines the rose's renewed possibilities for composition once the familiar associations of love have been removed, uncovering "the fragility of the flower / unbruised."

Williams's poetry seeks to tie the word anew to the object, as part of his insistence that the object be seen and described as it actually is. Williams's concern can be illustrated with an example he used to introduce a 1934 essay on Alfred Stieglitz, whose championing of American art Williams admired. The first settlers, Williams recounts, "saw birds with rusty breasts and called them robins." But the birds are thrushes, only faintly resembling the English bird of the same name. The example serves for Williams to demonstrate a lack of looking carefully, a nostalgia for what has been left behind, and a careless use of language. For Williams the first settlers, and too many American writers and readers since, have lacked the courage to face and recognize the new.

Williams's work of the 1920s reflects his continuing concern to delineate his relationship both to Europe and to his own culture. The end of the First World War saw the return of the European artists to France, to be followed by many American writers and artists attracted by the favorable exchange rates. Williams's resulting sense of isolation was compounded by the international success of *The Waste Land* in 1922, which he later termed "the great catastrophe to our letters," and argued "gave the poem back to the academics." In his letters to Pound Williams occasionally confessed to a temptation to join the expatriates, tired as he sometimes was of his neglect, and what he saw as the provincialism of the American audience. On a leave of absence from his medical practice he and Florence Williams visited Europe in 1924 for six months, and Williams's first novel *A Voyage to Pagany* (1928) illustrates his coming to terms with European achievement, through the thinly disguised autobiographical protagonist Dr. Dev Evans. The novel ends with the confrontation producing another of Williams's characteristic renewals, as the returning doctor views the Nantucket shore in the distance, again a pioneer: "So this is the beginning."

Lacking a regular publisher for his work in the United States in the 1920s, Williams was obliged to publish two books of prose and poetry arrangements, *Spring and All* and "The Descent of Winter," in limited editions in Europe. Neither book was reprinted in its original format in Williams's lifetime, although Williams did reprint most of the poetry. The unavailability of these texts—which some critics feel contain Williams's finest writing—helps explain Williams's late recognition as a major Modernist poet, and also explains why most of the earliest scholarly discussions, in the 1950s and 1960s, were of the more readily available *Paterson*, and the work of the 1950s. When J. Hillis Miller wanted to discuss the *Spring and All* prose in his important essay in *Poets of Reality* (1965), he had to return to one of the only three hundred copies of the book printed to find the text.

Both books were reprinted in their original form in *Imaginations* (1970), and also in the *Collected Poems: Volume I*, but many readers still only know such famous poems from *Spring and All* as "The Red Wheelbarrow," "To Elsie," and "Spring and All" ("By the road to the contagious hospital") as isolated anthology pieces. To read the poems in the full context of the twenty-seven poems and thematically related prose is to see Williams working to develop a poetics that, while still retaining a sharpness of pictorial immediacy, transcended the structural limitations of the short lyric.

In the "Prologue to *Kora in Hell*" Williams argued that a "loose linking of one thing with another has effects of a destructive power little to be guessed at." In addition to thematic connections one way this "loose linking" governs the arrangement of the *Spring and All* poems is through their titles being merely numbers—"I–XXVII." The device also ensures that the poems are read within the context of the arrangement and the world of imagination that the book's opening pages present, rather than through the expectations raised by a title. The book's prose arguments have their own dynamic, and are rarely presented logically. A sentence is as likely to suddenly stop with a dash or just blank space—sometimes after one word—as to complete the idea it had started to express. A poetics of immediacy will always seek to short-circuit analytical thought. Williams wants the self to engage the object world through a descent into the kind of preconscious energies that, for him, lie within the body, beneath the constructs of the mind and the logic of conventional discourse.

In "The Descent of Winter" the poems are also numbered. The numerical titles serve as dated journal entries, as the sequence moves from 9/27 to 12/18. The prose, as well as continuing the discussion of poetics, describes the people and landscape of the New Jersey towns of Williams's medical practice, while the poems, too, are largely concerned with local scenes. The poems are much more emotionally austere than those of *Spring and All*, matching the bareness of the landscape and the season that nevertheless serves the poet as the material of his art. Williams originally conceived "The Descent of Winter" as the first half of a book that would in its second half record the renewal of spring through the poetry and prose of "Della Primavera Trasportata al Morale" (Springtime translated to a moral). But he eventually separated the two and published the later sequence as ten poems without prose some years later.

In a 1925 book of essays entitled *In the American Grain*, which provides a helpful gloss on the poet's view of history in his poetry, Williams turned his attention to the schoolroom figures of American history. He searched for what he felt was the truth of such men as Columbus, Washington, Franklin, and Boone beneath the welter of legend and myth that had come to surround them. The figures are examined in terms of their commitment to, or rejection of, the rich possibilities of the New World. Using one of a variety of techniques for each essay, including straightforward quotation from documents, an invented monologue, or a discussion with a French critic, Williams rewrites history in his own terms. The inventiveness and sensitivity of Montezuma is destroyed by the Spanish. De Soto responds to the promise of the New World despite himself—its lure presented as a sexual invitation inevitable and ultimately destructive, for him, in its fulfillment. Boone resists the temptations of civilization, and understands the violence of the Indians, even toward his own family. Burr's attempt to bring about real change is thwarted by the totalitarian designs of Hamilton, and the false myths that cover their clash. The Puritans deny the sensual in themselves and attempt to repress it in others. A particularly important chapter for understanding the role of violence and the subconscious in Williams's poetry is his chapter on Poe. Williams sees Poe as a realist, and his tortured characters as representing the hell of repression within the American psyche. Poe himself Williams sees as the first American writer to recognize this hell of repression and to make it inform his work—only to fall victim himself, as man and writer, to its power. With the essays of *In the American Grain*, as in his poetry, Williams wants to recapture that "spirit" of Montezuma's lake city now buried in the soil, a city and people that recognized its "primal and continuous identity with the ground itself"—and also the spirit of all those figures in American history sensitive to its promise. In a way Williams's version of Eliot's "Tradition and the Individual Talent," the book also has clear affinities with D. H. Lawrence's *Studies in Classic American Literature*. (Lawrence, a writer Williams much admired, wrote a review praising the book, which Williams evidently was unaware of for many years.)

The 1930s did not see Williams turn to a more overtly political poetry. But he was always as concerned as Pound with the state of the culture, seeing a society's response to serious literature, especially poetry, as a crucial measure of that society's health. Williams's interest in economics is as much with the printing and publication of poetry as with the unemployment rate. But he wrote enough overtly political poetry to be accused of being sympathetic to communism when, in the early 1950s, he was nominated for the prestigious post of Consultant in Poetry to the Library of Congress. He was always interested in the social experiments of the Soviet Union, although he deplored totalitarianism. His interest can be seen in such poems as "A Morning Imagination of Russia," "Russia," and "Choral: the Pink Church." In 1927 he wrote "Impromptu: The Suckers" against the execution of Sacco and Vanzetti, but did not publish it for fourteen years. The 1935 poem "An Early Martyr," evidently begun in the 1920s, recounts the efforts of the courts to silence John Coffey, who shoplifted from department stores to protest the plight of the poor. In general, Williams was uncomfortable writing poems in response to particular public events, as one would expect from a poet who emphasizes the unexpected encounter with the object world.

Williams declined to join any radical party in the 1930s, and was attacked in the pages of some left-wing journals for his lack of full commitment to radical causes. He did, however, respond to Pound's directing him to the theories of Social Credit, an egalitarian system that attacked the central role of the banks in determining credit and ultimately costs. The role of economics becomes one of the central issues in *Paterson*, where Hamilton is presented as the advocate of a central bank that is one of a litany of exploiters of the landscape.

In the late 1930s Williams finally found a publisher who would regularly publish his books in commercial editions when James Laughlin started New Directions. Apart from a period in the early 1950s, Williams would remain with Laughlin for the rest of his life. One of the first projects Williams promised his new publisher was the first book of his long poem *Paterson*, but problems of how to structure his poem plagued Williams for some years. Some earlier shorter poems had marked a start on the main themes. In 1927 Williams published in the *Dial* a poem entitled "Paterson" of just under a hundred lines, and through the 1930s he published individual lyrics that came out of his work on the poem. But his first attempt to find an overall structure proved a dead end with the eighty-seven-page manuscript "Detail & Parody for the poem *Paterson*" that Williams sent Laughlin in 1939. The series of thematically related poems does highlight what became in the final version a central issue of the use and misuse of language. The abandoned arrangement became the source for many of Williams's periodical publications over the next five years, and supplied many poems for his 1944 volume *The Wedge*, titled at one point "The (lang)WEDGE."

By the middle of the 1940s Williams had finally worked out the form for *Paterson*. This form was a collagelike arrangement, in four books, of poetry that includes many different stanzaic forms, and prose excerpted from such diverse sources as contemporary and historical newspapers, nineteenth-century histories of New Jersey, oral histories of Rutherford residents, and letters Williams had received from such figures as Pound, Edward Dahlberg, and the then unknown Allen Ginsberg. The four books initially appeared in separate volumes in 1946, 1948, 1949, and 1951. While for some commentators the poem is only partly successful, and others have argued that the poem is a tardy attempt to match the achievement of *The Waste Land* and *The Cantos*, for many readers *Paterson* stands as Williams's most important and fully realized work.

At the center of the poem is the Passaic Falls, a geological feature of Paterson that was the cause of its boom in the nineteenth and early twentieth century as an industrial center. The roar of the Falls, exploited by industry, serves in the poem as a kind of hidden, unrecognized source of a potential language rooted in the landscape. The poem itself, and the residents of Paterson, must discover and express this source for relief from the violence and rootlessness of the past and present city that is revealed in the poetry and in the prose extracts. The protean figure of Paterson is at times a mythical figure connected to the history of the river, at others an embodiment of the city, and at still others a doctor-poet trying to find the means to write the poem that is itself recording his search.

The titles of the four books provide a geographical and thematic guide to the poem. The first book, "The Delineaments of the Giants," sets the themes into the context of local myths and history. Book II, "Sunday in the Park," records Dr. Paterson's largely unsuccessful search in the Garret Mountain Park of the city for any contemporary fulfillment of the landscape's promise. In Book III, "The Library," Paterson finds among the histories he reads an ossified language, trapped in its catalogued and classified place. But as Paterson reads of the actual fire, flood, and cyclones to hit the city at the beginning of this century, the landscape of his mind enacts the same destruction and reformation that the city itself went through, an action that also parallels the crashing descent and rebound of the Falls. The fourth book, "The Run to the Sea," offers no closure, but more examples of dissatisfied sexual energies, of murders—and of violence, particularly toward women. But at the end of the fourth book a male/female figure emerges from the sea to return inland, to begin again, with the knowledge gained from the journey recorded by the poem. The gesture is that of the courageous figures of *In the American Grain*. Like so much of Williams's poetry, the poem finally articulates a way to begin. In fact Williams originally intended to call the whole poem an "introduction."

Williams envisioned a fifth book of Paterson even as he was composing the fourth, but the short extract he published in 1952 as "Paterson, Book V: The River of Heaven" turned into his poem "Asphodel, That Greeny Flower," and *Paterson V* did not finally appear until 1958. Like "Asphodel, That Greeny Flower," Book V is much more of a memory poem than the earlier books, and reflects the sharp changes that had occurred in Williams's life and poetics in the early 1950s, as he suffered the first of what would be a series of strokes through the decade, which severely limited his mobility and his ability to type. Williams's next two books of poetry, *The Desert Music* (1954) and *Journey to Love* (1955), very much reflect the mood and circumstances of his strokes, his retirement from medicine, and his subsequent severe depression. Most of the poems are written in a three-step line, which brings a much more ruminative and personal voice to Williams's poetry, and which for some readers makes the poems of these years his finest achievement. Certainly the poems are more accessible than the more iconoclastic poems of such books as *Spring and All*, "The Descent of Winter," and most pages of *Paterson* I–IV. Williams gained in these years a much wider audience for his poems (these were also the two books published by the more commercial Random House), and his first important critical attention from scholars.

Williams claimed to have discovered the three-step line of *The Desert Music* and *Journey to Love* by looking again at a section of *Paterson*, Book II, written in the triadic form. Significantly, the lines concern recovery and the importance of revisiting memory, both couched in Williams's familiar motif of an inevitable descent that precedes an ascent. Williams presented the lines as the first poem of *The Desert Music*, entitled "The Descent." The poem begins:

> The descent beckons
> > as the ascent beckoned.
> > > Memory is a kind
> > of accomplishment,
> > > a sort of renewal
> > > > even

With the poet increasingly housebound, the encounters recorded by these poems are not only with the outside object world but also with memories of past experiences, sometimes from many years ago, that are now for the first time recognized for their full significance—as Williams had come to recognize the full significance of the lines from *Paterson*. The tension of the earlier poetry between the fully realized contours of the moment and its deep-seated continuity now appears within the sharp memories of a rich and deeply felt lifetime. In the best known of these poems, "Asphodel, That Greeny Flower," the long and sometimes troubled marriage of Williams and Florence is reexamined for the core of love embodied in their wedding more than forty years earlier. The rediscovery brings to the troubled present a salvation born of the renewal of love.

In a number of critical statements and letters to such interested younger poets as Richard Eberhart and Robert Creeley, Williams argued that his triadic line allowed him both the flexibility and discipline to capture the essence of American speech rhythms in his verse. This "American idiom" could be expressed through the "variable foot" of the triadic line.

Williams's theorizing is rarely to his or his correspondents' satisfaction, but this attempt to give authority to a more common speech and to a disciplined free form proved attractive to a number of poets seeking alternatives to the prevailing modes of dense, highly allusive verse. Williams, along with Pound—now confined in St. Elizabeths Hospital in Washington by the government—became important antiestablishment figures for poets seeking less formalist modes of expression. Both spoke from the authority of a considerable and respected body of work. Williams was standard reading at Black Mountain College, and at this time became the center of a correspondence that took in Charles Olson and Robert Creeley, whom he introduced to each other, Allen Ginsberg, Denise Levertov, and Robert Lowell, among others—all of whom to one degree or another were responding to his work, finding their own ways to build upon what they had learned from his poetry. For Olson, for example, *Paterson* showed a way to bring the local into an epic poem, and a way to avoid the problem of ego that for Olson was a flaw of Pound's *Cantos*. But he thought Williams's long poem concentrated too little on the city itself, and tried to bring Gloucester more to the fore in his own *Maximus* poems. Ginsberg's *Howl and Other Poems* (1956), which carried an introduction by Williams, shows in the earlier poems of the book Ginsberg's own experiments with the Williams lyric. Lowell responded to Williams's work in the composition of *Life Studies* (1959), while always retaining more formal qualities in his verse than Williams would have admitted.

By the middle of the decade Williams began to feel that he had worked through most of the possibilities of his triadic line, and *Paterson V* (1958) is his final major work in that mode as much as it is a fifth book of the long poem. Williams himself was uncertain that he had integrated the book with the earlier four, and critical opinion has generally been divided on whether he succeeded. Nevertheless, *Paterson V* is an example of the late Williams style at its best. The format follows that of the first four books, verse interspersed with prose—prose that includes a Mike Wallace interview with Williams, extracts from a short story Gilbert Sorrentino had sent the poet, and a third letter from an Allen Ginsberg about to become famous for *Howl*. The city itself, however, is much less present in this book. "I had to take the spirit of the river up in the air," Williams told his friend John Thirlwall, and the world of *Paterson V* is one of old age, of memory, and of ways to fight the pressure of time and loss. A central feature of the book is Williams's use of the unicorn tapestries in the New York Metropolitan Museum's Cloisters. The tapestries, created for the celebration of a royal marriage, become an artistic embodiment of the weaving, lacing waters of the river at the Fall's edge.

The final line of *Paterson V* celebrates "the tragic foot," a "measured dance" of both the poetic line and the poet's imagination. But *Paterson* is a poem that Williams never wanted to finish, his own struggle for constant renewal of language and form so intimately tied up with the poem's record of that struggle. He was soon thinking about a sixth book, and only his continuing debilitating strokes stopped him. Four sheets of the proposed sixth book, dating apparently from late 1960 and early 1961, were found among the poet's papers after his death and were included as an appendix to the collected *Paterson* in 1963.

Before completing the poems of the late 1950s that would form his final book of verse, *Pictures from Brueghel* (1962), Williams published a number of translated poems. Williams worked on translations throughout his career, often turning to them when he felt he had a particular problem to work out in his own verse. Writing to Nicolas Calas in the 1940s, Williams had told him: "If I do original work all well and good. But if I can say it (the matter of form I mean) by translating the work of others that also is valuable." Williams's translations, of this and the earlier periods of his career, have been little discussed, in part because many of them were never reprinted or collected. Apart from their own interest as poems, however, they make a valuable study of the writers who interested the poet. The translations are now available in the two volumes of *Collected Poems*, and their sheer quantity might cause a revaluation on the part of readers who still think of the poet as the maker of short Imagist pieces. Williams had proficiency in French (in 1929 he published a translation of Philippe Soupault's novel *Last Nights of Paris*) as well as German and Spanish. His translations also include poems from Greek and Chinese, where he worked from literal translations provided by others.

The translations also testify to the more complex attitude Williams held toward tradition, and toward Europe, than is sometimes recognized. This tireless proclaimer of the need to liberate American poetry from its adherence to European conventions would nevertheless take from Europe what was needed for his own cause. So too he would cite Kandinsky in the "Prologue to *Kora in Hell*" and Juan Gris in *Spring and All* as examples of artists whose strategies he saw as parallel to his own. In his last poems he would hold up Sibelius and Brueghel as artists who courageously broke with conventions, thus creating compositions that allow the artist's imagination to outlast the death that, as Williams neared his eighties, he knew was close for him.

The poems of *Pictures from Brueghel* return to the shorter lyric form of Williams's earlier verse, although they can also be seen as a concentrated form of his triadic line. The subject of many of the poems is the poet's family—his mother, his wife, his grandchildren, and objects around the house and their associations over the years. In May 1963, two months after his death, the book won Williams his only Pulitzer prize.

In the years since his death Williams has continued to serve as a mentor for many younger poets, his spirit of challenge as powerful a force as the work itself. His poetry has been the subject of numerous academic studies that have explored such topics as Williams's interest in the visual arts, his use of history, and his lineation and stanza form. New Directions, the publisher to whom Williams returned for his last books, have kept all his work in print and have made available the original versions of *Spring and All* and "The Descent of Winter," the over two hundred poems that were not reprinted in Williams's own collected volumes, and many of his essays and experimental prose pieces.

Williams is now generally, although not universally, acknowledged as one of the major figures of twentieth-century American poetry; one who demanded a thorough reassessment of many assumptions about the form, diction, and subject matter of poetry, and who argued for a characteristically American form and voice, of international standard rather than of merely local color interest. Among the dissenters some more formalist writers and critics argue that his contribution is greatly overvalued, the most recent salvoes being directed at the *Collected Poems* volumes of 1986 and 1988. The whole line of American poetry to which Williams is such an important figure, the line that includes such figures as Olson and Creeley, comes under similar attack from time to time. For some critics, in addition, a key refrain in *Paterson*, "no ideas but in things," points up the lack of intellectual content in Williams's poetry, but as Denise Levertov has pointed out, the phrase does not mean "no ideas." Williams's legacy continues to be a potent force in contemporary debate on American poetry.

Many high school and college poetry readers, unfortunately, get their impressions of Williams's work from the same half-dozen poems served up in anthology after anthology. Williams is a difficult poet to anthologize, however, because part of his attempt to move beyond the limitations of the sharply rendered Imagist moment lay with such strategies

as his prose/poetry arrangements and the amorphous man/city figure of
Paterson. The reader interested in an introduction to Williams's work
could look at the 1930 sequence of ten poems "Della Primavera
Trasportata al Morale," the late "Pictures from Brueghel" sequence, or
the opening pages of *Spring and All* or "The Descent of Winter" in their
original formats. Of the triadic line poems, "Asphodel, That Greeny
Flower," Williams's long love poem to his wife, has moved many readers, including W. H. Auden. The "Prologue to *Kora in Hell*" is a characteristically feisty statement by Williams on his poetics, and is reprinted in his *Selected Essays* and in *Imaginations* (1970). The essay is invalu-
able both as a record of where Williams saw his future direction and of
the sort of Modernism he was to set himself against for the next forty
years.

Christopher MacGowan

Further Reading

Breslin, James E. *William Carlos Williams: An American Artist*. New York: Oxford University Press, 1970.

Conrad, Bryce. *Refiguring America: A Study of William Carlos Williams' "In the American
Grain."* Urbana: University of Illinois Press, 1990.

Cushman, Stephen. *William Carlos Williams and the Meaning of Measure*. New Haven:
Yale University Press, 1985.

Diggory, Terence. *William Carlos Williams and the Ethics of Painting*. Princeton:
Princeton University Press, 1991.

Mariani, Paul. *William Carlos Williams: A New World Naked*. New York: McGraw Hill,
1981.

Miller, J. Hillis. "Williams." In J. Hillis Miller, *The Linguistic Moment*, pp. 349–389.
Princeton: Princeton University Press, 1985.

Sankey, Benjamin. *A Companion to William Carlos Williams' "Paterson."* Berkeley: University of California Press, 1971.

Sayre, Henry. *The Visual Text of William Carlos Williams*. Urbana: University of Illinois
Press, 1983.

Schmidt, Peter. *William Carlos Williams, the Arts, and Literary Tradition*. Baton Rouge:
Louisiana State University Press, 1988.

Tapscott, Stephen. *American Beauty: William Carlos Williams and the Modernist Whitman*. New York: Columbia University Press, 1984.

Wallace, Emily. *A Bibliography of William Carlos Williams.* Middletown, Conn.: Wesleyan University Press, 1968.

Weaver, Mike. *William Carlos Williams: The American Background.* Cambridge: Cambridge University Press, 1971.

Williams, William Carlos. *Collected Poems.* 2 vols. *Volume I: 1909–1939.* Ed. A. Walton Litz and Christopher MacGowan. New York: New Directions, 1986..

Williams, William Carlos. *Collected Poems.* 2 vols. *Volume II: 1939–1962.* Ed. Christopher MacGowan. New York: New Directions, 1988.

Williams, William Carlos. *Imaginations.* Ed. Webster Schott. New York: New Directions, 1970.

Williams, William Carlos. *In the American Grain.* New York: New Directions, 1956.

Williams, William Carlos. *Paterson: Revised Edition.* New York: New Directions, 1992.

Hart Crane's Difficult Passage

IN about one generation Hart Crane has moved from the position of a reader's guilty pleasure to the James Dean of American poetry, with a legend built on a slim masterpiece, *White Buildings*, and on that romancing of Modernism, *The Bridge*. But until the emergence in the sixties of a friendly critical idiom Crane's poetry was consistently subverted; critics opposed its ambitions, were deaf to its methods, and made much of his vices. Hart Crane was an enthusiasm, an adolescent crush whom Winters had already humiliated on canonical and on personal grounds, and whom Blackmur had lumped with Lawrence, saying "Each is a blow in the face but neither can hit you twice." Having outlived the dismissals and New Criticism, the Hart Crane that we currently read we read reverently, since, as Harold Bloom remarked, Crane "continues to bury his critical undertakers." Now our "Orphic voice," Crane's position has shifted from obscurity to ambiguity, confounding an America reluctant to embrace one whom we admit to loving less than unreservedly and sometimes hardly at all.

Crane's publication history is a logarithm of his reputation. At his death, Liveright hastily issued *The Collected Poems of Hart Crane* (1933), edited by Waldo Frank, to whom Crane had dedicated *White Buildings* (1926). Frank assembled Crane's two published volumes, inexplicably in reverse chronological order, added the working manuscript of *Key West: An Island Sheaf*, and included some uncollected poems and "Modern Poetry," a fussy, stilted overview with Crane's intelligence but none of his passion. Liveright then advertised this edition as "definitive" over

Frank's admissions that it contained neither *variora* nor important early fugitive works. In five years Norton had published a moralizing biography, Philip Horton's *Hart Crane: The Life of an American Poet* (long superseded by Unterecker's 1969 *Voyager: A Life of Hart Crane*). The "definitive" Frank edition of the poems meantime underwent a second "Black and Gold" impression (after the fancy black and gold stitching on the cloth editions) in 1946, then a third in 1958 titled even more misleadingly *Complete Poems*. By then the critical climate had improved: in 1960 there was a full-length treatment of Crane's total output (Hazo's) and another of *The Bridge* (Dembo's); in 1965 Monroe Spears was saying that "more than thirty years after his suicide, we can say that his work . . . will remain among the permanent treasures of American poetry in the twentieth century"; in 1967 R. W. B. Lewis's *The Poetry of Hart Crane: A Critical Study* recontextualized Crane's Modernism and got Blake, Keats, and Shelley back into the conversation, distancing itself at once from Winters and Blackmur.

Moreover, by 1966 the editorial situation was somewhat less of a mess. A new editor, Brom Weber, who in 1952 had made the first compilation of Crane's correspondence, reedited the text, returned to a sane chronological sequencing, contributed a cool-headed introduction, added a selection of reviews, letters, and short prose (including "Modern Poetry," from which Weber eliminated a solecism introduced by Frank), twenty-one pages of notes, an index (Frank's contained only a table of contents), and gave the whole a decisive title: *The Complete Poems and Selected Letters of Hart Crane.* Yet nothing close to an authoritative text would exist for twenty years. Weber's, the best, was neither complete nor completely correct: it omitted the significant four-line fragment "The Return" ("The sea raised up a campanile . . . ") and carried an uninherited typo on page 30, where the opening line of "The Marriage of Faustus and Helen" is given as "Brazen *hynotics* glitter there" (my italics). When, ten years later, and under what compulsion one can only speculate, Liveright brought out a slim reprint of *White Buildings* and corrected *hynotics* to *hypnotics*, Crane's faithfullest readers found the volume's prefacer, John Logan, effusively misquoting the fourth line of "Voyages II" ("Her undinal vast belly moonward bends") as "Her vast undinal belly moonward bends." Liveright finally, in 1986, got around to a standard edition of *The Poems of Hart Crane*, edited by Marc Simon and intelligently introduced by Unterecker. Simon fixed the blunders, numbered lines, justified punctuation, gathered work uncollected, unpublished, and fragmentary into separate sections, and tacked on a section of informative if somehow peremptory end notes. Over fifty years had elapsed before the specialists wrested Crane's poetry from his publishers and editors.

Crane's early poetry issued from an apprenticeship in Eliot and Pound carried on from Cleveland, Akron, and New York. It is work cluttered with the trendy artifice of the "new poetry" that was already old when *White Buildings* appeared in 1926, work encumbered with the circumstantial obscurities that an education carried on in public tends to attract. "C 33" (1916), his first published poem, is a thirteen-line elegy to Oscar Wilde, who is identified hyperbolically as "O Materna," and whose jail cell inspired the title, though neither the title's source nor the subject's identity is disclosed. There are third-generation Imagist takes like "October-November," gravid with the lunar imagery of Aldington via T. E. Hulme and the leaden cadences of Lowell; there are poems like "Echoes" or "Exile" (the latter carries the epigraph, "after the Chinese"), which betray a vaguely Poundian contouring of syntax and subject that chases the depth and complexity of either out; there is even a fairly strong set of "Three Locutions Des Pierrots" whose sentimentalism Crane later disavowed. All the Modernist gestures—the copybook Classicism, the tags from Seneca, Jonson, and Miss Peters' high school Latin ("O Materna!"), Eliotic grace notes, vers libre prosody, the lapses into Pound-speak—are there. R. W. B. Lewis smartly named this period "The Escape From Irony," when Crane was dividing his attention between "Pound and Eliot and the minor Elizabethans," to whom he had gone "for values," in order to achieve what he termed "[that] synthetic conviction of form and creation" of great poetry. Only five years later, in a prospectus he would prepare for Eugene O'Neill, who had originally volunteered to do an introduction to *White Buildings*, Crane's views would alter: "I put no particular value on the simple objective of 'modernity.'" The "calligraphic tricks and slang used so brilliantly by an impressionist like Cummings" bored him; the "fastidious whimpering" of "Laforgue, Eliot and others of that kidney" depressed him; his objective had become a poetry grounded in the organic "logic of metaphor" and "the truth of the imagination." Allen Tate's foreword to *White Buildings* was precisely right: "To the Imagists Crane doubtless went to school in poetry," he wrote, and "learned their structural economy." But Crane, a poet whose "spiritual allegiances are outside the English tradition," would be a modern but not a Modernist, and his early poetry would be a labor of distancing himself from his masters.

How much distance he could cover in a single year is measured in "The Bridge of Estador" and "Porphyro in Akron." The former is slight but worth remarking, if only because it signals the point when the bridge as symbol enters Crane's poetry. Estador is a place of productive indecision where young visionaries engage in serious but inconsequential reflection on the sensuous career before them. The persona, with forced casualness ("Do not think too deeply, and you'll find / A soul, an element in it all"), yearns for a Keatsian life of sensations rather than one of thought, where unchecked desire leads to disclosures of suddenly novel beauties ("I had never seen a hand before"). The bridge is named, in fact, so as to reflect Crane's sense of verging on the brink of his experience: Estador, according to Brom Weber, is a nonce word meaning "he who views or measures," a significant fusion (in Spanish) of visionary distance and scientific accuracy. As for "Porphyro in Akron" (1921), it is an odd triptych. Section 1 shifts through layers of arch Poundian observations of American culture ("Akron, 'high place,'" the speaker ominously instructs us in line 10); section 2 comprises gossip about a Sunday afternoon among working-class immigrant families, with homemade applejack on the table and fiddlers at the front door; section 3 returns the reader to the room and the moment that launched the poem's recollection—and to the poet himself, reading *The Eve of Saint Agnes*, remembering a line of a French lullaby sung to him by his mother ("One summer day in a little town / Where you had started to grow" [47–48]), and pulling his sentimentally educated, dreaming self firmly back from the brink of yet more reverie, with the self-mothering advice that "in this town, poetry's a / Bedroom occupation" (60–61).

Both poems record failed self-enactments, though in the second the failure is cushioned by the softly allusive ironies of section 3. The quest of the persona, Keats's Porphyro, reproduces the phases of ritual initiations—a separation, a transformation, and a return—but just as poetry has become a bedroom occupation, the Romantic quester has left the monastery of his imagination to become a habitually self-effacing ironist: Porphyro has been Prufrocked. Throughout the poems comes the unmistakable impression of Crane's reading, the first two sections especially defaced by Imagist signatures. The taut comparison of the "shift of rubber workers" to muddy water is the kernel of the Imagist poem this started out to be; the backhanded pedantry of "Akron, 'high place'" and the flat diction and the looped-in dialogue of section 2 is all Pound. The clearest give-away is the poem's cadence. Set a quatrain of Crane's—

> And some Sunday fiddlers
> Roumanian business men,
> Played ragtime and dances before the door,
>   And we overpayed [*sic*] them because we felt like it

—beside one from Pound's "Salutation" (*Lustra: 1913–1915*)—

> And I am happier than you are,
> And they were happier than I am;
> And the fish swim in the lake
>   and do not even own clothing.

—and you hear in both the genial paratactic ironies of Pound's mid-career.

But Crane, who would never be a vernacularist and whose most robust attempts at common speech ("The River," for instance) are painful, suddenly adjusts himself in section 3 and begins to sound like the poet of *White Buildings*. "Pull down the hotel counterpane / And hitch yourself up to your book," he says, as though pinching himself. The cool apostrophic ironies and paratactic diction are gone, replaced by a rhetorical attitude that eventually matures into a lyrical signature: an attitude of *epideixis*, of impassioned invocation, a habit of emphatically *pointing* to what is beloved. Rather than attaching things through the gathering embrace of narration or by aggressive impersonations, his language reaches out and grabs them. One could compile an impressive list of his epideictic outbursts, or overreachings—from this poem through "Bind us in time, O seasons clear, and awe" ("Voyages II") to "Sheer over to the other side,—" ("The Idiot")—occasions when the poet shouts at the world, wakes it to his speaking. Epideictic speech is as old as poetry; its purpose, the acquisition of phenomena by naming them correctly, is also primal, and aligned with magical beliefs about vocables and "genetic" theories of language that Crane espoused. But maybe just as important is the impression this habit leaves on readers: they are lifted out of their reading as the poem is taken off the page, out of the realm of the literary into that of spoken or presentational arts like drama or oratory. The decisive distance between Crane's poetry and nearly every other Modernist's is hardly in its obscurities, which are circumstantial, or its textual allegiances, which are trivial, but in its elected modality, in its incredible musical intelligence.

Section 3's spiritual drift from Keats to the mother's recollected lullaby identifies, moreover, a mnemonic bent, a constant, and what I would suggest are the two enduring spiritual attractors of his life—Keats, a synechdoche for Romantic faith in imagination, and Crane's mother, Grace Hart Crane, a synechdoche for all women, whose varied appearances, from "the lounged goddess" Aphrodite of "Voyages VI" to the densely configured Anima of *The Bridge* (commencing with the Virgin Mary of "Ave Maria," through Pocahontas and ending conclusively with the unnamed universal mother of "Indiana"), stabilize context and connect memory and desire. Here it's probably not unwise to remark a climactic event at the outset of Crane's career, his decision to substitute for a conventionally masculine first name (Harold) his mother's maiden name (Hart) as his professional first name—abridging the father's presence and replacing it with the mother's. Crane punned freely and often on both the words *heart* and *grace* in his poetry.

Finally, there is the poem's organization. The moment of enabling insight is staged as an *antiphonal* exchange (though "staging" may mistake for strategy a mental instinct). These antiphonies happen at least in six of the twenty-three poems in *White Buildings*, each a conventionally framed first-person meditation that erupts into punctuated dialogue between Hart Crane and his better or recollected or experimental selves. The rhetorical is too closely fused with the structural habit to peel away; but, and without making much more of it, these antiphonal episodes are to Crane's epideictic habit what Pound's *ideographic* method in the *Cantos* is to the *one-image Imagist* poem—the former the structural outgrowth of the latter. Crane's direction, moreover, was determined less by theory than by the need of any twenty-four-year-old lyric poet putting together his first book: a stable point of view, a place to stand in his poetry. It's a requirement both more serious and demanding when the subject's poetic faith is being undermined by practical and theoretical models. Everywhere Crane looked he saw retreats into *personae*, personalities reassembled in exploded dramatic monologues like *The Waste Land* or *Mauberley*; in place of traditional "unmasked" lyricism were observational vantages from which personality could be satirized, ironized, objectified, or decomposed into the grounds of culture from which Eliot, for one, believed the self eventually sprang. For Crane, however, personality was not what it was for Eliot—an artifact of a decadent culture—but the ongoing competition between desire, which is innate, and memory, which is not. The antiphonal frame must have impressed Crane as a way of organizing the competition. Among these enactments of it are some humiliatingly trivial or failed ones ("North Labrador," "In Shadow"), but Crane elaborates the conflict between these priorities and alters the opposing terms until one reaches the most complicated version of the same debate, the poem "Passage." By the time this structural discovery became a structural habit or instinct, the ironic objectivity and sham "realism" of the early poems had disappeared along with the associated rhetorical strategies.

With rhetorical and structural departures from Modernism come thematic ones. "My Grandmother's Love Letters," one of the lesser pieces in *White Buildings*, takes place in an attic, where the recollected stars of Crane's youth introduce the spirit of the spot, Crane's maternal grandmother, Elizabeth, represented by the packet of letters referred to in the title. The disposition of natural details is peculiar:

> There are no stars tonight
> But those of memory.
> Yet how much room for memory there is
> In the loose girdle of soft rain.

The Pound who announced that "the natural object is the adequate symbol" thought he was ruling out daring, overly subjective reifications like the "stars of memory" or faintly ridiculous literalizations of such subjective moves as one finds in lines 3 and 4, where remembered stars replace those sealed off by the "loose girdle of soft rain" and the attic itself starts to seem *nearly* a symbol for whatever a girdle holds. But Crane takes his metaphors seriously: they are all that separate him from ambiguity and juxtapositional irony. Among the stronger of Crane's Keatsian meditations on the pressure of imagination on the objective world, the poem also contains an antiphonal exchange between Crane and his better self—

> "Are your fingers long enough to play
> Old keys that are but echoes:

> Is the silence strong enough
> To carry back the music to its source
> And back to you again
> As though to her?"

—and a disturbingly tender associative logic that forces images of absence and presence to succeed each other. Absent stars summon living memory's presence; memory descends from rain to "girdling" attic to the packet, whose disintegration is the grandmother's absence blurring into a spooky presence; and absence of sound—the silence in the attic—brings Crane into the poem in his own voice, a presence who educates silence with his grandmother's absence. The poem's relaxing at last into a musical metaphor, where the poet's fingering of the fragile letters is compared to the fingering of piano keys, is unembarrassedly sentimental, and Crane's attempt to guarantee some legitimacy ("Yet I would lead my grandmother *by the hand*, / Through much of what she would not understand") only makes the poem's ending a cleverly bittersweet, slightly gruesome, semantic pun. Still, what makes the poem unusual is how it interrogates not so much the object itself but its own imaginative strength. And given how his every encounter with common things stimulates a lapse from the purely representational into metaphor, this is obviously a poet who has already put some distance between his work and what he disclosed, to friends like Munson, to be his reading at the moment: Pound's "*Pavannes & Divisions*, T. S. Eliot, Maupassant and *The L[ittle] R[eview]*."

Four poems follow "My Grandmother's Love Letters" in *White Buildings*. "Praise for an Urn" is the poem that Blackmur singled out for its amiable clarity and New Critical paraphraseability; "Stark Major" (1923) is heavily indebted to *The Waste Land*, which we know Crane to have read by at least November 22, 1922. In both his prosody and selection of details—

> And she will wake before you pass
> Scarcely aloud, behind her door,
> And every third step down the stair
> Until you reach the muffled floor—

Crane is thinking of the assignation between Eliot's Typist ("home at tea time") and her Young Man Carbuncular. The other two are indifferent vers librist word-paintings. "Sunday Morning Apples" from one point of view might actually qualify as a minor Imagist success since its representational surface is spared the savage complications of metaphor. "Garden Abstract," which Tate's introduction called "the perfectly written piece of Imagism," is a mythic calculus with clear designs on the reader: a girl's reaching up for an apple superimposes modern spontaneity over the eternally human longing of Daphne, "[t]he wind possessing her, weaving her young arms / Holding her to the sky and its quick blue" (lines 8–9). All four poems admit in theme or form the double influences of Pound and Eliot; none is Crane at the peak of his strength.

But I single out for exception the too-little attended "Pastorale" (1921), a calculatedly dense, beautifully figured elegy of five free-verse quinzaines that begins by negating something:

> No more violets
> And the year
> Broken into smoky panels.
> What woods remember now
> Her calls, her enthusiasms.

The negation of violets (which recalls the negated stars of "My Grandmother's Love Letters") announces the Orphically "broken year," and given that the first three lines are, to make a point of grammar, a fragment, the opening constitutes a complicated syntactic pun. What is puzzling is the relationship between that which is absent (violets) or broken (time) and memory, whose presence in this and so many of Crane's poems is not always welcome. What is it, asks the unpunctuated question of lines 4–5, that *nature* (the woods) remembers? We think of the year, now three-quarters' old, and visualize a set of "smoky panels"; in other words, we see a quantifiably *human* rather than qualitatively *natural* wholeness. Yet unless the woods themselves "remember . . . / Her calls, her enthusiasms," the beloved will vanish into the routine products of human resource, like triptychs—and what could be more desperately unnatural, or artier, than "smoky panels"? Natural processes alone matter—only the summer, or the near-sentience of the season's graduation from smallness (violets) into largesse (leaves, the "fallen harvest" [13])—but nature's way of remembering is brutal:

> That ritual of sap and leaves
> The sun drew out,
> Ends in this latter muffled
> Bronze and brass . . .

Autumn, in a noisy compounding of color on texture, shows up all "bronze and brass," savaging the summer sun's gentle, ritual invitations of "sap and leaves" into the open air, turning the green into gold.

In the antiphonal exchange that follows Crane evaluates the worth of whatever "image" (i.e., poem) he may carry "beyond this / Already fallen harvest." But the evaluation is, typically in these exchanges with his better self, a scolding: "Fool— / Have you remembered too long." The implications of that earlier superimposition of "bronze and brass" over "sap and leaves" are decisive influences upon whatever it is that the poet imagines: imagination is chained to memory. Yet what Crane's speaker wants, at least here, is memory without art, Keats's "unheard melodies," not "bronze and brass" or the monument outlasting time; what he bears off is a memory, a copy of what he really desires, the living violets. As a critique of Classical aesthetic faith as well as for the way it questions its own Romantic nostalgia the poem is impressive, and impressively independent of local technical-thematic influences (Imagistic, mythic, allusive), but what makes it valuable is its sheer moral intelligence. Crane seems irritated nearly to the point of worry over his indulgence in Romantic pathos.

I want to emphasize this point because the poem's unfolding drama of imagination's sublime alienation from memory has huge implications. The poem originates in a need to reproduce the natural unity of living violets, in an acknowledgment that something like intelligence exists in nature; the poem ends on a note of irresolution, backhanding the original provocation, the need itself, as the outcome of jejune faith in that peculiar Romantic habit of projecting feeling into nature, but unable to believe in the "image" that it is, or the Classical art-faith that backs the image. The poem's refusal to solve the world back into unity, its stubborn thematic earnestness, makes it a work of Crane's maturity. He understands the implications of Romantic faith: to assume that *Nature feels*—or that the "woods remember"—is the onset of the Romantic illness whose name is narcissism and whose earliest symptom, Ruskin teaches us, is the pathetic fallacy. Narcissus, in fact, is precisely the namesake: he was punished not because he was caught admiring himself in a river but because in the act of self-reflection he *forgot* what he was looking at. The old story is not quite a homily against physical vanity; its gist is that any behavior that annihilates *human memory* leads to a chain-reaction of loss—of self-consciousness, of personality, of the human itself to the level of the bestial, vegetal, or elemental.

The instinct to personify that compels man, paraphrasing Coleridge, "to fill all nature with himself" is essentially a condition of alienated perception and is usually carefully controlled in canonical Modernism. Pound's "The apparition of these faces in the crowd; / Petals on a wet, black bough" keeps the elements it compares distinct and leaves them just where it found them; the poem is designed to function like a visionary tool and *not* to reproduce visionary rapture. Likewise, when Prufrock sees in the evening sky himself aenaesthetized, we're supposed to delight in his sad but ultimately dangerous personification of the natural world—so dangerous, in fact, that the mermaids refuse to sing to him in the end. Whenever Modernism encounters the instinct to personify the natural it replaces it with a technique—of objective correlatives, allusions, juxtaposed images, carefully adjusted ironies, and mythic double-takes—all substitution strategies that restore the "objective" distance between subject and object. By comparison, Crane's decision to dramatize the problem as a tragedy of alienated instinct is backed by a Keats and, I suspect, Emerson. "The greatest delight which the fields and woods minister is the suggestion of an occult relation between man and the vegetable," Emerson says in "Nature" (1849), adding with self-correcting wisdom, "it is certain that the power to produce this delight, does not reside in nature, but in man, or in a harmony of both." Crane, failing to restore the harmony, would continue to attack his failure. Note, too, that the statement of the outcome is *not* intellectual ironies disposed as sets of related images but pained oxymorons of feeling— Keats's "Cold pastoral!"; Coleridge's "positive Negation"; Crane's "Infinite consanguinity."

Crane's sensitivity to Romantic phenomenology—a sensitivity that went utterly unperceived by critics like Winters—is one of the subplots of *White Buildings*, and two of the book's most difficult, most vigorously discussed (and dismissed) poems, "Lachrymae Christi" and "The Wine Menagerie," are antiphonal meditations on it. "The Wine

Menagerie" is ultimately done in by the preciosity of its allusions (Shakespeare, Keats, Stravinsky, probably Tennyson) and its language ("Each chamber, transept, coins some squint, / Remorseless line, minting their separate wills"). To me the poem communicates only some of the coherence that the resourceful exegete, Sherman Paul, confers on it (though more "cumulative force" than was apparent to Marianne Moore, who ran it in *Poetry* only after cutting it back to nineteen lines). Yet it does extend Crane's meditation on how human consciousness can successfully migrate into the inhuman, and contains—along with some jawbreakers—the central statement of American Negative Capability:

> New thresholds, new anatomies! Wine talons
> Build freedom up about me and distil
> This competence—to travel in a tear
> Sparkling alone, within another's will.

Visionary "competence," a belief in a faith without alienating irony, is the saving distance from ambient Modernist skepticism as it is the sign of closeness to Keats.

Yet by that much it signals a huge and important distance from Wordsworth. Wordsworthian imagination is always, as Bloom has said, a compensation for the lost immediacy of experience:

> I gazed—and gazed—but little thought
> What wealth the show to me had brought.
>
> For oft when on my couch I lie
> In vacant or in pensive mood
> They flash upon the *inward eye*
> That is the bliss of solitude . . .

It's amazing how separate are the faculties of reception and retention, of *gazing* and *thinking*, in what is still the most cogent statement of Romantic skepticism. The joy comes only *after* the recollected daffodils "flash upon" imagination, our "inward eye." How oddly static, too, Wordsworth's metaphor appears, how thoroughly un-Coleridgean this image of dynamic processes where imagination seems reduced to a simple staging area. Nor would I overlook the family resemblance between imagination in Wordsworth and the same rationally disabled faculty of Eliot's "Prelude":

> You dozed, and watched the night revealing
> The thousand sordid images
> Of which your soul was constituted;
> They flickered against the ceiling.

Behind imagination's paralysis is nothing but despair, a sense of the "soul stretched tight across the skies / That fade behind a city block," and the gathering desire for imagination's redemption (or renunciation) that is realized in the *Four Quartets*. Like Wordsworth, Eliot is a rational skeptic when the issue is what the imagination can actually *do*, and if the grandfather of the one's qualified joy and the other's unqualified despair is David Hume ("The most lively thought is still inferior to the dullest sensation"), past the melancholy fact of deferred pleasure is the potentially more unhinging one that we are *never fully conscious*, no matter how steadily or how long we gaze and gaze at the daffodils. All of which leaves Wordsworth weighing the disproportionate power of memory, which recovers the daffodils, and imagination, which makes them dance; it leaves Eliot weighing the value of poetry and culture against religion and sanctifying grace.

That Wordsworth equivocates over the stature of memory and imagination (which he also calls "fancy") interests me only inasmuch as Eliot inherits his attitude; that Keats's poetry is a constant courtroom where their status is arbitrated is of greater interest, for Keats—far more than Blake—seems to have been Crane's early spiritual guide. Yet though an inheritor of Keats's dilemma, Crane is always, and always impatiently, making an act of faith in imagination:

> Distinctly praise the years, whose volatile
> Blamed bleeding hands extend and thresh the height
> The imagination spans beyond despair,
> Outpacing bargain, vocable and prayer.

Crane, even more radically, declares the instinctive complement of imagination to be *physical*, amorous desire; Crane believed, moreover, that we could become fully conscious through imagination, whose logic was "the genetic basis of all speech, *hence consciousness* and thought-extension" (my italics). Thus here ("For the Marriage of Faustus and Helen") imagination, personified in Faustus, rescues memory or the past, personified by Helen, whom the Erasmian ironist with the "bleeding hands" and plodding Classical intelligence gets only in translation.

Imagination in Crane's poetry is forever running back to the body, to sensuous love; for if one way of avoiding narcissism is to surround the imagination in God as Coleridge did, another is to identify God with nature, embrace pantheism, and thus credit nature with an intelligence that is at least safely inhuman. Winters recognized the implications of Crane's choice and saw only "a void." Crane, indeed, is credited with a critical intelligence probably less than any poet except Shelley (though for essentially the same reasons), yet the record of his verse constitutes an astonishing insight into poetic choices and the morality, if one may call it that, of metaphor. His poetry is a constant, powerful unpacking of the content of Romantic subjectivity, weighing the value of what imagination knows, which is not a fixity, against the given imaginative act, which may or may not take the fixed shape of a poem.

I mention Shelley, but again it is Keats who compels Crane to frame issues of poetic priority, at times antiphonally, as competitions between imagination or desire and the faculty of memory. Memory's contents are brakes on desire, negations of nature (violets, stars), or possessions, like the "record" of "Paraphrase," violently "wedged in the soul": both the personal and historical "record" of a species whose descent into pure natural death is "systematic," terrifying, and cyclic, the context even teases out of the word suggestions of needles stuck in *phonograph records*. Positioned at the end of the poem between recollection and desire ("A few picked, the rest dead"), the same metaphorical logic forces us gloomily to reposition the violets of "Pastorale" between life as it is lived, "fallen harvests" of "picked" violets known to memory, and life as imagination verifies it, life known to desire, whose issue here is a starkly dead remainder ("the rest dead"). Memory looks backward to the products that desire wants to escape; desire looks forward to an endless, self-propelled career of successive embodiments. Neither one wants, or is worth much without, the other.

Out of the crisis of the helpfully titled "Passage," Crane's most Keatsian allegory of moral alienation, Crane emerged fully conscious. Or perhaps fully *self-conscious*: what he would bring to his work from this point on was that reflexiveness of language which strains critical patience and understanding. I've noted so far certain habits of enactment Crane had got into: the antiphonal habit is an index of honesty, of a curiosity and sincerity about technique. Another, also an outgrowth of his profound faith in the world, is the epideictic habit of addressing it as though it were an erotic object. With "Passage" a third thing enters his work: a habit of intuiting the psychic truths within his own personifications. He becomes less involved with Romantic mythology and, growing in strength, more implicated in sketching his own.

It opens peremptorily: a two-line gesture to the cedar leaf, the sky, and the sea, and then this couplet: "In sapphire arenas of the hills / I was promised an improved infancy." Harold Bloom, who finds in *sapphire* a pointer to the far more confident enlisting of the past, "Repose of Rivers," asks us to consider whether there is "a more outrageously American, Emersonian concept and phrase than 'an improved infancy.'" The phrase is an intersection of associations, from Keats's "life of sensations rather than of thought" through Emerson's "plantations of God" to Verlaine's *la vie opportune* ("Claire de Lune"): it is the Romantic promise of unific perception organized within what Frank Kermode calls "the Romantic *rêve*." But the hoped-for improvement is a lie—or at least an invitation to the conflict announced in the next line: "My memory I left in a ravine." Insectiform ("Casual louse"), memory is denied the mobility it gains from its host—desire itself—and mopes around, enthusiastically parasitic. This is typical of Crane, who will always assign memory a psychological location inferior to the one given desire, the parent of imagination.

The allegory of memory and desire begins to complicate itself in the next stanza, where Crane's mythic self is discovered among "the entrainments of the wind," a phrase charged with positive significance. The wind, for one thing, is the agency of change, in which it participates yet from which it is always distinct; hence its significance for Crane, as for Shelley, for whom it is *the* image of poetic voice. In "The Broken Tower" (1932) the wind is identified with "the visionary company of love," which Crane pursues:

> And so it was I entered the broken world
> To trace the visionary company of love, its voice
> An instant in the wind (I knew not wither hurled)
> But not for long to hold each desperate choice.

Voice, Crane urges us to consider, is a weird grafting of the human on the elemental; to join the wind's *entrainments* (or entourage), of which the visionary company is one, means risking *voice*, which is permanently human but lasts only "an instant" in our desire to join what is perfectly, eternally elemental and achieve that "improved infancy." Desire wins and all the warnings—summer's burning into fall, the shadows spilling into and elongating his own, and most ominously, the odorless evaporation of the rain in his grotesquely monumental cheeks, "bronze gongs"— are ignored. Everything points to oncoming change, trouble and sterility. Even the wind gives warning:

> "It is not long, it is not long;
> See where the red and black
> Vine-stanchioned valleys—"; but the wind
> Died speaking through the ages that you know
> And hug, chimney-sooted heart of man!

This could be Crane's response to Shelley's question at the end of "Ode to the West Wind": though spring is close behind, it will not last. Nothing does. The sudden wind-borne message wakes up consciousness: stay and die into inconscient nature; return and live the life of agonized consciousness. With its power, both physical and vatic, doubled, the wind assumes the role of the poetic agent of resolution: the paralyzed narcissist is "turned about and back, much as your smoke / Compiles a too well known biography" (21–22), a beautifully understated imaging of crematory smoke—a conclusively biographical form of sky-writing—on the poet's powerless "turning" from a life of sensation back toward the *paideia* of memory. The trip back to the ravine where memory was dumped in line 6 reveals a chastened landscape and evokes one of the most astonishing distiches in all of Crane: "The evening was a spear in the ravine / That throve through very oak" (23–24). The phrase ramifies: *throve*, past tense of *thrive* (and grotesquely homophonic of *throw*), may refer exclusively to the ravine, i.e., as a *thriving hole* that swallows up the oak's very wholeness; but I think the even more likely representational core here is the acuminated shadow of *an oak* lain like a tossed spear along the bed of a ravine. (The complexity of the figure becomes nearly rabbinical once you admit an allusion to the stars that threw down their spears in Blake's "Tyger." One can see why R. W. B. Lewis was led to cite Blake as Crane's major precursor.) The metaphor is a powerful synechdoche for what experience without recognition amounts to as well as the consequences of memory's recovery: nature (the oak tree) humiliated by nothing (ravine) or by one of its denatured *variora* (darkness, a spear)—signs of the loss of natural innocence.

The poem's third, unmarked phase is the return to chronological awareness, to aging. Desire, beaten or reeducated by its rejection of memory, now joins the allegorical antiphony that begins at line 26. The speaking self addresses memory, "A thief, my stolen book in hand," hiding beneath the heavily symbolic laurel tree:

> "Why are you back here—smiling an iron coffin?"
> "To argue with the laurel," I replied:
> "Am justified in transience, fleeing
> Under the constant wonder of your eyes—."

Memory's question is arrogantly paternalistic; desire's reply is adolescently flip and hyperbolic. The contest is over which configuration of psychic energies—backwarding memory or forwarding desire—will claim poetic priority, that stolen book. After two more lines the dialogue breaks off. Memory shuts the book, an apocalypse of consciousness buries both faculties "in a glittering abyss," and a serpent heads sunward, its ascent paired with its descent upon "unpaced beaches," where it leans its tongue and drums, its doubled motions signing the restoration of the competing human faculties to tragic but necessary doubleness. At last the poem can end:

> What fountains did I hear? what icy speeches?
> Memory, committed to the page, had broke.

I can think of no better image for the whole Modernist-Romantic agon than this Punch-and-Judy face off between suicidally principled memory and sensuously flirtatious desire. Memory's instrumentalist obsession with *written* record ("to the page") leads to the ultimate quasi-Biblical breakings of line 37, while desire looks on, incomplete, waiting for another flight into "transience." The poem ends almost exactly where it began—on a note of irresolution and division ("Where the cedar leaf divides the sky").

The title points to several *passages*: the psychological rite of passage the poem enacts; desire's textual-allegorical journey from innocence through chastened narcissism; most suggestively, the written passage from which recollection cannot rise without ending the dialogue—a point of interpretation I will return to momentarily. But the poem's most forceful recognition is that the relationship of historical memory to living desire is a perpetual competition. This recognition blocks our passing successfully from innocence to experience here or elsewhere:

Crane, striking off his own Romantic difference from Blake, must have understood that the implication of any such "successful" crossing is the essential completion (i.e., exhaustion) of desire itself, or literal death, which to the believer Blake was the onset of life. Such Blakean success, from the point of view of Crane's poem, is failure. Crane has begun to define the terms for his fabulous "allegories of rhetoric," to borrow Lee Edelman's phrase: desire, which leads us out of history into the unprecedented selfhood of "an improved infancy," enthusiastically androgynous, and essentially good; and memory, which is almost always a *male* principle in Crane's poetry, inevitably parasitic, always a drag on poetic enthusiasm.

From Crane's maturing idiom, moreover, "Passage" deletes the Modernist emphases. This and subsequent poems like it define the "visionary and apocalyptic" Hart Crane, whose "tortured complexities" will obliterate the pale literalist of "Praise for an Urn" and cause such trouble for New Critics looking for paraphrasable cores. "Passage" has to be read as a piece of developmental history, as one more entry in Crane's total mythology of desire. What's more, given the reciprocity of idiom and context, any historical or thematic decontextualizing renders the poem unreadable. The New Criticism's opening gambit was, of course, to decontextualize. That critics indisposed to credit (though empowered to evaluate) Crane's work had already discredited an entire dimension of referential significance—his Romantic debt—itself becomes critical in understanding what Crane is up to precisely in the period beginning around 1922, following his reading and rejection of Eliot's "philosophical pessimism" and the purge from his own prosody of the worrisome strategies of Modernism. He found his voice in the passage from the elliptical logic of Modernist irony to the passionately synoptic, metaphorical logic of his own neoromanticism. Given the climate, in gaining his voice Crane would logically have alienated his audience.

Crane shares some of the blame; another passage the poem makes is from relative simplicity to a complexity of syntax and diction that is enough to raise worrisome charges—of obfuscation, or simple sloppiness. Take line 36 and 37 of "Passage": "What fountains did I hear? what icy speeches? / Memory, committed to the page, had broke." Do we accuse Crane of using *broke* as a nonstandard past participle, or should I read lines 36 and 37 as I have—a compound interrogative object of *broke*? My sense of the line: the faculty of memory, its concentration invested solely in the instrumentality of writing and in fixed expressions of desire, "broke"—perhaps even "broke off"—"what[ever]" lasting impressions of "fountains" and "icy speeches" we bring down from Helicon or Mt. Sinai. Chastening as it is that Werner Berthoff, a brilliant and unapologetic explicator, reads line and poem differently, the grammatical exigency that admits *broke* as a conventional past participle stumps me. Nor am I reluctant to admit the presence of slang (if that is what it is) or some residual Clevelandism. My reading requires the noun-clause adjustment in part because I sense in the fountains and the icy speeches artifacts of Crane's reading in the English Romantics: the fountains come from the neighborhood around Kubla's pleasure dome; the "icy" speeches concentrate the gist of Keats's "Cold pastoral!" Thus the poem is an allegory of reading, and the "thief" is tradition masked as memory, the primary or collective memory that Eliot describes (under the mask of *tradition*) in "Tradition and the Individual Talent." The secondary echo in the finite, so to speak, of collective memory is personal memory, and in Crane it is dominated by associations with his father, on whom he blamed the wreck of his adolescence and his "sundered parentage." If the past as memory already knows us, our personality, driven by mothering desire, will always be "fleeing / Under the constant wonder of [our father's] eyes"; our originality will be a mere authorized representative (at times hired assassin) for collective history. The point is not personal ingenuity but the extent to which rhetorical miracles to one are muddles to others, circumstantial obscurities to me are willed obfuscations to Blackmur.

Not to be obtuse, but what does it mean for the poet to "sanction the sun" (line 5)? Is the word conditioned by the resonance of *sulking* so that it has the meaning we give to *sanctions passed against* another? Or is the correct reading Hazo's altogether different one, which detects a note of "renascence, purification, 'renewed [*sic*] infancy,'" and sees the poet's "sanctioning" of the sun as an *affirmation* and, in the "thief," sees death itself. And what about the distribution of cedars, oaks, and laurels along desire's route? Is it ranked or random? "To argue with the laurel" seems a clear statement of what poets do in their competition with Apollo, but the divided cedars and humiliated oaks look too rhetorically out of position to point to Greek myth, and source-hunters get no help from the immediate context. Cases like "Passage," in fact, where hauntingly allusive stuff gets absorbed into dense transumptive figures, constitute *essential* breaks with Modernist practice; cases like this define the characteristic anxiety of an audience trained to read *The Waste Land* and *Mauberley* and for whom, to paraphrase Johnson, there was always an appeal open from art to the reader's education. For though typically elliptical, a Modernist allusion guarantees ultimate accessibility to anyone with the intelligence or cultivation to "work it out"; poems are "impersonal" as crossword puzzles, "self-subsistent" (Leavis's word) microcultures that satisfy the cultural demand that art be meaningful. Crane takes a different tack; his use of myth is altogether idiosyncratic, hence subversive of meaningfulness, and unproductive of the sort of Wintersian moral clarities associated with the shared cultural objectives of the Modernist's mythic method.

The so-called Modernist mythic vision, last, often involves a form of what Alan Wilde calls *absolute irony*, where ambiguity is stilled into irresolution; such irony can take the reduced form of an image, a visual oxymoron where unlike objects are juxta- or "super-positioned," or a grander, structural form where the explicit connections between large narrative neighborhoods (sections of *The Waste Land*, chapters of *Ulysses*, the component lyrics of the *Cantos*) are suppressed. But Crane, again, was temperamentally incapable of being an ironist, something that Elizabeth Drew observed fifty years ago when with smartly worded accuracy she noted "his exasperating combination of the meritorious and the meretricious." The "penniless rich" palms of the sea that review (or *superscribe*) the waves, obediently "bent" as they strike the beach ("Voyages II"), are as wittily ironic as Hart Crane gets. Most decisively, his textual cruxes are not products of elliptical strategies but of a synoptic instinct that dismisses as inessential all differences. What "source-studies," then, of a poetics whose purpose is exactly to transcend rather than to analyze (Pound), ridicule (Joyce), or redeem (Eliot) the origins from which poetry itself wants to awake? What source-study when there is no "source"? A synoptic or transumptive poetic, whatever its purpose, leaves a traceless "theft," whereas as the inherent wisdom (and moral purpose) of a Modernist elliptical (juxtapositional, paratactic, imagistic) procedure is precisely never to leave the scene of the crime. Hence, a typically Modernist textual move, for example, such as the rhymed polyglot puns of section 3 of Pound's *Mauberley*—

> O bright Apollo,
> τίν' ἄνδρα, τίν' ἥρωα, τίνα θεόν,
> What god, man, or hero
> Shall I place a tin wreath upon?

makes us forget our originality and remember the cultural and historical realities to which our educations are mortgaged; it implies that to a
praise a poet is to praise our own ingenuity. Notice how Pound's quatrain, like living geography, phonically reacts to the imported lines from
Pindar and the drama of historical discontinuity that Pound is staging.
Massimo Baciagalupo has named "brutally mimetic" the way a Modernist text *remembers* things.

Discussions of the material origins of Crane's work, on the other
hand, are like comparisons of acorns and oak trees. To contrast any
Modernist's treatment of nature with any of Crane's is an education in
competing sensibilities.

> The sun beats lightning on the waves,
> The waves fold thunder on the sand . . .

These two lines from "Voyages I" make what I have always regarded,
since I first read them at age seventeen, as a perfect distich. All four
humors or elements—earth (sand), air (thunder), fire (the sun, the
lightning), and water—are compressed with majestic concentration,
neither "intellectual" nor "mythic," yet positively overwhelming.
Their power is such that exegesis may not know where to stop: the
succession of details, like the process they describe, is interconnected,
panoptic, even cyclic; the viewed totality is a huge descending gesture
(sun to water to shore) toward conflict (lightning and thunder), music
(the sun *beats* the water as one might beat a drum, and synaestheti-
cally the percussion produces brilliant light), and even food (*beating*
and *folding*). Restore the prosodic context, moreover, and the ear
hears

> And in answer to their treble interjections
> The sun beats lightning on the waves,
> The waves fold thunder on the sand

a loosely iambic alexandrine contracting sharply into a pair of eight-syl-
lable lines that retain their iambic identities because all that freight of
long vowels (*beats, lightning, waves*) and consonantal accents (su*n*,

thu*nd*er, light*ning*) works like a drag-chute. The power, moreover, is not on the order of that which was often thought but ne'er so well expressed. It is not that no poet ever *wrote* this way before Hart Crane but that no one has ever *thought* of natural processes the way he did. This is not to dispraise good technique or "good writing," but to invoke what I regard was at the core of Crane's poetics: a conviction that the poetic shape of an idea *is* at once "idea," or thought, and feeling. And nothing else quite like this conviction exists in the core curricula of Modernist poetics, which embraces an analytic lyricism of infinite discrimination but retreats from such connectedness, such "infinite consanguinity."

Crane's poetic theory was not entirely without precedent, however, something that Allen Tate spotted and encoded in his still sturdy introduction to *White Buildings*, mainly in three smart references to Baudelaire. I want to confirm Tate's intuition and suggest some of Baudelaire's importance to Crane by accessing one of the primary texts of French Symbolism, "Correspondences." I quote the first quatrain only:

> La Nature est un temple où de vivants piliers
> Laissent parfois sortir de confuses paroles;
> L'homme y passe à travers des forêts de symboles
> Qui l'observent avec des regards familiers.

The poem is about *connections*: Baudelaire's perception is different from the ordinary person's in that he senses in nature a realm of eternal correspondences, sensuous essences that reproduce themselves in ways that seem chaotic to most but that to him cohere profoundly. Nature is a resource of symbols both hieratic ("La Nature est un temple") and demotic ("L'homme y passe à travers des forêts de symboles") that Baudelaire says, lines later, encode "une ténébreuse et profonde unité," a "shadowy and profound order." Now here is Crane's opening to "Voyages II":

> —And yet this great wink of eternity,
> Of rimless floods, unfettered leewardings,
> Samite sheeted and processioned where
> Her undinal vast belly moonward bends,
> Laughing the wrapt inflections of our love;

That "great wink of eternity" issues from a clearly Baudelairean sense of corresponding values human and natural, brought into concord and orchestrated only by the poet possessed of the genius to allegorize the connection between humanity and nature. The sea that *winks* is communicating a shared secret (*eternity*) to the poet in his hieratic role as glimpser of eternity; at the same time the sea is *eternity winking* at anyone who passes by, who is open to these promiscuous glimpses "of eternity." The fourth line (which the late John Logan butchered in his preface) is a metonymic statement of the poet's penetration of nature's corresponding human form, the analogue to its eternal nature: of the sea's anatomy (*belly*), curvaciousness *(undinal*, literally "wave-like"), responsiveness (it *bends*), fecundity (the whole image suggests pregnancy), and gender. Speak the line aloud and it yields even more "senses." The line spoken *is* the living synthesis that Crane must have had in mind when he spoke of a "synthetic conviction of form and creation."

Crane's poetry has left behind it a history of defeated explications that has, at times curiously, become part of its author's too well known biography. A single line from "Lachrymae Christi," "Thy Nazarene and tinder eyes," and the stanza that succeeds it—

> (Let sphinxes from the ripe
> Borage of death have cleansed my tongue
> Once and again . . .

drove Blackmur, whose analysis crashes and burns after two pages, to insist coyly that Crane, "a great failure," demands that "we must make allowances for him," and even to raise the question of "duplicity," which Blackmur with even greater coyness identifies with what he terms "Crane's fundamental attitudes toward his work." And whether Cowley's description of Crane's compositional fury is related to what Blackmur means by "fundamental attitudes"—the poet gets drunk, disappears into an adjoining room, storms around and declaims poems, types in time with the record player—it notches a shared impression of Crane as a visionary drunk of occasional genius. Philip Horton, in a passage Hazo quotes approvingly, had company when he implied that Crane's suicide was the morally inevitable outcome and "violent issue of" a life of "debauchery"; likewise Hazo, who on the same page (and with far less respect for psychological complexity) factors a talk-show insight into his own condemnation of Crane's "dissipation."

I have already admitted that the difficulties, grammatical, syntactical, and lexical, are not always trivial. Like every true believer in Crane I have a top-ten list of brain- or jawbreakers: along with violations of idiom (*broke* for *broken*), fits of synaesthetic delirium ("Until my blood dreams a receptive smile"), strained allusions ("Holofernes' shins"), strained circumlocutions ("Above the feet the clever sheets / Lie guard upon *the integers of life*"), lame apostrophes ("O Darkly Bright," "O Materna!"), boneheaded puns ("And where was finally *borne* a chosen hero"), and unhelpful ambiguities ("But now there are challenges to *spring* / In that ripe nude with head / reared"), mine includes most of the "Cape Hatteras" section of *The Bridge*, all of "Voyages IV," and passages of pure mud like the damnably dense

> Immaculate venom binds
> The fox's teeth, and swart
> Thorns freshen on the year's
> First blood. From flanks unfended

from "Lachrymae Christi." And often when critical genius rescues Crane's more difficult poems from potentially crippling ambiguity commonsense can dissent, wondering if the work has been interpreted or invented. Not incidentally, Crane knew his work was hard to understand. In a moving letter to Tate (March 14, 1927), the context of which was "the subject of OBSCURITY" and the reputation that Crane had already earned for incomprehensibleness, Crane admits,

There is no place left for *our* kinds of minds or emotions. Unless we can pursue our futilities with some sort of constant pleasure there is little use in going on—and we must apprehend some element of truth in our mock ceremonies or even our follies aren't amusing.

Justifying his difficult poetry is the simple need to "go on" with a project inherently futile, and mocking the impossible goal of appealing to "the panting bosom of the generous reader" is his poetry's oddly validating density, inbred structural logic, and borrowings. But it is going too far, is in fact obfuscating, to accuse Crane of "duplicity" (Blackmur) or "obscurantism" (Winters). Crane's goal—full self-embodiment *in* language, a fully achieved secular *immanence* that is the opposite of the transcendence associated with Eliot, even Keats or Whitman—

accounts for his frustrated outcries as well as his critics' and others' stumped by the poems.

Let me acknowledge critical dissent of a different character, born in the moral anxieties of critics who saw his self-destructive behavior as the evil twin of a genius bedeviled into meanings of inordinate difficulty. As soon as attempts to get beneath the poems founder, it is not unusual to find the critic using failure as an excuse to go "beneath the myth"—that phrase is the title of the final chapter of Hazo's study—and blaming the defeat of rational interpretation on Crane's "vices," among which some, like Hazo, mention his "deviant" sexual orientation. Hazo and Horton, for instance, moralize a good deal about Crane's bad habits; neither is sympathetic, and both smell dissipation behind the opacities. Even the sympathetic critics, moreover, tend to cover their tails with high-handed correctives: "The thirty-three years of Hart Crane's troubled life were not sufficient to develop the genius that was within him," says the author of this high school textbook headnote. "[Crane's] emotional disintegration resulted from psychological disturbances probably personal in origin rather than reflections of the spiritual disillusionment which prevailed among the literary generation of the First World War." The diagnosis surgically separates Crane's "emotional disintegration" from Eliot's grander spell of "spiritual disillusionment," code for "nervous breakdown." Crane, in other words, was probably just an old-fashioned mess, whereas Eliot came down with a bad case of *impersonal* spiritual influenza.

The less kind assessments are Horton's, Hazo's, Spears's, and Cowley's (drunkenness, sexual excess), the last dragging his out through several interminably similar volumes of Panglossian recollections. Spears's monograph, whatever its acceptance of the poetry (which still seems somehow grudging), punishes the poetry for the excesses of the poet: according to Spears, Crane, or "St. Hart the Homintern Martyr," is an irrational contagion thankfully "disinfected by the passage of time." Weber seems the first to have argued that the binges followed Crane's loss of poetic faith, not vice versa. Crane's deterioration, Weber writes, had origins in the poetic crisis of his maturity, when he, "like Whitman, had turned away from capitalist materialism and found hope . . . in the concept of a spiritual democracy." Crane's loss of spiritual faith, like Keats's after *Hyperion*, came when *The Bridge* failed to attract wide acceptance. And finally there is Unterecker. More in love with the poet than his poetry, he evades the poems' difficulty but tends to support Weber's view that Crane had died as a poet before his suicide.

A new generation of critics (Berthoff, Edelman, Grossman, and others) finds the poetry no less difficult, and not only concedes the difficulties but validates them. In turn, it has become far more apparent how starkly, literally uncouth a genius Crane was, and especially to what extent the obscurity is the offspring of his theories about language. There is only one coherent theoretical description outside his correspondence, the essay "General Aims and Principles" (1926). In it Crane announces that a "logic of metaphor," his desideratum, is the "organic principle . . . which antedates our so-called pure logic, and . . . is the genetic basis of all speech, hence consciousness and thought-extension." He cites Shakespeare, Baudelaire, Rimbaud, Donne, and Blake, but behind this exalting of poetic power the theoretical godfather is Coleridge's theistic model of the imagination, which Coleridge calls, in the *Biographia*, "the echo in the finite" of God's act of speaking creation into being. To protect us, Coleridge organized our imaginations inside the infinitely creative Imagination—the originating *I AM*—of God: that way the self would radiate *outward*, this radiating being the self's consciousness of something bigger than it or its productions and driven by a longing for completion in God.

Crane of course departs from Coleridge, and starkly: imagination for Crane is not a *property* of consciousness but, or so the phrase "the genetic basis of all speech" suggests, is consciousness itself in the act of *reproducing itself* in language: "It is as though a poem gave the reader . . . a single, new *word*, never before spoken and impossible to actually enunciate, but self-evident as an active principle in the reader's consciousness." What an extraordinary claim. The poet becomes conscious within language's prerational, organic, and culturally indifferent consciousness of itself. What so troubled the poets of Modernism—the poet's role in society, in culture, its cognitive value—Crane resolves by an act of faith in metaphor. We became rationally conscious *of* words, he implies, either through or, more likely, after we came to consciousness *in* words. Metaphor, the bedrock of language, is the foundation on which reason and logic repose. Edelman paraphrases it this way: "In the beginning was neither word nor world, but the rhetorical logic of association that would call forth and shape them both." Consciousness is mothered by metaphor into the material world; conscious, rational speech is a kind of granddaughter.

> Nature is the incarnation of a thought, and turns to a
> thought again, as ice becomes water and gas. The
> world is mind precipitated.
> —Emerson, "Nature" (1849)

The grander implications of this strange theology of language—it has no analogue in twentieth-century American poetry that I know of— need spelling out. Its most uncanny requirement is a total belief in language as a physical medium for spiritual embodiment; if its final purpose was the incarnation of human identity in poetry, its formal purpose was that desire itself might not transcend but become *immanent in poetry*, one immediate result of which is renewed attention to poetry's presentational value, which Modernism's infatuation with semiotics has taught us to ignore. As John Yeats wrote to William Yeats, there is no critic like the memory, and nowhere else in the century do we find an American poetry equal to Crane's in its ability to apprehend some of the sensuous truth behind the words we name the world with. Not a line of his is not voice-centered; so very often one leaves it having gained a sense of what Berthoff named its "felt continuity," a sense that one has gained sensuous knowledge that outlasts understanding and precludes exegesis.

The problem is that aesthetic knowledge since Plato has always made way for the later *reinclusion* of exegetical intelligence because poetry's cognitive value has always been arbitrated by cultures. Since at the cultural level Crane's poetry is most ancient, even primal, what Crane called "the Word made flesh" would preempt cultural arbitration. If a poet's typical goal is the communication of meanings of things that exist outside of language through manipulations of language itself, Crane's goal, or so we could describe it, is to reverse this direction— even while understanding that failure to reinscribe the intelligence of the culture in the poem is tantamount to the assertion that there is no meaning, perhaps no identity, outside of poetry. This may be the most disturbing implication of the theory: that we have no life outside of language. Arguably, it is the greatest measure of the distance between

Crane and his master, Whitman. When Whitman declared that "creeds and schools" were to stand "in abeyance," he was not just preparing a creative shelter for his identity by making room for the "Me myself" who materializes from the pages of the book we read. Of the "Me myself," he says early on that it *stands apart* (*Song of Myself*, section 4) and later, that it "stops somewhere waiting for you" (52). Whitman also insists that the "meanings of poems" won't be found in books; the affiliation of book-learning and knowledge is spectral, and only weak cultural egos, hybrids of conscience and feeling, have their lives in texts. Whitman thought of himself, and maybe of the rest of us, as more than that:

> Speech is the twin of my vision, it is unequal to measure
> itself,
> It provokes me forever, it says sarcastically,
> *Walt you contain enough, why don't you let it out then?*

The Me myself cannot be measured because it always *wants out* of the materials that would embody it.

Yet Crane sought precisely such a sheltering identity: language in its fully embodied immanence, what he called, stealing a Roman Catholic reference to Christ, "the Word made flesh." There is exasperating rightness, therefore, in Winters's epigrammatic put-down of Crane as "a saint of the wrong religion." Crane, to borrow from Werner Berthoff, in the most literal sense is a *profane* poet, and *White Buildings* a profane gospel, a transumption of the Word of John. Crane may have recognized, uneasily, all that his inverted religiosity implied; one never satisfactorily explained dimension of his poetry is its religious allusiveness. To bring language fully to consciousness as though words were self-regarding intellections, "eidolons" that forget their origins in the things of the world, required daimonic faith in the spell-casting properties of language. His whole project—connectedness, not correlations, "infinite consanguinity," not knowledge that rules out forgiveness—was to further poetry's participation in our creaturehood, to occupy the body of language as spirit occupies flesh. Edelman makes the point pontifically:

Beyond the interconnected exigencies of remembrance and dismemberment, then, Crane's poetry achieves its "transmemberment of song" by virtue of a catachrestic extravagance that carries him always toward a new beginning—the "improved infancy" [of] "Passage."

A complete originality *is* an improved infancy, where we avoid the condemnation of having had fathers, real or poetic, and where deliberate violations suddenly become authorized usage. Crane's apparent obfuscations are in part the playing out of philosophical anxieties clearly religious in character.

Even if we address Crane's obscurities as what happens when imagination abandons heuristics for charismatics, they cannot be entirely explained. Dembo's enthusiastic claim, for instance, that "Crane is fundamentally not nearly so difficult a poet as Rimbaud or Thomas" does, I admit, hold a kerneled truth: that in the best of Hart Crane there is always something seen or felt, what Berthoff calls a solid representational core. On the other hand, what troubles lovers of his most troublesome poems is how the most perversely clever exegesis of the *poetry* often fails to get the *poem* to refer to more than itself. The music is so sensuously self-regarding it preempts occasional or circumstantial fitness: hence Eliot, and not Crane, is quoted at cocktail parties. Crane's poems want wholly, like Wordsworth's daffodils, to participate in the world—and he in them—so a reader ends up stunned by a sensuousness that only successive acts of the reader's imagination can, transposing Eliot's terminology, "catalyze." I imagine that Crane wanted it this way. "Praise for an Urn," where referentiality is inevitable (and obscurity impossible), a poem Blackmur overpraises before proceeding with attacks on others, concludes with peculiar self-disgust: "Scatter these well-meant idioms / Into the smoky spring that fills / The suburbs." Though I am not suggesting that a poem's lack of obscurity meant a poetic failure, with Crane "comprehensibility" hardly qualifies as a poetic success. The "well-meant idioms" that easily surrender their meanings belong to "suburban" sensibilities to whom words are the ashes of meaning. He wanted, to poach a line from an unfinished manuscript, to carry "invention / to the brink of intelligibility," where the central gist is the star seen only out of the corner of your eye, alive on the margins of rational disclosure. "What it enacts," Berthoff says of his poetry, "is a certain state of mind," outside of which the poem remains as incomprehensible as a burning bush to those who have eyes but are deaf to the voice within it.

In his *White Buildings* phase Hart Crane represents one of the extremes of American self-consciousness: an essentially Romantic imagination attempting to embody twentieth-century themes in twentieth-century forms. At the other extreme, implicitly, is the canonical Modernism he departs so drastically and continuously from in his early work. Crane's later work represents an even more bizarre departure. Because he embraced the traditional formalism that Modernism rejects, Crane ended by producing a poem that claims the major technical resources of Modernism, including some semiotic ones, while recovering the traditional technical resources of English prosody. The doubly alienated position that *The Bridge* occupies, without exploring the poem itself, is worth indexing.

In *In Defense of Reason* (1947) Winters attacked *The Bridge* by charging Crane with an ideological sin. "Most of Crane's thought," he says in the second paragraph, "derives from Whitman." Swept toward Whitman meant capture by Emerson, then conversion to the insane Romantic religion where change is "glorified" for change's sake and man abandons Reason, the source of the moral foundations of his institutions. The charge has substance. Crane's work is informed by Emerson and Whitman's enthusiasm for the physical. In Crane's enthusiasm Winters penetrated what is less *idea* than *creed*, whose central emphasis is upon the "glorification of change as change." This emphasis "we can find likewise . . . in Whitman; it is one of the most important ideas of *The Bridge*":

It should be observed that the glorification of change as change is a necessary part of a system in which every act is good, in which there is no way to choose between courses of action, in which there is no principle of consistency, and in which there is no conception of a goal other than to be automatically controlled from moment to moment.

Winters gives us his version of Yeats's charge against Shelley—Crane "lacked the vision of evil"—and makes it with crisp self-assurance, reproaching Crane for a failure of moral, then poetic, imagination. No sane poet would undergo a conversion to Emerson's Romantic religion and then undertake an epic celebration of twentieth-century America educated by what Winters called, with deep seriousness, the "[Henry] Adams-Eliot theory of Modern Art."

Even overlooking quibbles over terms (*system, idea*) and logical accuracy, what strikes one first is Winters's incapacitation before Crane's Romantic difference. It is no wonder that he introduces a confusion that is his and not Crane's into his reading; he assumes the poem's transitions are wild and woolly applications of "change for change's sake," mistakes its central synecdoche for "an unrestrained pun," and ignores its craft. He propounds charges: Crane "had no intellectual grasp" of his subject and was "a poet of great genius, who ruined his life and his talent" by following Whitman and Emerson. His march halts, once, to praise as "one of the purest and most moving lines of our time" one of the flattest and least moving lines in Crane, or of any time: "I could not pick the arrows from my side."

Winters's attempt to separate the lightning from the flash is absolutely fascinating. He is of course correct about the poem's technical sources in Eliot. Though no one can argue the extent to which Crane's Romantic faith influences its *actual* design, *The Bridge* is a throughly Modernist poem—no different from the *Cantos*, *Paterson*, or *The Waste Land*—in demanding of its readers an active literary intelligence that contributes to a coherent understanding: the reader participates in creating and communicating the impression of coherence. Crane used the approved Imagist-Modernist structural model— episodic lyrical narrative joined through paratactic rather than hypotactic means—to construct a celebratory epic. Its organization is therefore hardly unconventional but what the age demanded of a "major" long poem; it makes as much consecutive sense as one would desire in any long twentieth-century poem not written by Vachel Lindsay, Stephen Vincent Benet, or Edgar Lee Masters.

Winters is also correct about the poem's philosophical and rhetorical cores, which he also dislikes: we know that Crane went on to compose *The Bridge* in the central rhetorics of his maturity, Whitman and Emerson, the Marlowe of *Doctor Faustus*, Keats and the English Romantics—all departures from the approved rhetorics characterized by impersonality, objectivity, the variable foot, and paratactic structure. These rhetorical departures guaranteed that *The Bridge* would not make the first cut and that it would turn out to be such a complex homework assignment for the New Critics. That *The Bridge*'s prosody fails to sound Modern is obviously what has foxed many who read it.

What is most intriguing, nearly fifty years after he registered his disapproval of *The Bridge*, is the position that Winters's attack bought him—the moral center, rejecting the poem's philosophical and aesthetic axes, each of which, Romanticism and Modernism, are pushed to the extremes. There is a canniness, a comic inevitability, moreover, no matter how tacky the implications, in viewing both Modernism and Crane's twentieth-century Romanticism as extremes of a peculiarly

American self-consciousness—about form, technique, rhetoric, consciousness itself—that is arbitrated by professional moralizers like Winters, whose position is underpinned by one can only guess what canon. (Perhaps Masters's *Spoon River Anthology* or Benet's god-awful but awfully clear *John Brown's Body*.) Yet Winters foreshadows two generations of arguments advanced against either the poem's poetic architecture or informing philosophy. His discomfort with Crane's Romantic faith persists especially: the phrase "Romantic-Modernist sensibility," apparently a sudden coinage, appears not once but thrice in the back pages of a recent issue of the *Georgia Review*, part of a minor critical project to overcome precisely the ambiguity that Winters's attack on Crane enshrines. Readers are still attempting to wrestle with the ambiguity central to this somehow indispensible, if unbearably meanspirited, attack.

J. T. Barbarese

Further Reading

Berthoff, Werner. *Hart Crane: A Re-Introduction*. Minneapolis, Minn: University of Minnesota Press, 1989.

Blackmur, R. P. *Form and Value in Modern Poetry*. New York: Doubleday, 1957.

Bloom, Harold. "Hart Crane's Gnosis." In Harold Bloom, *Agon: Towards a Theory of Revisionism*. New York: Oxford University Press, 1982.

Bloom, Harold, ed. *Hart Crane: Modern Critical Views*. New York: Chelsea House, 1986.

Crane, Hart. *The Complete Poems and Selected Letters of Hart Crane*. Ed. Brom Weber. New York: Doubleday/Anchor, 1966.

——— *The Letters of Hart Crane*. Ed. Brom Weber. Berkeley: University of California Press, 1965.

——— *The Poems of Hart Crane*. Ed. Marc Simon. New York: Liveright, 1986.

Dembo, L. S. *Hart Crane's Sanskrit Charge: A Study of "The Bridge."* Ithaca: Cornell University Press, 1960.

Drew, Elizabeth. *Directions in Modern Poetry*. New York: Holt, 1941.

Edelman, Lee. *Transmemberment of Song: Hart Crane's Anatomies of Rhetoric and Desire*. Stanford: Stanford University Press, 1987.

Hanley, Alfred. *Hart Crane's Holy Vision: "White Buildings."* Pittsburgh: Duquesne University Press, 1981.

Hazo, Samuel. *Smithereened Apart: A Critique of Hart Crane.* Athens: Ohio State University Press, 1968.

Lewis, R. W. B.   *The Poetry of Hart Crane: A Critical Study.* Princeton: Princeton University Press, 1967.

Paul, Sherman. *Hart's Bridge.* Urbana: University of Illinois Press, 1972.

Quinn, Vincent. *Hart Crane.* United States Authors Series 35. New York: Twayne, 1963.

Spears, Monroe K. *Hart Crane.* University of Minnesota Pamphlets on American Writers Number 47. Minneapolis: University of Minnesota Press, 1965.

Tate, Allen. "Foreword." In Hart Crane, *White Buildings.* New York: Boni and Liveright, 1926.

Trachtenberg, Alan. *Hart Crane: A Collection of Critical Essays.* Englewood Cliffs, N.J.: Prentice-Hall, 1982.

Unterecker, John. *Voyager: A Life of Hart Crane.* New York: Farrar, Straus and Giroux, 1969.

Uroff, Marjorie D. *Hart Crane: The Patterns of His Poetry.* Urbana: University of Illinois Press, 1974.

Weber, Brom. *Hart Crane: A Biographical and Critical Study.* New York: Bodley Press, 1948.

Winters, Ivor. *In Defense of Reason.* Denver: Alan Swallow, 1947.

Yingling, Thomas. *Hart Crane and the Homosexual Text: New Thresholds, New Anatomies.* Chicago: University of Chicago Press, 1990.

The Poetry of the Harlem Renaissance

WHEN the Harlem Renaissance started, and when it ended, and—indeed—if it ever really happened, are questions sometimes debated by scholars and students of African American literary history. Most people would agree, however, that the 1920s was a decade of extraordinary creativity for black Americans in the arts, including the performing arts, so that these years marked a glowing moment of achievement in the troubled history of blacks in North America. There is agreement, moreover, that the second half of the decade saw an outpouring of published literature by Americans of African descent in New York so unusually rich that it possibly deserves the name *renaissance*. Most people would further agree that poetry, rather than fiction, drama, or the other literary arts, was either central to this literary movement or the foundation on which African American writers built as they attempted to establish themselves and their careers as part of the brave new world of African American culture in the 1920s.

To some extent, the term *Harlem Renaissance* is a metaphor for a movement that took place, with varying levels of intensity and success, in several parts of the United States and even beyond. Certainly by the early late 1920s African students in Paris and progressive young West Indians in the Caribbean were reading the work of black Americans and taking the first tentative steps toward what would be known as the Negritude movement in the case of Africa, and toward what would lead, in the Caribbean, to the outpouring of literature that would probably flower most brilliantly in the verse and drama of Derek Walcott and the fiction of V. S. Naipaul. But Harlem and New York were central to the movement in the United States. When Harper brought out Countee Cullen's book of verse *Color* in 1925, this apparently was the first book of poetry by a black American to be published by a major New York house (Harcourt, Brace had published the Jamaican-born Claude McKay's *Harlem Shadows* in 1922) since Dodd Mead's championing of Paul Laurence Dunbar at the turn of the century. Similarly, Jean Toomer's *Cane* in 1923 was probably the first novel—if novel it may be called—by a black American to appear from a New York publisher since Doubleday, Page had brought out Charles Chesnutt's *The Colonel's Dream* in 1905. From this point of view, the reality of the Harlem Renaissance cannot be doubted.

What factors lead to the Harlem Renaissance? Certainly New York had become one the main destinations—perhaps the destination of choice—for the swelling streams of blacks leaving the South, where nine out of ten black Americans had lived at the dawn of the century. Conditions for blacks there had so deteriorated in the preceding decade, as legal segregation hardened and lynch law became established, that migration appeared to many blacks to be the sole means of improving their lives in the long aftermath of slavery. Black migration was further accelerated by the demand for labor stimulated by industrial expansion in the major northern cities such as New York, Chicago, and Cleveland. When the United States entered World War I as a combatant thousands of jobs previously closed to blacks became open, and African Americans rushed to fill them.

To the black newcomers New York in particular was undoubtedly the epitome of freedom and opportunity. New York meant both the pleasures of Broadway and the sense of importance that came from living in the largest and most celebrated of American cities. New York also meant Harlem in Manhattan. Originally intended for upper middle-class and middle-class whites, then reluctantly opened to blacks by real estate interests responding to the effects of overbuilding, Harlem had been excellently laid out. Its fine avenues, broad sidewalks, and stylishly constructed houses promised blacks a standard of living far more refined than anything they could find elsewhere in the United States. As the national interest in African American culture grew, stimulated by a variety of factors, including the popularity of jazz and dance as developed by blacks (inaugurated to some extent by the spectacular success on Broadway of the musical production *Shuffle Along* in 1921), Harlem seemed destined to become soon, as one writer put it, "the Negro capital of the world."

In the struggle by blacks to assert their humanity in the face of laws, books, and even motion pictures (such as D. W. Griffith's *Birth of a Nation* in 1915) that seemed to deny it, the production of art became increasingly important. The basic supposition—or hope—was that the creation of a body of literature, painting, sculpture, and music—preferably of an "elevated" kind—would lead to a transformation in the way blacks were seen by whites, and perhaps also to a transformation in the way many blacks saw themselves. In this respect virtually all the principal cultural and political organizations, each based in New York, such as the National Association for the Advancement of Colored People, the National Urban League, and even Marcus Garvey's Universal Negro Improvement Association, with its back-to-Africa slogan, were united. And they were nowhere more directly influential on younger writers than in magazines and newspapers edited or owned by blacks and dedicated to African American progress.

Of these, the most important was almost certainly the official monthly journal of the N.A.A.C.P., the *Crisis*, founded in 1910 and edited by the scholar and propagandist W. E. B. Du Bois. No single journal was more important in stimulating literary activity among black Americans during this period, a fact underscored by the appointment of a literary editor, Jessie Fauset, between 1919 and 1926. In 1917 the *Crisis* was joined by the *Messenger*, edited by A. Philip Randolph and Chandler Owen, and in 1923 by *Opportunity*, the organ of the National Urban League, edited by the sophisticated sociologist and cultural entrepreneur Charles S. Johnson. Although the *Messenger* prided itself on being radical socialist in its politics, there was normally little or nothing ideologically different about the literature published in these three magazines. All were dedicated to black social uplift, and all were committed to the development of literature, and especially of poetry. Led presciently by Du Bois of the *Crisis*, all sooner or later identified a black artistic renaissance as a goal that would prove the genius of black America against its detractors.

One sure sign of the importance of poets to African American culture as the 1920s opened was the unprecedented appearance of anthologies devoted to their work. Most prominent among these was probably James Weldon Johnson's *Book of American Negro Poetry* (1922). In the following year, 1923, came *Negro Poets and Their Poems*, edited by Robert Kerlin, a white professor of literature who had become interested in African American poetic expression and culture before it became fashionable to do so—before, as Langston Hughes would put it, "the Negro was in vogue." In 1925 contemporary poets played a small but indispensable role in the most important anthology of the Harlem Renaissance, Alain Locke's skillfully edited *The New Negro*. Based on a special number of the nationally circulated *Survey Graphic* magazine earlier that year, this volume became quickly accepted as virtually the bible of the new movement and brought widespread recognition to the select group of poets it featured, including Claude McKay, Countee Cullen, Langston Hughes, and Jean Toomer. In 1927 Cullen, established by that point as perhaps the major poet of the movement (rivaled only by Langston Hughes), published *Caroling Dusk*, an anthology of almost three dozen poets of the age. A dozen younger poets were also represented, along with other kinds of writers, in *Ebony and Topaz*, described as a "collecteana" by its editor, Charles S. Johnson of *Opportunity* magazine. And when younger poets broke into "white" magazines, as Cullen did for the first time in 1923, or Hughes did in the prestigious *Vanity Fair* in 1925, the Harlem literary community reacted with pride and pleasure.

In James Weldon Johnson's anthology, *The Book of American Negro Poetry*, an expertly written introduction of almost forty pages traced the relatively thin but still praiseworthy history of black American poetry from the eighteenth century to the present time. Although Johnson was then the general secretary of the N.A.A.C.P., he was also known for previous successes as a poet, lyricist, diplomat, translator, and novelist. In addition, he had done graduate study in literature and drama at Columbia University. His artful preface to his anthology spelled out the terms of the essential debate concerning art, politics, and language for blacks in the United States, and framed that debate against a backdrop of similar cultural changes in other parts of the world.

What the colored poet in the United States needs to do is something like what Synge did for the Irish; he needs to find a form that will express the racial spirit by symbols from within rather than by symbols from without, such as the mere mutilation of English spelling and pronunciation. He needs a form that is freer and larger than dialect, but which will still hold the racial flavor; a form expressing the imagery, the idioms, the peculiar turns of thought, and the distinctive humor and pathos, too, of the Negro, but which will also be capable of voicing the deepest and highest emotions and aspirations, and allow of the widest range of subjects and the widest scope of treatment.

Thus Johnson linked what was happening among blacks in the United States to the Irish Renaissance that had produced Yeats, Synge, Lady Gregory, and the Abbey Theatre. In alluding to "the racial spirit," he was identifying a counterpart to the so-called Celtic muse that was seen as quite distinct from the English literary imagination. In calling for a form "freer and larger than dialect," he challenged black writers to disentangle themselves from the snares of stereotypes that had reached their highest form of art in the poetry of the African American writer Paul Laurence Dunbar, who had died in 1906. Above all Johnson set the manipulation of language and other signification, not the overt assertion of political ideals, as the heart of the African American poetic enterprise. And he did so while reminding the young black writers, through his anthology, that they were heirs to a tradition on which they could draw with a measure of confidence as they moved into the future.

With very few exceptions none of the poets of the new movement saw themselves as part of the most radical Modernist strain of verse set in motion in American poetry mainly through the efforts of writers such as Ezra Pound, T. S. Eliot, H.D., and Wallace Stevens. Such crucial tenets of this strain of Modernism as a learned allusiveness and necessary complexity of expression, which led to an exclusive poetic audience, attracted few African American writers. Like most white poets of the age, most black poets were enthralled by traditional forms of verse as established by the major British and American Romantic poets and their admirers. Modernist verse that resembled the work of Pound, for example, would not appear until the 1940s, and then on a highly restricted scale. Although several writers sometimes questioned the validity of the role of race and politics in poetry, most black poets sought the broadest possible audience, and imagined their role as poets to be the kind of moral and intellectual authority that had characterized the Fireside tradition of an earlier age in America.

For James Weldon Johnson (as he made clear in his 1933 autobiography *Along This Way*) and Langston Hughes—certainly two highly influential figures—Walt Whitman's *Leaves of Grass* was the volume that inspired their own flight from the old kind of dialect verse, and set in motion their search—in ways, to be sure, often contrary to Whitman's— for an aesthetic that reflected the realities of African American language, culture, and history. Among major American writers after Whitman, only E. A. Robinson and Carl Sandburg would exert any particular degree of influence on the Harlem Renaissance. In part this distance was owing, no doubt, to some inattentiveness by the younger writers; in part, however, they were after a different business altogether. Most could not be completely taken, for example, by T. S. Eliot's epochal figuring of the entire modern world as a "Waste Land." For many of them, the 1920s was a decade of unrivaled optimism; and, all through the generations of slavery and neoslavery, black American culture had of necessity emphasized the power of endurance and survival, of love and laughter, as the only proper response to painful circumstance.

Moreover, from black writers of the past the African American poet of the 1920s had something of a rival tradition to draw on. In 1773, Phillis Wheatley of Boston, born a slave in Africa, had become the second American woman (a hundred years after Anne Bradstreet) to publish a volume of verse. In the nineteenth century George Moses Horton had sung the sorrows of slavery. At mid-century and afterward, in the wake of the rise of the slave narratives, Frances Ellen Watkins Harper had given voice to black hopes in the years before and after the Civil War. Still later in the century Albery A. Whitman had acquired fame as a polished bard in books such as *The Rape of Florida* (1884). At the end of the century had come the towering figure whose fame in the writing of both standard and dialect verse still hovered over African American writing in the 1920s, the Ohio-born Paul Laurence Dunbar. Dunbar's dialect verse, in such volumes as *Majors and Minors* (1895) and, especially, *Lyrics of Lowly Life* (1896), had brought him the highest measure of national recognition ever accorded a black American poet. His images of black life, often humorous but also tender and poignant, had earned him the place of honor by the African American hearth just as white poets of an earlier age—Whittier and Longfellow, for example—had been so recognized by the nation as a whole.

The foundation of Dunbar's fame was dialect poems such as "A Negro Love Song" ("Seen my lady home las' night, / Jump back, honey, jump back"), "Little Brown Baby" ("Little brown baby wif spa'klin' eyes, /

Come to yo' pappy an' set on his knee"), "A Death Song" ("Lay me down beneaf de willers in de grass") and "When de Co'n Pone's Hot" (influenced no doubt by James Whitcomb Riley, the Indiana folk poet whose work powerfully appealed to Dunbar). Such work pleased blacks and whites alike. At least as proud of his work in standard English, Dunbar worked mightily to polish and adorn lyric set pieces such as "Ere Sleep Comes Down to Soothe the Weary Eyes," "Ships That Pass in the Night" ("O Earth, O Sky, O Ocean, both surpassing, / O heart of mine, O soul that dreads the dark!"), and "We Wear the Mask" ("We wear the mask that grins and lies, / It hides our cheeks and shades our eyes,— / This debt we play to human guile"). Many blacks interpreted "We Wear the Mask" as a poem about their historic endurance of suffering— although Dunbar was reluctant to express overt racial or political protest in his poetry.

Even before Dunbar died in 1906, however, the foundation of his greatest fame was under attack, and with it the art of his many admirers and imitators who depicted black life according to stereotypes born of the so-called plantation tradition, which sought to sentimentalize and even glorify the Old South. Indeed, Dunbar himself shared a sense of its inadequacy as an expression of African American culture. William Dean Howells, in a well-intentioned introduction to *Lyrics of Lowly Life*, had unwittingly pointed to this inadequacy in a way that wounded Dunbar. Howells identified "a precious difference of temperament between the races which it would be a great pity to lose." That racial difference was best expressed in Dunbar's dialect pieces, which seemed to Howells to reflect "the range between appetite and emotion, with certain lifts far beyond and above it, which is the range of the [black] race."

Torn between gratitude and a desire to be seen as more than a dialect poet (as well as chagrin at the possible slander of his race), Dunbar captured his painful dilemma—and the dilemma of the black poet and artist in a culture that demanded stereotypes of black life—in his brief poem "The Poet." There, the poet, unnamed and racially undefined, sings "eternal" themes ("He sang of love when earth was young"). However, his audience demands something else: "But ah, the world, it turned to praise / A jingle in a broken tongue."

A decade after Dunbar's death in 1906 black American poetry was virtually leaderless, its standards vague and sometimes contradictory. A few writers stood out, but none had produced work sufficiently accomplished to supplant the hold of Dunbar's verse, and his aesthetic dilemma, on younger writers. One was the Chicago-born and -bred Fenton Johnson, who published three volumes of verse, *A Little Dreaming* (1912), *Visions of Dusk* (1915), and *Sons of the Soil* (1916). Starting out as a fairly conventional versifier, Fenton Johnson was stirred by elements in the Modernist ferment that surrounded the founding in Chicago in 1912 of Harriet Monroe's *Poetry* magazine (though clearly not by Pound's standards as expressed in that magazine). He published several pieces in *Poetry* and elsewhere that—not unfashionably—declared a loss of confidence in civilization, and he did so in free verse. "Tired" is one example ("I am tired of work; I am tired of building up somebody else's civilization. / Let us take a rest, M'Lissy Jane"). He also sometimes struck an optimistic racial note, as in "Children of the Sun" ("We are children of the sun / Rising sun!") and "The Banjo Player" ("There is music in me, the music of a peasant people. / I wander through the levee"). But Fenton Johnson did not develop further as a poet, and indeed published virtually nothing in the 1920s.

These were not the first free-verse poems by a black. That distinction belongs—as so many distinctions belong in black American literary and scholarly culture—to the historian and sociologist W. E. B. Du Bois, whose rage against racism had led to a number of formally unchained poems published in obscure black journals. Notable among these is "A Litany of Atlanta" ("O Silent God, Thou whose voice afar in mist and mystery"), which had been directly inspired by a major riot in Atlanta (where he lived) in 1906, "Song of the Smoke" ("I am the Smoke King / I am black!"), and "The Burden of Black Women," later called "The Riddle of the Sphinx" ("The white world's vermin and filth: All the dirt of London; Valiant spoilers of women / And conquerors of unarmed men"). However, probably few writers in the 1920s knew most of these poems. Still, Du Bois's literary opinions were important not only because of them and his editorship of the *Crisis* but also because of the epochal significance of his classic text, *The Souls of Black Folk* (1903), in defining African American identity and in honoring learning and formal culture as the hallmark of black progress toward civilization.

The last significant figure—apart from James Weldon Johnson—among the older poets who would still be alive and acknowledged in the

Harlem Renaissance was William Stanley Braithwaite of Boston. Best known as a reviewer of verse and, starting in 1913, as an annual anthologist of American poetry published in magazines, Braithwaite also published books of his own verse, starting with *Lyrics of Life and Love* (1904) and *House of Falling Leaves* (1908). Later came *Sandy Star and Willie Gee* (1922). In his poetry, which was strongly influenced early by Swinburne and Ernest Dowson, and his criticism he resolutely avoided racial identification and instead quietly asserted his right to associate with what appeared to be the mainstream of American poetry. He also had little interest in the more adventurous forms of Modernism. His own major influence among American writers seems to have been Edwin Arlington Robinson, as in "Laughing it Out," from *Sandy Star*: "He had a whim and laughed it out / Upon the exit of a chance; / He floundered in a sea of doubt— / If life was real—or just romance." But irony of such a refined character would not move many of the new writers, and Braithwaite's influence on them did not reflect his national prestige. Pride in his national reputation coexisted side by side among several of the younger writers with regret about his conservative aesthetic and the listlessness of his racial sense.

To many of the younger writers probably the most compelling of the figures with something of a reputation by the time James Weldon Johnson's anthology appeared in 1922 was the Jamaican-born Claude McKay. After publishing two volumes of dialect verse in Jamaica McKay had come to the United States in 1912 to study at Booker T. Washington's Tuskegee Institute in Alabama. He soon moved on to Kansas, then to New York, where his work appeared in *Seven Arts* magazine, and later became coeditor of Max Eastman's avant-garde *Liberator* magazine. In 1919 he created something of a sensation among blacks with a sonnet published in the *Liberator*, "If We Must Die." Written in response to the "Red Summer" of that year, when deadly antiblack riots in Chicago and elsewhere underscored the tragic element in black hopes that the war and migration had permanently changed their roles in America, "If We Must Die" seemed to many blacks a clarion call to active resistance.

> If we must die, let it not be like hogs
> Hunted and penned in an inglorious spot,
> While round us bark the mad and hungry dogs,
> Making their mock at our accursed lot.
> If we must die, O let us nobly die,

Faced with death, blacks (in fact, the sonnet is devoid of racial reference) must fight, not submit: "Like men we'll face the murderous, cowardly pack, / Pressed to the wall, dying, but fighting back!"

In 1920, in London, McKay published *Spring in New Hampshire*, with an introduction by I. A. Richards; in 1922, in the United States, came *Harlem Shadows*. Together, these books showed an accomplished lyric poet working in traditional forms (especially the sonnet) but clearly also alert to urban, political, and racial themes. Several poems dealt with McKay's nostalgia for Jamaica (which he never saw again), as in "Flame-Heart" ("So much I have forgotten in ten years, / So much in ten brief years!"). In "The Tropics in New York," the sight of "Bananas ripe and green, and ginger-root, / Cocoa in pods and alligator pears" in a window is too much for the poet:

> My eyes grew dim, and I could not longer gaze;
> A wave of longing through my body swept,
> And, hungry for the old familiar ways,
> I turned aside and bowed my head and wept.

McKay also wrote poignantly about themes such as prostitution in Harlem ("I see the shapes of girls who pass / To bend and barter at desire's call"). But his impact was probably greater with the appearance of poems such as "The White House" ("Your door is shut against my tightened face; / And I am sharp as steel with discontent"); "To the White Fiends" ("Think you I could not arm me with a gun / And shoot down ten of you for every one / Of my black brothers murdered, burnt by you?"), and the defiant "America":

> Although she feeds me bread of bitterness,
> And sinks into my throat her tiger's tooth,
> Stealing my breath of life, I will confess
> I love this cultured hell that tests my youth!

He wrote about white mob justice that mocked black lives, as in "The Lynching" ("And little lads, lynchers that were to be, / Danced round the dreadful thing in fiendish glee"). He fearlessly challenged racism, but he could also be sardonic about political reality, as in "Africa" ("Thou art the harlot, now thy time is done, / Of all the mighty nations of the sun"). The combination of conservative form, radical socialist association, and political and racial aggressiveness made McKay a talismanic poetic figure for blacks in the 1920s, even though he left the United States in 1922 and did not return until the 1930s. (Because of its frankness, his novel *Home to Harlem* in 1928 became probably the most controversial book of fiction by a black writer of the 1920s.)

Another important writer to publish a brilliant book early in the 1920s, then absent himself from Harlem for the rest of the decade— in fact, for virtually the rest of his life—was the Washington, D.C.-born Jean Toomer. Sometimes called a novel, Toomer's *Cane* (1923) is in reality a genuinely Modernist, perhaps even avant-garde pastiche of intensely lyrical fiction, poems, and drama. The book was composed after a brief, stirring stay by Toomer, in 1921, in Sparta, Georgia, where he worked as a school administrator, followed by a visit to Spartanburg, South Carolina, the following year. *Cane* had a stunning effect upon the younger writers—perhaps the greatest impact of any single book on their writing. His formal poems there, including "November Cotton Flower" ("Boll-weevil's coming, and the winter's cold / Made cotton-stalks look rusty, seasons old"), "Song of the Son" ("Pour O pour that parting soul in song, / O pour it in the sawdust glow of night"), and "Harvest Song" ("I am a reaper whose muscles set at sundown") were matched and even surpassed by the overwhelming poetic language of his brief prose portraits of black men and women, such as "Fern" ("Face flowed into her eyes. Flowed in soft cream foam and plaintive ripples") and "Karintha" ("Men had always wanted her, this Karintha, even as a child, Karintha carrying beauty, perfect as dusk when the sun goes down"). Suffused by a sense of both the beauty and the tragedy of black lives in the South, *Cane* had something for the conservative and for the would-be avant-garde among the younger writers, for the racial militant and for those who would pursue "universal" themes. Echoes of Toomer may be found certainly in much of the lyric writing that followed; certainly, for all its lack of commercial success, the book set a new literary standard for African American writers of both poetry and prose. And its reputation endured, even after Toomer, following the siren song of G. I. Gurdjieff as one of the mystic's major American disciples, declared himself not a Negro and left for more sympathetic settings, including an artists' colony in Taos, New Mexico, and a Quaker community in Bucks County, Pennsylvania.

If writers such as McKay and Toomer abandoned Harlem, Langston Hughes was among those who came from elsewhere to stay.

Born in Joplin, Missouri, in 1902, Hughes had grown up in Lawrence, Kansas, and Lincoln, Illinois, before going to high school in Cleveland, Ohio; in 1921 he arrived in New York, ostensibly to attend Columbia University, but really, he later claimed, to see Harlem. Complementing his earlier influence by Whitman and Sandburg ("my guiding star"), McKay stood for Hughes as the embodiment of the cosmopolitan and yet racially confident and committed black poet Hughes hoped to be. Although his signature poem for the rest of his life, "The Negro Speaks of Rivers," appeared in the *Crisis* (June 1921) before Hughes set foot in Harlem, the young poet was already indebted to older figures such as McKay, Du Bois, and James Weldon Johnson when he penned this free-verse ode to the historicity and spiritual beauty of the black folk.

> I've known rivers:
> I've known rivers ancient as the world and older
> than the flow of human blood in human veins
>
> My soul has grown deep like the rivers.
>
> I bathed in the Euphrates when dawns were young.
> I built my hut near the Congo and it lulled
>   me to sleep.

His experience deepened by a year in New York, a voyage in 1923 down the west coast of Africa, and a stay of several months in 1924 in Europe (mainly in Paris, as a dishwasher in a nightclub), Hughes developed steadily as a poet. Images and sentiments such as that in "Poem" ("The night is beautiful, / So the faces of my people") and "Dream Variation" ("Night coming tenderly / Black like me") and the following, from "Youth," endeared his work to a wide range of African Americans, for whom Hughes delighted in writing:

> We have tomorrow
> Bright before us
>
> Like a flame
>
> Yesterday, a night-gone thing
> A sun-down name.
>
> And dawn today
> Broad arch above the road we came.
> We march!

His major step, encouraged in part by Sandburg's example (as in Sandburg's "Jazz Fantasies" of 1919) but anchored by his own near-worship of black music as the major form of art within the race, was his adaptation of traditional poetic forms first to jazz, then to the blues, in which Hughes sometimes used dialect but in a way radically different from that of Dunbar and his imitators. In these steps Hughes was well served by his early experimentation with a loose form of rhyme that frequently gave way to an inventively rhythmic free verse ("Me an' ma baby's / Got two mo' ways, / Two mo' ways to do de buck!"). His landmark poem "The Weary Blues" ("Droning a drowsy syncopated tune, / Rocking back and forth to a mellow croon, / I heard a Negro play") was the first by any poet to make use of the basic blues form.

> . . . In a deep song voice with a melancholy tone
> I heard that Negro sing, that old piano moan—
> "Ain't got nobody in all this world,
> Ain't got nobody but ma self.
> I's gwine to quit ma frownin'
> And put ma troubles on the shelf."

Written in 1923 after a visit to a Harlem cabaret, and revised over the next two years, the poem gained Hughes the first prize in poetry in a widely advertised literary contest offered by *Opportunity* magazine in 1925 in which Charles Johnson had shrewdly involved several prominent editors and publishers. This prize led directly to the publication several months later of Hughes's first volume of verse, *The Weary Blues* (1926).

Even more radical experimentation with the blues form led to his next collection, *Fine Clothes to the Jew* (1927). Perhaps his finest single book of verse, *Fine Clothes* was also his least successful in terms of sales and, in the black press (though not the white), its critical reception. Several reviewers in black newspapers and magazines were distressed by Hughes's fearless and, to them, tasteless evocation of elements of lower-class black culture, including its sometimes crude eroticism, never before treated in serious poetry. The book was "about 100 pages of trash [reeking] of the gutter and sewer," wrote one man; another found the poems "unsanitary, insipid and repulsing." These reviewers probably gave *Fine Clothes to the Jew* a harsher reception than that ever accorded any other book of American poetry with the exception of *Leaves of Grass*.

Many were affronted by "Red Silk Stockings" ("Put on yo' red silk stocking, / Black gal. / Go out an' let de white boys / Look at yo' legs") and by the brutality of "Beale Street Love," which speaks of love as

> . . . a brown man's fist
> With hard knuckles
> Crushing the lips,
> Blackening the eyes,—
> Hit me again,
> Says Clorinda.

Others poems were full of joy, but of a kind that embarrassed some readers:

> . . . When ma man looks at me
> He knocks me off ma feet.
> When ma man looks at me
> He knocks me off ma feet.
> He's got those 'lectric-shockin' eyes an'
> De way he shocks me sho is sweet.

In response to his critics Hughes was adamant about his determination to write about such people and to experiment with blues and jazz. The year before, 1926, he had published in the *Nation* an essay in defense of the freedom of the black writer, "The Negro Artist and the Racial Mountain." "We younger Negro artists who create now intend to express our individual dark-skinned selves without fear or shame," he had declared. "We know we are beautiful. And ugly too." This essay quickly became a manifesto for many of the younger writers who also wished to assert their right to explore and exploit allegedly degraded aspects of black life.

Around 1931, when Hughes began a major shift toward the left, his new poetry almost completely reflected that change, which took him far away from the typical themes and interests of the Harlem Renaissance. (On the other hand, Hughes had been writing some leftist verse from the start of his career.) His radical pieces were collected in the pamphlet *A New Song* (1938). During World War II he returned to a more centrist position (starting with *Shakespeare in Harlem* (1942), and, with important modifications, to the kind of blues- and jazz-influenced verse that had made his reputation in the 1920s. Until his death in 1967 he regularly brought out collections of verse. Despite his extensive publication in a variety of genres, including fiction, drama, and autobiography, Hughes continued to see himself as being essentially a poet. In hindsight he may be seen as without much doubt the foremost poet of the Harlem Renaissance.

Hughes's major rival as the leading poet of the Harlem Renaissance, Countee Cullen, was not one of writers who took "The Negro Artist and the Racial Mountain" as a manifesto. In fact, in opening this essay with a reference to an unnamed black poet who wished to be known simply as a poet, and who therefore (Hughes claimed) probably wanted to be white, Hughes was almost certainly alluding to Cullen. A degree of mystery surrounds Cullen's beginnings. Although he later claimed New York City as his birthplace, he was probably born as Countee Porter in Louisville, Kentucky (Baltimore has also been cited as his place of birth), under humble and perhaps humiliating circumstances; he may have grown up without knowing his mother or father. In the middle of his teenage years he was adopted by—or went to live with—the Reverend Frederick A. Cullen, the pastor of a prominent Harlem church, Salem Methodist Episcopal, and his wife.

An excellent student, Cullen was graduated almost at the top of his class at DeWitt Clinton High School, where he edited the school magazine and also created a sensation by winning a citywide poetry competition with "I Have a Rendezvous with Life." He then went on to New York University, where he earned a bachelor's degree before entering Harvard, from which he was graduated in 1926 with a master of arts degree in English. By this time he had already published his first volume of verse, *Color* (1925). In 1927 he published his second collection, *The Ballad of the Brown Girl*, as well as his anthology *Caroling Dusk*. In various ways, Hughes and Cullen were direct opposites as poets. Where Hughes was devoted to American poets, Cullen consciously admired English writers. He liked in particular Shelley and Keats ("To John Keats, at Spring Time": "I cannot hold my peace, John Keats; / There never was a spring like this"), as well his "beloved" contemporary, A. E. Housman, the author of *A Shropshire Lad*. A conservative craftsman, Cullen believed in the discipline of strict rhyme. Hughes's interest in blues and jazz meant little to Cullen, who once publicly expressed doubts that Hughes's blues and jazz verse was poetry at all. Where Hughes was drawn to Africa and the Caribbean above his interest in Europe, Cullen made much of his devotion to the classics and to his fondness for French culture (he later taught French in the New York public school system). His best known longer poem of the Harlem Renaissance, "Heritage," questions the meaning of Africa, asking if it is

> Copper sun or scarlet sea,
> Jungle star or jungle track,
> Strong bronzed men, or regal black
> Women from whose loins I sprang
> When the birds of Eden sang?
> . . . .
> . . . .
> Spicy grove, cinnamon tree,
> What is Africa to me?

The poem concludes with a wavering between satisfaction in the apparent triumph of Christian values over pagan impulses ("I belong to Jesus Christ, / Preacher of humility; / Heathen gods are naught to me") and the suggestion of passions and desires that Christianity cannot satisfy, and of which Africa is to some extent highly symbolic ("Not yet has my heart or head / In the least way realized / They and I are civilized").

"Heritage," in its oppositions of paganism and Christianity, tribalism and civilization, the jungle and domesticity, passion and refinement, suggests strongly elements of shame and guilt, perhaps connected to homosexuality. Other elements of Cullen's poetry also suggest the extent to which he was prey to these ambivalent and repressive feelings. Where Hughes seemed to glory in his color, and celebrated the beauty of blackness, Cullen either avoided the racial theme altogether or chose to emphasize the pathos of being black in a hostile white country, as in "The Shroud of Color" (" 'Lord, being dark,' I said, 'I cannot bear / The further touch of earth, the scented air'"). Identifying blackness with suffering and rejection, he saw it as diametrically opposed to the life of the poet. In "Yet Do I Marvel," he writes of the inscrutability of God and the difficulty of comprehending His ways: "Yet do I marvel at this curious thing: / To make a poet black, and bid him sing!"

Late in the 1920s the theme of religious doubt and an interest in the classics became increasingly important to Cullen. In 1929 came *The Black Christ and Other Poems*, published after a visit to Jerusalem, which had stirred Cullen. "The Black Christ" ("God's glory and my country's shame, / And how one man who cursed Christ's name / May never fully expiate / That crime") was Cullen's longest and most ambitious poem.

Ostensibly a narrative poem about a black man, Jim, who is lynched after killing a white man, the poem has deeper significance as a gospel-haunted (especially gospel accounts of the Crucifixion) rendering of Cullen's personal conflict between religious faith and doubt. Whatever the piece meant to Cullen, it received scant attention. In 1935 he attempted a translation or adaptation from the Greek that resulted in *The Medea and Other Poems*; this volume did even less to revive his fading reputation as a poet. Around this time he appears to have virtually abandoned the writing of verse.

One of the most acclaimed volumes of verse of the movement, and one of the most novel, appeared in 1927 from James Weldon Johnson. Busy as a civil rights leader, Johnson had not published a volume of poetry since his *Fifty Years and Other Poems* (1917), commemorating the Emancipation, had celebrated in conventional forms the hard-won progress of blacks since the Emancipation Proclamation of 1863. *God's Trombones* was his own major response to the challenge he had eloquently set down in the preface to his *Book of American Negro Poetry* in 1922. Johnson was among those who recognized the extraordinary rhetorical gifts of the black preacher, or—in a distinction he was careful to make—the Negro preacher of an era already bygone in the 1920s. As Sterling Brown put it, Johnson sought to recover in his volume "the dignity, the sweep and splendor" of this preaching tradition. In tribute Johnson composed seven sermons, or dramatic monologues, on a variety of themes and preacherly styles.

Probably the best known of these quickly became "The Creation" ("And God stepped out on space, / And he looked around and said: / I'm lonely"). With its intrinsic drama, its flashing changes of rhythm, its rousing images now awe-inspiring, now tender, "The Creation" soon became popular as a recitation piece, especially in the mouth of Johnson himself, who was a remarkable reader of verse. Building steadily to its climax, the poem finds God ("Who lit the sun and fixed it in the sky, / Who flung the stars to the most far corner of the night, / Who rounded the earth in the middle of His hand"), scooping up clay and kneeling down by the bank of a river:

> Like a mammy bending over her baby,
> Kneeled down in the dust
> Toiling over a lump of clay
> Till He shaped it in His own image;

> Then into it He blew the breath of life,
> And man became a living soul.

Another major voice attracted to black folkways was Sterling A. Brown—although like Hughes, Cullen, and Johnson, he was decidedly not one of the folk by birth. Born in Washington, D.C., Brown was graduated from Williams College in 1922 and, also like Cullen, received a master's degree from Harvard University (in 1923). Later, he taught for several decades as a professor at Howard University. Never a resident of Harlem, Brown would later play down the significance of the Harlem Renaissance and even raise doubts that it had ever occurred. And yet Brown was unquestionably close in spirit to some of the major initiatives and ideas of the renaissance, especially concerning the validity and beauty of folk culture and folk expressive forms, especially the blues.

As in the case of Hughes and Johnson, Brown's love of and devotion to folk culture was accompanied by a desire to find the most appropriate poetic forms and standards to transmute this culture. He wrote poems on more conventional themes and in standard English, but became best known for ballads, often written in dialect, that celebrated the suffering and heroism and the irrepressible joy of black lives lived out under harsh conditions in the South. "Southern Road," the title poem of his only book of verse (1932) takes its meter and rhythm from the sounds of the black chain gang:

> Swing dat hammer—hunh—
> Steady, bo.
> Swing dat hammer—hunh—
> Steady, bo;
> Ain't no rush, bebby,
> Long ways to go

"Odyssey of Big Boy" is an extended ballad tribute to a black roustabout and wanderer, a fighter and a lover who knows where he stands in the long line of black fighters and lovers:

> Lemme be wid Casey Jones,
> Lemme be wid Stagolee,
> Lemme be wid such like men
> When Death takes hol' on me,
> When Death takes hol' on me.

Big Boy recalls his work days and his loving days ("Had two fair browns in Arkansaw / And three in Tennessee") but regrets nothing ("Man done caught me wid his wife / His doggone purty wife"). He has made his peace with himself and the world. All that he wants in the end is the company of the ancestral heroes of the African American world: "Lemme be wid John Henry, steel drivin' man / Lemme be wid ole Jazzbo; / Lemme be wid ole Jazzbo."

Brown's poetry would command a small but committed following, particularly among those people who knew him as a charismatic professor at Howard University, where he championed the cause of folk culture. Perhaps his best known poem, a tribute to black men in slavery and what passed for freedom, is "Strong Men" (*They dragged you from homeland, / They chained you in coffles, / They huddled you spoon-fashion in filthy hatches*"). The poem alternates between what "they" did to "you," the black man, and the indomitable response of the black man, which derives from a mixture of mental toughness and sheer physical power:

> You sang:
>> Ain't no hammah
>> In dis' lan',
>> Strikes lak mine, bebby,
>> Strikes lak mine.

The refrain that binds the poem together is the image of enduring and irresistible energy and power of will in the black man:

> One thing they cannot prohibit—
>> The strong men . . . coming on
>> The strong men gittin' stronger.
>> Strong men . . .
>> Stronger . . ."

The last of the major poets who may accurately be associated with the Harlem Renaissance was the Missouri-born Melvin B. Tolson, although he lived in Harlem for less than a year (1931–1932) while he worked on his master's degree in English at Columbia University. Tolson did not publish a volume of verse until his socialist-influenced *Rendezvous with America* appeared in 1944. Later, after a major change in Tolson's approach to poetry, came *Libretto for the Republic of Liberia* (1953), with an introduction by Allen Tate that hailed the author as the first true Modernist African American poet, and *Harlem Gallery: Book 1, The Creator* (1965), introduced by Karl Shapiro. Between 1932 and 1936, however, Tolson wrote *A Gallery of Harlem Portraits* (not published until 1979, after Tolson's death in 1966). Modeled clearly on Masters's *Spoon River Anthology*, Tolson's *Gallery* drew its primary inspiration from the spirit and accomplishments of the Harlem Renaissance, which was the subject of his master's thesis (received in 1940, after almost a decade of work) at Columbia.

The work opens with the poem "Harlem" ("Diamond Canady / Was stabbed in bed by Little Eva Winn. / Deacon Phineas Bloom / Confessed his adultery on his deathbed"). Typical of Tolson's approach here, the piece moves through a kaleidoscope of Harlem sights, sounds, characters, and situations before concluding with a bold announcement of Tolson's larger intentions:

> Radicals, prizefighters, actors and deacons,
> Beggars, politicians, professors and redcaps,
> Bulldikers, Babbitts, racketeers and jog-chasers,
> Harlots, crapshooter, workers and pink-chasers,
> Artists, dicties, Pullman porters and messiahs . . .
> The Curator has hung the likenesses of all
> In *A Gallery of Harlem Portraits*.

Tolson's obvious desire to shock and amuse was not shared by the majority of the poets of the movement, who tended to prize dignity and decorum. One of these writers was Georgia Douglas Johnson. While it might seem inappropriate to see Johnson as a figure of the Harlem Renaissance since she never lived in Harlem but spent most of her life in Washington, D.C., her career illustrates the extent to which the term *Harlem Renaissance* was a metaphor for black American literary creativity, even when the writers involved never visited Harlem, avoided race as a theme, and wrote no blues or jazz verse. Running a salon of sorts in Washington, she was a vital, nurturing presence for younger writers, and her reputation was widespread within the black world. Her volumes—*The Heart of a Woman* (1918), *Bronze* (1922), and *An Autumn Love Cycle* (1928)—indicate an enduring if conventional lyric interest. Her verse treats the familiar themes of hope, love, and the tragic passage of time, as in "Youth" ("The dew is on the grasses, dear, / The blush is on the rose") and "Recessional" ("Consider me a memory, a dream that passed away; / Or yet a flower that has blown and shattered in a day"). More modern expression had little appeal for her, but the wide popularity of her poems within black America indicated that she knew her audience well and was happy to serve it.

Of the poets who failed to publish a volume during the Renaissance, Anne Spencer was—apart from Tolson—perhaps the most gifted and unusual. She was apparently never in Harlem; born in West Virginia, she was educated in Lynchburg, Virginia, and remained there, married but almost reclusive, for most of the rest of her life. But she participated in the renaissance, as did so many other writers, through the pages of magazines like the *Crisis*. She did not participate vigorously, however; forty when she published her first poem, her output remained unfortunately small in spite of the urgings of such admirers as Langston Hughes. Although it is difficult to trace specific influences on her work, Spencer seems to have been drawn to Anglo-American Modernism more strongly than was perhaps any of her contemporaries. At least one poem shows an old-fashioned touch. Her poem "Dunbar," ostensibly about Paul Laurence Dunbar, associates poetry with pathos and death in a conventional lyricism.

> Ah, how poets sing and die!
> Make one song and Heaven takes it;
> Have one heart and Beauty breaks it;
> Chatterton, Shelley, Keats and I—
> Ah, how poets sing and die.

Far more typical of her writing, however, is a distinctly Modernist density and compression of language, an allusiveness, and a general resistance to easy interpretation. In "At the Carnival," she appears to express a possibly feminist longing for a life of action. "Gay little Girl-of-the-Diving-Tank, / I desire a name for you," she begins this poem in tribute to someone she sees as "darling of spirit and form," admired and envied by the less adventurous in life. "The bull-necked man knows you—this first time / His itching flesh sees form divine and vibrant health / And thinks not of his avocation." Possibly more direct, in this respect, is "Letter to My Sister" ("It is dangerous for a woman to defy the gods; / To taunt them with the tongue's thin whip"), where the poet instructs her to "lock your heart":

And lest they peer within,
Light no lamp when dark comes down
Raise no shade for sun;
Breathless must your breath come through
If you'd die and dare deny
The gods their god-like fun.

Perhaps her most anthologized piece is "Before the Feast of Shushan," a shimmering if sometimes opaque dramatic monologue by the King of Persia about a maiden:

Garden of Shushan!
After Eden, all terrace, pool, and flower
                    recollect thee:
Ye weavers in saffron and haze and Tyrian purple,
Tell yet what range in color wakes the eye.

Jessie Fauset, a poet and the author of four novels during this period, would deserve a prominent place in any history of poetry in the movement simply because of her skillful performance as literary editor of the *Crisis* between 1919 and 1926 (her major discovery for the magazine was Langston Hughes). Born in Philadelphia and educated at Cornell and the Sorbonne, Fauset was also a poet, albeit one of unadventurous technique and a contained range of ideas. James Weldon Johnson characterized her work as *vers de société*; touching frequently on the theme of lost love, she almost completely shunned the racial themes and images that she admitted perforce to the pages of the *Crisis*. Perhaps her best-known poem is the two-stanza "Dead Fires" ("If this is peace, this dead and leaden thing, / Than better far the hateful fret, the sting").

Because of the significance of religion and religious feeling in his life and work, Arna Bontemps stands apart from most of his peers in the Harlem Renaissance. Born in 1902 in Louisiana but reared in Los Angeles, Bontemps grew up at home and in school under the tight discipline of the Seventh Day Adventist Church. Coming to Harlem from Los Angeles in 1924, he taught for seven years at the Harlem Academy run there by his church. Although his closest friend among the figures of the Harlem Renaissance was Langston Hughes, his poetic career in the 1920s developed largely independent of Hughes's standards and interests. Bontemps wrote neither dialect verse nor jazz and blues poetry, which would have offended his brethren in the church. Sometimes he expressed racial feeling (as in "A Black Man Talks of Reaping") but he did so only mildly, for the most part; a sense of decorum suffuses his work. His one break with tradition was in eschewing rhyme in favor of a restrained, often stately free verse well suited to his meditative utterances.

Most of Bontemps's published poems appeared in the 1920s, although a pamphlet of his verse, *Personals*, appeared in London near the end of his life. His most successful poem is almost certainly "Nocturne at Bethesda," from the twenties:

> I thought I saw an angel flying low,
> I thought I saw the flicker of a wing
> Above the mulberry trees; but not again.
> Bethesda sleeps. The ancient pool that healed
> A host of bearded Jews does not awake.

Without a specific allusion to time and place, the poem mourns the loss of spiritual values where once God was immanent. When, finally, it appears to turn, tentatively, on an optimistic note ("Yet I hope, still I long to live") the idea of a saving racial destiny enters the poem. If there is indeed an afterlife, and if the speaker returns to this world, "it will not be here; / If you want me you must search for me / Beneath the palms of Africa." Characteristically of Bontemps, however, the work ends on a doubting, even forlorn sound: "There is a simple story on your face; / Years have wrinkled you. I know, Bethesda! / You are sad. It is the same with me."

Most of the poets of the Harlem Renaissance never published a volume of verse and in fact published only a few poems. Yet because of the power of anthologies and the high prestige of poets within the African American world, several of these writers are well known. Helene Johnson of Boston brought a vigorous, independent spirit to her verse, as in "Sonnet to a Negro in Harlem" ("You are disdainful and magnificent— / Your perfect body and your pompous gait"). Gwendolyn Bennett of Texas, who came to New York to study, was primarily committed to the fine arts but made a name for herself as a poet with pieces such as "Lines Written at the Grave of Alexandre Dumas" and "To a Dark Girl" ("I love you for your brownness / And the rounded darkness of your breast"). A born New Yorker and an accomplished athlete, Frank Horne achieved an easy facility in his poems, applying casual Modernist techniques to his main themes—religious feeling, athletics, and a concern for racial justice. In 1925 he won first prize in the *Crisis* poetry competition with "Letters Found Near a Suicide." The section "To 'Chick'":

> Oh Achilles of the moleskins
> And the gridiron
> Do not wonder
> Nor doubt that this is I
> . . . .
> This is the same exultant beast
> That so joyously
> Ran the ball with you
> In those far-flung days of abandon.

Other writers fairly well known in the 1920s included Alice Dunbar Nelson, Leslie Pinckney Hill, Effie Lee Newsome, and Benjamin Brawley, who was also prominent as a scholar and literary critic—albeit one of almost glacial conservatism.

Pride of place among those who achieved a wide reputation with work of limited quantity must probably go to Waring Cuney, whose "No Images" once enjoyed an almost international vogue as helping to define the spirit of the Harlem Renaissance:

> She thinks her brown body
> Has no glory.
>
> If she could dance
> Naked,
> Under palm trees
> And see her image in the river
> . . . .
>
> But there are no palm trees
> On the street,
> And dish water gives back no images.

As the decade of the 1920s wore on poetry clearly became increasingly less significant to the Harlem Renaissance. The year 1928 saw an outpouring of novels at a rate never before witnessed in Harlem, or in black America; the presence of established poets among the novelists signaled a definite diminution in the prestige of verse. Of the poets, McKay brought out his first novel in 1928, Hughes in 1930, Bontemps in 1931, and Cullen his only novel in 1932. Among these writers only the dedicated Hughes continued to write and publish verse with any-thing like the zeal and zest—and the innovative drive—that had char-acterized their careers to this point. When a combination of factors (notably the Depression, which quickly devastated Harlem as a site of black aspiration) brought the glory years of the movement to a close—the Harlem Riot of 1935 may be taken as the absolute boundary of the renaissance—few poets were still singing in Harlem.

And yet the poets of the renaissance had played a major role—per-haps the central role—in defining the spirit of the age. In literature, as in music (that of Duke Ellington and Louis Armstrong, for example) and art (Aaron Douglas and Augusta Savage), the movement laid the foundations for the creative representation of African American social and cultural reality in the modern world. All subsequent African Amer-ican creativity in these fields has built upon that solid foundation, laid mainly by young men and women of lengthening vision who respond-ed affirmatively to the challenge and the opportunity best symbolized within black America in the decade of the 1920s by Harlem.

Arnold Rampersad

Further Reading

Honey, Maureen, ed. *Shadowed Dreams: Women's Poetry of the Harlem Renaissance.* New Brunswick, N.J.: Rutgers University Press, 1989.

Huggins, Nathan Irvin, ed. *Voices from the Harlem Renaissance.* New York: Oxford Uni-versity Press, 1976.

Hughes, Langston, and Arna Bontemps, eds. *The Poetry of the Negro, 1746–1970.* New York: Doubleday, 1970.

Lewis, David Levering. *When Harlem Was in Vogue.* New York: Oxford University Press, 1981.

Rampersad, Arnold. *The Life of Langston Hughes: I, Too, Sing America.* Vol. 1. New York: Oxford University Press, 1986.

Wagner, Jean. *Black Poets of the United States.* Tr. Kenneth Douglas. Urbana: Universi-ty of Illinois Press, 1973.

Warren, with Ransom and Tate

ROBERT PENN WARREN was only sixteen years old when he entered Vanderbilt University in 1921. He was born in Guthrie, Kentucky, fifty miles north of Nashville, on the border between Kentucky and Tennessee, in 1905. He had graduated from the Guthrie high school early (no great feat, he later said), but was then too young to be permitted to enter the university, so he took an extra year at a preparatory high school in Clarksville, Tennessee, until he was sixteen. His youthful plans did not, in fact, include attending Vanderbilt anymore than they included becoming a poet. His ambition at the time was to become a naval officer ("my desire was to be admiral of the Pacific Fleet of course"), and he had attained an appointment to Annapolis. But an accident caused him to lose the sight in one eye, and, unable to pass the Annapolis physical, he went instead to Vanderbilt, intending to become a chemical engineer. His freshman English teacher, the poet and critic John Crowe Ransom, swiftly put an end to that intention. In this period Ransom was also Allen Tate's teacher, and later, after moving to Kenyon College, taught both Robert Lowell and Randall Jarrell (the two shared a second-story room in Ransom's house in Gambier, Ohio, which may have given that particular house a greater concentration of poetic talent per cubic inch than any other in the country). Lowell remembered Ransom as "one of the best talkers that has ever lived in the United States," and surely Ransom was one of the great teachers as well. He believed that both poetry and literary criticism were of genuine cultural importance and taught his students that literary texture and technique were central to the significance of a work rather than merely decorative. In addition to his gifts as a writer Ransom's courtesy, his playfulness, and his generosity all made him a figure of enormous influence. After Warren had been in Ransom's freshman class for a term, Ransom announced that he didn't think Warren belonged there—he was moving him into his advanced class. "This was the greatest day of my life," Warren later remembered, "that he would give *me* some personal attention in another class of older people."

Of course what Ransom had noticed in the young Warren was visible to others as well. Allen Tate, who became Warren's roommate, remembered his first sight of "the most remarkable-looking boy I had ever laid eyes on. . . . When he walked across the room he made a sliding shuffle, as if his bones didn't belong to one another." This description not only communicates something of the young Warren's aura but also points toward the striking physicality—the bodiliness—that would come to mark Warren's finest poems. The sixteen-year-old "Red" Warren was, Tate said, the most gifted person he had ever known (Warren's lifelong nickname came from hair "red as a termater," as his poem "Homage to Emerson, On Night Flight to New York" puts it). When they became roommates, sharing a room in the old Theological School at Vanderbilt, Tate was six years older than Warren (he'd entered the university late while Warren had entered early) and Warren thought him a "genius." In the intensity of that time the talk was all passionate interest in art and ideas and poetry. If Warren left one of his poems in the typewriter and fell asleep, he later remembered, Tate (and Ridley Wills, another roommate) would come in and start revising it.

Warren, Tate, and Wills were among the precocious undergraduates invited to join the Fugitive group, which had originated before the First World War as a gathering of Vanderbilt faculty and Nashville citizens exchanging ideas on a wide range of political and artistic subjects. Revived in the 1920s under the leadership of John Crowe Ransom, the Fugitives were less a coherent "school" than a poetry club whose various members read and criticized one another's work (all of them were men. A later exception, Laura Riding, never attended regular meetings). From 1922 to 1925 the group published the *Fugitive* magazine, which gained a lasting reputation for the work it included—almost all of the poems Ransom produced, as well as poems by Donald Davidson, Tate, and Warren. The first edition (April 1922) contained a preface by

Ransom in which he said, "*The Fugitive* flees from nothing faster than from the high-caste Brahmins of the Old South." He thus targeted an overly genteel, sentimental southern literature and culture as the impulse for the group's flight; like other Modernists, they fled an enervated literary tradition that had come to a dead-end. The Fugitives have since come to be seen as fleeing modern, urban industrialism, in large part because they later espoused anti-industrial, Agrarian ideals, documented most famously in *I'll Take My Stand: The South and the Agrarian Tradition* (1930). Authorship of the manifesto was attributed to "Twelve Southerners," and Ransom, Tate, and Warren each contributed essays. Despite its important critique of industrialism's myth of progress, *I'll Take My Stand* is a problematic volume. Its assumptions about race are objectionable, and its advocacy of a return to the land and to traditional values as a cure for economic materialism was wildly off the point in 1930 for many who were hungry and unemployed. One consequence of the debates surrounding *I'll Take My Stand* has been to eclipse the original nature of the Fugitive group; as Warren remembered them, "many had totally different views, violently different views. They hung together because they were all crazy about poetry."

Nashville was a good place to be crazy about poetry in the twenties and thirties. Like Black Mountain in the fifties and Iowa City in the sixties and seventies, Nashville was a lively artistic community located in what the literary establishments of New York or Boston thought of as a backwater. At Vanderbilt there was an intense excitement about modern poetry; when new issues of the *Nation* or the *Dial* came out with poems by Hart Crane, Yeats, or Eliot, the copies sold out. A passion for Eliot's *The Waste Land* and the new experiments in poetic technique it represented was so strong that many students could quote the poem by heart. Warren was probably one of those students; not only had he memorized poems during his boyhood both at school and at home but his passion for *The Waste Land* manifested itself on the walls of the room he and Tate shared, decorated with Warren's murals of scenes from Eliot's poem. It is understandable that, even many years later, Tate would remember vividly the one of the typist putting the record on the gramophone, and the rat creeping through the vegetation.

To stand out as gifted in the company that surrounded Warren during his Vanderbilt years suggests an extraordinary gift, which the fruits of Warren's long and remarkable career bear out. If the stature of Ransom and Tate as poets seems to shrink somewhat under Warren's imposing shadow, it is not because the poems they produced aren't valuable. Rather, Warren emerges as a major if imperfect poet, his career vitalized by dynamic change, while Ransom and Tate are poets whose development is more static and more limited. Understanding something about the strengths and limits of Ransom's and Tate's poems helps to clarify the nature of Warren's unfolding achievement.

John Crowe Ransom was born in Tennessee in 1888, and his father was a Methodist minister. He attended Vanderbilt and then became a Rhodes Scholar at Oxford (as fifteen years later Warren also would) in 1913, where he studied Classics. After serving in Europe in the war, he returned to Vanderbilt to teach, until 1937 when he left to continue his long career of teaching and criticism at Kenyon College in Gambier, Ohio. There he founded *The Kenyon Review*, a journal that published an extraordinary number of the most important writers and critics in its time. Ransom served as its editor from 1937 until his retirement in 1959. By almost every criterion—birth, continued residence, and subject matter—Ransom can be called a southern poet. However, Ransom's southernness is worth interrogating, as it both illumines his own work and complicates our understanding of that term.

In a piece written for Ransom's eightieth birthday Warren described Ransom's southernness as a "drama of 'difference from' and 'identification with.'" Ransom resisted a modernity without stable values, values he believed endured in southern, communal traditions. At the same time, he also set himself against a southern literary tradition whose overgentility was a form of escape from the world, and against a romantic idealism equally deplorable ("heart's desire poetry," he called it, "the act of a sick mind"). Irony and paradox became Ransom's literary corrective, and Warren saw the mock heroic tone of many Ransom poems as an ironic reduction of "official Southern rhetoric." Arguably, this commitment to irony and paradox combined with an abbreviated poetic career kept Ransom from tapping the full power of the heart's desire, that "yearning" which fuels the poetic achievement of Warren and drives poetry into the world's embrace.

Almost all of Ransom's best poems were written in the short period between 1920 and 1927, when, essentially, he stopped writing poetry. An early collection, *Poems About God* (1919), was published while Ransom was an artillery officer in Europe (Henry Holt published the collection on Robert Frost's recommendation). But the poems of that volume are scarcely recognizable as the work of the poet who wrote "Captain Carpenter" or "Bells for John Whiteside's Daughter" or "Janet Waking" or "The Equilibrists," to name a few of the best poems that appeared in Ransom's second book, *Chills and Fever* (1924), and his third, *Two Gentlemen in Bonds* (1927) (not counting the English selection of his work, *Grace After Meat*, published in 1924 with an introduction by Robert Graves). Thereafter Ransom wrote only five more poems, although editions of his *Selected Poems* appeared over the years along with some disastrous late revisions that, as Tate remarked after Ransom's death, we may now safely ignore.

Ransom's decision to stop writing will always remain mysterious, especially since he was producing his best poems when, as Warren remembered it, Ransom turned to him and said, "I'm gonna quit writing poetry." Ransom's perplexing explanation was that he enjoyed being an "amateur," and doing what he did for pleasure alone. He did not want to become a "professional" poet, and he did not want to repeat himself. When Warren later tried to make his own sense of Ransom's decision, he turned to Randall Jarrell's comment, that "being a poet is like standing out in the rain, waiting for lightning to hit you. If it hits you once—that is, if you write one really fine poem—you are good; if it hits you six times, you're great." Ransom, Warren concluded, wouldn't stay out in the rain. The larger question of *why* Ransom didn't stay out in the rain is not, of course, answered by the description.

Perhaps the lightness and formal perfection in Ransom's best work provides some of the explanation. There is something beautifully balanced and achieved (Randall Jarrell called it "Mozartian") about Ransom's best poems. They do what they do with grace and ease, even as they move in complex ways between the heroic and mock-heroic, between irony and pathos, and between Ransom's distinctively latinate and his colloquial vocabulary. They are not poems whose scope widens to increase the possibility of lightning bolts. Indeed, part of the pleasure of Ransom's poems is that they rest at home within smaller boundaries.

Despite his dark themes—mortality, the transience of beauty, and the helplessness of much human experience—reading Ransom is a delight. His consistent stance may be irony, but, as Warren noted, there is always a tension in Ransom between irony and tenderness, between involvement and withdrawal. The tone of the poems often walks a tightrope, attaining a difficult and exhilarating balance. We experience that balance, sometimes with comic effect, in Ransom's rhythms. "Captain Carpenter," for example, tells the story of the good captain who, in search of fame and honor, rides out again and again undaunted, while each time a different adversary deprives him of yet another bodily part (his nose, legs, arms, eyes, and, at last, his heart). All the while the ballad music of Ransom's stanzas keeps its brisk pace and nothing disturbs the poet's own balance of observation and mild attachment. The result is wittily gruesome and comic (the poem resembles Edgar Arlington Robinson's "Miniver Cheevy," also wittily mock-heroic, but without Ransom's darker edge). The sixth stanza of this poem is a good example of the way Ransom balances high-toned and colloquial diction, and uses rhyme for a surprising effect: the captain exchanges blows with "the wife of Satan"—"Their strokes and counters whistled in the wind / I wish he had delivered half his blows / But where she should have made off like a hind / The bitch bit off his arms at the elbows." Ransom's work often contains little kicks of surprise, like the rhyme of "his blows" and its deliberately inelegant antiphon, "his arms at the elbows." In another Ransom poem, "Philomela," the surprising latinal, "I pernoctated with Oxford students once," provides an unexpected jolt.

All of Ransom's best poems have this sense of pleasure and play, no matter how sorrowful their subject. In "Janet Waking," which begins elegantly with "Beautifully Janet slept / Till it was deeply morning." we have that Ransom hallmark, the "transmogrifying bee" that comes "droning down on Chucky's old bald head." The surprising, comic concreteness unsettles the loveliness of the poem's opening and close. (Ransom's essay, "On Shakespeare's Language," attributed the strength of that language to Shakespeare's mixture of Latin and Anglo-Saxon vocabulary.) In "The Equilibrists" the poet's tone and description enact their own dazzling balance in a poem about two illicit lovers fatally balancing the claims of both desire and honor. There's playfulness too in the way the poem's beginning, with its open, liquid sounds, suddenly snaps at the arrival of the rhyme: "Full of her long white arms and milky skin / He had a thousand times remembered sin." Even the delicate and elegiac "Bells for John Whiteside's Daughter," about that most genteel of subjects, the death of a young girl, ends with a final stanza, and a witty final rhyme whose tone cuts short graver feelings:

> But now go the bells, and we are ready;
> In one house we are sternly stopped
> To say we are vexed at her brown study,
> Lying so primly propped.

Reading "Winter Remembered," the opening poem of the 1945 and 1955 *Selected Poems*, offers the fun of watching a poet pull off a poem about the pain of love in a high-toned rhetoric (Delmore Schwartz once linked Ransom and Stevens for their mutual love of a "dandyism" of surface, of a mock-grand style rendered playfully). The final stanza of that poem has the thrill of balanced excess flirting with imbalance. No one, Warren wrote of his former teacher, is so much the master of the withheld effect as Ransom. The stanza rounds the corner into a final image, down-shifting its gears.

> Dear love, these fingers that had known your touch,
> And tied our separate forces first together,
> Were ten poor idiot fingers not worth much,
> Ten frozen parsnips hanging in the weather.

Parsnips! Ransom thought of himself as a domestic poet, who attended to ordinary and small things (suggesting the work of his student, Randall Jarrell, some of whose poems imitate Ransom's subjects, and Ransom's tenderness, without the ironic stance). Ransom's self-description might seem to put a poem like "Captain Carpenter" or "Necrological" (where a friar visits a place of battle littered with bodies) somewhat to the side of poems like "Bells for John Whiteside's Daughter," "Here Lies a Lady," "Vision By Sweet Water" or "Janet Waking" which, with their focus often on women, seem to occupy a kind of bounded domestic space. But even "Captain Carpenter" and "Necrological" are domestic, because the poet's voice in these poems keeps the "heroic" scene a miniature. Things in the poem seem small because the poet's voice refuses to make too much of them (as in "Necrological," with its description of the stallion and rider: "The great beast had spilled there his little brain, / And the little groin of the knight was spilled by a stone."). As Randall Jarrell remarked, "his poems profess their limitations so candidly, almost as a principle of style, that it is hardly necessary to say they are not poems of the largest scope or of the greatest intensity." It is embarrassing to call Ransom's work "minor poetry," when it is so clear that Ransom himself never intends the poems to be great or encompassing. In this way he is the very opposite of his gifted student, Robert Penn Warren, whose work constantly aspires to what Warren himself called "glory." Perhaps Ransom's courtesy, harmony, and control prevented him from throwing himself, heart and soul, into poetic ambition ("Ambition is a terrible thing," Warren once heard him say). For all the pleasure of Ransom's poetry, in the end it is all too perfectly balanced and too little in scale. Yet each time one returns to reading the slim edition of Ransom's *Selected Poems* any clear-eyed assessment of his limitations seems rather beside the point.

"To expect Tate's and Warren's poems to be much influenced by Ransom's is like expecting two nightmares to be influenced by a daydream," Randall Jarrell wrote. The characteristics of Ransom's poetry are lightness and balance, and part of the pleasure of reading him is that he makes the difficult look easy. Allen Tate's poetry is knotted and weighty; it makes the difficult feel—well, difficult. Tate was self-consciously a man of letters, as his essays "The Man of Letters in the Modern World" (1952) and "The Profession of Letters in the South" (1935), among numerous others, make clear. He was also self-consciously a writer, and it was perhaps this characteristic that often prevented his poems from genuine, achieved feeling. His best work may be in his critical essays; "There is strength in his language superior to any idea that may be detached from it," R. P. Blackmur once said of Tate's criticism. Tate became an early admirer (and later friend) of another poet whose language is markedly difficult, Hart Crane; their friendship began when Crane read one of Tate's poems in the *Fugitive* and wrote him about it. Some of Tate's best poems remind us of Crane's language and imagery, especially "The Subway" (1927), which resembles Crane's "The Tunnel." For Tate strict form was a necessary "bondage of limitation" to which the poet willingly submits and he accepted that "bondage" in sometimes astonishingly complex forms throughout his career. "The Subway" is a Petrarchan sonnet; its sextet begins, "Till broken in the shift of quieter / Dense altitudes tangential of your steel, / I am become geometries, and glut / Expansions like a blind astronomer." Yet where Crane's complexity seems driven by complex feeling, Tate's seems the product of will.

Like Ransom, his teacher, Tate himself was an important teacher and model for younger poets, one of whom was Robert Lowell. In 1937, fleeing his New England origins, the young Lowell set off for Nashville; "My head was full of Miltonic, vaguely piratical ambitions. My only anchor was a suitcase, heavy with bad poetry." He arrived at the Tates', and, revisiting later when the house was crowded with guests, camped on their lawn for three months in a pup tent he bought at Sears, the sort of story that is perhaps doomed to seem apocryphal even though true. One can hear in the early Lowell the kind of weightiness and literariness one hears in Tate (Tate wrote the introduction to Lowell's *Land of Unlikeness*, 1944), along with a preoccupation with some of the same themes. Both share what Lowell called (speaking of Tate) "the resonance of desperation," the desperation of a hemmed-in ego fixed in its own reflective consciousness, trying to connect with the world. Tate believed the meaning of poetry is "its 'tension'" ("Tension in Poetry") and that the writer carries the conflicts and tensions of a complex society within him or herself, conflicts that often make meaningful action impossible. Lowell's early work (and that of his contemporary, John Berryman, as well) suggests some of Tate's poetic practice, and we can profitably read Lowell's "Quaker Graveyard in Nantucket" and even the later "For the Union Dead," next to Tate's "Ode to the Confederate Dead." Later Lowell wrote of Tate's poems that "no one has so given us the impression that poetry must be burly, must be courteous, must be tinkered with and recast until one's eyes pop out of one's head." But, he continues, "How often something smashes through the tortured joy of composition to strike the impossible bull's-eye!" Lowell points to a crucial moment in Tate's work, one we wish happened more often.

Such a moment occurs in the title poem of Tate's first book, *Mr. Pope and Other Poems* (1928), a meditation on the knotted figure of the hunch-backed Alexander Pope ("For Pope's tight back was rather a goat's than man's") and the enduring power of his art. The poem bears Tate's mark in its focus on something contorted, painful, and difficult (here, the body of Pope), accompanied by a language equally compacted. Tate here confronts the way Mr. Pope's contortedness and separateness—qualities that may belong to Mr. Tate as well—are painful and limiting (in the poem people fear rather than pity Pope, but in any case he is apart from them). What, in Lowell's phrase, smashes through the knots of composition is a genuine difficulty the poem leaves unresolved: the limits of what we can know of the personal sources of a writer's power and style (what "Prompted the wit and rage between his teeth /

One cannot say"). Tate and the reader both face that mystery as well as the mystery of art's power to rise up out of, and to transfigure, difficulty and pain. The poem ends, "Around a crooked tree / A moral climbs whose name should be a wreath." This poem from Tate's first book sets a standard Tate never developed beyond, although unlike Ransom he continued writing poems for more than forty years.

Like Ransom, Tate's identity as a southerner was proudly acknowledged but complicated. He was born in Winchester, Kentucky, in 1899, but he spent his summers in Fairfax, Virginia, the home of his mother's family. Too often we assume a single monolithic "South," ignoring the powerful differences between Kentucky or Tennessee, with their frontier ties and small-town, Methodist or Baptist communities, and Tidewater Virginia with its genteel history, its plantations, and its social and religious hierarchies. Louis Rubin has pointed out these distinctions, noting that when Tate entered Vanderbilt and was invited to join the Fugitives (he was twenty-one) his sophistication "was not merely intellectual but social as well." Part of his intellectual sophistication was a knowledge of the French Symbolists and literary Modernism. Ransom would later say that Tate's position in the group was "[a]s champion of the new literature," and, indeed, when Ransom attacked the pessimism and collage technique of *The Waste Land* (in the *Literary Review*, 1923), Tate wrote an immediate response denouncing Ransom's "ignorance" of Modernism, and sent his teacher, Ransom, a copy. "How he ever forgave me I do not know," Tate wrote on the occasion of Ransom's seventy-fifth birthday, "and I do not want to know." Warren also remembered Tate as the "most modern" of the remarkable Fugitive group, but perhaps more important, he also called Tate his own most powerful critic. Tate's embrace of Modernism was, in particular, an embrace of the work of T. S. Eliot as his Modern master. He wrote in a prefatory note to *The Swimmers and Other Selected Poems* (1970) that he defined his "early" work as "a poem written before 1922, when I read T. S. Eliot's *Poems* (1920)." Thereafter everything Tate wrote had Eliot as a model and Tate's search for values and order led him, like Eliot, to religion; he converted to Catholicism in 1951.

When Tate graduated from Vanderbilt in 1923 (his graduation was delayed for a year by tuberculosis), he went to New York City to make his life as a writer. Like another of his models, Edgar Allen Poe, the southern poet Tate saw as his spectral shadow ("He is so close to me,"

Tate wrote, "that I am sometimes tempted to enter the mists of pre-American genealogy to find out whether he may not actually be my cousin"), Tate became a southern writer exiled from the South even as he was connected to it. This is true even for the period in which Tate returned to live in the South (in 1930, after a Guggenheim to Europe), first in Tennessee, then in Memphis and Greensboro. In the 1940s he began a second long period of separation in various northern cities (Princeton, New York, Chicago, Minneapolis) until, on his retirement from the University of Minnesota in 1968, he returned to Tennessee. In Tate's self-understanding as well as in his vision of Poe, the larger meanings of exile and connection extended both to a divided self and to a fragmented culture in which this self might be stranded without connection.

While Tate was living in New York he began work on his most famous poem, "Ode to the Confederate Dead," which is preoccupied exactly with the dilemma of a "locked-in ego" (Tate's own description). First published in 1927 but revised over a ten-year period until it appeared in *Selected Poems* (1937), this is the one poem of Tate's that even readers who don't read Tate come to know. Much literary ink has been spilled in commentary on this poem, some of that ink Tate's own; his 1938 essay, "Narcissus as Narcissus," is an extended commentary on the "Ode." Tate began the essay by saying it was the first and probably last of his writing about his own verse, invoking Poe's "Philosophy of Composition." Part of the effect of reading Tate's essay is to have confirmed one's sense of the poem as overburdened. At one point Tate remarks that he has commented on a passage in the poem in detail "not because I think it is successful, but because I labored with it," recalling for us again Lowell's description of Tate's poetry. If Ransom's poetry suffers from being all delicate balance and too little, "Ode to the Confederate Dead" is all too labored and too much. And yet, the poem has power. The constrictive sense of the "you" in the poem, positioned by the wall of the cemetery, is *felt* constriction, and the speaker's (and reader's) separation from the Confederate dead—from the possibility of heroism they might represent, and from their conviction about the value of their own actions—is also vividly represented. The concerns of this poem—the burden of history, the place of memory, the question of what might be heroic—are also the animating motives in much of Warren's mature work. But in Tate these concerns are too hemmed in by form and too abstracted by intellect to become the passionate inquiry we find in Warren's poems of history, memory, and time.

"I often think of my poems," Tate said, "as commentaries on those human situations from which there is no escape." Poetic form functions for Tate as an emblem of what cannot be escaped, even when his submission to formal constraints comes at the cost of feeling. It is like Tate to write a sequence, "Seasons of the Soul," in ten-line stanzas with three beats a line and a complicated rhyme scheme. Likewise, three of his most interesting poems in later career—"The Maimed Man" (1952), "The Swimmers" (1953), and "The Buried Lake" (1953)—are written in *strict* imitation of Dante's terza rima (thereby making Eliot's imitation of Dante's form without the strict rhyme seem "loose," even if "Little Gidding" turned out to be a great and moving poem beyond what Tate's efforts could produce). One might imagine that Yeats had Tate in mind when he wrote the opening lines of "The Fascination of What's Difficult"—had that poem not been published in 1910—"The fascination of what's difficult / Has dried the sap out of my veins, and rent / Spontaneous joy and natural content / Out of my heart." That Tate made a body of poetry, even if a slim body, out of that fascination and emotional constraint is a tribute to his particular, genuine gifts.

"You hold your eager head / Too high in the air, you walk / As if the sleepy dead / Had never fallen to drowse / From the sublimest talk / Of many a vehement house." These are the opening lines of "To a Romantic," an early (1924) Tate poem addressed to Robert Penn Warren. Read now, with Warren's full achievement before us, Tate's poem seems remarkably in touch with some distinctive aspects of Warren's poetic temperament. There is Warren's characteristic poetic and bodily stance: the head held up to the sky or the stars while the poet (like the title figure in his *Audubon*) walks in the world. Tate's lines also anticipate the way history and memory reanimate "the sleepy dead" in the present of a Warren poem, which seeks, over and over again, the vital connection of now and then (the phrase itself is the title of one of Warren's collections). And yet the tone of Tate's poem, while clearly admiring the figure of the youthful Warren, also suggests that this romantic may have his head too much in the clouds, that Tate knows better than this Warren who, because his "clamorous blood / Beats an impermanent rest," is naive enough to think that "the dead arise / Westward and fabulous."

While it's certainly likely that nineteen-year-old Robert Penn Warren had his head too high in the clouds, the drama of renewal amidst what is lost or passing and the vigorous clamor in the blood are hallmarks not simply of Warren's youth but of his mature poetic accomplishment. These qualities are fully evident in the well-known "Heart of Autumn" (from the 1978 volume, *Now and Then*), a powerful example of Warren's achieved work that, set beside Tate's poem, revises and extends the promise Tate saw. In "Heart of Autumn" Warren stands, "my face lifted now skyward," watching the wild geese "head for a land of warm water." As the geese move across the autumn sky, some of them dropped from the air by rifle blasts, he asks:

> Do I know my own story? At least, they know
> When the hour comes for the great wing-beat. Sky-strider,
> Star-strider—they rise, and the imperial utterance,
> Which cries out for distance, quivers in the wheeling sky.

Those sky-striding, star-striding geese—one of a group of magisterial and invigorating birds that recur throughout Warren's work—are figures for what arises, "fabulous" (as Tate imagined it), amidst what falls and fails. Watching them—looking skyward but equally grounded in his body—and hearing their imperial utterance (a kind of clamor), the poet's own heart stirs until, at last:

> Hearing the high beat, my arms outstretched in the tingling
> Process of transformation, and soon tough legs
> With folded feet, trail in the sounding vacuum of passage
> And my heart is impacted with a fierce impulse
> To unwordable utterance—
> Toward sunset, at a great height.

This poem is one incarnation of Warren, the romantic, as major poet, whose heart resounds with the clamorous utterance he hears in the wild geese, whose body feels their wing-beat. "Fierce impulse" drives his lines out of the narrow margins of Tate's early poem, and the energy and passion of bodily perception drive him to forge his characteristic noun compounds within a rhythm that is tugged by gravity and rises beyond it. The moment of transformation in this poem comes from a yearning far beyond the boundaries of Ransom's ironies or the abstract and intellectual complexities of Tate, but that yearning is not narrowly "Romantic." The scope of Warren's feeling includes the knowledge of "pathlessness" and of "folly" (as we know from many other Warren poems and from his novels as well), yet it reaches toward joy. All Warren's powerful feeling and passionate aspiration in this poem—which, like the geese, falls, then rises again "Toward sunset, at a great height"—were for many years hemmed in by a narrow formalism and model of ironic paradox that dominated much of American poetry before 1945. We might say that Warren kept revising his own story until such time as he freed himself to be both a grounded, unblinking truth-seeker *and* the powerful, romantic yearner Tate glimpsed in 1924. In that same year Tate wrote in a letter to Donald Davidson, "That boy's a wonder—has more sheer genius than any of us; watch him: his work from now on will have what none of us can achieve—power." Tate was right, and the emergence of that power is the story of Warren's developing vocation.

The sources of a poetic vocation must always be partly mysterious, but it is clear that those sources begin in Warren's childhood. His maternal grandfather ("an idol," Warren called him), on whose farm Warren spent his boyhood summers, "read poetry and quoted it by the yard" and imbued Warren with the importance of history and memory. As a boy he also discovered a volume containing poems his father had written, although his father swiftly removed the book from Warren's sight ("Later, I found the poems. Not good," he wrote in "Reading Late at Night, Thermometer Falling"). Several of Warren's poems attribute to his mother (who died when Warren was a twenty-six-year-old assistant professor at Vanderbilt) a love of the natural world and a voice whose "undeclared timbre" ("Code Book Lost") suggests both joy and loss (see "The Only Poem"). Memory's repetitions, the dream enacted and reenacted, obsessed Warren all his life.

Significantly for both Warren's poetic identity and his identity as a southerner the dream he reenacts is not his alone. It is inherited—from the possibilities and failures of his own mother, father and grandfather, and from the deep sense of loss that marks southern history. As James M. Cox has said of Faulkner, Warren's poetic "I" begins in debt (a psychic form of the literal debt into which business failures and honorable character led both his father and grandfather). In Warren's poems we repeatedly feel we are entering into something that was there before the poem began, and that endures beyond the poem's close. Warren responded to this indebtedness with both resistance and a violent need to understand the meaning of what was remembered. As much as anything this violent need shaped Warren's poetic vocation; "I Am Dreaming of a White Christmas: The Natural History of a Vision," "There's a Grandfather's Clock in the Hall," *Audubon*'s "The Dream He Never Knew the End of," *Tale of Time*'s "Insomnia," and the early "Original Sin: A Short Story," to name only some of the strongest examples, all give expression to it.

Like all true poets, Warren felt called to speak as a response to what he heard speaking *to* him; the sounds of the world, the voices of the past and present, lay claim on Warren in poem after poem. The figure of Audubon (Warren's shadow double as Poe was Tate's), in Warren's great long poem of the 1960s, both walks in the world and listens; he discovers that "the world declares itself." The world declared itself likewise to Warren, and its sounds, even when untranslatable, became the music of poetry. In a poem Harold Bloom has linked to poetic identity, "Evening Hour" (from *Now and Then*), Warren remembers a boy who is clearly himself looking for arrowheads in a graveyard, suddenly distracted from his pursuit by something not quite utterable. An impulse without rational explanation comes upon the boy (and the poet remembering) to *claim* him. In the final stanza when the boy sees the lights of the town come on: "He did not know / Why the lights, so familiar, now seemed so far away, / And more than once felt the crazy impulse grow / To lay ear to earth for what voices beneath might say." The voices beneath the earth also form part of what Warren inherited, like it or not.

Of course, for the world to declare itself Warren had to do what the Audubon of his poem does—both walk in the world and love it. Walking means inhabiting, feeling one's connection to and and implication in time and history (walking, Kierkegaard said, is finitude). This inhabiting means that love of the world, in Warren's work, is never without the shadows of loss, loneliness, violence, guilt, and failure. Nonetheless, Warren's poems express a passion for existence that energizes and animates them even when the subject is grim. And it is often grim—with its skulls, carcasses, hangings, rifle blasts, taxidermy, decay. An embrace of the world was not readily available to Warren in his early models; Ransom was tender but too ironic and detached for passion, Tate, too cerebral and divided. Then there was the looming figure of Eliot, whose influence is palpable in Warren's early work (see, for example, section 3 of "Kentucky Mountain Farm," written in the twenties and thirties, with its "There are many ways to die / Here among the rocks in any weather." And, of course, there were those murals Warren drew on the walls of his room at Vanderbilt). But Eliot's temperament (repulsion, F. R. Leavis once said, is a "motive force" in Eliot's work) was much more compatible with Tate's than with Warren's. In Warren there is too much love for the sensuous world, too much bodily being-in-the world to be at ease in Eliot's tone, although, like many poets who began writing in the twenties and thirties, Warren had to write himself out of the burden of Eliot's influence. Throughout his career, however, Warren retained the power of some of Eliot's images and made his own distinctive blend of the descriptive and meditative modes Eliot joined in *The Four Quartets*. Like so many Warren poems, Eliot's *Quartets* seek to know the nature of time. But for Eliot, the "unattended moment" in which the real is apprehended lay outside an ordinary human time empty of meaning: "Ridiculous the sad waste time / Stretching before and after." Warren's acts of walking in the world, however, are grounded within the passage of ordinary time and within personal and national history. That Warren knew how to *use* time is apparent from the way his poems unfold on the page: the line extending itself and sometimes abruptly closing, as if a clock suddenly struck, the piled-up lines that give the time of the poem a plentitude. To the conjunction of the descriptive and meditative Warren added a third element largely absent in Eliot: narrative, the way a story unfolds itself in and through time. Warren's poems, like those of Ransom, tell stories ("Stories!" Jarrell exclaimed, in mock-horror, of Ransom's work).

Of course, as an undergraduate Warren was reading Eliot as well as the Metaphysical poets Eliot championed. In that period of his life poetry became consciously important to Warren: "The reading of it and the trying to write it," he said, "became simply matters of life and death." Many years later he speculated that the passion he developed for poetry then may have been intensified by his fear of blindness (having lost the sight in one eye, he feared a sympathetic failure of sight in the other eye; the injured eye was removed in the early 1930s when he was teaching at Vanderbilt). In that period poetry became, Warren said, a refuge. Perhaps we can see his acute visual gifts, his vivid and particular descriptions of the natural world as deepened and fired by that fear of blindness. He notices the way clouds move across the sky in different seasons ("Today, under gray cloud-scud and over gray / Wind-flicker of forest" in "Heart of Autumn") and sees the distinctiveness of trees ("high-tangled spruce night" in "Sunset Walk in Thaw-Time in Vermont"). Poetry remained at the center for Warren, even in the middle 1940s, when he entered a period in which he could not finish a short poem. In that period his most famous novel, *All The King's Men* (1945), was published, and he was also working on his book-length "verse drama," *Brother to Dragons* (1953, revised as a second version in 1979). Warren found himself able to return to poetry with renewed openness and energy in the mid-fifties. American poetry was loosening up (Allen Ginsberg's *Howl* appeared in 1956) and *Brother to Dragons* was behind him. After an unhappy first marriage he married the writer Eleanor Clark in 1952, and they soon had two children, Rosanna and Gabriel.

The poems of *Promises* (1957) come from this period, and the volume is filled with a capacity for happiness quite different from some of Warren's earlier work. For example, these lines from the sequence "To a Little Girl, One Year Old, in a Ruined Fortress," are not imaginable in the earlier Warren: "You leap in gold-glitter and brightness. / You leap like a fish-flash in bright air" or the sequence's closing invocation of "that joy in which all joys should rejoice." Warren himself described this book as "memories and natural events: the poems wander back and forth from my boyhood to my children," suggesting that the renewal of a happy remarriage, and of children, also revived his own earlier memories. The book was, he felt, "a fresh start." To an important degree Warren was right; *Promises* marked a loosening of emotional and formal constraints and led him forward to what many see as his breakthrough book, *Audubon: A Vision* (1969). On the other hand, Warren's capacity for self-renewal—for fresh starts—is clear throughout his long career. Indeed, that capacity for change, a capacity Warren admired in his list of American autodidacts in *Democracy and Poetry* (1975)—Lincoln, Mark Twain, Dreiser—allowed Warren to become the major poet he became. His career is best understood in the company of poets (even those very unlike him in other ways) who kept and keep remaking themselves, who possess what Charles Olson called "the will to change": poets from an older generation like Yeats, Williams, and H.D. (whose *Trilogy* shares Warren's love of the wild geese), and from a younger one, Adrienne Rich, Robert Lowell, and Robert Duncan.

While the "fresh start" of *Promises* and the achievement of *Audubon* can lead us to think of two discrete Warrens—early and late—the body of work as a whole is both more coherent and more diverse than that schema suggests. Appropriately, the work of this poet who thirsted to know the nature of time is work that must be seen as developing over, and changing within, time. A space of fifty years separates his first published collection and his last. The passage of time was in important ways a crucible for Warren, bringing him to rekindle and remake his poetic fires. His own habit of arranging his selected poems (there are several such volumes) with the newest work at the beginning enforces a constant reseeing of the earlier poems through the lens of the new.

If none of the poems before 1954 exhibit Warren's fullest powers, a number of them are explorations of experience to which Warren returned throughout his career. Although most of the poems in *Thirty-Six Poems*, for example, seem forced into awkward rhymes, rickety in tone, and caged in by form (he was a young poet after all), rereading them we now and then hear the distinctive sound of later work. "The Return," from that volume, is full of labored description (recalling Tate) but its twice repeated question, "Tell me its name," is a version of the urgent questioning that energizes Warren's work at its best. The often Eliotic "Kentucky Mountain Farm" comes to life when natural description and memory fuse in the last part of the third section:

> Grey coats, blue coats. Young men on the mountainside
> Clambered, fought. Heels muddied the rocky spring.
> Their reason is hard to guess, remembering
> Blood on their black mustaches in moonlight.
> Their reason is hard to guess and a long time past:
> The apple falls, falling in the quiet night.

This moment anticipates the dark and bloody ancestral ground reimagined in later poems like "American Portrait: Old Style," with its memory of a boyhood Kentucky landscape, so depleted of hope and of history that "we had to invent it all, our Bloody Ground, K and I." Warren's first *Selected Poems* (1923–1943) includes the powerful "Original Sin: A Short Story." Although that poem is also too self-consciously literary, the stumbling nightmare whose anguish trails the poet belongs to Warren's obsession with the dream reenacted. And the final stanza opens into a cleanness of language and fullness of rhythm that anticipates many poems to come:

Later you may hear it wander the dark house
Like a mother who rises at night to seek a childhood picture
Or it goes to the backyard and stands like an old horse cold
    in the pasture.

The loneliness in those lines, and the evocation of an action (leaving the house and wandering into a solitude) that repeats itself in various forms over generations, looks forward to poems like "What Were You Thinking, Dear Mother" (from *Tale of Time*, 1966), "Night Walking" and "The Moonlight's Dream" in *Being Here* (1980), the beautiful "Little Girl Wakes Early" from Warren's last *Selected Poems* (1985), and "Why A Boy Came to Lonely Place" in the same volume.

Like Tate, for whom exile was part of his southern identity, Warren once said he "became a Southerner by going to California and Connecticut and New England." After his graduation from Vanderbilt in 1925, he was a teaching fellow at the University of California, Berkeley, from which he received a master's degree. He then went on to do graduate work at Yale, and in 1928 (like his teacher Ransom earlier) went to Oxford as a Rhodes Scholar. In 1931 he returned to teach at Vanderbilt, but when his contract was not renewed he left in 1934 for Louisiana State University, where the following year with Cleanth Brooks he cofounded the *Southern Review*. Together the two friends and colleagues also published one of the most influential text books in modern American literature, *Understanding Poetry* (1938). In 1942, however, Warren went to the University of Minnesota, where Tate also came to teach in 1951; "I left [L.S.U.]," he said later, "under pressure of some kind or another. . . . I always felt myself somehow squeezed out of the South." Later, he took a position at Yale, and Warren never returned to the South to live.

Distance, Warren felt, intensified his conscious identity as a southerner (an identity that resembles his description of Ransom's drama of "difference from" and "identification with"). Warren's southernness was also complicated by his Kentucky origins, for Kentucky, with its frontier history and its Daniel Boone, represented for him both the South and the West. The importance of memory, the weight of loss, and a deep sense of history all belong to Warren's identity as a southerner. But another part of that identity emerges in the project of *Brother to Dragons*; in this long verse narrative, Warren meditates on an enduring and agonized inheritance, that of slavery and the violence surrounding the social fact of race. Warren had written about issues of race much earlier in an essay, "The Briar Patch," for *I'll Take My Stand*. This early essay makes the argument for separate but equal conditions for black and white southerners; it assumes racial segregation in the South as a permanent social structure. Warren later separated himself from what he had written there. More than twenty years after "The Briar Patch," he published *Segregation: The Inner Conflict in the South* (1956), a series of conversations that explore the costs both of social divisions and "self-division" in the South. In 1965 he published a collection called *Who Speaks for the Negro?* which contains his interviews with, among others, Malcolm X, Martin Luther King, and Adam Clayton Powell. Warren himself called this book a "record of personal discovery." Clearly the meaning and consequences of racial divisions for the South and for the republic were part of Warren's necessary thinking and rethinking throughout most of his life. The ways in which that thinking entered his poetry are most evident in *Brother to Dragons*.

While there are those who have admired it greatly, *Brother to Dragons* is difficult to love (*Audubon* is a much more inviting and engaging work). It staggers under the burdens of detailed historical documents and multiple personal agendas and is overwrought. It feels too long, in part because, for a verse drama, everyone sounds too much alike. But its very imperfectness is revealing, for it throws into relief the struggle in that work, which is Warren's most extended, explicit poetic confrontation with mortal racial conflict and its legacies. Meditations on race appear elsewhere in scattered poems (of uneven success) like the first section of the sequence, *Internal Injuries* (1968), "Old Nigger on One-Mule Cart Encountered Late at Night When Driving Home from Party in the Back Country" (1975), "Ballad of Mister Dutcher and the Last Lynching in Gupton" and "News Photo" (1974), and, perhaps most movingly, in "The Interim," a section from *Tale of Time* (1966). But the work of *Brother to Dragons* precedes these poems, and its flawed ambitiousness suggests the poet is working out something at his (and our) center. The poem tells the terrible story of the murder of a slave, George, hacked to death, in the presence of other slaves, for breaking a pitcher prized by his master's mother. The master was Liliburn Lewis, a nephew of Thomas Jefferson, and his brother, Isham, also participated in the horror. Warren based his poem on historical accounts, but added a contemporary frame in which a narrator, R. P. W., travels with his father to the site of the ruined Lewis house in Smithland, Kentucky (as Warren actually did). In conversation with the historical personages, including Thomas Jefferson, R. P. W. reimagines the murder and the events leading up to and following it. George, the murdered slave, is a crucial exception to these conversations; he never speaks in the poem, but his screams are an undercurrent throughout the narrative.

Brother to Dragons strains toward a metaphysical vision of a dark, violent human nature at odds with Jefferson's vision of perfectible humanity. But the poem's real subject is more specific and historical—the inherited violence of slavery that mutilates everyone in the poem, black and white. This violence forms a legacy laid across the present, which the narrator must confront and acknowledge. Indeed, part of the violence of the poem inheres in Warren's own violent need to come to terms with this legacy. The poem makes it clear that the distortions of slavery are so encompassing that all the poem's historical figures are somehow complicit in Liliburn's act (his brother Isham, his wife Laetitia, his mother Lucy, his uncle Thomas Jefferson, and even George and the domestic servant, Aunt Cat). But that complicity also extends to R. P. W., and likewise to every reader (northern or southern) of the poem as well; it is one of the lessons of Warren's poetry that the various meanings of "southern" comprise not only a geographical region but what James M. Cox calls "the South of our very selves." George's scream and the sound of Liliburn's axe-stroke reverberate in "the lash-bite" and in "the lost child's cry / Down in the quarters when the mother is sold," and reverberate in an American history that has tried to repress those sounds and their meanings. The violence at the heart of this poem has the quality of nightmare, and surely is linked to the unspecified and recurring nightmare that haunts Warren's work. For all the poem's sometimes hysterical tone ("bombast," Leslie Fiedler called it, admiringly) and the fact that characters often seem to be giving speeches, the anguish and horror are never resolved. They spiral out of *Brother to Dragons* into Warren's larger sense of personal and national history, making themselves felt elsewhere in his poems, in variants like *Audubon*'s nightmare hovel, full of guilt and terror, with its silent, wounded Indian (one of whose eyes is gone), or the mutilated sound of the Indian, Laughing Boy, in the powerful "Rattlesnake Country," whose "croupy laughter" is the dark undertone of the horseman's joyous "I-yee!" The repercussions of *Brother to Dragons* enter into what D. H.

Lawrence called the "menace" of the American landscape, "tense with latent violence and resistance," like the "fool pheasant" exploding onto the car windshield in Warren's "Going West" ("This is one way to write the history of America").

In *Brother to Dragons* Warren wrote, "The recognition of complicity is the beginning of innocence." Perhaps confronting the darkest aspects of his inheritance freed Warren when he once again returned to both historical materials and to the long poem in *Audubon: A Vision* (1969). Warren once described his younger self as one "who lived by the excitements and violences of life rather than by acceptances," and there are Warren poems, early and late, that support this portrayal (for example, "Folly on Royal Street Before the Raw Face of God"). But *Audubon* is about acceptance—the acceptance of one's fate:

> His life, at the end, seemed—even the anguish—simple.
> Simple, at least, in that it had to be
> Simply, what it was, as he was,
> In the end, himself and not what
> He had known he ought to be. The blessedness!—

If *Brother to Dragons* is nightmare, then *Audubon* moves out of nightmare's unending repetitions into a reverie that includes love and the possibility of joy. The American landscape in this poem reveals more beauty than terror. There's violence in *Audubon*, but its energies are channeled into creation (Audubon slays the birds in order to paint them). Warren's interest in the historical Audubon had begun twenty years earlier, when he was writing a novel (*World Enough and Time*) that required him to immerse himself in the nineteenth-century history of Kentucky and Tennessee (again, the South as also the West). He read the journals, the autobiography, the nature writings of Audubon (all his life Warren remained a voracious reader of history, an appetite instilled in him by his grandfather). But he could not, at the time, find a form for the narrative. In the 1960s he began work on a history of American literature (with R. W. B. Lewis and Cleanth Brooks), and Warren wrote the section on Audubon. As he told it later, one day "there popped into my mind a line that had been in the version of *Audubon* that I abandoned. I never went and hunted the rest of it up, so I only had that one line to go on. But I suddenly saw how to do it. I did it in fragments, sort of snapshots of Audubon."

The elliptical structure of *Audubon* ("snapshots") removed the burden of trying to integrate everything into a narrative (the burden that *Brother to Dragons* stumbles under) and opened up space for powerful questions and inexpressible feelings. In *Audubon* narrative, description, and meditation move fluidly in and out of each other and the poem's language responds to felt experience, to contact with the world (rather than with "literature"). Furthermore, in the figure of Audubon Warren was able to project himself with a wholeness absent in the divided speakers of *Dragons*, which is, after all, an agonized meditation on a literal and metaphoric splitting apart. Imagining the historical Audubon, Warren became him; he imaginatively reenacts Audubon's journey, as elsewhere he reenacts the flight of the wild geese ("Heart of Autumn") or experiences the movements of caribou across the snow fully within himself ("Caribou"). In his Audubon Warren could locate and accept destruction and creation, fear and courage, loss and joy. The result is one of the finest long poems in American literature since 1945.

As many of Warren's critics have noted, the Audubon of Warren's poems is a distinctly revised version of the historical figure. Although Warren began with historical documents, the Audubon he created was his own mythic double. This Audubon, artist and scientist, walks through woods and swamp, stands sometimes "in perfect stillness, when no leaf stirred." He longs to know the world's mystery and power, embodied for him in the birds, and yet accepts the impossibility of any final knowledge. Versions of Warren himself as such a figure appear in "Red-Tail Hawk and Pyre of Youth" (where he is a slayer and preserver of the hawk), "Heart of Autumn," "Vermont Thaw," "Sunset Walk in Thaw-Time in Vermont," "Preternaturally Early Snowfall in Mating Season," "Snowshoeing Back to Camp in Gloaming," and "Sila." The Warren of these poems, however, seldom has Audubon's serenity. Audubon is his *mythic* double precisely because Warren remains caught in the snares of history, and lives as much in "the excitements and violences of life" as in acceptance.

Among the important Warren techniques in *Audubon* is the intermingling of narrative sections with those of resonant description, so that the poem has both the power of story and of image. Warren's poetic line in *Audubon* moves between leisurely extension and the clipped syntax also characteristic of later Warren, as in the poem's opening: "Was not the lost dauphin, though handsome was only / Base-born and not even able / To make a decent living, was only / Himself, Jean Jacques, and his passion—." The elided syntax moves things along, sends energy forward, whereas the extended line suspends time, holds the image in a moment of stillness ("He slew them, at surprising distances, with his gun. / Over a body held in his hand, his head was bowed low, / But not in grief"). The poem is beautifully paced in its alterations between the energetic push forward (like walking) and the more liquid suspensions, and what Warren learned about rhythmic pacing in *Audubon* shows up in many of his finest later poems.

Audubon has intensity but also remarkable beauty and tenderness. The opening description of the birds in section 6, "Love and Knowledge," is one unforgettable example of the tenderness. "Their footless dance / Is of the beautiful liability of their nature. / Their eyes are round, boldly convex, bright as a jewel, / And merciless." The sudden shift into the surprise of "merciless" may show that Warren learned something from the withholding effects of his teacher Ransom. That final "merciless" also testifies to Warren's realism, his capacity to look things in the face. The combinations of this Warren poem—toughness and delicacy, energy and stillness, beauty and violence—call to mind our reading of Whitman, that other American poet who so combined manliness and tenderness. Such a combination subverts some of the standard oppositions used to describe American literature. Not enough attention has been paid to the way that Warren, like Whitman before him, offers a heroic model of tenderness, responsiveness, and gaiety as well as energy, intensity and strength.

It is certainly true that many of Warren's best poems have a ferocious and passionate energy; "Rattlesnake Country" (*Or Else*, 1974) crackles with it. But others are written in a quieter register, for example, the moving late poems, "After the Dinner Party" and "Little Girl Wakes Early," and the earlier "Evening Hour." An especially fine example of registers sometimes ignored in Warren's poetry is "The Birth of Love" (*Or Else*, 1974). The poem begins with one of Warren's acute visual descriptions: "Season late, day late, sun just down, and the sky / Cold gunmetal but with a wash of live rose." Warren once said of Faulkner's vivid natural background that "it is the atmosphere that counts, the infusion of feeling, the symbolic weight," and his words might well be turned on his own work here and elsewhere. The immediate focus of the poem is the body of the loved woman emerging from the water in which she has been bathing ("Her motion has fractured it to shivering splinters of silver"). The man watching her—clearly a figure of Warren himself—has swum out, and now hangs "Motionless in the gunmetal water, feet / Cold." Watching, he feels himself dissolve into a single (Emersonian?) "eye." "Birth of Love" is a love poem, and what is striking about it is the way the poet offers first a description of the woman's body "marked by his use, and Time's" and then, as the woman stands erect, catches the astonishment and mystery of her separate being. Her embodied presence is utterly apart from the poet's possession. Here, the figure that stands and gazes toward the sky is not Warren but the woman; in the poem's fresh and lovely image, her body "is / A white stalk from which the face flowers gravely toward the high sky" (an example of Warren's extended line as it holds the moment in suspension). The poem and its landscape are infused with feeling. At the end of the sixth stanza the woman disappears into the trees. The line dangles at its end, suspended above the stanza break, a final phrase ("Dimly glimmers, goes. Glimmers and is gone, and the man,"), as the man in the poem himself hangs inelegantly in the water, and is overcome, in the following stanza, by intense longing, looking for her in the trees where "he knows":

> She moves, and in his heart he cries out that, if only
> He had such strength, he would put his hand forth
> And maintain it over her to guard, in all
> Her out-goings and in-comings, from whatever
> Inclemency of sky or slur of the world's weather
> Might ever be.

In addition to love and acknowledgment this poem gives expression to the heart's desire to protect what it loves. The heart wants the impossible, and Warren knows that, yet knowing, still wants it (*if only*). The pace of Warren's lines here breaks up rhythm with clauses, so that a rhythmic longing to push forward keeps encountering and pushing past obstacles. "The Birth of Love" is a moving, humorous, self-aware poem, and it helps enlarge our understanding of the variedness of Warren's poetic achievement. Such variedness exists not only among poems but within individual poems. "Dead Horse in Field" (*Rumor Verified*, 1980), with its vivid and even brutal description of the horse's carcass preyed on by buzzards, also contains these lines: "A year later, I'll see /

The green twine of vine, each leaf / Heart-shaped, soft as velvet, begin-ning / Its benediction."

When Warren gave the Jefferson Lecture in the Humanities, pub-lished the following year as *Democracy and Poetry* (1975), he explored a vision of selfhood, vital to creativity, that links American democracy and art. Like Whitman, Warren understood his work as a poet and his love for the republic of American letters as part of a love for the larger Republic. This poet, we should remember, also engaged American his-tory in *John Brown: The Making of a Martyr* (1929), *The Legacy of the Civil War: Meditations on The Centennial* (1961), *Who Speaks for the Negro?* (1965), and acted out his love for American literature in impor-tant essays and introductions on Hawthorne, Twain, Hemingway, Faulkner, Dreiser, Melville, Whittier, Frost, and Katherine Anne Porter. Warren's feeling for the nation and its literature was as clear-sighted as it was deep; he wrote movingly of the strengths and imper-fections of both.

In *Democracy and Poetry* Warren said of poetry that "the 'made thing' becomes, then, a vital emblem of the struggle toward the achieving of the self, and that mark of struggle, the human signature, is what gives the aesthetic organization its numinousness." The achieved self that Warren describes in the lectures is constituted not by separateness but by vital relation—to a world, to a community, and to time. Memory, then, is an instrument in that struggle, linking as it does both *then* and *now*, implicating the poet's self in a development over time. His vital relation is not only to those in his present, like the loved woman in "The Birth of Love," but to those of his past, and not his personal past alone. In a culture of forgetting Warren is one of our poets of memory. But his is not simply the backward gaze. Memory in Warren's work intensifies and deepens the present, and opens into the future; this is what an "his-torical sense" means to him. The pace of Warren's lines is always enlarg-ing our sense of time, extending to recover the past, and slapping us back into the immediate now, as in "Reading Late at Night, Ther-mometer Falling" (*Or Else*), one of Warren's poems for and about his father, where the remembered image of the old man reading beneath "the bare hundred-watt bulb" appears "Thus— / But only in my mind's eye now." The *now* of the poem is like the "[p]istol-shot" sound of an oak bough snapping, like the moment when the poet, walking home, suddenly stops. And stares. "And there it is"—the presence of the past.

We find such a moment in another poem of memory, "Doubleness in Time" (*New and Selected Poems*, 1985), its subject the death of Warren's mother.

> *Then*
> Uncoils like *Now. Now*
> Like *Then.* Oh, it
> Was long ago—the years, how many?
> Fifty—but now at last it truly
> Happens. Only *Now.*

Then, now, Now, then. This is the doubleness that gives the poem its title and inhabits many other Warren poems. Here, the reach toward memory uncoils, then recoils, jerking us back from reverie, insisting on the way memory remakes identity *now.*

Even "American Portrait: Old Style" (*Now and Then*, 1978), which is flooded with the memory of childhood's spaciousness and enormity and with a mythic potency embodied in a boyhood friend, K., who "seemed never to walk, but float / With a singular joy and silence," moves, inexorably, into the passage of time toward *now.* Now, "some sixty / Years blown like a hurricane past!" both the poet and K. are old men, and the trench where they played at soldiers in boyhood is a "ditch full of late-season weed-growth." But if the clouds in the sky the poet watches, lying down in the trench on his back, are "drifting on, drifting on, like forever," that drift is not the motion that concludes Warren's poem. He will rise up again, for "I love the world even in my anger / And that's a hard thing to outgrow."

That love of the world opens Warren's poems up into the future, even when, like "Dead Horse in Field," or "Reading Late at Night" or "American Portrait," or "Rattlesnake Country" they are also elegiac. "All I can do is to offer my testimony," he wrote in "Rattlesnake Country," and that testimony is the poet's present witness to what he remembers. It isn't surprising that the testimony of Warren the poet and man of letters has been an inspiration for many younger writers. *Audubon* was published when Warren was in his sixties; there followed seven more books that include some of his finest poems: *Or Else, Can I See Arcturus From Where I Stand, Now and Then, Being Here, Rumor Verified, Chief Joseph of the Nez Pierce,* and *New and Selected Poems 1923–1985.* The last of these volumes appeared when Warren was eighty, and that same year he became the nation's first poet laureate.

The whole, dynamic career offers a model of ongoing creativity. Among those who have explicitly acknowledged a debt to Warren are Randall Jarrell, in his late poems, James Dickey, James Wright, Dave Smith, and T. R. Hummer. Each of these can be called a southern poet as well (Wright's Ohio is North and South simultaneously, just as Warren's Kentucky is West and South). It is also instructive to read Warren's work beside that of other younger poets whom he may have influenced: Sharon Olds and C. K. Williams, with their passionate intensity and use of the extended, forward-pushing line; Susan Howe, a New Englander whose historical imagination is as deep as Warren's; the southerner Charles Wright, with his meditations and his mixture of elegant and colloquial language; and Rita Dove, whose book-length sequence *Thomas and Beulah* owes something of its structure to Warren's *Audubon*.

A poet of Warren's aspirations runs a larger risk of failure than does a more guarded writer. As Warren wrote of William Faulkner, the southern writer with whom he has most in common, "Let us grant . . . Faulkner is a very uneven writer. The unevenness is, in a way, an index to his vitality, his willingness to take risks, to try for new effects, to make new explorations of material and method." When Warren writes about the strengths and imperfections of Faulkner, he also points to something distinctive about his own work, especially when it is seen against its Fugitive origins. Ransom is, in his way, a more polished poet than Warren, and Tate perhaps labored harder to write a perfect (and perfectly difficult) poem. But both Ransom and Tate hold something back in their poetry and thus neither is what Calvin Bedient has called Warren—our poet of "tragic joy." Warren's unevenness is a consequence of both his will to change and the wholeness with which he gives himself to his art.

In *Democracy and Poetry* Warren called poetry "an antidote to passivity." Warren asks us to enter his poetry bodily, to exert ourselves wholly as he does when he swims out into the water in "Acquaintance with Time in Early Autumn." (*Being Here*, 1980). Suddenly the water is "striped with cold," and something deep and chilling is encountered; this discovery of a "dark inwardness" is reenacted in poem after poem. Yet watching a "red-gold" leaf release itself from a tree and descend toward the water, Warren once again feels the heart's "ravening" response to "the world's provocation and beauty." This is his repeated encounter with what he elsewhere calls "the world's magnificence / To which the heart would answer if it could" (*Brother to Dragons*). The world—beautiful and terrible—declares itself and Warren struggles to answer. That struggle is the signature by which we know his poems.

Patricia Wallace

Further Reading

Conkin, Paul Keith. *The Southern Agrarians*. Knoxville: University of Tennessee Press, 1988.

Ransom, John Crowe. *Selected Poems*. New York: Ecco Press, 1978.

Stewart, John Lincoln. *The Burden of Time: The Fugitives and the Agrarians*. Princeton: Princeton University Press, 1965.

Tate, Allen. *Collected Poems: 1919–1976*. New York: Farrar, Straus and Giroux, 1977.

Twelve Southerners. *I'll Take My Stand: The South and the Agrarian Tradition*. Baton Rouge: Louisiana State University Press, 1930.

Warren, Robert Penn. *New and Selected Poems, 1923–1985*. New York: Random House, 1985.

Young, Thomas Daniel. *Waking Their Neighbors Up: The Nashville Agrarians*. Athens: University of Georgia Press, 1982.

American Auden

W. H. AUDEN's emigration from England to the United States in January of 1939 was both one of the most noteworthy literary events of that tumultuous, "low dishonest decade" and a decisive turning point in the career of a prodigiously gifted poet. Many of his British readers and critics accused him of moral cowardice for deserting his native country in a perilous time, while others interpreted his disengagement from radical politics as a form of evasion and a betrayal of his talent. But such views reflected an essential misunderstanding of the poet's complex and continuous development. Auden's embrace of America at that particular moment was absolutely necessary for him, both as a person and as an artist. Voluntary exile offered him the scope he needed to complete a project of refashioning himself and his gift that had begun earlier; it allowed him to create an American (or, as he would have described it, a New York) self significantly different from the persona in which his early fame had trapped him. Although one should not overstate the differences between early and late Auden or deny the dynamic continuity that links them, the process of remaking was a crucial enabling task. Not only did it facilitate his metamorphosis into a "minor Atlantic Goethe," as he too modestly described himself in his late years, but it also vitally contributed to his ultimately becoming, in the words of Edward Mendelson, "the most inclusive poet of the twentieth century, its most technically skilled, and its most truthful."

Born into an upper middle-class professional family in York in 1907, and educated at Christ Church College, Oxford, from which he received his B.A. in 1928, Wystan Hugh Auden was the third son of a physician and a nurse, from whom he imbibed scientific and musical interests and a love of the Norse sagas, as well as bourgeois values and an ideal of public service. Following his graduation he spent a year in Berlin, where he enjoyed the city's homosexual demimonde and absorbed German culture. He returned to teach in public schools in Scotland and England from 1930 to 1935, where he proved a popular if unconventional instructor. Thereafter, until his emigration, he supported himself mainly through literary commissions and intermittent work on documentary films. In 1938, he married Erika Mann, daughter of the German novelist Thomas Mann, in order to enable her to obtain a British visa and escape Nazi Germany; the two never lived together and the marriage was not consummated. As a young man Auden exuded an enormous self-confidence. Brilliant, outrageous, bossy, dogmatic, and eccentric, the poet impressed his friends as at once a genuine original and a precocious chameleon who tried on ideas as though they were masks. But behind his bravado hid a great deal of uncertainty and self-doubt. Throughout his youth the author of so many quest poems was himself continuously in search of honest feelings, genuine beliefs, and authentic styles.

Auden dominated the British literary scene of the 1930s, quickly emerging as the leading voice of his generation and as the heir presumptive to the Modernist mantle of T. S. Eliot, who recommended the publication of *Poems* (1930) and who, along with Hardy and Hopkins, was a significant early influence. With the publication of *The Orators* (1932) and the enlarged edition of *Poems* (1933), Auden became, by his mid-twenties, firmly established as an important literary presence. His early poetry breathed an air of revolutionary freshness, epitomized in the oblique energy of its deftly controlled but dissonant rhythms. In language at once exotic and earthy, alternately banal and elegant, colloquial yet faintly archaic, abstract and general but also obscure and reticent, Auden's verse diagnosed the psychic disturbances and social ills of his age with a curiously clinical detachment. In his allegorized landscapes, which encapsulate psychological perspectives and dilemmas, and in his striking images of fragmentation and isolation, the young poet explored personal alienation and estrangement, but so resonantly—so mysteriously—as to seem to voice the fears and uncertainties of his entire generation. "Consider this and in our time / As the hawk sees it or the helmeted airman," he enjoined his readers in an early poem that, against a vaguely military backdrop, calmly forecasts a threatening future of equally grim alternatives: "After some haunting migratory years / To disintegrate on an instant in the explosion of mania / Or lapse for ever into a classic fatigue." The disorienting syntax, the distant vantage point, the scientific and medical terminology, the minimal exposition, and the conspiratorial tone in these excerpts are typical of Auden's early work.

Although most of Auden's early poems have their origins in his personal anxieties—including especially those related to his homosexuality—and in his search for psychic healing, they adopted such a large perspective and incorporated so inclusive a vision as to achieve general applicability to the social malaise widely felt in the years of the great depression. Calling, on the one hand, for "New styles of architecture, a change of heart" and, on the other, threatening "Death to the old gang" as means of averting individual and global disaster, Auden's earliest works resonated with political implications even as they addressed public issues mainly as symptoms of personal distress and characteristically prescribed psychological cures for social problems. Revealing the incompletely harmonized and frequently contradictory influences of a wide variety of social thinkers, including Freud, Marx, D. H. Lawrence, and Gerald Heard, Auden's early poems forged links between personal wounds and public wrongs and implied connections between psychological, economic, and political conditions without specifically engaging in political analysis. During the 1930s, however, his poetry became increasingly public in reference and theme. Even *The Orators*, an ambitious but notoriously obscure surrealist experiment in prose and verse, is subtitled *An English Study* and takes as its subject the politically ambiguous role of leadership. Moreover, as the 1930s wore on and political turmoil and extremism of all stripes dominated European public life, the poetry came more and more to register the relationship between the personal and the public as problematic and to alternate expressions and rejections of political engagement.

Concurrent with its increased concern with public issues was the poetry's move toward greater clarity, directness, and (apparent) simplicity. This is not to say that Auden's poems suddenly became crystalline. In fact, they continued to suffer from what George Wright aptly describes as "blur." Intellectual mystification is a consequence of some of the most common elements of Auden's poetic imagination and procedure, including his reliance on arcane historical and psychological knowledge, his abstruse vocabulary, his penchant for telescoping vast stretches of human history, his characteristic interpretation of the external world as symbolic of the inner, his readiness to construct parables of human experience and to enact symbolic quests, and his elliptical style. The obliquity and abstractness of much of his poetry, a legacy perhaps of his interest in German literature and probably motivated in the first instance by the impossibility at the time of depicting homosexual love openly and concretely, continued for most of his career. But what changed and thereby permitted a greater degree of clarity was his attitude toward art, which resulted in his abandonment of coded language and deliberately obscure coterie references. He came to see poetry as a form of efficacious communication rather than as an autonomous structure of private feeling and intellect. That is, while retaining an interest in Modernist techniques and psychological complexity, he discarded one of the central tenets of Modernism, the conception of art and the self as isolated worlds. The immediate effect of this revised aesthetic was an increased specificity in the dramatic situations of the poems, a greater reliance on formal patterns (such as the Rilkean sonnet, the sestina, the art song), and a more personal and meditative tone.

As Auden's works of the mid- and late 1930s retreated steadily (but by no means invariably) from the Modernist obscurity and Romantic subjectivity that characterized the early poems, they reflected an increasingly charged tension regarding political issues. The new clarity of the poetry—as well as its experimentation with "popular" forms— may have itself been, at least partially, a response to its author's recurrent questioning of the role of the poet. Auden's public prominence in the 1930s made the question urgent, as he was cast as a spokesperson for left-wing artists, the leader of the "Auden Gang" that included Stephen Spender and C. Day Lewis, among others. Auden was never himself a committed communist; his Marxism was more a matter of sympathy with the downtrodden and a probing of middle-class values than a coherent economic or political program. Still, his collaboration with Christopher Isherwood on three overtly political, determinedly experimental plays (*The Dog Beneath the Skin* [1935], *The Ascent of F 6* [1936], and *On the Frontier* [1938]) earned him a reputation for ideological commitment, as did his brief (and disillusioning) participation in the Spanish Civil War, which led to the publication of his most explicit statement of sympathy for the communist cause, "Spain 1937," the most influential poem inspired by the antifascist movement of the era. In its invocation of a purposive history and its urgent refrain, the poem stirringly justified Auden's idealistic decision to participate directly in the defining confrontation of his age.

Auden's search for the Just City is a central component of his activity as poet and thinker, one that he modified but never abandoned. Hence, he was always to remain a political poet in the most generous conception of that term. His great themes of isolation, guilt, freedom, and choice have social implications even when they are figured forth in the restrictive terms of individual responsibility. At the same time, however, also discernible in Auden's poetry is a deep-seated suspicion of political rhetoric and of his own glibness as a sloganeer. He insisted that in a time of "external disorder, and extravagant lies, / The baroque frontiers, the surrealist police," truth demands the austere discipline of "a narrow strictness." Although Auden was later to disown "Spain 1937" on the grounds of its alleged dishonesty, even that masterpiece of political rhetoric actually adheres to a strictness of truth and embodies an awareness of the complexity and consequences of moral decisions that could not have entirely pleased his more fully committed or less self-questioning comrades. As a call to action it is considerably more equivocal than it may at first appear, and it conspicuously avoids praising the Republican cause in the utopian phrases common at the time. Indeed, its subject is not the glory of the Popular Front but the wrenching difficulty of commitment in a dubious age. Thus, even at the very height of his direct political involvement, Auden's poems resisted partisan engagement. Concomitantly, they revealed an increasing interest in the definition and power of love in both the private and public spheres. That interest more than any other most fully defines the distinctive continuity of Auden's canon as a whole.

Auden's insistent preoccupation with the varieties of love is apparent in *Look, Stranger!* (1936; published in the United States under Auden's preferred title *On this Island*, 1937), a collection of thirty-one lyrics nearly all of which focus directly or indirectly on the nature of love. Much of the volume is concerned with erotic love, but presents it reticently and obliquely, perhaps in an attempt to mask the homosexual nature of the relationships. The poems expand and deepen the exploration of romantic love by acknowledging moral conundrums and conscious choice as distinctly human complications of love and by juxtaposing the claims of Eros and Agape. Auden emphasizes not the satisfactions but the disappointments and limitations of Eros, whether in the individual (as in the sonnet subsequently titled "Who's Who," which anatomizes the unfulfilled passion of the heroic overachiever who wept his pints for the homebody who "answered some / Of his long marvellous letters but kept none") or in the aggregate (as in the guilt-shadowed landscape of "May with its light behaving" where the compensations of Eros are finally deemed "insufficient" for a world that has rejected divine love). Auden's earliest love poems complained of his lack of sexual success, but these lament an emotional isolation that accompanies physical intimacy. Erotic love is even limited as a refuge from the oppressive public world, which in the guise of fascism is itself infected with emotional excess. In the poem beginning "Easily, my dear, you move," erotic love and feverish political activity are both depicted as stemming from the identical impulse and as expressions of vanity and the desire for power.

Rather than seeing Eros and Agape as opposed, Auden implied in *Look, Stranger!* that the failures of Eros are a function of the failures of Agape, a position that will be even more prominent in the American poetry. He later explained that "Agape is the fulfillment and correction of eros, not its contradiction," but the interdependence of Agape and Eros is already stunningly explicit in the remarkable ballad "As I walked out one evening" (1937), one of several in which Auden radically enlarged the ballad form by investing it with abstract moral generalizations, as indeed he did with several popular genres, including the cabaret song. In "As I walked out one evening" the unsparing clocks rebuke the sentimental and selfish expectations of Eros by demanding the practice of Agape:

> 'O stand, stand at the window
>   As the tears scald and start;
> You shall love your crooked neighbour
>   With your crooked heart.'

Until his emigration to America, Auden treated romantic love warily, a reflection perhaps of the estrangement he felt as a homosexual and of his doubts about his ability to find a stable and mutually fulfilling relationship. Even the grave and tender "Lullaby" (["Lay your sleeping head"] 1937), which moves so nimbly and with such grace among abstractions evoked so subtly that it may well be regarded as the premiere example of the poet's intellectual lyricism, depicts mortal love as vulnerable and besieged. The luminous moment of fulfillment that the poem celebrates is placed in a context of mutability and decay that poignantly underlines the fragility of a love endangered from within by guilt, promiscuity, and betrayal, and from without by the "pedantic boring cry" of "fashionable madmen."

Look, Stranger! also considers various forms of nonerotic love, including love of friends, love of country, and Agape itself, as in the second poem in the volume, subsequently entitled "A Summer Night" and based on an experience that Auden later described as a "Vision of Agape." The first half of this straightforward, apparently simple, but richly orchestrated work commemorates a moment of happiness shared with friends and colleagues, which generates an enlarged sympathy for others. But the complacency implicit in the heightened enjoyment of personal contentment is dissipated in the poem's second half, which acknowledges the social and political injustices that make possible "our freedom in this English house / Our picnics in the sun." The poet foresees that "soon through the dykes of our content / The crumpling flood will force a rent" and hopes that after the cataclysm the force of love may survive as an agent of reconciliation, to "calm / The pulse of nervous nations" and to "Forgive the murderer in his glass." "A Summer Night" privileges the mundane contentments of private life yet refuses to deny or mystify the exploitation on which bourgeois happiness rests. In its recognition of economic and social inequities and its acceptance of the inevitability of revolution, the poem is certainly political; yet in its desperate invocation of love as an agent of reconciliation, it transcends the narrowly partisan to make a leap of faith. Written at the peak of Auden's brief tenure as left-wing ideologue, the poems of *Look, Stranger!* also contain the seeds of his later conversion to Christianity.

Auden's late manner is also adumbrated in the autobiographical "Letter to Lord Byron" included in the travel book that he wrote with Louis MacNeice, *Letters from Iceland* (1937). A discursive verse epistle in Byron's airy manner, reminiscent of the jauntiness of *Don Juan* but less satiric, "Letter to Lord Byron" offers autobiography not as Romantic self-indulgence but as illustrative of the dilemmas of a representative twentieth-century artist. The comic lightness of the poem should not obscure its seriousness as Auden's attempt to announce a new poetic credo and to resituate himself within literary history. Tellingly, he allies himself not with the Romantic Byron of *Childe Harold* or *Manfred*, but with the urbane, witty ironist of the late works. He thereby places himself within a nonromantic, antimodernist, Neoclassical tradition, seeing himself as a successor of Byron in the line of Dryden and Pope. He embraces as his credo the Neoclassic contention that the proper study of art is humanity:

> To me Art's subject is the human clay,
> And landscape but a background to a torso;
> All Cézanne's apples I would give away
> For one small Goya or a Daumier.

He looks back on his earlier Lawrentian instinctualism with wry amusement and renounces utopian ambitions, both for society and himself. He has "come only to the rather tame conclusion / That no man by himself has life's solution." In "Letter to Lord Byron," Auden rejects Romantic and Modernist conceptions of autonomous art and of the superiority of the artist, including most emphatically the idea of the poet as Shelleyan legislator or prophet. In denying these roles to which he himself had previously aspired, he in effect proclaims his refusal to be great.

After Auden's disillusioning experience in Spain, where he was shocked by the inefficiency, anticlericalism, and brutality of the Republicans, his poetry continued to express conflicting attitudes toward political action and the obligations of the poet. Despite his rejection of a Romantic, messianic role in "Letter to Lord Byron," he reverted to that guise in several works of 1937 and 1938, in which he speaks as a Freudian or Marxist prophet. Although he had grown disenchanted with partisan politics and with his pose as left-wing mouthpiece, he felt trapped by his reputation. He experienced acute discomfort with the increasingly wide discrepancy between what he actually believed and what he was expected to say. As he later explained, "I felt the situation for me in England was becoming impossible. I couldn't grow up." In July 1938, on his return from a trip to China with Isherwood to fulfill a commission to write a travel book about the Far East, he decided to leave England at least partly in response to this crisis of authenticity. Only with a fresh start in a new country could he gain maturity and speak truthfully.

The trip to China resulted in *Journey to a War* (1939), the only really distinguished product of the Auden-Isherwood collaboration. The title alludes to the Sino-Japanese war, which was accurately seen as a presentiment of the coming European conflict. Auden's principal contribution to the book was a sequence of twenty-seven sonnets, "In Time of War," accompanied by a verse commentary. Beginning with a familiar Audenesque survey of the entire history of humankind in the first half of the sequence, the second half focuses on the present time and the specific conflict. "In Time of War" emphasizes characteristic issues of freedom and choice, but constructs a moral universe in which to judge human action, one in which the word *evil* has serious theological rather than merely psychological significance: "maps can really point to places / Where life is evil now: / Nanking; Dachau." Not only does the historical survey include Christian events such as the Fall and expulsion, but the theological perspective gives resonance to the assessment of the rise of fascism and the outbreak of war as evidence of the persistence of Original Sin. The war itself, depicted unsentimentally but without disguising its brutality and suffering, is seen as a lapse of ethical choice by a flawed species "articled to error": "We live in freedom by necessity, / A mountain people dwelling among mountains." The coupling of existentialist and theological concerns in the sonnet sequence strikingly anticipates Auden's later poetry, yet the wordy and uninspired verse commentary recalls his least convincing Marxist phase. While the verse commentary is woodenly hortatory, the sonnet sequence eschews exhortation for a parable that analyzes past action. The conflicting methods of the sonnets and the commentary crystallize the painful position in which Auden found himself in 1938. He had moved beyond the utopian materialism of Marxism, yet he was unable to break completely with his old attitudes.

Before his departure to America Auden spent four weeks in Brussels, where he wrote an astonishing number of memorable poems, including "The Capital," "Brussels in Winter," "Rimbaud," "A. E. Housman," "The Novelist," "The Composer," "Edward Lear," and "Musée des Beaux Arts." The poems about art and artists allowed Auden to ponder his own possible future through the choices of others. Rimbaud and Housman function as negative exemplars, the one sacrificing his gift for a life of action, the other—"Heart-injured in North London"—retreating into petulant pedantry and "the uncritical relations of the dead." In contrast, "The Novelist" and "The Composer" function as positive examples, the former teaching how to identify with common humanity, the latter how to "pour out . . . forgiveness like a wine." But the most important lesson Auden learned in this series of poems is that recounted in "Musée des Beaux Arts," one of the most beautiful and quietly profound poems of the century. In subtle rhythms, irregular lines, unemphatic rhymes, and subdued tone, "Musée des Beaux Arts" meditates on the "human position" of suffering, "how it takes place / While someone else is eating or opening a window or just walking dully along." While it is perfectly ordinary to attempt to ignore or evade the dreadful martyrdoms and the forsaken cries of everyday life, we do so at our peril; for to be human, the poem suggests through its Christian allusions, is inevitably to be both implicated in the suffering of others and responsible for our own indifference. Auden's attribution to the "Old Masters" of an aesthetic vision that naturally includes both the mundane and the miraculous not only functions self-reflexively to describe "Musée des Beaux Arts" but also foreshadows his late poetry, in which he discovers in ordinary life the deepest questions of human existence.

Accompanied by Isherwood, his friend and frequent collaborator, who would soon settle permanently in southern California, Auden arrived in New York on January 26, 1939, the very day that the Republicans were decisively defeated in Spain and two days before the death of William Butler Yeats. Soon after his arrival Auden reached the conclusion that for the sake of his integrity he could no longer be involved in politics. Given the fact that his decision to emigrate reflected both disenchantment with the life he had been leading in England and his loss of political faith, the resolution was unsurprising. Nevertheless, it is significant as direct testimony of his view of the emigration as a quest for authenticity. He desperately needed to feel that both his poetry and his life were honest and that each was consistent with the other.

Auden took the occasion of the death of Yeats, whose work had influenced him variously but problematically, to resolve the question he had repeatedly posed about the relationship of poetry and politics. "In Memory of W. B. Yeats" is one of Auden's most justly famous poems, a superbly modulated and moving tribute to one great poet by another. At the same time, however, the elegy is less about Yeats himself (who was "silly like us") than about poetry, and in articulating the doctrine that "poetry makes nothing happen" it actually rebukes the cult of Romanticism that Yeats epitomized. Auden's position in the poem is consistent with his declaration of the same year that "the political history of the world would have been the same if not a poem had been written, not a picture painted nor a bar of music composed." But if poetry is merely "a way of happening, a mouth," that is not to say that it is insignificant nor even that it cannot indirectly affect politics. Indeed, precisely because of the political nightmare of Europe, where "the living nations wait / Each sequestered in its hate" and "intellectual disgrace / Stares from every human face," poetry is desperately needed. But the role of the poet is not that of propagandist or cheerleader; rather, the poet functions as reconciler of feeling and intellect, an agent who can "teach the free man how to praise" and "in the deserts of the heart / Let the healing fountain start."

Soon after Auden's self-exile to America two momentous events occurred that would alter his life altogether. The first is that he fell in love, the second is that he returned to the Anglicanism of his youth. The conversion to Christianity was a gradual process that would not be completed until the autumn of 1940, but his falling in love was quick and irrevocable. By the late spring of 1939 Auden had plighted troth with a precocious eighteen-year-old from Brooklyn, Chester Kallman, with whom he would maintain a relationship for the rest of his life, sharing apartments in New York and, later, summer residences in first Ischia and then Austria. A few weeks after meeting Kallman, Auden wrote to a friend that "for some years now I've known that the one thing I really needed was marriage, and I think I have enough experience and judgement to know that this relationship is going to be marriage with all its boredoms and rewards." The alliance was not to prove entirely happy (primarily due to Kallman's promiscuity), but it provided the poet with the stability, emotional security, and loving companionship that he badly needed. Auden's first flush of passion immediately inspired several poems of fulfilled erotic love, including "The Prophets," "Like a Vocation," "The Riddle," "Law Like Love," and "Heavy Date," in which he tells his lover, "I have / Found myself in you." With the possible exception of "The Prophets," none of these poems achieves the luminosity of "Lullaby" ("Lay your sleeping head"), but they added a missing dimension to the canon. To some of Auden's friends the quick-witted, irresponsible Kallman seemed utterly unworthy of the devotion lavished upon him, but the poet defended him against all criticism, declaring that "he was one of the three or four people who have had a profound and direct influence on my intellectual life." Kallman was also responsible for introducing Auden to opera, an interest that would exert an impact on several late poems and even shape the curve of his career. The partners were later to collaborate on several original libretti, including one for Stravinsky's *The Rake's Progress* (1951), and on translating others.

Auden's marriage to Kallman helped seal the permanence of his self-exile and helped transform him into a *New* Yorker. His involvement with the young American was also one of several factors that made his return to England at the outbreak of World War II impossible. Auden reacted to the beginning of the hostilities with "September 1, 1939," a controversial work that, like "Spain 1937" and several others, he later disowned. Although its author subsequently deemed it "infected with dishonesty," the poem is a powerful statement of the helplessness and dismay widely experienced at the onset of the long anticipated but repeatedly delayed war. It effectively captures both the despair Auden felt as he observed "the clever hopes expire / Of a low dishonest decade" and the muted optimism—akin to the visionary hope of "A Summer Night"—that he clung to almost as an act of will. The war itself is diagnosed as a failure of Agape and a perversion of Eros. In the face of the international wrong, all the poet can do is speak the truth. Yet even as the world lies in stupor, "defenceless under the night," still the Just (an allusion to E. M. Forster's aristocracy of the sensitive, the considerate, and the plucky as described in "What I Believe") exchange messages, "ironic points of light." The poem ends with the poet asking to be counted among the unquenchable lights of the Forsterian aristocracy:

> May I, composed like them
> Of Eros and dust,
> Beleaguered by the same
> Negation and despair
> Show an affirming flame.

The desire to "show an affirming flame" in the face of a world hell-bent on self-destruction is analogous to the poet's prescribed task in the Yeats elegy to "sing of human unsuccess / In a rapture of distress."

Auden's first American collection of poetry is *Another Time* (1940), which includes fifty poems, nearly all of which were written since *Look,*

Stranger! The volume contains some of the most acclaimed works of Auden's career. It is notably diverse in style and remarkable for its range and tonal variety, including not only songs, ballads, and satirical portraits (such as "Miss Gee" and "The Unknown Citizen") but also meditations on art and artists (including "Voltaire at Ferney," "Matthew Arnold," and "Herman Melville"), three elegies (including the beautifully felt tribute "In Memory of Sigmund Freud," perhaps the finest of all Auden's commemorative odes), love poems, and even an epithalamion. Although Auden's arrangement seems deliberately to discourage comparison of the works that were written before the emigration and those that were written afterward, nevertheless there are important but subtle differences. The later poems express more optimism than the former and they evince greater personal warmth and openness. In addition, the existentialist themes that were implicit in the sonnets of "In Time of War" are now the direct subjects of such abstract American poems as "Our Bias," "Hell," and "Another Time." For the rest of his career Auden would be absorbed by existentialist dilemmas, especially the question of human freedom in time, but with his conversion to Christianity he will finally be able to proffer a solution.

By the fall of 1940 Auden had taken the Kierkegaardian leap of faith and become a Christian. The poet's progress to Christianity had been incremental, variously influenced by his mother's devotion, his experience of a mystical "Vision of Agape" in 1933, his revulsion against the anticlericalism of the Republicans in Spain in 1937, his disenchantment with the various social gospels he had experimented with during the 1930s, and his search for a system of belief that could account for the personal and public pain of the war. In addition, the anguish he felt at the discovery of Kallman's infidelity in 1941 soon tested and solidified his Christian convictions. Despite the incredulity it occasioned among many of his long-time readers and critics, the conversion was not unpredictable. Christian ideas and concepts had, after all, informed some of the earlier poems. But Auden's new faith represented a philosophical renunciation, not only of the materialist perspective of his recent Marxism but also of the modified liberal humanism that he had embraced in 1938 and endorsed in "September 1, 1939." The poet was always to value the self-evident virtues of liberalism, but he came to see its failure to prevent the rise of fascism and the outbreak of the European war as indicative of its ineffectuality. Liberalism's trust in the innate goodness of humanity and its faith in progress had, he thought, been mocked by the reality of evil and the deterioration of life as manifested in world conflict. Auden had reached the conclusion that humanism and rationalism, while valuable in themselves, were insufficient. In contrast, Christianity offered a transcendent perspective that could account for evil in the world and a philosophy of history spacious enough to accommodate present failures. The redemption promised by Christianity did not depend on the Romantic utopianism that Auden had come to despise. Moreover, as filtered through Kierkegaard and the English novelist and theologian Charles Williams, Christianity could address Auden's habitual concerns with the nature of love and the responsibilities of choice.

The first major fruit of Auden's serious interest in Christianity was *The Double Man* (1941, subsequently entitled *New Year Letter*). The volume contains both a sequence of twenty sonnets, "The Quest," which recounts an implicitly Christian spiritual journey, and "New Year Letter," a verse epistle of some seventeen hundred lines in rhymed octosyllabic couplets (followed by eighty-seven pages of notes) addressed to Auden's friend Elizabeth Mayer, a German emigré who was to function as a mother figure to him. Though much more ambitious in scope and appropriately more serious in tone, "New Year Letter" recalls "Letter to Lord Byron" in its discursive fluency. Written in the "middle style" of Dryden, the epistle is a meditation on the history of civilization, approached from a moral rather than a political vantage point. Although it is enormously erudite, its learning is borne lightly, leavened by wit and infused with deep feeling. It contains the familiar sweeping summaries of history, yet it is never unaware of the decisiveness of its own particular moment in time, when the European war offered irrefutable evidence of the crisis of civilization. The three sections of the work correspond to Kierkegaard's triad of the Aesthetic, Ethical, and Religious categories of existence. Part 1 considers art and its limitations, concluding that "no words men write can stop the war," yet nevertheless hoping that heart and intelligence may "use the Good Offices of verse" to reach an accord. Part 2 exposes the falsity of dogmatic ideologies and utopian dreams, including Marxism, but sees them as forms of doubt that "push us into grace." Part 3, which offers both the most stunning intellectual survey and also the most autobiographical passages, attributes the parlous state of the present to the triumph of

Romanticism. Finding rationalism insufficient and Romanticism dangerous, Auden prays for instruction in the "civil art / Of making from the muddled heart / A desert and a city where / The thoughts that have to labour there / May find locality and peace / And pent up feelings their release." Despite the bleakness of contemporary civilization the author finds hope in the painful fact of each individual's isolation, because it motivates us to love others. Indeed, the "privileged community" of friends bound together by affirmative art and the spirit of Agape functions as an antidote to the despair induced by the war. Hence, the poem pays tribute to the dedicatee, who embodies the practice of Agape ("always there are such as you, / Forgiving, helping what we do"), and concludes:

> O every day in sleep and labour
> Our life and death are with our neighbour,
> And love illuminates again
> The city and the lion's den,
> The world's great rage, the travel of young men.

A major statement of Auden's intellectual history and his American attitudes, "New Year Letter" also marks his mastery of the Augustan manner that would become his trademark though by no means his only tone of voice.

During the early 1940s Auden taught at several American universities, principally the University of Michigan and Swarthmore College. After the war he continued to lecture at colleges and occasionally spent terms as writer-in-residence, but he earned the bulk of his income from his writing. He was rejected from military service on the grounds of his homosexuality, but in 1945 he was given the status of major in the U.S. Army as a member of the United States Strategic Bombing Survey, which toured Germany to assess the effects of Allied bombing. He became an American citizen in 1946.

The 1940s was the decade of Auden's long poems and a transparent attempt to reshape his canon. He followed "New Year Letter" with three other major works, "For the Time Being" and "The Sea and the Mirror" (published together as *For the Time Being* in 1944) and *The Age of Anxiety* (1947). In 1945 he published a volume entitled *The Collected Poetry of W. H. Auden*, which excised a number of important poems from the canon, significantly revised others, added (sometimes facetious) titles to many of the previously untitled works, and arranged the contents not chronologically but alphabetically by first line. The alphabetical ordering was an attempt to obscure his development and to disarm those who assumed that his earlier poetry was superior to his later. This tactic failed, for not only did the revisions and omissions infuriate many of his admirers but others scathingly denounced the changes in the poetry and its informing ideology. Still, the publication of *The Collected Poetry*, which included "For the Time Being" and "The Sea and the Mirror" as well as some fugitive poems not previously collected such as "At the Grave of Henry James," "Canzone," and "The Lesson," was an important event. The volume not only announced the thirty-seven-year-old Auden's status as a major poet to be ranked with his older contemporaries Eliot, Stevens, and Frost, but in the ruthless excisions of poems that now seemed to him dishonest it also demonstrated his continuing preoccupation with the authenticity of his work.

"For the Time Being," a Christmas oratorio written to memorialize Auden's mother who died in August 1941, was intended for musical setting by Benjamin Britten, with whom the poet had previously collaborated on an opera, *Paul Bunyan* (1941). Although, as it turned out, Britten did not provide a setting, Auden's expectation of one affected the composition; he created a simple but symbolic drama utilizing a range of verse forms and diction appropriate to the speakers of the choruses, arias, recitatives, and monologues. One of Auden's few works centered on an overtly religious subject, the oratorio tells the Christmas story from a variety of angles, corresponding to the traditional divisions in the Gospels but deliberately adding anachronisms to suggest that the nativity is at once historical and timeless and to encourage analogies between the past and present. The anachronisms recall the technique of medieval mystery plays, as do the simple language and the naive pageantry. At the same time, however, the poem is extraordinarily sophisticated theologically, incorporating the insights of Kierkegaard, Reinhold Niebuhr, and Paul Tillich, among others. The work includes serious wit and irony, especially in the section entitled "The Massacre of the Innocents," where Herod is presented as a humanist trapped in a situation for which rationalism is unhelpful. "I've tried to be good. I brush my teeth every night. I haven't had sex for a month," he complains, "I'm a liberal. I want everyone to be happy. I wish I had never been born." The oratorio is also often philosophically penetrating, as in "The Meditation of Simeon," and also frequently very moving, especially in the sections entitled "The Annunciation" and "The Temptation of St. Joseph." Although critical assessment of the oratorio remains sharply divided, it succeeds in rendering its sophisticated existentialism concrete and accessible and in making the spiritual issues inherent in the nativity universal and contemporary: "The Time Being is . . . the most trying time of all."

In "The Sea and the Mirror," subtitled "A Commentary on Shakespeare's *The Tempest*," Auden reimagines Shakespeare's characters after the play has ended and they have embarked on the journey homeward from Prospero's island, leaving the timeless world of artifice and entering the time-bound world of reality. The sea of the title symbolizes life, the mirror art, and the poem explores the complex relationship between the two. It is arranged into three parts, corresponding to the artist, the work, and the audience. In part 1 Prospero, representing the artist, explains to Ariel, who symbolizes the imagination, his future life without magic. In part 2 the "Supporting Cast" speaks, each in an appropriate verse form ranging from the sestina assigned to Ferdinand and the villanelle to Miranda to the quatrains given to Trinculo. All of the supporting characters except Antonio are repentant and are "linked as children in a circle dancing," with the recalcitrant Antonio standing apart and contradicting the expressions of forgiveness and unity. In the third section, Caliban, signifying the natural man and the author deprived of his imagination, speaks in prose that parodies the late style of Henry James. Throughout his career Auden was preoccupied with the role of art; the difference in this elaborate meditation is that his approach is now informed by his Christian existentialism. The poem illustrates the limitations of Kierkegaard's Aesthetic category of existence, seeing Prospero's farewell to art as a movement toward the Religious stage. Art's limitations are figured forth in a number of ways, including its illusoriness and its inability to deal with either the dualities of human existence or with death, "All the rest is silence / On the other side of the wall; / And the silence ripeness, / And the ripeness all." But even as the poem insists on the limitations of art, it equally acknowledges the power of art as an agent of reconciliation and a source of pleasure. The metrical tour de force of the various verse forms of the first two parts of the work itself affirms art, as does the brilliant (though sometimes tedious) Jamesian parody in Caliban's long monologue, later claimed by Auden to be "the poem of which he was most proud." "The

Sea and the Mirror" warns against the dangers of abusing the imagination, yet it also celebrates the world of art with full knowledge of its limitations. As Edward Callan has noted, the poem "occupies a unique place in twentieth-century literature: it is an existentialist work that is at once joyful, celebratory, and a festival of imagination."

Of Auden's four long poems of the 1940s, his final, the Pulitzer prize-winning *The Age of Anxiety*, is the most problematic. At first glance it seems a regression to the bafflingly obscure poetry of the early 1930s. Not only is its diction self-consciously arcane, but it also employs the Anglo-Saxon alliterative accentual verse common in Auden's early work, and it explores issues of subjectivity that also haunted the early poetry. But in *The Age of Anxiety* this exploration is guided by theological as well as psychological interests, and in its vividly realized contemporary setting and Joycean interior monologues the poem stunningly captures the dazed exhaustion of people in the midst of an uncertain war. Hence even as its obscurity and its verse forms are disorienting, the work nevertheless conveys a powerful sense of time and place. On one level the poetic drama depicts the interactions of four individuals—Malin, a medical intelligence officer in the Canadian Air Force, Rosetta, a Jewish businesswoman, Emble, a young enlisted man in the U.S. Navy, and Quant, an elderly clerk originally from Ireland—who meet in a New York bar one Night of All Souls during the war. They discuss the "seven ages of man" and then embark on a surrealist dream-quest through the "seven stages" of the unconscious. On awakening they leave the bar for a nightcap at Rosetta's apartment, where she and Emble enact a wedding masque but do not actually consummate the "marriage"; at daybreak, the four go their separate ways, each having attained a little more self-awareness than they originally possessed. On another level, however, the four characters are not individuals at all but symbols of the Jungian psychic faculties of Thought (Malin), Feeling (Rosetta), Intuition (Quant), and Sensation (Emble), and each episode of the drama is a movement toward integration and wholeness that is never actually accomplished. Subtitled a "Baroque Eclogue," *The Age of Anxiety* is a highly stylized, ornately wrought, and extravagantly ironic antipastoral. Some readers have found it self-indulgent and alienating, but others have seen it as a mythic work that successfully represents the dilemma of modern men and women, whose anxieties result from the consciousness of time and the divided self. As

one of the characters remarks, "We're quite in the dark: we do not /
Know the connection between / The clock we are bound to obey / And
the miracle we must not despair of." Dramatic productions of *The Age
of Anxiety* have been staged, and Leonard Bernstein based his Second
Symphony on it, which in turn inspired a ballet by Jerome Robbins.

After the 1940s Auden did not turn again to the long poem, though
he did create works of ambitious scope by linking together several related brief poems to form analyzed series ("Bucolics" and "Horae Canonicae" from *The Shield of Achilles*, and "Thanksgiving for a Habitat" from
About the House, for example). The abandonment of the long poem is
often attributed to the fact that Auden's opera libretti sapped his energy for work on large projects; but more probably he turned away from
the long form because the poems of the 1940s had performed a crucial
service that did not need repeating. Quite apart from their considerable
intrinsic merits as significant achievements, each in its separate way
also reoriented facets of Auden's art to his new philosophical and religious beliefs. "New Year Letter" is primarily intellectual in focus, "For
the Time Being" religious, "The Sea and the Mirror" aesthetic, and *The
Age of Anxiety* psychological. Taken together, they compose an impressively comprehensive account of a major poet's refashioning of the
foundations of his intellectual and artistic life. The long poems recorded the spiritual journey and artistic maturity of the questing poet.
Among other things, they embodied the theoretical positions that govern the work of American Auden. The Horatian poetry that followed
is the fruit of the remaking process that the long poems accomplished.

Late Auden may conveniently be divided into two periods based on
his summer residences. From 1949 until 1957 he divided his time
between winters in New York and summers on the island of Ischia in
the Bay of Naples, where he lived in the fishing village of Forio. In 1958
he bought a house in Kirchstetten, near Vienna, where he subsequently spent his summers. The Ischian period produced two important collections of poems, *Nones* (1951) and *The Shield of Achilles* (1955), while
the Kirchstetten period issued forth *Homage to Clio* (1960), *About the
House* (1965), *City Without Walls* (1969), *Epistle to a Godson* (1972), and
the posthumous *Thank You, Fog: Last Poems* (1974). In 1966 he published *Collected Shorter Poems, 1927–1957*. This volume, in which he
again rejected some of his most admired poems and revised others,
proved almost as controversial as the *Collected Poetry* of 1945. Again,

Auden justified his excisions on the grounds of honesty. When a friend objected to the omission of "September 1, 1939," he replied that it was exactly that kind of poem he left England in order to *stop* writing.

In the final quarter of his life Auden was internationally recognized as the foremost poet writing in English. He received numerous awards, including the Bollingen Prize in 1954, the Italian government's Feltrinelli Prize in 1957 (the proceeds of which he used to buy the house in Kirchstetten), the Guinness Poetry Award in 1959, the Austrian State Prize for European Literature in 1966, and the National Medal for Literature in 1967. He was elected to a five-year term as Professor of Poetry at Oxford in 1956, and was widely expected to be awarded the Nobel Prize in the 1960s, an award that did not materialize, allegedly because he refused to alter some comments in his introduction to Dag Hammarskjöld's *Markings*. For all the honors that came his way, however, Auden was a dubious figure in his later years, as he changed precipitously from the "lank, tow-headed, slouching boy" of the English poetry to the shuffling, prematurely and monumentally aged American "who looks at you with a lined, sagging, fretful, consciously powerful old lion's face," as Randall Jarrell described him. His later volumes were not universally acclaimed—his detractors repeatedly complained of his facetiousness and complacency, and attributed his putative decline to a waste of powers, a lack of inspiration, a failure of engagement, and a loss of will—but they constitute an achievement unique in American poetry.

Generalizations about a body of work as subtly various as late Auden are inevitably misleading, but some trends are apparent. The late poetry, for example, discarded almost entirely the prophetic note, self-dramatization, and violent imagery of the youthful work. Its imagery is less abstract, though no less richly suggestive. It most frequently converses in the relaxed, urbane voice of an assured, casual, highly civilized, and ironic observer who discovers in the sacralized world of nature and art small and large wonders. Although he is sometimes reticent and sober, he is more often garrulous and playfully self-mocking. He exhibits more personal warmth than the persona of the English poetry yet he feels no compulsion to entertain, believing that "never to be dull shows a lack of taste." He has reached "the stage / When one starts to dislike the young," but determinedly avoids "the lacrimae rerum note." His tone tends to be one of tolerant, wistful acceptance of himself and others; he knows that "the Love that rules the sun and stars / Permits what He forbids." Yet he is also acutely conscious of living in a debased era, inhabiting a "suburb of dissent" in which heroism and the "civil style" are no longer possible; and he sometimes expresses a Cavafyian sense of disillusionment, as in "Under Sirius," "We Too Had Known Golden Hours," "The Epigoni," or "City Without Walls." The sense of decline expressed in these poems is a reaction against such political developments as the triumph of mass-produced "Hobbesian Man," McCarthyism, the communist occupation of Eastern Europe, the cold war, and the possibility of nuclear annihilation; hence the late work is quintessentially public and social, but the poet's prescription for the Just City is not much more specific than the practice of Agape. A poetry of contemplation and interpretation rather than action, the late work ruminates on an amazing variety of subjects. It is capable of gravity and levity, and a complex mixture of the two. It also exhibits astonishing formal control and inventiveness, effortlessly employing a remarkably wide range of metrical and syllabic rhythms and forms as ordinary or exotic as the limerick, the haiku, the clerihew, the rime royal, the heroic couplet, and the Horatian ode.

The Ischian period produced a number of superb works, ranging from excellent songs and witty light verse to the celebrated moralized landscape poems. The latter include the humorous yet dignified and surpassingly moving "In Praise of Limestone" ("when I try to imagine a faultless love / Or the life to come, what I hear is the murmur / Of underground streams, what I see is a limestone landscape"), the "Ode to Gaea," and the seven-poem series of "Bucolics." These complex pastorals explore humankind's paradoxical relationship to nature as both a natural creature and a historically conscious being. The other major sequence of this period is "Horae Canonicae," which consists of seven meditations on the Crucifixion correlated with the canonical hours and the church offices associated with them. Throughout the cycle Auden superimposes an ordinary day in contemporary time on the historical Good Friday to make a typological point similar to that accomplished by the anachronisms of "For the Time Being"—we reenact the Crucifixion in our daily lives. Like "For the Time Being," "Horae Canonicae" is theologically sophisticated, but it more thoroughly and subtly infuses doctrinal perspectives into the texture of the human experience it depicts. The cycle moves from individual awareness and guilt, the conscious actions that express our implication in the Crucifixion and our attempt to evade responsibility, to a joyful communion in forgiveness, *"In solitude, for company,"* translating the humiliations of sin into the victorious Christian comedy. Like many of Auden's late poems, including "The Shield of Achilles," "Horae Canonicae" simultaneously acknowledges the failure of Agape in the world of experience and its ultimate triumph in the wonder of God's Grace. This position is not an expression of complacency; it is an active resolution of the existential dilemma in the light of Christian revelation.

Auden inaugurated the Ischian period with "Ischia," an affectionate celebration of the pleasures of Mediterranean life; he concluded the era with "Goodbye to the Mezzogiorno," a valediction that expresses gratitude to the South for the happiness it provided but that also makes clear that as a child of the "gothic North" he had never been completely at home there. His move to Austria was motivated by a desire to be near a major opera house and by distress over the increasing commercialization of the island, but also by his need to return to a Northern "Guilt culture" as a protection against the inertia that the South encouraged. He quickly became completely acclimated in Kirchstetten. Indeed, the poetry of this era is a decidedly domestic literature, its ruminations rooted in local experience and in the round of daily life. Intellectually less formidable than that of the Ischian period, the works of Auden's last phase are characterized by the same fineness of qualification and discrimination and by the same concern with existential and historical issues. Though rarely self-indulgent, the poetry of this period is self-absorbed; and it is increasingly focused on aspects of aging, often particularized in the poet's own decaying flesh. In this phase Auden writes with an unprecedented openness and directness. Without becoming solipsistic, he presents himself in all his eccentricities as a faithful mirror of the human condition, extrapolating from his own experience large generalizations and testing received wisdom by reference to his experience. The Kirchstetten poems include a series of meditations on history, an important cycle inspired by the beloved farmhouse he shared with Kallman, several interesting occasional works, elegies for a number of friends, and many epigrams and "shorts."

The signal achievement of the Austrian years is "Thanksgiving for a Habitat," the twelve-poem cycle that comprises the bulk of *About the House.* Proceeding through all the rooms of the Kirchstetten residence, the cycle celebrates the dailiness of an orderly existence. A meditation on the human creature as a domestic animal, the work is also a specific commemoration of a particular kind of life—indeed, of Auden's own life. The poem about the living room, for example, is a moving account of the Auden-Kallman relationship, and all the poems in the sequence are dedicated to friends. The dedications of the poems are not random; each room is assigned to the friend whose personality or interests make it especially appropriate to him or her (for example, the poem about the dining room is dedicated to the food writer M. F. K. Fisher, the one about the study, "The Cave of Making," is an elegy for Auden's fellow-poet Louis MacNeice, the one about the toilet is dedicated to Isherwood, whose novel *A Single Man* [1964] featured a scene with the protagonist reading Ruskin in the bathroom). "Thanksgiving for a Habitat" is, thus, social poetry. But, like Jonson's in the seventeenth-century, Auden's social verse is more serious and inclusive than it appears at first glance. It transcends the vividly realized particulars to articulate an ideal of civilized life. The meditations stress the practical functions of the rooms, but unpretentiously reach out from the functional to the larger social and spiritual concerns of mid-twentieth-century life, a time when the domestic sphere has increased in importance as the possibilities of significant action in the public sphere have decreased. Indeed, the failure of public life in the twentieth-century is itself an argument for the retreat into the domestic; "we shan't, not since Stalin and Hitler, / trust ourselves ever again: we know that, subjectively, / all is possible." Despite its appearance of cozy insularity, "Thanksgiving for a Habitat" expands to become a vehicle for the exploration of topics as diverse as the conception of the self, the history of eating, the distinctions between humans and animals, the nature of imagination, and the role of the artist. Each of the poems is successful in its own right, but taken together they offer both a fascinating glimpse of Auden's own life and an absorbing account of the domestic life of a civilized, thinking Western man.

During the Kirchstetten era Auden was preoccupied with aging and death, but the poems on such subjects are neither sentimental nor mawkish. In regard to age, he adopted the attitude of "The Horatians" and "learned to look at / this world with a happy eye / but from a sober perspective." He discovered that there are compensations in old age and he expressed gratitude for the unanticipated joys that came his way, especially those that alleviated the isolation he carried with him like a priest carries a breviary. Among the poems published posthumously is "Glad," a light but deeply felt account of his relationship with a paid companion, "for a decade now / My bed-visitor, / An unexpected blessing / In a lucky life." In "Since," a poem probably inspired by his relationship with Kallman, Auden suddenly remembers an August noon thirty years ago and "You as then you were." He juxtaposes the memory of his youthful love-making with an account of the failures of Eros and Agape in the world since and finds sustenance in the memory: "round your image / there is no fog, and the Earth / can still astonish." In a remarkable conclusion that bravely faces the issue of aging with unsentimental wit, he concludes, "I at least can learn / to live with obesity / and a little fame." Auden's attitude toward his own death is perhaps best illustrated by the body-soul debate, "Talking to Myself," which concludes with the Soul telling the Body: "Remember: when *Le Bon Dieu* says to You *Leave him!*, / please, please, for His sake and mine, pay no attention / to my piteous *Dont*'s, but bugger off quickly." One of his last poems was a haiku: "He still loves life / But O O O O how he wishes / The good Lord would take him."

Auden's death did come quickly. In the fall of 1972 he gave up his New York apartment to accept a position as Fellow of Christ Church, Oxford, where he planned to live half of every year. The return to Oxford was not altogether successful, principally because he did not find the convivial community that he expected. He spent the summer of 1973 in Kirchstetten, and, on September 29, after a poetry reading in Vienna, he died in his sleep in a hotel room. He was buried in Kirchstetten; memorial services were held in New York and Oxford; and a year later a tablet was unveiled at Westminster Abbey, with the inscription: "In the prison of his days, / Teach the free man how to praise."

The curious shape of Auden's career makes it difficult to assess his specific influence with much precision. The metamorphosis of the *enfant terrible* of English poetry into the religious, Horatian ruminator of American poetry complicates any sense of a clear line of influence. In the 1930s Auden spoke to his own generation with exceptional power, inspiring not only nearly all of his English contemporaries but also young American poets like Randall Jarrell and Anthony Hecht, who later bewailed his apostasy. Writing in 1945 Louise Bogan remarked that "Auden . . . has succeeded Eliot as the strongest influence in American and British poetry." This influence manifested itself in a number of ways. The violent imagery, the psychological perspectives, and the allegorized and industrial landscapes of the early poetry exerted a palpable impact, affecting the idiom and tone of Anglo-American poetry for two decades. More subtle, but longer lasting, was the influence of Auden's extraordinary craftsmanship and employment of a wide range of traditional and nontraditional forms throughout his career. His revitalization of the ballad, the art song, and the sonnet as well as his experimentations with the long line, syllabic rhythm, and a host of exotic genres, offered important new or rehabilitated models for younger poets. He illustrated the possibility of renewing exhausted forms and creating complex new patterns from the semblances of old ones, and of renovating ancient meters for twentieth-century themes. Similarly, his colloquial yet elegant language, his practice of deflating the portentous and the grandiose, and his discovery of symbols in the commonplace objects of the world were also influential, as was his seemingly effortless encapsulations of scientific and historical generalizations. Perhaps his most distinctive and imitated contribution to contemporary poetic practice was his creation of a brand of intellectual lyricism in which abstract ideas are subsumed within an aureate diction. But even the austere, antiromantic, measured, and controlled meditational voice of the later verse essays has attracted imitators.

Because fame came to him so early and because he assumed roles of leadership in the literary circles of both England and America, Auden's influence was profound, yet after the immediate impact of his poetry on his contemporaries in the 1930s, it tended to be diffuse. As editor of the Yale Series of Younger Poets for twelve years beginning in 1945, he helped bring to prominence several unknown American poets, including W. S. Merwin, Daniel Hoffman, John Ashbery, Adrienne Rich, James Wright, and John Hollander. Each of these betrays a general indebtedness to Auden, though only Hollander, who acknowledges him as an "onlie begetter" (in "Upon Apthorp House," where he also pleads "old W. H., get off my back!"), might be described as "Audenesque" in theme and manner. Among contemporary American poets who evince a clear debt to Auden are poets as diverse as Thom Gunn, Donald Justice, Daryl Hine, Richard Howard, James Merrill, Howard Moss, Theodore Roethke, Louis Simpson, and Richard Wilbur. But

Auden's presence affected American poetry more generally. Even Allen Ginsberg and Gregory Corso have acknowledged his influence.

For Merrill and Howard, and other gay poets intent on constructing gay genealogies, Auden's impact has been enormous, involving his personality as well as his poetry. In his series of adventures with the Ouija board, beginning with *Divine Comedies* (1976) and continuing in several subsequent volumes, Merrill presents Auden as a ghostly presence and source of wisdom, the embodiment of a homosexual artistic sensibility. Merrill's elegant diction, nimble command of the long line, relaxed narrative voice, and propensity for camp wit all owe something to Auden. For Howard, who twice addresses Auden as Hephaestos, the only one of the Olympian gods who ever worked, Auden functioned as a sometimes problematic poetic father and prior ego, as Howard both wrote self-consciously in an Audenesque manner and also struggled to find his own voice. In "For Hephaistos, with Reference to the Deaths in a Dry Year of Cocteau, Roethke and MacNeice" (*The Damages*, 1967), the younger poet tells the elder, "only now, at last / Free of you, my old ventriloquist, / Have I suspected what I have to say / Without having you say it for me first." And in his moving tribute, "Again for Hephaistos, the Last Time" (*Fellow Feelings* [1976]), he contrasts Auden's death with the deaths of Anna Magnani and Pablo Neruda, all occurring the same weekend, and concludes:

> The difference, then, between
> your death and all those others
> is this: you do not take a certain world away, after
> all. After you, because of you,
> all songs are possible.

For Howard, as for many English and American poets, Auden's was an "essential life— / one necessary to have been lived."

What Auden wrote of Freud is true of himself as well, "To us he is no more a person / Now but a whole climate of opinion / Under whom we conduct our differing lives." His great legacy lies not so much in the specific influence he exerted on particular poets as on a more general accomplishment, his dedication to an austere view of art as a secondary world. He believed that like speech, like "a shadow echoing / the silent light," poetry can at best "bear witness / to the Truth it is not." This aesthetic required his strict disciplining of an extraordinary lyric gift. In rejecting the example of Orpheus, who enchanted his hearers, for that of Horace, "the adroitest of makers," he declined to be great in the Romantic and Modernist tradition. His refusal, "like some self-proclaimed poets," to "wow an / audience, utter some resonant lie," was an affirmation of the quest for authenticity that led him to America in 1939 and that sustained his later career. Auden's canon is the largest of major twentieth-century poets and the most diverse. The first to incorporate modern psychological insights and paradigms as a natural element of his work and thought, Auden is the poet of that peculiarly twentieth-century affliction, anxiety. Yet he is also the foremost religious poet of his age, the most variously learned, and the one most preoccupied with existentialism. All the aspects of his canon are unified in his belief that the goal of poetry is not emotional transport or political transformation but the perception of truth and the affirmation of an imperfect world.

Claude J. Summers

Further Reading

Auden, W. H. *Collected Poems*. Ed. Edward Mendelson. New York: Random House, 1976.

―――― *The English Auden: Poems, Essays, and Dramatic Writings, 1927–1939*. Ed. Edward Mendelson. New York: Random House, 1977.

Boly, John R. *Reading Auden: The Returns of Caliban*. Ithaca: Cornell University Press, 1991.

Callan, Edward. *Auden: A Carnival of Intellect*. New York: Oxford University Press, 1983.

Carpenter, Humphrey. *W. H. Auden: A Biography*. Boston: Houghton Mifflin, 1981.

Fuller, John. *A Reader's Guide to W. H. Auden*. New York: Noonday, 1970.

Greenberg, Herbert. *Quest for the Necessary: W. H. Auden and the Dilemma of Divided Consciousness*. Cambridge: Harvard University Press, 1968.

Haffenden, John, ed. *W. H. Auden: The Critical Heritage*. London: Routledge and Kegan Paul, 1983.

Johnson, Richard A. *Man's Place: An Essay on Auden*. Ithaca: Cornell University Press, 1973.

McDiarmid, Lucy. *Auden's Apologies for Poetry*. Princeton: Princeton University Press, 1990.

Mendelson, Edward. *Early Auden*. New York: Viking, 1981.

Nelson, Gerald B. *Changes of Heart: A Study of the Poetry of W. H. Auden.* Berkeley: University of California Press, 1969.

Smith, Stan. *W. H. Auden.* Oxford: Basil Blackwell, 1983.

Spears, Monroe K. *The Poetry of W. H. Auden: The Disenchanted Island.* New York: Oxford University Press, 1963.

Spender, Stephen, ed. *W. H. Auden: A Tribute.* New York: Macmillan, 1975.

Wright, George T. *W. H. Auden.* Rev. ed. Boston: Twayne, 1981.

The Twentieth-Century Long Poem

DESPITE the powerful impact of Imagism and the accompanying prestige of the lyric in Modernist poetry, the long poem became a major form for Modernist experimentation and has remained a central form for later twentieth-century American poetry. Around 1910 those who would become the major innovators of the Modern long poem were composing brief poems based on a single image intended to fix a momentary apprehension. But, particularly in the aftermath of World War I, the Modernists' desire to reclaim for poetry the range and significance it had ceded to the novel—a breadth of subject and discursive scope that would insure poetry's social relevance—led them to invent extended forms, usually with some qualities of traditional epic in mind. Long poems enabled the Modernists to reach beyond the inward perspective of the postromantic lyric to include sociological, anthropological, and, with particular frequency, historical material.

Although the generic label *long poem* is well established, its exact meaning is not. Perhaps the term most readily calls to mind collage epics along the lines of Ezra Pound's *Cantos*, but it can also denote lyric sequences (including those using set forms such as sonnets), poetic meditations, or continuous verse narratives. Nor are there established conventions concerning length. Indeed, the lack of restrictive generic conventions is crucial to the identity of the long poem. Debates about the desirability of shapeliness and coherence have accompanied the form's history; recently these debates have been conducted in terms of "open" versus "closed" form, with "openness" identifying often organic conceptions of poetic form as an evolving process or as a reflection of a perceived disorderly unfolding of experience. Thus, poets' desires to innovate or to capture distinctly modern fragmentations sometimes contend with the desire to impose coherence. In combining elements of lyric and epic traditions along with the resources of various prose genres, the long poem has provided a vehicle responsive to a range of ambitions and perspectives. Although not always used experimentally, the form has been particularly important for poets who have shared Pound's belief that each poet and generation must, in their own way, "make it new."

While American literature often defines itself against Anglo-European traditions, the long poem emerges as a particularly contestatory form. Through its refusal of generic decorums it easily accommodates protest as well as innovative constructions of subjectivity, aesthetic value, or national identity. Whitman's "Song of Myself" (1855), an important precursor for many modern long poems, establishes a tradition of innovation. Whitman invented an extraordinarily inclusive form and a flexible, long free-verse line in which he could give voice to a distinctly American hero at once individual and collective. Discarding inherited notions of the grand style and subject appropriate to epic, he insisted on being the poet of democracy and embracing the full reality of the world around him; he celebrated even urban squalor and the nation's most downtrodden inhabitants. His catalogues, though less radically disjunctive than the Modernists' paratactic techniques, nonetheless pave the way for their surprising juxtapositions.

The poem begins with a defiant allusion to the opening of Virgil's *Aenead* ("Arms and the man I sing") as Whitman proclaims, "I celebrate myself, and sing myself, / And what I assume you shall assume." Rather than retelling the story of a recognized national hero in order to reaffirm the present social order, Whitman places "[c]reeds and schools in abeyance" and, generating a hero from a version of himself that includes his American readers, seeks instead to give voice to nature's "original energy" and to release the oppositional dynamics propelling "the procreant urge of the world." While the quasi-circular quest-journey structure of traditional epic is loosely retained, there is no specified end toward which the poem or its speaker is directed. The poem aims at an open-ended transformation of its readers; at its close, they are invited to take up the speaker's "perpetual journey." Like "Song of Myself," many Modern long poems enact a sense of poem-as-process that can incorporate private and public statement, individual self-construction and communal identity, social criticism and nationalistic celebration, epic breadth and lyric intensity. Whitman's celebration of homosexual experience is also exemplary: the innovative and rebellious aspects of American long poems often have to do as much with identity politics as with poetic form and scope.

However, Whitman is not the only important precursor for twentieth-century long poems. Among the Modernists, for example, those committed to an international transformation of the arts (often expatriates, such as Pound, Eliot, and H.D.) looked to Homer, Dante, and Browning, among others, often expressing ambivalence toward Whitman. Even those most interested in specifically American writing who call attention to their links to Whitman have also drawn on other traditions.

The survey that follows organizes the century's production of long poems around three sometimes overlapping chronological divisions. The first, in which collage-based texts dominate, extends from the first flowering of the Modernist long poem in the early 1920s through the late long poems of the High Modernists published after World War II. The longevity of that generation born in the 1880s and 1890s has insured their dominance in the history of the twentieth-century long poem despite the diversity of long poems produced by writers born after the turn of the century. This portion of the essay selects for focus works that have proved influential and that, at this moment in the evolution of the American literary canon, are widely thought worthy of critical attention. Some of these long poems have only recently entered the canon because of increased interest in traditions of women's writing, African American writing, and politically engaged writing. Not included are little known or less influential works of the period such Conrad Aiken's *The Divine Pilgrim* or the long narratives of Edwin Arlington Robinson, Stephen Vincent Benét, Archibald MacLeish, and—the most important among these—Robinson Jeffers.

The second portion of the essay discusses long poems written by poets born, roughly, between 1910 and 1930, works published from the late fifties through the early seventies as part of the widespread reaction among younger poets against the standards of the "well-wrought" lyric that dominated American poetry in the forties and fifties. These poems, which often reflect the social upheavals of the Vietnam era, I discuss largely in terms of four schools of writing important to the post-World War II renewal of American poetry: the Black Mountain or Projectivist group, which extended the examples of Pound's and William Carlos Williams's open-form long poems; the Beat poets, for whom Whitman was a particularly important model; the confessional poets, who explored open-ended autobiographical lyric sequences; and poets of the New York school along with other writers interested in discursive long poems.

The concluding pages of the essay consider long poems of the seventies and especially the eighties, an era in which poetic decentralization and pluralization render text selection particularly difficult. Currently identity politics surrounding ethnicity or sexual preference often are more important determinants of poetic groupings than shared ideas about form and language. Thus, distinctive uses of the long poem may be associated with the new formalists and with Language writers, but for the most part particular approaches to the genre are not identified with particular groups of poets, and a range of approaches is in evidence. I have chosen to mention more briefly a greater number of poems than in earlier decades, emphasizing works that continue the long poem's tradition of invention and renewal.

T. S. Eliot's *The Waste Land* (1922), arguably the earliest Modernist long poem, was, at 434 lines, considerably shorter than most that would follow. Nonetheless, Eliot's strategies for moving beyond the short lyric proved tremendously influential—most notably, his construction of the poem as a collage in which brief fragments or more extended passages in diverse voices, lexicons, and styles are juxtaposed without connective material. Yet the poem contains recurring motifs and mythological patterns that point to the possibility of ordered continuity. Thus, its structure demonstrates a tension, discernible in varying degrees in most Modernist long poems, between a belief in fragmentation and chaos and a desire for order. Just as the form of *The Waste Land* seems to struggle for unity against great odds, its content comprises an attempt to discover coherence beneath the apparent meaninglessness of modern life. The reader, understood to be a member of an educated elite, is positioned as a doubly active participant: in the very act of reading the reader necessarily generates meaning by teasing out associative links, unpacking allusions, and tracing motifs, yet, addressed as "You! hypocrite lecteur!—mon semblable,—mon frère!," the reader also takes part in the condition of meaninglessness the poem explores.

The poem's collage construction is in part mimetic: as a "heap of broken images" confronted by speakers who can "connect / nothing with nothing," the poem mirrors the desiccated ruin that Eliot sees as the condition of postwar Anglo-European civilization. Similarly, its predominantly ironic perspective reflects modern culture's alienation from the faiths and ideals of the past. Countering both the formal fragmentation and the psychic isolation dramatized by the inability of any of the fleetingly introduced personae to connect meaningfully, are allusions to mythic orders that might subsume the disjunctive details. Eliot invokes patterns of the Grail legend and the vegetation myths described in Frazer's anthropological study, *The Golden Bough*. The existence of degraded parallels to former exemplars of value—the Fisher King, for instance—not only marks the modern world's decline but also signals a tentative hope for its recuperation.

The work's ordering structures gain emphasis in the notes, added after the initial publication, in which Eliot announces dominant themes, explains motifs linking "characters," signals the presence of the Fisher King, and identifies the spectator Tiresias as "the most important personage in the poem, uniting all the rest." Such proclamations underscore the uneasy coexistence of Eliot's longing to impose the once viable organization of a unified perceiving consciousness or a coherent narrative and his desire to represent the chaos of a botched civilization.

A controversial splash in the literary scene, *The Waste Land* inspired others to explore the resources of extended poetic forms. Among those spurred on was the poem's early champion, Ezra Pound. The densely paratactic form so crucial to *The Waste Land*'s impact derived partly from Pound's drastic editing, which Eliot acknowledged by dedicating the poem to Pound as "*il miglior fabbro*" (the better craftsman). Regarding Eliot's poem as "the justification . . . of our modern experiment," Pound hoped it would help build the audience and the environment he wanted for the "poem of some length" on which he was already working. The first book-length installment of this project, which eventually ran to more than a hundred cantos totaling about twenty-three thousand lines, appeared in 1925 as *A Draft of XVI Cantos*.

As in Whitman's poem, the epic dimension of Pound's work is heralded in the opening line—"And then went down to the ship"—through its allusion, in this case to Homer's *Odyssey*. But where Whitman anchors himself in the present, Pound—like Eliot—looks to the past for lessons that may resuscitate the present and benefit the future. Indeed, in opening Canto 8 by addressing Eliot and his method—"These fragments you have shelved (shored)."—Pound acknowledges overlap, as well as divergence, between his allusive collage method and Eliot's. Pound's fragmentation is not mimetic, like Eliot's, but synechdochic; parts evoke wholes, and it is from parts—from "a rain of factual atoms"—that we build knowledge. Pound's palimpsestic arrangement of concrete bits provides a selection of empirical data from which the reader is to assemble a coherent understanding.

Pound is far more interested than Eliot in the specific historical and cultural contexts generating the modern malaise. Epic for him is by definition "a poem including history," and his long poem burrows into history to demonstrate through resonant examples principles of economics and proper government that could promise current cultural and spiritual renewal. Pound shares Eliot's belief, developed from Imagism, in the telling concrete image, in a nondiscursive approach to poetic communication; but his "luminous details" or energized "ideograms," presented in multiple languages and voices, function more didactically than Eliot's. He insists on the fusion of poetry and politics—that is, of responsible language use with responsible government. Notoriously, he defined responsible government in terms that led to fascist sympathies and to the pro-Mussolini radio broadcasts that prompted his arrest for treason during World War II.

The section of the *Cantos* widely regarded as Pound's greatest achievement, *The Pisan Cantos* (numbers 74–84, published in 1948), was composed during his recovery from the breakdown he suffered while caged in a military detention camp in Pisa. The apparent humility of this poetry, its reliance on the urgencies of memory rather than historical research, its seemingly heartfelt condemnation of his errors alongside the moving discovery of what could sustain him—"What thou lov'st well shall not be reft from thee / What thou lov'st well is thy true heritage"—give this section an emotional power unsustained elsewhere in the *Cantos*.

Critics disagree on the nature or presence of an overall design for the *Cantos*; Pound himself in the late cantos struggles with his inability to "make it cohere." The work does, however, cohere loosely around Pound's didactic design. It also gains some structure from the layered "rhyming" of people and events that emerges from Pound's distinctive reading of history and from the progress of his autobiography.

Hart Crane, who composed *The Bridge* (1930) as a conscious refutation of the pessimism of Eliot's *The Waste Land* and as a renewal of Whitman's visionary celebration of America, retreated in his "symphony with an epic theme" from the relative openness of the Modernist long poem. Rather than resisting the imposition of order, as Eliot and Pound did in different degrees, Crane carefully planned his poem to affirm a Romantic wholeness underlying the apparent fragmentation of modern America. In 1923, when the poem was in its earliest stages, he declared, "It concerns a mystical synthesis of 'America.' . . . The initial impulses of 'our people' will have to be gathered up toward the climax of the bridge, symbol of our constructive future, our unique identity, in which is included also our scientific hopes and achievements of the future." Rather than inviting the reader to construct an order, this work, like the Romantic lyric, asks the reader to follow the associations in the poet's mind.

Crane's method, while it follows Eliot's in employing multifaceted symbols as ordering devices, places no particular value on the concretion of Eliot's "objective correlative" or Pound's "luminous detail"; more mystical than they in his approach to language, Crane sought through the "dynamics of metaphor" to free words so that they might capture "another logic, quite independent of the original definition of the word or phrase or image." The results were mixed: sometimes his linguistic innovations are exciting in their defamiliarization and powerful in their synesthetic evocations; elsewhere his writing is overwrought, turgid, and contrived.

The poem begins with a stately address, "To Brooklyn Bridge," emphasizing the balance of tensions achieved by that personified triumph of modern technology, at once material and transcendent, still and in motion, bound to the city and spanning the entire nation. The proem closes with a prayer that the Bridge in its "unfractioned idiom" might provide a usable mythology, a vehicle of transport to the divine. Eight titled sections follow, each drawing upon a distinct region and portion of American history. The speaker's spiritual quest—and Crane's determinedly visionary plan—is fulfilled in the final ascent of

"Atlantis." There the bridge and the verbal imagination it symbolizes merge in upwardly "arching strands of song," connecting the speaker to eternity and godhead.

Six years after the publication of *The Bridge* Muriel Rukeyser, who would compose a great many extended poetic sequences over her long career, published in her first volume another response to Eliot, "Theory of Flight." This poem, too, in the tradition of such works of Whitman as "Passage to India," celebrates the achievements of modern technology. Its technique is markedly Modernist—jagged free-verse lines, densely allusive imagery, disruptive syntax and grammar capturing the disruptive movement of modern life. But where Eliot felt despair Rukeyser perceives possibility: "Fortuitously have we gained loneliness, / fallen in waste places liberated." With Eliot and Pound probably in mind, she rejects the idea that we may "replica / ourselves in hieroglyphs and broken things," proposing instead a flight available in the fullness of the present. Her concerns about contemporary commercial America and her determination to achieve an empowering vision of human possibility within the technological world overlap with Crane's, but her perspective is far more socially conscious. Her presentation of social ills involves analyzing power and its abuses, not just in general but in specific cases—Sacco and Vanzetti, Tom Mooney, the Scottsboro boys. Where Crane readily leaves behind the concrete details of modern life in his ascent to the absolute, Rukeyser seeks an exaltation of the human that invokes myth but does not require transcendence. Her poetic sequences of the later 1930s, such as "The Book of the Dead" (1938), demonstrate skillful poetic application of the techniques of cinematic montage. But this poem, which is based on Rukeyser's investigation of events surrounding miners' deaths from silicosis in Fayette County, West Virginia, and others that followed were pigeonholed as literature of social protest by an establishment that refused to see aesthetic merit in topical political work. Only recently have critics begun to explore Rukeyser's contribution to the development of the long poem.

Another socially concerned writer of long poems whose technique is heavily indebted to the Modernism of Pound, Eliot, and Crane is Melvin B. Tolson. Although this black Missouri-born college teacher lived in the United States, he was named poet laureate of Liberia in 1947. He therefore set out to write a poem to honor the centennial of that nation, settled by American freed slaves. Tolson conceived of his *Libretto for the Republic of Liberia* (1953) as an ode structured along the lines of *The Bridge*. Each of the work's eight metrically diverse but highly formalized sections is named for a note of the ascending scale (do, re, mi, etc.). Its treatment of Liberian history culminates in Whitmanian free-verse prophesies of the technological greatness of "The Futureafrique" and a coming era of global racial harmony. Claiming American, European, and African artistic roots, Tolson incorporates phrases in African languages—along with many translated African proverbs—as well as phrases in German, Spanish, French, and Hebrew. Throughout the language and imagery are so condensed, the manner so highly allusive and intellectually demanding, that Tolson added seventeen pages of notes.

Tolson's *Harlem Gallery, Book I: The Curator* (1965) also employs the techniques of High Modernism, which by this time were out of fashion among most black poets and many white ones. Tolson intended this stylized narrative ode to be the first section of a five-volume epic telling the story of the black man in America; he lived only to complete this first volume. Here, guided by the "Curator," a light-skinned black intellectual, the reader encounters African Americans of all social classes in twentieth-century Harlem. Still heavily allusive, this work incorporates more black vernacular and more of the ordinary details of black life than *Libretto*. Tolson's choice of a highly erudite style for works dedicated to strengthening and celebrating the black community, especially the black proletariat—that is, his use of a style whose politics are widely regarded as contradicting his message—has resulted in a small audience for his complex long poems.

The Objectivist poet Louis Zukofsky, a Jew whose political sympathies were for a time Marxist, also employs a difficult version of Modernist allusive collage, and the opacities of his work have limited his audience as well. His poem "*A*," composed between 1928 and 1974 and published between 1940 and 1978, is written in twenty-four movements of varying styles and lengths; "A 16" is four words long, while "A 24" is a two hundred and forty-page masque in which one of the voices is the musical score of Handel's "Harpsichord Pieces." The poems in "*A 1–12*" follow closely the paratactic manner of Pound's *Cantos*, incorporating in collage fashion considerable historical documentation; the later sections sometimes employ a less disjunctive manner and often treat autobiographical material. *"A"* often responds to topical events such as race riots and space flights or considers such historical phenomena as American imperialism, but Zukofsky does not propound a political program so much as he seeks harmony, political and otherwise, through language. He is very interested in musical form (especially baroque forms such as Bach's fugues), in musical analogues for the poetic forms he invents or adopts (such as ballades and canzones), and in the musical properties of language. Delighting in the materiality of words and playing with their potential permutations, Zukofsky sometimes anticipates the recent Language poets' desire to let language itself guide the sense of one's utterance.

The historically oriented collage-epic is not the only type of long poem that developed within Modernism. Over the course of his career Wallace Stevens composed a number of masterful extended poems in a meditative form. For Stevens the modern poem is "[t]he poem of the mind in the act of finding / [w]hat will suffice." Uninterested in American landscape, American history, modern mechanical triumphs, or the urban scene, his process-oriented long poems are speculative philosophical works exploring the relation of imagination to reality and the imagination's role in compensating for the modern loss of religious belief. He does not rely on multiple voices, fragmentary quotation, and erudite allusion as Pound and Eliot do. His technique is discursive rather than paratactic. Although enlivened by wit, by an exotic heterogeneity of diction, and by remarkably various manipulations of syntax, his impersonal, urbane voice is relatively consistent, as are his stanza and line lengths within a given poem. The aesthetics of his long poems might be summed up by the three principles elaborated in "Notes Toward a Supreme Fiction": "It Must Be Abstract," "It Must Change," "It Must Give Pleasure." Although Stevens approaches abstractions through ingenious metaphors and although his delight in change frequently yields disjunctive shifts between stanzas, his stately musings nonetheless provide a distinct alternative to Pound's or Eliot's paratactic models of the long poem.

Each of Stevens's volumes contains at least one longer poem, beginning with *Harmonium*'s "The Comedian as the Letter C," yet probably his greatest and most influential long poems were those of his last decade: "Notes Toward a Supreme Fiction" (1942) and "An Ordinary Evening in New Haven" (1949), along with the late longish sequences,

"Credences of Summer" (1947) and "The Auroras of Autumn" (1948). Indeed, a number of the major Modernists published important long poems after World War II, in the late years of their lengthy careers.

Eliot's greatest long poem, *Four Quartets*, was written between the mid-thirties and the early forties when Eliot—by then a devout Anglican and a British citizen—was no longer much concerned with social critique or pagan mythic archetypes. Instead, he explores how the person of faith can find meaning living within time, bridging the temporal world and the eternal. *Four Quartets* employs the language of conception and generalization in a discursive format. The four linked meditations gain imagistic grounding in autobiographical memories—of a rose garden Eliot visited in 1935, of a visit to an ancestor's village in England, of his childhood in St. Louis and near Gloucester, Massachusetts. Yet the speaker is also representative, concerned with the spiritual life of his community; hence the recent bombing of London provides images for the destruction that must somehow be redeemed in spiritual experience. As the title's allusion to musical form suggests, the work's structure depends on recurring images and themes analogous to musical leitmotifs. The work's governing rhetorical figure is the balanced one of paradox: e.g., "Time the destroyer is time the preserver" or "In my beginning is my end."

Many younger poets have been haunted by Eliot's achievement in *Four Quartets*, among them Theodore Roethke, whose "North American Sequence" (published posthumously in *The Far Field* [1964]) responds to the poem directly. Roethke, too, seeks experiences of timelessness within time—partly through memory—but his moments of spiritual enlightenment, unlike Eliot's, occur through union with the natural world. Where Eliot's visionary moment occurs in a formal English rose garden, Roethke's occurs in the dynamic wilderness. Roethke's speaker achieves spiritual awakening through a dissolving of the self's boundaries reminiscent of Whitman's dissolution into the sky and the grass at the close of "Song of Myself."

H.D. and William Carlos Williams were contemporaries of Pound and Eliot who, partly because of their deep allegiance to Imagist poetics, came late to extended poetic forms. Their long poems have been particularly important to poets coming of age since World War II who have sought alternative traditions to that of hegemonic Eliotic Modernism. H.D.'s *Trilogy* has affinities with both of Eliot's major long poems, since she responds to a fractured modern waste land—to experiencing the bombing of London—by turning to values from the past. But the past she seeks to recover is a largely erased matrifocal one, and the religion she reconstructs is a revisionary gynocentric one. Written between 1942 and 1944, the work's three parts, *The Walls Do Not Fall*, *Tribute to the Angels*, and *Flowering of the Rod*, attempt to reinterpret inherited myths in order to reveal ancient meanings that have been obscured. Each book is composed of forty-three sections, mostly in unrhymed couplets, and employs elaborate patterns of imagery. The first focuses especially on the recovery of female goddesses, particularly the story of Isis; the second replaces John's vengeful vision of the Apocalypse in Revelation with a vision of salvation and rebirth through the Lady who is goddess, muse, and female psyche; the third tells of the coming together of Kaspar and Mary Magdalene, a depolarization of the male and the female accomplished through reverence for the recuperative powers of female fertility and creativity.

In *Helen in Egypt*, written in the early 1950s and published in 1961, H.D. more directly takes on the tradition of male epic by retelling from Helen's point of view the Trojan War story central to the Homeric tradition. Adopting the version of the myth according to which Helen of Troy was a phantom and the real Helen spent the war years quietly in Egypt, H.D. dramatizes through Helen's thoughts her own psychic history. The poem invokes the psychoanalytic process of calling up memories in order to recover repressed aspects of the self. The speakers can be linked to figures in H.D.'s own life, yet the personal growth Helen achieves, in part through a reconnection with the mother, models a process by which women may give birth to and empower themselves. Similarly, Achilles' development from martial figure into a worshipper of Eros who is the perfect brother-mate for Helen implicitly models a transformation of patriarchy that would heal our splintered world. The poetry has a far more lyrical character than Pound's *Cantos*; H.D.'s later addition of a copious prose gloss, often more obfuscating than illuminating, dramatically diverges from the Poundian technique of thoroughly integrating prose and poetry.

H.D.'s identification of *Helen in Egypt* as "my own *Cantos*" points not only to her work's indebtedness but also to its defiant revision of Pound. In composing *Paterson*, Williams, too, built upon and challenged the achievement of Pound's *Cantos*. He extended the tradition of what Michael Bernstein calls the "modern verse epic"—didactic works that narrate their audience's cultural, historical, or mythic heritage, and in which the dominant voice speaks not as a private individual but for an entire community. Williams follows Pound in presenting documentary prose passages as part of his poetry, yet he also sets his project in opposition to Pound's and, quite vehemently, to Eliot's. Rejecting the expatriate poets' allegiance to what he regards as exhausted European traditions, Williams writes "a reply to Greek and Latin with the bare hands." He struggles toward an adequate American speech and focuses on a specific American locality—Paterson, New Jersey—where he seeks exemplary behavior among ordinary men and women in daily life. The work was originally conceived in four books, published between 1946 (when Williams was sixty-three) and 1951. A fifth book was added in 1958, and Williams made notes for a sixth.

Assembled as a collage of flexible, generally short-lined free-verse and prose passages drawn from historical documents and personal correspondence, *Paterson* is held together largely by symbolic patterns. The master trope of the poem identifies the city Paterson as a sleeping giant whose identity is linked to that of the (sometimes) narrator, Dr. Paterson, while the course of the Passaic River is linked to the movement of the poem. Each book is loosely centered on a particular site (e.g., the Falls in book 1, the Park in book 2) and on particular themes (e.g., Paterson's historical inheritance in book 1, the failures of love in book 2). Like Eliot and Pound, Williams perceives a shattered world; his central term is "divorce"—of people from their history, from geography, from others, and from language. As in their works, ideas gain vitality by being conveyed through concrete examples. But in contrast to Pound and Eliot, Williams insists that renewal, which will be achieved through open-ended "invention" and "discovery," depends on defiance of received authority and wholesale destruction of old forms and traditions.

Langston Hughes, a major voice of the Harlem Renaissance, also did not publish a long poem until late in his career, and he too insisted that his long poem assume an American form and idiom. His portrait of contemporary Harlem, *Montage of a Dream Deferred*, appeared in 1951, and while the open-ended improvisatory character of Hughes's free verse is indebted to Whitman and Carl Sandburg, his long poem is structured by the distinctly African American, consciously rebellious forms of jazz. In a prefatory note Hughes likens the poem to be-bop:

marked by conflicting changes, sudden nuances, sharp and impudent interjections, broken rhythms, and passages sometimes in the manner of the jam session, sometimes the popular song, punctuated by the riffs, breaks, and disctortions of the music of a community in transition.

Hughes's use of scat singing, black vernacular, and forms like the blues and the ballad emphasizes the oral and folk roots of this work. The dominant theme of *Montage* is the deferred fulfillment of African American people's themes. Taken together the poem's many voices highlight the injustices and economic restrictions blacks experience in racist America as well as the resourcefulness of the black community. The original version was divided into six titled sections of thematically related poems; in the 1959 *Selected Poems* version one poem follows immediately after another, heightening the effect of rapid montage, of nonhierarchical perception, and of a cumulative energy pressing toward that explosion which "Harlem" warns us is the likely consequence of long-deferred dreams. Hughes adapts Modernist juxtaposition to convey a people's vitality rather than their fragmentation and to emphasize the expressive empowerment gained from the conflux of high and low traditions.

When Pound began his "long poem" those two words in proximity made him uneasy. Since the 1930s, thanks largely to the achievements of Pound and his Modernist colleagues, the long poem has been an available option for aspiring writers, and increasingly various, sometimes less experimental, uses of the form have developed, both in the United States and in Great Britain. The parameters of this volume preclude discussion of such British long poems as David Jones's *In Parenthesis* (1937) and *Anathemata* (1952), Basil Bunting's *Briggflatts* (1966), or Geoffrey Hill's *Mercian Hymns* (1971), which have contributed to the long poem's diversity and importance. W. H. Auden's long poems of the 1930s and 1940s, especially, diversified the generic analogues available to authors of this form. Instead of revising epic models, in his long poems "Letter to Lord Byron" (1936), "New Year Letter" (1941), "The Sea and the Mirror" (1944), *For the Time Being* (1944), and *The Age of Anxiety* (1947), Auden taps the resources of epistolary, dramatic, and essayistic forms. Auden's interweaving of wit and playfulness with serious material, his use of prosaic conversation-al language, of single narrative threads, and of discursive continuity offer alternatives to the disjunctive image-centered intensities of the High Modernist epic.

After mid-century more and more American poets essay some extended form. The only major group of poets whose members eschew the long poem are the Southern Agrarians and the other practitioners of tightly crafted lyric popularized by Eliot and the New Critics. (Robert Penn Warren, as author of *Brother to Dragons* [1953, rev. 1979] and *Chief Joseph of the Nez Perce* (1983) is the exception.) Since their standards dominated American poetry during the forties and fifties, their disinterest in the long poem proved significant for the genre's sub-sequent history. Writers reacting against the constraints of New Criti-cal doctrine and seeking to revitalize poetry in the fifties and sixties often looked to long poems, as their early Modernist predecessors had, as vehicles for renewal and expansion of poetic possibility.

Contesting the closure of the hegemonic lyric, with its carefully bal-anced ambiguities, tidy symbolic patterns, metrical and rhythmic regu-larity, and controlled tonalities, young poets in the fifties turned to "open forms" and to the example of the more open Modernist struc-tures. Thus, when Charles Olson, one of the earliest advocates of this development, identified himself and his cohorts in Projectivist writing as "sons of Pound and Williams," he was thinking particularly of the methodology of the *Cantos* and of *Paterson*—of lines developing with apparent spontaneity in response to immediate apprehension and of extended forms with no predetermined shape. Olson's epic, *The Max-imus Poems*, written in elliptical and allusive cantolike units identified often as "letters," follows *Paterson* in focusing on a particular locale: the fishing port of Gloucester, Massachusetts, where Olson had spent childhood summers. It adapts to that place Pound's interest in histori-cal exploration and economic analysis; Gloucester's history, examined in a documentary fashion, is a microcosm for the nation's. Following Whitmanian tradition, the hero, Maximus, is in part the poet himself and in part a mythicized aggrandizement; his goal is the reawakening of community. The work has no plot or guiding plan. It evolved along-side its author's interests and appeared in installments—the first ten Maximus poems in 1953, the final ones in *The Maximus Poems: Volume Three* posthumously in 1975. The later parts show diminished concern with local history and increased preoccupation with mythic magnifications and archetypes.

Other poets associated with Projectivist or Black Mountain writing who have produced major long poems are Robert Duncan and Ed Dorn. The title of Duncan's "Passages," in suggesting movement, transition, and parts of an evolving literary whole, points to the open-ended character of this varied sequence, which began appearing in the 1960s. The first thirty "Passages" appear in *Bending the Bow* (1968) and smaller sets appear in subsequent volumes. "Passages" was not collected as a single work, however, and Duncan asserted that the poems belong in the volumes where they appear. Individual poems often elliptically develop interpretations of works by others, as the erudite poet ruminates on passages from Hesiod, Verlaine, or Kipling, as he contemplates the revelations of historical studies or ideas projected in paintings such as Bosch's "Christ Bearing the Cross" or Piero di Cosimo's "A Forest Fire." Duncan adapts Pound's and Olson's allusive collage method to emphasize the artist's participation in the thoughts and creations of others as well as the links between artistic creation and cosmic design. Like Olson he is concerned with community, but his orientation is more spiritual, mystical, and (homo)erotic, and he is more consistently involved with mythological and occult lore. While Duncan's writing is often very personal, the private self he posits is a microcosm of the conflicts and the interconnections of the external world. Thus he addresses more directly than Olson the political concerns of his day, exploring at length, for instance, his opposition to the Vietnam war. Through his sometimes visionary art he attempts to contribute to a pattern and to enlarged notions of selfhood that would make possible a redemptive world order.

Ed Dorn's *Slinger* (1975) continues the Pound-Olson tradition of didactic intellectual exploration, but his didacticism is expressed through sarcasm and the ironies of poetic deconstruction rather than through Olson's mode of explanation. In the fantastic fractured (anti)narrative of his long poem, Dorn puts into play innumerable myths and stereotypes of the American frontier derived from popular culture. These he subjects to mutation via puns and wordplay in a mock-heroic tale of a "semi-dios" Gunslinger, an outlaw inclined to metaphysical pronouncement who may also be the robber-baron Howard Hughes. This distinctly postmodern quest-epic, which incorporates a great variety of verse forms, is distinguished by its thorough rejection of personality and inwardness and by the hilarious ingenuity of its critique of entrepreneurial capitalism.

The West Coast Beat poets published in some of the same small magazines as the early Black Mountain writers and shared their interest in open forms. A cornerstone of the Beat movement was Allen Ginsberg's 1956 long poem, "Howl." The epigraph to *Howl and Other Poems* (a volume for which Williams wrote the introduction) is from Whitman—"Unscrew the locks from the doors! / Unscrew the doors themselves from their jambs!"—and announces the iconoclastic tradition in which Ginsberg places his work. In "Howl" he looks directly to Whitman's model of long-lined inclusive free verse to catalog examples of the anguished quest for vision and connection undertaken by "the best minds of [his] generation." Ginsberg's madmen heros, committed to erotic and spiritual connection, fight the deadly forces of conformist fifties America. The poem is an outpouring at once of sympathy and outrage, prophetic righteousness and surreal comedy, concrete particularities and visionary insight. In 1961 Ginsberg published a second important long poem, "Kaddish" (named for the Jewish prayer for the dead), his harrowing elegy for his mother. Exploring his grief at her death and at her painful life, he recounts his history with her in order to forgive and to heal the scars left on him by her mental illness.

The five books of Ginsberg's *The Fall of America: poems of these states, 1965–1971* reflect epic ambitions without anxiety about unifying form. Many of the shorter poems that make up each part are transcriptions of sometimes slack and self-indulgent tape recordings. The sprawling whole is organized chronologically and geographically to follow the poet's travels throughout the nation, volubly recording his own shifting states of consciousness and physical being and the desperate political state of the union in those years.

Ginsberg is one of our frankest celebrants of homoerotic experience. His daring to depict in intimate detail madness, sexual promiscuity, and a sexuality then widely regarded as deviant—and to claim these experiences as his own—contributed to the development of confessional writing in the late 1950s. In the breakthrough confessional volume, *Life Studies* (1959), Robert Lowell let go of the tight metrics and gnarled symbolic densities of his earlier work in the New Critical style, partly because of his experiences reading before West Coast audiences accustomed to the accessible speech rhythms and speech idiom of Beat writing. But the confessional long poems of Lowell and John Berryman do not pursue radically open forms as the Beats and Projectivists do. Both men use sequences of sonnets or sonnetlike lyrics to record the continuing turmoil of their psychic lives, their marital difficulties and extramarital affairs as well as contemporary political upheavals. They combine "closed" forms with "open" structures; the fixed-length short lyric provides a comfortable unit for capturing immediate experience, while such lyrics can accumulate without any fixed end. For these confessional poets poetic form serves as a vehicle for previously tabooed content rather than, as for the Projectivists, an organic extension of content.

Lowell's *Notebook 1967–68* (1969), which he identified as "one poem, jagged in pattern," records in unrhymed, often elliptical sonnets the events of a year when Lowell was active in the antiwar movement. The volume includes poems depicting his participation in the October march on the Pentagon and in Eugene McCarthy's presidential campaign, and treats such political events as the deaths of Che Guevara and Martin Luther King. Preoccupied with the way history reflects human imperfection and psychology, Lowell explores the role of violence in past and present events and in his own manic-depressive psyche. He reveals the moral ambiguities of his own behavior, exposing his own "cowardly / foolhardy heart."

Diary or notebooklike forms were popular at this time (e.g., Denise Levertov's "From a Notebook: October '68–May '69," Robert Creeley's *A Day Book*), but Lowell did not remain satisfied with the arrangement of *Notebook 1967–68*. From this volume he selected poems, revised and rearranged them, while adding other blank verse sonnets to produce three subsequent books: *Notebook* (1970), *History* (1973), and *For Lizzie and Harriet* (1973). The last of these, named for his second wife and daughter, contains the poems recording the drama of his troubled domestic life. The fourteen-liners of *The Dolphin* (1973) provide a sequel to *For Lizzie and Harriet* incorporating passages from his wife's letters, transcriptions of telephone conversations, and the like. Lowell's exposure of personal material—even when others are also exposed—is relentless. *History* moves closer to the genuinely public focus of epic, tracing in chronological order events and figures of Western history. Many of the 368 lyrics are dramatic monologues, so that the autobiographical emphasis is diminished. Yet, as is often the case in modern "poems containing history," the recurrence of past patterns in the present renders history and the poet's life inextricable.

John Berryman's first long poem, which was his third volume, *Homage to Mistress Bradstreet* (1956), began his movement toward confessional poetry. That poem, in fifty-seven rhyming stanzas, enters into the rebellious consciousness of the Puritan poet who describes the difficulties of her life on this continent. Summoned by the modern poet, she speaks out against the constraints imposed on her by her religion and her God, her society, her gender, her body, and by life itself. Although *Homage* rests on extensive historical research, its emphasis is psychological, and Berryman himself is a key presence engaged in passionate communion with Bradstreet.

In *The Dream Songs* Berryman fully enters the confessional mode, documenting the processes of his own mind and his own anguished history of mental breakdowns, alcoholism, and failed marriages through his multifaceted persona, Henry. The 385 poems, mostly in three six-line stanzas, were written between 1955 and 1968 and published in two volumes. Like Lowell's sequences, the work's structure is open in that it follows the evolving circumstances of Berryman's personal life. Its innovations lie in its portrayal of the divided self through Henry's many manifestations—Henry Pussycat, Henry House, Henry Hankovitch, Mr. Bones—and in its bizarre comic language. Feeling battered by the world, obsessed with death—especially his father's suicide—longing for sex and love, Henry uses disrupted and frequently inverted syntax and diction that outrageously combine high and low—erudite polysyllables, minstrel show talk, nursery rhymes, baby talk, profanity—to give kaleidoscopic brilliance and poignancy to work that might otherwise seem merely self-pitying.

While confessional aesthetics encouraged open-ended autobiographical sequences, the image-based and archetypal focus of so-called deep image writing of the same period lent itself primarily to shorter poems. Yet the pressures of political events in the late 1960s pushed some deep image writers toward longer forms that could engage history. Robert Bly's *The Teeth Mother Naked at Last* (1970) is one such poem; Galway Kinnells' *The Book of Nightmares* (1971) is better known and more accomplished. Kinnell's speaker confronts a personal fear of death that is deepened by awareness of humankind's apparent addiction to human slaughter. To work through his fears and regain a sense of union with the natural world, the speaker (in Whitmanian fashion, at once collective and individual) journeys through nightmares of loss and fragmentation and through "our history of errors," particularly the horrors of contemporary Vietnam. The poem's ten books (modeled partly on Rilke's *Duino Elegies*) are linked by recurring heterogeneous motifs—e.g., the births of Kinnell's children, his recent parting from a lover, a hen's death, an old man's shoes, a burning corpse. The value of these images shifts as the speaker struggles to accept death and loss so that he may embrace life. While historical bloodshed remains unredeemed, interpersonal connection, the sensory wealth of earthly experience, and the enduring powers of language enable a qualified rejoicing that "*the wages / of dying is love.*"

In the sixties and seventies writers associated with the New York school of avant-garde writers such as Kenneth Koch and John Ashbery were generating discursive long poems, as was their contemporary A. R. Ammons. These poems rely little on personal narrative and semiautobiographical quests. Ammons and Ashbery combine Williams's interest in open forms that refuse a finality of vision with Stevens's meditative, apolitical uses of the long poem to record acts of mind. Ammons's *Tape for the Turn of the Year* (1965) is, arbitrarily, "a long / thin / poem" composed on the "narrow, long, / unbroken" surface of an adding-machine tape in entries dated from December 6 to January 10, when the tape runs out. A conversational record of the poet's immediate thoughts and observations, *Tape* aims to be "a / running with, fleet / recorder at the crest of / change." This poetry aspires at once to participate fully in temporal flux and to arrest time's flow by giving it more permanent form. *Sphere: The Form of a Motion* (1974) uses longer free verse lines employing frequently abstract and scientific diction in a similar quest to render the "shapes nearest shapelessness" in the apprehending mind.

John Ashbery, the most celebrated writer of the New York school, has included at least one long poem in almost every volume he has published: "Europe," a collage text in *The Tennis Court Oath* (1962), "The Skaters" in *Rivers and Mountains* (1966), "Fragment" in *The Double Dream of Spring* (1970), the long prose poems comprising *Three Poems* (1972), the title poem of *Self-Portrait in a Convex Mirror* (1975), "Fantasia on 'The Nut-Brown Maid'" in *Houseboat Days* (1977), "Litany" in *As We Know* (1979), the title poem in *A Wave* (1984), and all of *Flow*

Chart (1991). He regards long poems as "logbooks of a continuing experience or at any rate of an experience that continues to provide new reflections and therefore . . . gets to be much closer to a whole reality than shorter ones do." "The Skaters" establishes the playful, disorienting expansiveness that characterizes most of Ashbery's long works, which represent the processes of consciousness. Mental process as Ashbery portrays it is more subject to interruption, distraction, and the action of chance than Stevens's rendition of "the mind in the act of finding," so that even as Ashbery's syntax progresses logically, his pronouns, levels of diction, and semantic focus shift unpredictably. "Self-Portrait in a Convex Mirror," Ashbery's best known—and most conventional—work, records the poet's responses to a mannerist self-portrait by Francesco Parmigianino, who painted on a hemispheric surface the self-image he saw in a convex mirror. More often long poems are experimental vehicles for Ashbery. For instance, *Three Poems* explores the resources of prose for negotiating the territory between the two impossible extremes of "put[ting] it all down," and "leav[ing it] all out." A quite different experiment, "Litany" presents two columns of text intended to be heard simultaneously, dramatizing our ordinary experience of having to process data selectively from a polyphonic barrage of stimuli. Throughout his long poems Ashbery is interested in the "inaccuracies and anomalies of common speech"; with a kind of torquing of usual usage he renews the resources of banal and clichéd language as he tries to get at "a general, all-purpose experience . . . in which anybody can see reflected his own private experiences without them having to be defined or set up for him."

Humor, subtly present in Ashbery's works, is a marked characteristic of Kenneth Koch's long poems, including his zany semisurreal narrative, *The Duplications* (1977), and the two more autobiographically based (but nonconfessional) sequences comprising *On the Edge* (1986). Koch also discursively explores the poetic resources of the banal, refusing to impose hierarchies on experience, and instead celebrating with apparent spontaneity, zest, and irreverent inventiveness all the "many factors engaging our attention" in modern urban life.

Recently, somewhat younger poets have taken discursive writing in rather different directions with poems of personal quest. Fred Chappell models his autobiographical *Midquest* (1981) on the American artform of the sampler. James McMichael's *Four Good Things* (1980) offers a discursive exploration of suburban life centering on his own childhood in Pasadena, California. In his more intellectually ambitious discursive long poem, *An Explanation of America* (1979), Robert Pinsky draws upon ideas from diverse thinkers (e.g., Gogol, Malcolm X, Horace) and images from his own middle-class life to explain to his daughter his idea of the nation and how one defines individual identity in relation to it.

Like his contemporary Ashbery, James Merrill is indebted to Stevens, but Merrill's allegiance to received forms and his love of condensed wit remove his work from the often flat discursive expansiveness embraced by Ashbery, Koch, Ammons, Pinsky and the others just mentioned. In his astonishing epic, *The Changing Light at Sandover* (1982), Merrill integrates Stevens's love of illusion and lush language with Auden's formalist and dramatic approach to the long poem. This massive work was initially published in three books, each structured in imitation of a portion of the ouija board: "The Book of Ephraim" (1976, in *Divine Comedies*) has a section for each letter of the alphabet; *Mirabell: Books of Number* (1978) follows the ouija board numbers from zero to nine, with decimal subdivisions; *Scripts for the Pageant* (1980) has three large, subdivided sections, "Yes," "&," "No." The forms are various: ABBA quatrains, blank verse, syllabic fourteeners, sonnets, sestinas, a canzone, etc., with different forms and styles assigned to different voices. The work purports to be autobiographical and centers around the experiences Merrill and his lover, David Jackson, have contacting the spirit world via the ouija board. Intertwined in "The Book of Ephraim" are the narratives of Merrill's and Jackson's twenty-five-year companionship, the story told in Merrill's lost novel (itself a version of the couple's relationship as well as the life stories of their parents), and the tale of the poem's composition in 1974. This first book—in which the couple's guide to the spirit world is the witty, sophisticated Ephraim, once a favorite of the emperor Tiberius—is very much a celebration of homosexual love. In subsequent books Merrill is required by the spirit world to record for humanity a series of lessons. The guides are more challenging, and greater space is given to direct transcriptions of information from the other world, with increasing focus on the danger of nuclear annihilation. Making these lessons more comprehensible are spirits of dead friends, especially W. H. Auden and Maria Mitsotaki, who assume roles for Merrill analogous to those Virgil and Beatrice played for Dante. The information they present is a pastiche of myths, just as Merrill's style becomes at times a pastiche of the great voices of English literary tradition. Despite the work's sometimes urgent didacticism the poet retains a skeptical stance, a camp sense of humor, and an urbane tone; *Sandover* offers yes-and-no ambiguities along with constantly shifting levels of metaphor rather than fixed truths.

Merrill's epic is one among many recent long poems signaling a revived interest in narrative, both among formalists and free-verse poets. In some of the texts by the younger generation of new formalists the turning toward narrative entails a turning away from the innovations of Modernist writing, its paratactic techniques, and its exploration of fragmented perception in a fractured world. Such works include Vikram Seth's "novel in verse," *The Golden Gate* (1986), and Frederick Turner's futuristic verse epic, *The New World* (1985).

Less traditionally formalist writers interested in narrative have employed flexible forms of lyric sequences in nonlinear explorations of imagined history. Albert Goldbarth's "novel/poem," *Different Fleshes* (1979), centers on a historical figure, Vander Clyde, who was born in 1904 in Round Rock, Texas, left work as a field hand, and traveled to Paris in the early twenties to become the famous female impersonator and acrobat, "Barbette." Relying heavily on Modernist juxtaposition, the poem shifts among eras and styles; its historical reach extends backward to a nineteenth-century Texas outlaw who robbed banks dressed as a woman and forward to contemporary gay bars in Austin, where Clyde lived in the thirties and Goldbarth lives while writing.

Many others who have turned to historically focused long poems in the 1970s and 1980s have adopted to a single historical focus tamer forms of the Modernist long poem's incorporation of found documents and of parataxis. Examples of these lyric-based documentary histories include Donald Finkel's *Adequate Earth* (1972), *Endurance: An Antarctic Idyll* (1978), and *Going Under* (1978), which chart Antarctic exploration, especially Shackleton's voyage, and exploration of the Mammoth Caves to examine human adaptability and endurance; Daniel Hoffman's presentation of William Penn's history, *Brotherly Love* (1981); and Marc Kaminsky's sequence based on the testimony of survivors of the Hiroshima and Nagasaki bombings, *The Road From Hiroshima* (1984). Ruth Whitman's sequences stick less closely to historical sources and focus instead on imaginative entrance into the consciousness of historical women in situations of extremity. *Tamsen Don-*

ner: A Woman's Journey (1977) recreates in alternating passages of prose and lyric the lost journal of the wife of the leader of the Donner Party. *The Testing of Hanna Senesh* (1986) portrays the last nine months of the young Jewish poet who joined the British National Intelligence Corps in 1944 and returned to her native Hungary to assist the Resistance but was captured and killed by the Nazis. Jill Breckenridge, in her sequence of poems and lyrical prose, *Civil Blood* (1986), uses the voices of various characters to depict the life of her ancestor John Cabell Breckinridge, vice president under Buchanan and a Confederate general. Rita Dove, too, has effectively used the lyric sequence to represent ancestral history; *Thomas and Beulah* (1986) presents her grandparents' lives through two sets of chronologically arranged lyrics that "tell two sides of a story and are meant to be read in sequence."

The number of women poets named in the preceding paragraph reflects the increasing interest in extended poetic forms shown by women in recent decades. This is a marked contrast with the period before World War II, when few women either wished to or felt empowered to attempt the long poem, associated as it was with epic's traditionally male spheres of historically significant action. Gwendolyn Brooks, whose work has been consistently concerned with public issues surrounding race, was among the first young women to take up long poems in the postwar era. *Annie Allen* (1949) contains a compressed mock-epic in forty-three seven-line rhyming stanzas, "The Anniad." Here Brooks echoes epic conventions and subversively employs traditional metrics to expose both white society's oppression of black men and black men's oppression of black women. Her long poem, "In the Mecca" (1968), depicts life in Chicago's old Mecca Building, a slum tenement that was once an elegant apartment complex. Influenced by the Black Arts movement, Brooks in this poem abandons tight formalism for lines of varying length with random rhyme. Its narrative depicts Mrs. Sallie Smith's search for her missing daughter Pepita, describing her encounters with a host of characters inhabiting the building. Several characters express hope for an empowered and unified African American community, but the grim discovery that Pepita has been murdered by a resident of the Mecca suggests how far that dream is from the violent realities of urban poverty.

Whereas Brooks's awareness of the political dimensions of her characters' experience is typical of minority writers, white women poets have generally been slower to recognize the political dimensions of their lives and the consequent importance of their treating public material. The political upheavals of the sixties, including the growth of the women's movement, produced in many white women an increased awareness that, as feminism argues, "the personal is the political." One poetic consequence was poetry that combines frank treatment of intimate material with analysis of the social, political, and ideological contexts of personal experience. Adrienne Rich's sequences, "Twenty-One Love Poems" (1978) and *Sources* (1983), insist on the social contexts of their personal subject matter. Opening her sequence of lesbian love poems with a vision of the violence and misogyny of urban America, Rich asserts the inseparability of her lovers' experience from "those rancid dreams, that blurt of metal, those disgraces." Similarly, her sequence meditating on the sources of her own identity and strength focuses on her Jewish heritage (and that of her dead father and husband) considered in historical and class contexts.

Sharon Doubiago also exemplifies recent women poets' gender-conscious politicized treatment of intimate material in her ambitious woman-centered epic, *Hard Country* (1982). Combining a mythic scale with a personal one in the tradition of Modernist epic, Doubiago portrays herself "as an American Isis" who wanders the land "in search of the lover strewn in pieces across it, buried in it." Her private quest for a balanced relationship with a male lover merges with a quest for understanding of, and escape from, the violence of our nation's history.

Contemporary women poets often self-consciously modify predominantly male traditions to represent female perspectives and to accommodate feminist agendas; in so doing they reinforce the tendency toward change essential to the American long poem's paradoxical traditions of innovation. Formalist lesbian poet Marilyn Hacker, for instance, in *Love, Death, and the Changing of the Seasons* (1986) revises the Petrarchan tradition of the love-sonnet sequence by depicting the course of a lesbian relationship within a social world composed almost exclusively of women. Like Rich in her love poems, Hacker celebrates and gives explicit representation to lesbian sexual experience, while she gives fuller subjectivity to the beloved, herself a poet, than is usual in the Petrarchan tradition. Hacker's outrageously heterogeneous diction and unorthodox rhymes call attention to the sonnet's conventionality so as to reinforce her story's exposure of the conventional, constructed nature of gender itself.

Working-class lesbian poet Judy Grahn, extending the example of H.D., modifies Eliot's "mythical method" by focusing on feminist revisionary mythmaking in the first two books of her projected quartet, *A Chronicle of Queens*. In three sections of titled lyrics and one section of prose notes about goddess figures from various cultures, *The Queen of Wands* (1982) explores the history of El-ana, goddess of beauty, fire, love, light, thought, and weaving, who was stolen from her temple and whose power was eradicated to make way for the gods of patriarchy. Weaving together crosscultural strands of the goddess's nearly forgotten history, Grahn seeks the restoration of her power. *The Queen of Swords* (1987) reworks the myth of the perilous descent of the goddess—here called Inanna—into the underworld and her confrontation with its queen, Ereshkigal, goddess of death, rebirth, and the spirit world. Most of the volume is devoted to a sometimes humorous dramatic poem set largely in an underground lesbian bar. Beat-associated poet Diane di Prima is similarly engaged in feminist revisionary mythography in *Loba, Parts I–VIII* (1978).

As increasing numbers of poets of color have gained access to publishing venues in the seventies and eighties, they, too, have begun to explore and expand the resources of the long poem, often by fusing its predominantly Anglo-European traditions with forms and languages distinct to particular minority cultures. Langston Hughes's already mentioned use of African American musical forms as the basis for his *Montage* is an earlier example of this phenomenon. Jay Wright turns, not to improvisation, but to African rituals—particularly the Komo initiation rite among the Bambara—to provide a formal structure and a system of values enhancing African American identity in *The Double Invention of Komo* (1980). N. J. Loftis—responding especially to Eliot's poetry, including his use of Frazer's *Golden Bough*—revises mainstream epic traditions to suit African American history; the quest for rebirth in *Black Anima* (1973) involves a journey into hell for contact with both black and white dead and the history of slavery and racial struggle they embody.

For some Chicano poets the folk song narrative form of the *corrido*, which traditionally focused on intercultural border conflict, has provided a culturally specific basis for long poems. Rudolfo Gonzales, for example, draws upon the *corrido*'s conventions of compressed narration of men's battles for their cultural community in his politically programmatic poem, *I Am Joaquín / Yo Soy Joaquín: An Epic Poem* (1967). In facing English and Spanish versions of the text accompanied by photographs and by reproductions of Mexican or Mexican-American art, Joaquín speaks as a modern Chicano who must choose between the economically fruitful, spiritually destitute ways of gringo culture and the spiritually enriching path of reviving the values of his Mexican and Indian heritages. Jimmy Santiago Baca seems not to draw upon the *corrido* in his autobiographical long poems *Martín and Meditations on the South Valley* (1987); the cultural conflict martially enacted in those narratives is internalized in Baca's lyric sequences. In portraying his disinherited protagonist's quests for a sense of community and cultural identity, Baca often incorporates Chicano Spanish, while his imagery depicts with vivid particularity western landscapes and life in the barrio.

The best-known text by a Native American that can be considered a long poem, Simon J. Ortiz's *From Sand Creek* (1981), demonstrates an interest in narrative and in oral tradition characteristic of recent Native American writing. Ortiz (from the Acoma Pueblo) may typify Native American writers in focusing on poetry as something vitally connected to ritual tradition and possessing social force. Regarding language and story as efficacious, Ortiz hopes his work will generate political change. Here Ortiz's speaker is a hospitalized Vietnam veteran in the mid-seventies whose repression of his war experience mirrors the (white) nation's dangerous repression of its violent historical errors. Juxtaposing brief prose statements with chiseled lyrics, the poem combines compassion and anger as it attempts to understand the history of white and Native American relations and thereby to move beyond that history's destructive powers. Native American writers, including Ortiz in *Going for the Rain* (1976) or Wendy Rose in *Builder Kachina: A Home-Going Cycle* (1979), are also experimenting with traditional models of the Native American ritual song or prayer cycle as the basis for shapely sequences of lyrics, particularly ones tracing quests for spiritual regeneration.

These sequences are in fact typical of much poetry published since the 1960s in that volumes in this era are frequently so carefully organized and thematically coherent as to be barely distinguishable from poetic sequences. This tendency along with the tremendous popularity of mid-length sequences, usually in numbered sections gathered under a single title, suggests a widespread desire to escape from the limitations of the isolated lyric. The pervasiveness of impulses toward expanded forms—even if not exactly long poems—may well reflect a general sense that the tradition of Romantic lyric expressing a single speaker's feelings in an epiphanic moment is exhausted.

Certainly that is the perspective of some of today's self-consciously avant-garde and oppositional writers, particularly those associated with Language writing, a vital literary network since the early seventies. Whether any of their works should be classified as long poems is arguable, given the writers' determination to disrupt literary conventions, including those constituting genres. But because the modern long poem combines the strengths of prose, epic, and lyric in a genre with extremely fluid conventions, and because the Language writers trace their evolution centrally from Pound and Zukofsky as well as from Ashbery and Stein (some of whose works, such as *Tender Buttons* and *Stanzas in Meditation*, might well be considered long poems), it seems appropriate to consider their long works as one extension of the collage tradition of the *Cantos* and *"A."*

A number of works by these experimental writers are written in prose with a collage of lexicons from various high and low discourses. Yet classifying the works as poetry accords with the theories behind such writing. For the Language writers, even when composing prose, disrupt the illusions of language's transparency to highlight how language constructs rather than reflects or refers to reality. In so doing they regard themselves as interiorizing within their sentences poetry's external devices (such as rhyme and meter) that keep the reader's attention on the materiality of language and counter tendencies to regard language as referential. Consequently Language writers often identify their works as poems. Their extended works—including Clark Coolidge's *The Crystal Text* (1986), Ron Silliman's *Tjanting* (1981) and *Paradise* (1985), Bernadette Mayer's *Midwinter Day* (1982), Lyn Hejinian's *My Life* (1980, 1987), Carla Harryman's *Vice* (1986)—are too numerous to characterize here. Although varied, they all demand that the reader, deprived of the conventional ordering systems of consistent grammar, syntax, theme, and voice, participate in the construction of the work. Wanting to foster consciousness of the commodification of language within capitalism, these Marxist-affiliated writers strive to make readers active producers, not just consumers, of the text.

Rejecting structures generated either by literary conventions or by conventions of individual subjectivity, these writers have embraced various arbitrary structuring systems. Silliman, for instance, has relied on the Fibonacci number sequence. Hejinian composed *My Life* by first writing a one-sentence paragraph, then writing a separate two-sentence paragraph and adding a sentence to the first, then composing a three-sentence paragraph and adding a new sentence to each of the two preceding paragraphs, and so on. The total number of paragraphs and the number of sentences in each paragraph coincided with her age. Such intentionally arbitrary structures and compositional methods render language and form, rather than the desire for a coherent narrative or a unified subject, generative forces.

Some experimental women writers loosely affiliated with Language writing are also associated with a specifically feminist avant-garde; their gender-conscious works interrogate the ways in which literary and discursive forces interact with structures of patriarchal power. These writers include Beverly Dahlen and Rachel Blau DuPlessis, whose long poems-in-progress, *A Reading* and *Drafts*, respectively, extend the serial tradition of the *Cantos*, *The Maximus Poems*, and *Passages*, as well as Susan Howe, who has composed a number of radically experimental extended texts. Howe's "The Liberties," for instance, from *Defenestration of Prague* (1983), opens with a straightforward prose summary of the life of Hester Johnson, who appears in Jonathan Swift's work as Stella. Asserting that "no authentic portrait exists" of this woman who was Swift's unacknowledged companion for twenty-seven years, Howe proceeds to develop one from the aporias and silences surrounding Stella's history, the history of Ireland, and histories of other real and fictional women. Fragments of various genres—including an extended masque—function in this sometimes minimalistic collage text; later sections present grids of isolated words that may be read vertically or horizontally. Such experiments—in which nondiscursive patterns give renewed substance to words left as traces from earlier works and to white spaces of silence—point to a language in which women and colonized people might achieve liberty and self-portraiture.

Howe's work provides a suitable stopping point because it embodies several characteristics that typify the varied and experimental history of the twentieth-century long poem: a liberating mixture of genres, an enlargement beyond the postromantic lyric's focus on a moment of subjective experience, and an accompanying exploration of social and historical materials, often in service to a fresh understanding of the self and its construction. In addition, the unpredictable structure of Howe's poem engages the ongoing tension between open and closed form, in which the quest for the poem as an open process has predominated.

Lynn Keller

Further Reading

Baker, Peter. *Obdurate Brilliance: Exteriority and the Modern Long Poem*. Gainesville: University of Florida Press, 1991.

Bernstein, Michael. *The Tale of the Tribe: Ezra Pound and the Modern Verse Epic*. Princeton: Princeton University Press, 1980.

Dickie, Margaret. *On the Modernist Long Poem*. Iowa City: University of Iowa Press, 1986.

Friedman, Susan Stanford. "Gender and Genre Anxiety: Elizabeth Barrett Browning and H.D. as Epic Poets." *Tulsa Studies in Women's Literature* (1986), 5:203–228.

——— "When a 'Long' Poem Is a 'Big' Poem: Self-Authorizing Strategies in Women's Twentieth-Century 'Long Poems.'" *LIT* (1990), 2:9–25.

Gardner, Thomas. *Discovering Ourselves in Whitman: The Contemporary American Long Poem*. Urbana and Chicago: University of Illinois Press, 1989.

Kamboureli, Smaro. *On the Edge of Genre: The Contemporary Canadian Long Poem*. Toronto: University of Toronto Press, 1991.

Miller, James E., Jr. *The American Quest for a Supreme Fiction: Whitman's Legacy in the Personal Epic*. Chicago: University of Chicago Press, 1979.

Pearce, Roy Harvey. "The Long View: An American Epic." In Roy Harvey Pearce, *The Continuity of American Poetry*, pp. 59–136. Princeton: Princeton University Press, 1960.

Ridell, Joseph N., ed. *The Long Poem in the Twentieth Century*. Genre (1978), 11:459–687.

Rosenthal, M. L., and Sally M. Gall. *The Modern Poetic Sequence: The Genius of Modern Poetry*. New York: Oxford University Press, 1983.

Public Music

A S EARLY AS 1913, in his essay "Patria Mia," Ezra Pound affirmed that a work of art does not have to contain "any statement of a political . . . conviction, but it nearly always implies one." He had begun writing the *Cantos* around 1904, adapting epic form to suit his own ends, which were not only to give passionate intelligible shape to political conviction but also to dramatize the movements of a mind holding such conviction. His view of epic as "a poem containing history" has obvious precedents in antiquity, but we should not presume too much continuity with the past. The Mycenean civilization from which the Homeric poems issued recorded and preserved its traditions, its identity, and consequently its political coherence and stability through the oral transmission from generation to generation of facts and myths recited in the rhythmic orders of verse. Poetry was essentially encyclopedic, archival, conservative. It constituted a shelf of reference works on astronomy, medicine, social convention, and religion and therefore contributed crucially to the knowledge needed to preserve and improve the social order. The Mycenean palace complex and the Greek polis that evolved from it, Eric Havelock tells us, *used* poetry as an unofficial table of contents of the tribe. Without the oral practice they called poetry the early polis could not have survived. Poetry from the archaic period to around the sixth century was not literature with a political theme or element, and it was unimaginably far from the prerogatives of self-expression we now take for granted. Poetry was instead a political necessity.

The encyclopedic didactic procedures of the *Cantos* convince me that Pound wanted his poem to be a political stabilizer as poetry had been in antiquity. He takes over prose documents like Adams's letters to recover and conserve the process of judicious deliberation just as oral performers once preserved the protocols of tribal oratory that we hear in the *Iliad*. Pound's epic boils over with quoted testimony, cited documents, a carnival of raised voices installed in wisdom booths. As the log of a journey into knowledge, which Pound called periplum ("not as land looks on a map / but as sea bord seen by men sailing"), the poem is an idiosyncratic Modernist *paideia*, a system and log of developmental learning. Its instructiveness is irritatingly present, although the instruction is aimed as intently at the poet himself as it is at us. The poem is meant *at least* to demonstrate what a person needs to know to be an informed responsible world citizen. The amassed slabs of erudition serve this end, and even the lyric passages so often singled out for their beauty are usually encoded in some kind of historicized speech, whether it derives from Tyndale's translations of scripture, the Edwardian mannerisms of Pound's youth, or the Anglo-Saxon and troubadour idioms Pound contrived in his translation work. Much of the *Cantos* is as antiqued, as artificially pitched, as anything in *The Fairie Queen*, but for very different purposes. It's not a recovered purity of diction or romance that Pound wants, but rather a tone and idiom of pastness conserved as a guide to Good Mind. The antiqued idioms are, in any event, hammered, chopped, cut up, collaged, and rorschached into the emergent periplum patterns of the poem. Pound knew that the poem's manner as well as its matter would play a role in determining our own *paideuma*, which he glossed (out of Frobenius) as "the mental formation, the inherited habits of thought, the conditionings, aptitudes of a given race or time." The spastic turns of attention, the long ribbons of information unfurled in the cantos treating Adams, Van Buren, Chinese history, and monetary theory, the eruptions of religious feelings and sacred visions, the flashing voices (we hear Chinese emperors, arms manufacturers, writers and philosophers, American presidents, the guards and detainees at Pisa, the poet's wife and child and neighbors, and on and on) all combine to make a private memory store into a public archive. The *Cantos* may not be a political necessity as poetry was thought to be in antiquity, but its formal plying of fact and vision insists on the essential relation between the political order and the poetic imagination.

Pound was most Dante's pupil in understanding that formal invention is exercise and expression of political sense. Unlike Dante's lengths of processional narrative, Pound's formal means are congestive, incremental, and reiterative, all utterance so much on a level, so apparently nonhierarchical, that what readers like myself experience as a tedium of warehoused facts and collaged stories may be finally a kind of democratic delirium of statement. The formal ideal for Pound, I suppose, would be to say everything at once yet have every thing said distinct. But we also feel the poet acting as an all-gathering and willful governor of that incipient chaos, whose vigor of address and headstrong assertions are instances of what Pound called *directio voluntatis*.

The opening of Canto 38 is representative of this method. The epigraph is Dante's denunciation of Philip the Fair for debasing coinage to finance a military campaign:

> il duol che sopra Senna
> Induce, falseggiando la moneta.
> —Paradiso 19:118

The subsequent lines stack facts that seep and bleed into one another. Metevsky (Pound's name for Sir Basil Zaharoff) was a successful arms manufacturer early in the century, a reference keyed to the money-for-arms content of the epigraph. Then Pound introduces two acquaintances, Pope Pius XI (whom Pound knew before his ascendancy) and James Joyce. Papal manners, it seems, are learned from arrogant, impoverished Irish artists:

> An' that year Metevsky went over to America del Sud
>   (and the Pope's manners were so like Mr Joyce's,
>   got that way in the Vatican, weren't like that before)

Marconi is likened to the American politico Jimmy Walker.

> Marconi knelt in the ancient manner
>   like Jimmy Walker sayin' his prayers.

Lucrezia Borgia's rabbits are like those "electric shakes" Marconi chased through the atmosphere and which so amazed the Pontiff:

His Holiness expressed a polite curiosity
    as to how His Excellency had chased those
electric shakes through the a'mosphere.
    Lucrezia
Wanted a rabbit's foot,

And the guns-and-bombs industry can be made more efficient by borrowing the labor techniques Dexter Kimball introduced to rollers of big cigars:

    and he, Metevsky said to the one side
· ·
        . . . the other boys got more munitions
    (thus cigar-makers whose work is highly repetitive
    can perform the necessary operations almost automatically
    and at the same time listen to readers who are hired
    for the purpose of providing mental entertainment while they
    work; Dexter Kimball 1929.)

The idioms race from pokey vernacular to mock ceremonial to instructive drone. The lines storm with gossip. The data, flooding the poet's consciousness, suggest the menacing fluidity and indiscriminate massiveness of that salient force in modern politics: the crowd. Pound is not so much interested in differentiating the facts as he is in similitudes, match-ups, correspondences, the associative orders by which he can hold in a simultaneity of occurrence the dazzling heterogeneous instants of his experience. (This way of making political poetry is also the mechanic of paranoia.) He even suggests allegorical equivalences between men and professional activity: Metevsky = Commerce; Pius XI = Organized Religion; Joyce = Art; Marconi = Science; Walker = Ward Politics; Kimball = Labor Technology. That, at any rate, may be the formal pattern, though it's not the way I actually experience the poetry. Pound tumbles personal anecdote with the historical record in such a way as to make me feel I'm coming into an awareness of something that may at any moment, now or later in the poem, be radically revised or fragmented. The log of the coastline journey gets bulkier as the work progresses, and its entries become more obsessive and bullying. One of them is announced in the epigraph above: the use of money.

Canto 38 dates from the early 1930s, by which time Pound was convinced that the proper use of money was a determining factor in the civil order and therefore determinant in the intellectual, moral, and artistic orders. He believed that the expressions of the soul of an age in its painting, sculpture, music, and writing were exact indicators of the political balance. And that balance was determined by the degree to which money functioned as evidence and extension of natural abundance. Money is "a ticket for the orderly distribution of WHAT IS AVAILABLE . . . it is NOT in itself abundance." *Usura*, strictly speaking, was the practice of renting money; generally, it was any use of money that violated the appropriation of natural abundance for moderate, necessary human use. Given Pound's view of *paideuma* as the interrelatedness of all values and actions in a culture, he believed that usura inevitably shaped the products of consciousness. He could read the process of usura in the history of art. In 1938, he explained to his Italian translator what he meant by the phrase in Canto 45, "with usura the line grows thick": "means the *line* in painting and design. Quattrocento painters are still in morally clean era when usury and buggary were on a par. As the moral sense becomes . . . incapable of moral distinction . . . painting gets bitched. I can tell the bank-rate and component of tolerance for usury in any epoch by the quality of *line* in a painting." Pound always preferred the Italian Primitives and Florentine painting to the mess-of-shadows colorism of later Venetian and Baroque art. He put his preference into practice. The *Cantos* is a poem of perspective manipulations, vectors, cross-hatchings, the allegorical clarities of good *disegno*. Pound was an anticolorist. His remarks make clear that he believed style was political expressiveness, and that a politics grounded in usura, in the unnatural exploitative creation and circulation of money, violates Good Mind.

I read the *Cantos* as an image of economy. The natural wealth of learning in the poem is presented as an active, patterning exemplum of complete consciousness, which in an instant can connect a corn kernel to a commodity exchange to a supper to an ear-shaped sculptural form to the slow presence of Demeter among us. The poem insists on relatedness and on the political need to constantly review and adjudicate relatedness. In this respect it's a political instrument, I mean an instrument for political effect, for Pound saw how in the modern period the intent of bankers, industrialists, politicians, and of certain intellectuals, artists, and impresarios, has been to break down the consciousness of relatedness. Specialization, isolation, "individual initiative," and special interests distract a populace from an awareness of patterns that connect natural abundance and labor to the processes of work and the circulation of money. Pound detested abstraction because it estranges us from the actuality of shared destiny. Usura was a representative outrage because it abstracted wealth from the nature wherein the gods revealed themselves to us. Usura—abstraction generally—could thus set human action at vicious odds with nature. It's grotesquely apt, therefore, that Pound's most vicious error was in abstracting race from individuals, the Jew from Jews, and worse, to do so in service to another abstraction: Authority.

Pound loved the roughneck improvisations and rakehell moodiness of the American character. I often think he loved especially what he could never get quite right, the dialectical and regional colorism of American speech. (His celebrated "great ear" was mostly a bookworm's literary contrivance, not the great ear of someone who listens with affectionate criticism to what's actually said.) His intellectual formations and predilections, however, were elitist, hierarchical, and sectarian, from the Gnostic Cathar brotherhood and the teachings of Kung, to the money policies of C. H. Douglas and the initiation rites of Eleusis. His apparently egalitarian all-at-once style was rooted in, and often takes as its subject, the pedagogical hierarchy of master and pupil, adept and neophyte. As a poet of wanton intellectual appetites he welcomed heterogeneity, but as a political thinker within the poetry he was wary of the cultural and social instabilities created by a contentious, racially pied, inarticulate populace. His mixed attitudes toward authority are a source of unrest throughout the *Cantos*. While he sought in some ways to undermine established authority—by criticizing the efficacy of capitalist economies, by advocating a complete overhaul of money policies, by insisting on the actual presence in the material world of deities—the poem itself stands as a directory of authority and masteries.

Most of the raw experience in the *Cantos* is fippled by magisterial texts. In 1911 Pound described his procedure as "the method of luminous detail . . . certain facts give one a sudden insight into circumjacent conditions, into their causes, their effects, into sequence and law." The luminous details come as often from source material as from Pound's invention: from the Jefferson-Adams correspondence, Confucian analects, Malatesta's mailbag, Martin Van Buren's autobiography; and from translations of translations, of Divus's Latin version of the *nekuia* from the *Odyssey*, for instance, and of French versions of Chinese documents. Even gossip, the fabulous gossip that rushes in and out of the poem, is a patterning of authority. Pound reports Yeats's report of Beardsley's deathbed remark, "Beauty is difficult," to defend his own stylistic adventures in the *Cantos*. Pound's admiration for Dante has always been apparent. More important is what he refused, or what the age (and kind of art it necessitated) refused him. The *Comedy* has serial, lucid, conclusive confrontations between the pilgrim and his instructors. The *Cantos*, however, is mostly second- or third-hand transmission; the passion of confrontational engagement so consistent in Dante's poem is deflected, baffled, and rechanneled by mediating authorities, intervening texts. The result is not processional interrogation of the history of a consciousness but an encyclopedist fever dream.

Pound's judgments of historical figures were often based on homologies. He came to a late appreciation of the Italian reformer Mazzini when he perceived in Mazzini theories of social credit later advocated by Douglas. He was similarly impressed by something in Mazzini's character that he admired in other powerful figures: *directio voluntatis*. Around 1941 he writes: "What counts is the direction of the will." He saw the same quality in Italian Fascism: "The name of the Fascist era is *Voluntas*." The directed will is the destiny-forging element in the *Comedy*, wherein sinfulness is the act of directing the will toward an inappropriate object or allowing the will to be deflected from the good, proper object. Sin is not so much a bad act as it is a wrong way. *Directio voluntatis* can decide the fate of an individual or of a populace or nation. Dante describes it in *De Vulgari Eloquentia* as the opposite of *abuleia*, paralysis of the will, a condition Pound detested. (That Pound, a declared non-Christian, should take over and adapt to his own purposes a Christian, indeed Thomistic, moral philosophy is one of the many kinds of intellectual colonizing perpetrated in the *Cantos*.) Pound was convinced that Mussolini would be remembered for his personal *voluntas* and his passion for order: "The Duce will stand not with despots and the lovers of power but with the lovers of ORDER." Pound's sense of good order, derived from Confucius, is set out early in the famous lines of Canto 13: "If a man have not order within him / He can not spread order about him; / And if a man have not order within him / His family will not act with due order; / And if the prince have not order within him / He can not put order in his dominions."

Pound was so intent on instructing us in the ideal polity of the mind, himself acting (as he felt, I think, historically obligated to do) as master teacher, that he ignored particular occurrences. In the interests of order Mussolini imprisoned or confined many of the best, most independent minds of his time, Gramsci being the most conspicuous and tragic instance. Cesare Pavese and Carlo Levi were, along with many other writers and artists, banished to the south and put under house arrest, and politically aloof poets like Eugenio Montale lost their jobs for refusing to join the party. Pound may have been unaware of these events, but he was not unaware of the derangements of order that artists often incite by challenging the normalcies and niceties of established values. Formally at least he was doing just that in the *Cantos*, even while the poem in part argues for the importance of political order under strong leaders. The poem would be politically less volatile, however, if it were mostly a brief for steely hierarchy sustained by voluntas. But the *Cantos* also argues that a renewed vision of wholeness requires incoherence, confusion, and obscured destinies, and that the process of defining a polity shares the dissonance and chaos and indefiniteness that goes into the making of art: "Wilderness of renewals, confusion / Basis of renewals, subsistence, / Glazed green of the jungle." Essential to the wilderness and to the renewals is a vision of sacred presence in the world.

In the *Cantos*, especially in the Pisan sequence and the agonizing meditations of the final drafts and fragments, gods and goddesses—Pound believed most passionately in Aphrodite and Dionysus/Zagreus: intoxicators, chaos-bringers, sweeteners of sense, light-bearers, leaders, disturbers of good order—materialize as data of consciousness pulled into the poem with all the particularity, substantiality, and abrupt selective decisiveness of the contents of Sigismundo's mail pouch. Though for long stretches of the poem we are allowed to forget it, Pound's political thinking was inseparable from his Neo-Platonic religious vision. In secular terms the directed will of a populace, governed by leaders with a sense of order sustained throughout the body politic, can make for a balanced state. This can succeed, though, only if grounded in a vision of human origins, and Pound's vision was that Athenian one which held we are children of the earth, and that earth may be our paradise: "the forms of men rose out of $\gamma\bar{\epsilon}\alpha$ / Le Paradis n'est pas artificiel." Human intellect refracts divine intelligence, which is itself embodied or embedded in the things of the world, in the materiality of the eucalyptus pip he pocketed on his way to the Disciplinary Training Center in 1944, in the visionary forms of Dread Aphrodite that he sees from his prison cage at Pisa, and in the moth of smoke rising from his smoke hole.

This Neo-Platonic way of regarding the physical world takes shape fairly early in the poem, where it is already associated with government and the artist's place in the polity: "Forms, forms and renewal, god held in the air, / Form seen, and then clearness, / Bright void, without image." This comes in the midst of Canto 25's narrative of the history of Venetian government and the disputed contract for Titian's decorations of the Doge's palace in the early 1550s. Very late in the poem, in Canto 113, Pound says "there is something intelligent in the cherrystone," a principle of order, but principle in process of growth and change, articulated in material presence. These are instances when the poet's imagination holds the world's harmonious order, its spirit and matter, in a pattern of words. There are other instances when I want to shake the poem and, taking up its own methods, instruct *it*: that the gods may also appear to human beings whose obsession with control and order, guided by *directio voluntatis*, might lead to genocide or the tolerance or calculated ignorance thereof; and that no complete political vision, no actual political wholeness, can be founded on selective or edited relatedness. Pound's own viciousness converged on his spurious distinction between the big Jew (banker, usurer types like Rothschild) and the little Jew (like, presumably, Zukovsky and Oppen). He would have us believe, and would have himself believe, that he nursed murderous hatred toward the abstract Jew but not toward real, ordinary, artistic sorts of Jews. This is not an example of temperament fouling intelligence, but of the desire for a deliberate, discriminating purity, borne along by rhapsodic authority, contaminating the possibility for a useful, practical whole community made up of real human beings.

Pound finally situated his imagined world, his politically whole earthly paradise, "between KUNG and ELEUSIS," between a balanced civil order constellated around familial and social order as articulated by Confucius, and the secret, exclusionary, initiatory, transformational, ecstatic mystery religion where the gods are airborne presences materialized in the things of the world: "That butterfly has gone out thru my smoke hole." Deity does not sponsor the world of things, it floods and saturates it and is the ordinary visionary aspect by which relations are seen. In the last fragmentary chunks of the poem the political is clearly inseparable from spiritual relatedness and continuity. There are moments when Pound's vision quest is achieved, when he *saw*:

> And for one beautiful day there was peace.
>   Brancusi's bird
>   in the hollow of pine trunks
> or when the snow was like sea foam

His aspiration "To make a church / or an altar to Zagreus" remains with him. Pound conceived of his work, however, not as prophecy but as agency, voluntas operating through the forms of art. When at the end he declares in sorrow "that I lost my center / fighting the world. / The dreams clash / and are shattered— / and that I tried to make a paradiso / terrestre," he's announcing the failure of his attempt, not the inadequacy of the vision. Pursuing the vision of wholeness, he lost his way by becoming snared in the very confusion his poem presents as a matrix for renewals.

In his most important work, *Illusion and Reality*, Christopher Caudwell describes the fantasy element in the harvest dance of native peoples. The dancers' objective, the harvest, does not yet exist; it lives only in the imagination of the participants. "The violence of the dance, the screams of the music and the hypnotic rhythm of the verse," Caudwell says, alienate the dancers from the present moment and expand their consciousness to include the fantasy harvest image as something present. That world, in the frenzy of the dance, becomes real. When the dance is over that object stays fixed in the mind as a sustaining purpose so that the tribe can make the fantastic harvest a reality. Though Caudwell does not pursue this, it seems to me that in poetry the instinctual claims of cadence, diction, sonority, repetition, rhythm, and emergent spectral structure are equivalent to the singing and pulse of the harvest dance. In formal terms these powers or "primitive elements" create an image, a fantasy image, of a political reality. Apart from the statements a poem makes, its blood powers and formal appetites create an imaginative pattern—that is, an image—which is as essential to the political content of the poem as any statement the poem makes. Indeed, when these powers are interdicted or suppressed or censored by a poet's desire to make statements that are unimpeachable, correct, or opportunistic, the poem turns into propaganda, which requires a puritanical curtailment of the hunger for formal invention. The imagination in pursuit of political vision has to follow its own unstable ways, must sometimes be caught up in impolitic concerns and headstrong formal impulses. No modern poet can produce the equivalent of harvest dance music. Our shared public music is fated to be idiosyncratic in origin, and our vision one not of fixed tribal relations but of the process of relatedness.

Poetry can, of course, be a form of political activism, or a sign of it, a cry, a shout, the voice raised on or against occasion. But that does not make it political in the sense I'm after here, as a constant inquiry into relatedness, as the torment of affects and sympathies induced by concern for the destiny of the polity—which is the destiny of a structure as well as of the human beings who define, inhabit, and realize the structure. To cry out against atrocity, against any outrage to our shared sense of the good, is one of poetry's most important offices. What we find in a poet like George Oppen, however, is that sort of cry muffled, scissored into pieces, and transmuted into an intensely personal inquisitiveness, an interrogating regard for the relation of the individual to the human collective. For him it is finally a question of an ethic, one in which moral value is grounded in an awareness of the destiny of the species.

Oppen once tried to explain to Hugh Kenner the reasons for the long silence that followed his first book of poems, *Discrete Series*. Kenner interrupted, "In brief, it took twenty-five years to write the next poem." Oppen relished the story and retold it many times, not because of the hard differences in the two men's political views but because Kenner's remark really does account for the break between Oppen's political and poetic activity. He was not abandoning poetry, he was setting it aside until he learned things he felt he needed to learn. He did not believe in political poetry. "If you decide to do something politically," he insisted, "you do something that has political efficacy." And so, beginning in the mid-1930s he spent more than twenty years in political activity, first helping the poor and dispossessed during the Great Depression, then working as a communist party organizer. After serving in World War II he fled to Mexico in 1950 to escape harassment by the McCarthy committee. He began writing poetry again in 1958.

The book that marked his return, *The Materials*, bore an epigraph from Maritain's *Creative Intuition and the Art of Poetry*: "We awake in the same moment to ourselves and to things." Such waking is a pure Objectivist moment, when consciousness cleanses perception and objectifies its subjects. It's also a moment of pure relatedness. The notion of "the Things" is very important for Maritain. They are the elements that make up the world that the poet both inhabits and confronts; they are "that infinite host of beings, aspects, events, physical and moral tangles of horror and beauty." The Things, moreover, possess the chaotic force of feeling that an artist experiences, "the feelings of primitive men looking at the all-pervading force of Nature, or of the old Ionian philosophers saying that 'all things are full of gods.'" This is a description of radical imaginative sympathy, when the poet finds himself or herself a consciousness apart from the Things *and* dispersed among them, elemented there. Oppen told that experience as an act of witness: "What I've seen / Is all I've found: myself."

A poet's intelligence feeds on the desire for analogue, correspondence, and likeness, even when such desire distracts from political actuality. Metaphor can be frivolous diversion or mere illustration. But the search for correspondence in its purest ambition is a search for wholeness, an imagined restoration of completeness. To the eye of Ezra Pound, imprisoned in the Disciplinary Training Center in Pisa, the mountain he sees nearby is in likeness of the holy mountain of Taishan in China, and both are in likeness of Mount Chocuroa in New Hampshire, which was a favorite place for William James, who meditated there on the divided soul suffered by an American who must choose between Europe and America. Metaphor may seditiously set the mind against itself, or it may promise a new order and unity. Oppen's great theme is naturally his most political: the singular and the numerous—the one in and of (or against) the many. Likeness is both vehicle and tenor of his theme. In "Population" the numerous is represented by the conceivable but unimaginable expanse of the sea. (A seadog all his life, Oppen spoke of these things with real expertise.) The singular mind coming into awareness is born not to a true solitude but to a tenacious conviction of its solitude: "Like a flat sea, / Here is where we are, the empty reaches / Empty of ourselves." That *we*, the collective, already releases what the poet in his sincerity must acknowledge, that while the mind "born / alone to ocean" feels itself a solitude, it is, *we* are, a mass, a crowd, "the moment's / Populace sea-borne and violent."

Consciousness generates likenesses of its own structure and functions. The mind is a mansion, a data base, a machine or cyberspace or wilderness. Part of the work of poetry is to reveal or invent (only to then question and correct or demolish) such models. We allow them, for a while anyway, to shape our vision of ourselves, our capacities and destiny. The title of one of Oppen's poems, "The Crowded Countries of the Bomb," is a rubric for this situation. The image the title composes could not have existed before the invention of nuclear firepower, though Oppen is also drawing on the knowledge that bombs generally, their shape and sound and effects, live in the modern imagination as deeply and as ordinarily as helmets and swords lived in the minds of Homeric singers. The poem suggests that one new model for public space, for the space of politics, is the shelter; not a fallout shelter (or not only that) but the shield created by chance—almighty chance that, "as if a god," has so far spared our species from nuclear annihilation. Oppen wants a name for this place we have entered: "Despair? Ourselves?" The country of the bomb is, by his reckoning, the country of ourselves, the shelter made "of each other's backs and shoulders / Entering the country that is / Impenetrably ours." The new thing in the world, the nuclear bomb, forces us to revise all our previous mental images of human community. The new country is impenetrably ours because although we ourselves element it, it's a shelter we cannot in fact enter, for it is finally no shelter at all from what we ourselves have made. We might just as well try to ward off disease by hiding inside our bodies. The poem is not grim soothsaying. Oppen does not go in for prophecy. Oppen's poem is rather an inquiry into newly fashioned likeness, a provisional definition of the generations, of the more-than-one. Like so much of Oppen's work, it seems nearly toneless, though one never feels it's aloof or noncommittal. The music it makes is that of a mind scrutinizing its own imaginings and the source of those imaginings in the changing Things.

Anecdote is an instrument of political vision. Oppen's experience of conscience, played out from the 1930s to the 1950s (later, too, in his witness of events in the 1960s), lives in his poems but is not displayed as a glamor-object. His own sort of heroical will has the appearance and tone of diffidence, of witness-as-forebearance. He doesn't announce the vividness of his experience or proclaim its privileges, he simply writes poems that express its knowledge, nowhere more intensely than in "Of Being Numerous," where words and their political values are tested against the public space, a speech place where values may take hold in words used efficaciously. Language needs a public space where words like "the fortunate" and "the People" will have shared meaning and sense. The modern city, however, is built of "walled avenues / In which one cannot speak." It's not for lack of an agora; rather that the entire city has become an impenetrable facsimile of an agora, a simulacrum, a corporate center, "city of the corporations." How then do we develop politically efficacious speech, grounded in the fact of the existence of a plenitude of human beings, in a city whose images are all abstractions from elemental facts? The crisis in Oppen's poem—"How talk / Distantly of 'The People'"—is precipitated by anecdote, by his recollection of being *among the many* during his army service. When words cannot contain or recover or heal over the relation of individual experience to the *site* of mass organization, to that place called the "crowd," poetry becomes feckless and surrenders to abstraction. Abstraction in this sense is the worst kind of existential divisiveness because it sets up as a desirable mental object an antihuman idea of the human separate from actual biological and social necessity. Quite recently we've lived through these consequences, during the war in the Persian Gulf, with our arsenal of computer lights, pulsing beeps, and smart bombs, where death is imitated, mocked, by transitory perceptual stimuli. If, as Engels said, freedom is the recognition of necessity, then abstraction starves freedom. To Oppen the poet's task is to treat words as ghosts run wild in subways, the poet a kind of spook-catcher chasing words underground in the hope that once caught they will bring meaning and sense. Aboveground, as the elemental regard of words rooted in necessity diminishes, public speech becomes more and more rootless; it becomes what Oppen calls "a ferocious mumbling."

A private task it is, but for public effect. And a tragic task in at least one respect. The American poet knows well, and can recognize, a divisiveness that cannot be healed over. In section 20 of "Of Being Numerous" we're riding the subway in the 1960s. The passengers, the "they" that includes the poet regarding them, are waiting for war, more war, news of war, knowing the passion of that expectation and the passion of the destruction to come. The mood of the passage is tense, sick with the blend of exhilaration and dread. Then there is a turn: "They know / By now as I know / Failure and the guilt / Of failure." And Oppen remembers it is like the nervous anticipation in "Hardy's poem of Christmas," where we imagine and hope to find "in the sheds of a nation / Farm animals, / Draft animals, beasts for slaughter." Hardy's "The Oxen" is about the migratory imagination seeking refuge in familiar (though no longer tenable) images of devotional unity. For Oppen, if we were to find the animals there, it would mean they have forgiven us, "or which is the same thing, / That we do not altogether matter." The first degree of political tragedy is that the mind holds and the body feels as true that which both at once realize to be dream dust. The second and intenser degree is described in remarks made not long ago by Claude Lévi-Strauss. Asked to define myth, he said that an American Indian would say a myth tells of time before humans and animals became distinct beings. "No situation seems more tragic, more offensive to heart and mind, than that of humanity coexisting and sharing the joys of a planet with other living species yet being unable to communicate with them." Failing to recover that lost time, yet feeling in our deepest sense the desire for such unity, we would wish forgiveness from the other orders of life on earth even while we pulse with dread and thrill over more war. That's the terrifying compound a poet of political intelligence confronts and struggles to express.

"Of Being Numerous" ends with a prose bit cribbed from Whitman's letter to his mother, describing the Capitol and the Genius of Liberty figure recently mounted atop it. Oppen's work generally is a criticism of Whitman's headlong expansionist poetics. He sets off from the prose paragraph (dated 1864, after Whitman had served as a volunteer medic and had written about the heaps of amputated limbs around the hospital camp) its final word:

> "The sun when it is nearly down shines on the [Genius of
> Liberty's] headpiece and it dazzles and glistens like a
> big star: it looks quite
>
>
> curious . . . "

Oppen, who once said that Whitman's "deluge and soup of words is a screen for the uncertainty of his own identity," distributes the historicized material so that it conforms to his own halting, deliberative, probing idiom. He makes use of Whitman's own language to revise, rhythmically, his celebratory project. Oppen's own project is not vocative or expansionist. His language does not summon or shout. His words, as public offering, calibrate consciousness as it secretes its crucial sentences about love, perception, and destiny. In a note on Thomas McGrath and other Old Left poets he wrote: "It can be observed . . . that when we say 'moral' we mean that which concerns the destiny of humanity." His own intention was to make poems that had moral purpose and therefore, as he says elsewhere, would express a concept of humanity, "something we want humanity to be or to become, [which] would establish the basis of an ethic."

Poets have an austere sense of being singular subjects (Oppen's "the singular / Which is the bright light of shipwreck") confronting the indiscriminate feelings of a crowd. A useful poetic language, however much evolved from tradition, is essentially an idiolect, and that sets poets apart from the crowd for whom or toward whom they write. Modern poets have had to live maybe more self-consciously than their predecessors with the fact of linguistic estrangement as a necessary condition for making statements that will be directed ultimately at the communal good, statements that are exemplary attempts at moral discrimination. This estrangement may be what Yeats had in mind when he said that poets are good citizens turned inside out. In the public sphere politicians have not so much coopted a common language as they have shown with grotesque verve that any speech purporting to be common idiom, as a voice of the people, is Geryon's speech. This, too, is a poet's proper subject, the imposture and fraudulent sincerity of public speech. In fact, the complete political poet is probably one who dares to allow into poetry Geryon's smoothie voice or soapbox sincerities or delusional outcries as necessary poisons immunizing poetry against the falsehood of self-interested speech.

Anything a poet writes measures some estrangement between the poet and the polis. For the true idiolect, moreover, there can be no correct or acceptable point of view. During the antihierarchical rage of the counterculture in the late 1960s, whose efforts as a mass against the Vietnam War he entirely supported, Oppen knew that the death of singular art in favor of "art for the people" meant the death of individual meditative dissent and therefore the weakening of political intelligence in society at large. Poets cannot finesse idiosyncrasy so that it seems populist or communal. (Or if they can, it's tribute paid to Geryon.) All one can do, finally, is to eat the contradiction and make it part of one's materials. Better that than improvised solidarity or heat-seeking sloganeering. For Oppen the political lay in writing truthfully one's perceptions, not arguing one's beliefs. Bad poetry, he said, is poetry "tied to a moral or a political (same thing) judgment."

And yet the most idiosyncratic verse, if it is political, has something in it that aspires to choral crowd music. I sometimes think the intense personalism of American poetry in recent decades, with its psychological fussiness and maniacally modest self-absorption, is one sign of the failure of belief in the possibility of poetry as truly public music. In a 1969 letter Oppen says that before putting words down he thinks of his daughter, already twenty-seven years old, and knows she will read what he writes. This engages the scrupulous sense of a future, of the truth of a record kept and passed on. In those days he felt that the only real safety for him or her or any of us was to put the poems "in the public record And in the public music." Poetry thus adds to the store of moral deliberation, to specific imaginative concern for the destiny of humanity. Although his method of composition owed much to the precisionist example of Pound, Oppen admitted that the masculine energy of Pound's work and personality appalled him. In the poems he wrote after those twenty-five years of silence, Oppen went round and round the question of being numerous, "of being part of a human unity, a human entity." Sometimes his moral authority is a little oppressive (he is much esteemed as a "moral presence," but within famous moral presences lurk moral police) and it is mostly humorless. But the question of poetry's agency in the world was and is a real one. Oppen insisted that the poet's work is to see the one thing, not the thousand things. I would add that to see the one thing in consciousness of the world is always to see *in relation*—to the polis, to the Things, to the annals of anecdote, to poetry's formal past. And it's a happy task to intensify poetry's response to relatedness, not out of a gray somber sense of poetical obligation, but rather out of fevered uncertainty and anxiety about its efficacy. I often think the first image of the poetic imagination is one of its own disappearance—words written on a fogged window, words lost in a passing car. Out of that original separation comes the need to put words in whole arrangements that have meaning and that adequately express the sense and meaning of existence.

W. S. Di Piero

Beat Poetry and the San Francisco Poetry Renaissance

T HE TERMS *Beat poetry* and the *San Francisco Poetry Renaissance* refer to two different literary movements created by two loose ly associated groups of writers in New York City and San Francisco who first gained a national audience for their work in the mid-1950s. Although reviewers and critics sometimes used the terms interchangeably, not all Beat poets were associated with the San Francisco Renaissance poets, and not all San Francisco Renaissance poets were associated with the Beats.

As the critic Michael Davidson has said, "Despite the obvious centrality of the Beat movement to the San Francisco literary scene, it was . . . only one strand in a much more diverse and eclectic movement." Among the group of writers often included in both categories at mid-century were Allen Ginsberg, Jack Kerouac, and Gregory Corso, members of the original Beat group in New York City, and Lawrence Ferlinghetti, Gary Snyder, and Michael McClure, three West Coast writers participating in the San Francisco Poetry Renaissance who also befriended the Beats.

Gary Snyder later made clear that

The term Beat is better used for a smaller group of writers . . . the immediate group around Allen Ginsberg and Jack Kerouac, plus Gregory Corso and a few others. Many of us . . . belong together in the category of the San Francisco Renaissance. Both categories fall within, it seems to me, a definable time frame. It would be from sometime in the early fifties up until the mid-sixties when jazz was replaced by rock and roll and marijuana by LSD and a whole new generation of youth jumped on board and the name beatnik changed to hippy. Still, beat can also be defined as a particular state of mind . . . and I was in that mind for a while. Even the state of mind belongs to that historic window.

Like the clusters of the Lost Generation writers of the 1920s and the Proletarian writers of the 1930s, the Beat poets and their fellow travelers in San Francisco are associated with a specific time frame and a "particular state of mind." While there was no shared formal aesthetic beyond their practice of experimental free-verse forms and their interest in poetry as performance, frequently with jazz accompaniment, there was often a recognizable quality that distinguished their work from other experimental poetry of the time.

This was the poets' rebellious questioning of conventional American cultural values during the cold war. The Beat poets were determined to put the idealism of the American dream of individual freedom to its ultimate test. They rebelled against what they saw as their country's social conformity, political repression, and prevailing materialism by championing unconventional aesthetic, sexual, and spiritual values. They insisted that Americans could find an alternate life-style despite the prevailing conformism of their time, and—like Emerson and Whitman before them—they reaffirmed the essential sanctity of individual experience. While the term *San Francisco Poetry Renaissance* is linked to a specific locale and time period (San Francisco poetry in the 1950s and 1960s) and suggests a definite literary context, the word Beat is weighed with nonliterary associations for most readers. The *Random House Dictionary* credited the writer Jack Kerouac for defining the term *Beat Generation*, which means "members of the generation that came of age after World War II who, supposedly as a result of disillusionment stemming from the Cold War, espouse mystical detachment and relaxation of social and sexual tensions." Emerging at a time of significant postwar cultural changes, the Beat literary movement was absorbed into the more turbulent counterculture movement in the late 1960s. It was both a social and a literary movement. At its heart were its writers, who included some of the most widely read American poets of the last half-century.

Although the earliest published writing by the New York Beat authors was autobiographical fiction—John Clellon Holmes's *Go* in 1952, William Burroughs's *Junky* in 1953, and Kerouac's excerpt from

On the Road titled "Jazz of the Beat Generation" in *New World Writing* in 1955—it wasn't until 1957 with the publication of Allen Ginsberg's long poem "Howl" and Kerouac's novel *On the Road*, that Beat writing received widespread attention. Ginsberg, Kerouac, Burroughs, and Holmes first formed friendships in New York City in the mid-1940s. According to Ginsberg, they first heard the word *beat* from Herbert Huncke, a Times Square hustler, in 1944. Ginsberg understood the word to mean "exhausted, at the bottom of the world, looking up or out, sleepless, wide-eyed, perceptive, rejected by society, on your own, streetwise." Kerouac remembered that in 1948 he and Holmes "were sitting around trying to think up the meaning of the Lost Generation and the subsequent Existentialism, and I said, 'You know, this is really a Beat Generation,' and he leapt up and said , 'That's it, that's right!'" To Holmes, the term "beat generation" had the "subversive attraction of an image that just might contain a concept, with the added mystery of being hard to define. . . . It was a vision, not an idea."

The group of earliest Beat writers in New York City was united by their close friendships and their interest in experimental writing. According to Ginsberg, they shared an awareness of "the phantom nature of being," the transitoriness of existence. "Beatness" to Ginsberg was

looking at society from the underside, beyond society's conceptions of good and evil, which in those days [1948] of human emotion, sexuality, poetry, censorship and drugs, were medieval compared to what common judgment and opinion offers now as a standard understanding. Then Henry Miller's books and D. H. Lawrence's *Lady Chatterley's Lover* were banned and illegal. You couldn't smoke marijuana without being considered a "dope fiend." These conditions produced a certain revolutionary insight into the hallucinatory nature of official government classifications and terminology. After the horrors of World War II and the concentration camps and atomic bombs, Americans had a desire for normalcy, but we felt it was a facade.

In 1954, after graduating Columbia College, Ginsberg left New York City for San Francisco. He had read the literary magazines *Circle* and *Ark*, published by anarchist groups on the West Coast, that featured the poetry of Robert Duncan, William Everson, and others, and he understood that the community of writers in the Bay Area was supported by an ongoing tradition of radical politics, including a more open and tolerant acceptance of homosexuality. There had been a thriving poetry scene in the East Bay cities of Oakland and Berkeley since the end of the Second World War, centering around the activities of the poets Robert Duncan, Jack Spicer, Robin Blaser, William Everson, Mary Fabilli, Thomas Parkinson and Josephine Miles. In the late 1940s their success in establishing a literary community gave rise to the term the *Berkeley Renaissance.* By the early 1950s many of the Berkeley poets had moved to San Francisco. As Michael Davidson recognized, their "ideas of community were formative in generating the group affiliations of North Beach, and it was within such enclaves, with their shared social and sexual programs, that a new poetics emerged." After Ginsberg moved to San Francisco with a letter of introduction from William Carlos Williams to Kenneth Rexroth, a poet, translator, and political activist who was at the center of cultural events in the city, Ginsberg soon felt himself in sympathetic company. Through Rexroth he met many "interesting types," among them Duncan, Kenneth Patchen, and a young poet named Gary Snyder who was studying Asian languages and philosophy at the University of California at Berkeley. First living in a furnished apartment in San Francisco, then settling in a cottage in Berkeley, Ginsberg wrote the poem "Howl" in August 1955. Two months later he organized a poetry reading at the Six Gallery with Snyder, another young poet named Michael McClure who had come to San Francisco from Kansas to study painting, the young San Francisco Surrealist poet Philip Lamantia, and one of Snyder's friends from Reed College, Philip Whalen. Rexroth agreed to be master of ceremonies, and the event—advertised as "Six Poets at the Six Gallery"—occurred on October 7, 1955. The reading marked what Rexroth later described in his book *American Poetry in the Twentieth Century* (1971) as the most important development in American poetry since World War II, a "change of medium—poetry as voice not as printing. The climacteric was not the publication of a book, it was the famous Six Gallery reading, the culmination of twenty years of the oral presentation of poetry in San Francisco." Michael McClure has described the Six Gallery reading in his book *Scratching the Beat Surface* (1982). He understood that all of the poets participating in the event felt oppressed by

the pressures of the war culture. We were locked in the Cold War and the first Asian debacle—the Korean War. . . . As artists we were oppressed and indeed the people of the nation were oppressed. There were certain of us (whether we were fearful or brave) who could not help speaking out—we had to speak. We knew we were poets and we had to speak out as poets. We saw that the art of poetry was essentially dead—killed by war, by academies, by neglect, by lack of love, and by disinterest. We knew we could bring it back to life.

The Six Gallery reading was the first time that Ginsberg read his new poem "Howl" in public. To McClure and the others listening to him, it seemed that "in all of our memories no one had been so outspoken in poetry before." Jack Goodman, one of the listeners in the audience, was also taken with the performance of Ginsberg's friend Kerouac, who

sat on the floor downstage right, slugging a gallon of Burgundy and repeating lines after Ginsberg, and singing snatches of scat in between the lines; he kept a kind of chanted, revival-meeting rhythm going. Ginsberg's main number was a long descriptive roster of our group, pessimistic dionysian young bohemians and their peculiar and horrible feats, leading up to a thrilling jeremiad at the end, that seemed to pick up the ponderous main body of the poem and float it along stately overhead as if it were a kite . . . the people gasped and laughed and swayed, they were psychologically had, it was an orgiastic occasion.

As McClure later wrote in *Scratching the Beat Surface*, the audience was left "standing in wonder, or cheering and wondering, but knowing at the deepest level that a barrier had been broken, that a human voice and body had been hurled against the harsh wall of America."

In the audience at the Six Gallery that night was the San Francisco poet and publisher Lawrence Ferlinghetti. He was so impressed by "Howl" that he copied Emerson's message to Whitman a century earlier in a telegram to Ginsberg: "I greet you at the beginning of a great career. When do I get the manuscript?" Two years before, in North Beach, Ferlinghetti had started the City Lights bookstore and publishing company in what he called "an anarchist, civil libertarian, antiauthoritarian tradition." Published as number four in the City Lights Pocket Poets series, *Howl and Other Poems* was seized by the U.S. Customs in San Francisco on March 25, 1957, with the charge that Ginsberg's language describing homosexual acts was obscene. Ferlinghetti strongly defended the poem, saying that "it is not the poet but what he observes which is revealed as obscene. The great obscene wastes of *Howl* are the sad wastes of the mechanized world, lost among atom bombs and insane nationalisms." Six months later, after convicing testimony by Mark Schorer of the University of California, Henry Rago, editor of *Poetry* magazine, and James Laughlin of New Directions (among several witnesses called by the defense), Judge Clayton Horn ruled that Ginsberg had not written an obscene poem. His decision established judicial precedent by stating that if the printed material has social importance, it is protected by the First and Fourteenth Amendments of the United States Constitution. What had been the private cultural rebellion of an obscure literary group in New York was energized and given political focus by the contact of the East Coast Beats with the West Coast poets, who were sustained by a flourishing tradition of radical poetry and small press publication. When East Coast met West Coast, the whole was suddenly larger than the sum of its parts, and the formation of a broad new poetry front entered the course of American literature at mid-century.

In the late-1950s after the *Howl* trial most readers considered San Francisco to be the center of the new activity in poetry, which was widely perceived as not only an aesthetic revolt but also a radical assault on mainstream cultural values. The historian Rebecca Solnit understood that

a poetic rebellion was taking place. Ezra Pound and T. S. Eliot had established a modernist tradition of erudite, impersonal poetry. . . . There was no single reaction against that orthodoxy, but there were some widespread tendencies— the assertion of the personal, a grounding in the details of everyday life, and a desire to return to a genuine, American speech. . . . Walt Whitman's free-wheeling rhapsodies and William Carlos Williams' taut, lucid verse became the foundation for a new tradition, in which Allen Ginsberg could write about supermarkets and homosexual encounters . . . in which humor and imperfection, confusion and confession were possible.

Early articles on the new literary phenomenon such as Kenneth Rexroth's "San Francisco's Mature Bohemians" in the *Nation* on February 23, 1957, focused on the radical tradition of protest literature on the West Coast. Rexroth included Kerouac and Ginsberg with the San Francisco poets. When *Time* magazine reviewed *On the Road* on September 16, 1957, it recognized that although the novel had a Madison Avenue publisher, it was an attack on Madison Avenue values. The reviewer said that Kerouac "was a member of the San Francisco group (whose disciples do not necessarily stay put in San Francisco)."

But it was also clear from the start that something had jarred American literary sensibilities far beyond the city limits of San Francisco.

Rexroth's article was followed in the same issue of *Nation* by M. L. Rosenthal's sympathetic review of *Howl* as "poetry of genuine suffering. . . . [Its] dynamic lies in the way it spews up undigested the elementary need for freedom of sympathy, for generous exploration of thought, for the open response of man to man so long repressed by the smooth machinery of intellectual distortion." Ginsberg had "brought a terrible psychological reality to the surface with enough originality to blast American verse a hair's breath forward in the process." Besides Ginsberg and Kerouac so many other gifted writers associated with the San Francisco Poetry Renaissance were publishing at this time that their literary achievement could not be easily dismissed. In the early years (1955 and 1956) there were such notable titles as Ferlinghetti's *Pictures of the Gone World*, Gregory Corso's *The Vestal Lady on Brattle and Other Poems*, Michael McClure's *Passage*, and the City Lights edition of Ginsberg's *Howl and Other Poems*. In 1957 came the celebrated second issue of *Evergreen Review* that featured the San Francisco scene and the work of Rexroth, Henry Miller, Ferlinghetti, McClure, Snyder, Whalen, Kerouac, and Ginsberg, among others. In 1958 Ferlinghetti's *A Coney Island of the Mind*, Corso's *Gasoline* and *Bomb*, McClure's *Peote Poem*, and Diane di Prima's *This Kind of Bird Flies Backwards* appeared. Small presses published most of these works, but some were so popular they were widely distributed in editions of thousands of copies in America and translated into a steady stream of publications in Europe and Asia as readers throughout the world recognized that a new, vital phenomenon was energizing American poetry.

The poet Thomas Parkinson later observed that "when the Beat writers emerged in 1956 they struck so responsive a chord that they became the most widely discussed phenomenon of the late 1950s." Spontaneity of feeling and expression as well as social protest were the characteristics of their writing, as when the San Francisco poet Bob Kaufman wrote that "Every time I open my big mouth / I put my soul into it."

If there were a few sympathetic reviewers such as Rexroth and Rosenthal who supported the early work of the Beat poets in the 1950s and 1960s, there were scores of journalists defending the status quo in America who attacked and belittled the "new writing" in such articles as "America's Angry Young Men: How Rebellious are the San Francisco Rebels?" (Dan Jacobson, *Commentary*, December 1957), "The

Know-Nothing Bohemians" (Norman Podhoretz, *Partisan Review*, Spring 1958), and "Epitaph for the Dead Beats" (John Ciardi, *Saturday Review*, February 6, 1960).

Harsh reviews failed to stem the flow of Beat writing, which struck responsive chords in poets throughout the country. As Solnit recognized, the territory of the new poetry "was unmistakably American. Kerouac hunted down the Dharma on freight trains and on Skid Road; while Ginsberg wrote of 'the drunken taxicabs of Absolute Reality,' of 'Mohammedan angels staggering on tenement roofs,' even of 'Zen New Jersey.'" In 1958 two issues of the *Chicago Review* featured "ten San Francisco poets" (Burroughs, Kirby Doyle, Duncan, Ferlinghetti, Ginsberg, Kerouac, Lamantia, McClure, Whalen, and John Wieners), and a symposium on Zen with writing by Allen Watts, Kerouac, Whalen, and Snyder. These two issues tripled the circulation of the magazine, but the winter 1959 *Chicago Review* was suppressed by the chancellor of the University of Chicago. He refused to publish experimental writing by Kerouac (his prose poem "Old Angel Midnight") and William Burroughs (excerpts from his novel *Naked Lunch*) because a columnist in the *Chicago Daily News* had attacked the 1958 issues of the *Chicago Review* under the headline "Filthy Writing on the Midway." When the editor, Irving Rosenthal, refused to "tone down" the contents of the *Review*, a new magazine called *Big Table* was started to publish the complete contents of the suppressed winter 1959 *Chicago Review*. *Big Table* continued for four more issues under the direction of the poet Paul Carroll.

Also published in 1959 were McClure's *Hymns to St. Geryon*, Snyder's *Riprap*, Whalen's *Self-Portrait from Another Direction*, and LeRoi Jones's Totem Press edition of *Jan. 1st 1959: Fidel Castro*. In 1960 some notable books of poetry by Beat and San Francisco Renaissance authors included Corso's *The Happy Birthday of Death*, Snyder's *Myths and Texts*, and Donald M. Allen's widely discussed anthology *The New American Poetry*, which grouped poets sharing "a total rejection of all those qualities typical of academic verse" into geographical categories like Beat (East Coast), San Francisco Renaissance (West Coast), Black Mountain College poets, and New York poets. In 1961, among other titles, Ginsberg published *Kaddish and Other Poems*, one of his most important works. The poem's thirty-year anniversary was celebrated in 1991 by the Modern Language Association, but during the 1960s the work of the Beat and San Francisco Renaissance poets continued to be subjected to vicious attacks by reviewers as in any avant-garde literary movement.

A typical establishment dismissal, written for the *National Review* on November 18, 1961, by Ralph De Toledano, characterized the poetry of the Beats as being "an overflow as accidental as a bathtub running over." The Beat writers' "artistic revolt" was "as graceless and unproductive as the copulation of mules." Admonishing "Mr. Ferlinghetti and Company" for not writing with the disciplined sensibility and reverence for tradition shown by T. S. Eliot, Wallace Stevens, and Marianne Moore, the reviewer concluded by saying that "the bumps and grinds of the Beat school may appeal to the blunted tastes and stunted sensibilities of our times, but they have as little connection with poetry as a strip act does with the sex act."

The insults didn't stop the poets; if anything the allegiances among the writers were strengthened by the attacks. The list of names of writers associated with the Beats on the East Coast and the San Francisco Renaissance poets on the West Coast continued to grow in the proliferation of poetry readings and new little magazines and small presses. The scholar George Butterick has listed 235 periodicals begun in the 1950s and 1960s inspired by the Beat and San Francisco Renaissance literary movements.

As the 1960s progressed the growing number of dissident writers and small press publishers became recognized as the development of an American "counterculture." In this decade of disruptive social changes, the complacency of the 1950s evaporated as the civil rights movement took on a new militancy in the South, the resistence to war in Southeast Asia grew when United States troops were sent to Vietnam, LSD became more readily available than peyote as a "consciousness expander," and rock music developed as an art from from earlier folk roots and black rhythm and blues.

By the 1970s the Beat and San Francisco Renaissance poets were recognized as a vital part of American culture. Their attitudes had become part of a complex series of self-renewing changes in America, the liberalization of many social and sexual attitudes they had challenged earlier. In 1973 the playwright Arthur Miller described "the revolution of the fifties and sixties" as not being a revolution in any classic sense—a transference of power between classes—but nevertheless, in Miller's words, "it partook of the revolutionary process of overturning certain attitudes of people toward what a human is and what he might be."

Most poets participating in the literary cluster weren't sorry to see the Beat and Beatnik labels go, as the word *hippie* gradually took over as the media's favorite name for the participants in the counterculture. The poet Gregory Corso understood that the Beat label stood for a "generation of outlaws." While some of the poets continued to be identified as avant-garde literary figures (Gregory Corso, for example, was the American representative in the first impromptu "Poetry Olympics" held in Westminster Abbey in September 1980), the leading writers were also gradually accepted into the literary establishment.

In 1974 Ginsberg became a member of the National Institute of Arts and Letters and won a National Book Award for *The Fall of America*. In his acceptance speech he signaled the end of the Beat Generation as a literary movement. In its place he said he hoped for the survival of what he called the sovereignty of the individual mind in post-Vietnam America. "There is no longer any hope for the Salvation of America proclaimed by Jack Kerouac and others of our Beat Generation, aware and howling, weeping and singing Kaddish for the nation decades ago, 'rejected yet confessing out the soul.' All we have to work from now is the vast empty quiet space of our own Consciousness." When Gary Snyder won the Pulitzer Prize for his 1974 collection of poetry, *Turtle Island*, he said he hoped the dust wrappers for his books could finally drop the "Beat Poet" label and describe him as a more honored "Pulitzer Prize-winning poet."

The allegiances of many of the writers continued in their personal friendships long after the labels *Beat* and *San Francisco Renaissance* passed into history. The last twenty years has witnessed definitive editions and significant collections of the major work of several poets in both literary groups as the writers established identities that went beyond their earlier affiliations: Amiri Baraka's *The LeRoi Jones/Amiri Baraka Reader* (1991), Corso's *Mindfield* (1989), Di Prima's *Pieces of a Song* (1990), Ferlinghetti's *Endless Life* (1981) and *When I Look at Pictures* (1990), Ginsberg's *Collected Poems, 1947–1980* (1984) and *White Shroud Poems, 1980–1985* (1986), McClure's *Rebel Lions* (1991), and Snyder's *Left Out in the Rain* (1986) and *No Nature* (1992).

In addition, four of the poets—Ginsberg, Baraka/Jones, Ferlinghetti, Snyder—have entered the literary canon as respected figures in contemporary American poetry, indicated by their continuous inclusion in the anthologies of American literature used as textbooks in our colleges. Their work and the major poems of several other writers in the two literary groups represent a significant contribution to American poetry at mid-century. The large sales figures over the last thirty-five years for books of poetry like Ferlinghetti's *Starting From San Francisco* (New Directions, 1961), 170,000 copies; Snyder's *Axe Handles* (North Point Press, 1983), 100,000 copies; and Ginsberg's *Howl and Other Poems* (City Lights, 1956), 825,000 copies, also signals a healthy and enduring interest in poetry among a large group of American readers. A sample of representative poems by the major authors in the two literary groups suggests some of the reasons why their work has found such a receptive and loyal audience.

In 1956 Allen Ginsberg's "Howl" in its publication as a black and white generic pamphlet in the City Lights' Pocket Poets series, was the earliest representative of Beat poetry to most readers. Almost four decades after the first public reading of the poem, its opening lines sound a voice both unique and unforgettable:

> I saw the best minds of my generation destroyed by madness, starving
>   hysterical naked,
> dragging themselves through the negro streets at dawn looking for an
>   angry fix,
> angelheaded hipsters burning for the ancient heavenly connection to
> the starry dynamo in the machinery of night,
> . . . .
> who bared their brains to Heaven under the El and saw
> Mohammedan angels . . . .
> who passed through universities with radiant cool eyes hallucinating
> Arkansas and Blake-light tragedy among the scholars of war

In 1986 Ginsberg with his editor Barry Miles prepared a new volume of "Howl" modeled on Valerie Eliot's facsimile edition of T. S. Eliot's *The Waste Land* (1971). This work, titled *Howl: Original Draft Facsimile, Transcript and Variant Versions, Fully Annotated by Author, with Contemporaneous Correspondence, Account of First Public Reading, Legal Skirmishes, Precursor Texts and Bibliography*, offers a unique insight into the evolution of his long, four-part poem protesting the hysteria and destruction he linked to the materialist values and repressive American social attitudes of his time. Among what he called the

"Model Texts: Inspirations Precursor to *Howl*," are Christopher Smart's "Jubilate Agno," Percy Bysshe Shelley's "Adonais" and "Ode to the West Wind," Guillaume Apollinaire's "Zone," Kurt Schwitters's "Primiitittiii," Vladimir Mayakovsky's "At the Top of My Voice," Federico García Lorca's "Ode to Walt Whitman," Hart Crane's "Atlantis," and William Carlos Williams's "To Elsie."

With the completion of "Howl" in 1955, Ginsberg entered into an inspired period, creating some of his best short lyrical works, including "A Supermarket in California," "Sunflower Sutra," and "America." His humor and self-confidence along with the emotional support of his friends among the Beat and San Francisco Renaissance writers enabled him to address the problems he saw in his contemporary cold war society with a spontaneity and authority unparalleled in American poetry in his time. For example, in "America," he wrote,

> America you don't really want to go to war.
> America it's them bad Russians.
> Them Russians them Russians and them Chinamen. . . .
> The Russia wants to eat us alive. The Russia's power mad. She wants
>   to take our cars from out our garages.
> Her wants to grab Chicago. Her needs a Red Reader's Digest. Her
>   wants our auto plants in Siberia. . . .

Ginsberg concluded his poem by a humorous reference to his homosexuality:

> That no good. Ugh. Him make Indians learn read. Him need big
> black niggers. Hah. Her make us all work sixteen hours a day. Help.
> America this is quite serious.
> America this is the impression I get from looking in the television set.
> . . . .
> I'd better get right down to the job.
> It's true I don't want to join the Army or turn lathes in precision parts
>   factories, I'm nearsighted and psychopathic anyway.
> America I'm putting my queer shoulder to the wheel.

"Kaddish," Ginsberg's next successful long poem, was a formal elegy written as a tribute to his mother Naomi, who had been a communist sympathizer during his boyhood and who had died in a mental hospital in 1956. As the critic Harvey Shapiro realized, in "Kaddish" Ginsberg was able "to capture a story and a period of American-Jewish life, a fat novel-full, in verse that never slides under the material it has to carry while it keeps the long breath that is his signature and the pure impulse that is his gift." Writing fifty-eight pages in an inspired forty-hour stretch, Ginsberg completed "Kaddish" in November 1958. It was the culmination of his early work, a deeply compassionate portrait of his mother's mental illness and its devastating affect on Ginsberg and his family.

During the summer of 1955, while Ginsberg was writing "Howl" in San Francisco, his friend Jack Kerouac was living in Mexico City, at work on his major long poem, *Mexico City Blues*, published in 1959. Kerouac's poem is less well known than are his descriptions of his youth in Lowell, Massachusetts, and his adventures with Neal Cassady, Allen Ginsberg, William Burroughs, Gregory Corso, Gary Snyder, Michael McClure, Lawrence Ferlinghetti, and other writers in the dozen novels comprising his fictional autobiography. (He describes the October 1955 Six Gallery reading, for example, in an early chapter of his novel *The Dharma Bums*.) Kerouac felt that "in poetry you can be completely free to say anything you want, you don't have to tell a story." As the critic Robert Gaspar recognized, "Poetry provided Kerouac a forum for the impressionistic, experimental writing that his fiction couldn't always accommodate."

Kerouac's *Mexico City Blues* is the most successful work of jazz poetry written by an American, a landmark achievement in a tradition begun by Paul Lawrence Dunbar, Vachel Lindsay, and Carl Sandburg in the early years of the century and continuing into the present in the work of the poets associated with the Black Arts movement like Amiri Baraka, Michael Harper and Ishmael Reed. In Kerouac's prefatory note to *Mexico City Blues*, he said,

I want to be considered a jazz poet blowing a long blues in an afternoon jam session on Sunday. I take 242 choruses; my ideas vary and sometimes roll from chorus to chorus or from halfway through a chorus to halfway into the next.

Kerouac's poetry was an extension of his individual prose style, developed in 1951, that he called spontaneous prose and described in two accounts, "Essentials of Spontaneous Prose" and "Belief and Technique for Modern Prose." These statements were regarded as the basic aesthetic of Beat writing. Ginsberg recalled that he pinned a typescript of Kerouac's description of his spontaneous prose method on the wall beside his typewriter when he began to write "Howl."

Although Kerouac was an influence on Ginsberg's poetry, Kerouac was primarily influenced by jazz musicians like the legendary bebop saxophonist Charlie Parker, who died in the spring of 1955. Kerouac's 239th, 240th, and 241st choruses in *Mexico City Blues* are a tribute to Parker, as in the 240th chorus, where he argues that Parker, as a musician, is:

> . . . as important as Beethoven,
> Yet not regarded as such at all,
> A genteel conductor of string
>   orchestras
> In front of which he stood,
> Proud and calm, like a leader of music
> In the Great Historic World Night.

Each of the 242 choruses in *Mexico City Blues* is the length of one of Kerouac's notebook pages, usually about twenty-five lines of free verse on different subjects. Kerouac said he conceived his poetic form as comparable to the practice of a jazz musician, using "the size of the notebook page for the form and length of the poem, just as a musician has to get out, a jazz musician, his statement within a certain number of bars, within one chorus." Typically Kerouac's memories of the past in Lowell mingled with present images seen on the streets of Mexico City as he free associated in the 100th chorus:

> I remember one day being parked in the
>   wickerbasket
> Baby carriage, under huge old tree,
> In family photos we've preserved it,
> A great elm rising from dust
> Of the little uphill road—

At the end of the chorus, Kerouac reflected on how the creation of the poem took precedence over the memories that prompted it:

> —that tree is still standing
> but the road has moved over,
>   Such is the might of the baby
>   in the seat
>   He hugens to re-double
>   the image, in words

In his "Essentials of Spontaneous Prose" Kerouac explained that he was guided by associational rather than linear poetics.

Not "selectivity" of expression but following free deviation (association) of mind into limitless blow-on-subject seas of thoughts, swimming in sea of English with no discipline other than rhythms of rhetorical exhalation and expostulated statement, like a fist coming down on a table with each complete utterance. . . . Blow as deep as you want—write as deeply, fish as far down as you want, satisfy yourself first, then reader cannot fail to receive telepathic shock and meaning-excitement by same laws operating in his own human mind.

Kerouac believed that "the best writing is always the most painful personal wrung-out tossed from cradle warm protective mind—tap from yourself the song of yourself, blow!—now!—your way is your only way—'good'—or 'bad'—always honest . . . interesting, because not 'crafted.' Craft *is* craft." Alluding to two Whitman poems in this statement ("Out of the Cradle Endlessly Rocking" and "Song of Myself"), Kerouac acknowledged Whitman as an important predecessor.

The Beat poet Gregory Corso was befriended by Allen Ginsberg in a Greenwich Village bar in 1950. Corso had begun writing poetry in prison, and he fit easily into the New York Beat group, as one commentator has recognized, having in common "that he was a misfit, self-invented, rebellious, and blessed by the Muse." Corso's first book *The Vestal Lady on Brattle and Other Poems* was published by a group of Harvard and Radcliffe students in 1955. Four years later City Lights published his long poem *Bomb* as a multiple-paged broadside, with the text shaped as a mushroom cloud. *Bomb* was the poet's powerful address to the atomic bomb, cataloging the evolution of mankind's destructive tendencies, culminating in the bomb as "Death's extravagance."

> Budger of history Brake of time You Bomb
> Toy of universe Grandest of all snatched-sky I cannot hate you
> Do I hate the mischievous thunderbolt the jawbone of an ass
> The bumpy club of One Million B.C. the mace the flail the axe
> Catapult Da Vinci tomahawk Conchise flintlock Kidd dagger

Reining in his apocalytic vision in "Bomb," Corso found a brief respite in humor:

> There is a hell for bombs
> They're there I see them there
> They sit in bits and sing songs
> mostly German songs
> and two very long American songs

He continues the joke:

> ... they wish there were more songs
> especially Russian and Chinese songs
> and some more very long American songs
> Poor little Bomb that'll never be
> an Eskimo song

The menace of the bomb was never far distant, and Corso faced the horror squarely in his poem:

> You are a paean   an acme of scream
> a lyric hat of Mister Thunder
> O resound thy tanky knees
> BOOM BOOM BOOM BOOM BOOM
> BOOM ye skies and BOOM ye suns
> . . . .
> nights ye BOOM ye days ye BOOM
> BOOM BOOM ye winds   ye clouds ye rains
> go BANG ye lakes   ye oceans BING ...
> Yes Yes into our midst a bomb will fall.

In 1957 the young poet LeRoi Jones moved to New York City and affiliated himself with the Beat writers after marrying Hettie Cohen and starting, with her, *Yugen* magazine and Totem Press. After the assassination of Malcolm X in 1965 he left his white wife and children and founded the Black Arts Repertory Theatre in Harlem. He adopted the name Amiri Baraka after embracing the Kawaida branch of the Muslim faith in 1966, when he committed himself to creating what he described as "an art that is recognizably Afro-American." Although this new art was to be shaped by certain aesthetic principles also found in Beat writing—what Baraka characterized as "an art that is mass oriented that will come out the libraries and stomp" and "an art that is revolutionary"—its strongest qualities were to be its black identity and its purpose of helping to promote social transformation in the elimination of racism.

During what Baraka has called the "Beat Period (1957–1962)" of his career, he published his first book, *Preface to a Twenty Volume Suicide Note* (1961). The previous year he visited Cuba and met politically committed third world artists who forced him to question his apolitical stance. Baraka has said that the Cuban revolution impressed him as an alternative to the "unanchored rebellion" of his bohemian friends in New York.

"In Memory of Radio," a frequently anthologized poem from *Preface to a Twenty Volume Suicide Note*, is an eloquent evocation of the unnamed but pervasive evil sensed by the poet from the time of his childhood as being present at the heart of American life:

> Who has ever stopped to think of the divinity of
>   Lamont Cranston?
> (Only Jack Kerouac, that I know of: & me.
> The rest of you probably had on WCBS and Kate Smith,
> Or something equally unattractive.)

After referring to "Lamont Cranston," the hero of the radio program "The Shadow" in the 1940s, when Jones was growing up in Newark, New Jersey, the poet continues evoking a sense of the inadequacy of his middle-class upbringing:

> What can I say?
> It is better to have loved and lost
> Than to put linoleum in your living rooms?
>
> Am I a sage or something?
> Mandrake's hypnotic gesture of the week?

He refers to other popular radio programs, suggesting the shallowness of revivalist religion that dominated the airwaves yet failed to disperse the destructive shadow of racism blighting every aspect of American life:

> (Remember, I do not have the healing powers
>   of Oral Roberts . . .
> I cannot, like F. J. Sheen, tell you how to get
>   saved & *rich*!
> I cannot even order you to gaschamber satori
>   like Hitler or Goody Knight

Then, midway in his poem, Jones explicitly names his subject, brilliantly turning language inside out to reveal the implication of a dark double meaning hidden inside a familiar word:

> & Love is an evil word.
> Turn it backwards/see, see what I mean?
> An evol word, & besides
> who understands it?
> I certainly wouldn't like to go out on that kind of
>   limb . . .

The poet Diane di Prima was one of the few women associated with the Beat literary movement in the late 1950s who has continued writing to the present day. In 1958 Hettie and LeRoi Jones's Totem Press published her first poetry collection, *This Kind of Bird Flies Backward*, with an endorsement by Lawrence Ferlinghetti: "I don't know her, never saw her, never heard her. In the middle of the street is a manhole with a portable iron fence around it. And a sign: Poet At Work. . . . Here's a sound not heard before. The voice is gutty. The eye turns. The heart is in it." The title poem of the collection established di Prima's tone of rueful surrender to the stubbornly ungovernable emotional forces controlling her life:

> this kind of bird flies backward
> and this love
> breaks on a windowpane
> where no light talks
>
> this is not time
> for crossing tongues

The last two lines explain parenthetically that "(the sand here / never shifts)."

In "Three Laments" di Prima flaunted the mock-cynicism she adopted as an emotional shield to help her survive as a poet in a bohemian community tolerant of homosexuality but inclined to regard women as "minor characters" in men's lives. In the first lament she explains that she would have been:

> a great writer
> but
> the chairs
> in the library
> were too hard

She jokes, in the second lament, that she has "the upper hand":

> but if I keep it
> I'll lose the circulation
> in one arm

And finally, she reveals that she is "the coolest in New York," but:

> what dont swing I dont push
>
> In some Elysian field
> by a big tree
> I chew my pride
> like cud.

Di Prima's twelve-part poem "Brass Furnace Going Out: Song, After an Abortion," originally published as a broadside, was one of her most eloquent works. It captured the pain of her feelings of regret over the loss of her unborn child and her reluctant acceptance of her difficult, irrevocable decision.

> forgive, forgive
> that the cosmic waters do not turn from me
> that I should not die of thirst.

In San Francisco Kenneth Rexroth was the strongest and most active presence in the cultural renaissance of the 1950s. His unshakable belief in an anarchist tradition gave rise to his vision of an "alternative society" where acts of civil disobedience could effectively oppose capitalism. His long poem "Thou Shalt Not Kill," written as a memorial for Dylan Thomas after the Welsh poet's death in November 1953, was a precursor of Ginsberg's *Howl*, especially in its evocation of a long line of martyred American, European, and Russian poets sacrificed to the indifference of their materialistic governments, willing to allow human creativity, in Rexroth's words, to be "stuffed down the maw of Moloch."

Rexroth's interest in Asian literature and philosophy also contributed to the Beat writers' study of what Ginsberg later called "Buddha consciousness." Rexroth's sensitive, supple translations of Japanese and Chinese poetry, published by New Directions, were a seminal influence on Gary Snyder and other young poets like Philip Whalen and Lew Welch, as in Rexroth's version of a poem by Onakatomi No Yoshinobu in his book *One Hundred Poems from the Japanese* (1955):

> The deer on pine mountain,
> Where there are no falling leaves,
> Knows the coming of autumn
> Only by the sound of his own voice.

The critic Sanehide Kodama understood that Rexroth's lifelong study of Japanese poetry was scholarly and profound. In *American Poetry and Japanese Culture*, Kodama pointed out that Rexroth's long poem *The Heart's Garden, The Garden's Heart* (1967), written after his first visit to Japan, ingeniously incorporated his translations from classical Japanese poets into his own descriptions of the landscape. In *The Silver Swan* (1979), published a few years before his death in 1982, Rexroth's enduring interest in Japanese culture resulted in one of his best short poems, what Kodama read as "a tableau of transcendence, esoteric beauty and religious truth."

> As the full moon rises
> The swan sings
> In sleep
> On the lake of the mind.

Gary Snyder's interest in ecological issues and Japanese culture was present in the poems he read at the Six Gallery in 1955. As Kodama perceived, Snyder has always been suspicious "of the values and morals of a too highly developed, affluent, and materialism-oriented society," and has always felt the need "to urge his readers to reconsider their civilization, and to search for values outside the Western norms to obtain a new kind of spiritual liberation and contentment by 'penetrating to the deepest non-self Self.'"

Snyder wrote that "there is a haiku influence in my poetry. It runs through *Myths & Texts* [written between 1952 and 1956], the use of a number of very short precise images within longer poems." His early poem "Mid-August at Sourdough Mountain Lookout," inspired by his summer job as a lookout ranger in the mountains of Washington, achieved visual intensity through crystal-clear images.

> I cannot remember things I once read
> A few friends, but they are in cities.
> Drinking cold snow-water from a tin cup
> Looking down for miles
> Through high still air.

Some of Snyder's short poems echo Rexroth's brilliant translations from classic Japanese sources, as in "Pine Tree Tops." He guides the reader's eye from the sky

> in the blue night
> frost haze, the sky glows
> with the moon
> pine tree tops
> bend snow-blue, fade
> into sky, frost, starlight.

And then we are thrown down to the ground, as Snyder combines sonic and visual images:

> the creak of boots
> rabbit tracks, deer tracks,
> what do we know.

As the critic Tim Dean has recognized in his study of *Gary Snyder and the American Unconscious* (1991), Snyder's "materialising of language . . . represents the effort to link poetry to the body, to work, and thus to what is taken as the immediacy of the real."

Snyder's later books, like *Turtle Island* (1974), exhibit a more mature fusion of Mahayana Buddhist ideas and Western literary tradition. In a poem like "Avocado," which begins "The Dharma [truth] is like an Avocado!," he playfully described the difficulty encountered by an American student searching for final enlightenment:

> The great big round seed
> In the middle,
> Is your own Original Nature—
> Pure and smooth
> . . . .
> It looks like
> You should plant it—but then
> It shoots out thru the
>   fingers—
> Gets away.

Michael McClure has, like Jack Kerouac, an identity separate from his achievement as a poet. He has written two Obie-winning experimental plays, *The Beard* and *Josephine the Mouse Singer*, in addition to his several books of poetry and fiction. His most influential poetry in the late 1950s was his "Peyote Poem" (1958), which he wrote as a deliberate exercise, taking peyote as a means of psychic liberation. In his autobiography *The Mad Cub* (1970) McClure explained the connection between his interest in ecology and his early peyote experiments, which taught him "the separate consciousness of my being. . . . In reading biology I hope to make the discoveries that will liberate man to exist in timelessness and a state of superconsciousness."

"Peyote Poem" invited the reader to join in the psychedelic experience, with McClure evoking a Whitmanic sense of the passage of his extraordinary sensations:

> Clear—the senses bright-sitting in the black chair—
> Rocker—
> the white walls reflecting the color of clouds
> moving over the sun. Intimacies! The rooms
> not important—but like divisions of all space
> of all hideousness and beauty. I hear
> the music of myself and write it down.

Closely involved with the California artists of the cold war era, McClure contributed poems to Wallace Berman's experimental *Semina* series, like his "Dallas Poem" for *Semina Nine* in 1964, which had a cover photograph of Jack Ruby shooting Lee Harvey Oswald after Kennedy's assasination:

> DOUBLE MURDER! VAHROOOOOOOOHR!
> Varshnohteeembreth nahrooohr PAIN STAR.
> CLOUDS ROLL INTO MARIGOLDS
> nrah paws blayge bullets eem air.
> BANG! BANG! BANG! BANG! BANG!
> BANG! BANG! BANG! BANG!
> . . . .
> BANG! BANG! BANG! BANG! BANG!
> BANG! BANG! BANG!
> Yahh oon FLAME held prisoner
> DALLAS!

In a later short poem "Song" from his collection *Fragments of Perseus* (1983), McClure evoked a shamanistic sense of the intricacies of his creative process:

I WORK WITH THE SHAPE
of spirit
moving the matter
in my hands

He goes on to explain that his work is shaped from:

the inner matrix.
Even a crow or fox
understands.

Lawrence Ferlinghetti's early lyrics, like "Constantly Risking Absurdity," from *A Coney Island of the Mind* (1958), were an instantly recognizable blend of wit and elegance. Here he addresses the nature of the poet.

Constantly risking absurdity
                    and death
        whenever he performs
                    above the heads
                        of his audience

Ferlinghetti compares the poet to an acrobat who:

climbs on rime
        to a high wire of his own making

Continuing, he argues that the poet is a "super realist":

who must perforce perceive
    taut truth
            before the taking of each stance or step
in his supposed advance
            toward that still higher perch
where Beauty stands and waits.

Ferlinghetti's political poems, like "Tentative Description of a Dinner to Promote the Impeachment of President Eisenhower" (1958) and "One Thousand Fearful Words for Fidel Castro" (1961), reflected his belief in the triumph of personal vision over the dangerous follies of American cold war politics and his faith in poetry as an agent of enlightenment. As he wrote in "Populist Manifesto,"

Poetry the common carrier
for the transportation of the public
to higher places.

American poetry at mid-century was characterized by a breaking away from the dominant modes of Modernist verse developed after World War I by Pound and Eliot and their contemporaries, and later canonized in the postwar years by academic critics. In the Beat poets' insistence on finding and using their own voices to express what Snyder has called the "playful, serious defiance of the whole generation," they were faithful to the spirit of Pound's dictim "Make it new," while in their subject matter they insisted on the social commitment of an earlier radical American literary tradition. Their achievement, along with the work of other experimental poets of the San Francisco Renaissance, the Black Mountain poets, and the poets of the New York School, revitalized American poetry and served as an inspiration for the generations to come.

Ann Charters

Further Reading

Allen, Donald M., ed. *The New American Poetry*. New York: Grove Press, 1960.

Allen, Donald M., and George F. Butterick, eds. *The Postmoderns: The New American Poetry Revised*. New York: Grove Press, 1982.

Bartlett, Lee, ed. *The Beats: Essays in Criticism*. Jefferson, N.C.: McFarland, 1981.

Charters, Ann, ed. *The Beats: Literary Bohemians in Postwar America*. Vol. 16, parts 1 and 2. *Dictionary of Literary Biography*. Detroit: Gale Research, 1983.

Charters, Ann, ed. *The Portable Beat Reader*. New York: Viking, 1992.

Charters, Samuel. *Some Poems/Poets: Studies in American Underground Poetry Since 1945*. Berkeley: Oyez, 1971

Corso, Gregory. *Elegiac Feelings American*. San Francisco: City Lights, 1970.

Davidson, Michael. *The San Francisco Renaissance: Poetics and Community at Mid-Century*. Cambridge: Cambridge University Press, 1989.

DiPrima, Diane. *Pieces of a Song*. San Francisco: City Lights, 1990.

Faas, Ekbert. *Toward a New American Poetics*. Santa Barbara: Black Sparrow, 1979.

Ferlinghetti, Lawrence. *Endless Life: Selected Poems*. New York: New Directions, 1981.

Ginsberg, Allen. *Collected Poems, 1947–1980*. New York: Harper and Row, 1986.

McClure, Michael. *Selected Poems*. New York: New Directions, 1986.

Meltzer, David, ed. *The San Francisco Poets*. New York: Ballantine, 1971.

Snyder, Gary. *No Nature: New and Selected Poems*. New York: Pantheon, 1992.

Solnit, Rebecca. *Secret Exhibition: Six California Artists of the Cold War Era*. San Francisco: City Lights, 1990.

Stephenson, Gregory. *The Daybreak Boys: Essays on the Literature of the Beat Generation*. Carbondale: Southern Illinois University Press, 1990.

John Berryman, Theodore Roethke, and the Elegy

DESPITE a number of parallels in the lives of John Berryman and Theodore Roethke, the two poets and their works are seldom paired in critical discussions. Even Bruce Bawer's *The Middle Generation* (1986), a critical study and collective biography that examines the works and lives of Roethke's contemporaries Delmore Schwartz, Randall Jarrell, John Berryman, and Robert Lowell, does not include analysis of Roethke and his poetry. Bawer connects the other four through the influence on their work of poetic forebears, namely, T. S. Eliot and W. B. Yeats, and through their shared experience of "turbulent childhoods," absent or dead fathers, domineering or manipulative mothers, and "alienated adulthoods" characterized by depression, alcoholism, manic phases, series of breakdowns, and preoccupation with suicide. Although Roethke's experience roughly correlates with that of the other four in many of these areas—and certainly he shares with Berryman the early influence of Yeats on his work, the premature loss of his father, and an "alienated adulthood"—Bawer notes that his "poetry and his attitude toward poetry" is significantly different.

While the same distinction could be made among the poets of Bawer's study, counterposing Roethke and Berryman's aesthetic points of departure—given their personal difficulties and the despairs common to that generation—enlarges our sense of their relationship to the elegiac tradition and of the role in that relationship of what was, for them, a fundamental experience—early loss of the father. An elegiac sensibility pervades the works of Roethke and Berryman, though the tone, expressiveness, and affectiveness of their poems differ dramatically, and their specific elegies are likewise variously achieved as both works, or "texts," and as works of mourning.

Berryman's achievement of the work of mourning—that difficult expression of the inexpressible in the movement from grief toward consolation—is evident in his short story "Wash Far Away" collected in *Freedom of the Poet*, and in the sequence of poems for Delmore Schwartz in *The Dream Songs*. To some extent, however, his elegiac work is a repetitive staccattolike reenactment of the early stages of grief—denial, rage, bitterness, and the attempt to arbitrate for a satisfactory but somehow mysteriously unattainable emotional equilibrium. From the earlier poems gathered in *Collected Poems: 1937–1971* through much of *The Dream Songs* and later poems, many—particularly those for the father—do not evolve, poetically or psychically, toward the acceptance necessary for release from stultifying grief into the liberating vision and embrace of the world and self that allows for the poet-mourner's healthy return to the community of life and the living.

Roethke's work, on the other hand, exhibits a wider range of the responses associated with loss, both in individual poems and sequences and throughout his work as a whole, from his first volume *Open House* (1941) to *The Far Field*, published posthumously in 1964. Although the most striking elegiac achievements are "The Lost Son" poems (from *The Lost Son*, published in 1948), the short but exquisite "Elegy for Jane" (from *The Waking*, published in 1953), and "The Dying Man" sequence (from *Words for the Wind*, 1958), Roethke's entire poetic production enacts the desire for and movement toward recuperative release and empowerment. As with Berryman, early loss of the father is the central figuration in Roethke's work, but—unlike Berryman—Roethke endeavors to transform the search for understanding and acceptance into a psychic and spiritual journey anchored in the phenomenal world as remembered from childhood and reexperienced in the present, his "lost son" a mythic hero who embraces the anguish and beauty, the terror and ecstasy of the journey.

That the lives as well as the work of the two poets are marked by a similar and devastating loss is undeniable. John Allyn Smith, Jr., Berryman's name for his first twelve years, was born on October 25, 1914, in rural Oklahoma to John Allyn Smith, a small-town banker, and Martha ("Peg" and later "Jill") Little, a school teacher. Another son, Robert Jefferson, was born in September 1919. The family moved from one small

Oklahoma town to another until hopes of making good on the Florida land boom sent the adult Smiths and Martha's mother to Tampa in the fall of 1925. They left the boys behind in boarding school, sold the land Martha's mother owned in Tampa, and bought a family restaurant, the Orange Blossom, that the three of them ran together. In December Martha returned to Oklahoma to bring the boys back, and in early spring 1926 the land crash forced the family to sell the business for a third of their original investment. In June 1926 John Allyn Smith, Sr., shot himself in the chest with a .32 in the early hours of the morning outside the house of his recently estranged family.

Whether the failure of the Orange Blossom or his wife's attachment to a married neighbor, the successful and older John Angus Berryman, or both are responsible for Smith's alienation and depression is speculation; that the young John never forgave him the act is repeatedly recorded in the poet's life and work. The violence and finality of his father's suicide staggered John Allyn's older son, whose struggle with the incomprehensibility of such a shocking act and ravaging loss soon translated into anger with his father for abandoning him, literally, and leaving him helplessly vulnerable to the chaos and turmoil of life. Berryman's efforts to grasp the complexities of John Allyn's suicide and to negotiate his way through a "fatherless" life plagued him to the point of obsession. Evidence of that obsession recurs throughout *The Dream Songs* and later poems as the poet relentlessly investigated the legitimacy of the alternative guiding principle his father's suicide had provided.

The vicissitudes and troubles of Berryman's own life later enabled him to reconsider more objectively and compassionately—"I put him down / while all the same on forty years I love him / . . . / . . . I repeat: I love him" (143)—what may have compelled his father to that last irrevocable act. Forgiveness never quite materialized, however, though the "figure" of suicide, as a seductive siren calling to the man and as a tropic motif in his creative work, dominated Berryman's inner life and poetry. Reconciliation with his father's death was further complicated by Berryman's ambiguous and conflicted relationship with his mother. Her villification, unreliable as her testimony may have been, of the man Berryman remembered only "dreamily" haunted the poet, as did his suspicion over the years that his mother had driven John Allyn to suicide, or may even have killed him herself.

Theodeore Huebner Roethke was born on May 25, 1908, in Sagi-
naw, Michigan, to Helen, née Huebner, Roethke, from a German
immigrant family, and Otto Roethke, who with his brother Charles
(originally Karl) owned and operated The William Roethke Greenhouses established by their father Wilhelm, an immigrant from Prus-
sia. The young Roethke grew up in the greenhouse world of his
father—"The rose, the chrysanthemum turned toward light. / . . .
Moved in a slow up-sway"—that he first celebrated in *The Lost Son*
and returned to in subsequent volumes—his connection to that world
later translated into heightened attention to and expressive evocation
of the phenomenal world he viewed and experienced as an adult. The
twenty-some acres on which Roethke's grandfather established the
garden market included a number of buildings and greenhouses
beyond which were Roethke's "field" and a tract of woods. Both Otto
and Charles built homes near the greenhouses, and the families were
close, their business a family one. While Charles handled the financial side, Otto maintained, with devotion and attentive efficiency, the
greenhouses.

The daily routine of the greenhouse—the young Roethke "[w]atch-
ing hands transplanting / Turning and tamping"—was a natural part
of the boy's life, as was his father, about whom Roethke felt both
awe—for his father's meticulous and loving artistry—and fear—of
Otto's austere presence, his short temper and impatience, his expectations of the awkward child. Roethke repeatedly recorded the ecstatic
beauty of his greenhouse childhood—"everything blooming above me,
/ Lilies, pale-pink cyclamen, roses"—and its seductive terrors—"So
many devouring infants! / . . . Loose ghostly mouths / Breathing." In
a mid-1940s entry from his notebooks collected in *Straw for the Fire*
(1972) he asks, "What was the greenhouse? It was a jungle, and it was
paradise; it was order and disorder: Was it an escape? No, for it was a
reality harsher than reality."

If John Allyn Smith's suicide was the most potent and life-affecting
event in Berryman's youth, it was for Roethke the loss of the greenhouse and of his father. A series of quarrels between Charles and Otto
in the fall of 1922 resulted in Otto's sale of his interest in the business
to Charles in October 1922. In February 1923 Charles committed suicide, and in April, after months of extreme ill health, Otto died of cancer in the family home, his wife and children witness to the pain and

agony of his last weeks. In a few short months the fourteen-year-old Roethke lost the greenhouse, his uncle, and his father.

That both poets subsequently suffered alienated or difficult and troubled adulthoods is well-documented in their work and discussions of it, and in their biographies and interviews. Previous to their marriages both maintained lengthy relationships with women who provided inspiration, stability, and the possiblity of intimacy, though Berryman and Roethke failed to make lasting commitments to them. In a list Roethke made, analyzing his character during his recuperation at Mercywood Sanitarium in December 1935 after his first breakdown, reprinted in Allan Seager's *The Glass House* (1968), note 29 is uncannily appropriate to both poets: "Afraid of marriage, of what it will do to the girl, etc. etc." Roethke did not marry until January 1953, a few months before his forty-fifth birthday, although Berryman married three times, the first time in 1942, a few weeks before his twenty-eighth birthday, to Eileen (née Mulligan) Simpson, and the last time in 1961 to Kate Donahue. Both were comparatively strong and stable marriages, his separation from Eileen occurring in 1953 (although their divorce, necessitated by Berryman's desire to marry Ann Levine, who was pregnant, was not finalized until 1956), and his commitment to Kate lasting until his death in 1972. Berryman's second and third marriages occurred swiftly after meeting the women to whom he proposed and Roethke married Beatrice O'Connell after courting her for only a few weeks, though she had been one of his students at Bennington a few years earlier. Although Roethke did not and Berryman did have children, Berryman was deeply troubled by his responsibility to fatherhood and both he and Roethke were conflicted about "fathering" children.

Both poets were notorious womanizers, often creating awkward and embarrassing scenes in public, their outrageous behavior exacerbated by excessive drinking. Berryman's famous account of his first meeting with Roethke at a 1952 Christmas party in Princeton—which details Roethke's aggressive social banter and his climactic tweeking of Edmund Wilson's jowls with the exclamation that Wilson was "all blubber"—could easily be a narrative of Berryman's own frenzied antics on any number of occasions throughout the years. Alcoholic, subject to depression, and half in love with the heightened experiences created by extreme self-abuse, Berryman and Roethke also suffered a series of breakdowns the severity of which often required hospitilization. Both were apparently capable of self-inducing the mental states that would eventually lead to temporary periods of emotional and mental disintegration, though Roethke was formally diagnosed a manic-depressive, with varying qualifications. While it is difficult to assess which of the two more consciously courted disaster as they matured, Roethke was not driven, as was Berryman, by an obsession and infatuation with suicide. Vivid as the parallels are between the final leaps into water that led to their deaths, Berryman purposely sought his death while Roethke did not. As his poetry attests, he desired and experienced affirmation of life, and his later poetry, in which the poet actively seeks illumination and reconciliation with the father/Father, indicates Roethke's imperative to shape productively and creatively the trauma and ecstasy of his life into a mystical quest.

That the different and singular effect on the two poets of their fathers' early deaths significantly influenced their aesthetics—not only in poems directly responsive to the event but in their elegiac work and artistic endeavors in general—distinguishes Berryman and Roethke, both as distinctive yet representative voices of their generation and as distinct from one another. A divisive factor between them is their relationship to childhood, their memory—or lack thereof—of childhood and their use of the remembered experience of childhood in their aesthetic and psychic development. After burying her husband and returning to Minnesota to visit John Allyn's family, Martha Smith took her children to New York and on September 8, 1926, married John Angus Berryman, thus beginning a new life, for herself and the two boys, completely severed from the still recent past. The young John took his stepfather's name and, at least for the time, effectively erased his childhood and any persisting connection to it. No such erasure occurred with Roethke. From his first volume *The Open House* and its catalogue of experience as tainted by the agony and rage of loss, into *The Lost Son* with the "greenhouse" poems of childhood and "The Lost Son" sequence, through to the late meditations in *The Far Field*, Roethke recounted "each childhood pleasure"—and terror—his attachment to the physical world of his youth enabling him to claim, "I live in air; the long light is my home; / I dare caress the stones, the field my friend."

Berryman found it difficult to access the "feeling" of his childhood—except for the anguish and disorientation elicited by his father's suicide—and sometimes even confused literal experience. Though it was the younger son Robert Jefferson whom John Allyn roped to himself when, shortly before his suicide, he swam so far out into the gulf that his wife and mother-in-law became distraught, Berryman recalls, "My mother was scared almost to death. / He was going to swim out, with me, forevers" (143). Berryman's "mismemory" of the event is startling, though the poet's technique throughout *The Dream Songs* of conflating literal experience with reinvestigation into the "feeling" of a particular experience often results in the discovery of a psychic truth, in this case Berryman's conviction that the experience of "that mad drive wiped out my childhood." Despite the conviction that his childhood had been effectively and irrevocably erased, Berryman nonetheless exhibits in his elegiac work a propensity for a return not so much to child*hood* but to the child himself. *The Dream Songs*, in particular, are characterized by a fragmentation of syntax, "nonsense" diction, playful rhythms, and the intermittent allusions, relatively rare, to a pristine and unrecoverable past when "above the lindens tops of poplars waved" (178), the poet recalling the beauty of "the phosphorescent Gulf" (143) into which his father swam, wishing for himself—"Soon you'll see stars / you fevered after, child, man" (92). Presence of the child is also evident in the grousing and quibbles—motivated by affection, competition, and clever one-upmanship—among the *Dream Song* voices of its persona, of Henry—"a white American in early middle age sometimes in blackface, who has suffered an irreversible loss"—and of Henry's unnamed friend who sometimes addresses him as Mr. Bones.

Berryman's devices can seem just that—devices—when contrasted with the "natural," organic, strategies of Roethke, who embraced in his poetry a wholly and deeply experienced return to childhood, to both its beauty and its terror—and the myriad nuances of emotional and spiritual response in between, ever conscious of reclaiming somehow the rich territory of its disturbing agitations and nurturing ecstasies. He regenerates the child in himself—". . . I'm five / Times five a man; I breathe / . . . / A man, a man alive"—and indulges it, again and again, exploring the multiplicity of his youthful experience in an effort to rediscover a way of anchoring himself in a drifting, mutable, and chaotic world. Where Berryman repeatedly ponders the idea that a "fatherless" world perhaps signifies a godless one—or at least one in which he is "cross" with whatever sort of god "has wrecked this generation" (153),

Roethke neutralizes and transcends his bleakest moments of doubt with immersion in the material, physical world—"I love the world"—and his poems through the years enact an incantatory affirmation—"I believe! I believe!"

However differently early loss affected their lives and, hence, their aesthetics, Berryman and Roethke have a common ground as well—and not just by virtue of their corresponding experiences or their mutual love of tennis or their reputations as the most striking and brilliant teachers of their generation. For both the life project was to investigate and, God or world willing, assimilate and articulate the significance of loss. They both embraced the lived and "worked" notion presented in the opening lines of "Meditation at Lagunitas" by Robert Hass: "All the new thinking is about loss. / In this it resembles all the old thinking" (from *Praise*, 1979). Echoing Berryman's observation about himself and those poets closest to him who "coughed & sang / the new forms in which ancient thought appears" (282), these lines allude both to the self-conscious and characterisitically elegiac disposition of our century and to recognition that human history is a history of our sense of continuous loss punctuated by moments of specific loss. Certainly Berryman and Roethke, as surgeons of and spokesmen for that sensibilty, provide us with two of the strongest, most vibrant, elegiac voices of our time, each identifying the impetus for his poetic enterprise in similar terms. In a 1970 interview with Richard Kostelanetz Berryman remarked, "All the way through my work is a tendency to regard the individual soul under stress." Quite a few years earlier, in the essay "Open Letter" first published in 1950 and later collected in the 1965 publication of *The Poet and His Craft*, Roethke had written that the poet must speak in a "compelling and immediate language," using "a kind of psychic shorthand when his protagonist is under stress." Upholding the aim of their enterprise with novitiate dedication, Berryman and Roethke excavated the dark regions of the soul or psyche "under stress," their elegiac work offering us distinctive yet representative and resonant expression of the inexpressible.

A formal poem traditionally occasioned by the death of a particular person, the elegy is, as Peter Sacks elaborates in his groundbreaking critical study, *The English Elegy*, also a manifestation of the "work" involved in the process of mourning—that is, of the psychological, spiritual, and creative energy the poet-mourner must summon and enact in order to move from grief to consolation. No twentieth-century American poet has more than John Berryman so ardently and devotedly engaged in an unrelenting study of "the epistemolgy of loss." His persistent attention to that study spans his entire poetic career, throughout which he brings to his "complex investigations of death" (335) a stunning range of voices and perspectives.

The early published poems, most of which were written between 1938 and 1947, are characterized by a melancholic presentiment of loss, the poet's agitated despair over the disintegration of Europe and the horrors of war, and Berryman's first allusions to his father's death. The inherent sense of loss that prevails in any number of the early poems—among them, "Winter Landscape," "The Statue," "A Point of Age," and "Parting as Descent"—is more "elusively" direct in the early 1938 poem "The Possessed," in which the poet reminds himself, "discomfortable dead / . . . . This is what you have inherited." Berryman's acknowledgment of that inheritance and the irrevocability of loss is most perfectly captured in "The Ball Poem," an accomplished 1941 lyric that begins, "What is the boy now, who has lost his ball, / What, what is he to do? / . . . . No use to say 'O there are other balls.' " The boy's first and sudden realization, his "ulitmate shaking grief," is sharpened both by Berryman's juxtaposition of a playful, childlike language and rhythm—"Merrily bouncing, down the street, and then / Merrily over"—with a more reflective commentary, and by the harder adult perspective on the recurrent nature of loss:

> He is learning, well behind his desperate eyes,
> The epistemology of loss, how to stand up
> Knowing what every man must one day know
> And most know many days, how to stand up

Berryman's antennaelike sensibility with regard to his subject—"losses and crisis"—also informs his poems in response to social and political events, most particularly the devastations in Europe during the late thirties and throughout World War II, as recorded in "World Telegram"—"News of one day, one afternoon, one time / . . . . might / Curry disorder in the strongest brain, / Immobilize the most resilient will"—and in a number of other poems from this period, among them "1 September 1939," "The Moon and the Night," and "White Feather." For the most part, however, Berryman imposes an already existing perspective and mind-set on that larger arena, and his deepest concerns continue to be, increasingly so in the middle and late work, more immediate and inescapable. The hauntings of his own "discomfortable dead" are evident throughout the early poems, and they persist even in such poems of goodwill as one Berryman composed in August 1938 for his brother's nineteenth birthday, in which he wishes for the younger man

> Whatever bargain can be got
> From the violent world our fathers bought,
> For which we pay with fantasy at dawn,
> Dismay at noon, fatigue, horror by night.

Although "Letter to His Brother" is in part a sociopolitical poem, any reference or epithet related to the word "father" has for Berryman a more personal context. John Allyn Smith's suicide when Berryman was eleven remained at the core of his life and work, and in the 1939 poem "World's Fair" the poet prophesies his lifetime relation to what he perceives as an unforgivable abandonment:

> Suddenly in torn images I trace
> The inexhaustible ability of a man
> Loved once, long lost, still to prevent my peace,
> Still to suggest my dreams and starve horizon.

Poems addressing the loss of the father punctuate *The Dream Songs* and later poems, and in one of the various outlines Berryman made for arranging his copious dream songs he noted that *The Dreams Songs* centered on the father. Though the poet moves through a series of emotions from guilt over his father's suicide, anger with the father for abandoning him, anger with his mother for perhaps having driven the father to his suicide, "Father being the loneliest word in one language" (241) epitomizes Berryman's most persistent and consistent attitude. From his continued examination of that early and damaging loss spiral out the poems obsessed with an ever present foreboding about the "dying" self and Berryman's extension of that obsession to an eventually realized preoccupation with suicide.

Berryman's "complex investigations of death" also include laments for lost love and the equation of disappointed love with death as well as specific elegies occasioned by the deaths of friends and fellow poets. Indeed, Berryman's poetry represents a number of the impulses toward the elegiac, and from his lifetime movement through "pockets of grief" (358) arises a variety of articulations, reiterated, interwoven, and circled back upon as the poet examines and reexamines—excruciatingly lives and relives—any number of given points within the broad spectrum of response to loss and the subsequent experience of grief. Repeatedly evocative of an elegiac self-consciousness, the poems call attention to themselves as "works" of mourning informed by the social and cultural, personal, and aesthetic pressures brought to bear on the poet's imagination in relationship to the psychic disturbance and turmoil generating a particular poem.

Demonstration of those pressures can be found in Berryman's short story, "Wash Far Away," first published posthumously in 1975 (it was originally drafted in the spring of 1947, and revised both early in the fifties and again in the mid to late fifties). The central character, a Berryman-like professor at what appears to be a small liberal arts college, recalls a revelatory experience some years back when, encumbered by a pervasive sense of deflation, ennui, and disenchantment, he had been revitalized while teaching John Milton's "Lycidas"—a poem the professor once revered and that Berryman himself considered a literary touchstone. The experience leads him to a new and inspired understanding of the poem, his preparation for and performance in the classroom underscored as they are by his intermittent drifts into reverie about his dead friend Hugh, the fictional counterpart to Berryman's friend, fellow poet, and colleague Bhain Campbell, who at the age of twenty-nine died of cancer in 1940.

The two subtexts—the renascent interpretation of "Lycidas" through which Berryman apprehends that "magnificent" poem's impact on him both poetically and personally and the elegiac movement in the story toward a life-affirming consolation with regard to Campbell's death—are intricately meshed in a narrative of thematic complexity. The professor's recollections parallel events in Berryman's own life, from the early years of friendship with Hugh/Bhain Campbell, the friend's early death, the subsequent marriage of the professor and Berryman's to Eileen Mulligan (later Simpson), to the dissolution of the marriage and the revelatory moment of teaching "Lycidas." Firmly grounded in the experience and anguish of Berryman's own life, "Wash Far Away" recreates, through its intertexuality, the work involved in the process of mourning, employing not only the traditional machinery and conventions of the pastoral elegy as appropriated from the text it seeks to elucidate but its structural, rhetorical, and imagistic strategies as well.

The double invocation of the opening paragraphs parallels Milton's invocation, for Edward King and Lycidas, and in both texts the dead friend is associated with the vegetation deity. Through the professor's awareness of and response to the profusion of spring around him and his recurrent references to the pastoral world of "Lycidas," Berryman provides a pastoral context for the story. Recurrent images of light, the hopeful figurations of possible consolation and resurrected life, are woven into a narrative that records the fluctuating range of emotions experienced after great loss—from paralyzing grief, anger, and self-deprecation, to fleeting joy with life, bitterness, and fear, to lament, renewed belief in the self, and liberating acceptance and consolation.

That "Wash Far Away" is an achieved work of mourning becomes clearest in the exchange between the professor and his students, whose "inquisition" of the text reenacts the "trial" in "Lycidas"—a stunning moment when the questions tormenting the professor in his earlier reflections on his life, on Hugh, arise poised in the classroom, palpable and undeniable. By their very interrogations of the text the professor and his students join in a performative trial of their own, one that for the professor dramatizes and activates his participation in confronting the losses that have so debilitated his imagination and energy. The students, then, become the "procession of mourners" who, like the various figures in "Lycidas," accompany the bereaved, their presence necessary for urging the mourner to temper sorrow and rejoin the community of the living, their multivocality essential for effecting the dialectic from grief to consolation. The professor's charged interaction with the students is itself evidence of his return to that community of the living, the last paragraph signaling the moment at which he is revitalized through release from the paralyzing emotions of grief. The professor's acknowledgment earlier that "consistently Lycidas was Hugh" is transformatively crystallized as he ponders after class, in the healing quiet of his office, "the transfiguration of Lycidas," his meditation enabling him to move toward a tentative consolation vibrant with "the trembling of light on the page."

What Berryman ascertained critically, aesthetically, and intuitively from his "deeper-deepest-acquaintance" with "Lycidas" is perhaps no more evident than in the sequence of poems in *The Dream Songs*

(146–157) for the friend and fellow poet of his youth, Delmore Schwartz. Of all Berryman's elegies the sequence for Schwartz is the most potent, accomplishing the complexity, beauty, and range of emotion first manifested in "Wash Far Away." It opens with a double invocation, first in 146, which names the subject of the poems that follow—"Delmore specially, the new ghost / haunting Henry most"—and then in 147, which summons the dead poet in a doubled chant that appears once in each of the three stanzas: "Delmore, Delmore." Except for "these lovely motions of the air" and Henry's "bird-of-paradise vestures" (146), followed by "High in the summer branches the poet sang" (147) and "His death clouded the grove" (151), Berryman replaces pastoral detail with evocation of those haunts in which the early friendship between Schwartz and Berryman flourished and suffered its numerous misunderstandings and enigmas—the cheap hotels and shoddy apartments of their youth.

Appropriately, the few allusions to light come not from the external, natural world but from evocations of the light emanating from Delmore's creative genuis, "his electrical insight" (155). While the poet celebrates Delmore's virility—"he was young & gift strong" (149), "Flagrant his young male beauty" (154), "the whole young man / alive with surplus love" (155), and laments that he died "too soon" (151), "fallen from his prime" (148), Berryman reminds us that Schwartz "hid his gift" (150) and lived long enough to have suffered "the awful years / of the failure of his administration" (151). In fact, the elegiac work in these poems is complicated somewhat by Berryman's double-edged despair over Delmore's death—his regret for the waste brought about by death and the waste Delmore willfully indulged in life:

> I'd bleed to say his lovely work improved
> but it is not so. He painfully removed
> himself from the ordinary contacts
> and shook with resentment.
>
> (150)

Although lamentation dominates these poems—"O and O I mourn / again this complex death" (156) and, "We suffer on, a day, a day, a day" (153)—and occasionally bursts into moments of rage—"I'm cross with god who has wrecked this generation" and "never again can come, like a man slapped, / news like this" (153), the poems are neither repetitive nor emotionally one-dimensional. Through Berryman's loving evoca-

618   Berryman, Roethke, and the Elegy

tion of Delmore's life and genuis he becomes a living and vital presence in the songs. The funerary flowers dismally absent in these poems become unexpectedly present as the poet gathers the verbal significations of place in an incantatory integration of reference after reference to sites of shared experience and the various modes of traveling—taxi and ambulance—between them: Harvard, Brooklyn, Warren House, Manhattan, NYU, hotel rooms, Bellevue, Providence, police stations, Cambridge. Throughout the sequence the poet gathers, as well, his procession of mourners—Berryman's mother and brother, the gossips of Harvard, the police in Washington, the "Jews bereft" (151), the children Delmore never had, the girls at NYU, Delmore's wife and friends—as he moves into the consolatory last poem.

Where in 1941 Berryman writes of Bhain Campbell's death, "Both of us at the end. / Nouns, verbs do not exist for what I feel," here he tells us, of Delmore, "one solid block of agony, / I wrote for him, and then I wrote no more" (157), the poet reenacting the necessary letting go, first articulated in "Wash Far Away," in this last song for Delmore:

> His sad ghost must aspire
> free of my love to its own post, that ghost,
> among its fellows, Mozart's, Bach's, Delmore's
> free of its careful body

Although he longs to join that company of "fellows"—Mozart, Bach, and Delmore—"high in the shades which line that avenue / where I will gladly walk, beloved of one," Berryman concludes the song with that consolatory directive of elegy necessary to both the subject, Delmore, and the poet himself: "I hope he's sitting with his peers: sit, sit, / & recover & be whole."

In the years between the composition of "Wash Far Away" and Delmore Schwartz's death in July 1966, Berryman suffered an astounding number of losses that, except for Dylan Thomas's death in 1953, followed one upon the other in the few years before Delmore's death: Ernest Hemingway in the summer of 1961, William Faulkner the following July, Robert Frost in January 1963, Sylvia Plath in July, Theodore Roethke in August, T. S. Eliot in January 1965, R. P. Blackmur in February, Randall Jarrell in October. Most of these deaths and many more are recorded in *The Dream Songs*, although few of the works Berryman was compelled to wrestle into being achieve the same transformative experience of the Schwartz sequence, in part because of the sustained attention Berryman brought to bear on that "one solid block of agony." By their very brevity the others often seem more occasional, as if he had dashed them off immediately, unwilling to dwell too long or too deeply on his grief. They do resonate more fully, however within the context of *The Dream Songs* as a whole, which collects Berryman's "losses and crisis" and relentlessly catalogues both the deaths and their nearly unbearable weight.

Although Berryman did not write his songs for Jarrell in "one solid block," they nonetheless constitute an affectionately incisive portrait of the poet-critic, and gestures toward consolatory release appear—"Let Randall rest" (90) and "Peace to the bearded corpse" (121). The poems record, as well, Berryman's agitation and struggle with Jarrell's suicide: "Again his friend's death made the man sit still / and freeze inside" for it

> had been adjudged a suicide
> which dangles a trail
>
> longer than Henry's chill, longer than his loss
> (127)

Nearly a year later he wrote, "When worst it got, you went away I charge you," prophesying that "we will wonder over this in Hell / if the circles communicate" (259). Although he concedes in the same poem that "[my] desire for death was strong / but never strong enough," the poem concludes with Berryman's request to Jarrell—"Come hunt me, ancient friend, / and tell me I am wrong." Indeed, their "lovely friendly rivalry / over a quarter of century" concerned more than Berryman's appreciation of his friend's brilliant mind and talent. Jarrell's suicide elicited yet another return to Berryman's questions about willingly continuing to live in the midst of so much death—"All those deaths keep Henry pale & ill / . . . a disadvantage of surviving" (191). For Berryman, "It all centered in the end on the suicide," his declaration "in which I am an expert, deep & wide" (136) immediately traceable to its source, his father's suicide. Though his return to that crippling loss opens *The Dream Songs* and continues through to the final poems, it is in the songs for his father that Berryman fails to recover emotional equilibrium.

As early as the first song Berryman credits his fall from the Edenic world of childhood—"Once in a sycamore I was glad / all at the top, and I sang"—to his father's abandonment, "then came a departure," after which "nothing fell out as it might or ought." Although most of *The Dream Songs* are characterized by confrontations with loss, the dying and the dead, and meditations on suicide—all of which are attributable to that first "departure"—nearly thirty of the poems refer specifically to John Allyn's death and the poet's efforts to come to terms with it. From "his unforgivable memory" (53) Berryman retrieves the details of the event for such songs as 143 in which the poet proposes to "sing you now a song / the like of which may bring your heart to break." In 145 the poet proclaims love for his father and admits "me he's done no wrong / for going on forty years—forgiveness time," trying to "touch now his despair," that is, of John Allyn, and arguing that when his father "rose with his gun and went outdoors by my window," he was doing only "what was needed." For all that the poet longs for a "forgiveness time" he cannot somehow "read that wretched mind" of his father, in 121 confessing

> I've always tried. I—I'm
> trying to forgive
> whose frantic passage, when he could not live
> an instant longer, in the summer dawn
> left Henry to live on.

The telling line here is the last: nothing alters for the poet the one irrevocable and unforgivable fact that he is left "to live on" alone in "the whole humiliating Human round." Indeed, the lines "in a modesty of death I join my father / who dared so long agone leave me" (76) couple Berryman's desire for death—and his pursuit of a self-willed death—with his unalterable and unforgiving anger.

In 384, composed in the late sixties a few years before Berryman's suicide, the poet's inability to comprehend John Allyn's action and forgive it translates into an anger so violent that it results in an imagined assault on the father's corpse. Open to rather intensive Freudian interpretation, the poem is stripped of all the hopeful figurations of light and usual funerary offerings—"The marker slants, flowerless, day's almost done." The poet announces, "I stand above my father's grave with rage," revealing that he has made this imagined "awful pilgrimage" more than once "to one / who cannot visit me,

who tore his page / out." The assault begins in the middle stanza—
"I spit upon this dreadful banker's grave"—as he professes his desire
to "scrabble till I got right down / away down under the grass" in
order to "ax the casket open." He proposes to "tear apart / the moul-
dering grave clothes," after which Henry "will heft the ax once more,
his final card, / and fell it on the start." The last line articulates a
desire to destroy the starting point, that is, both the father himself
and the fact of his suicide. As progenitor, the father is thus Berryman's "start"; the father's suicide is the "start" of the poet's lifelong
misery and the beginning of his residence in "the country of the
dead" (279). The irony in that desire to fell too late "the start"—that
is, the corpse of the father who has lived, begat, and willfully ended
his life—compounds the rage and impotency the poet experiences in
response to what is irreversible.

The two poems for Ernest Hemingway recapitulate this response,
and indeed it is easy to mistake 34 as a song for the father. The poet
refers to the "crack / of the dooming & emptying news" and portrays
the figure with a shotgun as

> One man, wide
> in the mind, and tendoned like a grizzly, pried
> to his trigger-digit, pal.

While the poet concludes here that Hemingway / the father "should
not have done that," in 235 he excavates the sources of "Hemingway in
despair," associating himself, after the heightened lament in the first
stanza, with those sources: "Save us from shotguns & fathers' suicides."
He argues that it is "a bad example, murder of oneself, / the final death,
in a paroxysm, of love." As in many of the poems in which the father
intrudes, Berryman turns from his first subject, here Hemingway, and
although in the third stanza he attempts to correct the digression—
"But to return, to return to Hemingway"—the song ends with a lament
for the self:

> Mercy! my father; do not pull the trigger
> or all my life I'll suffer from your anger
> killing what you began.

The prayer not only encapsulates Berryman's lifetime relationship to his
father's suicide but alludes, as well, to Berryman's increasing sense of a
painful responsibility: the burden of his own fatherhood. "Killing what

you began" uncannily correlates not only with the last line of the penultimate song, "and fell it on the start," but with its paired relationship to
the final song, which begins "My daughter's heavier. Light leaves are
flying." For as the daughter grows heavier so too does the poet's burden
of fatherhood—most specifically the burden of continuing to live. That
Berryman was unable to carry that burden much more than a few years
after the completion of *The Dream Songs* is evident from his suicide in
early January 1972—though perhaps he saw his action, throwing himself from the Washington Bridge in Minneapolis on his way to his
office, as somehow like the one he had made years before with Bhain
Campbell into the dunes, that exhilirating and liberating leap he recalls
in "Wash Far Away."

Theodore Roethke's movement toward reconciliation, however,
became a lifetime objective he arduously pursued in the search for and
experience of redemptive insight and acceptance, although his early
losses were as potentially crippling as Berryman's. The young Roethke's
confused perception of the relationship between the "disappearance" of
the greenhouse and his uncle's suicide with his father's death, which in
the context of the other two losses appeared to be itself a suicide and
hence a betrayal and willful abandonment, was further complicated by
his conflicted yet natural, from an adult perspective, feelings for his
father: his love, admiration, and awe somehow undermined, unforgiv-
ably in the boy's mind, by his guilt—hating at times the father for his
impatience and abrupt castigations, and at other times fearing Otto's
austerity, resenting his authority. Nevertheless, Roethke's early losses
produced a significantly different lens on the world and inner psyche,
the poet transforming personal trauma into an aesthetic of individual
and mythic quest. As Peter Balakian elaborates in *Theodore Roethke's Far
Fields* (1989), Roethke's poetry mythologizes the family past and melds
it with an archetypal and cultural vision of a "larger" past, the poet
absorbing and celebrating the natural world and appropriating it as his
objective correlative.

From *Open House*, which rehearses the griefs at the core of the poet's
experience, to *The Lost Son* and *Praise to the End*, which manifest his
leap into the mythic, mystical, and phenomenal through which he
endeavors to validate personal apprehension of reality, to *The Far Field*
with its complexly rendered meditations evocative of the poet's increasing urgency and sense of impending death, Roethke creates an elegiac

body of work that excavates and addresses our most fundamental relation to loss and mortality. The title poem and program piece of *Open House* announces the very contradictions that inform requisite performative response to loss: while the poet / mourner must experience grief fully, he must also enact a psychological and spiritual movement toward communion with life. Although the speaker in "Open House" claims that "my heart keeps open house," the doors "widely swung," he also acknowledges that, while his "secrets" and "truths" are loudly proclaimed, the speaker "naked to the bone," his reality is one of "anguish self-revealed." In such a state of anguish "the anger will endure," for, as the speaker confesses, "Rage warps my clearest cry / To witless agony." In a number of ways the subsequent poems in *Open House* elucidate both the effects of the emotions cited—anguish, vulnerability, anger, rage, agony—and the pervasive elegiac sensibility to which Robert Hass alludes in the opening lines of "Meditation at Lagunitas." While some of the poems, with varying degrees of aesthetic and psychological success, project forward to a possibility of release from the paralysis of anguish—among them "To My Sister," "The Premonition," and "Ballad of the Clairvoyant Widow," it is not until "Night Journey," which concludes with the lines "I stay up half the night / To see the land I love," that the poet anticipates his liberating immersion in the greenhouse and open field worlds of childhood, where the personal, mythic, archetypal, mystical, and phenomenal intersect.

In the poems of *The Lost Son* and *Praise to the End* Roethke uncovers for himself and develops the major tropes, symbols, and figurations that activate the aesthetic and psychological potency of his work in these and subsequent volumes. As Jay Parini notes in *Theodore Roethke* (1979), the whole of Roethke's work can be interpreted through the light of "The Lost Son" and the poems associated with it. Here the external landscape is transformatively experienced internally, the greenhouse rooting the poet to the "order and disorder" of the phenomenal as he explores man's physical and psychical relationship to the unknown, the eternal, and the sublime. In these poems Roethke resurrects, as he will continue to do, the figure of Papa as father-God, the inaccessible but peripherally constant figure of the mother-lover, and the figurations of light and wind as kinetic forces in the landscape and journey. The symbolic and mystical significance of water becomes fully developed only later, in *The Far Field*, when the Puget Sound landscape of Roethke's last years correlates to what Parini calls the "long journey out of the self," as the poet seeks illumination and embarks on what is, for Roethke, a curiously idiosyn-cratic mystical / phenomenal quest for the sublime.

It is reductive to isolate the specific elegies of a poet whose works exhibit not only elegiac proclivities but, as with Roethke, an overall movement through the various stages of grief, both within sequences and through an entire canon, from the first poems of rage and anguish to the later meditations through which the poet resolutely seeks a con-solatory and redemptive reconciliation. While the longer sequences, "The Lost Son" and "the Dying Man," are Roethke's most achieved elegies, of the shorter ones the two entitled "Elegy" and "Otto" are characteristically occasional and anecdotal, relatively stiff and self-con-sciously distant. "Elegy for Jane," however, is a remarkable and stun-ning poem—perhaps for the very reasons we suspect it should not be.

Written for a student Roethke knew only slightly, the poem never-theless exemplifies the aim of the traditional elegy in that it responds to an occasion—the death of a young and vital person to whom the poet may not have been particularly close, though the loss is real and deeply felt—the poet exercising both the objectivity inherent in the somewhat distant relation to his subject and the emotional investment the occasion, in connection with his own "psyche under stress," pro-vokes. Appropriating material from what the poet knows best, Roethke renders the character and physical presence of Jane by associ-ating her with the phenomenal world—her "quick look" is "a sidelong pickerel smile"; she is a "wren," her "song trembling the twigs and small branches"—and in the final stanza she is a "maimed darling," the speaker's "skittery pigeon." In the second stanza, which moves from impressionistic characterization of the young woman into evocation of the inner Jane, the poet remarks that her sadness was so deep that "even a father could not find her." The poem moves from the third-person observations of the first two stanzas to apostrophe in the final two, the poet directly addressing "my sad sparrow," who is "not here." Nothing from the organic and known world, however, can console the poet—not "the sides of wet stones . . . / Nor the moss, wound with the last light."

By connecting the dead girl to the organic world, and invoking the apostrophe, the poet both animates her and acknowledges the irrevoca-bility of her death—the damp tendrils of the first line resonant in the "damp grave" of the final stanza, the natural world through which the poet experiences her youthful vitality and presence unable, finally, to provide the consolation the poet requires as he faces the loss and his sense of Jane's unfullfilled promise "waiting like a fern." Having symbolically substituted language for the living girl, "not here," the poet laments his powerlessness—"If only I could nudge you from this sleep"—recognizing the attempt at revivification for what it is, substitution, the failure of language painfully apparent in the poet's failure to describe and name the relationship between himself and the mourned. Just as Tennyson's "widowed" is no more precise than the alternative "orphaned" in his lament for Arthur Hallam, Roethke finds his available vocabulary altogether inadequate. Though he wishes to "speak the words of my love," he is "neither father nor lover" and has "no rights in this matter." The "pure depth" of the living Jane's sadness—"Even a father could not find her"—becomes the weighty grief of the poet, the impossibility of recovering her wrenchingly clear—he is himself not even a father.

In "The Lost Son" the subjectivity of the poet's remembered experience of the greenhouse and the far field intersects with the larger field of myth and archetype as the poet journeys into and through the external and internal landscapes associated with ecstasy, terror, and traumatic loss. Parini's discussion of the poem as a monomyth in which the hero/boy/poet embarks on a Freudian descent into the depths—a ritualistic enactment of separation, ordeal, symbolic death, resurrection, and illumination—brilliantly explores the psychic dimension of "The Lost Son." His elaboration of the cycles of regression and progression the poet-traveler experiences also provides an applicable construct for the elegiac impulse that initiates the poem and activates the elegiac "work" operating within it. That loss of the father is the central psychic imperative is announced in the first line, "At Woodlawn I heard the dead cry," which refers to the cemetery where Otto was buried and to the speaker's bondage; attuned to hear the cry of the dead, "not here," the poet is so enervated by grief that his is a "dead cry," his lament powerless, his psyche static—"lulled by the slamming iron." Although the poet is both "fished in an old wound" and fishing in it, he calls for assistance and guidance, "Snail, snail, glister me forward," as he turns to the phenomenal, natural world and invokes bird, worm, dark hollows, moon, salt, sea—an incantatory gathering that enlarges as the poem progresses, each element a being to which the poet poses the elegist's questions, the elements together becoming the poet's requisite procession of mourners.

The first three movements of the poem are punctuated by the unanswerable questions the poet must ask, from the conventional "Which is the way . . . ?" to the Roethkean melding of the organic and psychic in such gestures as "Where do the roots go?"—"Who put the moss here?"—"Has the worm a shadow?"—"Hath the rain a father?"—"Do the bones cast out their fire?" They are characterized as well by the confusion and alienation the mourner experiences—"This is my hard time"—and the anguish that accompanies his failed attempts at consolation, "The moon would not have me" and, worse, "The cows and briars / Said to me: Die."

By the end of the third movement, however, the hopeful figurations of light to which the poet increasingly turns in the fourth and last sections finally appear, "These sweeps of light undo me." In the fourth movement the poet returns to the landscape of his father, "the long greenhouse" where "the roses kept breathing in the dark." Though it is night and "dark all the way," he keeps his vigil and is rewarded—"The light in the morning came slowly," and with it the presence he had hoped to evoke: "Papa is coming!" The section ends with elegiac demarcations between the living and the dead—"The rose, the chrysanthemum turned toward light."

The fifth and last movement opens at the "beginning of winter," the stillness of that "in-between time" the central trope in a section through which light travels: "The light moved slowly over the frozen field." Although the series of questions in the fourth stanza

> Was it light?
> Was it light within?
> Was it light within light?
> Stillness becoming alive,
> Yet still?

suggests the still tentative relation of the poet-mourner to possible consolation, he has observed that "light traveled over the wide field; / Stayed." Imagining that light is "stillness coming alive, / yet still," he recalls that a "lively understandable spirit / Once entertained" him and reminds himself that it "will come again," his last instruction—the consolatory directive of elegy—"Be still. / Wait."

Roethke's elegiac work in "The Lost Son" reverberates in the context of all the poems that comprise "The Lost Son" sequence—the three poems that follow it in the last section of *The Lost Son*, all the poems of *Praise to the End*, and the first poem in *The Waking* (1953). The very titles of these volumes reconstruct the process of mourning worked through within individual poems and throughout the entire sequence: the anguish, grief, alienation, and uncertainty associated with loss as the poet returns, again and again, to what he can and must praise in order to move toward a redemptive consolation that allows him to reawaken to the self, the world, and the living. His task in "The Dying Man," a later poem from *The Far Field*, is a different and perhaps more difficult one, though the work and working through to which he dedicated himself in "The Lost Son" poems provided him with the mettle to meet that challenge—to dare, as he confesses and laments in "The Dying Man," "to question all," "to fix his vision anywhere," "to bleed," and "to live."

The subtitle of "The Dying Man"—"In Memoriam: W. B. Yeats"—suggests that, at the least, the poem is an homage, if not an elegy, for that poet whose cadences, language, and versification influenced Roethke's apprentice work and whose experimentations with masks and personae provided him with an example for the unifying device that generates and shapes "The Lost Son," in particular, and a number of the later poems. After the opening invocation of Yeats's music, images, and vision of eternity, however, the poem metamorphoses into an elegy for a father figure triadically comprised of the poetic-progenitor, Otto-Papa, and the divine. This triadic figuration as guide is not surprising. Roethke admired the poignant nobility of Yeats as aging man and as aging poet, desiring himself to achieve the insights of Yeats at that stage in his life and of his own father in his search for the experience of the sublime. As the poem evolves it is transformed yet again into a pre-elegy for the self as the poet, increasingly burdened by the weight of mortality and the premonition of death, explores what guidance his fathers, phenomenal and organic life, and the quest for the sublime can and cannot provide.

Employing the five-part structure he discovered and imposed in "The Lost Son" and repeated in a number of other poems from the sequence, Roethke opens with instruction from the poet to whom the poem is dedicated—or so he would have us believe from his announcement in the first two lines and the first section's title, "His Words." The dying man claims that though "the flesh deserts the bone / . . . a kiss widens the rose." Both a symbol for the imagination in Yeats's mystical system and Roethke's referent for return to the greenhouse, the rose—when kissed— signifies that embrasure of the world and imagination opens up to the possible sublime: "Eternity is Now." The closing lines of the first movement—"I am that final thing / A man learning to sing"—not only derives from the dying man/Yeats's example but asserts, as well, the poet's instruction to the self.

This self-instruction fails to satisfy or console, however, for the poet feels caught in "the dying light." Although "[w]hat's done is yet to become"—one need only kiss the rose—the poet is worn by the "leaden weight" of his mortality, of "what I did not do." Only when he returns to "places great with their dead" is he reminded "to stay alive," but those places are desolate ones—"the mire, the sodden trees"—and he is a "clumsy man" who has "burned the flesh away" and "dared to question all." Where in the second movement the poet had once thought himself to be reborn, in the third, entitled "The Wall," he "moans to be reborn" again. The father returns to him only when he "works," but he loses himself too often and too easily in "this small dark." The wall—associated with the ghost of the father and those things that obscure or cannot be penetrated—"has entered." Both an obstacle and the means by which the poet may experience revelation, the wall by its very presence transforms the poet into "a madman staring at perpetual night / A spirit raging at the visible." That these two lines modify both the poetic "I" and the wall doubles the poet's sense of it as both a barrier and the way to what he longs for, and he necessarily counsels himself, "I must love the wall."

The fourth movement, "Exultation," returns the poet to his childhood landscape where he is able to claim, "I love the world." Exultation in that world is, however, a "dangerous thing," and the poet desires more "than the world / Or after-image of the inner eye." The Yeatsian and Otto figures of the earlier movements collapse into a larger figure—poetic, human, and divine—who dares "to fix his vision anywhere." The poet, who acknowledges only what he knows—"I have the earth"—wishes to enact that dare, and in the fifth movement ponders the possibility of doing so in a "dying light."

In some respects the poem comes full circle, the title of the last movement—"They Sing, They Sing"—in conjunction with its first line—"All women loved dance in a dying light"—serving as a reminder of that first instruction—"I am that final thing, / A man learning to sing." The poet accedes—"I love the moon"—and invokes in their most primordial forms the figures from Yeats's more intellectualized and systemized visionary tableaux—the dolphin, the beast, the bird as bird, singing and ungilded. He wonders, nonetheless, if he is "but nothing, leaning towards a thing," and appeals to the eternal, "Descend, O gentlest light, descend, descend. / O sweet field far ahead." Acknowledging that "what's seen recedes; Forever's what we know!," which echoes the lines from the first movement, he claims also that eternity is "strewn with straw, / The fury of the slug beneath the stone." Though he dreads the "thing I am" and though "[t]he edges of the summit still appall / When we brood on the dead or the beloved," he "dares to live." The affirmation that closes the poem and brings it full circle has been at great cost, however, for the one "who dares to live" is one "who stops being a bird, yet beats his wings / Against the immense immeasurable emptiness of things." For Roethke the challenge of living in a "dying light" requires that he be one who abandons the self—"stops being a bird"—while activating the imagination—"yet beats his wings"—and does so without visible proof "against the immense immeasurable emptiness of things."

Although Roethke and Berryman had in common a similar traumatic loss and a central burning and finally unanswerable question that compelled each of them in the life of experience and the life of poetry, the affects and effects of their elegiac work is strikingly different. That two such singular temperments would generate such intersecting yet contrastive elegiac responses is neither surprising nor problematic. Read against each other they richly inform our own relation to loss, grief, and the work of mourning, together widening and articulating the ecstatic and terrifying territory of the "psyche under stress." Of the two, Berryman—with the frenetic, nervous, fragmented qualities of both his language and life, his resistance to closure and resolution—perhaps speaks more directly to the postmodern sensibility, though Roethke's noble struggle—and he succeeds to a nobility like that of his poetic father—is a qualified high note in an age of disbelief.

Roethke's achievement in his elegiac work is in part due to his richly experienced journey into memory—the landscapes and psychic reality of childhood—as well as to his attentive celebration of the organic, phenomenal world. Berryman had no such unifying ground except the self in constant fission, his tropes and syntax remarkable for their divisive and splintering effects. The natural, organic world at the edge of a far field world opening up to eternity that Roethke resurrected again and again, even in "dying light," is not central to Berryman's poetry, as he himself declares:

> I don't know one damned butterfly from another
> my ignorance of the stars is formidable,
> also of dogs & ferns

(265)

Not surprisingly, one of the few poems strikingly responsive to that world so alien to Berryman is his elegy for Roethke, with its "cadenzas of flowers," its "bluebells, pool-shadows," and "friendlier ground" (18). Although Berryman failed in his elegiac work for the father, "Strut for Roethke" not only commemorates with loving detail the man, his music, and his sublime "high note," but yearns for the things Roethke revered, always elusive to Berryman and irrevocably lost once again, "The Garden Master's gone."

Lea Baechler

Further Reading

Balakian, Peter. *Theodore Roethke's Far Fields: The Evolution of His Poetry.* Baton Rouge: Louisiana State University Press, 1989.

Bawer, Bruce. *The Middle Generation: The Lives and Poetry of Delmore Schwartz, Randall Jarrell, John Berryman, and Robert Lowell.* Hamden, Conn.: Archon, 1986.

Berryman, John. *Collected Poems, 1937–1971.* Ed. Charles Thornbury. New York: Farrar, Straus and Giroux, 1989.

Berryman, John. *The Dream Songs.* New York: Farrar, Straus and Giroux, 1969.

Berryman, John. *The Freedom of the Poet.* Ed. Robert Giroux. New York: Farrar, Straus, and Giroux, 1976.

Bloom, Harold, ed. *Theodore Roethke.* New York: Chelsea House Publishers, 1988.

Haffendan, John. *The Life of John Berryman.* Boston: Routledge and Kegan Paul, 1982.

Mariani, Paul. *Dream Song: The Life of John Berryman.* New York: William Morrow, 1990.

Parini, Jay. *Theodore Roethke: An American Romantic.* Amherst: University of Massachusetts Press, 1979.

Roethke, Theodore. *The Collected Poems.* New York: Doubleday, 1966.

Roethke, Theodore. *On the Poet and His Craft: Selected Prose of Theodore Roethke.* Ed. Ralph J. Mills, Jr. Seattle: University of Washington Press, 1965.

Roethke, Theodore. *Straw for the Fire: From the Notebooks of Theodore Roethke, 1943–1963.* Ed. David Wagoner. New York: Doubleday, 1972.

Sacks, Peter. *The English Elegy: Studies in the Genre from Spenser to Yeats.* Baltimore: Johns Hopkins University, 1985.

Seager, Allan. *The Glass House: The Life of Theodore Roethke.* New York: McGraw-Hill, 1968.

Simpson, Eileen. *Poets in Their Youth: A Memoir.* New York: Farrar, Straus and Giroux, 1982.

Thomas, Harry, ed. *Berryman's Understanding: Reflections on the Poetry of John Berryman.* Boston: Northeastern University Press, 1988.

What Was Confessional Poetry?

A father's no shield
for his child
—Robert Lowell, "Fall, 1961"

ON July 21, 1969, Neil Armstrong stepped through the opened hatches of the American spacecraft *Apollo 11* and became the first human being to set foot on the moon. In politics the moon landing provided an American cold war victory and in popular culture, an excuse for carnival. Apollo—the moon—this was poet territory! A banner on the cover of *Esquire* queried, "What words should the first man on the moon utter that will ring through the ages?"; the story, headed "Fifty Helpful Hints," pictured the poet Anne Sexton (among others) in a space helmet. The fashion magazine *Harper's Bazaar* asked a number of famous people to ponder what should be placed in a time capsule on the moon, and the novelist Joyce Carol Oates replied, "The confessional poems of Anne Sexton, Sylvia Plath, Robert Lowell and W. D. Snodgrass."

The confessional poems of Sexton, Plath, Lowell, and Snodgrass— not just because they were thought of as works by lunatic artists— appear in retrospect as peculiarly suitable for placement on the moon as cultural icons of their times, cold war politics and all. The label *confessional* was first applied, disapprovingly, to Robert Lowell's *Life Studies*, a collection of autobiographical prose and poetry published in 1959. Within a very short time confessional poetry established itself as a poetic type that could not be dismissed or ignored. This was thoroughly middle-class postwar art—produced by WASP writers—that violated the norms of decorum for subject matter prevailing in serious literature; its influence forced a mutation of critical standards. Specifically, *confessional* referred to content, not technique. But how did readers come to care about what American poets put into their poems? Answers can be sought in the relevance of the themes of confessional poetry to other areas of culture that had obvious influence on middle-class life at the time: psychoanalysis as a mode of address to postwar existential misery, anticommunism as a pressure on American artists and intellectuals, and television as a solvent of boundaries between public and domestic life.

To the selective vision of retrospect the first part of this century appears dominated by a very few figures, the poets of High Modernism: W. B. Yeats, T. S. Eliot, Ezra Pound, Wallace Stevens, and their ideologically American rival, William Carlos Williams. The next generation of American poets, born during the twenty-year period beginning with World War I, were heirs of Modernist poetry and of its high valuation of technical finish. Anybody's short list of that cohort would probably include the following:

1914   John Berryman, David Ignatow, Randall Jarrell, Weldon Kees, Dudley Randall, William Stafford
1915   Isabella Gardner, Ruth Stone, Margaret Walker
1916   John Malcolm Brinnin, Theodore Weiss
1917   Robert Lowell, Gwendolyn Brooks
1919   Robert Duncan, Lawrence Ferlinghetti, Edwin Honig, William Meredith, May Swenson
1920   Howard Nemerov, Amy Clampitt
1921   Richard Wilbur
1922   Howard Moss
1923   James Dickey, James Emanuel, Mari Evans, Alan Dugan, Anthony Hecht, Richard Hugo, Denise Levertov, John Logan, James Schuyler, Louis Simpson
1924   Edgar Bowers, Edward Field, Lucien Stryk
1925   Donald Justice, Carolyn Kizer, Kenneth Koch, Maxine Kumin, Jack Spicer, Gerald Stern
1926   A. R. Ammons, Paul Blackburn, Robert Bly, Robert Creeley, Allen Ginsberg, James Merrill, Frank O'Hara, W. D. Snodgrass, David Wagoner

1927   John Ashbery, Paul Carroll, Galway Kinnell, W. S. Merwin,
        James Wright
1928   Maya Angelou, Peter Davison, Donald Hall, Philip
        Levine, Anne Sexton
1929   Edward Dorn, Thom Gunn, John Hollander,
        Richard Howard, Adrienne Rich
1930   Gregory Corso, Joel Oppenheimer, Gary Snyder
1931   Jerome Rothenberg, George Starbuck
1932   Allen Grossman, Michael McClure, Linda Pastan,
        Sylvia Plath
1933   Etheridge Knight
1934   LeRoi Jones/Imamu Amiri Baraka, Ted Berrigan,
        Audre Lorde, Sonia Sanchez, Mark Strand

By 1959 the last High Modernist poets were dead or dying, and dying, too, was their influence on the idea of the poet's role in culture. As the poet Allen Grossman put it, the High Modern poets had "used up the idea of greatness" or compromised it by ideas about civilization that were appallingly consistent with the human abuses perpetrated by World War II. Modernist aesthetic values held strong in academic criticism, however, having been displaced into what was called the New Criticism. Its principal tenets were that valid interpretations had to avoid the Intentional Fallacy—searching for presumed intentions of the author—and the Affective Fallacy—crediting emotional effects produced in the reader. To arrive at correct or "universal" meanings the reader had to approach the poem as an ahistorical, self-enclosed system, an object made of language: in the words of its major theorists, Monroe Bearsley and W. K. Wimsatt, "a verbal icon." All of the poets listed above served apprenticeships in the formalist techniques to which New Critical principles were the analytical antiphon, and some continued to write traditional verse, distinguishing themselves, as poets always have, by the skill of making room in the tradition for a voice distinctly their own. As Robert Lowell observed, "Poets of my generation . . . write a very musical, difficult poem with tremendous skill, perhaps there's never been such skill." Berryman, Stafford, Weiss, Swenson, Nemerov, Wilbur, Moss, Hecht, Bowers, Justice, Wagoner, Merwin, Gunn, Hollander, Rich, and Strand were among the most accomplished poets of this sort.

But during the late 1950s and throughout the 1960s some members of their generation went on—in some poems—to oppose formalism, devising ways to readmit both Intention and Affect to the discussion of poetic value. The most important pathbreaker out of academic formalism was Allen Ginsberg's *Howl* (1956). Ginsberg adapted the comic and incantatory rhythms of Whitman to write long-line free-verse invective against the horror of living in money-mad postwar atomic age America. *Beat* was the term proposed by Ginsberg's pal Jack Kerouac to account for this poetic. Beat poetry was visionary ("Beatific"), rhythmically "hip" to the beat of jazz, and disaffected, antibourgeois. It described a decadent way of life shared by poet friends of Ginsberg and Kerouac in San Francisco and New York: Lawrence Ferlinghetti, Jack Spicer, Paul Blackburn, Robert Creeley, LeRoi Jones, Gregory Corso, Michael McClure. Their poetry was not taken seriously by contemporary academic critics, but its accessible, rebellious, shocking subject matter attracted mass audiences.

Beat poetry, however, proposed no changes in material social conditions. *That* poetic project was undertaken, eventually, by the artistic wings of two progressive political movements: black civil rights, and women's liberation. By the mid-sixties the poets of a New Black Aesthetic—prominently, Gwendolyn Brooks, Maya Angelou, Etheridge Knight, Audrey Lorde, LeRoi Jones/Amiri Baraka—were defying the precepts of New Critical universalism by making African American difference the subject of the poem itself: are you or are you not a Brother, *mon semblable*? Establishing the reader's cultural relation to the first-person speaker was often the entire point of the poem: a "universal" reader cannot *be*. A similar artistic impulse motivated the women—mainly white women—who began writing women into poetry as makers and readers. Swenson, Kizer, Kumin, Sexton, Rich, and Plath were among the first to evoke in their women-centered poems the definitive ways that gender difference shapes the social experience of persons, and inescapably situates readers in a gendered position vis-à-vis the poetic text.

Confessional poetry was not overtly political, but it participated in the protest against Impersonality as a poetic value by reinstating an insistently autobiographical first person engaged in resistance to the pressure to conform. The most distinctive confessional poems located the pressure in family life, specifically in the relations of parents and children. Once the label gained currency it was applied to a number of poets, though indeed it was a term more properly applied to certain poems published in a handful of books that appeared between 1959–1966: in addition to Robert Lowell's *Life Studies* these were W. D. Snodgrass's *Heart's Needle* (1960), Anne Sexton's *To Bedlam and Part Way Back* (1960) and *All My Pretty Ones* (1962), and Sylvia Plath's *Ariel* (London, 1965; New York, 1966). The work was technically proficient, like the best academic work of the day, but its subject matter made critics publically recoil. M. L. Rosenthal set the tone in a review of *Life Studies* for the *Nation*: "It is hard not to think of *Life Studies* as a series of personal confidences, rather shameful, that one is honor-bound not to reveal." Especially troubled by Lowell's "public discrediting of his father's manliness and character" in this book, Rosenthal, applying a core New Critical concept, condemned the autobiographical work as "impure art"—"magnificently stated but unpleasantly egocentric." Lowell, at forty-two, was one of the few poets of whom the nation took much notice, so this perceived artistic misdirection mattered. Other poets would also sometimes be reviewed as confessional: John Berryman, Randall Jarrell, Weldon Kees, Richard Hugo, James Merrill, and—from a slightly earlier generation—Theodore Roethke. But the quartet of Lowell, Snodgrass, Sexton, and Plath that Oates singled out provides the type.

What they had in common were several definitive social conditions. First, they had developed close personal affiliations. Lowell was the teacher and mentor of Snodgrass, Sexton, and Plath, who also knew each other's work very well. Second, they had all been through psychological breakdowns and treatment, following rather early marriages. Third, all four poets had become parents—of daughters, as it happens—not long before writing their confessional poems. Finally, they understood the dynamics of family life in terms of Freudian psychoanalysis. Their confessional poetry investigates the pressures on the family as an institution regulating middle-class private life, primarily through the agency of the mother. Its principal themes are divorce, sexual infidelity, childhood neglect, and the mental disorders that follow from deep emotional wounds received in early life. A confessional poem contains a first-person speaker, "I," and always seems to refer to a real person in whose actual life real episodes have occurred that cause actual pain, all represented in the poem.

Life Studies—written between 1954–1959—issued from a period of jolts in Robert Lowell's life: his father died in 1950, his mother in 1954; he had two severe recurrences of manic-depressive illness, in 1952, and in 1954 immediately following his mother's death; and he became a father in 1957. *Life Studies* drew its themes from these experiences: midlife scrutiny of ancestors, disappointment by parents, the formative imprint of childhood traumas.

Lowell had established a reputation as a skilled formalist in the two books that preceded *Life Studies*, but while on a reading tour of the West Coast in 1957 had discovered that even *he* couldn't understand his old poems while reciting them to audiences: his syntax was too dense, his method too allusive. Noting the contrast between his effectiveness and that of Allen Ginsberg and Dylan Thomas, Lowell formed a new goal for his poetics: "to write poems as pliant as conversation, so clear a listener might get every word." Yet, as he told William Carlos Williams, he wanted nonetheless to write poetry that retained the "carpentry of definite meter that tells me when to stop rambling." The poetics he developed for *Life Studies* permitted a proselike flow of reminiscence with movement in and out of meter and rhyme. He began drafting new work in prose, versifying it later. Technical complexity was meant to be the partner of plainspeaking in *Life Studies*; Lowell wanted nothing to "ruin the honesty of sentiment" and the directness possible in prose.

Life Studies was deeply personal: in part a book of elegies. Its centerpiece was a prose memoir of his family, "91 Revere Street," that grounded the confessional poems in an explanatory narrative focused with relentless disdain on his father. In both the poetry and prose of *Life Studies* Lowell's witty, scathing portraiture of his "unmasterful" father is placed in relief by memories of Grandfather Winslow, his mother's father, mourned as "all I could ever want to be: the bad boy, the problem child, the commodore of his household." After his father's death Lowell, who had been undergoing psychoanalysis off and on for many years, began reading Freud voraciously; "Every fault is a goldmine of discoveries," he reported. "I am a walking goldmine." The contrast between the father figures in "91 Revere Street" is self-consciously Freudian, framed to position his mother as the object of an oedipal struggle in the generation preceding him, whose consequences have deformed his own psyche. Notably the idealized figure of Grandfather

Winslow is troped as a naughty *boy*: neither branch of the family tree produces "real" men, only one or another version of domestication by strong women.

The advent of fatherhood released many of the splendors of *Life Studies:* in January 1957 Harriet Winslow Lowell was born to Elizabeth Hardwick and Robert Lowell. Preoccupied with family and lineage, Lowell begain writing her into the book—perhaps under the influence of his brilliant students W. D. Snodgrass and Anne Sexton. Two poems ("During Fever" and "Home After Three Months Away") focused on this baby daughter and inevitably lead back into the subject that motivates all of the confessional poems in *Life Studies*: the problem of Lowell's unresolved oedipal rage. "During Fever" begins in sympathy: "my daughter in fever / flounders in her chicken-colored sleeping bag. / 'Sorry,' she mumbles like her dim-bulb father, 'sorry.' / / Mother! Mother!" The naming, "father," produces a stanza break and a guilty memory of scoffing with his mother at his own ineffectual father. The irruption of recall—"Mother!"—inaugurates a dizzying number of elided identifications: mother is regressed back to daughter of a guardian father who blocks her from suitors. The poem never returns to the sick baby daughter but dreamlike stays fixed in Lilliputian fury, apostrophizing a distant Mother whose desire is invariably fixed on an inappropriate object: "Mother, you smile / as if you saw your Father / inches away yet hidden." The poem tries to diffuse this memory of Grandfather Winslow with a joke about a "Freudian papá." But a peculiar lack of conceptual closure in the poem points to an unbearable identification, Lowell's daughter with Lowell's mother as the fearsome female creature who instinctively ("Sorry") engulfs and emasculates the men around her. He sees it coming—backward.

Lowell's other poem in *Life Studies* about his daughter is equally surreal in its technique, slipping inexplicably from one vivid image to another along the logic of a dream. "Home After Three Months Away" commemorates the babyhood that passed while the father absented himself in a mental hospital, returning "frizzled, stale and small" while the baby has bloomed: "Dimpled with exaltation, / my daughter holds her levee in the tub. / Our noses rub. / Each of us pats a stringy lock of hair— / they tell me nothing's gone." But something *feels* gone: subtracted from him, added to her. "When / we dress her in sky-blue corduroy, / she changes to a boy." In this low-key poem of convalescence the sense of shrinkage is displaced everywhere: glancing out the window, Lowell sees the pedigreed spring tulips flattened by snow, and this too seems emblematic of his own losses: "I keep no rank or station." In this phase of his life studies Lowell finds everywhere the repeating pattern of damage to masculinity that domestic life exacts through daughters. Sovereignty, rank station is hers (the levee in the tub); he is resigned, even grateful, to be "cured."

Lowell's confidence in this revelatory mode of writing about family life had been strengthened by meeting up with Snodgrass's "Heart's Needle" in the pages of an anthology, *The New Poets of England and America*, that caused a great stir when it appeared in the fall of 1957. Though the term *confessional* was first applied to Lowell's poetry, Lowell himself credited the example of W. D. Snodgrass's poem "Heart's Needle." Snodgrass, a returning veteran of World War II, had been Lowell's student at the University of Iowa writer's workshop during Lowell's stints of teaching there in 1950 and again in 1953. Lowell kept a rather paternal teacherly eye on him—in Lowell's case this would always be a rivalrous eye—and was thus more than usually interested in Snodgrass's accomplishments.

"Heart's Needle" is a narrative in ten poems about the breakup of the speaker's marriage, balancing images of the Korean War, begun the winter of his daughter's birth, against images of caretaking. The context of the cold war functions to illuminate the plight of loveless men doomed to banishment and violence and useless labor. The war exists in the poems as evidence for the failure of a masculine ethos; the divorced father feels as helpless and lonely as the soldiers freezing in a foreign country, longing for home: "I've gone / As men must."

The emotional center of the sequence is the claim the speaker makes to his daughter that "I am your real mother." Discharged from the armed services and from marriage at the same time, the speaker seizes the opportunity to remake his social identity through relation to his child. He wishes most to divest himself of old notions of manhood that underlie the will to make war. "Like the cold men of Rome, / we have won costly fields to sow / in salt, our only seed. / Nothing but injury will grow" in the space between himself and his former world, his former wife. To the conventions of masculinity prevailing in the cold war era "Heart's Needle" opposes a dialogic human relation dependent on cycles of visitation. In the seventh poem of the sequence he finds a resolving trope for relationship: a playground swing. "You keep my constant time / to bob in blue July / where fat goldfinches fly / over the glittering, fecund / reach of our growing lands. / Once more now, this second, / I hold you in my hands."

In Lowell's poems to his daughter the speaker is enfeebled by fatherhood. In contrast, Snodgrass's speaker is authorized by his caretaking role; it restores his manhood without putting him at sexual risk or in competition with other males. Notably, this speaker does not measure his masculinity against family models. There are no other fathers in the poem he addresses to his daughter: her sheer animal existence provides his chance to gestate a fatherhood in response. Snodgrass displaced into natural imagery the erotic components of this bond, and diffused its pressures by designing into the relationship a periodicity of absence and return.

Though Lowell paid sincere tribute to Snodgrass's model, his own confessional poetry confronted directly and through a Freudian paradigm the complex libidinous connections between fathers and daughters that are elided in "Heart's Needle." Moreover, the confessional poetry Lowell wrote mattered more to critics who were attempting to evaluate this kind of work, because of the cultural meanings that had already accrued to the name *Lowell* before he received it. ("He is, after all, a *Lowell*," Rosenthal protested in his review of *Life Studies*.) Lowell's patrimony held for him the cultural resonance of an older order of things, in which, being the only child, the son and heir, his masculine identity should have been secured at birth. His youthful rebellions—as a boarding school tyrant, as a Harvard drop-out who went South to complete a splendid education, as a renegade Episcopalian who briefly but fiercely adopted the Catholic faith—tested not so much what kind of man he was going to be but what kind of Lowell he was going to be. More: what kind of poet named Lowell he was going to be—James Russell Lowell and Amy Lowell having already pressed the family signet deep into the wax of American poetry. In *Life Studies* Lowell broke new ground by finding a way to make the self-reflexive gaze both personal and cultural. His name, his technical mastery, and the shock of his subject matter all worked together to elicit from critics a revisionary look at the limitations of New Critical standards when confronted by the firmness of artistic purpose conveyed by *Life Studies*. It was Lowell's pedigree that gave rank and station to confessional poetry as a genre. It was the stance of painful truth-telling about the instability of gender identity that provided the model.

For the women poets, predictably, the institution of family had other meanings than the continuity of a name or a patrimony. As mothers who were poets, poets who were mothers, Sexton and Plath introduced into thinking about poetry a deconstruction of the core of male-oriented concepts of poetic inspiration that characterized High Modernism. In the culture as Sexton and Plath received it two obstacles in particular stood in the way of women's acquisition of poetic authority. One was the belief that, for one reason or another—by nature or through culture—women lacked the cognitive powers required for the production of serious art. The other obstacle was the female body, objectified in poetry as Woman: the site of Man's mythic connection to the largesse of Nature, and the source of his distraction from the work of civilization.

The poetry written by Sexton and Plath attempts the construction of a poetics from within the woman's position. It dismantles the cultural icon of the idealized and despised Freudian Mother to reveal the mere woman occluded by projections. And it retrieves the female body, particularly the female breast, from objectification by the male gaze, reconfiguring it as a principle of connection both physical and cultural in the scheme of generation.

Anne Sexton began writing poetry in 1957, when she was twenty-nine years old, during recovery from a mental breakdown. While she was separated from her children her doctor prescribed writing as a form of psychotherapy. Sexton quickly discovered and then developed an impressive talent. A resident of the Boston area, she joined Robert Lowell's graduate poetry seminar at Boston University in 1958, after spending a week under the tutelage of W. D. Snodgrass in an intensive writing workshop at the Antioch Writer's Program the preceding summer.

One of the poems Sexton worked on in Lowell's class was "The Double Image," a long autobiographical poem addressed to her younger daughter, Joy, that dealt with the circumstances of their separation through Sexton's mental illness. Modeled on Snodgrass's "Heart's Needle" (from which it borrows a few rhymes, too) the poem summarizes the breakdown, suicide attempts, and serial hospitalizations that underlay Sexton's development as a poet and that divested her of motherhood during the first three years of Joy's life. Within the narrative, autobiographical line of the poem is a second network of meaning that broadens its reference to the field of feminine psychology. Sexton commented on this larger set of meanings herself. "The mother-daughter relationship is more poignant than Romeo and Juliet," she observed, "just as Oedipus is more interesting." The intense attachment of infant to mother underlies all of these relations; in the Freudian paradigm, successful development requires that the female child repress and redirect the prolonged erotic attachment to the mother ("my overthrown / love, my first image"), replacing Mother and Daughter eventually with a heterosexual attachment founded on erotic bonding with Father. The loss of a girl's earliest love image is presumably "more poignant" because it cannot be avoided. But "The Double Image" gives the story another twist, by seeing through "mother" as a social construction.

The poem is an analysis of the resistance by means of illness to the feminine roles available to women, figured in the poem's title. The "double image" is the outcome of the socialization process that makes the daughter into a "restyled" version of her mother, a reproduction that cancels possibility. "This is the cave of the mirror," Sexton writes, "that double woman who stares / at herself, as if she were petrified." The poem shows the ways that feminine socialization places the mother and daughter in a hall of mirrors where authentic individuation occurs with the greatest difficulty.

A central trope in the poem is the mother's breast as a gift that can be withheld as well as offered. The two generations of mother/daughter pairs are configured as ill and well in terms of relation to the breast. The speaker's mother renounces her in the middle of the poem: " . . . she looked at me / and said I gave her cancer. / They carved her sweet hills out / and still I couldn't answer." The daughter's previous "answer" has been regression through mental illness to an imperfectly infantile state of dependency. Now life has offered her a temptation to assume the mother-role in turn. "You came like an awkward guest / that first time, all wrapped and moist / and strange at my heavy breast," the speaker says to her own daughter. "I needed you. I didn't want a boy." The rhyme-word in this stanza, significantly, is "Joy"—the state of mind the speaker deludedly hopes to produce in herself by assigning it to her own potential "double." Drawing back from the vertigo of mother/daughter identifications, the speaker arrives at a saving clarity: "This was my worst guilt; you could not cure / nor soothe it. I made you to find me." The poem culminates in this protest against the notion of the mother-role as a naturally occurring moral relation.

"The Double Image" is not manifestly about the making of a poet. But Sexton fit this separation story into a larger frame in "The Fortress," her central poem on the poetics of the mother-daughter bond. It was written for presentation at the Radcliffe Institute in 1962 to a group of women scholars and artists.

"The Fortress (while taking a nap with Linda)" is a dramatic monologue addressed by a mother to a young daughter, making images from what they can see out the window. "Outside, the bittersweet turns orange. / Before she died, my mother and I picked those fat / branches, finding orange nipples / on the gray wire strands." The bittersweet of memory colors the poem, for "The Fortress" has to do with dangerous hidden connections between mother and daughter. "I press down my index finger— / half in jest, half in dread— / on the brown mole / under your left eye, inherited / from my right cheek: a spot of danger." The poem balances images of the body's mortality against the transformative power of image-making that enables the "finding" of "nipples." This skill cannot be inherited because it is not of the body, but it can be taught to a daughter as a gift that combats death. "The Double Image" expresses hope of becoming a "good" mother: protective, nurturing, responsible; but the symbol of the double image strongly implies that the daughter is doomed to replicate the mother's failures. In "The Fortress," addressed by Anne Gray Harvey Sexton to her older daughter, Linda Gray Sexton, the poet acknowledges the writerly legacy in her mother's family, encoded in the name Gray (which was also part of her mother's name): the "gray strand" that binds the generations in the realm of symbolisms. Death undoes the mother's breast, but its permanent influence inhabits a multiplicity of metaphors.

Taken together, Sexton's poems propose a most un-Freudian resolution of the oedipal struggle by which the daughter gains from the mother the power of image-making. The daughter's task, the opposite of the task of Oedipus, is to find the adult woman concealed within the overwhelming presence of the mother. The demystification of the mother permits the exchange of the breast by other means: language, the voice, the spoken word. And, indeed, Sexton went on to develop two talents as a poet: forming acoustically complex stanzas and performing them. Moreover, Sexton's performances put her body onstage in a manner foundational to the poetics of female performance art during the 1970s and 1980s. Sexton read her confessional poems as if they were scripts, not speech: she was the polished, urbane, well-rehearsed medium of emotions that had come from somewhere else. By the mid-1960s she had organized what she called a "chamber rock" group to perform her poems to music. Her freedom as an actress may have been linked to her mental illness; Sexton was in awe of the workings of unconscious processes and recognized the ways they entered into the making of poetry. She also recognized that it was only when a poem engaged the unconscious of an auditor that a deep response was possible.

The career of Anne Sexton was linked to that of Sylvia Plath in 1959, when Plath joined Sexton in Robert Lowell's seminar at Boston University. The women became friends after Lowell began comparing them as poets. The works often singled out as "confessional" in Sylvia Plath's oeuvre are "Lady Lazarus" and "Daddy": the former as an apparent forecast of Plath's suicide, the latter because it seems to articulate a link between the poet's loss of her father in childhood and her catastrophic abandonment by her husband after the birth of their second child. A good case can be made, though, for poems that make symbolic use of her children as Plath's most original contribution to confessional poetry: "Morning Song" and "Ariel" in particular.

"Morning Song" recreates the psychological resistances through which a postpartum woman moves toward forming an emotional and moral bond with her infant. "Love set you going like a fat gold watch," the poem begins, "and your bald cry / Took its place among the elements." The baby's hunger and rage resonate in the poem with the mother's fear of "effacement"—a word that occurs often in Plath's poetry. A metaphoric thread woven through the poem permits a denouement of delayed maternal attachment in the poem's last stanza: the infant's "bald cry" in stanza 1 repeats in stanza 5, where the infant mouth "opens clean as a cat's" to take the mother's breastmilk. "One cry, and I stumble from bed, cow-heavy": the mother's unwilled, instinctual response through her body leads on to another connection: "and now you try / Your handful of notes; / The clear vowels rise like balloons." Vowels make syllables distinct from one another and are the building blocks of communication: where cry was, there language shall be. The mother responds to the baby's contented postfeeding babble with a flow of interpretive acknowledgment: a transfer of the maternal nurture from nature to culture. Plath's poem makes of motherhood not a biological relation but a social relation engaged first through the body but crucially renegotiated in the realm of language.

In this Plath was very radical, and she took poetry with her. "Morning Song," the poem that opens the volume *Ariel*, establishes a new analogue between poetry and creativity, a wholly feminine analogue. Human identity is not one of the "elements"—an interpretation proposed in the first stanza. By the end of the poem, humanity has been *conferred*, in a dialogue that begins with the infant's address to the mother's body through a cry, and that body's recognition of the infant's message as a message. The poem shows how the semiotic powers evolve in dialogue with the mother's body; the infant's separation has been accomplished with a cry that situates its being, and motherhood is troped as the reengagement enabled by separation. At the poem's ending night has been swallowed, the vowels rise.

Plath's "Ariel"—another morning song—reverses this trajectory: "The child's cry / / Melts in the wall. / And I / Am the arrow / / The dew that flies / Suicidal, at one with the drive / Into the red / Eye, the cauldron of morning." Mastery is troped as the forceful, willed withdrawal of energy from "dead stringencies," specifically as a withdrawal of mother's attention from child's demand and from all else that impedes concentration. The forceful ending symbolism of "Ariel" proposes immolation as a consequence of such flight, but it is blissfully embraced; "suicidal" cannot mean a depressive death wish such as the woman herself appears to have suffered at the end of her life. What must be extinguished for the moment is a sense of self as beholden to the natural and social claims of the mother's role. Stripped of distractions, the poet's "I" grows one with "the cauldron of morning," the place of ecstatic singularity, the cookpot of poetry.

"Ariel" contains in a sense a Romantic poetic in asserting solitude and self-transcendence as the ground of poetic activity, but it may be read with "Morning Song" as one of a pair of poems that together exemplify the woman poet's specific and dangerous relation to the demands of inhabiting a female body claimed by others for nurture. In these poems the Romantic poetic is adapted to the context of the life circumstances of an adult woman. The trope of connection is breastmilk, the paradigms are attachment and separation within the human world of symbolic making.

The confessional poetry of Plath and Sexton opened the way for the woman-centered poetry of the 1970s, but it would have been impermissible without the models provided by Lowell in emulation of Snodgrass. In homage that was possibly unconscious the poetry of both Plath and Sexton recirculates a number of Lowell's phrasings. Lowell's image in "For the Union Dead" (written by June 1960)—"the drained faces of Negro children rise like balloons"—resurfaces in Plath's "Morning Song" (written February 1961): "The clear vowels rise like balloons"; while a phrase from Lowell's boyhood recollections in "My Last Afternoon with Uncle Devereux Winslow" ("What in the world was I wishing?") echoes in poems by Anne Sexton written in the early 1960s: "What could I have been dreaming as I sat there" ("The Double Image"); "Child, / what are you wishing?" ("The Fortress"). When Plath was asked in an interview for the BBC to evaluate the influence of Robert Lowell's class on her development as a poet, she designated his "breakthrough into very serious, very personal emotional experience which I feel has been partly taboo." Plath singled out as equally important the model of Anne Sexton, whose writing "as a young mother" she also viewed as experience that had previously been "partly taboo."

The emphasis on decorum, or of breaking taboos in the case of confessional poets, can hardly be understood, however, without reference to the ethos of the cold war years, during which decorum developed extreme political significance. The House Unamerican Activities Committee, formed in 1938 to promote "internal security," went into high gear following World War II in attempts to identify and weed out communists in public life. Under the leadership of J. Edgar Hoover the FBI established in 1945 a Custodial Detention Program for emergency use in case of an attack by the Soviet Union; compiling lists of those to be arrested and detained formed a major part of the bureau's work during the 1950s. During the Eisenhower presidency, under pressure from Hoover, government employees of many kinds were required to swear a loyalty oath; this included employees of many institutions of higher learning.

Hoover believed strongly that the key to internal security was the institution of the family. Hoover's biographer, Richard Gid Powers, notes that throughout his long career Hoover preached the gospel that the early formation of character was the responsibility of the parents in the home. "When the home is destroyed, everything in our civilization crashes to its doom," he told a graduating law school class. And those principally responsible were fathers. Hoover, a bachelor himself, saw the "virile leadership" that fathers could offer in their communities as crucial to the development of strong citizenship in their sons: the answer both to crime and to soft attitudes toward communism. In the interest of deterrence, ordinary citizens were encouraged to keep an eye on their neighbors and report deviant behavior or suspicious activity to the FBI. Family and security were ideologically linked.

During the same era thousands of American homes were invaded by another influence: television technology. Programs that gained mass audiences were frequently comic representations of the vicissitudes of family life: "The Honeymooners," "I Love Lucy," "Father Knows Best." Their plots deployed extreme stereotypes of the American Mom against whom men struggled to maintain control and assert authority in the home. Sex was unmentionable on TV, but outrageous cross-dressing was a frequent device, frustrated male rage a common frisson in the story line. Like confessional poetry, the fifties sit-com was a showcase for anxiety about what a later age would label "gender malad-justment": women farcically pushing male dominance to the point of collapse, until put back in their place.

The confessional poems of all four of these poets participated in the concerns with social hygiene that inflected popular culture. Confessional poets wrote about the instability of the institution of the family from the inside, and in analytical language partially supplied by psychoanalysis. They conducted their poetic scrutiny of parent-child relations in a manner licensed by psychoanalytic theories regarding the formation of significant memories in early life, looking to childhood as the era when the elders hold unassailable authority and the value of one's individual life is assigned by the terms on which love is bestowed and withheld by Mother and Father. The sphere of this psychosocial formation is the middle-class home, its bedrooms, bathrooms, and staircases, its kitchens. The structure of the confessional poem, whether technically formal or free, juxtaposes moments drawn from common life in a manner that invites the psychoanalyst's approach to dreams. Manifestly ordinary and accessible, the images of the confessional poem encode the whole culture's shame-making machinery.

Confession has a double meaning, however. On the one hand, confession is an act of expiation for sins, one that restores the shriven person to membership in a community of the like-minded. Contemporary reviewers explained confessional poems as acts of self-accusation performed in public by poets as a way of accounting for their nonconformism to American ideals. The gifted daughters were viewed as doomed to womanly unfulfillment; their suicides made the case incontestable. The gifted sons were praised for acts of repatriation through self-surveillance: in the same year that Snodgrass's *Heart's Needle* won the Pulitzer Prize, *Life Studies* won the National Book Award—the most public prizes awarded to poets, and recognition of the closest thing to popular appeal that books of poems can achieve.

But an older usage links confession to a quite different meaning: the public avowal of a point of view, as in the confession of faith. The faith affirmed in confessional poetry is Freudian, secular, and critical; Robert Lowell reduced the formula to eight syllables, two lines, a faltering rhyme: "a father's no shield / for his child." Confessional poems sought to expose the poverty of the ideology of the family that dominated postwar culture and to draw poetic truth from the actual pain given and taken in the context of family life, especially as experienced by children. During the 1960s and 1970s "The personal is political" became a slogan of progressive politics, and madness was glorified in some quarters as a mode of resistance to repressive socialization. The confessional poets had been there first, in their own spaceships and time machines. In all ways fit matter for a capsule on the moon.

Diane Wood Middlebrook

Further Reading

Conte, Joseph. *Unending Design: The Forms of Postmodern Poetry.* Ithaca: Cornell University Press, 1991.

Halliday, Mark, ed. *Against Our Vanishing: Winter Conversations with Allen Grossman on the Theory and Practice of Poetry.* Boston: Rowan Tree, 1981.

Hamilton, Ian. *Robert Lowell: A Biography.* New York: Random House, 1982.

Lowell, Robert. *Collected Prose.* Ed. Robert Giroux. New York: Farrar, Straus and Giroux, 1987.

———— *Life Studies and For the Union Dead.* New York: Farrar, Straus and Giroux, 1964.

Ostriker, Alicia. *Writing Like a Woman.* Ann Arbor: University of Michigan Press, 1983.

Perloff, Marjorie. *Poetic License: Essays on Modernist and Postmodernist Lyric.* Evanston: Illinois University Press, 1990.

Plath, Sylvia. *The Collected Poems.* Ed. Ted Hughes. New York: Harper and Row, 1981.

Powers, Richard Gid. *Secrecy and Power: The Life of J. Edgar Hoover.* New York: Free Press, 1987.

Rosenthal, M. L. *The Modern Poets: A Critical Introduction.* New York: Oxford University Press, 1960.

Sexton, Anne. *The Complete Poems.* Boston: Houghton Mifflin, 1981.

Snodgrass, W. D. *Selected Poems, 1957–1987.* New York: Soho Press, 1991.

Von Hallberg, Robert. *American Poetry and Culture, 1945–1980.* Cambridge: Harvard University Press, 1985.

Wimsatt, W. K. *The Verbal Icon: Studies in the Meaning of Poetry.* New York: Noonday, 1954.

The Postconfessional Lyric

A LTHOUGH the postconfessional lyric, as its name implies, comes into its own in the second half of the twentieth century, it is a variant on the autobiographical dramatic lyric. Many of the best and strongest American poems are in this mode. It is, in fact, one of the main threads of American poetry, running from Anne Bradstreet to Louise Glück.

When in 1840 Alexis de Tocqueville considered the prospects for important American poetry, he professed himself skeptical since "the language, the dress, and the daily actions of men in democracies are repugnant to conceptions of the ideal," and the purpose of poetry was just such a "search after and delineation of the Ideal." But the astute Frenchman goes on to propose that the ideal might have a more local habitation in democratic climes: "I need not traverse earth and sky to discover a wondrous object woven of contrast, of infinite greatness and littleness, of intense gloom and amazing brightness, capable at once of exciting pity, admiration, terror, contempt. I have only to look at myself." American poets who do so will, he predicts, "enlarge and throw light on some of the obscurer recesses of the human heart."

In some sense de Tocqueville is simply asserting that America is the right place for Romanticism to prosper, the proper home for the Romantic lyric of the self. If de Tocqueville imagines his poet *looking in* to the self in order to speak, then Thoreau, on the opening page of *Walden*, demands that speech emanate *out* from that same self:

In most books, the "I," or first person, is omitted; in this it will be retained; that, in respect to egotism, is the main difference. We commonly do not remember that it is, after all, always the first person that is speaking. I should not talk so much about myself if there were anybody else whom I knew as well. Unfortunately, I am confined to this theme by the narrowness of my experience.

Although Thoreau is urging a moral imperative of authenticity, he blends it with ironic humor. No such detachment is available to Whitman, in whose poems the ethos and aesthetics of self-revelation take on a passionate earnestness. Though the precise content of Whitman's "confession" is elusive, his claim for the centrality of self-revelation to his work is so emphatic in the poem "Trickle Drops" (from "Calamus") that it can be said to be the poem that establishes the confessional mode in American poetry:

> Trickle drops! my blue veins leaving!
> O drops of me! trickle, slow drops,
> Candid from me falling, drip, bleeding drops,
> From wounds made to free you whence you were prison'd,
> From my face, from my forehead and lips,
> From my breast, from within where I was concealed, press
>   forth red drops, confession drops,
> Stain every page, stain every song I sing, every word
>   I say, bloody drops,
> Let them know your scarlet heat, let them glisten,
> Saturate them with yourself all ashamed and wet,
> Glow upon all I have written or shall write,
>   bleeding drops,
> Let it all be seen in your light, blushing drops.

By the same token, Emily Dickinson, the other great American poet of the nineteenth century, also gives us important poems in her own version of the personal lyric centered in urgent autobiography. In the poem "I cannot live with you" readers don't need to know who Dickinson's "you" is. What is needed of biography is set forth and established in the poem itself as dramatic context.

In following the thread of the poem of self in American poetry, I must note that the American High Moderns (Pound, post-Prufrock Eliot, Stevens) are not part of the story. They are, in fact, an aberration from the American theme. Their very "height"—their interest in grand schemes, their rejection of Romanticism, their interest in the impersonal and the "carved"— all these led them away from the personal lyric and the autobiographical mode.

A preference for system over self distinguishes both Pound and Eliot. Even Stevens's self is abstract and impersonal—not one Thoreau would have recognized. From the perspective of American individualism, the great system makers proved to be out of touch with the realities of the twentieth century—rigid in their systems, cold and distant from the human fates being suffered around them. Some of them seem indifferent (Stevens), others actively identified with the century's transpersonal destructive forces (Pound's fascism, Eliot's reactionary politics and anti-Semitism), perceiving them as forces of "order."

I would also like to consider the connection between Pound's and Eliot's expatriation and their susceptibility to the abstraction of system making. Even Stevens, who evolves a system of the sublime Self, was an internal exile. In contrast, one thinks of the one major American poet of that generation who resisted both the charms of Europe and the charms of system, William Carlos Williams. Williams knew full well that his resistance to ideology and abstract schemes was a positive consequence of his commitment to the local, to what someone living in a particular place, among its people, might see and say.

Perhaps de Tocqueville is right when he says the people in democratic nations are "excited in reality only by a survey of themselves." Perhaps this naive egoism explains in part how the confessionals came to reject the grand and inhuman schemes of Pound, Eliot, and Stevens and instead returned American poetry to an individual scale, a poetry of the self.

In such works as Snodgrass's *Heart's Needle* (1959), Robert Lowell's *Life Studies* (1959), Ginsberg's *Kaddish* (1961), Ann Sexton's *To Bedlam and Part Way Back* (1960), John Berryman's *77 Dream Songs* (1964), and Sylvia Plath's *Ariel* (1966), the confessionals injected into poetry an enormous intensity of self. Not only did the confessionals react against the system making of the High Moderns and reinstate the poetry of self but they also hauled in enormous and startling new areas of subject matter including madness, promiscuity, divorce, the violence of sexuality and relationships, alcoholism, women's rage against victimization, hymns to suicide, and unsentimentalized portraits of immediate family members.

All these new subjects were presented as personalized drama, all as implicit or explicit autobiographical encounter. When one considers that there was little precedent for ordering such volatile personal material in poetry, the genuine courage of the confessionals becomes apparent.

Who are the postconfessional lyric poets? The best way to understand them is in terms of three generational groupings emerging around roughly the same time (the sixties and early seventies), each with its characteristic concerns. The first group could be called the elders and includes the Randall Jarrell of *The Lost World* (1965), the Stanley Kunitz of *The Testing-Tree* (1973), and the Elizabeth Bishop of *Geography III* (1976). Alhough their authors were contemporaries and friends of a number of the original confessional poets, these books represent radical departures for their respective authors, departures that were a delayed and even a reluctant response to the example of the confessionals. Prior to this, these elders survived in part by keeping a real distance from autobiographical material. As a result of such distance from personal circumstance their early work can be chilly (Bishop), or somewhat mannered and obscure (Kunitz). Jarrell's personal concerns are typically deflected through personae in his earlier work. Nevertheless, late in their careers, these poets accepted the challenge to take more risks, to write closer to the bone.

At the same time a second, much younger group of poets was publishing important work in the postconfessional mode. This group includes James Wright, with *The Branch Shall Not Break* (1963) and *Shall We Gather at the River* (1968), Philip Levine, with *They Feed They Lion* (1972), and Adrienne Rich, with *The Dream of a Common Language* (1978). In addition, postconfessionalism can be seen to have affected other poets in this generation more peripherally.

Although the postconfessional influence in the youngest generational grouping is pervasive, certain books represented significant contributions to this generation's version of the postconfessional lyric. Among them were Frank Bidart's *Golden State* (1973), my own *Gathering the Bones Together* (1975), Louise Glück's *Descending Figure* (1980), and Sharon Olds's *The Living and the Dead* (1984). Using a variety of literary and psychological strategies, the youngest generation has assimilated the autobiographical encounter into the mainstream of

American poetry to such an extent that, thirty years after the confessionals, it is one of the dominant modes of writing.

There are two ways of exploring the relationship between the confessionals and the postconfessionals. The first stresses continuity and focuses on subject matter. According to this approach the postconfessionals are best understood as extending and expanding the implications of the original confessional enterprise. The second emphasizes transformation and focuses on how the postconfessionals bring lyric strategies to bear on autobiographical material. I will consider each approach in turn.

Both confessional and postconfessional poetries are solidly in that tradition by which poetry is seen to change through its desire and ability to incorporate new subject matter—hitherto unarticulated manifestations of disorder that it orders and thus restores to human meaning.

This is what Keats celebrated in Wordsworth's poetry and what he aspired to himself—a poetry "explorative of the dark passages" of human consciousness, one that "think[s] into the human heart" (letter of May 3, 1818). Shifting centuries and metaphors, I might also invoke Freud's dictum: "where id was, let ego be," with its accompanying metaphor (derived from Goethe's *Faust*) of the heroic struggle to claim land from the sea with dikes, dams, drainage—to explore, to reclaim. In this scheme of things, the poet is the person who assimilates new and previously taboo or unsayable material (either psychological or experiential) into that most irreducible and intense of encounters between the self and experience: the personal lyric.

Although the protagonist of confessional poems was occasionally a child, for the most part such topics as madness, alcohol, violence in marriage, and sexuality were dealt with from an adult viewpoint. By contrast, the elder group of postconfessionals oriented a number of their most powerful and important poems toward childhood and adolescence. In such poems as Jarrell's "The Lost World," Kunitz's "The Portrait," "The Testing-Tree," and "The Magic Curtain," and Elizabeth Bishop's "In the Waiting Room," they explored how a child feels, lives, survives; how a child interacts with parents and world in its struggle to assume an identity.

These reinhabited childhood memories are sometimes celebratory, as when the boy Kunitz sees, behind his solemn and preoccupied mother at the breakfast table, "Frieda with the yellow hair, / capricious keeper of the toast, / [who] buckled her knees, as if she'd lost / balance and platter, then winked at me, blue-eyed" ("The Magic Curtain"). Sometimes they are unsettling, as when Jarrell as a boy watches his grandmother enter a chicken coop: "She chooses one, / Comes out, and wrings its neck. The body hurls / Itself out—lunging, reeling" ("The Lost World"). Sometimes the memories are terrifying, as when the six-year-old Bishop experiences a kind of existential vertigo in a dentist's office: "The waiting room was bright / and too hot. It was sliding / beneath a big black wave, / another, and another" ("In the Waiting Room").

Of the three "elders" Stanley Kunitz is the only one who extensively explores the postconfessional lyric. But Kunitz occupies an even more peculiar position in relation to the autobiographical personal lyric. With his poem "Father and Son," published in 1934, Kunitz could well be said to be the progenitor of the confessional mode as well as his own precursor as a postconfessional lyric poet. "Father and Son" establishes itself as a dream poem in which the lyric protagonist pursues his dead father's fleeing ghost. The poem climaxes in the son's anguished pleading for guidance, only to have the ghost at last turn to him "the white ignorant hollow of his face." All the ingredients of a postconfessional lyric are present in this poem, although Kunitz is not yet ready to descend into the detail that will authenticate such encounters as autobiography. Nevertheless, "Father and Son" inspired other precursor autobiographical poems, such as Kunitz's friend Theodore Roethke's "The Lost Son" and poems in Lowell's *Life Studies*. Still, it wasn't until the poems of *The Testing-Tree* (1973), appearing when he was sixty-eight years old, that Kunitz firmly established his version of the autobiographical lyric. There, in such poems as "Journal for My Daughter," "Three Floors," "The Portrait," "Robin Redbreast," "River Road," "The Magic Curtain," and "The Testing-Tree," the postconfessional lyric received strong and varied expression. By then Kunitz had devised a strategy of "converting life into legend" that allowed him to be both autobiographical and impersonal. The life material that demanded such conversion centered in childhood trauma: the death by suicide of Kunitz's father while Kunitz was still in the womb (conflated for literary purposes and emotional truth with the later loss of a beloved step-father), a cold mother, and a pervading longing for the idealized father.

In such pivotal poems as "The Portrait" Kunitz was able to address these painful issues directly while simultaneously dramatizing the intense interactions of the family triad: "My mother never forgave my father / for killing himself / especially at such an awkward time / and in a public park / that spring / when I was waiting to be born." In "The Magic Curtain" the interaction of the child protagonist, the unresponsive mother, and a coquettish and friendly governess unfolds the "legend" of a boy arriving at affectionate and life-affirming attitudes despite a destructive mother. In the long title poem, "The Testing-Tree," the child protagonist seeks those spiritual principles he associates with his father in a wilderness that is both a scrub woods outside Worchester, Massachusetts and the Dark Woods of quest and myth. In that same poem the protagonist as adult must struggle with guilt about the father's death and must resist a destructiveness that characterizes both his family (the accusing mother) and the larger political landscape of this century ("That single Model A / sputtering up the grade / unfurled a highway behind / where the tanks maneuver, / revolving their turrets."). Again and again the poems of this volume are haunted by guilt, trauma, and impossible longing. Throughout there is an insistence on the way that past trauma persists and periodically asserts itself with great intensity in the life. The poem becomes the arena where the agon takes place—self wrestles its demons, seeking a difficult blessing and tenuous, passionate affirmations: "I dance, for the joy of surviving, / at the edge of the road."

Randall Jarrell's last book, *The Lost World* (1965), contains the ten-page title poem and "Thinking of the Lost World," Jarrell's first "factual autobiographical poems" (as his wife characterized them). Based on letters he had written his mother from California when he was twelve and staying with his grandparents, the title poem's three sections, set in the present tense, reinhabit an Edenic world. Its opening images establish the fusion of matter-of-fact and fantastical that characterize the poem: "On my way home I pass a cameraman / On a platform on the bumper of a car / Inside which, rolling and plunging, a comedian / Is working; on one white lot I see a star / Stumble to her igloo through the howling gale / Of the wind machines. On Melrose a dinosaur / And pterodactyl . . . look over the fence / Of *The Lost World*." The poem's child protagonist moves through a complex world of grandparents, great-grandmother, and a mysterious aunt ("young, tall, brown"), vaguely aware of desires, acutely aware of pleasures and apocalyptic fears.

"Thinking of *The Lost World*" draws on the same imagery and incidents as the title poem but involves an adult self going back à la Proust: "Swallowing that spoonful (of chocolate tapioca), I have already traveled / Through time to my childhood." In his longing for the lost objects and lost loved ones ("All of them are gone / Except for me; and for me nothing is gone—"), the poet arrived at a kind of visionary desolation, which, paradoxically, he calls happiness. The incantatory repetitions of negative absolutes with which the poem ends ("nothing" and "nowhere") are reminiscent of the conclusion of his early poem "90 North" (1942), but where the earlier poem's concluding repetitions of "nothing" and "pain" conjure an apocalyptic ecstasy, the later poem, grounded in the details of cherished autobiography, achieves a grim serenity.

A close friend of Robert Lowell's, though in most ways his temperamental opposite, the reticent Elizabeth Bishop found her way to the autobiographical personal lyric late, and even reluctantly, in such poems as "In the Waiting Room," "One Art," and "The Moose," from *Geography III* (1976), and the later poem "Santarém." It was extremely difficult for Bishop to put herself forward as a protagonist whose subjectivity is a part of the poem's drama. She can be seen to be inching toward it in such poems as "Under the Window: Ouro Prêto" (1966), where the speaker is clearly the poet talking about what she sees from her house in Brazil. But the gaze is outward; the self, a shrewd and humane observor, looks and listens, but does not reflect on itself and its emotions nor interact with the world it observes. What a distance is covered between "Under the Window: Ouro Prêto" and "In the Waiting Room," the first poem in *Geography III*. The latter poem opens with details and an anchoring context ("In Worcester, Massachusetts, / I went with Aunt Consuelo / to keep her dentist's appointment."). Like the adult observer she would become, curious and precise, the child-Bishop reads a *National Geographic* and notes its photos. Then, "suddenly, from inside came an oh! of pain"—Aunt Consuelo's voice, which quickly becomes confused with her own—and we see that "from inside" constitutes a pun and the pain marks the entrance of subjective feeling into the poem and Bishop's work generally. "In the Waiting Room" and, to a lesser extent, "One Art" and "The Moose," continue the book's engagement with autobiographical subjectivity. But, in fact, the poem in *Geography III* that most lays bare the fundamental issues and agonies of Bishop's life, "Crusoe in England," is not in the postconfessional mode. Adopting a persona, Bishop writes an extraordinary poem (a spiritual autobiography, really) that is both elegy for a lost lover and dramatization of the primary themes of her personality, including such painful issues as her sense of abandonment, her alcoholism, and her homosexuality.

If the elder postconfessionals focused on childhood and adolescence with great success, the younger group, consisting of James Wright, Philip Levine, and Adrienne Rich, characteristically moved their poems' autobiographical encounters further into the political and social world than either the elders or the original confessional poets.

James Wright's anguished poems have explored the degradation and humiliation of the self and the natural world, but always by linking the self to others and a surrounding landscape. Some of his poems are set in his childhood in blue-collar southwestern Ohio, where his father labored in mills, others in Minnesota, where he himself taught and suffered. The rages and fears he expressed are both personal and political, and alcohol and drunkenness accompany him each step of the way. When in "Stages on a Journey Westward," from *The Branch Will Not Break* (1963), he accompanies the "half-educated sheriff of Mukilteo, Washington" to the continent's edge, his personal despair fuses with a despair at his nation's destiny as he stares down, drunk to where "at the bottom of the cliff / America is over and done with. / America, / Plunged into the dark furrows / Of the sea again."

By the time of his next book, *Shall We Gather at the River* (1968), titles and the opening lines of poems insist on anguished autobiographical encounters. "Inscription for the Tank" is a poem about being incarcerated in the drunk tank, and "In Terror of Hospital Bills" begins, "I still have some money / To eat with, alone / And frightened," and proceeds toward a fusion of his identity with that of "a full-blooded Sioux Indian" in equally desperate circumstances. A haunting, haunted sense of loneliness and inadequacy permeates the book. "Before a Cashier's Window in a Department Store," begins, "The beautiful cashier's white face has risen once more / Behind a young manager's shoulder. / They whisper together, and stare / Straight into my face."

A theme of power and powerlessness runs through Wright's work. The poems embrace and endorse victims of system, victims of bureaucracy, and worse, but the poems are also populated by victims of addiction and despair, himself among them. The poor and homeless, the suicidal and addicted earn a place in poems (and thus in consciousness) when they act out their stories with a dignity that is only occasionally tinged with sentimentality. The relationship of the large and impersonal power structure to its most powerless members is a persistent theme of his work. "How does the city keep lists of its fathers / Who have no names?" he asks of the drowned derelicts Minneapolis hauls out of its river in "The Minneapolis Poem" (1968). His mystical brotherhood of the powerless combines with a reverential awe of nature in the image that culminates that same poem—his wish to be "carefully hidden / Modest and golden as one last corn grain, / Stored with the secrets of the wheat and the mysterious lives / Of the unnamed poor."

As early as "My Poets" (from *On the Edge*, 1963), Philip Levine identifies outward from his person. After enumerating four desperate characters ("One was put in the lockup / in Toledo, Ohio / for ever and ever"), he connects himself with them through a unifying image ("And we, we number the five / fingers of our fists and try / anything to stay alive."). Nor is he reluctant to bring in the personal in his first book: "My living wife, Frances Levine, / Mother of Theodore, John, and Mark" ("For Fran"). And the poem "A New Day" from his second book, *Not This Pig* (1968), features an autobiographical encounter on the shores of the Great Lakes: "The old champion in a sweat suit / Tells me this is Chicago, this." Nevertheless, these poems lack sufficient autobiographical weight and focus to qualify as postconfessional lyrics. Levine has also in his first two books written a kind of visionary autobiography in such poems as "Saturday Sweeping" and "Salami," or "Silent in America," but the visionary seems to dominate. It is with the poem "Detroit Grease Shop Poem" (from *They Feed They Lion*, 1972) that the autobiographical can be felt to take hold, to take on the visceral urgency that will continue to characterize Levine's postconfessional lyrics.

In his sixth collection, *1933* (published in 1974), the autobiographical engagement becomes dominant with such poems as the title poem, "Zaydee," "Late Moon," "Goodbye," and "Hold Me." "1933" begins with personal memories of his father ("the hands that stroked my head / the voice in the dark asking . . . he brought Ray Estrada from Mexico."), then moves to the present, where both the descriptive ("I climb the tree in the vacant lot") and the visionary ("I find the glacier and wash my face in the Arctic dust / I shit handfuls of earth") fuse in a sustained litany. Gradually, as the litany progresses, the visionary becomes local again, attaching to specific family members. This exploration of the autobiographical fused with the visionary continues into the next collection, *The Names of the Lost* (1976), with such poems as "Belle Isle, 1949," "My Son and I," "New Season," "No One Remembers," "And the Trains Go On," and "Ask the Roses."

Levine's characteristic autobiographical material calls for an encounter with family in childhood (a father who died when he was five, grandparents, an uncle, his mother), or with blue-collar workers with whom he labored as an adolescent ("And the Trains Go On," "Making it New," "Gift for a Believer"). The self in these poems is sometimes tender, sometimes angry. The anger can be directed at the destruction, oppression, and exploitation of industrialism ("We burn this city every day" ends "Coming Home, Detroit," 1968) or at those who are personally brutal (Uncle Joe of "No One Remembers"). The tenderness is directed toward family, then outward with significant intensity toward fellow laborers, prisoners, fighters in doomed, noble causes like the Spanish Civil War, residents of ethnic ghettos—until such identification rises or generalizes to include "all the holy names of the lost." The litany is a favored mode—it can celebrate or lament. These litanies incorporate imagery from the elemental world: stars, stones, wind, sea, earth, night, moon—all invoked to bind together human destiny and the life of the planet in what could be characterized as tragic exultation.

Adrienne Rich, like Bishop, does not arrive easily at the use of personal and autobiographical material in her poems. The enormous detachment of Bishop's early poem "The Imaginary Iceberg" has its miniature equivalent in Rich's "The Diamond Cutters" (1955), her poem about poetic process in which "intelligence" is the tool that cuts the icy facets. Yet as early as 1964 there are exceptions—poems in which an autobiographical encounter structures the poem, such as "After Dark," her elegy for her father. That poem opens with the clear, embodying context dramatic lyrics demand ("You are falling asleep and I sit looking at you / old tree of life / old man whose death I wanted / I can't stir you up now.") and moves through its difficult feelings with feeling. For Rich, as for Bishop and Kunitz, the descent into the autobiographical encounter is a descent into feeling as well as thinking, into intimacy and vulnerability. In the sixties this risk of the personal is sporadic in Rich's work. She prefers to speak in ideas or, later, in myths. Along with this detachment there is a reliance on the plural pronoun *we*. Perhaps, maturing as a political engagé in the fifties and sixties, she shared the leftist distrust of the person as a bourgeois encumbrance, preferring the plural pronoun *we* that permits those with whom one is in conflict to be located as a *they*. *Us* against *them* is a powerful concept, and it liberates from the personal. Certainly it has stood Rich in good stead in her role in the seventies as literary spokesperson for a radical feminism.

But I would argue that to lose the self through the extensive use of *we* is also to lose contact with the personal sources of pain and joy, of feeling in general. It is Rich's poems that engage personal sources that I would choose to emphasize as being powerful instances of the postconfessional lyric and important expansions of autobiographical subject matter. Such poems would include "After Dark" and "From a Survivor" (1972), a poem addressed to her husband who committed suicide in 1970. Certainly her strongest and most sustained work in this mode is in the 1978 book, *The Dream of a Common Language*, especially in its central section of twenty-one poems addressed to her gay lover. Again and again, the poems explore their territory by beginning (not necessarily ending) with an *I* and a *you*. Now the ideas and principles so important to Rich are set to the side, and the poems begin in the experiences of a lived life:

> We crouched in the open hatchway
> vomiting into plastic bags
> for three hours between St. Pierre and Miquelon.
> I never felt closer to you.

(14)

Such a poem may well arrive at Rich's desired ideas and principles, but they will emerge from experience, from the interaction of self and world.

In another poem in the book, "Sibling Mysteries," the poem moves through four sections of mythologized sisterhood ("Remind me how . . . we made fire / scooped clay lifted water . . . / and how we drew the quills / of porcupines between our teeth") before, in section 5, it engages an actual sister by way of an excerpt from Rich's 1963 journal in which she notes her feelings of estrangement from her sister, who has just had a child. The section proceeds to unfold as postconfessional lyric:

> There were years you and I
> hardly spoke to each other
>
> then one whole night
> our father dying upstairs
>
> we burned our childhood, reams of paper,
> talking till the birds sang . . .

In a later book, *Your Native Land, Your Life* (1986), she confronts her father and husband in the sequence "Sources"—writing of her background growing up in "a castle in air." In another sequence from that same book, "Contradictions: Tracking Poems," she writes about longing for lyric absolutes ("you long for one idea / one simple, huge idea to take this weight") and of her physical pain from rheumatoid arthritis and how it impinges intensely on her life and hopes ("I feel signified by pain"). Yet her goal is never to arrive at the self but always to connect outward from self to other in a social and political context: "The problem is / to connect, without hysteria, the pain / of any one's body with the pain of the body's world / For it is the body's world / they are trying to destroy forever."

Among the younger postconfessionals Frank Bidart's work, and especially his first book, *Golden State* (1973), occupies a special place. An admirer of Lowell's and a student of his at Harvard, Bidart nevertheless registers a lyric critique of Lowell's *Life Studies*, faulting their "static" quality and their presentation of "a world that refuses knowledge of the causes beneath it, [and is therefore] without change or escape." Seeking all those things his mentor evaded, Bidart, in "California Plush," confronts his father in a coffee shop decorated in the style of the poem's title. Poetry as a therapeutic quest reaches a kind of apotheosis of self-awareness in Bidart's poem: "The need for the past / / is so much at the center of my life / I write this poem to record my discovery of it / my reconciliation." Among the bric-a-brac of a California coffee shop he encounters his father and his own feelings and thoughts as he quests for his sense of self. Against the oppressiveness of the immediate surroundings and the burden of personal history ("The past in maiming us, / makes us), the poem's lyric possibilities are few: a memory of riding the Hollywood Freeway "at midnight, windows down and radio blaring," references to culture figures (Proust, Oedipus) that grant him a brief transcendent perspective on his plight—and the poem, for all its longing for "change" and self-transformation, ends on a questioning, uncertain note.

The title poem of the volume addresses the dead father and again the poet-speaker searches for the sources of his malaise in the details of his father's life, fearing that beneath the father's trivial disappointments lies "a radical disaffection / from the very possibilities / of human life." The poem itself becomes an enacting drama in the son's quest for "release" from his father: "When I began this poem: . . . / I sensed I had to become not merely / a speaker, the 'eye,' but a character." Against this longing is set the conditional world symbolized by photos of his father: "they stare back at me / with dazzling, impenetrable, glitter of mere life." Homosexuality becomes a central subject matter in *The Book of the Body* (1977). In the powerful poem, "Confessional," from *The Sacrifice* (1983), Bidart records his rage and struggle to reconcile with his now-dead mother. By and large, a longing for transcendence or reconciliation is powerfully present in Bidart's work, but it often goes unappeased.

In the seven sections of the title poem of my second book, *Gathering the Bones Together* (1975), I confront a childhood trauma—my responsibility for a brother's death in a hunting accident. Writing in a compressed lyric mode that is at times flatly descriptive, at times dreamlike or surrealistic, I struggle to assimilate the death and its manifold emotional consequences into the ongoingness of survival. My brother's death and the equally sudden death of my mother a few years later ("the last tear / turns to glass on her cheek; / it isn't ice because / squeezed in the boy's hot fist / it doesn't thaw" ["Song: Early Death of the Mother," 1980]) become loci for such recurring themes as guilt, terror, abandonment, and grief. Continuing to work in the postconfessional lyric mode, I have written about my involvement in the Civil Rights movement in such poems as "On a Highway East of Selma, Alabama, July 1965" and "Solitary Confinement."

With the title sequence of *Descending Figure* (1980) Louise Glück begins to incorporate autobiographical material into her stark, oracular lyrics. In this poem, she dramatizes the persisting anguish associated with the childhood in which a sister died: "Far away my sister is moving in her crib. / The dead ones are like that, / always the last to quiet." In the same book the poem "Tango" centers on the rivalrous relationship between the speaker and her sister. Family is a central theme in Glück's work. Her childhood in the suburbs, her relationship with her parents, sisters, relatives—these are clearly autobiographical issues, but rendered in almost mythic terms. "Dedication to Hunger," a poem in five sections, is a stunning exploration of anorexia nervosa. Each section dramatizes an aspect and moment of the phenomenon itself—its origins, its enactments, or its analogues and implications in art, love, and life. The whole sequence is like the lucid, concentric rings from a pebble dropped in a dark pond.

The Triumph of Achilles (1985) continues with poems about Glück's father's death, a subject that will become a central theme in the book-length probing of a family and its interactions that constitutes *Ararat* (1990). Sexuality and the relationship between the sexes is another recurring theme in her work. These relationships are seldom easy since behind them is a sense of male violence (of a man's kiss to his young bride: "clearly tender— / / Of course, of course. Except / it might as well have been / his hand over her mouth.") coupled with a fierce estrangement from one's own body ("because a woman's body / is a grave; it will accept / anything."). Nevertheless, sexual passion provides a powerful if ambiguous vision of self-transcendence. Glück possesses the rare power of concentrating image and concept in the same compressed lyric, creating poems that are a triumph of tone and intelligence.

Sharon Olds, in *The Dead and the Living* (1984), demonstrates a commitment to exploring and dramatizing primary relationships in an autobiographical mode that makes her a true descendent of Anne Sexton. She shares with Sexton a concrete imagination, one that in her case is often visceral. She says of parents, haunting her adult room and life, "I dream the inner parts of your bodies, the / coils of your bowels like smoke, your hearts / opening like jaws, drops from your glands / clinging to my walls" ("Possessed"). In poem after poem she describes the dynamics of life with an abusive, alcoholic father and a passive mother. A primal anger at victimization animates a number of the poems, such as "The Victims," which begins, "When Mother divorced you, we were glad," and goes on to exult over the father's further defeats and "annhilations." We feel again and again that we are invited on a Dantesque descent into an Inferno with no guide but numerous grisly punishments and grim metaphors. In a later section of the book entitled "The Men," poems such as "Ecstasy" and "The Connoisseuse of Slugs" are hymns to female sexuality and desire. Another section, "The Children," celebrates and describes her son and daughter as they pass through various phases of childhood, some violent, some sexual or presexual. Though they sometimes verge on the sensationalistic, the poems are always striking.

Bidart, Olds, Glück, and I are members of a generation that grew up or entered adulthood during the sixties. By far the largest grouping of postconfessionals, this generation has pushed the mode in diverse directions. Those among it who have focused on childhood and adolescence have explored the complex and anguished interactions of families far more extensively than their elders. In poems by such poets as Olds, Glück, Bidart, Molly Peacock, Michael Ryan, Stanley Plumly, Cleopatra Mathis, Ira Sadoff, and Marie Howe the "dark passages" of family life have yielded such themes as sexual abuse, violence, alcoholism, and madness, all of which are explored in an autobiographical mode fraught with personal urgency. At the same time, the affirmation of cultural diversity since the sixties has created audiences and poetries focused on ethnic and sexual orientation issues, and in each of these poetries there are strong postconfessional presences. Both Marilyn Hacker and Bidart, among others, have extensively dramatized and probed homosexuality as a subject. Racial tensions and awarenesses have entered the arena of the postconfessional lyric in such poems as Audre Lorde's "Cables to Rage or I've Been Talking on This Street Corner a Hell of a Long Time" (1969), and Rita Dove's "Crab-Boil" and "After Reading *Mickey in the Night Kitchen* for the Third Time Before Bed" (both 1989), and in Yusef Komunyakaa's remarkable book *Dien Cai Dau* (1988), which, along with the work of W. D. Erhart, Bruce Weigl, and others, also powerfully extends the postconfessional lyric's territory to include autobiographical experience of the Vietnam War.

By the late seventies and early eighties the postconfessional lyric's influence is so powerful that even when a poet's primary work is not in the postconfessional mode, some of their most important individual poems are. In this regard, one thinks of such early instances as Robert Hayden's "Those Winter Sundays" (1962), Frank O'Hara's "The Day Lady Died" (1964), Louis Simpson's "My Father in the Night Commanding No" (1963), James Merrill's "The Broken Home" (1966), Robert Penn Warren's "Tale of Time" (1966), James Tate's "The Lost Pilot" (1966), and Diane Wakoski's "Thanking My Mother for Piano Lessons" (1971). Other instances of outstanding poems in the postconfessional lyric mode by poets who didn't necessarily continue in that direction are Richard Wilbur's "Cottage Street, 1953" (1972), Donald Hall's "Kicking the Leaves" and "Maple Syrup" (1978), Donald Justice's "First Death" and "Childhood" (1979), Mark Strand's "Elegy for My Father" (1973), C. K. Williams's "My Mother's Lips" and "Tar" (1983), Robert Pinsky's "History of My Heart" (1984), and Bill Knott's "The Closet" (1983).

In addition, a number of younger poets have explored this mode intensively rather than extensively with such poems as Robert Hass's "Songs to Survive the Summer" (1979), Carolyn Forché's "Kalaloch" and "Burning the Tomato Worms" (1975), Michael Ryan's "Switchblade" and "Milking the Mouse" (1989), Dave Smith's "Nekkid: Homage to Edgar Allan Poe" (1981), Molly Peacock's "Those Paperweights with Snow Inside" (1984) and "Buffalo" (1989), Albert Goldbarth's "Before" (1983), Ira Sadoff's "My Father's Leaving" (1978), Ellen Bryant Voigt's "The Chosen" and "At the Movie: Virginia, 1956" (1987), Charles Wright's "Lonesome Pine Special" (1984), Tom Lux's "The Milkman and His Son" (1986), Stanley Plumly's "Cows" and "Two Poems" (1977), Heather McHugh's "I Knew I'd Sing" and "Unspeakable" (1988), and Larry Levis's "My Story in a Late Style of Fire" (1985). The poet who did not work, even briefly, in the postconfessional lyric mode during the late seventies and eighties is the rare exception rather than the rule.

If the postconfessional poets are an extension and even an expansion of the confessional mode, they must nevertheless be understood as a significant modification of the confessional. Elizabeth Bishop's remark in a letter to Robert Lowell, who was both her close friend and one of the principle poets of confessionalism, signals the shift and distance between the two: "In general, I deplore the 'confessional.' "

The postconfessional critique centers around a potential danger of the confessional mode seen perhaps most clearly in the work of Lowell and Berryman. When the confessional poets transformed and extended American poetry by courageously engaging an enormous amount of autobiographical material, it had the effect of ensnaring the self in the conditional, circumstantial world. The self in Berryman and Lowell is typically an ego seething with drives, desires, conflicts, and rationalizations, but with almost all expression of these intensities confined to the surrounding, material world. Such a situation can be seen from another perspective also—the lives of the confessional poets were characterized by emotional instability, addictions, breakdowns. A number of them were rightly fearful of madness and therefore they may well have longed to cling to the circumstantial, to the "real" and palpable world, as a means of stabilizing a precarious identity.

When we consider the childhoods and adult lives of the postconfessionals we see a misery and unbalance commensurate with that found among the confessionals, but somehow the postconfessionals were survivors who brought their survivors' skills to bear on their autobiographical material. Chief among these skills was access to the transcendent, to what, in poetry, could be called the lyric mode. What the lyric mode brings to the drama of self and the conditional world is a way out, or, in that version of the lyric known as the dramatic lyric, a series of strategies by which self and the conditional world can be reconciled.

The basic notion behind the dramatic lyric is that the poet's self experiences two powerful principles at once. The first principle could be called "lyric longing," and manifests as the desire to transcend the conditions of being, to attain, in Keats's words, "fellowship divine, / A fellowship with essence; till we shine, / Full alchemized, and free of space." Lyric longing can be imaged as a vertical line bisecting the self. The second principle, an awareness of the conditional world, can be thought of as passing through the self horizontally, at right angles to the vertical lyric axis. This horizontal axis conceived as an arrow moving from left to right represents how the self moves through time and space in the conditional world.

The lyric premise in its pure form is that we are not of this world (transcendence). The dramatic premise (horizontal arrow) is that this world and its forces and how they act on us and we on them are all that we are. The dramatic lyric records the interplay of these two premises: lyric longing and the reality of the contingent world—how these two principles impinge on the self.

The dramatic lyric can be experienced without reference to the poet's biography—for example, Keats's "Ode to a Nightingale" is a quintessential dramatic lyric that has little need of biographical context. But the dramatic lyric takes on a particular urgency and intensity when autobiographical material is allowed to enter the poem and comes to represent the demands of the conditional world, whether it be Emily Dickinson's "I cannot live with you," or Elizabeth Bishop's "In the Waiting Room."

Perhaps one of the most inadvertent gifts of the confessionals was to blur the distinction between art and life. Such a blurring can have destructive and self-destructive consequences but can also have salutary effects: what can't be resolved in life can be brought over into art, where it is again engaged, again encountered by a self struggling to extract sustaining meaning from experience.

The postconfessional lyric can be thought of as proposing or enacting various strategies of sustaining the autobiographical self in its encounter with the conditional world. Although these strategies are part of the traditional repertoire of the lyric mode and are even utilized by the original confessional poets, it is a matter of emphasis. Employed sporadically by the confessional poets, they are central to the postconfessional lyric, indeed, can be said to give the postconfessional lyric its identity as a distinct phenomenon in the autobiographical tradition. The four strategies that follow, while not the only ones available, seem to me the most significant.

Eros. Eros as a strategy in the dramatic lyric could use as a touchstone Blake's proverb: "The most sublime act is to set another before you." Eros proposes the erotic couple, the bonded couple as a situation in which each partner focuses on the other, thereby escaping his or her self and perhaps creating in the process a two-person world, set apart from the conditional world. In the literary version of eros, it is, of course, the poet who speaks and who is concerned with his or her transcendence, although the implicit premise remains one of mutuality and reciprocal release.

Eros is at the heart of Stanley Kunitz's "The Magic Curtain," where the boy protagonist bonds with his governess behind his prim mother's back—a poem that can be simultaneously tongue-in-cheek Freudian and profoundly poignant. In Louise Glück's "Mock Orange," eros, release from the self, is as brief as the sexual act, more a haunting than a hope, since its "premise of union," which is capable of producing "one sound / that mounts and mounts," must ultimately "split into the old selves / the tired antagonisms." In "Twenty-One Love Poems," the central section of *The Dream of a Common Language*, eros becomes a crucial premise of Adrienne Rich's poetry. When, in poem 10 of that sequence, she says "without tenderness we are in hell," we might think of the isolated and alienated self of Lowell's "Skunk Hour," who, echoing Marlowe and Milton, announces "I myself am hell." Although this world of personal intimacy is hard won for Rich, whose prior work is more committed to idea than feeling, she cannot rest content there. In another poem in the same book, "Origins and History of Consciousness," Rich again celebrates "the secret circle of fire" that is the "tiny world" of the erotic couple: "I want to call this, life, / / But I can't call it life until we start to move / beyond this secret circle of fire." Rich insists we must interact with the world, be socially and politically as well as erotically bonded. Nevertheless, it's important to see that in her later work the erotic bond is what gives hope—where the politics starts. And, of course, since the couple is lesbian, its eros is inherently political in our culture.

Sympathy. In the midst of that extensive litany of things to be celebrated which is "Song of Myself" Whitman pauses, "I am he attesting sympathy, / (shall I make my list of things in the house and skip the house that supports them?)." Whitman's chilling image of the individual self without sympathy shows what is at stake. "Who walks a furlong without sympathy walks to his own funeral drest in his shroud." Such an alienated being is cut off entirely from the human community. By contrast, the sympathetic self is constantly extending outward in identifications with the other: "I do not ask the wounded person how he feels, I myself become the wounded person, / My hurts turn livid upon me as I lean on my cane and observe" ("Song of Myself," section 33).

Among the postconfessionals we see such sympathy in Philip Levine's identification with blue-collar laborers in the factories of Detroit, an identification that clearly emerges from autobiographical experiences: "We're all here to count / and be counted, Lemon, / Rosie, Eugene, Luis, / and me, too young to know / this is for keeps" ("Detroit Grease Shop Poem").

The same strategy permeates James Wright's work, where his experiences of humiliation and degradation permit him to transcend his own plight and join a brotherhood of suffering that involves the poor, the exploited, the ignorant, and others whose lives are overwhelmed by the world of circumstance.

Sympathetic identification provides the emotional turning point in Robert Hayden's "Those Winter Sundays" as the son-speaker becomes the father from whom he was alienated and takes on his desolate knowledge in the final lines: "What did I know, what did I know / of love's austere and lonely offices?" And sympathetic identification and its rejection animate the protagonist's anguish in C. K. Williams's "My Mother's Lips" from the remarkable book *Tar* (1983).

Symbol. There is a tendency among poets of the lyric persuasion to experience symbol as a means of escape from the conditional world. Oppressed by conditions of being, the lyric poet cries out in the spirit of Baudelaire's title: "Anywhere Out of This World!" Although the lyric symbol often signals transcendence, it can also signal reconciliation, even in such a compulsive lyric transcender as Yeats, who, at the end of "Circus Animals' Desertion," proposes a disparaging symbol for the world ("the foul rag and bone shop of the heart") only to acknowledge his reluctant reconciliation with it. Likewise Yeats's image of erotic love in "Crazy Jane Talks with the Bishop" functions as a symbol for a central reconciliation of self and world through the sexual body: "But Love has pitched his mansion in / The place of excrement."

In short, symbols don't have to take us out of the world—they satisfy lyric longing if they take us out of the self and its anguished moment. Often this involves solitary transcendence, the self losing its burden through identification with an object (Keats's nightingale, say, or the Grecian urn). But object as symbol can also function as a bridge of communion between isolated or separate selves, as in Elizabeth Bishop's great poem, "Santarém," where the Brazilian pharmacist gives her a wasps' nest she has admired and both the object (a symbol of aesthetic beauty as a natural product of this world) and the pharmacist's gesture affirm the possibilities of the self being reconciled to the conditional world. In Bishop's late work the conditional world seems to nominate such reconciling symbols from its vast array of objects—one thinks of "The Moose," how the poem culminates in the animal's sighting and the awed focus generates a brief communion of strangers. Or in C. K. Williams's "Tar," a poem that struggles to localize and cope with the nuclear accident at Three Mile Island, the chunks of leftover roofing tar used by neighborhood kids to make grafitti, and the ensuing "obscenities and hearts" that cover the sidewalks symbolize a precarious yoking of the destructive and affirmative possibilities within us.

Proportionate Ego. In a review of Robert Lowell's *The Dolphin* in the September-October 1973 issue of the *American Poetry Review*, Adrienne Rich attacked Lowell's incorporation and alteration of letters from his ex-wife into poems. Outraged at this excess, at what seemed to her an instance of a self so narcissistic as to devour everything and turn it into literary material, Rich spoke of Lowell's "unproportionate ego." If I were to turn Rich's phrase of condemnation around, I might propose "proportionate ego" as an essential element in a number of postconfessional lyrics. In a poem where a proportionate ego is protagonist the competing claims of self, other, and world are all honored, and an important aspect of the poem is dramatizing how (and how powerfully) each asserts itself.

We might look to William Carlos Williams's late poem "Asphodel, That Greeny Flower" (1955) as an important presursor poem that seems especially sensitive to the competing claims of self, other, and world. For all his egotism, Williams always saw himself as a part of a community, committed to a place and a people, and it may be this which allows him to dramatize so gracefully this encounter with his wife that ranges over such topics as infidelity, old age, and the atom bomb.

It would be erroneous to claim that the strategy of proportionate ego is lyrical, but when combined with other lyric elements it becomes an important element in many postconfessional lyrics. It can be especially useful to poets who are by nature reticent about autobiography in poetry, skeptical about the lyric's potential narcissism. For example, it is at the heart of Richard Wilbur's "Cottage Street, 1953," a moving poem about his awkward meeting with the young and desperate Sylvia Plath shortly after one of her suicide attempts. Perhaps the most distinctive and widespread characteristic of the postconfessional lyric, the strategy of proportionate ego calls for a complex balance of forces. Each poet and each poem must present a proportion of self, world, and/or other capable of generating a convincing and urgent enactment of autobiographical themes.

To enter into an intense engagement with autobiographical subject matter can be one powerful means of exploring Keats's "dark passages," but it can also lead to a self-involvement that alienates the poet from the surrounding world and even to "a radical disaffection from the very possibilities of human life" (to use a phrase from Frank Bidart's "Golden State"). Keats himself was tormented by this problem, and in "The Fall of Hyperion" postulated a distinction between the "dreamer" and the "poet." The dreamer is not at peace with the world (which he "vexes") nor with himself: "Only the dreamer venoms all his days / Bearing more woe than all his sins deserve." The poet, by contrast, is a "physician to all men" who "pours out a balm upon the world." Though poet and dreamer are opposites in Keats's scheme, they are easily mistaken for each other, and Keats himself, at various times in his career, is unsure of his true identity. At the end of "Ode to a Nightingale" he asks, "Was it a vision, or a waking dream?"—that is to say, was the experience a revelation of a higher reality or a hallucination: Am I a poet or a dreamer?

Although they were clearly anguished vexers of their own lives it would be simplistic to say that the confessional poets belong, by and large, to Keats's category of dreamers. But it is credible and necessary to assert that the postconfessional lyric poets have constantly and consciously aspired to Keats's notion of the poet. The postconfessional lyric, in its various incarnations, again and again models an engagement with fundamental issues of personal life, an engagement in which the survival value of transcendence is asserted. One of the major contributions of the postconfessional lyric is to show how the self survives the miseries and trials in which it finds itself—both its own personal anguishes and what Keats calls "the giant agony of the world."

Gregory Orr

Further Reading

Bidart, Frank. *Golden State*. New York: Braziller, 1973.

Bishop, Elizabeth. *Geography III*. New York: Farrar, Straus and Giroux, 1976.

Glück, Louise. *Descending Figure*. New York: Ecco, 1980.

Jarrell, Randall. *The Lost World*. New York: Farrar, Straus and Giroux, 1965.

Kunitz, Stanley. *The Testing-Tree*. Boston: Atlantic-Little, Brown, 1973.

Levine, Philip. *They Feed They Lion*. New York: Atheneum, 1972.

Olds, Sharon. *The Dead and the Living*. New York: Knopf, 1984.

Orr, Gregory. *Gathering the Bones Together*. New York: Harper and Row, 1975.

Rich, Adrienne. *The Dream of the Common Language*. New York: Norton, 1978.

Wright, James. *The Branch Shall Not Break*. Middletown, Conn.: Wesleyan University Press, 1963.

—— *Shall We Gather at the River*. Middletown, Conn.: Wesleyan University Press, 1968.

The Black Arts Poets

I N *Mumbo Jumbo*, a roman à clef published in 1972, Ishmael Reed depicts the Black Arts movement of the 1960s as an extension of two earlier eruptions of African American creativity in the 1890s and the 1920s. The appearance in Addison Gayle, Jr.'s *The Black Aesthetic* (a text that attempted to define the movement) of Alain Locke and Langston Hughes, both prominent figures in the Harlem Renaissance of the twenties, testifies to the accuracy of Reed's linkage of these movements. Gwendolyn Brooks, in *Report From Part One* (published also in 1972), describes her encounter with the early stages of the Black Arts movement and its effect on her as an artist. Brooks dates her own contact from the Fisk University Writers' Conference in the spring of 1967. One of the principal figures, and the clear sensation of that conference, was Imamu Amiri Baraka, who in 1967 still retained the name LeRoi Jones. The movement, which received its first coherent sense of mission at the Fisk University conference, differed from earlier flowerings of African American creativity in the real sense that it was marked by a more unified and coherent ideology and aesthetic than were the more loosely cohesive movements that preceded it. An understanding of the nature of its ideology and aesthetic is necessary to a full appreciation of the poetry that played such a central role in the Black Arts movement.

Five texts that appeared in the years following the Fisk conference are central to the development of the Black Arts movement. *Black Fire*, a 1968 anthology edited by LeRoi Jones and Larry Neal, introduced a number of new voices to the public. Clarence Major's *The New Black Poetry* (1969) sought to displace the "deadweight" anthologies of predecessors like Arna Bontemps, Langston Hughes, and Rosey E. Pool. Addison Gayle, Jr., in *The Black Aesthetic* (1971), assembled thirty-three essays defining both the movement itself and its place in music, poetry, drama, and fiction. *Black Poets and Prophets*, edited in 1972 by Woodie King and Earl Anthony was more pan-African in its approach and more radical in its politics than was the more "balanced" Gayle volume. Stephen Henderson's *Understanding the New Black Poetry* offered a detailed analysis of the poetics of the movement and an anthology of its principal poets.

The shifts first evident in Alain Locke's *The New Negro: An Interpretation* (1925) are heightened in the above reflections on the art of the sixties. Langston Hughes's "The Negro Artist and The Racial Mountain," first published in 1926, is reprinted in Gayle's *The Black Aesthetic*. In that essay Hughes argues for an art focusing on "the low-down folk, the common people." The mountain to which his title refers symbolized the resistance of African Americans to the authentic voice of their own unique cultural experience and a destructive valorization of "the drab melodies in white folk's hymnbooks." Hughes argues that a new poetry will come that will reflect "the beauty of dark faces," that will counter the efforts of "the Nordicized Negro intelligentsia." This new poetry will be "racial in theme and treatment." It will use as its metrical base jazz, "the inherent expression of Negro life in America." It will speak without shame or fear of the experience of the African American on the streets of those communities that have not abandoned the sound of the tom-tom in such a way as to open the "ears of colored near-intellectuals" to the blare and bellowing voice of the African-American reality. Hughes's 1926 prophecy appears in *The Black Aesthetic* because it insists, in spite of the absence of the ideological base of the later movement, on many of its aesthetic principles.

More representative of the ideological base of the movement would be essays found in part 1 of *The Black Aesthetic*. This section, devoted to theory, includes ideological treatises by Hoyt Fuller, Larry Neal, and Ron Karenga. Fuller, in "Towards a Black Aesthetic," argues that the new movement must not be concerned with so-called mainstream theories. Rather, writers are to turn "their backs on the old 'certainties' "; they must strike out "in new if uncharted, directions." He sounds a note common to the movement when he emphasizes the sharp differences between the "two separate and naturally antagonistic worlds" of black and white America and the colonial reality in which black Americans live. Fuller emphasizes the "we are black and beautiful" theme of the movement, situates that movement in the ghetto, and pronounces as irrelevant the cultural products of those who do not "reflect the special character and imperatives of black experience." Larry Neal's contribution to the volume is his rap "Some Reflection on the Black Aesthetic." The subtitles of the work and the heroes evoked in it reflect Neal's ideological construction for Black Arts poetry. He organizes the rap according to principles of mythology (African-based belief systems) and neomythology (African American continuities with the homeland). Preacher, hustler, seer, and teacher are linked to Legba, Oshun, Yemaya, and Erzulie. Malcolm X, Rap Brown, Charlie Parker, James Brown, and Bessie Smith are one with Nat Turner, High John the Conqueror, and the Signifying Monkey. The Black Arts movement is the final stage in a five-step historical process:

1. Race Memory
2. The Middle Passage
3. Transmutation and Synthesis
4. Blues God/Tone as Meaning and Memory
5. Black Arts Movement/Black Aesthetic

Ron Karenga's "Black Cultural Nationalism" centers on the place of Black Arts in revolutionary struggle. Art must satisfy requirements other than those of form and feeling. Technical skills and the artistic considerations that so dominate literary criticism are not sufficient guides for validating work that aspires to the label "black aesthetic." Black art, Karenga argues, must possess three qualities: it must "expose the enemy, praise the people and support the revolution." The new Black art must also be a collective art, one that "must move with the masses and be moved by the masses." Individuality, like art for art's sake, is both nonexistent and a luxury. Black collective art will be marked by diversity within unity: the artist is free to do his or her art but is never free from the people who both provide the occasion of that art and who reward and validate the true collective artist. Finally, the Black art described by Karenga will be committed to revolution and change. It should revive and inspire rather than teach defeat and resignation. Such an art, as the arm of "revolutionary war," will focus on a future rather than rehearse romanticized notions of the past.

Imamu Amiri Baraka's "A Black Value System" appeared first in the November 1969 issue of the *Black Scholar* and was reprinted in King and Anthony, *Black Poets and Prophets*, a volume that had as its subtitle the following: "The Theory, Practice, and Esthetics of the Pan-Africanist Revolution." In his essay Baraka focuses on the seven principles of the Nguzo Saba a belief system that unites all people of African descent no matter where they may live, a belief system that privileges black sovereignty and separation, and one that restores art to the center of revolutionary activity. Such a system is crucial to the liberation of black people caught in the web of an "absolutely detrimental "Euro-American value system." The seven principles with which Baraka opens his essay are the Kawaida (customary or traditional black practices): Umoja (unity), Kujichagulia (self-determination), Ujima (collective work and responsibility), Ujamaa (cooperative economics), Nia (purpose), Kuumba (creativity), and Tmani (faith). These principles are offered as a constructive alternative to Euro-American destructive constructs; they still remain the center of Kwanzaa, an African celebration that has displaced or at least rivaled Christmas in many African American communities. The seven principles of Nguzo Saba, Baraka argues, are to be used as the standards against which all ideas and acts of African American life is measured. Used in this way, they will engender the cultural revolution that must precede violent revolution, i.e., only when the minds of the people are freed will they be able to contribute to the revolution in a positive way. Culture—and particularly the arts—are at the center of this emancipation. "You must have the cultural revolution, i.e., you must get the mind before you move another futha." Kuumba is concerned solely with the unity, self-determination, collective work and responsibility of black people and, as such, it is Nguzo Saba's central principle. Baraka's "black ideology in toto" has nationalism as its direction, but that nationalism is clearly pan-African in its substance rather than concerned solely with the United States. This new value system offers salvation and an alternative to "crazy America."

It should be noted that an essay by Karenga titled "Black Art: Mute Matter Given Force and Function" does appear in the 1972 *Black Poets and Prophets*, but this essay is not substantially different from an earlier *Black World* (April 1968) version or the version that appears in *The Black*

Aesthetic under the title "Black Cultural Nationalism." It represents an important aspect of the theory of a black aesthetic that was developed in the late sixties by a group of artists, most of whom were in very active collaboration on the development of that aesthetic. Emphases may differ however as we move from one artist to another. Ishmael Reed's idiosyncratic and fascinating turn on this theme was suggested in *The Black Aesthetic* by a brief excerpt from his introduction to *19 Necromancers from Now* (1970). His subsequent development of neo-Hoodooism in the poems included in *Conjure* (1972), and in a series of stunning novels, represents his unique version of a new Black art. Neo-Hoodooism as developed by Reed in the late sixties and early seventies shares many of the cultural concerns of the Black Arts movement, even though Reed would later sever ties with that group, accusing it of too narrowly constraining the creative freedom of the African American artist.

Three anthologies are noteworthy among those that treat the new black poetry, each offering its special perspective on ideology and poetics. Clarence Major's *The New Black Poetry* (1969) presents poems born of the tension caused by "the crisis and drama of the late 1960's." They represent for him a revolutionary art, one concerned with the very "education" Gwendolyn Brooks received and one based in "the genesis of our African spirit." The poems that he selects are the work of poets "aligned with the social and political struggles of visionary peoples who seek ultimately to renew the world, especially to authenticate this society." They are the product of a collective experience, an "ethical-aesthetic" revolution that parallels the political revolution he saw. Major's agreement with Black Arts' goals is further exemplified by his castigation of "escapist" poetry and his dedication to a poetry aimed at consigning "capitalist oppression to some museum of time, to leave it 'out there' somewhere as a relic of western space." He selects for inclusion poems that reflect the Kekima (wisdom) and the Shauku (strong desire) of black people; such a selection is reflective of both artistic quality and "the *quantity* of the poets' social black consciousness." The poems are representative of a "new means of seeing," one echoed in the music of "John Coltrane, Pharoah Sanders, James Brown, Aretha Franklin, Wilson Pickett, Sam Cooke, Sun Ra, Cecil Taylor, Ray Charles, et al.," and are the creations in the main of poets born after 1930.

Black Fire, published a year earlier than Major's anthology, attempts a much broader coverage. In a brief incantatory introduction by Ameer

Baraha (a.k.a. LeRoi Jones/Amiri Baraka), writers are identified as "the founding Fathers and Mothers, of our nation" and as "wizards, bards, the babalawo, the shaikhs . . . of the constant striving (Jihad) of a nation coming back into focus." The reader is told to find, not the voice of another in the anthology, but "yr self . . . is you . . . your vehicle . . . your various selves . . . a tone, your own." The essays in this volume are representative of a more consistent ideology than that governing Gayle's *The Black Aesthetic.* They constitute the first section of the anthology and center on pan-African themes, black liberation, the corruption of the black bourgeoisie, revolution, black rage, and black power—themes that dominate the poetry of the movement. Peter Labrie, in "The New Breed," argues that changes in the music of black America are reflections of "a new breed of black man making his influence felt over the black ghetto." Labrie goes on to argue that internal forces in the ghetto are the catalyst for the changes in the new breed and its music. He foregrounds the decline since World War II of twin forces of oppression, the Christian church and the white authority that he links to that church. Countering this influence is that of the Nation of Islam and its repudiation of Christian values, white authority, and their surrogates—black preachers. Black pride has not only redefined the way in which black people see themselves, under leaders like Malcolm X it has demystified the legendary superiority of white America, clarifying and exposing the "treachery, hypocrisy and deceit" that has made possible exploitation of black men and the diminution of their significance in a nonwhite world. Using Arna Bontemps's complaint that Harlem in the 1940s was not the place it was in the Harlem Renaissance as an example of that poet's misconstruing of cultural and political forces, Labrie sees the very violence deplored by Bontemps as a necessary precursor to new life.

New folk ways, new moves are being developed. But before they become structured the old ones must be vomited up. This means a process of shock, disruption, and transformation. It can be a violent and frightening process.

The violence of riots results in " steady growth in community," people "become more polite to each other . . . there is a steady growth in their sense of community and a profound realization that they are sharing a common cause and a common destiny." Labrie's positive reading of the violence of the ghetto, his insistence that the new black knows too much "to be moral in any conventional sense," will be a hallmark of the Black Arts poetry found in *Black Fire*. Because the view is most readily expressed by New Breed music, it will be to that music and its per-former-creators that the poet must look. Further, the New Breed are the "field Negroes," not the privileged house servants of the past or the new bourgeoisie—"the preachers, lawyers, and entertainers." They are "ripe for militant black leadership," a leadership that will rise form the ghetto streets and not from office, pulpit, or suburban split-level.

Calvin Hernton, in his essay "Dynamite Growing Out of Their Skulls," elaborates on the theme of false consciousness and the failure of traditional black leadership. His targets include Martin Luther King, Jr., a member of "the Negro Leadership Class," those whom E. Franklin Frazier dubbed the "Black Bourgeoisie," so-called Black Anglo-Saxons according to Nathan Hare and all those whose conduct, marked by "restraint and refinement," is nothing more than a reflection of their alienation from "run-of-the-mill Negroes." Hernton sees the nonviolent movement headed by King not as a progressive movement but as an object of "utter contempt," as a grave breach of responsibility.

The species of the non-violent Negro, as a progressive social force towards the liberation of black people in America, has been eclipsed by the very forces that have called the species into being and yet prevail against it—the forces of com-promise, corruption, hate and violence.

The movement is dominated by a "new species of the House Negro . . . the bastard descendant of his master." The dynamite growing out of the skulls of the black masses is an angry response to betrayal and an accep-tance of the necessity and rationality of violence, a violence that will result in new birth: "the world will be changed."

After the opening group of essays the editors of *Black Fire* turn to the poetry, fiction, and drama of the New Breed, closing with Larry Neal's afterword, "And Shine Swam On." Neal recovers this traditional figure of black power and resistance to the temptations of white America to further define the New Breed. He will not repeat the Harlem Renais-sance, for that was "a fantasy-era for most black writers and their white friends . . . an illusion, a kind of surrealistic euphoria." Unlike Wright, they will construct a black ideology. "New constructs will have to be developed" and "dead forms . . . destroyed, or at best, radically altered." The   sources of such new construction will be found in Malcolm's speeches and in black music, which "has always been far ahead of our literature." Such a reconstruction of ideology and art will be linked to the struggle for liberation and will destroy the double consciousness of which W. E. B. DuBois spoke in *Souls of Black Folk*. When it reappeared in *Black Poets and Prophets* Neal's essay departed further from discursive prose; it exploded into a rap on the death of the double consciousness.

Because her fame as a poet and her acceptance by a general American public preceded the Black Arts movement, Gwendolyn Brooks can serve as a first exemplar of the changes in black poetry that the movement wrought. Brooks refers to her poetry written before 1967 as the product of a "Negro" fraction. The Black Arts movement led her to a redefinition of herself and her poetry. The "fraction" became, in 1950, the winner of the Pulitzer Prize for poetry—the first African American to do so—and was the creator of poetry with a clear integrationist ideology, one frequently shaped by European ballad and sonnet traditions. Note the following exchange with Ida Lewis in 1971.

Lewis: During the 1940's and 1950's, how did you view the black world?

Brooks: I thought that integration was the solution. All we had to do was keep on appealing to the whites to help us, and they would. . . . I relied heavily on Christianity. People were really good, I thought.

George Stavos in 1969 quoted for Brooks a statement she had made in 1950.

No real artist is going to be content with offering raw materials. The Negro poet's most urgent duty, at present, is to polish his technique, his way of presenting his truths and his beauties.

Brooks's reply suggests the shifts that had occurred in her thinking.

I said something there about the Negro poet, and that's not acceptable; black is the word. . . . Something different is happening now . . . black poets are becoming increasingly aware of themselves and their blackness; they are interested in speaking to black people . . . the whole concept of what "good poetry" is is changing today, thank goodness.

In the same interview Brooks sounds the central note of what will be her new black woman's poetry. That poetry will not only be different, it will speak to and for a different audience.

There is something different I want to do. I want to write poems that will be non-compromising. . . . I want to write poetry—and it won't be Ezra Pound poetry, as you can imagine—that will be exciting to people. And I don't see why it can't be "good" poetry.

The changes noted above were not limited to the content, audience, and formal properties of her poems. Two events reported by D. H. Melhem in *Gwendolyn Brooks: Poetry and the Heroic Voice* (1987) point to the actual scope of the transformation that had taken place in this poet. In 1969 Brooks shifted her allegiance to Dudley Randall's Broadside Press, a black-owned and -controlled press founded in the late 1960s. She also sent her Harper editor a new "photo of herself with her hair natural, a style she had adopted in February" of that year. Brooks also severed connections with her literary agent and her editor at Harper's after *The World of Gwendolyn Brooks*, the last work by her published by that press. Her insistence that Harper's include *In the Mecca* in that book was predicated on her concern that the "omission would disregard her development and ignore her contemporary vitality."

The changes wrought in Brooks's work by the experience of a new black poetry and the turbulent events of the sixties most sharply defines the distinction between the Negro poetry of the forties and fifties and the new Black Arts poetry that developed out of and in opposition to it. A single contrast between lines from *Annie Allen* (1949) and *In the Mecca* (1968) will serve to clarify the differences between the pre- and post-Black Arts movement Gwendolyn Brooks.

> Men of careful turns, haters of forks in the road,
> The strain at the eye, that puzzlement, that awe—
> Grant me that I am human, that I hurt,
> That I can cry.

She notes that she is not begging for acceptance, or ashamed; she asks only that the hegemony

> Admit me to our mutual estate.
> Open my rooms, let in the light and air.

> Reserve my service at the human feast.
> And let the joy continue.
> (*Annie Allen*, "The Womanhood," 14)

The poem is a plea to those in power, those who have failed to note their shared humanity with the black suppliant—their mutual estate. They hate change and difference and are unaware that inclusion of the black in the human feast will not alter that celebration. The diction and imagery are the common stock of English poetry—"ask alms," "the loud and sumptuous gate," "the human feast"—as is the elliptical compression, the Hopkinsian rhythms and the subtle rhyme scheme. America is also the subject of *In the Mecca*, but the subject of the conflicting views of two black speakers, Alfred, the gradualist, and Amos, whose views more nearly approximate the purgative violence and the immediacy of the poetry of the Black Arts movement, a violence and immediacy couched in language more proximate to that of speech. Amos prays for America:

> Bathe her in her beautiful blood.
> A long blood bath will wash her pure.
> . . . .
> Let this good rage continue out beyond
> her power to believe or to surmise.
> Slap the false sweetness from that face.

Brooks continues, arguing that the "Great-nailed boots"

> must kick her prostrate, heel-grind that soft breast
> remove her fair fine mask.
> Let her lie there, panting and wild, her pain
> red, running roughly through the illustrious ruin—
> . . . .
> Then shall she rise, recover.
> Never to forget

The signature alliteration is here—"red, running roughly," "rise, recover"—but what we see in imagery, diction, and metrics is a poetic voice that approaches the goal Brooks spoke of in 1969, "that business of abandoning lyricism, et cetera." This less lyrical voice does not issue from a suppliant who prays for membership. Brooks's Amos, like the Biblical prophet, speaks from a position of moral superiority, demanding the necessary destruction precedent to a new dispensation. The following Biblical passages illustrate Brooks's debt to the prophet.

> Wailing shall be in all streets; and they
> shall say in all the highways, Alas! Alas!
> . . . and in all vineyards shall be wailing. . . .
> I hate, I despise your feast days, and I will
> not smell in your solemn assemblies.
> (Amos 5:16–21)

> Let judgment run down as waters, and
> righteousness as a mighty stream.
> (Amos 5:24)

Brooks turns from the image of the meek, suffering victim so well loved in earlier poetry to that of the raging, threatening avenger.

If Brooks experienced a change in her poetic mission as a result of the example of LeRoi Jones at the second Fisk University Writers' Conference, the younger poet, who would later become Imamu Amiri Baraka, Ameer Baraha, and later Amiri Baraka, was also the product of development and change. In 1978 Baraka pointed up the distance between himself then and the self responsible for *Slave Ship*.

It was the petty bourgeois of the oppressed nationality opposing national oppression, but oblivious that capitalism is the material base, the root of all national oppression.

The play was a product of a nationalist phase in Baraka's development. At that point in his career his ideological comprehension of struggle was at best limited and at worst erroneous in its perception of the cause of oppression. The play in this respect was ideologically flawed, as was another work, *The Sidney Poet Heroical*, published in 1979 by Ishmael Reed's I. Reed Books after rejections by a number of publishers. That play "saw only 'black alternatives' to 'white sterility,'" rather than the proletarian alternative to bourgeois rule, which is revolution and socialism." The changes noted here are indicative of the progression from LeRoi Jones the poet to Amiri Baraka the poet.

In February 1965 LeRoi Jones left Greenwich Village where he had been a successful part of an alternative movement in American poetry;

left the Village and his wife and moved to Harlem to found the Black Arts Repertory Theater School (BARTS).

Jones/Baraka comments on stylistic as well as ideological differences between his artist self at different stages in his development. The recording of his development is clearly identified as a central purpose in the closing poem, "The Liar," of *The Dead Lecturer* (1964). The function of poetry is

> Publicly redefining
> each change in my soul, as if I had predicted them
> and profited, biblically, even tho
> their chanting weight,
>   erased familiarity
>   from my face.

The "chanting" of this man "who is loud/ on the birth / of his ways," is not the usual voice of mainstream poetics in the United States; rather, such chanting is more representative of the Beat poetry with which Baraka was associated during his Village period. It hearkens back to the "barbaric yawp" of Walt Whitman, one of the idols of the Beat poets. One result of such chanting will be the bequeathing of a multiple self to his readers.

> When they say, "It is Roi
> Who is dead?" I wonder
> Who will they mean?

Baraka saw the various "schools" of poetry as "a point of departure from the academic, from the Eliotic model of rhetoric, formalism, and iambics. He lists the "Jewish Apocalyptic" of Ginsberg and Kerouac, the bohemians of "turn on, drop out" fame, the Black Mountain poets (especially Creeley and Olson, "who touched me deeply"), William Carlos Williams, the New York school and Pop Art, Kenneth Koch, and John Ashbery. "Whitman and Williams and Pound and Apollinaire and the Surrealists were our prophets." "To A Publisher," first published in *Combustion*, bears the clear marks of Ginberg's brand of outrageous spoofery of the powerful.

> Watch out for Peanuts.
> He's gonna turn out bad / A J.D. / A Beatnik / A
> Typical wise-ass N.Y. kid.

The poem is marked by a crazy blend of cartoon characters (Peanuts, Charlie Brown, Little Orphan Annie), Seurat, DuBarry, Raymond Chandler, Uncle Don, and Olson and Johnson's *Hellzapoppin*. The helpless poet thumbs his nose at the powerful publisher by trashing high culture, elevating popular culture—confusing the very language of the two. Jones's dedications clarify further his early influences. *The Dead Lecturer* opens with a dedication to Ed Dorn and includes the "Crow Jane" sequence, a take-off on William Butler Yeats's "Crazy Jane" poems.

In his autobiography, other influences are clear. "I am not nonviolent. . . . I knew I rejected King's tactics," but "the Cuban Revolution under Castro, the Cuban trip was a turning point in my life . . . I carried so much back with me that I was never the same again. The dynamic of the revolution had touched me." Jones was impelled by this experience to seek a more distinct and personal voice, one "more rooted in my deepest experience." This led to his attempt to escape the "ready-mades, the imitations of Creeley (or Olson)" by turning to the methods used by Aimé Césaire to escape French Symbolist poetry. In preparation for his new poetry of "deepest experience" he began *Blues People* and a study of African American music and history.

It was like my loose-floating feelings, the subordinated brown that was hooked to the black and the blues, were now being reconstructed in the most basic of ways.

Miles Davis, Pharaoh Saunders, Albert Ayler and especially John Coltrane were powerful musical *and* ideological influences on his new consciousness: "It is no coincidence that people always associate John Coltrane and Malcolm X, they are harbingers and reflectors of the same life development." If Malcolm's life represented the new cultural nationalism and non-Western political thought, Coltrane expressed and defined those same forces in his art.

Trane was leaping away from "the given" and the troops of the mainstream were both shocked and sometimes scandalized. . . . The cry of "freedom" was not only musical but reflected what was going on in the marches and confrontations, on the streets and in the restaurants and department stores of the South.

Malcolm and the new music were, for Jones, a movement beyond the nonviolent, integrationist Civil Rights movement, substituting for its epideictic rhetoric the black voices of young black revolutionaries. Jones took part in the protests at the United Nations over the murder of Patrice Lumumba, a protest that heightened the connection between African American concerns and those of emerging independent African nations.

Other sixties influences are present in the new poetry and new sensibility Jones was developing.

A major node or point of change for us came with John Kennedy's assassination. Kennedy, for many of us, even unconsciously, represented something positive.

Malcolm X was a powerful voice of the new African American: "He charged me in a way no one else had ever done. He *reached* me. His media appearances made my head tingle with anticipation and new ideas." The March on Washington and the murder of young black girls in Birmingham were, for Jones, not the beginning or the flowering of the Civil Rights movement headed by King. These events marked its end and the beginning of a new phase of the movement, which did not see itself dedicated to "peace and love."

LeRoi Jones, having earned an M.A. in German Literature, having married the Jewish writer Hettie Cohen in a Buddhist ceremony, and, through his skillful poetry, drama, fiction and editing, having earned a place in the major journals of the avant-garde, came to a crossroads. He left Greenwich Village and his wife, married his present wife Amina in a Yoruba ceremony, and began the cultural nationalist project that was to change African American poetry in substantial ways. If movements can be dated by the appearance of a single book, Black Arts poetry can date its birth from the appearance of *Black Magic* in 1969. This work was the result of a developmental rather than a sudden Saul/Paul shift in sensibility. It was the culmination of his search for an ideology and an art reflective and supportive of a new black America. When *It's Nation Time* appeared a year later, published by Third World Press, a black press, it appeared as the work of a new man—new but continuous with the earlier man. That work was the product, not of LeRoi Jones, but of Amiri Baraka, whose new work would be submitted to Third World Press, to Jihad Publications, and to black journals.

Black Magic contains poems that serve as useful models of Black Arts poetry. "W.W.," a humorous love poem to black women, is a direct repudiation of the earlier "For Hettie," a humorous love poem to a beat-nik—a bohemian in black stockings. If Gwendolyn Brooks sent her publishers a new publicity photo of herself with her hair worn natural, "W.W." calls on all black women to recognize their own beauty and to doff their imitation-Caucasian wigs. Two other poems in the collection must be mentioned here because they have had such broad influence and publicity. "Black Art" is as close as the poet came to an ars poetica for the new poetry; such a poetry must avoid "artiness," and the poem demonstrates this in its avoidance of the lyrical voice and of stock poetic diction, and in its use of ideophones.

> Airplane poems, rrrrrrrrrrrrrrr
> rrrrrrrrrrrrrrr . . . tuhtuhtuhtuhtuhtuhtuhtuh
> . . . rrrrrrrrrrrrrrr . . . Setting fire and death to
> whities ass.

The poem employs suggestions not only of the poem as airplane strafing the enemy but also the death of that enemy.

> Agggh . . . stumbles across the room . . .
> Put it on him, poem. Strip him naked
> to the world!

Poetry is not, as art form, separate from the violent struggles of the people; it is and must be a weapon in that struggle.

> We want live
> words of the hip world live flesh &
> coursing blood. Hearts Brains
> Souls splintering fire.

Poems must be fists, daggers, and poison gas. They are the weapons of the warriors who will accomplish that destruction which will usher in a new world. They will "clean out the world for virtue and love." They will be about love only when the new day arrives, that day on which

> Black People understand
> That they are the lovers and the sons
> of lovers and warriors and sons
> of warriors Are poems & Poets &
> all the loveliness here in the world.

Neither language nor form here can be directly attributed to early models (Creeley, Olson, Ginsberg). The language is that of the black community ("put it on him," "girdle mamma mulatto bitches," "red jelly stuck / between 'lizabeth Taylor's toes.") and, shockingly for many readers, names the enemies of that community ("wops or slick half white / politicians," "the Liberal / Spokesman for the Jews," "a Negro leader pinned to / a bar stool in Sardi's," "cops and niggers"). This is hardly the lyrical effusion of the postromantic divided and alienated self of the first two volumes. Popular culture remains a reference, but it is no longer a site for nostalgic musings on the Green Lantern, the Shadow, and other popular figures (see "In Memory of Radio"), now becoming source and justification of a violent resistance central to new life.

"Black People!" the poem from which Judge Kapp read before sentencing Jones/Baraka during the Newark rebellion, made the line "Up against the wall mother fucker" a motto of the black nationalist movement, and, like Calvin Hernton's "Jitterbugging in the Streets" referred to the urban riots of the period in terms borrowed from Martha and the Vandellas' recording. They were "Dancing in the Streets."

Martha and the Vandellas' "Dancing in the Streets" was like our national anthem. Their "Heat Wave" had signaled earlier, downtown, that the shit was on the rise. But "Dancing in the Streets" which spoke to us of Harlem and the other places, then Watts and later Newark and Detroit, seemed to say it all out. "Summer's here and time is near / for dancing in the streets!"

Baraka sees these songs and Dionne Warwick's "Walk On By," Marvin Gaye's "Stubborn Kind of Fellow," and especially Curtis Mayfield's "Keep on Pushing" as part of the new era for black music that he had developed as a "Black Arts core" and a "word from the black." The voice of revolution was heard not only in the music of avant garde artists like Coltrane but also in rhythm and blues and in black pop music. "Black People!" uses this musical model to celebrate the urban insurrections.

> Dance up and down the streets, turn all
> the music up, run through the streets with music, beautiful radios on
> Market Street

Looting becomes not a crime but an act of rebellion, a recovery of what "he (the white man) already stole."

The name of Sylvia Wilson, Baraka's new wife, was changed to Amina (Faithful) and LeRoi Jones's to Ameer Baraka (Blessed Prince)—a name that he changed to Amiri Baraka in order to Bantu-ize or Swahilize the Arabic. The name change signals the coming into being of the new poet LeRoi Jones had struggled toward through a number of changes and influences. This is the poet who galvanized Gwendolyn Brooks and a generation of Black Arts poets.

Gwendolyn Brooks's *In the Mecca* (1968) interrupts its depiction of life in an urban housing development and the search for a murdered girl with a tribute to Don Lee. She says that he does not want a "various America." Rather, he desires

> a new nation
> under nothing;
> a physical light that waxes; he does not want to
> be exorcised, adjoining and revered;
> he does not like a local garniture
> nor any impish onus in the vogue

He rejects candlelight for

> . . . the auspices of fire
> and rock and jungle-flail;
> wants
> new art and anthem; will
> want a new music screaming in the sun.

The poems in *In the Mecca* are dedicated to "Langston Hughes, and to James Baldwin, LeRoi Jones and Mike Alexandroff, educators extraordinaire," but as the Don Lee section indicates, this poet, too, is one of the educators extraordinaire to whom Brooks is indebted.

Don Lee (later Haki R. Madhubuti, "Precise Justice" in English) was a member of Gwendolyn Brooks's writers workshop and a founder with Johari Amini and Carolyn Rodgers of Third World Press (1967). He also founded the Institute of Positive Education and its educational arm, New Concept Development Center, and has served as editor and publisher of *Black Books Bulletin*. He popularized Kwanzaa (a creation of Maulana Karenga), has held a series of retreats under the aegis of his National Black Wholistic Retreat Foundation, and has remained since the publication of his third book, *Don't Cry, Scream* (1969), one of the most influential and popular Black Arts poets, a position awarded him by critics as varied as Gwendolyn Brooks, his mentor-disciple, who includes him as one figure in her triptych "Young Heroes" (*Family Pictures*, 1970), and Helen Vendler, who saw that "in him the sardonic and savage turn-of-phrase long present in black speech as a survival tactic finds its best poet."

In his introduction to Brooks's *Report from Part One* (1972) Lee cites a passage that might well be as representative of his own as of Brooks's poetic mission.

> My aim, in my next future, is to write poems
> That will somehow successfully "call" (see Imamu
> Baraka's "SOS") all black people . . . Not always
> to "teach"—I shall wish often to entertain,
> to illumine.

Lee's "But He Was Cool" is both a hilariously entertaining put-down of those blacks whose lives are marked by empty posturing and au courant fads and a "call" to blacks to abandon coolness.

> he had a double-natural
> that would put the sisters to shame.
> his dashikis were tailor made
> his beads were imported sea shells
> (from some black/country i never heard of)
> he was triple-hip
> . . . .
> he didn't know,
> after detroit, newark, chicago & c.,
> we had to hip
>   cool-cool/super-cool/real-cool
>   . . . .
> to be black
> is
> to be
> very-hot.

Lee's popularity is linked to his brilliant performance of his poems, his close attention to black music, and his flawless ear for black speech. Few poets have had the power to move audiences possessed by this poet. *Black Pride* (1968) is dedicated to Malcolm X (religious and political model), Langston Hughes (poet and black cultural model), and John Coltrane (musician and master manipulator of black music and sensibility). The title poem of *Don't Cry, Scream* (1969) exemplifies the thematic, stylistic, and political concerns of Madhubuti. The poem derives its title from his mother's admonition, "nigger, if u is goin ta open yr / mouth Don't Cry, Scream" and is dedicated to John Coltrane. The poem rejects the crying of the blues—

> i cried for billie holiday.
> the blues. we ain't blue
> the blues exhibited illusions of manhood.

—for the screaming of Coltrane's saxaphone riffs. Screaming here connotes not simple sounds of anguish and pain. Screaming is rage and defiance; a refusal to beg. Screaming is the dozens, screaming on the enemy and his blind collaborators.

> blonds had more fun—
> with snagga-tooth niggers
> who saved pennies & pop bottles for week-ends
> to play negro & other filthy inventions.
> by-bop-en to james brown's
> Cold Sweat—these niggers didn't sweat,
> they perspired

For such "Niggers" (Madhubuti, like Baraka uses the terms *nigger, negro,* and *faggot* to represent the traitor, the deluded, and the impotent) he has

>   instant hate.)
> they didn't know any better,
> brother, they were too busy getting
> into debt, expressing humanity &
> taking off color.

The poem, dedicated to Coltrane, featuring him as hero also recreates his musical style. Performance directions are included in the margin:

Sing
loud &
high
with
feeling
. . . . .
sing
loud &
long with
feeling
. . . . .
sing loud
& high
with
feeling
letting
yr/voice
break
. . . . .
improvise
with
feeling
. . . . .
very
soft

The performer vocally recreates the sounds of Coltrane's instrument and riffs lines in the manner of that model black artist.

& that BLIND man
i don't envy him anymore
i can see his hear
& hear his heard through my pores.
i can see my me it was truth you gave,
. . . .
it had to come.

The performer (the poem is not intended for a reader), progresses from the loud screaming of the middle portion of the poem to the subdued, soft reassured sounds of the closing. Only when he opens the ears of his deaf audience can this musician chance closing on a softer note.

That softer note is found in the beautiful love poem to black women "A Poem Looking for a Reader (to be read with a love consciousness)."

> a fifty minute call to blackwomanworld:
>> hi baby,
>> how u doin?
>> need u.

It is a song, a riff on "Please Sunshine, Please" but it is also a love rap, one assured of its success.

> she will come as she would
> want her man to come.
> she'll come,
> she'll come.

Though he "never wrote a love letter,"

> that doesn't mean
> i
> don't love.

Typography here, as in most poems, is used as a guide to performance. The distribution of lines is used to create the rhythms and asymetrical moves of jazz performance.

For Madhubuti black poetry is political, and he includes poems not only to black liberation but also to women's liberation; he celebrates the heroes and martyrs of the movement dealing with Malcolm X and Martin Luther King, Jr. His "Black Poetics / for the many to come," an essay that opens *Don't Cry, Scream*, makes this political focus clear.

I've often come across black artists . . . who feel that they and their work should be apolitical; not realizing that to be apolitical is to be political in a negative way for black folks. There is no neutral black art; either it is or it isn't, period.

Madhubuti closes the volume with "A Message All Blackpeople Can Dig (& a few negroes too)."

> now is
> the time, the best
> while there is something to save (other than our lives).
> we'll move together
> . . . .

> blackpeople
> are moving, moving to return
>   this earth into the hand of
> human beings.

The transformation recorded in "The Self-Hatred of Don Lee" (*Black Pride*, 1968) is clearly in evidence in *Don't Cry, Scream*, the work that positioned Don Lee/Haki R. Madhubuti as a central figure in the development of Black Arts poetry. He moves from division, ignorance, and silence to unity, awareness, and a calling. The initiating experiences are his reading of DuBois, Rodgers, Locke, Wright, and others. They move him to an "us, we, me i / awareness," where he begins "to love / only a / part of" himself, the "inner / self which" is "black." Thus Madhubuti

> developed a
> vehement
> hatred of
> my light
> brown
> other.

He can be the poet of love as well as the poet of hate. He can blur the boundaries between poetry and music, reading and performance, the lyrical and the vatic.

Jones/Baraka's *Home* (1966) records in twenty-five selections the journey of consciousness that brought him home, not to a place, but "toward the thing I had coming into the world, with no sweat: my blackness." It closes with a call to black artists ("state-meant") to "aid in the destruction of America, . . . to report and reflect . . . the nature of the society . . . to draw out of his soul the correct image of the world," and to use this image to "band his brothers and sisters together." "The Black Artist must teach the White Eyes their deaths, and teach the black man how to bring these deaths about.".

In his autobiography he recalls one of the poets of the Black Arts Movement, "a wide-eyed young woman, quiet and self-deprecating, was herself coming out of a bad marriage and she came to our programs announcing very quietly and timidly that she was a poet." This was Sonia Sanchez, who was instrumental in organizing one of the first black studies programs in the United States and who made her first guest artist at San Francisco State Amiri Baraka.

Like Baraka and Madhubuti, Sanchez traveled widely in the "third" world; her 1979 trip to Cuba echoed the 1960 experience of Baraka. *Homecoming* (1969), her first book of poems reflects thematically and stylistically the Black Arts aesthetic and its focus on the theme of cultural and consciousness development. Her ability to command the attention of ordinary black people in the streets and in the taverns was a part of the new poetic mission that Brooks set for herself. Sanchez was determined to be the artist called for in Jones/Baraka's "State-Meant."

In the title poem of *Homecoming* she contrasts her earlier "tourist style" detachment to her second return to a black identity and solidarity. Sanchez leaves behind

> . . . those hide and
> seek faces peeling
> with freudian dreams
> this is for real.
>
> >   black
> >   Niggers
> >   my beauty.

The "niggers" she once watched kill each other are no longer disconnected others, they are her self and her beauty. In her first book she celebrates homecoming and black unity.

Sanchez knows the power of humor and of tenderness, qualities not often associated with Black Arts poetry. Both love and comedy are to be found in "To Chuck" a poem parodying e. e. cummings's use of unusual typography. The purpose of the poem is to provide her lover who is

>   3
>   0
>   0
>   0
>   mi
>   awayfromme
>   my   MAN
>   with a sexual object.
>   i'
>   m
>   go
>   n n
>   a   sc
>   rew
>   u on   pap er

She chooses cummings as a model because

> heknewallabout
> SCR
>   EW
> ing
> on   WH
>   ite pa per.

We are left to wonder if this is tribute or mockery. Did cummings know how to screw or did he screw up on white paper?

Madhubuti describes Sanchez as "the poet-revolutionary whose sole aim is liberation, peace, love, and effective writing." That sole aim of liberation is clear to him as a reader of Sanchez's poetry.

> she wants Blackpeople to grow and
> develop so that we can move toward
> determining our own destiny. She wants
> us not only to be responsible for our
> actions but to take responsible actions.

Madhubuti calls attention to Sanchez's rightful place among the ranks of those who should be credited with "legitimizing the use of urban Black English." This language has been combined with the internal and the external music of black people. Note her use of both the language and the music of urban Black America in "to Blk / record / buyers," a poem in which she attempts to reeducate her people, to deafen them to cheap negro delineators in the music world.

> don't play me no
> righteous bros.
>   white people
> ain't rt bout nothing
> no mo.

These imitations sing meaningless songs:

>   cuz no blk /
> people are grooving on a
> sunday afternoon.

In the place of this false, plastic music she demands authentic black sound.

> play blk / songs
>   to drown out the
> shit / screams of honkies. AAAH.
> AAAH. AAAH. yeah.   brothers.
>   andmanymoretogo.

The poem does more than cite black songs. In its closing lines it moves toward the very condition of song.

"Poem at Thirty" appeared in *Homecoming* and this poem, like "Homecoming" focuses on her own transformation, one that she presents as a model for all becoming black people. The midnight journey is not depicted as easy; the way is not clear.

> did i know
> then where i
> was going?
> traveling. i'm
> always traveling.

Although the journey is marked by darkness and terror, it must be made. Successful completion of such a journey demands reaching out to those brothers and sisters who may appear both threatening and completely lost. To the black man "stretching scraping / the mold from [his] body," she reaches out.

> here is my hand.
> i am not afraid
> of the night.

The above poem marks one of the unique contributions of Sanchez to Black Arts poetry. She returns blues, repudiated by Karenga, Baraka, and others, to the center of poetic discourse. (One may argue that she turns later to haiku and tanka because they are like blues lyrics in their compression and obliqueness.) Sanchez goes back not only to a blues form but to a blues sensibility. If her poetic mission is to support and exhort her black brothers and sisters, it is also to report the pain she has felt when they have failed to realize their beauty and their best. "Prelude to Nothing" is a remarkable poem for the tightly controlled dialogue that holds in the rage and frustration of the speaking voice, emotions that shout for attention

> what's that you say?
> NOW HEAR THIS. NOW HEAR THIS.

but finally lapse into an enigmatic and, given the power of the need expressed, tragic resignation. The question on which the poem closes suggests its own negative answer.

The desire for "a man who fucks without hating" expressed in "Prelude to Nothing" comes to full realization in "Blues, a conversation with Bessie Smith, the only other woman who could understand the wonder and power of good sex." (Sanchez, like Giovanni, is not content to be the idealized spiritual Black Madonna. She insists on the full expression of her sexuality.) The poet remembers that wonderful moment in the midst of what is now loss. The absence is greater because of that one fleeting moment.

> won't someone open
> the door for me? won't some
> one schedule my sleep
> and don't ask no question?
> noise.

Sanchez juxtaposes this need and emptiness to the fullness expressed in the lines lifted from Bessie Smith.

> Yeah, bessie he put in the bacon
> and it overflowed the pot.

But like the great blues singer Bessie Smith, her music can move from regret and sorrow to rage and condemnation. Blues were more than sorrow songs, they were a vehicle used to put people's business in the street, to sound on the worthless. "A Poem for My Father" is vicious in its condemnation of those men who use and abuse women, whose "makeshift manhood" demands frequent verification, verification found only in the subjugation of women. Sex here is not an act of love. It is

> so many black
> perfumed bodies weeping
> underneath you

or

> you slapped some
> wide hips about in
> your pvt dungeon.

Sanchez draws attention to the absence of love within the community, an absence that makes revolution impossible; an absence resulting not only from black brothers and sisters hating each other, but from a very corrosive self-hatred. Both "Blk / Rhetoric" and "Indianapolis Summer / 1969 / Poem" are raps that clarify this illness using a form borrowed not from mainstream poetics but from the black oral tradition. "Blk / Rhetoric" opens on a note of complaint, one aimed at the empty rhetoric of so many so-called black revolutionaries.

> Who's gonna make all
> this beautiful blk/rhetoric
> mean something

To mean something the rhetoric must effect real change in the lives of black men and women. It must result in economic change "more real then blk / capitalism." It must teach brothers and sisters that they are important and must move them "in straight / revolutionary / lines." Most of all, such rhetoric must bring into being true heroes as opposed to the negative and destructive who are the subject of Sanchez's corruption list. The poet turns at the end to that device used by Baraka

> Like. this. is an SOS
> me. calling . . .
> calling . . .
> some / one
> pleasereplysoon.

Her "SOS," like her "NOW HEAR THIS," are military terms and the desperate call of an embattled warrior hoping for relief, demanding comrades, and refusing to accept anything short of full engagement. "Indianapolis / Summer / 1969 / Poem" draws us closer to the corruption that prevents love and revolution (an inseparable pair for Sanchez). This rap deals with the corrupt economic system that results in black men and women prostituting themselves for a few coins. It skewers black men who fail to program

> sistuhs fo love
> instead of
> > fucken / hood,

mothers who do not teach their daughters to love black men, black fathers who substitute sexual dominance for true manhood. We have failed.

> if we programmed /
> > loved / each
> other in com / mun / al ways,
> . . . .
> > it wud all
> come down to some
> > thing else
> like RE VO LU TION.

R. Roderick Palmer closes his essay "The Poetry of Three Revolution-ists" with the following prophecy.

The path depicted by the poetry of Lee (Madhubuti), Sanchez, and Giovan-ni—depending upon circumstances and future developments—could lead in either of two directions, the direction of revolution or evolution.

If revolution was a clear mark of Nikki Giovanni's first books, *Black Feeling Black Talk and Black Judgment* (published as one volume in 1970), evolution toward a different view of the poet's function is more clear in the body of her later work than in that of Madhubuti and Sanchez. Giovanni shares with Sanchez a concern with woman's voice, woman's experience, and woman's concerns, but she moves closer to an individual and domestic thematics than does her sister poet. The personal in Sanchez is more easily read as a representative self than is found in Giovanni's poems after *Black Feeling Black Talk and Black Judgment*. In "Poem at Thirty," discussed above, Sanchez may be referring directly to her tragic marriage to drug-addicted Etheridge Knight (a marriage Baraka referred to in his description of his first meeting Sanchez), but the poem is so constructed that we may read in it the experience of all black people, all black women. The very titles of Giovanni's works in the 1970s signaled a different kind of focus. *My House* (1972), *The Women and the Men*, (1975) and *Cotton Candy on a Rainy*

Day (1978) do not sound like titles for a Black Arts poetry of revolution.

Giovanni was the fourth member of that quartet of young Turks (Jones/Baraka, Lee/Madhubuti, and Sanchez were the others) that so galvanized Gwendolyn Brooks at the Fisk University Writers' Conference, but the other members of the group have not been wholly positive about her powers or her excellence as a poet. Baraka felt that she was an opportunist and Madhubuti castigated her for the absence of what he termed sophistication of thought in her poetry. A younger writer, Michelle Wallace (*Black Macho and the Myth of the Superwoman*, 1978, and *Invisibility Blues*, 1990), labeled her a black Rod McKuen. Giovanni studied at Fisk, where she was part of J. O. Killens's famous writers' workshop and was the first of the younger Black Arts poets to be published by a mainstream publisher. Her work—unlike the later work of Brooks and Baraka and almost all of the work of Madhubuti and Sanchez—has appeared under the names of publishers like Bobbs-Merrill and Morrow rather than black houses like Jihad, Broadside, or Third World.

Two sides of Giovanni are already present in her first book. "The True Import of Present Dialogue, Black as Negro" is a clear product of the Black Arts aesthetic. The poem exhorts its reader to acts of murder, necessary murder, a revolutionary act.

> can you kill nigger
> Huh? . . .
>
> . . .
> Do you know how to draw blood
> Can you poison
> Can you stab-a-Jew
> Can you kill huh?

Two themes are present: the necessity of violence and the necessity for desertion of the status of nigger or Negro. The killing of the poem is extended to the murder of the "white-washed" mind that prevents one from murdering white oppressors. Not to be overlooked is the presence in the poem of that other popular target of early Black Arts poetry, the Jew as quintessence of the white man. Kill them but kill also the intestine enemy, the nigger.

> Can you kill the nigger
> in you
> Can you make your nigger mind
> die
> Can you kill your nigger mind
> And free your black hands to
> strangle
> . . . .
> Learn to kill niggers
> Learn to be Black men

The poem as chant, as rap, is clearly illustrated here in the patterned repetition and in the plays on words as well as the jazzy rhythms.

"The true Import . . ." was one of the most frequently anthologized of Giovanni's early poems. A second poem from this first collection also found its way into the anthologies. "Nikki-Rosa" is related to black revolution in an oblique manner if at all. The concern here is the happiness of growing up in a black home; the images are domestic rather than militant.

> how good the water felt when you got your bath
> from one of those
> big tubs that folk in Chicago barbecue in
> . . . .
> it isn't your father's drinking that makes any difference
> but only that everybody is together and you
> and your sister have happy birthdays and very good
> Christmasses

The "racial" confrontation in the poem is situated in the regret that white biographers will assess her happy life only in terms focused on poverty and lack of status. None of these were important enough to cloud her happiness. Regret at white blindness seems tacked on as an afterthought to a poem centered on domestic bliss. Later in this volume she offers a gloss on her own militant poem, a gloss that calls into question the Black Arts insistence on the centrality of the artist to black revolution. "My Poem" argues that nothing that she can do or say will stop the "revolution in the streets"; Giovanni as poet is irrelevant to that Armegeddon.

and if i stay on
the 5th floor
it will go on
if i never do
anything
it will go on.

Her relationship to an audience develops not only along domestic lines, it turns from exhortation to love. In *Re: Creation* (1970) "Kidnap Poem" does not purport to move a reader to revolution, rather, the goal is joy and love. She will "meter" a reader to Jones Beach or Coney Island,

alliterate the beach
to complement my see

Play the lyre for you
Ode you with my love song.

We encounter here the lyre and the ode rather than the sax of Coltrane or the rap. The appearance of the red black and green (black liberation colors) in the closing lines does not radically disturb the lilting tone of this lyric. "Poem for Aretha," while seeming to follow the direction in which other Black Arts poets moved—i.e., the adoption of the method of musicians of both liberation music and rhythm and blues artists— does something else. Giovanni is interested here in the exhaustion of the musician, her inability to enjoy a home, the exhaustion that comes from "the strangers / pulling at you cause they love you but you having no love / to give back." Aretha's singing, like Giovanni's poetry, may have no real power to stop

chickens from frying
eggs from being laid
crackers from hating

Aretha is "more important than her music." "She needs / a rest." She is in danger of suffering the same fate as Billie Holiday or Dinah Washington. Here again the poem shifts its focus to argue that "Aretha was the riot was the leader," but the riot to which Giovanni refers is not equated to "dancing in the streets" and urban violence. Giovanni's Aretha led a riot in music. She brought black crossover artists back into the mainstream of authentic black music.

Giovanni does not begin as a Black Arts poet and then desert the movement. From its first appearance her work is marked by an ambivalence toward the ideology though not the aesthetics of the Black Arts movement. She may have delivered the final word on her ambivalence in *Gemini* (1971). In an essay that first appeared in *Negro Digest* she asserts: "I like all militant poems that tell how we're going to kick the honkie's backside and purge our new system of all honkie things. . . . I mean, I wrote a poem asking, 'Nigger, can you Kill?' " Yet she argues that listening to black music results, for her, in a different experience. Smokey Robinson and the Miracles remind her of the wonder and necessity of love. "There is a tendency to look at the Black experience too narrowly."

In his introduction to *Modern Black Poets* (1973) Donald Gibson argues the uniqueness of Black Arts poetry. "Never before has there been any significant body of literature by black writers so closely resembling a unique black literature." The work of Baraka, Giovanni, Madhubuti, and Sanchez in the sixties and seventies is central to an understanding of the contours and dimensions of that movement.

William W. Cook

Further Reading

Baraka, Imamu Amiri (LeRoi Jones). *The Autobiography of LeRoi Jones/Amiri Baraka.* New York: Freundlich, 1984.

——— *Black Magic: Collected Poetry, 1961–69.* New York: Bobbs-Merrill, 1969.

——— *Selected Poetry of Amiri Baraka/LeRoi Jones.* New York: Morrow, 1979.

Brooks, Gwendolyn. *Blacks.* Chicago: David, 1987.

——— *Report from Part One.* Detroit: Broadside, 1972.

——— *Selected Poems.* New York: Harper-Collins, 1992.

Giovanni, Nikki. *Black Feeling Black Talk and Black Judgment.* New York: Morrow, 1970.

——— *Cotton Candy on a Rainy Day.* New York: Morrow, 1980.

——— *Gemini: An Extended Autobiographical Statement.* New York: Penguin, 1976.

——— *Spin a Soft Black Song.* New York: Morrow, 1987.

——— *THe Women and the Men.* New York: Morrow, 1979.

Madhubuti, Haki R. (Don L. Lee). *Directionscore: Selected and New Poems.* Detroit: Broadside, 1971.

———— *Don't Cry, Scream.* Detroit: Broadside, 1969.

———— *Earthquakes and Sun Rise Missions: Poetry and Essays of Black Renewal, 1973–83.* Chicago: Third World, 1984.

———— *Killing Memory, Seeking Ancestors.* Detroit: Lotus, 1987.

Sanchez, Sonia. *homegirls & handgrenades.* New York: Thunder's Mouth Press, 1984.

———— *I've Been a Woman: New and Selected Poems.* Sausalito: Black Scholar, 1978.

———— *Under a Soprano Sky.* Trenton: Africa World, 1987.

Nature's Refrain in American Poetry

A RIDGE of the Green Mountains runs between Lincoln, Vermont and Ripton, where Robert Frost maintained a home for many years. When migrating glaciers raddled the crest-line here and scraped away the topsoil, a disorienting terrain of spurs, cliffs, and bogs was left behind. This is the landscape of Robert Frost's poem "Directive," where one can only go forward through a process of reversals and roundabouts, and where one only finds one's way by getting lost. Walking up onto this ridge, densely reforested now yet harboring still the cellar holes and stone walls of last century's marginal farms, the poet sought a retreat from the complexities of the present. It was a trajectory

> Back out of all this now too much for us,
> Back in a time made simple by the loss
> Of detail . . .

"Directive" expresses a central impulse in American nature poetry: toward a retreat that is at the same time a return. "All this" represents the pressures of modern society, while the turning "back" reflects a desire to regain intimacy with the earth. Our poets have attempted to retreat not just from the realm of "getting and spending" but also from prevailing *ideas* of nature and "the good place"—to come back down to earth in a way that is less a recollection of past gardens than a renewal of natural vividness in the present. This dynamic of therapeutic simplification and regrounding is summed up in a line from section 10 of

A. R. Ammons's *Sphere: The Form of a Motion*, "Things go away to return, brightened for the passage." In its celebrations of the local and the present, American nature poetry completes a grounded circuit of separation and recovery.

This poetry of strategic retreat grows out of the Puritan sensibility, as may be illuminated by looking at Anne Bradstreet's "Contemplations." Probably written in 1666, this is the major work of our nation's first important poet in English. In such elements as its classical allusions to Phoebus, Neptune, and Philomel—the nightingale whose voice was never heard on *this* continent—"Contemplations" reflects Bradstreet's own background in sixteenth- and seventeenth-century English literature. Her Puritan education and outlook are also evident throughout, of course, as may be seen in the twentieth of her thirty-three stanzas. After an opening that celebrates the beauty of the late-afternoon hour and laments humanity's mortal state, she asks:

> Shall I then praise the heavens, the trees, the earth,
> Because their beauty and their strength last longer?
> Shall I wish there or never to had birth,
> Because they're bigger and their bodies stronger?
> Nay, they shall darken, perish, fade, and die,
> And when unmade so ever shall they lie,
> But man was made for endless immortality.

The most remarkable effect of the poem, though, is that just as she retreats from *one* vision of earthly paradise, Bradstreet steps into a new, more *vivid* landscape. While her theological viewpoint is unaffected, the dynamic of retreat has nonetheless refreshed her senses and stimulated her emotions. She begins actually to see the world, as in the celebrated lines when she turns to watch the jumping of fish:

> Look how the wantons frisk to taste the air,
> Then to the colder bottom straight they dive

It is at this point, too, that she hears birdsong break forth:

> a most melodious strain,
> Which rapt me so with wonder and delight,
> I judged my hearing better than my sight,
> And wished me wings with her a while to take my flight.

Such heightened sensibility on the heels of renunciation is a distinctively Puritan reflex, strengthened in America by the wild abundance of a new continent and by the myth that in the founding of a New Jerusalem history could be reversed.

Though the religious assumptions of later poets diverge wildly from Bradstreet's, this psychological rhythm of retreat and restoration echoes through three centuries of American poetry. In "Autumn Refrain" Wallace Stevens describes the nightingale, Bradstreet's Philomel, as

> not a bird for me
> But the name of a bird and the name of a nameless air
> I have never—shall never hear.

Yet he still hears a "skreaking and skrittering residuum" and perceives his Connecticut present *through* "evasions of the nightingale." The act of turning away from the past, and "the stillness of everything gone," opens a clearing where America's grackles can grate their own unmellifluous song before flying away themselves. Perceiving nature, and even experiencing a particular moment, is always a process of rejection for Stevens—a continuous act of erasure rather than a blankness. As he writes in "Notes Toward a Supreme Fiction," "You must become an ignorant man again." The "refrain" of "Autumn Refrain" thus expresses both the necessity of a witholding or separation before one can come freshly to nature and the *recurrence* of such "evasion" as the most consistent element in our perception of nature's music.

Gary Snyder's poem "For Nothing," from *Turtle Island,* dramatizes this process of retreat from our known earth. In the age of space exploration as in the era of colonization in New England, relinquishment is the first step toward renewing vision and strengthening love.

> Earth a flower
> a phlox on the steep
> slopes of light
> hanging over the vast
> solid spaces
> small rotten crystals;
> salts.
>
> Earth a flower
> by a gulf where a raven
> flaps by once

a glimmer, a color
forgotten as all falls away.
a flower
for nothing;
an offer;
no taker;

Snow-trickle, feldspar, dirt.

With its depiction of the smallness and isolation of our blue-green, cloud-swirled orb, when viewed from orbit as in the famous NASA photograph, the poem reads as an elegy. This distanced perspective of earth provides an external corollary for Bradstreet's inward withdrawal. And as her renunciation, does, Snyder's poem generates a heightened responsiveness to our planet. The effect of separation in "For Nothing" is reinforced by the poet's own tactful distance from his picture; there are no personal pronouns, no grammatically complete propositions casting their human claims across the image. Here the celebration of a flowering planet is spoken in a language resonant yet remote. Such simplification clears the ground for new growth. Once, in a discussion of "For Nothing" in a Middlebury College seminar on the poetry of nature, a geology major exclaimed: "Look at that last line—'snow-trickle, feldspar, dirt'—it's the genesis of soil!"

Retreats are both *from* and *to*. In evading conventions, including those that govern our perceptions of nature, America's poetry of nature also swarms toward the bliss of presentness. For modern poets the Puritans' City Set Upon a Hill is a fulfillment that may be entered into most directly through the sensory experience of one's own body as an integral part of the physical universe. This is a matter of faith, of opening one's spirit to the joyful austerities of natural providence. David Wagoner's "Sitting by a Swamp," from *In Broken Country*, begins with an apparently dead scene. Then, as the speaker settles in to listen and watch, life flows into both the swamp and the human subject. The third and last stanza reads:

From a thicket a fox sparrow
Taking me in, one eye
At a wary time, where I wait
To be what they want me to be:
Less human. A dragonfly
Burns green at my elbow.

To enter into the wholeness of nature one must give up one's sense of human specialness. In effect, one must separate oneself from one's own sense of separateness. This is the logic of religious paradox: the will for will-lessness, or dying to be born again. Recoiling from ideas of nature, letting go of clearly perceived designs, the poet momentarily touches the earth.

In one section of the poem "Music," from her collection *American Primitive,* Mary Oliver discovers the wholeness of human experience within the most immediate natural impulses. She asks if "the heart / is accountable," if a person's body is really anything "more than a branch / of a honey locust tree":

> hunting water,
> hunching toward the sun,
> shivering, when it feels
> that good, into
> white blossoms?

She goes on to ponder whether there is a type of music

> that lights up the otherwise
> blunt wilderness of the body—
> a furious
> and unaccountable selectivity?

"Hunching toward the sun" is a wry and modest line, like "Snow-trickle, feldspar, dirt." They both possess the quality William Hazlitt attributed to Wordsworth in an early review—"proud humility." A process of scouring their experience and their verse down to images less adorned than "imagery" aligns these poets with forces grander than any immediate aesthetic design. Soil builds up in crevices of a granite face, preparing for another flourishing of Snyder's alpine phlox. A branch, wet and black in the uncertain vicissitudes of spring, makes ready to blossom.

From our present perspective, in the last decade of the twentieth century, three poets seem to have exerted special influence upon America's poetry of nature: Walt Whitman, Emily Dickinson, and Robert Frost. Each of them, through the conduit of Emerson, registers the Puritan impulse of retreat. At the same time in their own distinctive qualities, such as optimism, patriotism, humor, and scientific curiosity, they contribute to a diverse new language in our nature poetry. Since World War

II other voices from quite distinct traditions have also gained prominence. An upsurge of Native American poetry written in English has made more generally available a mythic view of nature that is not predicated upon a conflict between humanity and nature. East Asian poetry, especially haiku, has also become part of our literary landscape. Such poetry from Buddhist cultures both presents an alternative to the providential Christian view of nature and confirms in its different way the visions of immediacy within our Western tradition.

Descending into the present moment of nature our poets have discovered another familial form of descent as well—a kinship with others who have dedicated themselves to the same discipline of retreat. In the final section of "Song of Myself" Whitman addresses the way in which, by coming down to the ground level in his poetry, he has made himself available to all who seek ecstatic communion with this world:

> I depart as air, I shake my white locks at the runaway sun,
> I effuse my flesh in eddies, and drift it in lacy jags.
>
> I bequeath myself to the dirt to grow from the grass I love,
> If you want me again look for me under your boot-soles.

Just as relinquishment offers the gift of presentness, so too does it make available a community rooted in the earth, arising in each new season as it flourishes over the centuries.

Whitman experiences the beauty of nature as an ecstasy that both overwhelms and intensifies his own sense of individuality:

> Smile, O voluptuous cool-breath'd earth!
> Earth of the slumbering and liquid trees!
> Earth of the departed sunset—earth of the mountains misty-topt!
> Earth of the vitreous pour of the full moon just tinged with blue!
> Earth of shine and dark mottling the tide of the river!
> Earth of the limpid gray of clouds brighter and clearer for my sake!
> Far-swooping elbow'd earth—rich apple-blossom'd earth!
> Smile, for your lover comes.

This rhapsody from section 21 of "Song of Myself" turns on the sense of *mutual* love between the poet and the earth. He can come down to earth confidently and joyfully because of his deep faith: nature will always be meaningful for him—not simply a blank or, in any emotional sense, a wasteland. This faith, like the basic dynamic of retreat and return, once more echoes a Puritan strain in American culture—a sense that individual natural facts are at the same time "types," or spiritual facts. As Perry Miller has pointed out, Emerson's essays transported and transformed such Puritan perspectives into the American Renaissance.

Whitman begins section 25 of "Song of Myself" with these lines:

> Dazzling and tremendous how quick the sun-rise would kill me,
> If I could not now and always send sun-rise out of me.
>
> We also ascend dazzling and tremendous as the sun,
> We found our own O my soul in the calm and cool of the daybreak.

Behind Whitman's verse one can hear chapter 1 of Emerson's *Nature*.

The sun illuminates only the eye of the man, but shines into the eye and the heart of the child. The lover of nature is he whose inward and outward senses are still truly adjusted to each other, who has retained the spirit of infancy even into the era of manhood. His intercourse with heaven and earth, becomes part of his daily food. In the presence of nature, a wild delight runs through the man, in spite of real sorrows.

While this oneness with nature represents an article of faith for many poets in Emerson's wake, it is also continually ratified for them by experience—or "experimentally," as the first generation of English Puritans would have expressed it. To the glossary of retreat and return one might thus add the world "recourse." Poets turn back to nature in perplexity and find in it comfort and sustenance.

Because of his belief that nature and culture reflect each other, Whitman finds a wholeness in the world, allowing him to identify with every human condition as well as with nonhuman life. One of the distinguishing traits of American nature poetry, even before the prominence of Native American motifs in our own century, is its inclusion of animal voices. In "Out of the Cradle Endlessly Rocking," Whitman both describes the song of the mockingbird calling for his mate and imitates the mockingbird's own song. Its whistled reiterations are echoed and elaborated in the lines' living pulse:

> Hither my love!
> Here I am! here!
> With this just-sustain'd note I announce myself to you,
> This gentle call is for you my love, for you.

Through birdsong, subsequent American writers too have opened their poetry to the voice of nature. In "Claritas" Denise Levertov evokes the piercing hymn of the white-throated sparrow whose high, pure notes ring across the wooded margins of northern New England at dawn and dusk:

> Sun
> light.
> > Light
> light light light.

Including the voices of birds also distills A. R. Ammons's strategy in "Corsons Inlet," a poem that ends with the words "tomorrow a new walk is a new walk." Daily the poet ventures forth into the world in order to be renewed as well as to convey, through the openness of his poetry, nature's own "news":

> the news to my left over the dunes and
> reeds and bayberry clumps was
> > fall: thousands of tree swallows
> > gathering for flight:
> > an order held
> > in constant change . . .

The birds, described by Ammons as "a congregation / rich with entropy," burst singing into the poem:

> cheet, cheet, cheet, cheet, wings rifling the green clumps,
> beaks
> at the bayberries
> a perception full of wind, flight, curve,
> sound

In counterpart to the human abstractions of "congregation" and "entropy" rings the swallows' honed and immediate utterance.

Emily Dickinson's poetry confirms the fact that, while America's poets of nature seek to begin history again in each vivid present, they are not without antecedents either in England or in America. Her sly appropriation of Puritan terminology acknowledges that she, like Emerson and Whitman, is a child of the Pilgrims—one who seeks and finds divine revelations in the physical details of her world. Like Whitman, too, she reveals an affinity with the English Romantics. For him, the closer association with this lineage seems to be with Wordsworth, the grand walker of *The Prelude;* Dickinson, by contrast, resembles the Keats of the great odes. Both her American and her English affinities are conveyed in the poem, "The Gentian weaves her fringes." Like Keats's "To Autumn," it evokes with densely sensual and emotional images the fruitful ending of the year.

> The Gentian weaves her fringes—
> The Maple's loom is red—
> My departing blossoms
>   Obviate parade.
>
> A brief, but patient illness—
> An hour to prepare,
> And one below this morning
> Is where the angels are—
>
> It was a short procession,
> The Bobolink was there—
> An aged Bee addressed us—
> And then we knelt in prayer—
> We trust that she was willing—
> We ask that she may be.
> Summer—Sister—Seraph!
> Let us go with thee!
>
> In the name of the Bee—
> And of the Butterfly—
> And of the Breeze—Amen!

Dickinson's dashes, no less than A. R. Ammons's use of colons, suggest a world of correspondences. The autumn is at once a bereavement and a consummation; the poet's voice is identified with the dying one ("My departing blossoms"), with the mourners at the funeral, and with the colorful beauty of trees and fields. "Summer—Sister—Seraph" further equates the seasons here on earth both with those of a human life and with eternity. The engaging quality of her final three lines comes from its union of religious language with the immediacy of insects and autumn. Her doxology under the sky, in celebration of the autumnal equinox, brings a distinctively playful note into American nature poetry, complementing the somber voices with which other poets have often sounded their strategic retreats to earth.

Like other American authors on the trajectory that runs from Edwards to moderns like Frost, Dillard, and Ammons, Dickinson is often drawn to the vivid world of spiders and insects. As she writes in one poem,

> Bees are Black, with Gild Surcingles—
> Buccaneers of Buzz.
> Ride abroad in ostentation
> And subsist on Fuzz.

Natural providence is then affirmed with a wholehearted laugh in the phrase, "Fuzz ordained—"

> not Fuzz contingent—
> Marrows of the Hill.
> Jugs—a Universe's fracture
> Could not jar or spill.

The mystical solemnity that often accompanies poetry's returns to nature is balanced by the wryness of Dickinson and her successors. Marianne Moore's meditation on the armored anteater, or "pangolin," invites a reader to see that remarkable beast as a "near artichoke." Describing the overlapping pattern of its armor, scale by scale, she celebrates an entrancing strangeness—"ordained," yet almost unbelievable. Exactness of observation testifies to nature's intricacy. Theodore Roethke, who sometimes recalls Dickinson with his short lines and rhyming quatrains, begins his poem "The Minimal," "I study the lives on a leaf: the little / sleepers." Detail, clearly apprehended, is intoxicating, hallucinatory.

Often, dreamlike precision fills Dickinson's world with a giddy significance.

> I'll tell you how the Sun rose—
> A Ribbon at a time—
> The Steeples swam in Amethyst—
> The news, like Squirrels, ran—

Stripping away to reach the surface of experience is here less like Stevens's "evasion of the nightingale" than it is a press of strange *new* images, registered as real and accurate because they are so vivid and unexpected. Dickinson is alert to the seasons within seasons, the incongruities between patterns we look for in nature and the immediate sensory information. She focuses on the more precise transitions within our broad understanding of the year's progression:

> 'Twas later when the summer went
> Than when the Cricket came—
> And yet we knew that gentle clock
> Meant not but going home—
>
> 'Twas sooner when the Cricket went
> Than when the Winter came
> Yet that pathetic Pendulum
> Keeps esoteric Time.

"Esoteric Time" is *natural* time: outside our conventional expectations because more particular; a "sister" whom we may recognize in both summer and seraph.

The twentieth-century poet who holds as central a place in American nature poetry as Whitman and Dickinson do is Robert Frost. Because he comes later in the life of the nation, he understands that poets' continous retreat to the earth enacts a prominent pattern in American *history* as well. "Directive" invites its reader "back out of all this" to a place where ancestors in the *land* also attempted, and temporarily succeeded in finding, a passage "back." For Frost the repetition of rising up into the light then falling into darkness again is a grand and tragic pattern. No less than Dickinson, he celebrates nature's entrancing details as "play for mortal stakes." "In Hardwood Groves" he finds in the cycle of deciduous foliage that same "pathetic pendulum" Dickinson hears in the crickets of late summer:

> The same leaves over and over again!
> They fall from giving shade above,
> To make one texture of faded brown
> And fit the earth like a leather glove.

Frost identifies both upward and downward trajectories here, in a way resembling Dickinson's "The Gentian weaves her fringes."

> Before the leaves can mount again
> To fill the trees with another shade,
> They must go down past things coming up.
> They must go down into the dark decayed.

But on an emotional level his poem struggles against the necessity of fall and decay even as it affirms that it "must" be so.

> They must be pierced by flowers and put
> Beneath the feet of dancing flowers.
> However it is in some other world
> I know that this is the way in ours.

Frost's vision of human oneness with nature is a tragic one. Such unity is only accomplished in a fall through seasons of failure and mortality; any resulting renewal will be experienced in subsequent cycles that are beyond the individual lives and consciousness of the fallen.

Frost's awareness of entropy as a force in nature reflects the fact that, though he shares with Whitman and Dickinson a knowledge of the Bible and an affinity with Transcendentalism, he also is intensely interested in the disclosures of twentieth-century science. Modern science's much vaster perspective on time, especially, makes nature less of a secure retreat for him. The depopulation of Frost's northern New England, with the mountains reverting from farms to woodlands, accorded for him with the prevailing scientific view. The earth sciences showed mountains themselves rising and falling, while biology presented a spectacle of species evolving and going extinct and cosmology disclosed a constantly altering universe with stars exploding and cooling across an immense emptiness. Nature was no safe haven, but a panorama of decay.

One of Frost's main contributions to nature poetry is his vision of human meaning in the context of, but *counter* to, the general entropic drift. "Stopping by Woods on a Snowy Evening" evokes a world in which coldness and darkness prevail—"Between the woods and frozen lake / The darkest evening of the year." The poem acknowledges the beauty of universal entropy, as manifest in the fall of snow and the silence and cold of the woods, and admits the human desire, having "stopped" in this frozen beauty, to stay. Yet, while recognizing the allure of inertness, the poet still ventures forward, energized by the sublime world beyond his little human projects even as he continues on to fulfill them:

> The woods are lovely, dark, and deep,
> But I have promises to keep,
> And miles to go before I sleep,
> And miles to go before I sleep.

Frost's nature expands to include much beyond the human scale, much beyond our enduring. Stepping into the woods for him is an encounter with mortality by which our human possibilities are renewed. But such reaction and renewal themselves are attuned to something essential in nature. In "West-Running Brook" a couple engages in conversation about, and across, a brook that represents mortality and entropy for the husband:

> It flows between us, over us, and *with* us.
> And it is time, strength, tone, light, life, and love—
> And even substance lapsing unsubstantial;
> The universal cataract of death
> That spends to nothingness . . .

But the overwhelming *downwardness* of these lines is counteracted both in the brook and in the poem. Amid the current, where "the black stream" meets a submerged rock, white water sends a wave continually back against the "universal" flow:

> Not just a swerving, but a throwing back,
> As if regret were in it and were sacred.
> It has this throwing backward on itself
> So that the fall of most of it is always
> Raising a little, sending up a little.
> Our life runs down in sending up the clock

Both the brook and the sun run down; the brook sends "up our life" as the sun sends "up the brook":

> And there is something sending up the sun.
> It is this backward motion toward the source,
> Against the stream, that most we see ourselves in,
> The tribute of the current to the source.

No less than Whitman, Frost has faith in the meaningfulness of nature. His corresponding sense of *reciprocal* creativity, however, comes from the energy of reaction or recoil, in the discovery of momentary connection even as "our life runs down." Thus, he is true both to his psychological and spiritual experience, in which dark brooding establishes a sky that may be pierced by sharp moments of clarity, and to the insights of a science that reads the unfolding of the universe as the broken syntax of entropy.

More recent poets, too, have found in the breakdown of natural and human orders a context for healing vision. In "Identity" Ammons praises the world for its

> disorder ripe,
> entropy rich, high levels of random,
>   numerous occasions of accident

Each spider web reveals at its center a pattern that is characteristic of a given species. But such predictable designs lapse, Ammons points out, at the edges where a web is moored into the contingencies of tree and rock. Through improvisation lives make a place for themselves in this disorderly world. Because such preordained designs are relinquished at the points of mooring, connection holds, the internal order is sustained, and the world's richness is replenished.

> order
>   diminishes toward the
> periphery
>   allowing at the points of contact
>   entropy equal to entropy.

The opening poem in Wendell Berry's *Sabbaths* offers a similar affirmation of letting go, and of the way a closer relationship with the world may come when we relinquish the projects and preferences that had organized it for us up until that point:

> I go among trees and sit still.
> All my stirring becomes quiet
> around me like circles on water.
> My tasks lie in their places
> where I left them, asleep like cattle.
>
> After days of labor,
> mute in my consternations,
> I hear my song at last,
> and I sing it. As we sing
> the days turn, the trees move.

Ceasing his ordinary, purposeful activity, the poet begins to open himself to the *world's* activity and to a harmony including and amplifying his own song.

While Whitman, Dickinson, and Frost may all be related to an Emersonian line in American nature poetry, the second half of the twentieth century has seen influxes from other traditions as well. Through poets like Kenneth Rexroth and Gary Snyder the poetry of China and Japan has become much more widely known in America. Snyder's "For Nothing," cited in the first section of this essay, can be heard to echo the resonant simplicity of the ancient Japanese poet Saigyō

> Waking me up
> To the spring that's come,
>   Water trickles down
> The valleys and long crag-bound ice
> Now cracks open, slides free.
>   (tr. William LaFleur)

The seventeenth-century haiku master Bashō conveys the essence of a season even more succinctly:

> On a bare branch
> settles a crow—
>   the end of autumn.
>   (tr. mine)

The condensed quality of Japanese verse hones American poets' evocations, as they experiment with a voice largely devoid of pronouns, operating by suggestive sentence fragments, and with no explicit authorial *presence* in the scene. Though such a direction affirms Whitman's vision of oneness with nature, it may in some cases act to mute his exuberant *persona*. One further effect of haiku on today's poetry may be to tilt our sense of the line away from longer breaths and towards Dickinson's gnomic brevity.

American poets have long been deeply interested in the culture of Native Americans. Writers such as Longfellow did their best to understand the spiritual and aesthetic life of this continent's original peoples; however, there was little poetry composed in English by Native Americans until after World War II. Now, though, such writing is flourishing, and the oldest stories and myths of North America flow into current nature poetry along with Dickinson and Frost. Trickster and creator, Coyote dodges through poems like "Saint Coyote," by the Chickasaw poet Linda Hogan:

> Luminous savior
> wise to traps,
> eyes shining like the electric bones
> of street lamps

The poet hears Coyote throwing a rock in the water, "singing"

> to the disappearing moon
> that walks on water.
> He was telling lies about people.

Acknowledging the power and personhood of the nonhuman realm, the Native American imagination opens new vistas in our poetry.

The *narrative* dimension of much Native American poetry also offers new visions of unity between humanity and nature. In an essay called "Landscape, History, and the Pueblo Imagination" Leslie Silko has written about how a deer hunting story becomes a "map" for her people, containing information about topography, animal behavior, water, and other matters crucial to human survival in an arid region. Conversely, the landscape encompasses each *story*, calling to mind both the narrative and its ethical implications: "Stories are most frequently recalled as people are passing by a specific geographical feature." In her poem "Where Mountainlion Laid Down with Deer" Silko suggests how a traditional tale, with its magical transformations, can make the landscape more fully human, the teller more wholly natural.

> I climb the black rock mountain
> > stepping from day to day
> > > silently.
> I smell the wind for my ancestors
> > pale blue leaves
> > > crushed wild mountain smell.

The memory and magic central to such a poetic narrative locates humanity in a wider terrain, enchanting the senses and disclosing unsuspected relationships.

> Returning
> > up the grey stone cliff
> > where I descended
> > > a thousand years ago.
> Returning to faded black stone
> > where mountainlion laid down with deer.

Humanity's degradation of the natural environment has increasingly concerned American poets. Early in the twentieth century Robinson Jeffers developed his own fierce polemic. Love of nature led him to rage at the casual destructiveness of "development" along his California coast—rage so insistent that it finally would not let him rest until he made his way back to the bedrock. "Life from the Lifeless" expresses a desire to pass not only beyond humanity but even beyond all organic life:

> Spirits and illusions have died,
> The naked mind lives
> In the beauty of inanimate things.
>
> Flowers wither, grass fades, trees wilt,
> The forest is burnt;
> The rock is not burnt.

And in the face of death

> Men suffer want and become
> Curiously ignoble; as prosperity
> Made them curiously vile.
>
> But look how noble the world,
> The lonely-flowing waters, the secret-
> Keeping stones, the flowing sky.

"Noble," "lonely," "secret," "flowing." The first three of these adjectives limn a monolithic, aristocratic nature, remote from the corruptions of humanity. But "flowing" brings the waters and sky back into a living circuit, a process within which new lives, new visions, new harmonies between humanity and the nonhuman can be engendered. These are the agents of erosion and release, crumbling rotten crystals into the medium of life.

Jeffers, then, can be seen as enacting the circuit of retreat and renewal described in the first two sections of this essay. He is a "reducer" in the ecological sense, breaking down corrupt forms and making available both cleared ground and the resources from which new relationships with the earth may flower. In this regard there is a similarity between Jeffers's work and "The Waste Land." Eliot, too, scours the ground, until there is only

> A heap of broken images, where the sun beats,
> And the dead tree gives no shelter, the cricket no relief,
> And the dry stone no sound of water.

Both poets could be seen as undertaking a search—akin to the Native American vision-quest, in which an individual departs from the human community in pursuit of totemic or ancestral wisdom that will sustain the whole tribe. Jeffers's polemic finally testifies to faith in a larger "balance." In "Point Joe" he writes that

> Man gleaning food between the solemn presences of land and
>   ocean,
> On shores where better men have shipwrecked, under fog and among
>   flowers,
>
> Equals the mountains in his past and future

Since Jeffers wrote, however, a rupture has been caused in the continuity of American nature poetry. There is growing evidence of grave injury to the biosphere by human beings. While Jeffers's contemporary Frost, from the perspective of modern science, saw a world of vast impersonal processes in which human settlements subsided back into the reforested mountains, he also found a basic consistency within change, lending familiarity to the challenges of each new moment. Today, as the trees of Latin America, Southeast Asia, and the Pacific Northwest are being cut wholesale, as damage to the atmosphere and the oceans becomes more widely understood, and as commercial exploitation and the destruction of their habitats plunge countless species into extinction, there is a widespread sense of an environmental holocaust. Such a sense of global peril troubles poets who might otherwise find refreshment and solace in nature. In a 1989 *New York Times* eulogy for the nature writer and novelist Edward Abbey, Edward Hoagland praised that writer's polemic energy on behalf of the earth. We need more furious defenders of nature's sanctity like Abbey, he wrote, rather than more "mystical Transcendentalists" engaging in "Emersonian optimism." "Emerson would be roaring with heartbreak and Thoreau would be raging with grief in these 1980's. *Where were you when the world burned? Get mad for a change, for heaven's sake!*"

   Christopher Merrill's important collection, *The Forgotten Language: Contemporary Poets and Nature*, includes a large number of poets who, though instinctively drawn to the heart of natural wholeness, now share Hoagland's grief and rage. Today's extinctions, they find, represent an evil far different from Frost's "universal cataract of death." James Dickey's "For the Last Wolverine" ends with the lines, *"Lord, let me die but not die / Out.*" There is an essential difference between the downward cycle in hardwood groves, where new life rises back out of the dark, and the *end* of that whole cycle. With extinction the imaginative world of the poet, too, is impoverished. Dickey writes to the last wolverine, "How much the timid poem needs / / The mindless explosion of your rage." Impaired, too, is Whitman's faith in the creative goodness of humanity, reciprocal to the bounty of natural creation. Instead, poetry often now conveys a sick sense that nature is *violated*, over and over, by our human heedlessness. In such violation poetry itself is damaged. Robert Pack, in "Mountain Ash Without Cedar Waxwings," writes,

> But now, dishonored and demeaned,
> language itself, like ravaged earth, betrays
> its own betrayers

Earlier, poets could be reinvigorated by identifying their own creative powers with nature, but in our own day, in contemplation of wounds to the earth, they become filled with bitterness and disgust. In his poem "For a Coming Extinction," W. S. Merwin writes,

> Gray whale
> Now that we are sending you to The End
> That great god
> Tell him
> That we who follow you invented forgiveness
>
> And forgive nothing

We don't send forth the sunrise to greet the sunrise, as in Whitman's vision. Instead, as Merwin's poem records, we dismantle the world. Addressing the whales in his poem's final stanza, he concludes,

> When you will not see again
> the whale calves trying the light
> Consider what you will find in the black garden
> And its court
> The sea cows the Great Auks the gorillas
> The irreplaceable hosts ranged countless
> . . . .
> Join your word to theirs
> Tell him
> That it is we who are important

The poet's task in an age of global catastrophe is one of creative grieving. Moving through the stages of denial and anger, and acknowledging that no external solution can be negotiated for a crisis to which we human beings are integral, poetry's task now is to generate images of deep grieving. This must be a poetry of identification with the wounded biosphere whose violation we have carried out ourselves. It must teach us to refrain from our habitual and careless exercise of power. In Bruce Weigl's "Snowy Egret" the poem's speaker awakens at midnight to a neighbor boy in his backyard, burying a dead egret that he has killed with a shotgun. Although he wants to shake out of the boy his lies about how he shot the bird by *accident*, the speaker ends up saying instead,

> I don't know what to do but hold him.
> If I let go he'll fly to pieces before me.
> What a time we share, that can make a good boy steal away,
> Wiping out from the blue face of the pond
> What he hadn't even known he loved, blasting
> Such beauty into nothing.

Weigl's poem feels like a dream—one of recognition and connection in the context of slaughter. At a time of environmental holocaust poets can offer the dreams through which we might confront, relive, and move beyond the basic destructiveness in our treatment of the earth. They haunt us with the countenance of grief.

Louise Erdrich's poem "I Was Sleeping Where the Black Oaks Move" begins with another charged image—at once describing a particular natural phenomenon and evoking a compounded dream of grief. She tells how a whole forest, and the heron rookery it housed, washed away in a flooding river. Her concluding stanzas mourn that world in details that suggest a larger cataclysm.

> We walked among them, the branches
> whitening in the raw sun.
> Above us drifted herons,
> alone, hoarse-voiced, broken,
> settling their beaks among the hollows.

But in the face of this catastrophe, too, there is a circuit of return, and of patient encounter with the earth.

Grandpa said, These are the ghosts of the tree people,
moving above us, unable to take their rest.

Giving herself over to a shattered world, in an act of memory and longing, the poet affirms a wholeness that endures within imagination, though occasionally obscured by the violations of the present.

Sometimes now, we dream our way back to the heron dance.
Their long wings are bending the air
into circles through which they fall.
They rise again in shifting wheels.
How long must we live in the broken figures
their necks make, narrowing the sky.

John Elder

Further Reading

Elder, John. *Imagining the Earth: Poetry and the Vision of Nature.* Urbana: University of Illinois Press, 1985.

Merrill, Christopher. *The Forgotten Language: Contemporary Poets and Nature.* Salt Lake City: Peregrine Smith, 1991.

Paul, Sherman. *Hewing to Experience: Essays and Reviews on Recent American Poetry and Poetics, Nature and Culture.* Iowa City: University of Iowa Press, 1989.

Vendler, Helen. *Part of Nature, Part of Us: Modern American Poets.* Cambridge: Harvard University Press, 1980.

Waggoner, Hyatt. *The Heel of Elohim: Science and Values in Modern American Poetry.* Norman: University of Oklahoma Press, 1950.

Native American Poetry

THE appearance of a discrete chapter on Native American poetry in a volume devoted to a survey of poetry in the United States is an event worth remarking. Only within the last few years has Native American writing attracted sufficient notice to earn it a distinct place in texts devoted to American literature or in the curricula of academic departments where American literature is taught. The reasons for the belated appearance of this literature are many, and certainly one reason has been the reluctance of the academy to enlarge the definition of American literature to include the productions of writers living in the United States whose work has deliberately foregrounded their specific racial or ethnic identities. Another (not unrelated) reason, however, is that only recently have we had a critical mass of published writing by Native Americans that fits the generic categories that have traditionally been used to organize academic texts and courses.

The cultural traditions in which Native American poetry is still grounded are the oldest indigenous traditions in North America; at the same time, Native American poetry itself is, in the strictest sense, almost entirely a twentieth-century phenomenon. Like Native American novelists, short story writers, and playwrights, the contemporary poets have elected to use a generic form that would have been foreign to their forebears who sang, chanted, orated, prayed, prophesied, told stories, and participated in communal rituals. For those precursors the forms of public expression were largely governed by function and occasion rather than by the internal formal features that, in other traditions, have usually served to distinguish poetry from prose, lyric from narrative, dramatic from nondramatic.

The formal features that have come to distinguish genres are, to at least some extent, the result of the spread of print culture—when we look at a printed text, we can usually tell quickly whether it is poetry or prose, short story or novel, sonnet or epic poem. The appearance of the text on the page gives the reader a general idea of how the text will proceed: what conventions it will employ, what its pace will be, what expectations it will raise in the reader. The process of printing also removes a text from the context in which it was originally produced. In an oral culture, on the other hand, in which texts are spoken (and heard) and the speaking of them is always performative, the context of the performance serves much the same function as the visual appearance of the printed text, raising expectations in the audience about what they will hear, how long the performance will last, and which familiar conventions will be evoked.

Therefore, to call some of the productions of an oral culture "poetry" is, essentially, to analogize. When parts of the Navajo Blessingway Rite are translated and printed, for example, they look like poems on the page, and their appearance invites us to read them as if they were as self-contained and discrete as poems. For the participants and observers at a Blessingway Rite, however, the significance of any part of the ritual has everything to do with its placement and use within the ritual—its function as part of a communal healing ceremony—and almost nothing to do with the appearance it may assume when it is extracted from its context and written down or printed.

This distinction, between oral productions that are distinguished by their performative context and their use, and written productions that are distinguished by internal formal features, is an important one to make in approaching Native American poetry. It explains, in the first place, why the term "Native American poetry" is most appropriately applied only to the recent productions of writers who have chosen to work in a form that is, from the Native perspective, nontraditional. The great majority of these writers have also chosen to write in English rather than in a Native language, further emphasizing the significant shifts in traditional cultural practices that the writing of poetry represents.

Those shifts have been accomplished gradually. While most Native American writers publishing today are poets, the productions of earlier Native writers most often took such forms as autobiography or historical narrative or political commentary, forms that tend to gradate more easily into fiction than into poetry. The earliest published collections of poetry generally came from writers who were better known, during their lifetimes and after, for their work in other genres. The Cherokee writer John Rollin Ridge, for example, whose collected *Poems* (1868) were published after his death, is known primarily as the author of the first published novel by a Native American, *The Life and Adventures of Joaquin Murieta* (1854). The Mohawk writer Emily Pauline Johnson published two volumes of poetry during her lifetime, *The White Wampum* (1895) and *Canadian Born* (1903), but readers knew her best as the author of short stories that appeared in *Mother's Magazine* and *Boy's World*; a collection of her fiction was eventually published as *The Moccasin Maker* (1913). The reputation of Lynn Riggs, a Cherokee writer whose volume of poetry, *The Iron Dish*, was published in 1930, derives largely from her play, *Green Grow the Lilacs* (1931), which became the basis for the musical *Oklahoma!*.

The work of these earlier poets is important in that it marks the entry of Native American poets into the American literary "mainstream"; these writers are, to some extent, the enabling precursors of the contemporary Native poets. Significantly, however, many contemporary writers, no matter what the genre in which they are working, cite the publication of a much later work, N. Scott Momaday's novel *House Made of Dawn*, as the real watershed event that made it possible for them to take themselves seriously as writers. When Momaday's novel won the Pulitzer Prize for fiction in 1969, the prospects suddenly changed for other Native writers; the awarding of the prize to a work that was written by a Native American and that directly addressed some of the political and social issues that were of serious concern to other Native American writers opened up the possibility that the American public might be receptive to Native American writing and, more important, that publishers might recognize the existence of a commercially viable market for Native writing. The success of Momaday's novel also coincided with a resurgence of political awareness and activity on the part of many younger Native Americans, as indicated by the formation of the American Indian Movement (AIM) in 1968, the occupation of Alcatraz Island in 1969, the "Trail of Broken Treaties" march that culminated in the occupation of the Bureau of Indian Affairs in 1972, and the occupation of Wounded Knee in 1973.

All of these events signaled, on the one hand, a new determination on the part of many Native Americans to articulate their own concerns in their own voices, and, on the other hand, an increased interest on the part of non-Indian Americans in listening to those voices. It is understandable, then, that in most anthologies of Native American poetry available today nearly all of the poets represented are still living and writing, and most are still under fifty. These younger poets represent a generation whose experiences have given them both a stronger motivation to write and a greater access to the means of publication than their parents and grandparents had. These poets were influenced by the political movements of the sixties and seventies; most now live off-reservation, even though many spent their early lives on a reservation; many are college-educated, and some now hold college or university teaching appointments; and, significantly, most grew up speaking and writing English as a second language or even as their first language.

Because Native American literature has so recently been introduced into the curricula of schools and colleges, most of the poets writing today first encountered poetry through the work of non-Native writers. In a recent collection of interviews with Native writers, Laura Coltelli's *Winged Words: American Indian Writers Speak*, the interviewer frequently asked the poets to name the writers whose influence on their own work had been strongest. The poets mentioned include William Carlos Williams, John Keats, Elizabeth Bishop, Pablo Neruda, James Wright, Galway Kinnell, the Black Mountain poets, and Amiri Baraka—as well as Scott Momaday and Leslie Marmon Silko.

In some ways, then, the experiences of the contemporary poets place them in closer proximity to non-Indian Americans of similar age than to previous generations of Native Americans. And while the generational differences help to account for the success of the poets in finding (or creating) an audience for their work and in making their work accessible to non-Indian readers, these differences have also meant that each poet has had to confront the issue of his or her relationship to the oral traditions that defined and sustained Native American cultures in the past. This confrontation, in fact, is a frequently recurring subject in Native American poetry; while accepting the name of *poet* for themselves, and thus identifying themselves as practitioners of an art that is not, strictly speaking, indigenous, many Native American writers have been careful to emphasize that their work does not constitute a disruptive break with oral tradition but is, instead, a necessary if complicated extension of older traditions. Scott Momaday, for example, has specifically identified his writing as belonging to the "verbal tradition" of his Kiowa ancestors, thus conflating the orality of his forebears and his own literacy into a single, continuing tradition. Similarly, Leslie Marmon Silko (Laguna Pueblo) has situated her writing in a cultural continuum that relies on keeping alive what she calls "the long story of the people," an essential story that Silko insists can be spoken or written, in any of many languages including English, and that can be augmented and perpetuated in many forms. The Acoma Pueblo writer Simon Ortiz has spoken often of the necessary relation between his writing and the stories that constitute much of the oral tradition of the Acoma people. His poetry, Ortiz insists, is always grounded in the storytelling tradition—a tradition that shifts and grows as the world changes and as the lives of the storytellers change with it.

The commitment of Native writers to the perpetuation of tribal traditions is reflected even in the titles of some of the major anthologies of Native American poetry published in this country: Duane Niatum's *Carriers of the Dream Wheel* (1975); Kenneth Rosen's *Voices of the Rainbow* (1975); Joseph Bruchac's *Songs From This Earth on Turtle's Back* (1983); and Robert K. Dodge and Joseph B. McCullough's *New and Old Voices of Wah'Kon-Tah* (1985). These titles contextualize the poetry for the reader right away, announcing its cultural *difference* and distinguishing these anthologies from other collections of American poetry. The titles themselves are reminders that the writing contained in the anthologies is presented as an extension of established oral traditions, that these poets are adding their "voices" and their "songs" to those of their predecessors and joining them as "carriers" of an inherited body of beliefs, values, and perspectives.

Two other recent anthologies, however, have been published under titles that suggest a shift in the strategies of editors and publishers, and perhaps in the attitudes of the poets themselves. Rayna Green's collection of poetry and prose by Native American women, *That's What She Said* (1984), and *Harper's Anthology of Twentieth-Century Native American Poetry* (1988), edited by Duane Niatum, both use titles that reflect the concurrent shift in attitudes toward the place of Native American poetry on bookstore shelves, in academic curricula, and in volumes (such as this one) that offer a survey of major writers and major movements in American poetry. The poets who are included in these volumes still make it clear that their roots are in tribal traditions and that their poems are meant to affirm and extend those traditions, but the titles of the collections suggest a new effort to present these poets as writers with a real claim on the attention of that part of the American reading public that is interested in strong poetry, no matter what the ethnic identification of the poet; they also suggest a move on the part of editors and publishers to retreat from the association of Native American poetry with the exotic and esoteric and to focus instead on the accessibility of the poetry to the general reader.

For many of the poets themselves the legitimizing of their work that all of these anthologies represent has brought with it some concerns about the possibilities of *mis*representation and *mis*understanding of the particular histories, experiences, and motivations that lie behind the poetry. Many have been careful to point out, for one thing, that Native American poetry, because of its continuity with oral traditions, is always grounded in a fundamental sense that the purpose of language is never simply aesthetic or ornamental, that language always functions not only to signify but also to create or to destroy; as the Laguna Pueblo writer Paula Gunn Allen has noted, in Native traditions the beautiful and the useful are usually synonymous.

While this perspective has been articulated in various ways by many other writers, it has been given an especially consistent and forceful treatment by the Cherokee poet Carroll Arnett (who also uses his Cherokee name, Gogisgi). Arnett begins his poem "The Old Man Said" with the statement that "Everything, / Every single thing / matters." For Arnett the language of poetry clearly matters in a very particular and very political way. In his poem titled "Bio-Poetic Statement: Instruction to Warriors on Security," Arnett compares the purposes of his own poetry to those of a trained soldier or warrior who is taught to aim for an enemy's belly or legs in order to "stop him"; to hit the enemy in the head or chest would be to kill him, which is not the desired object, while to hit him in any other place or to miss him would only be a waste of ammunition, and "we have none to waste."

Arnett's identification of the poet with the warrior who is given an urgent, defensive mission—whose skills are used to protect something that is valuable and under constant threat—is an especially strong expression of an attitude that underlies the aesthetic of most contemporary Native poets: the shared conviction that their poetry has an urgent political and social function, and that what is at stake for the poet is nothing less than the survival of the entire community for whom the poet speaks. As Joy Harjo (Creek) suggests in her poem "Anchorage," the fundamental impetus behind all Native poetry is, necessarily, the need to keep telling "the fantastic and terrible story of all our survival, / those who were never meant / to survive."

In his poem "Survival This Way" Simon Ortiz contends that the way of survival for the contemporary Native person can only be a continuation of the old way, a reinforcement of belief in a way that is both a map and a method, passed on from one generation to the next: "We travelled this way, / gauged our distance by stories / and loved our children." For a contemporary writer like Ortiz the history of "the way" still constitutes an imperative, still maps the only route to the future: "Survival, I know how this way. / This way, I know." This sense of the significance of the cultural map is reiterated, in language similar to Ortiz's, by Wendy Rose (Hopi/Miwok) in "Walking on the Prayerstick": "We map our lives this way: trace our lineage / by the corn, find our words in the flute, / touch the shapes that feed us with dry seed." In these poems Ortiz and Rose represent the Native poets' language as given rather than chosen, their words as part of a discourse that allows the past to be brought forward into the future: the saving of their history depends upon the poets' ability to find the new words that inhere in the old traditions, to locate their poetry within what they know about the old ways of survival.

In his introduction to the *Harper's Anthology of Twentieth-Century Native American Poetry* Brian Swann observes that "more than most poetry being written today, Native American poetry is the poetry of historic witness." While a reading of the poetry clearly confirms that observation, it is also clear that the project of bearing historic witness is a complex one for the Native poet. For one thing, the general American audience has not been eager to hear tribal histories repeated, especially from a Native perspective. More important, the contemporary poet's relationship to his or her cultural history has become complicated by the many social and political pressures that have worked to separate the modern Indian from his or her historical roots. The history to which the poetry bears witness includes the painful histories of removal, dispossession, relocation, and the many forms of attack on tribalism mounted by church and state in America.

The range of attitudes toward the effects of that history on tribal identity could be marked, at one end, by the very skeptical stance taken by James Welch in his 1971 volume, *Riding the Earthboy 40*. In many of the poems of this volume Welch (Blackfeet/Gros Ventre) expresses a strong distrust of the possibility of retrieving a tradition and a history that have been, in his view, irremediably changed by the events of the not-so-distant past. In the most frequently reprinted (and perhaps the bitterest) poem from the collection, "The Man from Washington," the speaker acknowledges that a single man, an agent of the federal government, could bring about "the end" for an entire community of people simply by making an extraordinary promise to them—the promise that everyone "would be inoculated / against a world in which we had no part, / a world of money, promise, and disease." The failure of that earlier promise is reflected in Welch's reiterated images of contemporary reservation life as a self-defeating attempt to revive and defend a moribund way. In "Getting Things Straight," for example, Welch speculates about the implications of his knowledge that "history ended when / the last giant climbed Heart Butte, had his vision, / came back to town and drank himself / sick." The towns of Welch's poetry, like "Harlem, Montana: Just Off the Reservation," are places where "Booze is law / and all the Indians drink in the best tavern," where white entrepreneurs know that it is possible to "peddle / your hate for the wild who bring you money." To those who come to places like Harlem, looking for ways to reinsert themselves as Indians in a world of money and false promises, Welch's advice is, finally, to "let glory go the way of all sad things" ("Blackfeet, Blood and Piegan Hunters").

A markedly different response to the pressures of recent history is represented in the poetry of Simon Ortiz, a writer who acknowledges that optimism and hopefulness characterize all his work, even the work that begins in anger and bitterness. The sources of Ortiz's optimism are reflected in many ways in his poetry—in his tributes to the wisdom and constancy of his forebears, especially his father, in his confidence in the children of the next generation, in his delight in storytelling, and in his faith in the enduring and stabilizing values represented by the physical landscape in which the Acoma have lived for generations. All of these sources are present in a representative poem, "A Story of How a Wall Stands," in which the speaker recalls his father's instructions to him about how to repair a four-hundred-year-old hillside wall made of stone and mud. In explaining how the stones of the wall are woven together the father weaves his own fingers as illustration, and the speaker recognizes that it is the father's story, the story of the wall, that brings together past and present, place and person, father and son. As he tells the story, the father is also using his hands, "working the stone / and the mud until they become / the wall that stands a long, long time." The wall of the poem becomes an emblem of the interconnectedness of landscape, history, family, and—most important—the stories that keep the connections alive.

In his 1981 volume *From Sand Creek* Ortiz addresses a different set of connections. The title of the volume refers to a specific event in 1864 when more than a hundred Cheyennes and Arapahoes who were encamped along Sand Creek, flying a flag of truce, were massacred by a contingent of the Colorado Volunteers. Ortiz relates this event to other violent episodes in American history, especially its most recent wars. In doing so he claims the whole of American history as his own and cites his experience, as a Native American and therefore as the product of a history of violence and oppression, as the quintessential American experience. The two primary sites of reference in the collection are Sand Creek and a VA hospital in Colorado, home to the damaged veterans of World War II, Korea, and Vietnam. Both of those sites are peopled, in the poet's memory and in present reality, by the victims of what Ortiz calls "the dream called America." The poems constantly attribute American violence to the deliberate repression of historical memory: the early white settlers "crossed memory" in crossing the continent, learning to substitute "plans" and "designs" for memory; their descendants, refusing to recognize their own complicity in violent designs and their own victimization by those designs, continue to "deny regret / for the slaughter / of their future." Memory, in these poems, is embodied in the muted victims of history, the buried dead of Sand Creek as well as the "stricken men and broken boys" of the VA hospital, especially those who are most closed off from public view: "the basement speaks / for Africa, Saigon, Sand Creek." In this book Ortiz gives the basement a voice, claiming for its inhabitants—Indian and non-Indian—a significant place in a consistently violent American history that continues to claim many victims.

Ortiz's own personal memories form the basis for the series of poems that make up his 1977 volume, *A Good Journey*. Among these autobiographical, meditative, often prosy poems is one entitled "How to make a good chili stew—this one on July 16, a Saturday, Indian 1971." The poem begins with a basic instruction, "It's better to do it outside / or at sheepcamp / or during a two or three day campout. / In this case, we'll settle / for Hesperus, Colorado / and a Coleman stove." The qualifying phrase, "in this case," becomes a refrain in the poem, as Ortiz gives directions for using traditional ingredients and methods—dried chili pods, homemade hominy, a cast iron pot—while, at the same time, acknowledging that contemporary conditions may not allow the chili maker to replicate the traditional recipe exactly. In some cases powdered chili and store-bought hominy will have to do. However, Ortiz insists that certain parts of the process are not variable: smelling the stew, listening to the cooking sounds and thinking of a song to go with them, looking around at the landscape, being patient, paying "the utmost attention to everything." These things are vitally important, Ortiz cautions, and "all these go into the cooking."

In a poem called "How to Make Good Baked Salmon from the River," the Tlingit poet Nora Dauenhauer replies in kind to Ortiz, offering her own recipe for creating a traditional feast under contemporary conditions. Once again, the poem constantly turns on the phrase "in this case," as Dauenhauer acknowledges that the alder-wood fire may have to be replaced by an electric oven, seal oil by Wesson oil, fresh berries by fruit cocktail—and the traditional practice of disposing of the fish bones by offering them to the ravens and seagulls and mosquitoes may have to be replaced by wrapping the bones in plastic and placing them in the dumpster. However, as in Ortiz's recipe, Dauenhauer's instructions make it clear that certain parts of the process of cooking the salmon cannot be changed: "Smell how good it smells while it's cooking, / because it's soooooooo important." And if it is no longer feasible to make the ritual gestures to the raven and the mosquitoes, who "are known to be the ashes of the cannibal giant," one can and must still "think how good it is that we have good spirits / that still bring salmon and oil."

In this exchange of recipes Ortiz and Dauenhauer both acknowledge the changes and diminishments that contemporary life has forced on traditional practices. At the same time both recognize that feasting on chili made on a Coleman stove or salmon cooked in an electric oven is still feasting, still a means of bringing traditions forward into the pre-

738 *Native American Poetry*

sent and preserving the essential rituals, stories, and memories that give the traditions their personal and cultural significance. The adjusted recipes are, in both cases, the result of the poet's negotiations with the material realities of contemporary life, and both offer one way of defining the poet's position as a Native American and as a writer within contemporary American society. That position is one that many other poets have continued to negotiate in their poetry, especially as their audience has expanded to include those who might be inclined to see them only as exotics or as helpless victims of history, or both. According to Paula Gunn Allen the very process of negotiation, of writing frankly about their sense that history has put them into a psychologically and politically liminal position, has been a crucial source of empowerment for many Native writers and for the people they represent.

In her poem "Recuerdo" Allen speaks of one source of her own difficult struggle to find a confident, empowered voice in which to speak as a poet. The poem recalls her childhood experience of climbing a mountain with her family and hearing in the air the voices of the gods, voices that "the old ones" expected to hear because they knew that gods lived on that mountain. Believing, the child also heard—with awe and with fear—voices that the adult poet now strains to hear again: "Lately I write, trying to combine sound and memory, / searching for that significance once heard and nearly lost." The adult poet can only "climb the mesas in my dreams," but the need to climb back to family and to belief in the spirit voices that brought both "terror and comfort" still impels her writing and still keeps her inescapably attached to the landscapes and the people of her home.

The haunting voices of "the old ones," both the human voices of her Laguna family and the spirit voices that speak in and through the landscape near Laguna, are perhaps the most real presences in Allen's poetry, even though the poems track her movement through the parts of contemporary America, especially its cities, that seem the most hostile to the old voices. In "Kopis'taya, A Gathering of Spirits" Allen speaks as an urban Indian, one of the "women of the daylight, of clocks / and steel foundries," who live in an environment that interposes cement, plastic, pollution, sunglasses, and polyester between the Indian body and the earth and air to which it still instinctively inclines. The result is that, for these women, "nagging doubt is the false measure / of our days." The poem ends with a call to recognize that the spirit voices still sing in the city, that the real danger is doubt itself, that the challenge is to continue to believe that the urban Indian can still hear the voices through the urban noise, can still "dance the dance of feathers / the dance of birds."

The doubt that Allen identifies as a major threat to contemporary Native identity, both individual and communal, is a recurrent motif in the work of many other poets, especially those who are living and working in nonreservation settings. The poems of Linda Hogan (Chickasaw), for example, have consistently addressed Hogan's own sense of living a divided life, of trying to find a way to balance the "pull" of her Native ancestry and heritage with the demands and patterns of life in urban America. Like Paula Gunn Allen, Hogan frequently writes of the importance, and the difficulty, of hearing the voices that speak for a homeplace and a tradition that seem antithetical to modern life. In "Me, Crow, Fish, and the Magi," for example, Hogan speaks of the "lure" of escape from tradition, the temptation to simply plunge into the future, crowing like a rooster and leaping like a fish, bearing the past as a pattern of bodily scars that testify to one's successful escape from entrapment. But the poem ends with the assertion that "the odds are good" that moments will come when the pace slows and all those who have elected to crow and to leap suddenly "hear the pull of our own voices / like the Magi with their star," moments when they are capable of "believing their inner songs" and recognizing that those songs can restore them to the sources of faith and constancy, to "the beginning of life."

Those moments of listening and believing are often associated in Hogan's poetry with the image of light, especially the light of dawn. In "First Light" Hogan celebrates the dawn light in which, traditionally, prayers were always offered; the poem affirms that it is still possible at certain dawn moments to "know the old ones are here" and to remember the songs they sang. In "To Light" the collective "we" of the poem testify to hearing, "at the spring," the subterranean sounds of waters that course through the graveyards of history and break out of the earth, carrying "the stories of life to air." For the living as well as the dead, for all those with "noisy tongues that once were silenced," the sound of the waters brings not only consolation but also the sure promise of the resurrection of a repressed history, the promise of "all the oceans we contain / coming to light."

Hogan's poetry is frequently concerned with pan-American political issues, especially with the political repression of Native people outside the United States. In some of her more overtly political poems the inversion of the usual celebratory associations with light is used to make a powerfully ironic statement. In "Seeing through the Sun," for example, the "we" of the poem inhabit a "country of light" where the only safety, the only opportunity for speaking the truth, is in the darkness. The light of the sun illuminates "the men's uniforms with shining buttons" and scorches the skin of the speakers with the heat of fear. In such a place, where light is so dangerous that "we are polite in the sun / and we ask for nothing," the public light of day allows one to speak only in covert apology: "Never mind. I was just passing through / the universe. It's nothing." For the poet who would like to use her voice to speak for those who fear and apologize, who would like to bring their repressed stories to light, the only possibility is an empathic gesture, an offer to enter imaginatively into the darkened place where the truth can be spoken: "There is light entering a keyhole. / Cover it with your hand / and speak, tell me everything."

Hogan's emphasis on the self (especially the female self) that is divided between daylight and darkness, between the "pull" of ancestral voices and the "lure" of modern noise, or between the wish to deny a painful history and the conviction that the history must be brought to light, is an emphasis that is also found in the work of two other younger poets, Joy Harjo (Creek) and Wendy Rose (Hopi/Miwok). In Harjo's poetry the sense of the divided self, the self that is still in search of a confident and unambiguous voice, is reflected in the multiplicity of voices and personae that speak in the poems; it is also, at times, reflected in the objectifying of aspects of the self who speaks in the poems. In "I Give You Back," for example, the speaker of the poem addresses her "beautiful and terrible fear" as if the fear had its own separate existence or as if the constant naming of the fear as "you" might, by the end of the poem, have produced a successful exorcism. The fear that the speaker dissociates herself from, through the incantatory repetition of "I release you," has both personal and historical sources. It was originally a legacy from those who "burned" and "raped" and "stole," but the speaker acknowledges that she has adopted the fear as her "beloved / and hated twin," that the fear "devoured me, but I laid myself across the fire." The end of the poem records a significant shift of power, as the exorcised fear becomes a thing to be pitied and consoled by the empowered speaker. "But come here, fear / I am alive and you are so afraid / of dying."

In "The Woman Hanging from the Thirteenth Floor Window," the speaker of the poem, in a chillingly calm voice, relates the history of the anonymous woman who hangs by her fingertips from a tenement window on "the Indian side" of Chicago, the woman who "thinks she will be set free." She is a woman who has had two husbands, who has children and wants the comfort of more children, who hears in the night the voice of her grandmother as well as the voices of men telling her "to get up, to get up, to get up," who has memories of "waterfalls and pines" as well as of Chicago streets and northside bars, who sees other women hanging from their own windows while she hangs from hers. Most important, she is a woman who "would speak" but does not. She can only listen to the voices that speak for her, including those that "scream out from below / for her to jump" and those that "cry softly / from the sidewalks."

The inarticulateness of this composite woman who hangs suspended, not knowing whether freedom lies in the will to live or the wish to die, is shared by the speakers of many of Harjo's other poems for whom the language available to them is not sufficient to make meaning clear or, in a more crucial sense, to make them feel any more comfortably at home in the world they must inhabit. In "Anchorage" the speaker recounts the experience of visiting Alaska and seeing in the city "someone's Athabascan / grandmother, folded up, smelling like 200 years / of blood and piss." The image of the silent old woman becomes a powerful icon for the speaker, who sees written on the woman's body the history of Native people in North America but who does not have the words to speak what she knows: "What can we say that would make us understand / better than we do already?" What the speaker understands but does not have a way of telling to anyone else who is not already included in the "we" of the poem, is no less than "the fantastic and terrible story of all our survival / those who were never meant / to survive."

In "Transformations" the silent, iconic woman, the woman who has the potential for speaking the clarifying and transformative words, is represented as the speaker's own shadow self: "On the other side / of the place you live stands a dark woman. / She has been trying to talk to you for years." This dark woman, like the woman who hangs from the tenement window and the huddled Athabascan grandmother, can speak only through the indirection of metaphor or through her own visibility as a symbol, and, therefore, only through the imprecision of the poet's language. Others of Harjo's poems speculate about the possibility of discovering a more precise and more significant language. In "Resurrection" the only choice offered is to wait and watch "for all the fallen dead to return / and teach us a language so terrible / it could resurrect us all," while in "Eagle Poem" the circling flight of an eagle leads the speaker to recognize that there are things that can never be known except in moments of silent attention and "in languages / That aren't always sound but other / Circles of motion."

The struggle toward articulation, toward an authentic and significant voice, is also characteristic of much of the poetry of Wendy Rose. The most confident and unambiguous voices in Rose's poems are also the most unself-conscious, and they seldom belong to the writer. They belong instead to those whose impassioned utterances the poet can only imagine—to Eskimo throat-singers, for example, whose songs imitate the sounds they hear in nature; to an erupting volcano, personified as a raging old woman who "no longer cares / what we think"; to Rose's Hopi ancestors, who sang at dawn with prayersticks in their hands; to the outraged spirits of the dead, those who died at places like Wounded Knee and those whose skeletons have been disinterred, invoiced, sold, and stored in museums. When Rose speaks in her own voice it is often to lament her inability, as a writer, to replicate the strong voices of the old ones whose songs confirmed their place in the natural world. In "Poet Woman's Mitosis: Dividing All the Cells Apart," Rose admits that her own writerly voice "can do no more than mimic / the sound heard while my hand danced on paper / looking for the rattle of old words." Rose's sense of disengagement from a traditional past, her consciousness of the act of writing as ultimately inauthentic for the Native poet, further separates her from those old ones whose authenticity she trusts and whose songs and stories gave wholeness to their lives: "I would tell this like a story / but where a story should begin / I am left standing in the beat / of my silences."

When Rose does write about the uses of her own voice, as she does in "Vanishing Point: Urban Indian," she describes herself not as singing or telling stories but only as "making noise." As a city dweller separated from her tribal roots, she is one who "vanishes, who leans / under-balanced into nothing." However, as the title of the poem suggests, the vanishing urban Indian can serve a function analogous to that of the vanishing point of a painting: though she may be invisible, even her implied presence establishes a perspective that draws the eye, the attention, to the important figures in the foreground. Unseen, the poet-as-urban-Indian continues to make her noise "so as to protect your fragile immortality / O Medicine Ones."

Many of Rose's strongest and angriest poems are those in which she speaks in the voice of another, someone whose story has not been told or, frequently, someone whose story has been, in Rose's view, grotesquely misrepresented. Among these poems are "Truganniny," spoken in the voice of a Tasmanian aborigine woman whose body was stuffed, mounted, and put on display as the last of the Tasmanians; "Julia," in which the speaker is a Mexican Indian woman who, because of her deformities, was exhibited in a circus and who, after her death, was also stuffed and mounted; "I Expected My Skin and My Blood to Ripen," spoken by a woman who died at Wounded Knee and whose clothing was stripped from her body and sold to collectors; "The Day They Cleaned Up the Border," the meditation of a Salvadoran woman whose children were killed by government soldiers. The horrific nature of these stories testifies both to Rose's own horror at the history of violence done to nonwhite people and, more specifically, to her frustration with written history's indifference to the inscription of violence on the individual body. In these poems the human body is where the significant record of history begins and ends, and the wounded or mutilated body provides Rose with a metaphor for the disfiguring of many histories, especially the histories of Native peoples: "Our skin loosely lies / across grass borders; / . . . we struggle until our blood / has spread off our bodies / and frayed the sunset edges. / It's our blood that gives you / those southwestern skies." For those who know the history of violence the landscape becomes a terrible reminder of the personal histories that have been buried in the national consciousness.

In the poetry of Ray Young Bear (Mesquakie) history is also recorded on the landscapes of particular places, but in Young Bear's poetry the route to understanding the process of history is not through records or statistics or testimonials, as it often is for Wendy Rose, but through attention to myths, prophecies, and dreams. In the opening poem of his 1990 collection, *The Invisible Musician*, Young Bear recounts succinctly the Mesquakie creation myth: the muskrat's dive through primordial waters to bring up the dirt that would become the earth; the appearance of *O ki ma*, the first human being, who was formed from the flesh of the Creator's heart; and the subsequent appearance of "the rest of us," the Mesquakie or Red Earth people. Young Bear's understanding of the myth comes through his grandmother, whose words of warning conclude the poem: "Belief and what we were given / to take care of, / is on the verge / of ending."

In the rest of the collection Young Bear's own continuing belief—in the mystical nature of all creation, in the participation of nonhuman creatures in the mystical movements of history, and in the prophetic significance of natural events—is constantly juxtaposed to his perception of the undeniable material realities of contemporary life. This juxtaposition gives to Young Bear's poetry its persistently surreal quality. The messages from the spirit world are no longer easy to read, and the messengers themselves are no longer entirely reliable: jet lights and fireflies become indistinguishable in "the spotted night," and Moonwoman now "rests her body and leg / on a communication tower" ("Two Poems for Southeastern Washington"). The new world that the young poet inhabits is still governed by spirits who make themselves known through dreams and visions and the appearance of fireflies and stars, but the significance of their messages is confused by the static of intrusive machines. Similarly, the lives of those who were traditionally the keepers and conveyers of belief have been irrevocably changed: a tribal elder now sleeps with headphones on, intent on finding old tribal prophecies borne out by what he hears in the newscasts, and young warriors know they will be honored only by having their names carved on the Vietnam Memorial in Washington. In "Race of the Kingfishers: In Nuclear Winter" Young Bear offers an especially nightmarish vision of the ultimate apocalyptic result of the intrusion of technology into a world once ordered and made familiar by a coherent mythology. In the eerie darkness and cold of an imagined nuclear winter, belief disappears with the light of the sun— "We question which myth foretold / of this neverending storm." The prediction of Young Bear's grandmother is fully realized in this poem in an ironic and surrealistic validation of the visionary power of Mesquakie elders and the truth of Mesquakie prophecy.

The poetry of Louise Erdrich (Chippewa) is also frequently mysterious, often ghost-haunted, sometimes mystical. In Erdrich's poetry, however, the sources of mystery are usually located within the individual, in the dark psychic space between human desire and human understanding. The people of Erdrich's poems, moved by desire and need, make their way through the ordinariness of the world looking for ways to comprehend, to articulate, even to sacralize their sometimes violent needs. In her volume *Baptism of Desire* (1989) Erdrich brings together Christian saints, madwomen who kill their husbands or children, and the poets' own family of husband and children in a series of meditations on the many ways that human need is expressed and channeled, or frequently, repressed and disfigured.

The natural, nonhuman world, as Erdrich represents it in this collection, is driven in sometimes terrible ways by the sheer energy of need: newly fledged birds leave the nest when they are "no longer hindered by the violence of their need"; young frogs rise to the surface of a pond and contribute their voices to the "one clear unceasing note of need"; and owls scream in the night, reminding the wakened human listener that "there is nothing in the sound but raw need / of one feathered body for another" ("Saint Clare"; "The Sacraments"; "Owls"). The articulation and satisfaction of need, which consume much of the lives of birds and frogs, are more complicated matters for human beings, for whom justification and approval are needs sometimes as imperious as hunger or sexual desire. In these poems those who crave justification most are female, and the sources of justification to whom they turn, whether in supplication, fear, anger, or trust, are usually male: husbands, fathers, God.

In "Mary Kroger" the childless woman who is the speaker of the poem divides her anger between her profligate husband and a profligate God "who in your pity made a child / to slaughter on a tree." The speaker of "Fooling God" makes a list of things she "must" do in order to appease a god who is the disapproving husband/father writ large. She must be unobtrusive, careful, secretive, and cunning: "I must remain this person and be no trouble. / None at all. So he'll forget." In "Mary Magdalene" the woman who bathes the feet of Christ and dries them with her hair also knows that her ministrations mean little to the man she serves; she determines, in her frustration, to find more susceptible males—"boys"—whom she can drive to "smash empty bottles on their heads" by the offer of her body: "It is the old way that girls / get even with their fathers— / by wrecking their bodies on other men."

In the final section of the collection the fierce needs that drive the women of the previous poems (primarily women who are unmarried and/or childless) to rage or madness or self-destruction find a more pacific outlet in the energies given to creating and sustaining a family. As in most of Erdrich's poetry and fiction this collection ends with an affirmation of the family as perhaps the one human institution that is "natural" enough to contain and channel human need in ways that are generative rather than destructive. In this section men and women make love with the lustiness of owls, children enter the world as wild, inhuman creatures, and a woman leaves her sleeping husband in the night, "in the hour of the wolf," to prowl the house alone ("The Ritual"). But here the lust of men and women produces children whose moments of birth transform their parents: "I was on the other side ready with milk to lure them, / And their father, too, each name a net in his hands" ("Birth"). And the woman who prowls at night returns to sleep in the marital bed with its wedding quilt, bearing the pattern of "the twelve-branched tree of life." Within the family desire and need become shaped into a fierce guardianship of those whom one loves, those whose own needs may be as strong and as imperious as the needs of the owl or the wolf.

With one or two exceptions the poems of *Baptism of Desire* treat subjects that are not uniquely Native American; many of the political and cultural issues addressed by other Native American poets are present only indirectly, when they are present at all. In this respect Erdrich's success in finding major commercial publishers for her poetry (Holt for her first collection, *Jacklight*, and Harpers for *Baptism of Desire*) marks a significant departure from the experience of most of the other poets discussed in this chapter, for whom small presses and journals have provided the major means of publication. As Andrew Wiget and others have noted, many Native American poets have found that their poetry is most marketable when it is most overtly of the "beads-and-feathers" kind. While Native poets have had difficulty finding publishers, especially for their "non-Indian" work, however, some non-Native poets have, ironically, been more successful in publishing poems on "Indian" themes. In general, the response of Native writers to the non-Native poets who attempt to explain or to celebrate Native perspectives (poets often referred to as "white shamans" by the Native writers) has been at best cool. It may not be coincidental that Duane Niatum's anthology

Carriers of the Dream Wheel ends with a poem by Ray Young Bear that is specifically addressed to one of the "white shaman" poets. Young Bear's attitude is made clear in the opening lines of the poem: "your blood does not flow, not even a little. / the spinning of fathers is useless— / you weave no patterns, not even a word." More recently the Menominee poet Chrystos in her book *Dream On* has castigated those non-Indians who pursue, interrogate, or imitate Native people in hopes of absorbing their "spirit" and learning their "magic"; in Chrystos's poetry, these would-be shamans are reduced, through an exasperated pun, to "shame men" and "shame women."

The resistance to white shamanism is only one manifestation of Native writers' general reaction—sometimes angry, sometimes ironic or even laconic—to what many perceive as a frustrating pattern of shifts in attitudes and tastes on the part of the American public: sometimes Indians are "in," and sometimes they are "out." In either case, the status of the Native American person, whether that person is a writer or not, becomes subject to changing intellectual and aesthetic currents that are beyond the control of the Native population. In a poem called "At the Door of the Native Studies Director," the Tlingit poet Robert H. Davis eloquently traces the effects of recent attitudinal shifts through his meditations on the life of one man, the father of the speaker of the poem. As a child, the father, like many others of his generation, was put in a white-run Indian school where the object of education was to erase the children's ties to their families and to their cultural inheritance: "In this place years ago / they educated old language out of you, / put you in line, in uniform, on your own two feet." Years later the same school calls the father back, this time because his residual knowledge of traditional ways is seen as a valuable resource and qualifies him as a "native scholar." "They give you a job, a corner office. / Now you're instructed to remember old language, / faded legend, anything that's left." The results of these psychological and cultural disruptions are devastating not only for the father but also for the son, who now watches and listens as his father retreats more and more into memories and the inarticulate mutterings of sleep, leaving the son to imagine what his father dreams—and in what language he dreams: "Your sleep speech / grows guttural and I feel something pull / that when you wake I want to ask you about." The whimsical swings in American attitudes toward the value of "Indianness" have left this father and his son groping in dreams and in a half-remembered, half-heard language for the very sources of their identity.

The writers discussed in this chapter represent only a fraction of the Native American poets who are actively writing, publishing, and teaching today. Many are still finding an outlet through small presses and journals, but many are also being represented in anthologies. The 1988 edition of *Harper's Anthology of Twentieth-Century Native American Poetry*, for example, represents the work of thirty-six poets, none of whom is published there for the first time and most of whom have substantial publishing records. There are many accomplished poets who have not been discussed in this chapter and whose work deserves a much wider audience; among these are Mary Tallmountain (Athabaskan), Maurice Kenny (Mohawk), Elizabeth Cook-Lynn (Sioux), Carter Revard (Osage), Jim Barnes (Choctaw), Peter Blue Cloud (Mohawk), Jimmie Durham (Cherokee), Gladys Cardiff (Cherokee), Duane Niatum (Klallam), Charlotte DeClue (Osage), Gail Tremblay (Iroquois/Micmac), Roberta Hill Whiteman (Oneida), Anita Endrezze (Yaqui), Nia Francisco (Navajo), Diane Glancy (Cherokee), and Darryl Babe Wilson (Pit River).

The work of these and other poets constitutes a body of significant writing that is, fortunately, steadily increasing. Their poetry not only offers the general reader insight into the complex and varied cultures of Native America, past and present; it also offers the reader, especially the non-Indian reader, a new perspective from which to view his or her own relationship to American history, to American literary traditions, to the American landscape, even to the very definition and configuration of America. The particular histories to which this poetry bears eloquent witness have for too long been obscured; in the work of the contemporary Native American poets the "long story of the people," a story of survival, continuance, and celebration, is now available to all of us. We have only to listen.

Lucy Maddox

Further Reading

Bruchac, Joseph, ed. *Songs from This Earth on Turtle's Back*. Greenfield, N.Y.: Greenfield Review Press, 1983.

Coltelli, Laura. *Winged Words: American Indian Writers Speak*. Lincoln: University of Nebrask Press, 1990.

Dodge, Robert K., and Joseph B. McCullough, eds. *New and Old Voices of Wah'Kon-Tah*. New York: International Publishers, 1985.

Evers, Larry, ed. *The South Corner of Time: Hopi, Navajo, Papago, Yaqui Tribal Literature*. Tucson: University of Arizona Press, 1980.

Green, Rayna, ed. *That's What She Said: Contemporary Poetry and Fiction by Native American Women*. Bloomington: Indiana University Press, 1984.

Niatum, Duane, ed. *Carriers of the Dream Wheel: Contemporary Native American Poetry*. San Francisco: Harper and Row, 1975.

———— *Harper's Anthology of Twentieth-Century Native American Poetry*. San Francisco: Harper Collins, 1988.

Rosen, Kenneth. *Voices of the Rainbow: Contemporary Poetry by American Indians*. New York: Seaver Books, 1975.

Ruoff, A. Lavonne. *American Indian Literatures: An Introduction, Bibliographic Review, and Selected Bibliography*. New York: MLA, 1990.

James Merrill and John Ashbery

THOUGH Merrill's and Ashbery's primary poetic antecedents—Stevens, Auden, and Bishop—are nearly identical, their descendants hardly recognize each other. The Language poets, a diverse group of experimentalists named for the journal *L=A=N=G=U=A=G=E*, claim Ashbery in their criticism and their poetic practice as a major influence and encouragement. Incited by the lyric disjunctions of *The Tennis Court Oath* and "The Skaters" and by the prosaic conjunctions of *Three Poems*, poets such as Charles Bernstein, Michael Palmer, Susan Howe, and Lyn Hejinian all show his influence. Beginning in the mid-seventies, the Language poets have grown into the most significant experimental movement since the New York school (including Kenneth Koch, Frank O'Hara, and James Schuyler) in which Ashbery found himself enrolled. Few of the new formalists, a group of young poets (Brad Leithauser, J. D. McClatchy, Mary Jo Salter, Marilyn Hacker, among others) emerging in the eighties, would omit Merrill, arguably the best formalist poet America has yet produced, from their heritage. But neither group recognizes the other's significance. While Language poets dismiss the new formalists as retrograde versifiers created to fill the vacuum of conventional journals and awards, new formalists reject the Language poets as lineated literary theorists created to fill the vacuum of academic articles. Moreover, many (though by no means all) new formalists label Ashbery as a sloppy postmodern sham, and nearly all Language poets revile Merrill as an elitist premodern prosody manual. How did things come to such a pass?

After all, both Merrill and Ashbery are innovative, ambitious, prolific, cultivated, demanding, casually formal poets. Their differences, apparent from the beginning, arise from their different responses to their common traditions.

Ashbery began writing as an innovative formalist. *Some Trees* (1956), chosen by W. H. Auden for the Yale Younger Poets series, contained an eclogue, a hymn ("He"), a pantoum, a canzone, two sestinas, and two unrhymed poems entitled "Sonnet." Auden's influence is evident in Ashbery's sestina "The Painter," written in 1949 while he was a senior at Harvard. Here is Ashbery's coda alongside the close of Auden's "Musée des Beaux Arts":

> They tossed him, the portrait, from the tallest of the buildings;
> And the sea devoured the canvas and the brush
> As though his subject had decided to remain a prayer.
>
> . . . the expensive delicate ship that must have seen
> Something amazing, a boy falling out of the sky,
> Had somewhere to get to and sailed calmly on.

Auden's ironic perspective is matched by Ashbery's critical distance from those on the building who crucify the difficult painter. Where Auden describes the painting of a fall (Brueghel's *Icarus*), Ashbery narrates the fall of a painting; and where Auden's practical witnesses remain indifferent to miracles, Ashbery's spectators are coolly hostile to experimental art. Ashbery wrote his senior thesis at Harvard on Auden, and has continued in his debt. The prose poems in *Three Poems*, for instance, are indebted to Caliban's address in *The Sea and the Mirror*, and the talkative *Flow Chart* borrows from Auden's chatty New York lyrics. In general, Auden introduced Ashbery to eclectic urban poetry and taught him that daily and miraculous experience and language appear side by side.

Stevens, as several readers have noticed, casts a large shadow over Ashbery's early poetry. "The Idea of Order at Key West" is distinctly audible in Ashbery's "*Le Livre est sur la table* ": "We can only imagine a world in which a woman / Walks and wears her hair and knows / All that she does not know." Like Merrill, Ashbery learned from Stevens (and others, such as Marvell) how to write a fully blooded poetry of ideas. But above all, Stevens (and Eliot) showed Ashbery how to leave the scene of his own poetry so that the verse itself could represent him.

Of the few characters in Stevens's poetry, fewer are autobiographical (Crispin in "The Comedian as the Letter C" is perhaps the closest). Yet Stevens's ample mind seems embodied in his long poems, as in this expressive thesis from "An Ordinary Evening in New Haven": "The poem is the cry of its occasion, / Part of the res itself and not about it." Ashbery is no less present in this counterthesis from his long poem "A Wave" (1984): "It is true but also without knowing out there in the dark, / Being alone at the center of a moan that did not issue from me."

But Stevens's influence on Ashbery's poetry is often mediated by another personally reticent poet, Elizabeth Bishop. For Merrill and Ashbery, writing under the paranoid gaze of Senator Joseph McCarthy, there were good practical as well as aesthetic reasons for keeping their published life under wraps. Bishop and Auden showed both young poets how to let their homosexuality shine covertly through. Ashbery's early poem, "The Instruction Manual," and its further development, "The Skaters," both derive from Bishop's painting and travel poems (Bishop's late poem "Crusoe in England" is influenced in turn by "The Skaters"). Ashbery's on-the-scene tour guide is on loan from Bishop: "Let us take this opportunity to tiptoe into one of the side streets. / Here you may see one of those white houses with green trim / That are so popular here. Look—I told you!" Bishop's "The Monument" also puts us in the midst of things: "Now can you see the monument? It is of wood / built somewhat like a box. No. Built / like several boxes in descending sizes." This self-contained container makes everything look queer: "But that queer sea looks made of wood, / half-shining, like a driftwood sea." The instruction manual also makes everything look sexually strange, as the satisfied guide concludes: "How limited, but how complete withal, has been our experience of Guadalajara! / We have seen young love, married love, and the love of an aged mother for her son." What we haven't seen of course is love of one man or woman for another, an omission that renders his tour of Guadalajara an exotic instruction manual in heterosexual love.

For the young Merrill and Ashbery, writing in New York in the fifties, Auden must have been a formidable presence. Not only his poetry but his creased self could take you by surprise. Some such real or imagined encounter must have given rise to Merrill's sonnet "Marsyas," named for the Phrygian satyr who, after losing a fluting contest with Apollo, was flayed on a pine tree. While he is writing in a café someone brings the upstart poet a new book (*The Shield of Achilles* appeared in 1955). "I opened it—stiff rhythms, gorgeous rhymes— / And made a face. Then crash! my cup upset." Before him stood the author, "that gold archaic lion's look / Wherein I was my wiry person skinned / Of every skill it labored to acquire." A contemporary poem such as "Nocturne" would have sweetly vanquished most novices with its formal charm and play with rhyme and stress: "Make this night loveable, / Moon," begins the bedside prayer, "and with eye single / Looking down from up there, / Bless me, One especial / And friends everywhere." In his rematch with Auden in *Sandover* Merrill writes (or transcribes) lines and even poems for the departed poet. In "Mirabell" the "SINGLE FLAW" of Auden's New York poetry is isolated, "THE MISMARRIAGE / OF LYRIC TO BALD FARCE SO THAT WORK BECAME A PASTIME." But Auden's style as well as his voice inhabits *Sandover*. Merrill sets a celebration in "Scripts" to the tune of Auden's libretto for Stravinsky's *The Rake's Progress,* and Auden's formal lightness and colloquial quickness make the hardest lessons easier to take.

Of Stevens Merrill recalls first admiring his "great ease in combining abstract words with gaudy visual or sound effects." The difficulty in achieving this dynamic tension shows in this oval mirror poem from the forties, "The Blue Eye." In an earlier version, "The Cosmological Eye," the myopic gaze doubles back: "His cloven gaze withdraws and all at once / Upon the pure expanse of dream begins, / Fluent in the idiom of blue." "Notes Toward a Supreme Fiction" (1942), the Stevens poem Merrill first studied, ended with an address to *the* convex mirror: "I call you by name, my green, my fluent mundo. / You will have stopped revolving except in crystal." Merrill's revised version, "The Blue Eye," consolidates its influence with a full Stevensian rhyme: "The vanes of seeing veer back, forth to sound / An iris-deep epitome, dream bound, / Fluent in the idiom of blue." Though he seldom appears in the trilogy (in "Ephraim," Merrill notes that the Ouija sessions began in 1955, the year Stevens died), Stevens helps shape that fluent mundo. The first lesson of "Scripts for the Pageant," for instance, is an utterly Stevensian formulation: "THE MOST INNOCENT OF IDEAS IS THE IDEA THAT INNOCENCE IS DESTROYED BY IDEAS." In "Auroras of Autumn" Stevens theorizes that if "innocence" is "not a thing of time, nor of place, / Existing in the idea of it, alone, / / . . . it is not / Less real." The original innocence of ideas and of forms, the Latin equivalent, is central to Merrill's poetry.

In Merrill's lyrics as in Ashbery's the innocence comes primarily from Bishop. Merrill acknowledges having picked up "Elizabeth's way of contradicting something she's just said" (cf. "The Monument," quoted above). Both Ashbery's and Merrill's favorite among Bishop's ideas of innocence is that of representation. Like Keats's frozen lovers on the Grecian urn, Bishop's representatives do not know they're represented. In "The Map," for instance, "Labrador's yellow, where the moony Eskimo / has oiled it." So too, in Merrill's homage to Bishop, "The Victor Dog," the RCA logo must accept his world as he finds it: "Adamant [i.e., diamond] needles bear down on him from / Whirling of outer space, too black, too near—." The needle and whirling globe will also remind readers of the Bishop of "In the Waiting Room." With its childhood remembrances, its translations through life and history into death and art, Merrill's marvelous jigsaw-puzzle, "Lost in Translation," reassembles Proust. Yet Bishop helps Merrill translate his Proustian remembrances with her innocent perspectives—for example the confused Page, not yet pieced together: "He wonders whom to serve, / And what his duties are, and where his feet." Bishop's idea has its darker, grander implications. In *Sandover* we mortals play befuddled representatives, characters in a divine comedy not of our making. The revelation that we are, after all, only pieces of a puzzle is the encompassing, difficult idea of Merrill's trilogy.

What of Merrill's and Ashbery's mutual influence? For readers acclimated to their serious playfulnesses, common features are scarce. Their different ways of proceeding may be illustrated by a pair of poems from the seventies with nearly identical titles, Merrill's "Syrinx" and Ashbery's "Syringa." Unlike "Marsyas," Merrill's "Syrinx" has less to do with art than with love, sexual maturity and potency in particular. Though Bishop's representations and Stevens's blooded abstractions are evident, the primary influence on "Syrinx" is Whitman—a free-verse democrat seldom recognized in his elegant comrade—who would recognize it as another Calamus poem. Like Whitman's sexually explicit marsh plant, Merrill's "thinking reed" pipes pleasure and pain: "Who puts his mouth to me / Draws out the scale of love and dread," until Pan, written as "Pain," shrivels the "sunbather's precocious apricot." "Syrinx" is a love poem sent from "I" to "you" (Whitman's shifting erotic other), pledging lifelong constancy. But the more urgent question is whether the "I" is a constant or a variable. The poem ends hazardously, not with reeds gathered but with music scattered to the "four winds," arranged on the rhyming compass points:

> Or stop the four winds racing overhead
> Nought
> Waste   Eased
> Sought

Playing "He loves me, he loves me not," the poet ends up, fortunately, still sought. Ashbery's longer and more ambitious "Syringa" is equally loved and equally anthologized. Yet the syringa, a genus of shrub or tree including the lilac (probably Merrill's route to Whitman), appears only briefly in Ashbery's poem, which takes the Orpheus myth as its mythological topic. In "Syrinx" Merrill's syringa appears in the first person as a Bishop-like rebus: "Illiterate—X my mark—I tremble, still / A thinking reed." Ashbery's syringa is more subject to the passing current. To hold to the shore is "to become the tossing reeds of that slow, / Powerful stream, the trailing grasses / Playfully tugged at, but to participate in the action / No more than this." Ashbery flows where Merrill takes root. Like "Marsyas," Ashbery's "Syringa" concerns art, specifically artistic innovation and immortality. As in "Marsyas," the potentially erotic other (Eurydice plays almost no part in "Syringa") is a poetic father: "Then Apollo quietly told him: 'Leave it all on earth. / Your lute, what point? Why pick at a dull pavan few care to / Follow, . . . / Not vivid performances of the past.' " The narrator answers quickly for Orpheus: "But why not? / All other things must change too." As Merrill's reeds end up scattered but sought, Ashbery's Orpheus (torn limb from limb by the Bacchantes) has "disappeared into libraries, onto microfilm." Merrill's metamorphosis occurs at the level of characters, with his beautifully transmuted winds. Ashbery, who changes *syrinx* to *syringa* and *flute* to *lute*, concludes with the same idea, as the subject is conjured by "But they lie / Frozen and out of touch until an arbitrary chorus / Speaks of a totally different incident with a similar name." The "hidden syllables" themselves, if not their meaning or original reference, will carry the author's name downstream.

For a slice of the comparative history of these two incomparables I will turn to their long poems: Merrill's trilogy, *The Changing Light at San-*

dover (1982), three of Ashbery's contemporaneous long poems—*Three Poems*, "Self-Portrait in a Convex Mirror," and "Litany"—and finally, Ashbery's recent summation, *Flow Chart*. Merrill's immense tripartite volume, most recently entitled *The Changing Light at Sandover: A Poem*, will probably be regarded as the culmination of his career. It is certainly one of the strangest poems in the history of American literature. *Sandover*, a place combining a Palace of Art with Merrill's palatial childhood home in Southampton (Merrill's father helped found the Merrill Lynch firm), is based on Ouija board transcripts taken down between 1955 and 1979, in Stonington, Connecticut, and in Athens by Merrill and his longtime partner, David Jackson, known in the poem as "the hand" (Merrill once thought of crediting Jackson as coauthor). The trilogy is laid out itself like a grand Ouija board: "The Book of Ephraim" (1976) contains twenty-six chapters, going from *A* to *Z*, "Mirabell's Books of Number" (1978) has ten sections, numbered zero through nine, and "Scripts for the Pageant" is divided into three suggestive parts, Yes & No. Merrill is still taking dictation. *Sandover* included "Coda: The Higher Keys," his next book, *Late Settings*, gathered more transcripts "From the Cutting-Room Floor," and most recently the *Paris Review* (Spring 1992) published "The Plato Club," a multipersonality interview and a raunchy symposium including various (dead) writers insufficiently present in *Sandover*.

Even without these codas (more tales are sure to wag), *Sandover* is immense. The 560-page poem is universal in scale and scope, extending from the atom to its outer space creator, from the creation to the apocalyptic present, from this world of the living to the other world of the dead and the supernaturals, whose speech appears in alien, telegraphic capitals. *Sandover* is a consolatory elegy (in this mirror world people enter at death and exit at rebirth), an ecological argument, an exotic formal garden, a cosmology updated with modern science, a gay mythology, an austere theodicy, and a contemporary drama of its own composition. Its leading characters are JM and DJ, as the board members are abbreviated, Ephraim, an eighth-century Greek Jew, Mirabell, a bat turned peacock, the angels Michael and Gabriel, who largely supercede Ephraim and Mirabell in "Scripts," and W. H. Auden and Maria Mitsotáki (known from Athens), the poem's ghostly parents.

Merrill has suggested that WHA and MM are his poem's Virgil and Beatrice. More than the work of Plato, Auden, Stevens, Proust, Moore, and Bishop, *The Divine Comedy* of Dante (whom JM and DJ dare not call up) provided the impetus for *Sandover*. Dante's manifold design, austere pronouncements, and dramatically revised revelations concerning our supernatural world all find their counterpart in Merrill's trilogy (Merrill's title of the volume first containing "The Book of Ephraim," *Divine Comedies* , has modestly disappeared from the trilogy). In "Divine Poem," the best poet's essay on Dante since Eliot's, Merrill regards Dante as he does himself, as a mystic receiving otherworldly signals. Dante would surely agree, with reservations. Is *Sandover* also to be taken on faith? The simple but obvious question whether Merrill "believes all this," along with the increasingly pressing question whether Merrill wrote, and hence authorizes, all this, must be answered "yes and no." Merrill mentions in an interview with J. D. McClatchy, without a trace of irony, that "I can't pretend to have known Wystan terribly well in *this* world," yet later admits that one "exchange with Wystan is largely contrived." Mirabell postulates that his kind "ARE THE INSTRUMENTS OF REPLY. ALL / THESE OUR CONVERSATIONS COME FROM MEMORY & WORD BANKS / TAPPD IN U." And as for the sweet and bitter dicta of "Mirabell" and "Scripts," they are dramatically bracketed but poetically ascribed to. *Sandover* is best read as it was written, with two minds.

One thing the cosmically scaled *Sandover* isn't is historical. In this synchronic roundtable, where Auden chats with Plato and Frost sits next to Goethe, history is a delusion, a predestined unraveling. Even Clio demeans her province: "LORDS, WHAT IS HISTORY? / NOT MUCH. / YESTERDAY'S BLANK PAGE HAPHAZARD- LY / COLORED IN." American history and culture hold little interest for JM and DJ. When, amid a discussion of geological time in Mirabell, America's anniversary passes, the cloistered pair take momentary interest in history's parade: "Whistles and bells. We run to the window—why, / It's the Bicentennial, it's the Fourth of July!" upon which Mirabell notes, "U ARE NOT UNLIKE HEAVEN LOOKING DOWN ON TIME PASSING," a deadly accurate observation. *Sandover* may be read as an introspective retreat into certainty following the disastrous foreign and domestic policies of Vietnam and Watergate. But for Merrill the American psychohistorical context of *Sandover* would be insignificant, dwarfed by its timeless, cosmic truths.

Unlike the epic histories of Homer, Virgil, and Milton, little of consequence happens in *Sandover*. The drama of Merrill's poem instead involves the continuing revelation of conflicting ideas. If *Sandover* invites comparison with the great classical and modernist epics (which it has often received), Merrill sent out the invitations. There is nothing unusual in this; the self-canonizing gesture of epic works is by now generic. Eliot quotes Dante in *The Waste Land* and Joyce structures *Ulysses* on Homer's *Odyssey*. Even classical Western epics have claimed their high lineage; Dante lodged Homer and Virgil in his *Inferno* and Virgil's *Aeneid* revised Homer's narratives. The Latin epic poet Ennius recounted a dream in which Homer told him that his soul had passed into a peacock and then into Ennius, a coincidence Merrill's peacock Mirabell would surely say was no accident. *Sandover*, we learn, was commissioned not only by the scribes but by God. DJ, who often anticipates negative criticism of *Sandover*, frets, "The part about our being chosen / Won't sound complacent? Do the poem harm?" to which Michael replies that few are chosen. In the concluding poem, "The Ballroom at Sandover," Merrill begins reading his divinely inspired scriptures to an exclusive literary circle encompassing the alphabet from Austin to Yeats (no Zola or Zukofsky). But in spite of the fact that Merrill has reserved his seat among the immortals, the immortality of *Sandover* will depend on the very history the poem dismisses. Poems are canonized by readers and reciters, other writers, critics and editors, and librarians. No modern epic can mean to the culturally diverse population of the United States what *The Iliad* and the *Divine Comedy* or even *Paradise Lost* meant to their nations. But by its magnitude and astonishing conception and grace *Sandover* has already earned its place in the history of America's post-Vietnam poetry.

For many readers (myself included), "Ephraim" is not only the most successful part of *Sandover* but the best thing Merrill has written to date, rivaled only by "Lost in Translation." Its brisk, diversified narratives, parceled out among compact chapters, help maintain the suspense of its daring conception, when DJ and JM are not sure who or what they've tapped into. The early transcripts are employed sparingly; seldom do more than five capitalized lines appear without some reaction, question, or antipication from JM or DJ intervening. Like Dante's damned, Ephraim's first concern is with his life's unfinished business: "There was a buried room, a BED / WROUGHT IN SILVER I CAN

LEAD U THERE / IF If? U GIVE ME What? HA HA YR
SOULS." With these quick midline changes, the tempo of Merrill's
state-of-the-art pentameters is sometimes closer to Shakespeare's than
Pope's.

The mechanics of transcription plays its own part. One of the most
likeable characters in *Sandover* is the cup upon which DJ's and JM's
coupled hands ride around the Ouija board. The unnamed cup is an
expressive, antic mime reminiscent of Harpo Marx; Merrill's Disney-
vintage speaking unicorn, Unice, pales in comparison. The cup plays DJ
and JM as it picks up its first signal: "The cup twitched in its sleep. 'Is
someone there?' / We whispered, fingers light on Willowware, / When
the thing moved. Our breathing stopped. The cup, / Glazed zombie of
itself, was on the prowl." As an unidentified party breaks through,
"HELLP O SAV ME scrawled the cup," it is instantly characterized
both by Merrill's idiosyncratic spelling and by the cup's handwriting.
Merrill's receptive cup and erogenous-zoned board make a refreshing
break from the too often dully phallic pen.

On the first page of "Ephraim" Merrill wonders, "Best after all to do
it as a novel?" In a delightful poem on a fateful mishap entitled "The
Will" Merrill relates how he actually left an early draft of the novel that
might have been "Ephraim" in a taxi. This novel, lost in translation, hovers nevertheless over "Ephraim" as a shadowy subtext. Merrill wishes
"Ephraim" to be a "limpid, unfragmented" story with "conventional
stock figures" rather than the kind of "Nouveau roman" in vogue in
France in the fifties and in South and North America in the sixties and
seventies. But "Ephraim," the detective, magically realist novel of its
own recovery, is no artless tale. In fact, its most interesting idea, on the
nature of representation, is derived from the novelistic structure. Every
person, Ephraim explains, is the representative of a heavenly patron, a
kind of airy godparent fussing over the successive, unremembered lives
of its charge. The relation between patron and representative is analogous to that between author and character (an analogy Ashbery has also
frequently mined). The slow process of character development from
chapter to chapter, life to life, is itself akin to evolutionary change. The
metaphor is extended in chapter "F," nearly devoid of otherworldly caps:
"Flash-forward: April 1st in Purgatory, / Oklahoma. Young Temerlin
takes me calling / On his chimpanzees." "Flash-forward" aptly
describes, not only the narrative, but the evolutionary leap from chimp

to human. The chimp Miranda on her tempestuous island makes "the 'happy' sign" upon the arrival of her guest, which prompts Merrill's wonder over her silences: "regret? foreknowledge? Who / Can doubt she's one of us?" Such speculation also fueled contemporary debates between behavioral psychologists and linguists such as Jane Goodall over the language acquisition of primates; were chimps using language or merely imitating us? When Miranda seals her greeting with a kiss, Merrill feels their relation, resembling "that whole / Fantastic monkey business of the soul / Between lives, gathered to its patron's breast." Not only science but science fiction took an interest in language evolution; both the famous opening sequence of Stanley Kubrick's *2001* (select apes enlightened by a humming pyramid) and the devolutionary allegory *Planet of the Apes* (with multiple sequels) captivated the American screen. Though Merrill professes his "Horror of Popthink" with their "chosen apes," chapter "F" was spooned from the same cultural soup.

It is always instructive in *Sandover* to follow the spinal narrative across changes in scene and topic; there is rarely (if ever) such a thing in literature as pure, causeless sequence. After Miranda and JM kiss the narrative switches to Ephraim's search for a new home for his representative. JM and DJ suggest promising pregnant women, as they "stride roughshod / Past angels all agape." The allusion to Pope ("For *Fools* rush in where *Angels* fear to tread") nominates "Fools" as another candidate for the chapter heading. "Fathers" is another. (Several chapters conceal their proper names: *H*ypnotism, *I*, *W*endell, *S*ergei, etc.) Soon, in a pregnant stretch, Ephraim's representative is audibly placed: "out of the womb forthcoming / Late in the sixth month, a MELODIOUS HUMMING / —Which, heard there, would do much to clarify / Another year's abortion talks in Rome." These lines, beginning with a nod to Whitman's "Out of the cradle," join in America's budding abortion controversy over the passage of Roe v. Wade, giving birth to the potent coalition of Protestant and Roman Catholic fundamentalists. Merrill's impish sanctification of abortions into the second trimester tweaks the nose of the "pro-lifers" (as they misnamed themselves) as well as of the creationists and the moralists disapproving of artificial insemination and surrogate birthing. Though *Sandover* would be timeless, it is born of its time.

Another narrative sequence provides a more dramatic explanation for the rebirth of Ephraim's representative (as JM's nephew Wendell). In

"H," DJ is put under hypnosis and, possessed by Ephraim in his trance, makes love to JM. Then in "I" (the fallacy "post hoc propter hoc" doesn't hold for *Sandover*) Wendell is born, and JM confides in his shrink. Who are Wendell's (god)fathers? Who are Ephraim's? JM theorizes a Freudian explanation. To assuage a blaming "Father Figure," the gay sons "can both proclaim / And shuffle off the blame / For how we live." The vast otherworldly universe of *Sandover* may also be read as the other world of the gay male. *Sandover* by and large is a gay man's world. Even the female lead, Maria Mitsotáki, turns out to be a reincarnation of Plato, who notes that "THESE ESCAPES INTO A FEMALE LIFE ARE VAST / REFRESHMENTS." We are told in this defense that "Platonic" coupling between men, "A UNISEXUAL ONE PRODUCING ONLY LIGHT," fosters superior poetry and music. Unlike straight male disseminators, JM and DJ are "more the docile takers-in of seed": "No matter what tall tale our friends emit, / Lately—you've noticed?— we just swallow it." In Merrill's baudy Platonic dialogue, "The Plato Club," written during the resurgence of homophobia as arts censorship (Robert Mapplethorpe's homosexually explicit photography exhibit was attacked by Senator Jesse Helms and shut down by police in Cincinnati in 1989), the apologist goes on the offensive. In a surprising exchange, DJ locks horns with William Carlos Williams, who turns out to be a reluctant ally of Helms. Williams, who confesses that "I have long felt that American literature has given too much attention to homo-poets," claims that straight poets can only regain their edge through "Censorship. As is now being debated in Congress." Though Williams, who introduced Ginsberg's *Howl* in the mid-fifties, cannot simply be labeled a homophobe, his poetics is markedly heterosexual. Yet Merrill's own sexual theories are biased toward inherently upper classes. For all the good cheer of Merrill's gay science, its rigorous natural selections will create uneasiness among gay and straight readers alike.

Although "Mirabell's Books of Number" (1978) is twice as long as "Ephraim," it represents less than half the Ouija board transcripts taken during the busy summer of 1976. Its immensity is largely due to its complex doctrine, as *Sandover* moves away from lowercase narrative and toward uppercase argument. The poem is divided into ten books (0 through 9), each subdivided into ten, resembling Aquinas's *Summa Theologica* or a science textbook. It is embedded with formal gems: sonnets, odes, couplets, hendecasyllabics, terze rime, and invented rhyme schemes. Mirabell (named for Congreve's heroine and echoing "Merrill"), or 741, is one of fourteen vampire bats communicating in fourteen-syllable lines. During the discussion of homosexuality he metamorphoses into, or comes out as, a peacock. Lessons on universal dualism, hierarchy, and determinism are delivered primarily in this new measure. Unlike Chapman's or Blake's accentual fourteeners, these unheard syllabics must be counted. Merrill's choice was surely influenced by the syllabic scientific inquiries of Marianne Moore.

"Mirabell's Books of Number"—number also meaning verse—is an apt title. Like the new formalists, Merrill uses formalism for looking through the mirror of the self, hoping that arbitrary form will better reflect objective reality. Merrill's fourteeners, for instance, take on a life of their own as they move in with human-measured pentameters in split-level lines:

> Peacock, peacock—
> MAY I ASK A ? DO TEARS PAIN ONE?
> Yes. No. Pain and bless.
> MY EYES BURN RED

Mirabell's syllabics usher in the world of science, a world Merrill freely admits he knows little of. His goal is not to explain science but to mythologize and personify it: "What can you and I profitably learn from a neutrino? Yet give it a human mask and it will, as Oscar Wilde said, tell the truth. Read science this way." Scientists, like the dead, would communicate in absolutes. But some theories age and lose their predictability. Today's consensus is that dinosaurs evolved into birds rather than sank "coil by coil / Concentrated to deep coal, to oil." Mirabell's 1976 global forecast "WE SEE NO MAJOR FOOD / OR AIR PROBLEMS" was soon shown to be woefully myopic. But much of Merrill's science is animated and engaging myth. Like Lucretius, Merrill begins with the atom: "THE ATOM IT IS ADAM & THE UNIVERSE / LEAVE IT TO ITSELF & LET IT BREATHE." Nuclear fission and radioactivity ignite a cosmic holocaust, destroying not only bodies but souls. *Sandover* takes its place alongside the work of Ginsberg and Snyder as part of a growing antinuclear poetry in the seventies. Merrill also endows the life sciences with Miltonic wonder. In the sestet of a sonnet on his growing understanding Merrill looks back to his Satanic avatar in our "reptilian / Inmost brain" from which we sprang: "A small, tree-loving snake's / Olfactory lobes developed. Limbs occurred / To it, and mammal warmth, music and word." Merrill's latinate use of "occurred" (meaning "to run") also looks back to Milton's lost Paradise.

Merrill's formalist universe is deterministic, the filling-in of preordained measures and rhyme schemes. This gospel of formalism is epitomized by the oft repeated motto of *Sandover*, "NO ACCIDENT." Merrill's fatalism, though rooted in the diverse American transcendentalisms of Emerson, Whitman, and Dickinson, is itself alien to contemporary American readers. Merrill himself acknowledged difficulty in taking his medicine: "For me the talk and the tone—along with the elements of plot—are the candy coating. The pill itself is another matter. The reader who can't swallow it has my full sympathy. I've choked on it again and again." Serious readers of *Sandover* will have to ruminate on the explicit and implied content of its form. "Don't tell us that the heavenly Academy, like the earthly one nowadays," Merrill exclaims in "The Plato Club," "requires political correctness from its faculty." To be sure, some readers of the nineties—who want more agreement from their culture than they get from the rest of life—will dismiss *Sandover* out of hand as a Great Book on dead white males by a live rich one. Yet few of the rest of its readers will stand in mute admiration before its sweeping inequities.

"A BASIC PRECEPT U WILL NEED TO TAKE ON FAITH: THERE IS NO ACCIDENT / DJ: Not so fast there! JM: Whoa!" This unpalatable principle applies to everything that happens, "not just the gross event / But its minutest repercussion." What comes to be called the "NO ACCIDENT clause" (after no-fault accident insurance for automobiles) comprises the theodicy of *Sandover*. Mass deaths, we are told, are no accident. Gabriel chortles over African starvation: "JUNGLES? WE'LL THIN! THIN! THIN!" The Black Death in Europe "WAS PLANND FOR 2 EFFECTS: THIN POPULATION / KEEP IT PREDOMINANTLY RURAL." Mirabell's pseudoscientific explanation is that cities breed heat, "WHICH ALARM[S] GOD B" (God Biology, as the Creator is known in *Sandover*), and must be cooled by thinning. The contemporary implications of this theology are frightening. In 1982, the year *Sandover* was published, a growing incurable global plague received its capitalized acronym, AIDS. "No accident," say any number of religious and political fundamentalists. These self-sanctified dimwits espousing divine retribution are certainly among the darkest of Mirabell's and Gabriel's current representatives.

The NO ACCIDENT clause pertains to life as well as death. We are told in "Mirabell" that "Soul falls into two / Broad categories: run-of-the-mill souls . . . / / Whom nothing quickens" and "an elite," a distinction that Merrill admits, in a Popean expression, "Leaves the snob proud, the democrat perplexed." Both the "OLD LIBERAL" DJ and Auden object to what Auden calls "THE INFLEXIBLE ELITISM OF IT ALL." Yet the justified hierarchies of *Sandover* overcome their initial objections, which anticipate ours. Everybody in this intellectual hierarchy is really somebody; WHA will return as a great Eastern philosopher, MM turns out to be Plato, George Cotzias is a ground-breaking scientist, and Robert Morse will be the next major composer. Even chatty Ephraim is Michael, archangel of light and intellect, in disguise. Merrill recalls E. M. Forster's "TOUCHING THEORY THAT GOD WANTS EDU-CATED HIGHCLASS QUEERS / TO MAKE A DIFFERENCE"; in this play the rude Whitman, virtually absent from *Sandover*, has no speaking part.

With its capital(ist) letters, board meetings, private boarding schools, and souls commodified as precious metals, *Sandover* bears an uncanny resemblance to the speculative universe of Merrill Lynch. Those who make it, or have it made, were meant to. In "The Plato Club" Merrill wonders, "I've tried always to think of poetry—of all art—as the only clean use for power. Have I been naive?" For some readers, the answer would have to be, simply, "yes." There is in *Sandover* a failure to imagine other kinds of lives. Merrill regards a neighboring factory with Jamesian detachment: "Roseblush factory which makes, upstreet, / Exactly what, one once knew but forgets— / Something of plastic found in lun-cheonettes." When Gabriel claims that talent "IS THE GIFT MAN EARNS (OR NOT) WITH HIS LIFE," Merrill forgets that some are given considerably more opportunity to earn their gifts than others. But is this too no accident? Are the disadvantaged necessarily the untalent-ed? In *Sandover* privilege is seen as a necessary precaution. The blue-chip Robert Morse will be reborn in Minnesota: "NO RISK / OF LOSING ME IN SOME 'EMERGING' NATION," while Chester Kallman, as poetic justice for his apparent racism, will return black: "HIS ARTICU-LATE (SCRIBE) QUALITIES / WILL BRING COHERENCE TO

A RACE LARGELY WITHOUT SPOKESMEN." Neither ironic quotes nor liberal sentiment can conceal the moral and imaginative paucity of these lines. Mirabell exposes himself as a bird of Thomas Love Peacock's feather.

Elemental strife rages on Mirabell's side of the board as well, amply illustrating Frost's definition of poetry as a momentary stay against confusion. The universe of *Sandover* is fundamentally dualistic, formed of hierarchical oppositions. In this Manichean universe, God B and Chaos, matter and antimatter, positive and negative charge, good and evil, light and darkness, white and black struggle for dominance. And the privileged few fend off the many. Unice guards the schoolroom door "AGAINST THE BILLIONS THEY WD EXPLODE YR EARS!" God B himself is locked in immortal combat (an impotence making the NO ACCIDENT clause unnecessary and incoherent) against "IT." God's only speech is a stunning 10X10 syllabic tape loop: "I AND MINE HOLD IT BACK BROTHERS I AND / MINE SURVIVE BROTHERS HEAR ME SIGNAL ME." God's imagination holds more back than the Stevensian pressure of reality. George Cotzias hypothesizes that "THE ELEMENTS FROM A 'WHITE' SOURCE / RESISTED THOSE OF A 'BLACK' OR 'SHADOW' FORCE," and that "WE MUST ASSUME THAT GOOD / MATTER RESISTS BAD." What are we to make of this metaphorical meaning? Is the color choice of vehicles accidental? The image, implicit but inextricable, of God B and his elite white legions holding back billions of low-class whites and nonwhites will make many readers flee this cool Paradise for the warmth of the other place.

Near the end of "Mirabell" Merrill introduces a new character with his own grand measure and diction—the sun god Michael: "AND SO AS YOU FACE THIS SETTING SUN YOU FACE YOUR ANCESTOR, AND THE SUN LOOKS THROUGH YOUR EYES TO THE LIFE BEHIND YOU. / EACH OF YOUR SUN-CYCLES IS A STEP ON YOUR WAY TO YOUR ANCESTOR / AND THAT IS ALL YOU NEED TO KNOW OF YOUR PHYSICAL INCARNATE HISTORY." With these freely versed, immeasurable lines Merrill finally makes his pact with Walt Whitman. As the echo in the last line suggests, the gnomic script of Keats's Grecian urn also shapes Michael's voice. Other models, such as the Old Testament, come to mind. One unexpected model, a master of American prose (and Whitman's hero), is acknowledged in Michael's recreation story, one of the mythopoetic triumphs of *Sandover* : "NOW WHEN IN THE COURSE OF HIS PLAN THE ARCHITECT FROWNS ON HIS WORK, HIS MERCY ALLOWS IT TO DESTROY ITSELF." For visionary concision Merrill could do no better than turn to Lincoln's Gettysburg Address. Michael's address sets the sunny stage of "Scripts for the Pageant" (1980), in which the scales are tipped in favor of pageantry and grandeur. Though "Scripts" has its dark turns (some of which are quoted above), they are personified and characterized in the ghoulish speeches of Gabriel, who is hungry for death rather than taken with its sublimity. With its swelling cast, the 250-page "Scripts" is the longest and most intricately designed poem of the trilogy. Its own tripartite structure, Yes & No, reverses Carlyle's eternal nay, center of indifference, and eternal yea, yet Merrill struggles against allowing negation and incredulity the last word. Like the spirits of Pope's "The Rape of the Lock," many of the speakers in "Scripts" ask only to be taken poetically ("Yes and no" being a Platonic definition for metaphor). The four angels, the muses, the five immortals, and four religious sages are embodiments of ideas. Nature herself (a.k.a. Psyche and Chaos) joins the angels to personify the four elements and the five senses. Unlike Dante's rarefied "Paradiso," Merrill's "Scripts" is a poem of the earth and incarnation. WHA and MM, the most humane of the personae, serve as JM's and DJ's divine sensors. Michael's appearance, for instance, is thankfully left to Auden's imagination instead of ours: "A GREAT ORIGINAL IDEA A TALL / MELTING SHINING MOBILE PARIAN SHEER / CUMULUS MODELED BY SUN TO HUMAN LIKENESS." Yet even their descriptions are transfigured midway through "Yes" into unattributed italicized settings. Still, the celestial couple remain congenial parents and ardent defenders of their earthly kin, saying "no" as often as "yes." Whether we say "yes" and/or "no" to the lessons of *Sandover*, the wondering innocence attending them is undeniably refreshing.

Although Ashbery has written a number of long poems throughout his career, he has composed no single work to match the variegated dramatic verse of *Sandover*. Yet his extended productions of the seventies (I am skipping the collaged dialogue "Fantasia on 'The Nut-Brown Maid' ") are comparable in scope and conception. *Three Poems* (1972), two fifty-page prose poems and a ten-page coda, is less formally diversified than *Sandover*. "The New Spirit" is divided into unindented prose blocks punctuated occasionally by informal free verse, "The System" is entirely in prose blocks, and "The Recital" is in prose paragraphs. Ashbery's trilogy develops an undemonstrative dialectic. Various theses and antitheses, comparable to those generated by the symbiotic strife between God B and Chaos, surface in "The New Spirit" and "The System" respectively, and are partially resolved in "The Recital": old and new, present and past, actual and potential, physical and spiritual love, among others.

The styles of *Three Poems* are likewise indistinct. But Ashbery's new, plain, often hackneyed American has fundamentally altered not only his own later verse but also the poetry of innumerable younger poets. *Sandover* is aptly praised for its range of dictions, from the sonorous pronouncements of Michael to the gaily inflected gossip of JM, DJ, MM, and WHA. The voices of *Three Poems*, though perhaps equal in range, are generally lower in register, passing from rapt Proustian reflections down to trite homiletics and clunky journalese. Moreover, whereas the lowercase verse of JM, rarely oscillating beyond its fields of witty conversation, playful narration, and tender meditation, is insulated from the highs of Michael and the lows, for instance, of DJ's deceased parents, the unfenced stylistic terrain of *Three Poems* changed Ashbery's lyric style itself.

The shifting character—and latent characters—of *Three Poems* may be charted by its pronouns. Consider one of the interpersonal messages that set the key of "The New Spirit":

You are too close to this happy state for it to matter for you. But meanwhile I am to include everything: the furniture of this room, everyday expressions, as well as my rarest thoughts and dreams, so that you may never become aware of the scattered nature of it, and meanwhile you *are* it all, and my efforts are really directed toward keeping myself attached, however dimly, to it as it rolls from view, like a river which is never really there because of moving on someplace.

The initial problem with reading this passage, which no context will solve, is the identity of "you," a fluid, changing mixture of lover, alter ego, and reader. As "it" appears, it seems to be the poem but seems also to stand in for the departing "you." The prose changes slightly and unexpectedly from paradox to self-reflexive statement to Jamesian idiom ("and meanwhile you *are* it all") to an explicitly and awkwardly phrased simile. The echo of Heraclitus's famous dictum that you can't step into the same river twice leaves no verbal traces (as Merrill does with Keats and Lincoln) to mark it as conscious allusion. Yet the passage is surely and quietly Heraclitean, as the repeated "meanwhile" reveals, with writer and reader, narrating and narrated lover, dipping simultaneously and differently into the same river of prose.

"The System," which begins "The system was breaking down," records the "inner necessity" of the religious and cultural revolts against the system during the Vietnam war, and then seeks to convert its own generation to a philosophy of life and love. Writing contemporaneously with his subject, Ashbery's historian gives bemused, hilarious Chaucerian credence to cosmic love: "Not an atom but did not feel obscurely compelled to set out in search of a mate; not a living creature, no insect or rodent, that didn't feel the obscure twitchings of dormant love." He concludes, as many did at the time, that "this cosmic welter of attractions was coming to stand for the real thing." The problem with this mystical peace and love movement was its passivity: "It could not proceed unless the generalized shape of this nirvana-like state could impose its form on the continually active atoms of the moving forward which was the price it exacted." For the historian, certain unspecified members of this younger generation committed the Hegelian sin of assuming they had reached "the logical last step of history." This nirvana of bliss and enlightenment was really a nadir of bad faith.

At this point in the progression of *Three Poems* Ashbery's historical perspective would seem to take a dim view of the otherworldly enlightenment of *Sandover*. Yet Ashbery is neither an existentialist nor a historical relativist. His alternative to the apocalyptic raptures of his younger contemporaries entails its own purpose and inner necessity. The historian of "The System" soon merges with the preacher who delivers a long-winded, threadbare sermon that nonetheless provides us with the most extended discussion of Ashbery's own experiments in life and art until *Flow Chart*. As Merrill's universe divides into order and chaos, Ashbery's system is arranged around the poles of "two kinds of happiness . . . : the frontal and the latent." The first may be associated with the vertiginous joy of the last canto of Dante's *Paradiso* or the aesthetic intensity of the final pages of Merrill's "Scripts for the Pageant": "Its sudden balm suffuses the soul without warning, as a kind of bloom or grace." Though transient, this privileged, Proustian, climactic influx nevertheless directs us "as an ideal toward which the whole universe tends and which therefore confers a shape on the random movements outside us." The second kind of happiness—dormant, latent, expectant—is precipated by the passing of the first kind into the past, and, potentially, into the future: "its *nearness* is there, tingeing the air around them, in suspension, in escrow as it were, but they cannot get at it."

If Merrill's burden was to derive evil from good or hazard from necessity, Ashbery's was to derive latent from frontal happiness, historical from momentary awareness. Ashbery's argument, much less elaborated than Merrill's, hinges on the reality of the initial experience: "But if it was indeed as real as all that, then it *was* real, and therefore it *is* real. . . . But you must try to seize the truth of this: whatever was, is, and must be." This urgent message of dormant historical determinism is not far from Mirabell's precept that "THERE IS / NO ACCIDENT." The skeptical member of Ashbery's congregation may propose that the present on the contrary gives meaning and shape to the past, that one (or more) of an indefinite sequence of moments accumulates significance as a fateful, critical, (un)fortunate crossroad, depending on the significance we give to the life or history that follows. But Ashbery's system demands absolute assent. What practical significance does this happy faith hold for him? In a crucial new figuration Ashbery imagines his two kinds of happiness no longer as earlier and later points along life's way but as divided yet related ways of proceeding: "But it is certain now that these two ways are the same, that we *have* them both, the risk and the security. . . . So that this second kind of happiness is merely a fleshed-out, realized version of that ideal first kind"; that is, latent happiness paradoxically fleshes out frontal happiness by giving it a lived, historical circumstance. As becomes clearer in *Flow Chart*, itself a more fleshed-out version of *Three Poems*, this other way, necessarily the only choice, is the route of artistic and homosexual experimentation. The sexual choice (if it is one) is so fundamental, so meaningful, that it cannot be understood otherwise than as no choice, as the way it was meant to be. Merrill's determinate other side is Ashbery's fated other way; each side or way justifies its existence by subsuming the other so that nothing of significance is really lost.

Since Ashbery's and Merrill's necessary ways diverge into formal and informal poetry, it seems likely that Merrill would admire Ashbery's mannered "Self-Portrait in a Convex Mirror" (1975). Ashbery, however, has sought to distance himself from his first critically acclaimed poem, which he believes garnered the awards belatedly intended for *Three Poems*. Entitled after the mannerist Parmigianino's rounded mirror portrait (1523–24) with its recessed face and looming, oversized hand, Ashbery's poem keeps its readers at bay, but at a cost. "The soul establishes itself," the art-critical persona observes:

> But how far can it swim out through the eyes
> And still return safely to its nest? The surface
> Of the mirror being convex, the distance increases
> Significantly; that is, enough to make the point
> That the soul is a captive . . .

This verse, oscillating between five and six stresses a line, is more concise and "formal" than most of the communications of *Three Poems*. The line breaks show the face in "eyes" and "surface," but is the face painted on the surface or swimming up from its foreshortened depths? The playful enjambment "the distance increases / Significantly" reveals that "deeper" meaning makes its own space. The frontal look, to incorporate Ashbery's earlier terminology, is latent in the embodied surface. Similarly, the author's urgent point lies behind his academic manner ("manus" means "hand").

The private room with its distended bare protuberance is also a homosexual closet with the pointed gaze as its key: "But the look / Some wear as a sign makes one want to / Push forward" toward communication and engagement "since the light / Has been lit once and for all in their eyes / And is present, unimpaired, a permanent anomaly." This experimental "anomaly" refigures the persistant frontal look dormant in the hand's career. For this reason, and for the general reason that the more perfected one's manner or style is the more confining it becomes, the prophylactic surface between lovers or between readers and writers occasionally needs to burst. The circumferential self of Ashbery's "Self-Portrait" is a creation of other people, even though the buried center sheds its dormant influence. Like Sartre, in vogue in the seventies, Ashbery claims: "This otherness, this / 'Not-being-us' is all there is to look at / In the mirror." The limitation for Ashbery of the mannerist achievement—and, by extension, of the formalist project— is its perfected finish. Parmigianino made himself into a globe "So as to perfect and rule out the extraneous / Forever. In the circle of your intentions certain spars / Remain that perpetuate the enchantment of self with self." The word "extraneous" is cognate with "strange," as in the distorted appearance of Pargianino's extended hand, and "stranger," as in another's "shield of a greeting." In his sexual mythology Freud rooted homosexuality in an arrested narcissism, latent in everyone and frontal in some. In the hermetic reflective globe of Ashbery's "Self-Portrait" it is as important—and pointless—to tell self from other as it is for JM and DJ in the mirror board of *Sandover* to distinguish themselves from their conjured counterparts.

"Self-Portrait in a Convex Mirror" is a study in formal perfection, like Ashbery's early sestina "The Painter" or Browning's "Andrea del Sarto." While not a parody, "Self-Portrait" was meant to reveal the confines of errorlessness. Ashbery broke out of his Stevensian academicism dramatically in a long double-columned poem called "Litany," named after the antiphonal ritual of the Episcopal Church, of which Ashbery (like Auden before him) is a member. Unlike a text and its translation or the minister's call and the congregation's response, the parallel columns rarely correspond, though their simultaneous occurrence leads the reader across the margin in either direction for help or support. Since Ashbery seems to have been careful not to align stanzas or sentences, simultaneously beginning and ending passages are a rarity. Here is a necessarily fragmentary stretch:

Some in underwear stood around	*Outnumbering the sheaves,*
Puddles in the darkened	*Even the ants on the anthill,*
Cement and sodium lights	*Black line leading to*
Beyond the earthworks	*The cake of disasters*

"Litany" presents us with a number of mysterious rituals of irretrievable significance. The group on the left, dressed in an American mistranslation of primitive garb, wait (absently or expectantly) in a circle around a reflecting puddle beyond a margin. Beyond the text's margin the parallel text records another primitive, yet peculiarly American, ritual: ants instinctively ruining the picnic. In each case attention centers around an object of worship or desire, which is unattained. The parallel columns of antlike letters thus form a circumference, like a cross section of a cylinder, around what Ashbery later calls *"the whiteness / That was there."* What is this whiteness? The missing common ground that would connect people to each other, to their creative writer, and to themselves, around which everything revolves. The figuration of "Litany" thus resembles that of Parmigianino's "Self-Portrait," "which organizes everything / Around the polestar of your eyes which are empty." Since Ashbery is usually regarded as speaking to himself or to an unnamed erotic other, little attention has been focussed on the often invisible, intervening spirit. But reading "Litany" alongside *Sandover*, one discerns ghostly outlines that might have escaped notice. In one otherworldly moment of frontal happiness "we" find ourselves at a "strangely rewarding" New England oceanside party in which no wine or food appear but communion is partaken. "Presently," Ashbery begins, in muted Whitmanian tones,

> Out of this near-chaos an unearthly
> Radiance stood like a person in the room,
> The memory of the host, perhaps. And all
> Fell silent, or stayed at their musings, silent
> As before . . . .

As with Merrill, it takes two to commune. The communicants are nameless, as is their "host," so that only the diagrammatic structure of communion remains. But the common sense of a radiating central spirit, as with Merrill, is proof enough that there is something more between them than themselves.

Like Merrill's, Ashbery's spirituality too has its bias:

For so long	*Yet there are silent beginnings*
	of beginnings
	Nothing but prayers, though it seems
The lovers saunter away.	*That we can now feel with our minds*
It is a mild day in May.	*Which is someplace between prayers*
With music and birdsong alway	*And the answer to prayers.*

The italized antiphony responds most closely to Eliot's *Four Quartets*. Meanwhile, roman types stage an open-air orgy in Skeltonic doggerel, an antiformalist version of lyric gaiety that continues: "The sleeve detaches itself from the body / As the two bodies do from the throng of gay / Lovers on the prowl that do move and sway." Ashbery's solution to the mind-body problem is an equally liberating parallelism.

One hundred pages in typescript and over two hundred in print, *Flow Chart* (1991) is Ashbery's longest poem, comparable in length with Merrill's "Scripts for the Pageant." It is illuminating to compare their modes of composition. "With Scripts," Merrill recalls, "the

Lessons you see on the page appear just as we took them down. . . . [T]he design of the book just swept me along." *Flow Chart* too appears almost as it was taken swiftly down, over a period of nearly eight months ending on Ashbery's birthday (July 27, 1988). But the mere current of daily activity rather than any predetermined multifaceted design swept Ashbery's writing along (the six section breaks were added afterward as rest areas for the reader). Compared with Merrill's Ashbery's project was relatively undefined; he decided to write a poem one hundred pages long on his mother, who had died in 1987. It is no accident, we might imagine, that Merrill began "Ephraim" within days of the death of Maria Mitsotáki, who became (without Merrill foreseeing it) the mother figure of the trilogy. Ashbery's idea suggested to him a Wordsworthian project of figuring his mother as a river's temporal flow (like Wordsworth's Derwent, the Hudson, which flows by Ashbery's apartment in Chelsea and house in upstate New York, was his prototype) and charting it as an autobiography. A flow chart, of course, is an outline that maps not a river but a system of repeatable, programmed events. *Flow Chart* is anybody's autobiography; Ashbery characteristically omits the names and dates with which we could chart his own life or else he substitutes others. But as with *Three Poems*, the contours in *Flow Chart* of one who went another way slowly emerge.

"Jack" Ashbery tells about childhood as a fairy tale: "Early on / was a time of seeming: golden eggs that hatched / into regrets, a snowflake whose kiss burned like an enchanter's / poison; yet it all seemed good in the growing dawn." With each turn the lines uncover reality beneath the seeming, but the regrets are minor. Ashbery uses Wordsworth's "correspondent breeze" as a compass, the "breeze that always nurtures us . . . / / pointed out a way that diverged from the true way without negating it, / to arrive at the same result by different spells." As in "The System," the magic of this alternate route is that it goes one way without giving up the other. This autobiographical flow chart diverges subtlely from Mirabell's. Though it was not fated that Ashbery turn away from the right path (he is left-handed), having done so makes his choice unnecessary.

Ashbery learned the term "flow chart" from watching the Iran-Contra hearings on television, where the shadowy structure of Reagan's National Security Council was pieced together from what documents Oliver North had neglected to destroy: "And it turned out that the inquiry was silenced, / deliberately erased from the file." *Flow Chart* maps not only Ashbery's history but also the history of its composition: the 1988 Presidential campaign, the hostage crisis, and so on. But Ashbery, like Merrill, seeks to separate these private and public worlds. One verse paragraph begins with the not-so-new news: "Latest reports show that the government / still controls everything but that the location of the blond captive / has been pinpointed thanks to urgent needling from the backwoods constituency / and the population in general is alive and well." But with himself in particular Ashbery draws the line: "But can we dwell / on any of it? Our privacy ends where the clouds' begins, just here, just at / this bit of anonymity on the seashore." Like Merrill, Ashbery resents the censorious among the politically correct trying to ban the great books from the syllabus: "Otherwise there'll be such a scare / in the curriculum as only the oldest ones will want to get out, the others / impeded or impeached by the books they have a right to read / in this our own time." Neither Ashbery nor Merrill is an explicitly political poet; both tend to write within a circle of interpersonal privacy. But increasingly, as the AIDS epidemic grows, their personal poetry becomes inextricable from repressive governmental ideologies and policies. The elegiac cast of much of *Flow Chart* gathers in more victims than Ashbery's mother.

Near the end of *Flow Chart*, the poem jells as a "double sestina," its single fixed form. The jewel is set in a discussion of the real and the tenuously separated dream world. Ashbery waves away the concerned, "I'll be all right when the government goes away," and swears that "as usual life is a dream." But this dream involves a visitation, from the neglected Romantic poet Thomas Lovell Beddoes: "Yet the spirits are still angry that you woke them, if that's what you did. / *Dreaming a dream to prize*—way to go, Thomas L. It matters not how puke-encrusted / the areaway, how charged with punishments the jazz-inflected scroll—this is your time, by golly, / so change your clothes and get it right." The italicized phrase is taken from Beddoes's haunting lyric "Dream-Pedlary," in which the regretful poet dreams of conjuring "my loved longlost boy," a phrase cited as evidence of Beddoes's homosexuality. Ashbery awakens Beddoes's spirit by reciting from his poem. In the double sestina Ashbery calls up another gay precursor, Algernon Swinburne, by using the end-words from his double sestina, "The Complaint of Lisa," the only other poem in this hybrid form. In Ashbery's hands Swinburne's end-words (breath, her, way, death, sunflower, sun, day, bed, thee, dead, done, me) accrue a dreamy realism. The auspicious wind early on in *Flow Chart* turns out to be contagious. "The breath," Ashbery tells himself and us,

> you decide to catch comes at the far end of that day's slope,
>   when her
> vision is not so clear anymore. You say goodbye to her anyway,
>   for the way
> gleams up ahead. You don't need the day to see it by. And though
>   millions are already dead
> what matters is that they didn't break up the fight before I was able to
>   get to thee,
> to warn thee what would be done
> to thee if more than one were found occupying the same bed.

The transitory presences of Ashbery's aged mother and of the dead multitudes; of their courage, the hazards, and the puritanical punishments; all go without mentioning by name but are all the more keenly felt. As Eliot taught us, tradition inhabiting the individual talent is most like the dead possessing the living. In their grandly differing ways, so worn as to show no great traces of mutual influence, both Ashbery and Merrill have drawn the long lifeline a little further on.

John Shoptaw

Further Reading

Ashbery, John. *As We Know*. New York: Penguin, 1979.

——— *Flow Chart*. New York: Knopf, 1991.

——— *Selected Poems*. New York: Penguin, 1986.

——— *Three Poems*. New York: Penguin, 1972.

Bloom, Harold, ed. *James Merrill*. New York: Chelsea House, 1985.

——— *John Ashbery*. New York: Chelsea House, 1985.

Kalstone, David. *Five Temperaments: Elizabeth Bishop, Robert Lowell, James Merrill, Adrienne Rich, John Ashbery*. New York: Oxford University Press, 1977.

Labrie, Ross. *James Merrill*. Boston: Twayne, 1982.

Lehman, David, and Charles Berger, eds. *James Merrill: Essays in Criticism*. Ithaca: Cornell University Press, 1983.

McClatchy, J. D. "James Merrill." In Lea Baechler and A. Walton Litz, eds., *American Writers: A Collection of Literary Biographies*, supplement 3, part 1, pp. 317–338. New York: Scribner's, 1991.

Merrill, James. *The Changing Light at Sandover*. New York: Macmillan, 1983.

——— *Recitative*. New York: Macmillan, 1986.

——— *Selected Poems*. New York: Macmillan, 1986.

Shoptaw, John. *On the Outside Looking Out: John Ashbery's Poetry*. Cambridge: Harvard University Press, 1994.

Yenser, Stephen. *The Consuming Myth: The Work of James Merrill*. Cambridge: Harvard University Press, 1987.

The Visionary Poetics of Philip Levine and Charles Wright

THE tradition of American Romanticism in the second half of the twentieth-century has been complicated and renewed in different ways in the work of Philip Levine and Charles Wright, two indispensable contemporary poets. Both writers have been engaged in an agnostic quest for some visionary power or transcendental grandeur in a skeptical, secular age. In Levine's case that quest has taken the shape of a restless search for human communication and communion; in Wright's it has taken the form of a metaphysical search for spiritual meaning. Both of these free-verse poets—Levine with his incantatory urban rhythms and narrative drive, Wright with his luminous country music and associative structures—have helped to extend the range and define the character of American poetry in our era.

Levine and Wright take fundamentally different stances toward human reality in their work. Levine is an earth-centered and social poet of justice and memory, an heir to Walt Whitman and William Carlos Williams. The drama of his development has been his struggle to become a poet of joy as well as of suffering, to move through what he portrays as a dying industrial America and nonetheless find "the true and earthy prayer," the basis for genuine solidarity and community with other people. He has most often turned to Spanish poets for models—especially García Lorca, Miguel Hernández, and Antonio Machado—and to Spanish anarchist heroes for his political ideas. Like his contemporaries Adrienne Rich and Gerald Stern, he is a Jewish American storyteller with a utopian dream of equality and freedom.

Wright, on the other hand, has an essentially religious sensibility that was formed during an Episcopalian childhood in the Christian South. He is a poet of privileged moments rising out of time, a nonbeliever with a tremendous longing for belief, which continually fuels his work as he moves through the immanent natural world looking for signs and wonders, for emblems of the sacred and transcendental. In his disquieting quarrel with himself about permanence and impermanence, about the possibility (or impossibility) of salvation, in his focus on "the other side" he is an heir to Emily Dickinson who, as he has said, allowed him "to write what was in my heart and not just what was on my mind." Wright adapted most of his specific technical ideas about imagery, lineation, and poetic structure from Ezra Pound, and he has most often turned for imaginative models to poets from Italy (especially Eugenio Montale and Dino Campana) and China (especially poets of the T'ang Dynasty). The Italian landscape, like his native countryside, has served him as a talismanic source of renewal, but everything he writes aspires to shine under an eternal light.

Here, then, are two exemplary, divergent, and vital paths to a visionary, late twentieth-century American poetry. Philip Levine has created a memorializing poetics of human separation and connection. Charles Wright has defined a radiant metaphysics of absence and aspiration, of the longed-for presence of the divine.

In his essay, "Thinking Against Oneself," E. M. Cioran argues that "we measure an individual's value by the sum of his disagreements with things, by his incapacity to be indifferent, by his refusal as a subject to tend towards the object." Philip Levine's poetry is characterized by just such a profound disagreement with things as they are, by an incapacity for indifference and a rage against objectification. Throughout his work his first and most powerful commitment has been to the failed and lost, the marginal, the unloved, the unwanted. His primary impulse has been to summon the details and remember the exploitations. The dedicatory seventh section of "Silent in America"—his largest and most summary early poem—is explicit:

> For a black man whose
>   name I have forgotten who danced
>   all night night at Chevy
>   Gear & Axle,

for that great stunned Pole
who laughed when he called me Jew
   Boy, for the ugly
     who had no chance,

  the beautiful in
body, the used and the unused,
   those who had courage
     and those who quit—
Rousek and Ficklin
numbed by their own self-praise
   who ate their own shit
     in their own rage;

  for these and myself
whom I loved and hated, I
  had presumed to speak
    in measure.

Levine is a poet of the night shift, a late ironic Whitman of our industrial heartland, a Romantic anarchist who repeatedly proclaims, "Vivas for those who have failed." His life's work is a long assault on isolation, an ongoing struggle against the enclosures of suffering, the private, hermetic, sealed-off nature of our lives; indeed, he is a poet of radical immanence who has increasingly asserted a Keatsian faith in the boundlessness of human possibility. One might say that his work begins in rage, ripens toward elegy, and culminates in celebration. All three moods—rage, sorrow, and wry hopefulness—appear and reappear in his work, sometimes in complex tonal combinations. One lyric points forward, another backward, yet the overall drift and progress of his poems is clear. What starts as anger deepens into grief and finally rises into joy.

Levine's early work follows a stylistic and thematic arc from *On the Edge* (1963) to *They Feed They Lion* (1972). These poems are written under the sign of the thistle and the fist, what one poem evokes as the "bud of anger, kinked / tendril of my life" ("Fist"). Levine has always written with special concentrated fury about the so-called "stupid jobs" of his youth, and his first books established and developed his working-class loyalties and themes. They evoke three distinct but related cities: Detroit, Fresno, and Barcelona, all of which are defined as landscapes of desolation, rugged cities of the enraged, the exhausted, the exploited. One of the motivating premises of his early work was his determination to create a poetry of the urban landscape. In this regard the poem that reverberates through all his work is Wordsworth's sonnet, "Composed Upon Westminster Bridge, September 3, 1802," which eventually provided the title for his book, *Sweet Will*. Wordsworth's last line— "And all that mighty heart is lying still!"—has special resonance in Levine's case because his work begins in silence and failure: indeed, one of the persistent themes of the early books is voicelessness, the desperate silence of "Silent in America," the failure of poets who don't write in "My Poets." Speaking into a historical vacuum, seeking an absent but sympathetic listener, he has increasingly insisted on the defiant transformation of blankness into language, refusing to be quieted. This theme of the necessity of violently breaking silence peaks in "They Feed They Lion," a poem that celebrates the communal insurrection of the Detroit riots of 1967. All that mighty heart is no longer lying still.

Levine's first volume, *On the Edge*, published when he was thirty-five years old, was a book of free-floating despair, hampered by its own formalism, alienated even from itself. Levine has said that these were the poems of someone on the verge of despair and breakdown, on the edge of his own culture, even of his own life. The poems are too tightly controlled; they are rhyming iambic pentameter lyrics whose underlying subject matter is mostly suppressed and in conflict with the tradition of "pure poetry" out of which they emerge. The sole exception is "The Horse"—a devastating poem about the survivors of Hiroshima—which anticipates the idiomatic and controlled free-verse style of Levine's later work. The title poem is a skillful eighteen-line lyric that sounds a brooding note of defiance from the poet's alter ego: "My name is Edgar Poe / and I was born / In 1928 in Michigan. / Nobody gave a damn." The poem projects a certain hip bravado but also suggests the depth of the writer's alienation. "I did not write, for I am Edgar Poe, / Edgar the mad one, silly, drunk, unwise." *On the Edge* was a striking debut stymied by its own pent-up rage: it is about being on the margins, close to breakdown, hedged in by despair.

Levine's second book, *Not This Pig* (1968), exchanged despair for determination, digging in its heels. It is a volume of contained, well-wrought lyrics where the urban furies reign. In this world no one wants to remember who he is, happiness and despair are a "twi-night double-header," the eight o'clock factory whistle comes "blasting from heaven," and there are no fresh starts. Edgar Poe has been replaced by the under-dog "Baby Villon," a punch-drunk Algerian prizefighter who is every-where and at all times victimized but continues to fight back, a version of the poet as Baudelairean outlaw. But the book's key figure is a preter-naturally self-conscious pig being driven to market who staunchly refuses to squeal or break down. The pig in the elegiacally titled poem "Animals Are Passing from Our Lives," a Bartleby of the animal world, can already smell "the sour, grooved block . . . / the blade that opens the hole / and the pudgy white fingers / / that shake out the intestines / like a hankie," but he refuses to fall down in cowardice or terror, resolutely keeping his dignity, proclaiming "No. Not this pig." In a way, the pig is a tough, metaphorical stand-in for his human counterpart, the worker who refuses to give up his dignity or be objectified.

The bud of anger blossoms into full flower in *They Feed They Lion*, the culminating book of Levine's early work. In his two previous small-press books, *Red Dust* and *Pili's Wall* (both published in 1971), Levine began to abandon his early formalism, the syllabic poetry he once called "the language of princes." He developed an increasingly narrative and supple free-verse style, a more open and self-questioning approach to the dramatic lyric. One poem is entitled "Holding On," another, "How Much Can It Hurt?" Stylistically, he linked a quasi-surrealist imagery to a street-wise American idiom. "Clouds" is representative:

> The clouds go on eating oil, cigars,
> housewives, sighing letters,
> the breath of lies. In their great silent pockets
> they carry off all our dead.

In these poems Levine has turned from a descendant of Poe into a grandson of Whitman. One feels the influence of such Spanish lan-guage poets as Pablo Neruda, César Vallejo, and Rafael Alberti in the elliptical, disjunctive style, the hyperreal atmosphere, the catalogue of iron days and sleepless nights. These poets also turned him homeward with renewed vigor, and thereafter his poems seem to have grown from the gritty soil of William Carlos Williams. They became larger and more inclusive, representing the rugged, impure, democratic side of our poetry.

They Feed They Lion reaps the fruit of that labor. It is Levine's most eloquent book of industrial Detroit, evoking the world of Dodge Main and Wyandotte Chemical, grease shops and foundries, the city "pouring fire." The poems remember the "unburned" Detroit of 1952 ("Saturday Sweeping") as well as the "charred faces" of Detroit in 1968 ("Coming Home, Detroit, 1968"). Some are set in California ("Renaming the Kings"), some in Spain ("Salami," "To P. L., 1916–1937"), but all record a nightmare of suffering, what "To a Fish Head Found on the Beach Near Málaga" calls "the burned essential oil / seeping out of death." Yet their author is also capable of thorny affirmations, celebrating his own "angels of Detroit." The magisterial title poem is Levine's hymn to communal rage. It fuses a host of influences into a daring and brilliant new whole. One hears behind it the driving rhythms of the biblical prophets, the anaphora of Christopher Smart's "Jubilate Agno" and Whitman's "Out of the Cradle Endlessly Rocking," the wildly inventive, mixed diction of Dylan Thomas and John Berryman, the splendid verbal twists and turns of colloquial black speech. The poem inventively uses the word "Lion" as both noun (as in "the Lion") and verb (as in "to Lion"). The word "They" becomes both subject (as in "They Feed") and possessive pronoun (as in "They" or their "Lion"). This gives the poem a sinuous syntactical energy and ambiguity. Altogether it has a sweeping musical and rhetorical authority, a burning sense of "the acids of rage, the candors of tar," a psychological understanding of what motivates people to move from "Bow Down" to "Rise Up," and it builds to an apocalyptic conclusion:

> From my five arms and all my hands,
> From all my white sins forgiven, they feed,
> From my car passing under the stars,
> They Lion, from my children inherit,
> From the oak turned to a wall, they Lion,
> From they sack and they belly opened
> And all that was hidden burning on the oil-stained earth
> They feed they Lion and he comes.

Both in stylistic and thematic terms Levine's next two books, *1933* (1974) and *The Names of the Lost* (1976), are a single unit, a major turning point in his work, the books where he becomes a poet absorbed by memory and preoccupied by the deep past. *1933* is first and foremost haunted by the death of the father, ritualizing its suffering, asking the question, "Where did my father go in my fifth autumn?" ("Zaydee"). The fundamental psychological shock at the heart of Levine's work—

its first reverberating loss—is the death of the father: indeed, the dead father stands as the authoritative absence at the heart of his poetry. Thus the year 1933 is not—as so many have assumed—the date of his own birth, but the year of his father's death—his true baptism into the world. The title poem is simultaneously a letter to a man who died long ago ("Father, the world is different in many places" and "You would not know me now, I have a son taller than you") and a Roethkean elegy to a man who "entered the kingdom of roots / his head as still as a stone" when the poet was only a child. The poem typifies much of Levine's later work in the way it alternates between the present tense ("I go in afraid of the death you are") and an irretrievable past ("I would be a boy in worn shoes splashing through rain").

As a book, *1933* powerfully evokes "the blind night of Detroit" in the 1930s. It enlarges the first loss of the father to include a series of family elegies: "Zaydee," "Grandmother in Heaven," "Goodbye," "Uncle," and the centerpiece, "Letters for the Dead." Written in ten parts separated by asterisks, "Letters for the Dead" is a series of loosely linked and cumulative moments, a structure of fragmented ideas that address the dead serially. Its looser and more associative structure anticipates other such long poems as "A Poem with No Ending" (a twelve-part sequence in *Sweet Will*) and "Burned" (a twenty-part sequence in *What Work Is*). After *1933* all of Levine's work has one eye on the past, gathering its losses into "the basket of memory" ("28"). His poems become less protected and defended, emotionally riskier, more exposed. Wholly characteristic is the book's final poem, "Hold Me," which concludes with a mysterious image of time collapsed and closing back in on itself, of love transfigured into transcendental ecstasy:

> I am the eye filled with salt,
> his child climbing the rain, we are
> all the moon, the one planet, the hand
> of five stars flung on the night river.

As Levine's work has progressed, a dominant tone of ferocious anger has evolved into a more vulnerable and elegiac tenderness. His poems have developed a softer edge while maintaining their brooding intensity. Almost everything he has written has been characterized by a determination to witness and remember, to memorialize people who would otherwise be forgotten. His middle period begins neither with outrage nor with an Adamic impulse to name the swarming fullness of things;

it begins not with presence but with absence, with a stubborn determination to remember what has already been lost. These are books more concerned with memory than imagination, defining the poet as someone who names and recovers, who recalls the victimized, the disenfranchised, the fallen. Nowhere is this sense of the writer's task more clearly defined than in *The Names of the Lost* .

Mostly written in narrow two- and three-beat lines that have characterized much of his subsequent work, these poems explicitly link the people of his childhood "no one remembers" with his doomed heroes from the Spanish Civil War, especially the anarchists Buenaventura Durruti (to whom the book is dedicated) and Francisco Ascaso (who becomes the subject of the later elegy, "Francisco, I'll Bring You Red Carnations"). These martyred figures are deemed exemplary because they struggled against injustice and exploitation and kept alive a vision of the self freed from tyranny. As models they offer the American poet an escape from self-lacerating irony and paralysis.

In *Names of the Lost* the dead are continually singled out and called back. They are addressed, listed, bound together by imaginative sympathy—those the poet knew, those he glimpsed and admired from afar, those he summons across the gulfs of distance and history: Uncle Joe, Aunt Tsipie, Teddy Holmes, Ray Estrada, Art Tatum, Lieutenant José del Castillo, the poets of Chile. There is a sacred aspect to this catalogue as he speaks of "the stained refectory of the breath" and "the chalice of the air," even the "holy names / of the lost." "Gift for a Believer," dedicated to the Italian anarchist painter Flavio Constantini, makes clear that the poems originate with a personal oath to remember ("When old Nathan Pine / gave two hands to a drop-forge / at Chevy, my spit turned to gall / and I swore I'd never forget"), but they also take up the anarchist dream of justice, the biblical chant of "We shall inherit," the world that Durruti said "is growing here / in my heart this moment."

The political image of human growth and renewal is echoed in the recurrent garden imagery. Indeed, it finds a natural correlative in the garden itself where the poet's wife is repeatedly glimpsed kneeling in the earth and devotedly tending her plants ("New Season," "Autumn Again," "The Falling Sky," "Another Life," "My Son and I"). Detached from the garden himself, the poet is engaged in a dialectical internal quarrel about burning and blossoming, decay and renewal, isolation and community. His own vocation is defined by the trust of memory. As he puts it in "For the Poets of Chile": "Someone / must remember it over / and over, must bring / it all home." In the end the anarchist struggle for a new world as well as the romantic sense that "the human is boundless" provided Levine with a political as well as personal way to understand the past.

Levine's next book, *Ashes: Poems Old and New* (1979), is a transitional volume that looks back toward the two previous books of death as well as forward to the poems of regeneration. It begins by addressing the dead father, "a black tooth planted in the earth / of Michigan," asking him not to return ("Father"). The whole book is animated by the recognition that certain losses are final, death and childhood. And yet the book ends on the resolutely affirmative note that "for now / the lost are found," and that father and son, the living and the dead, can enter the world together ("Lost and Found"). What began with the death of the father has been converted into a dream of possibility. The silence and failure of people turning away from each other has been transformed into an ideal of communal inheritance. Out of the ashes names are given back to the lost.

The motif of regeneration and rebirth resounds through Levine's next three books: there is a plaintiveness in *7 Years from Somewhere* (1979) that turns into dark optimism and even hopefulness in *One for the Rose* (1981), and bittersweet acceptance in *Sweet Will* (1985). These books begin with the playful assertion, "I could come to believe / almost anything" ("I Could Believe"), and conclude on the image of the late sunlight "promising nothing" and overflowing "the luminous thorns / of the roses," catching fire "for a moment on the young leaves" ("Jewish Graveyards, Italy").

Many of the poems in *7 Years from Somewhere* have the intimate character of prayers half-addressed to the interior self, half to the darkness. Poems such as "I Could Believe," "Hear Me," "Let Me Begin Again," "Words," and "Let Me Be," have the tone of a man talking either "to no one or myself," disavowing wisdom, asking unanswerable questions. The old angers burn and crackle in "You Can Have It," perhaps the book's single greatest poem. Here Levine remembers being twenty in 1948 in Detroit, a city "founded / by de la Mothe Cadillac for the distant purposes / of Henry Ford"; he recalls his twin brother dropping into bed in exhaustion, working by night and sleeping by day while he worked by day and slept by night; he cries out with unrestrained intensity against the intervening years:

> Give me back my young brother, hard
> and furious, with wide shoulders and a curse
> for God and burning eyes that look upon
> all creation and say, You can have it.

Most of the poems, however, turn away from the hard fury of such a renunciation, accepting the flawed earth as it is, returning to the here and now, celebrating a mortal world "drowning / in oil, second by second" ("The Life Ahead"). The speaker in "Francisco, I'll Bring You Red Carnations" returns to Ascaso's grave not only to remember the dream of a city "where every man / and every woman gives / and receives the gifts of work / and care" but also to affirm that the dream "goes on in spite of all / that mocks it," and to celebrate "the unbroken / promise of your life that / once was frail and fresh."

This more celebratory mood of acceptance—self-questioning, darkened by doubts—continues to animate many of the more playful, narrative poems of *One for the Rose* and *Sweet Will*. In these books Levine weaves fuller and larger stories, mixing imagination and memory, creating fictive phantasmagorias of the past. He refuses to be pigeonholed, announcing with wry irony, "I was born in Lucerne," and "I think I must have lived / once before, not as a man or woman / but as a small, quick fox pursued / . . . by ladies and gentlemen on horseback" ("The Fox"). These poems are sometimes exaggerated and comic, sometimes brooding and sadly hopeful (as in the reflection after Keats "Having Been Asked 'What Is a Man?' I Answer"). Behind all of them, however, even the most playful, there is a powerful tension at work between the longing for flight and the need to stay grounded, the fantasy of escape and the recognition of actuality. Fantastic images of flight recur often ("The Poem of Flight," "Ascension," "Roofs," etc.). Yet transcendence also entails a terrifying loss of self, the obliteration of the consciousness. Memory, too—the reigning force in Levine's poetry—is destroyed. Thus the miraculous has to be countered by the quotidian, the unknown by the familiar. In "Rain," for example, Levine describes the sky by reversing a famous Platonic image of Shelley's: "This is not . . . the dome / of heaven or hell, many colored, splendid," he writes, "This is an ordinary gray Friday after work / and before dark in a city of the known world." There is a strong anxiety about mortality in these books, a complex of feelings about human limits and the reality of living in time, about the life one has actually had and the life one might have experienced.

In the title poem, "One for the Rose," the poet returns twenty-seven years later to a destroyed corner in Akron, Ohio (the past has been physically obliterated), and recalls an exhausting bus ride across the "sickened farms of 1951" to the "smeared air" of Detroit. "I could have been / in Paris at the foot of Gertrude Stein," he fantasizes, "I could have been drifting among / the reeds of a clear stream / like the little Moses." Instead, however, "born / in the wrong year and in the wrong place" he has had a less heroic and more real life, one filled with mistakes. He remembers every single turn in his experience and declares that each one smells like "an overblown rose, / yellow, American, beautiful, and true." Thus is the miraculous reconciled to the ordinary, the local deemed astonishing, and memory privileged.

The actuality of remembering—and what he actually remembers— always has political overtones and consequences in Levine's work. It is also nudged, shaped, changed, and reimagined for purposeful ends. For example, in the greatest poem in these two books, "To Cipriano, in the Wind," the poet recalls an Italian immigrant and anarchist who worked in the back of Peerless Cleaners and enunciated the word *Dignidad* for him. In fact, Levine has conflated into one person the composite identity of two Italian cleaners who ran a cleaning and dyeing operation in Detroit and Cipriano Mera who commanded an anarchist militia unit in Barcelona in 1936. The new Cipriano Mera becomes a tutelary spirit, a man who assured him, "Some day the world / is ours" and "Spring, spring, it always come after." Cipriano's idealism and faith haunt him and, years later, beset by doubts, he calls upon him to "enter my dreams / or my life" and to "come back / out of the wind." In a sense Cipriano is a spiritual kin and anarchist precursor to the emblematic black workers in "Sweet Will" and "A Walk with Tom Jefferson." Levine's politics are utopian, and the hard-won affirmation of his work is a Keatsian faith that the poet's breath can be passed on "to anyone who can / believe that one life comes back / again and again without end / and always with the same face" ("Belief"). His vision is humanistic; he concludes by embracing the earth as his own home ("The Voice").

Levine's two most recent books, *A Walk with Tom Jefferson* (1988) and *What Work Is* (1991) are both concerned with the issues, problems, and memories of working, with a country that seems to be going up in flames and the quest for a sustaining faith in a ruined America. Their recurring subject is—as Levine said of the twenty poems in *A Walk with Tom Jefferson*—"the way we work and don't work in a society that has abandoned so many of its citizens." Largely set in Detroit, rural California, and New York City, these poems are preoccupied with the problem of faith and faithlessness. The poet recalls being nineteen and "going nowhere," being twenty-eight and "still faithless." In "Picture Postcard from the Other World" he imagines the absent reader as a kind of distant cousin, a middle-aged wanderer like himself who has "lost whatever faiths he held" and continues on "with only the faith that even more / will be lost."

The question of what to believe in informs both *A Walk with Tom Jefferson* and *What Work Is*, books of radiant personal memories that ramify outward to tell the story of buying and selling, of laboring in America. "I am in my element," the poet asserts, "urging the past / out of its pockets of silence." He remembers with comic relish some of the depressing jobs of his youth and early adulthood (selling copper kitchenware, Fuller brushes, American encyclopedias, working the swing shift at a Plumbing and Plating Company, etc.). He thinks back to waiting with his brother for work in a tedious line outside Ford Highland Plant ("If you're / old enough to read this," he addresses the reader, "you know what / work is"); he remembers a woman behind a polishing wheel putting a dirty hand upon his white shirt and thus marking him "now and forever," sealing his calling. He writes of an intermediate school teacher, a tree trimmer, a boxing coach, of fire fighters and assembly line workers and various others who work at obscure jobs, who fuel the economy and enter the daily fires. These poems ferociously condemn the brutality of so much of working life, speaking with genuine indignation and moral authority against what is most corrupting and exploitative in American life, celebrating the gritty heroism of people who survive against the odds.

"A Walk with Tom Jefferson" is the long-braided narrative and the centerpiece of these two collections. It tells of an emblematic walk through Detroit with an unsung black man (another of Levine's composite heroes), a retired factory worker who shares "the fierce spirit of independence and originality of his namesake." Tom Jefferson acts as the poet's Virgilian guide—tough, unbowed, faithful, humane—leading him through a neighborhood that had been devastated in the late sixties. In the aftermath of the destruction, amid the vacant lots and condemned property, the poet discovers that people are leading quasi-rural lives— keeping gardens and animals, mustering their resources, cultivating new life. Their triumphs are small but real: they have the courage of survivors. As Levine said in an interview, "The poem is a tribute to all those people who survived in the face of so much discouragement. They survived everything America can dish out." This long poem takes its place in an American lineage that includes such other poems as Hart Crane's "The Bridge," Robert Hayden's "Middle Passage," and Galway Kinnell's "The Avenue Bearing the Initial of Christ into the New World."

The great subject behind *A Walk with Tom Jefferson* and *What Work Is* is the sustaining dream of liberty, the stubborn will of the dispossessed to dig in and endure. This determination is at the heart of Levine's central vision. His life's work sounds what Wallace Stevens called "the No that precedes the final Yes," and for all its furious renunciations it ends by being a poetry of praise for "a world / that runs on and on at its own sweet will."

Charles Wright is a poet of lyric impulses, of what Pound termed "gists and piths." His poems are structured associatively rather than narratively, and he has created a poetics of luminous moments, what Wordsworth called "spots of time," Joyce termed "epiphanies," Virginia Woolf labeled "moments of being." Such moments, fleeting and atemporal, rupture narrative and loosen bonds of continuity and consequence. They mark and isolate the self, transporting it to another realm, weakening its boundaries. They are inchoate and asocial—defying language, destroying time. Thus they have to be seized and contained, described and dramatized in words, reintegrated back into temporal experience. The epiphanic mode creates linguistic demands upon the poet, and Wright has responded to these demands conclusively. Over the years his work has become larger and more inclusive, with narrative overtones rather than undertones, though from the beginning he has written a poetry of flashes and jump-starts, of radiance glimpsed and noted down—transcribed, transfigured. There is a bright, ahistorical, diamondlike kernel of Neo-Platonism at the core of his writing.

The question of Wright's stylistic development has been how to get greater scope and complexity—more of the impure world itself—into his lyrics without forsaking his commitment to the pure image or resorting to discursive content. His work shows an ever-enlarged capacity to incorporate not just the results—the epiphanic moments—but also the quest for the divine itself. At times that quest seems permanently impaired. In this mood he quotes Novalis's aphorism, "We seek everywhere the Absolute and always find only things." At other times, however, Wright reads the things of this world as emblems of the beyond. In this mood he affirms the Dantesque ideal that "the true purpose and result of poetry is a contemplation of the divine and its attendant mysteries." There is an obsessive internal argument in Wright's work about the possibility of transcendence.

Wright combines an American Romantic sensibility—part Emily Dickinson, part Hart Crane—with the image-centered poetics of Ezra Pound. As to the *how* of his work, the verbal means and method of transport: he has adapted and revised the free-verse line of Pound's *Cathay* with the structural unfolding and imagistic layering of the *Cantos*. As to the *what* or the underlying thematics of his work: he has brought to that poetics a series of persistent concerns, nothing less than the idea that, in Wallace Stevens's aphorism, "The poet is the priest of the invisible." Or to cite Wright's own formulation, "The ultimate duty and fate of the poet is visionary."

Wright's work to date is neatly divided in half, collected in two retrospective volumes: *Country Music: Selected Early Poems* (1982) and *The World of the Ten Thousand Things: Poems, 1980–1990. Country Music* brings together eighty-five poems from four volumes. It includes five poems from his first book, *The Grave of the Right Hand* (1970), which serve as a quasi-prologue to the triptych of works that follows: *Hard Freight* (1973), *Bloodlines* (1975), and *China Trace* (1977). In a loose way these represent the present, the past, and the future. The title "Country Music" refers to the "white soul" music of Wright's childhood in Tennessee; indeed, one hears in his work, translated into a new key, the faint echoes of colloquial southern music, especially wandering songs and gospel hymns, with their recurring themes of departure and loss, death, and salvation. *Country Music* also has an epigraph from Ernest Hemingway—"The country was always better than the people"—that asserts the primacy of landscape in this poet's work. And it concludes with a quotation from T'u Lung that suggests how the land-

scape is borrowed and used as the site of a restless yearning and journey: "Therefore, strange were my travels." The landscape in Wright's
work is not a residence but a composite locale, an imaginary place that
has been composed and recomposed to situate and calm the wandering
spirit.

Wright began writing poems in 1959 in the army in Italy—"the
metaphysics of the quotidian," as he has called it. Ever since then the
metaphysical part, Italy, has been inextricably associated with poetry in
his work. The triggering literary experience for him was reading
Pound's "Blandula, Tenella, Vagula" where it was composed, Catullus's
villa—or what is thought to be Catullus's villa—on the tip of the
Sirmione Peninsula. This later became the location of "Nocturne," the
strongest piece in *The Grave of the Right Hand*. Here the poet speaks of
himself in the third person as a "strayed traveller" or "misguided pilgrim" who stands quietly on a summer night and imagines "he hears the
slight off-rhythm of some hexameter line deep in the olive grove, as the
slither of night birds moves toward the darker trees." The pilgrim who
seeks the presence and intimation of the spirit—of poetry—in a dark-
ening landscape would become one of the central figures in Wright's
work.

The Grave of the Right Hand is a stylistically hampered, conventional book of the late sixties. It is apprentice work. The sole exception is
the group of prose poems that comprise the second section, "Departures." These modest, descriptive poems signal his preoccupation with
a trinity of subjects: "Holy Memory," lost childhood, sacred and broken
landscapes. Wright is first and foremost a poet of leavetakings and wanderings, of pilgrimages to haunted terrain.

Wright's work begins in earnest in *Hard Freight* , a symmetrically
shaped collection of disparate lyrics that commences with four
homages—to Pound, Rimbaud, Baron Corvo, and an unnamed
Kafkaesque "X"—and concludes with four fragmentary endpapers. The
title section and main body of the text consists of thirty-two closely
honed short poems of the enigmatic statement and deep image. The
new poem "will not reveal its name," the opening programmatic lyric
asserts, it won't "attend our sorrow," "console our children," or "help us."
These secretive antidiscursive poems of paradox and mystery seem
indebted to Mark Strand's early poetry, especially his book *Darker*
(1970), and W. S. Merwin's middle work, especially his volume *The*

Lice (1967). Wright's poems of this period are elusive and closed, scrupulous in their erasures, peopled by traces, ghostly in their absences. An image from "White" is characteristic:

> I write your name for the last time in this mist,
> White breath on the windowpane,
> And watch it vanish. No, it stays there.

The question of what vanishes and what remains is at the core of Wright's poetry.

There are few narrative values in *Hard Freight*. The poems eschew character and plot. Some present stanzas separated by asterisks ("One Two Three," "White," "Tongues"), others are compressed lists of riddling assertations and knotty images ("Nouns," "Slides of Verona," "Negatives," "Yellow," "Synopsis"). Both stylistically and thematically the book's pivotal piece is "Dog Creek Mainline," a signature poem that opens out into "Blackwater Mountain," "Sky Valley Rider," "North-hanger Ridge," and "Clinchfield Station." These poems are rooted in Wright's southern region, mixing memory and abstraction, summoning the vague cutouts of a few people in remembered landscapes. Here the poet begins to bring back places where memory intersects with locale, as if the places themselves retained the vestiges and outlines of the people who once lived there.

Bloodlines is one of Wright's most directly personal and autobiographical collections, the breakthrough work in which he hits a new note and becomes an authentically southern poet determined to mine his sources and recapture moments from the past. As David St. John notes in his appreciative foreword to the second edition of *Country Music*: "*Bloodlines* is a fiercely elegiac book, detailing the losses of people, places, and times that have passed out of the poet's life." It is a book of reckonings, of mourning and reclamation, of severe losses mingled with lush landscapes.

Like each of Wright's individual collections, *Bloodlines* is constructed symmetrically. Containing ten poems in all, it is framed by two lyrical narratives, "Virgo Descending" and "Rural Route," and turns on the complementary poles of two ambitious twenty-poem sequences, "Tattoos" and "Skins." The middle of the book consists of parallel elegies for his father ("Hardin County") and mother ("Delta Traveller"). The death of his parents reverberates out from the heart of the volume, haunting his subsequent work.

The individual lyrics in "Tattoos" and "Skins" are opaque, elusive, aphoristic. Something is glimpsed and withheld, seen but not explained. The numbered sequences—one personal, one conceptual—were directly influenced by Montale's "Mottetti," a group of twenty poems Wright translated in the sixties. Wright's poems, like Montale's, are "flashes and dedications," coded fragments, dreamlike montages of allusive lines and cryptic images.

Each poem in "Tattoos" invokes a moment that indelibly marked the poet, a crisis point, a psychic tattoo. Accordingly, each is affixed with a specific year at the bottom. The experiences, ranging from 1940 to 1973, are not arranged chronologically but tonally, one leading to and juxtaposed against the next. Each consists of three five-line stanzas, a linear form (presentation, complication, release or refutation) for a nonlinear series. This form recalls Berryman's "dream songs," but whereas Berryman's poems are all voice, all repartee and talk, Wright's dream songs are all sensation—phenomenological, hallucinatory. Wright indicates that there are actual occasions or events behind these sensations by appending notes to the end of the sequence. These notes supply the literal ground of each poem—what the subject is, where it takes place, etc.—and represent one way of tackling the problem of referentiality. In the more journal-like poems of *China Trace* Wright would begin to integrate such quotidian information into his texts.

In addition to commemorating the deaths of his parents, the majority of "Tattoos" is connected to religious rituals and episodes. The poet calls back a snake-handling service in East Tennessee, he recreates a moment of evangelical certainty at school in North Carolina, he remembers what it felt like to be an acolyte fainting at the altar in Kingsport, Tennessee. There are echoes of the language of testifying as he jumps forward to Italy and summons up "the old scaffolding, old arrangements" of Venice ("I have seen what I have seen"), *The Resurrection* by Piero della Francesca in Borgo San Sepolcro ("And what pulls them pulls me"), the radiant image of a Jewish friend praying in the early morning in Positano ("And everything brilliance, brilliance, brilliance"). These assertations are testimonies to the epiphanic moment of apprehension.

Such moments also inform the twenty poems of "Skins," each a single fourteen-line block, blooding an abstraction (Beauty, Truth), illustrating a process (Metamorphosis), or embodying an element (Fire,

Air, Earth, Water). The sequence is structured as a ladder of knowledge, beginning at "Situation Point A" in the red earth, ascending to a
peak of Aether (10) and descending back to the original point on the
ground. The final lines point forward to the contemplative stance and
position of *China Trace* :

> And what does it come to, Pilgrim,
> This walking to and fro on the earth, knowing
> That nothing changes, or everything;
> And only, to tell it, these sad marks,
> Phrases half-parsed, ellipses and scratches across the dirt?
> It comes to a point. It comes and it goes.

China Trace is an aspirant's book, pushing itself toward the future,
orienting itself toward the spiritual. It might have been called, as
Wright has suggested, "The Book of Yearning." It is also an attempt to
write a book of "Chinese poems" in the tradition of *Cathay*. Pound's
versions of Chinese poems were based on Ernest Fenollosa'a notebooks, and indeed Fenollosa's Emersonian essay, "The Chinese Written Character as a Medium for Poetry," stands behind Pound's—and
hence Wright's fundamental conception of Chinese poetry. Pound's
versions fuse an intense lyricism, a firm commitment to the line as a
unit of composition, and a primary aesthetic of Imagism—all three germane to Wright's own musical and imagistic free verse. So, too, in
China Trace Italian hermeticism hooks up with Chinese poetry, but the
linkage is informed by an American Transcendental sensibility.

China Trace consists of fifty short poems divided into two sections of
equal length. Each commences with the same quotation from Italo
Calvino's novel *Invisible Cities* about someday becoming "an emblem
among emblems." The method throughout is compressed and ideographic, and each poem is a kind of emblem or brushstroke, a quick
fusion of energies. No single poem is longer than twelve lines. There is
a one-line poem ("Bygones"), a two-line poem ("Death"), a three-line
poem ("Scalp Mountain"), a four-line poem ("Guilt"), etc. These lyrics
don't sound like Chinese poetry so much as follow the road—the
trace—of the Chinese method. The protagonist is a fallen-away Christian who stands in the ongoing natural world with an eye fixed on the
everlasting.

China Trace can be read as a single book-length poem consisting of
different abbreviated "chapters," a type of contemporary pilgrim's

progress. The ghostly pilgrim is initially an "I," sometimes a "you," finally a "he." The book turns on the wheel of two seasons. As Wright has described it, "The 'character' going from religious release (childhood) through an attempted ascension, ends up stuck in the Heaven of the Fixed Stars (in the Dantescan cosmology), a man-made heaven." There is no divine guidance and the assumption is "willed" or arbitrary. Time and again the poems press forward toward the speaker's own death. The images are startling and audacious as he looks at himself buried and decomposing at the age of one-hundred ("Self-Portrait in 2035"), rising as dust and coming down again as snow ("Snow"), transfigured into wind and smoke ("Dog"). He foresees looking back without recognition from the other side ("January"), describes where they'll take him after the end ("Remembering San Zeno"), pictures his ghost hanging "like a noose in the night wind" ("Snapshot"). At one Merwinesque moment he pauses in mid-life, bewildered, looking for something to believe in, "Not knowing what sign to make, or where I should kneel" ("1975"). The overriding desire to pray is matched only by an uncertainty about how, where, and what to pray to.

In the course of *China Trace* the poet comes to describe his poems as prayers and hymns, refiguring a Christian terminology into a secular epiphanic aesthetic. "I write poems to untie myself," he writes in "Reunion," "to do penance and disappear / Through the upper right-hand corner of things, to say grace." The concepts of penance, grace, and redemption occur often, though here—as elsewhere in Wright's work—the beads of the rosary are broken and the religious hymns have fallen. Faith is elusive, redemption thwarted. "I live in the one world, the moth and rust in my arms," he grieves in " 'Where Moth and Rust Doth Corrupt.' " "I look up at the black bulge of the sky and its belt of stars," he declares in "Noon," "And know that what I have asked for cannot be granted." There is a pervasive sense that God, the supreme fiction, exists in the moment and the moment is eternally unavailable. It cannot be grasped. Thus, "Heaven, that stray dog, eats on the run and keeps moving" ("Sentences"). God is not so much a figure or presence as "the sleight-of-hand in the fireweed, the lost / Moment that stopped to grieve and moved on" ("Invisible Landscape"). *China Trace* may be the most Transcendentalist book of short poems in contemporary American poetry (James Merrill's *The Changing Light at Sandover* is the most Transcendentalist long poem), yet in the end it denies any full-scale transcendence. In this culminating work of his early period Wright has become a religious poet without the benefit or consolation of a saving religion.

The World of the Ten Thousand Things: Poems, 1980–1990 is a capacious volume that gathers in entirety and fuses into a single unit *The Southern Cross* (1981), *The Other Side of the River* (1984), *Zone Journals* (1988), and *Xionia* (1990). The book is an extended metaphysical meditation on the past and the present, memory and oblivion, continuity and change, purity and impurity, the quotidian and the archetypal, what is daily and improvisational and what is fixed and permanent. It consists of a series of spacious, ruminating poems that consider the nature of what the Chinese call the world of the ten thousand things under heaven. In Wright's work the road to the infinite can only be tracked through the natural landscape.

> —Everyone wants to tell his story.
> The Chinese say we live in the world of the ten thousand things,
> Each of the ten thousand things
>   crying out to us
> Precisely nothing,
> A silence whose tune we've come to understand,
> Words like birthmarks,
>   embolic sunsets drying behind the tongue.
>   ("Night Journal")

A vanishing world voices itself in an everlasting silence; nature speaks eloquently; the void engulfs us.

Wright's metaphysics of absence take on greater fullness, a more expansive shape and form in *The Southern Cross*. Here he puts things in rather than leaves them out, relaxing the compression of line and image that marked *China Trace* and letting loose his full intoxification with the grandeurs of language. There is a verbal texture and richness that is at times as breathtaking as Hopkins or Crane. "This is the story line," he writes in "Hawaii Dantesca":

> And the viridescent shirtwaists of light the trees wear.
> And the sutra-circles of cattle egrets wheeling out past the rain showers.
> And the spiked marimbas of dawn rattling their amulets . . .

The splendor of a world in transit is equaled only by the sense that the dead are looking back at us from some other place. "Thinking of Dante is thinking about the other side," he writes in the title poem, "And the other side of the other side." Our worlds touch at the edges. The physical world is shot through with ghosts.

The Southern Cross is a complex gesture to the past bracketed by two complementary long poems, "Homage to Paul Cézanne," a hypnotic, highly figurative litany for the unnamed dead, and the title piece, an interweaving series of specific places in time, moments really—typographically set apart—that repeatedly swim into and out of memory.

> There is an otherness inside us
> We never touch,
>   no matter how far down our hands reach.
> It is the past,
>   with its good looks and *Anytime, Anywhere* . . .
> Our prayers go out to it, our arms go out to it
> Year after year,
> But who can ever remember enough?

Trying to touch that otherness, praying to it, is the motor that powers this book.

"Homage to Paul Cézanne" is an attempt to amplify voices that have become too faint to hear. In eight unnumbered sections, each sixteen lines long and given a separate page, the poem postulates a wide range of things the dead do, refusing to individuate them. "At night, in the fish-light of the moon, the dead wear our white shirts / To stay warm, and litter the fields," it begins. "We pick them up in the mornings, dewy pieces of paper and scraps of cloth." In the elusive and cumulative imagery of this poem, the dead are always with us, an ancestral presence—refracted and transfigured, moving and unsettled, fading and returning, evasive, unrecognizable, nudging "close to the surface of all things." They slip under our feet and twist like stars over our heads. They are mist on the mirror, a gap in the wind, a space we enter in dreams, what we will become. Until then, however, "We sit out on the earth and stretch our limbs, / Hoarding the little mounds of sorrow laid up in our hearts."

Wright's "Homage" is a nonlinear poem in an oracular mode, an attempt to bring a series of painterly techniques to the poetic sequence. Cézanne is the magnetizing presence and guiding example, especially the sixty paintings of Mont Sante-Victoire that he made between 1882 and 1906. Wright's idea is to treat words like pigment, to build the poem by tonal units and blocks, by layering lines and stanzas the way Cézanne used color and form. The fourth section recalls Cézanne's commitment to significant form, his determination to seek in nature the cylinder, the sphere, and the cone, to penetrate its masses and planes, to use the color blue as a way of defining space, an intercession between earth and heaven:

> The dead are a cadmium blue.
> We spread them with palette knives in broad blocks and planes.
>
> We layer them stroke by stroke
> In steps and ascending mass, in verticals raised from the earth.
>
> We choose, and layer them in,
> Blue and a blue and a breath,
>
> Circle and smudge, cross-beak and buttonhook,
> We layer them in. We squint hard and terrace them line by line.

For Cézanne technique was itself spiritual ("What we are given in dreams we write as blue paint") and there is an exaltation to his work that is sometimes linked to the pantheism of Chinese painting. That's one reason he becomes "The Black Château"—the title of one of his greatest paintings—at the end of Wright's fourth self-portrait.

Each of the poems in *The Southern Cross* is a technical experiment. The forms are arbitrary and sometimes hidden. In one poem, for example, reminiscent of Georg Trakl, every line is a sentence ("California Spring"), in another there are no verbs ("Dog Yoga"). There is an ars poetica, a reel, a blues, etc. And there are five self-portraits. These fifteen-line poems are not confessional so much as painterly and meditative, poems that give a sense of the self displayed and dispersed, stopped for a moment and then released. Allusions to painting and photographs recur frequently in this book of nonce forms. In addition to the self-portraits there are two imaginary portraits of the artist (one with Hart Crane, one with Li Po), a "Composition in Grey and Pink," a "Spring Abstract," the description of an imaginary photograph, "Bar Giamaica, 1959–1960," a portrait of Ezra Pound called "Landscape with Seated Figure and Olive Trees," a poem entitled "Dead Color" that ends with the ecstatic cry, "Windows, rapturous windows!" In all these poems, what is seen is a touchstone, but one that has to be transmuted into emblems. Language is figuration.

The determination not to particularize the dead in "Homage to Paul

Cézanne" is complemented and mitigated by the particulars that characterize "The Southern Cross." The poem begins under the ambiguous signs of the eternal as an evasive night turns into an empty day:

> Things that divine us we never touch:
>
> The black sounds of the night music,
> The Southern Cross, like a kite at the end of its string,
>
> And now this sunrise, and empty sleeve of a day,
> The rain just starting to fall, and then not fall,
>
> No trace of a story line.

In Wright's poem the Southern Cross is both a constellation in the sky, an illumination above, and a constellation of sacred landscapes—in the American South, in his beloved Italy—that glisten in memory. The poem divines what it can from the past, recreating a series of moments that come into the mind and just as quickly disappear. It flashes on a few moments in childhood but soon jumps ahead to a more ample recreation of specific moments in Italy in the late fifties and early sixties before circling back to Tennessee and concluding in 1935 in Pickwick, the year and place of his birth. Places range up and recede as he evokes himself as a figure in a landscape. What fuels these memories is the sense of just how much evades memory, how much sinks back and is lost, how days disappear and edges grow indistinct. Experience is porous. "I can't remember enough," he confesses, "It's what we forget that defines us, and stays in the same place, / And waits to be rediscovered." All the poet can do is resurrect the word against the villainy of time. Thus does his autobiography accrue intermittently and in fragments, a necklace of luminous moments.

The activity of remembering goes on unabated in *The Other Side of the River*, Wright's most narrative- and human-centered book. Here he adds a number of vignettes to the method of "The Southern Cross," wherein he spliced moments from the past, landscapes in time, with the romantic terminology of awe that he has remade as his own. He also relies on the staggered line that he perfected in the earlier poem. This dropped line is a long declarative unit with a lower rider, an additional rhythmic kick. It's a way of packing the iambic line, extending its reach while isolating and intensifying a phrase at the end. It is a horizontal poetic of syntactical modification and progressive music.

It's linkage I'm talking about,
>   and harmonies and structures
And all the various things that lock our wrists to the past.

Something infinite behind everything appears,
>   and then disappears.
>   ("The Other Side of the River")

The strategy of such lineation is Poundian. In his well-known poem of reconciliation addressed to Whitman, "A Pact," Pound wrote, "It was you that broke the new wood, / Now is a time for carving." Wright has similarly carved the Whitmanian line to his own specifications. He has arranged and spatialized it to bring more of the whole page into his compositions in the manner of the Cantos and *The Maximus Poems*. Wright uses that spatial poetic for ends that are spiritual and autobiographical. He has written that, "Each line should be a station of the cross." And:

My father wrote out his dreams on lined paper, as I do now,
And gave them up to the priest
>   for both to come to terms with.
I give you mine for the same reason,

To summon the spirits up and set the body to music.
>   ("Lost Souls")

All of Wright's work is theologically haunted.

The Other Side of the River consists of twenty poems divided into four sections. The book is situated at the edges of the known world, on *this* side of the river, but the speaker repeatedly looks off with yearning toward "the other side":

I want to sit by the bank of the river,
>   in the shade of the evergreen tree,
And look in the face of whatever,
>   the whatever that's waiting for me.
>   ("The Other Side of the River")

This longing for essence, "the whatever," is balanced by an equivalent grief over the loss of a sustaining faith in the absolute. The reality of a faith that can no longer obtain or provide informs these poems, whether the poet is thinking about his heritage in the Christian South

When Jesus walked on the night grass
                    they say not even the dew trembled.
Such intricate catechisms of desire.
Such golden cars down the wrong side of the sky.
                                        ("Arkansas Traveller")

or speaking from California where he was living at the time of this collection:

I have nothing to say about the way the sky tilts
Toward the absolute,
                    or why I live at the edge
Of the black boundary,
                    a continent where the waves
Counsel my coming in and my going out.

I have nothing to say about the brightness and drear
Of any of that, or the vanity
                    of our separate consolations.
                    ("Three Poems for the New Year")

Each of the poems in *The Other Side of the River* functions as a variation on a theme. The title acts as frame for what follows. Such titles as
"Lost Bodies" or "Lost Souls," for example, or "Italian Days" and "To
Giacomo Leopardi in the Sky" don't delimit a subject so much as key
and create a narrative space for it. They are structured, to use Wright's
own word, synaptically, one image sparking another. Anecdotes are
enfolded into these associational structures, adding up to a group of
understories, the shadow of a story line. One of the best poems, "Lonesome Pine Special," is basically a catalogue of favorite roads and high-
ways where the poet has admired the views. These roads intersect with,
and lead to, a number of stories, some personal and anecdotal, some
akin to tall tales: about a mysterious figure from the poet's childhood,
Old Lone; about seeing the house in Idaho where Pound was born ("It
was all so American"); about a place in Montana where a man named
Doagie Duncan "killed three men some seventy years ago"; about spinning out on a slick patch of road in Sam's Gap, North Carolina, and
almost going over a mountainside in 1955. These disparate stories leave
their traces in landscapes where they wait to be rediscovered—remembered, imagined. In the end the landscapes are interiorized and become

territories in the mind. "What is it inside the imagination that keeps surprising us / At odd moments," Wright asks, "when something is given back / We didn't know we had had / In solitude, spontaneously, and with great joy?"

One trigger for these poems is the idea that salvation can only be found in the natural world. They assert that "radiance comes through the eye / and lodges like cut glass in the mind" ("Cryopexy") and that "what gifts there are are all here, in this world" ("Italian Days"). In Wright's romantic thematics death midwifes beauty and the world is loved most when threatened with extinction. What fades needs to be held, and sensuous beauty exists most strongly in fugitive moments of transfiguration. As he explicates in "Lonesome Pine Special":

> It's true, I think, as Kenkò says in his *Idleness*,
> That all beauty depends upon disappearance,
> The bitten edges of things,
>   the gradual sliding away
> Into tissue and memory,
>   the uncertainty
> And dazzling impermanence of days we beg our meanings from,
> And their frayed loveliness.

Yet Wright's aesthetic isn't objective or immanentist: it's unabashedly Transcendental. The gifts may all be here in this world, but salvation is momentary. For him the finite world must always bear traces—inscriptions—of the infinite. The mystic quests for the inorganic. In "Looking at Pictures," for example, the poet describes his assembled collection of photographs and reproductions "of all I've thought most beautiful / in the natural world." The postcards he catalogues, however (that which is most lovely in the *natural* world) are all religious: St. Francis, for example, "who saw the fire in the pig's mouth," and "the last half-page of the Verse of Light in Arabic / torn from the Koran," and an agonized Adam and Eve "ushered out through the stone gates of Paradise." In Wright's cosmology, Adam and Eve exist on this side of the river—partly on shore, partly in water—longing to find their way home to the Light.

The relationship between the seen and the unseen is at the heart of *Zone Journals*, a collection of ten verse journals. It also animates the shorter companion volume, *Xionia*, an epilogue of fifteen additional journal poems. As Wright has explained it, *Zone Journals* is "about language and landscape, and how they coexist in each other, and speak for, and to, each other." It is also about the ways they separate, embodying different domains. Language names, divides, encodes, evokes. Does it incarnate? "Words, like all things, are caught in their finitude," Wright concludes in one poem. In another he speaks of being "lashed to the syllable and noun, / the strict Armageddon of the verb," of lolling for seventeen years over a California bay:

> If nothing else
> It showed me that what you see
> both is and is not there,
> The unseen bulking in from the edges of all things,
> Changing the frame with its nothingness.
> ("A Journal of True Confessions")

The recurring problematic and tension of these poems of process, of descriptive quotidiana and metaphysical speculation, is how the unseen, the unvisible and abstract, can be attained by way of the visible and concrete. "Exclusion's the secret," Wright declares in the first poem, "Yard Journal." "What's missing is what appears / most visible to the eye." The paradox of "nothing on everything" recurs in different forms throughout the work, whether the poet is recalling an argument with army buddies "that what's outside / The picture is more important than what's in" ("A Journal of the Year of the Ox") or summoning his favorite Italian painter as an exemplar of the "Chinese" method he himself aspires to:

> In 1935, the year I was born,
> Giorgio Morandi
> Penciled these bottles in by leaving them out, letting
> The presence of what surrounds them increase the presence
> Of what is missing,
> keeping its distance and measure.
> ("Chinese Journal")

This defines Wright's own verbal project by analogy with drawing.

Zone Journals takes as its starting point the intersection of time and space. The poems are diaristic—each entry begins with a dash and each poem consists of many entries—though the immediacy and informality of the journal form is balanced and at times countered by the sense of individual poems as artfully composed sequences. The poems push the staggered line toward prose, often specifying an exact time of day, usually delineating the month and season of the year. Individual dates figure prominantly. Specific days of the year first began to appear in Wright's work with some frequency in *China Trace* and there is an improvisational character to the unfolding of "The Southern Cross" that prefigures the entries in *Zone Journals*. The layering of image, anecdote, and speculation that distinguished *The Other Side of the River* is developed even further in *Zone Journals*, especially in the book's centerpiece, "A Journal of the Year of the Ox." Wright's journals work by juxtaposing lines, stanzas, sections.

The dates in Wright's work are often used to mark personal pilgrimages, ritual occasions of his own devising. "A Journal of English Days," for example, takes place in London over four months in fall 1983. The poem begins in September with the speaker at Kensington Church Walk trying to piece together what it was like for Pound in 1908. As he walks the city over the next months the memorials accumulate around birthdays and death dates. One section is titled "Short Riff for John Keats on his 188th Birthday." The pilgrim is back in Kensington Gardens on October 17, "Sir Philip dead / 397 years today." Five days later he looks out at the blurred green trees without his glasses and thinks of Cézanne dying in Provence seventy-seven years to the day. Eight days later he feels the month running down, "Pound's birthday ninety-eight years ago." These memorials are interwoven with minute descriptions of the weather as the luxuriance of September pares down to a wintry December. And the whole is punctuated by moments of tremendous theological longing: "There is no sickness of spirit like homesickness / When what you are sick for / has never been seen or heard / In this world."

The structural method of such poems as "A Journal of English Days" and "A Journal of True Confessions" is developed fully in "A Journal of the Year of the Ox." This ambitious forty-page poem covers the period from January to December 1985, the year of the poet's fiftieth birthday. The pilgrim who sets out at the beginning of the year progresses through a detailed cycle of four seasons. He brings forth two sacred landscapes from Wright's past: the Long Island of the Holston River, in Kingsport, ceremonial ground of the Cherokee and a place near where he grew up, and the region of northern Italy where he first started writing poems. The four entries about the defeated Cherokee nation are intermixed with the memory of visits to the houses of two American precursors, Dickinson and Poe, and two Italian luminaries, Petrarch and Dante. The centerpiece of the journal is a two-month summer sojourn in a farmhouse in Italy. The peak moment is the description of a room of Renaissance frescoes in Palazzo Schifanoia of the Duke of Este in Ferrara. These allegorical frescoes depict an ascending structure of existence: the civic and social activity of daily life, the signs of the zodiac, and the triumph of the gods. "Reality, symbol and ideal / tripartite and everlasting," is how Wright describes it. All of Wright's landscapes, whether he is entering the zones of the aesthetic or the natural, are landscapes of desire.

In "December Journal," a key poem in *Xionia*, Wright once more refigures his Christian inheritance ("God is not offered to the senses, / St. Augustine tells us") in terms of his own descriptive concerns: "I keep coming back to the visible," he says, "I keep coming back / To what it leads me into, / The hymn in the hymnal." At the conclusion of the poem he declares that "from somewhere we never see comes everything we do see," and speaks of "the immanence of infinitude." But the yearning for the inviolate, which defines Wright's overall project, is elsewhere refuted, as when he decides that "it is not possible to read the then in the now" ("A Journal of One Significant Landscape"), or that "God is an abstract noun" ("A Journal of English Days"), or even that "language, always, is just language" ("Vesper Journal"). The longing for purified silence is countered by the materiality of language, its rhythms and textures. There is an unresolved argument in the journal poems as to what extent the gap between words and things, language and landscape, the flesh and the spirit, is transgressible. This work inscribes a dual commitment, however doomed, to what we say and what we see. Or as he puts it in the "Last Journal": "Lust of the tongue, lust of the eye, / out of our own mouths we are sentenced . . . "

Charles Wright has written some of the most hauntingly beautiful individual lines and poems in contemporary poetry, but they should be understood as part of a profound spiritual dialectic and project. His poetry is ultimately a form of worship. He has created a singular body of work that both rejoices in, and mourns for, the mutable world.

Edward Hirsch

Further Reading

Buckley, Christopher, ed. *On the Poetry of Philip Levine: Stranger to Nothing*. Ann Arbor: University of Michigan Press, 1991.

Levine, Philip. *Don't Ask*. Ann Arbor: University of Michigan Press, 1981.

—— *New Selected Poems*. New York: Knopf, 1991.

—— *What Work Is*. New York: Knopf, 1991.

Wright, Charles. *Country Music, Selected Early Poems*. 2d ed. Middletown, Conn.: Wesleyan University Press, 1991.

—— *Halflife: Improvisations and Interviews, 1977–1987*. Ann Arbor: University of Michigan Press, 1988.

—— *The World of Ten Thousand Things: Poems, 1980–1990*. New York: Farrar, Straus and Giroux, 1990.

Contributors

Lea Baechler teaches at Columbia University and, with A. Walton Litz, coedited the 1990 edition of *Personae: The Shorter Poems of Ezra Pound.* Her essay on John Berryman and the elegy will appear this year in a collection of essays on Berryman.

J. T. Barbarese heads the English Department at the Friends Select School in Philadelphia, and he is a visiting professor of literature, journalism, and poetry at Rutgers University, Camden. His books of poems are *Under the Blue Moon* (1985) and *New Science* (1989).

Lawrence Buell is Professor of English at Harvard University. He is the author of *Literary Transcendentalism and New England Literary Culture.* His essays and reviews have been widely published in journals.

Ann Charters is Professor of English at the University of Connecticut. She is the author of *Kerouac: A Biography* (1987) and *Olson/Melville: A Study in Affinity* (1968), and she has edited *The Portable Beat Reader* and *Scenes Along the Road*, a collection of photographs from the Beat era.

William W. Cook is Professor of English at Dartmouth College, where he chaired the program in African-American Studies for many years. A poet and critic, his collection of poems, *Hudson Hornet*, was recently published.

Margaret Dickie is Professor of English at the University of Georgia. Her books include *Hart Crane: The Patterns of His Poetry* (1974), *On the Modernist Long Poem* (1986), and *Lyric Contingencies: Emily Dickinson and Wallace Stevens* (1991).

W. S. Di Piero is the author of several books of poetry, the most recent of which is *The Restorers*. He has also published two collections of essays, *Memory and Enthusiasm* (1989) and *Out of Eden* (1991).

John Elder is Professor of English and Environmental Studies at Middlebury College. He is the author of *Imagining the Earth: Poetry and the Vision of Nature* (1985), and he edited, with Robert Finch, the *Norton Book of Nature Writing*.

Dana Gioia is the author of two books of poetry: *Daily Horoscope* (1986) and *The Gods in Winter* (1991). His critical essays are collected in *Can Poetry Matter? Essays on Poetry and American Culture* (1992). He has contributed widely to periodicals, including the *New Yorker* and the *New Criterion*.

Carolivia Herron has held professorial appointments in African American literature, comparative literature, and English at Harvard University and Mt. Holyoke College. She edited the *Selected Works of Angelina Weld Grimké* (1991), and is the author of *Thereafter Johnny*, a novel.

Edward Hirsch is a poet and Professor of English at the University of Houston. His books of poetry include *For the Sleepwalkers* (1981), *Wild Gratitude* (1986), and *The Night Parade* (1989). He won the National Book Critics Circle Award for poetry in 1986. His critical essays appear regularly in the *New Yorker* and elsewhere.

Lynn Keller is Professor of English at the University of Wisconsin, Madison, and the author of *Re-making It New: Contemporary American Poetry and the Modernist Tradition* (1987).

Jeanne Larsen is Professor of English at Hollins College. She is a poet, translator, and the author of two novels, *Silk Road* and *Bronze Mirror*. She has also published essays on H.D., Dickinson, and medieval Chinese poetry.

Christopher MacGowan is Professor of English at William and Mary. He coedited the *Collected Poems of William Carlos Williams*, with A. Walton Litz, and has recently published a new edition of *Paterson*.

John McWilliams is Abernethy Professor of American Literature at Middlebury College. His books include *Political Justice in a Republic: Fenimore Cooper's America* (1972), *Hawthore, Melville, and the American Character* (1984), and *The American Epic: Transforming a Genre* (1989).

Lucy Maddox is Professor of English at Georgetown University and the author of *Removals: Nineteenth-Century American Literature and the Politics of Indian Affairs* (1991). She also teaches at the Bread Loaf Graduate School of English of Middlebury College.

Jeredith Merrin is Associate Professor of English at the Ohio State University. She is the author of *An Enabling Humility: Marianne Moore, Elizabeth Bishop, and the Uses of Tradition* (1990). Her poems have been published in several national magazines.

Jeffrey Meyers, a Fellow of the Royal Society of Literature, has written biographies of Katherine Mansfield, Wyndam Lewis, Ernest Hemingway, Robert Lowell and his circle, D. H. Lawrence, Joseph Conrad, and Edgar Allan Poe.

Diane Wood Middlebrook is Professor of English at Stanford University. She is a poet and the author of *Anne Sexton, A Biography* and *Walt Whitman and Wallace Stevens*. With Marilyn Yalom she edited *Coming to Light: American Women Poets in the Twentieth Century* (1985).

Frank Murphy is Professor of English at Smith College. He edited the Puritan section of the *Norton Anthology of American Literature*, and is the author of *Yeats' Early Poetry: The Quest for Reconciliation* (1975).

Gregory Orr is Professor of English at the University of Virginia. He is the author of several books of poetry, which include *The Red House* (1980), *We Must Make a Kingdom of It* (1986), and a volume of selected poems. He has also written a critical study of Stanley Kunitz.

Jay Parini is Professor of English at Middlebury College. His books include three volumes of poetry: *Singing in Time* (1972), *Anthracite Country* (1982), and *Town Life* (1988). He has also written four novels, most recently, *The Last Station* (1990) and *Bay of Arrows* (1992). He published a critical study of Theodore Roethke in 1979.

Donald E. Pease is Professor of English at Dartmouth College. Among other books, he is the author of *Visionary Compacts: American Renaissance Writings in Cultural Context* (1987). He has edited several volumes of critical essays.

William H. Pritchard is the Henry Clay Folger Professor of English at Amherst College and the author of many books of criticism, including *Lives* *of the Modern Poets* and biographies of Robert Frost and Randall Jarrell. He is a frequent contributor to the *Hudson Review* and other periodicals.

Arnold Rampersad is the Woodrow Wilson Professor of Literature at Princeton University and directs the Program in American Studies there. He is the author of the two-volume *Life of Langston Hughes*, and of books on Melville's *Israel Potter* and W. E. B. Du Bois. He is a recent recipient of a MacArthur Fellowship.

John Shoptaw teaches English at Princeton University. He has written a critical study of John Ashbery and has published poems and reviews in several magazines and journals.

Claude J. Summers is Professor of English at the University of Michigan, Dearborn. The author of a recent study of gay literature, he has also written books on Christopher Isherwood and E. M. Forster. His critical articles on poetry and fiction have been widely published in journals.

Helen Vendler is Professor of English at Harvard University. Her books include major studies of Wallace Stevens, John Keats, and George Herbert, and she has published two influential collections of essays: *Part of Nature, Part of Us and The Music of What Happens*. She is currently at work on a study of Shakespeare's sonnets.

Patricia Wallace is a Professor of English at Vassar College. She has published work on a variety of modern and contemporary American poets, including Robert Frost, Elizabeth Bishop, and Rita Dove. She is the editor of the contemporary poetry section of the *Norton Anthology of American Literature*.

Cynthia Griffin Wolff is Professor of English at M.I.T. She is the author of critical biographies of Emily Dickinson and Edith Wharton as well as *Samuel Richardson and the Eighteenth-Century Puritan Character*.

Index